Benchmarks in Time and Culture

American Schools of Oriental Research
The Society of Biblical Literature
Archaeology and Biblical Studies
Philip J. King, editor

Number 01
BENCHMARKS IN TIME AND CULTURE
An Introduction to Palestinian Archaeology
Edited by
Joel F. Drinkard, Jr., Gerald L. Mattingly,
J. Maxwell Miller

BENCHMARKS IN TIME AND CULTURE

An Introduction to Palestinian Archaeology

Dedicated to
Joseph A. Callaway

Edited by
Joel F. Drinkard, Jr., Gerald L. Mattingly,
and J. Maxwell Miller

SCHOLARS PRESS
Atlanta, Georgia

Benchmarks in Time and Culture

Library of Congress Cataloging-in-Publication Data

Benchmarks in time and culture.

(Archaeology and biblical studies / Society
of Biblical Literature ; no. 1)
"Festschrift for Joseph A. Callaway"—Pref.
Bibliography: p.
Includes indexes.
1. Syria—Antiquities. 2. Palestine—Antiquities.
3. Archaeology—Methodology. 4. Bible—Antiquities.
5. Callaway, Joseph A. I. Drinkard, Joel F.
II. Mattingly, Gerald L. III. Miller, James Maxwell,
1937– . IV. Callaway, Joseph A. V. Series:
Archaeology and biblical studies ; no. 1.
DS94.5.B46 1987   933   87-20513

ISBN 1-55540-172-4 (alk. paper)
ISBN 1-55540-173-2 (pbk. : alk. paper)

Printed in the United States of America
on acid-free paper

CONTENTS

Part One
Archaeologists: The Practitioners

Part Two
Archaeological Methodology: The Techniques

Part Three
Integrative Archaeological Studies: The Synthesis

Epilogue

EDITORS AND CONTRIBUTORS

Pierre Benoit, O.P.
École Biblique
Jerusalem, Israel*

Roger S. Boraas
Upsala College
East Orange, NJ

Oded Borowski
Emory University
Atlanta, GA

Graham I. Davies
Cambridge University
Cambridge, England

John J. Davis
Grace Theological Seminary
Winona Lake, IN

William G. Dever
University of Arizona
Tucson, AZ

Joel F. Drinkard, Jr.
Southern Baptist Theological
  Seminary
Louisville, KY

J. Kenneth Eakins
Golden Gate Baptist Theological
  Seminary
Mill Valley, CA

Avraham Horowitz
Tel Aviv University
Tel Aviv, Israel

James R. Kautz, III
Department of Health and
  Human Resources
Baton Rouge, LA

Philip J. King
Boston College
Chestnut Hill, MA

Øystein S. LaBianca
Andrews University
Berrien Springs, MI

John McRay
Wheaton Graduate School
Wheaton, IL

Gerald L. Mattingly
Cincinnati Christian Seminary
Cincinnati, OH

Amihai Mazar
Hebrew University
Jerusalem, Israel

J. Maxwell Miller
Emory University
Atlanta, GA

Anson F. Rainey
Tel Aviv University
Tel Aviv, Israel

Eric C. Rust
Professor Emeritus
Southern Baptist Theological
  Seminary
Louisville, KY

Thomas L. Sever
National Space Technology
   Laboratories
NSTL, MS

James F. Strange
University of South Florida
Tampa, FL

Gus W. Van Beek
Smithsonian Institution
Washington, D.C.

James M. Weinstein
Cornell University
Ithaca, NY

Manfred and Helga Weippert
University of Heidelberg
Heidelberg, West Germany

*Deceased

PREFACE

In an address delivered at the Southern Baptist Theological Seminary on October 19, 1965, Joseph A. Callaway referred to the "emerging role of archaeology in biblical studies."* Callaway explained his use of the term "emerging" by saying that the relationship between these two disciplines "is not new, nor is it fully developed." Indeed, the role that archaeological research plays in biblical studies has been defined and redefined almost continously in the two decades that have passed since Callaway's address. Callaway's perspective was not as open-ended as it may sound, since he expressed himself with more certainty on a number of points, two of which stand out more clearly than all the rest. First, regarding the methodology employed in archaeological excavations in the Middle East, Callaway saw that the "introduction of scientifically respectable techniques" would change the ways in which fieldwork would be carried out *and* the ways in which biblical scholars would utilize the data recovered in archaeological fieldwork. More specifically, Callaway understood that the influence of Albright, Wright, Wheeler, and Kenyon would push the discipline of archaeology to new heights of professionalism, resulting in better methods of digging and recording and in more balanced interpretation. Naturally, the techniques introduced by these scholars have been developed and improved by many others, including Callaway himself. Second, Callaway advocated one positive and indisputable way in which archaeology should relate to biblical studies: "The real business of archaeology is to establish factual benchmarks in the world of the Bible to guide interpreters." Although we know that some "archaeological facts" change with the passage of time, or are subject to interpretation, Callaway's emphasis continues to warn us against the misuse of archaeological data in biblical studies. Once again, Callaway's writing demonstrates that he is involved in this search for integrity himself.

This volume is a *Festschrift* for Joseph A. Callaway, a field archaeologist and biblical scholar whose career has been characterized by a concern for methodological advancements and by a desire to establish factual benchmarks. All of the contributors have had the privilege of being associated with the honoree in some way during his productive

*The full text of Callaway's address was printed in *Review and Expositor* 63(1966): 200–209.

and respected career as teacher, dirt archaeologist, administrator, and writer. The essays are divided into three major sections: (1) historical summaries of the major national "schools" that have shaped Syro-Palestinian archaeology; (2) introductory surveys of some of the important techniques that are currently used in archaeological research; and (3) selected studies that illustrate ways in which archaeological data can be integrated into historical-cultural syntheses. Naturally, these essays do not exhaust the volume's overall theme; many subjects are left untouched, and there is probably room for several such volumes. It is our hope that this collection of essays will lead many students to understand the development of and methods used in Syro-Palestinian archaeology and to appreciate the contributions that this discipline can make to biblical, cultural, and historical studies.

We wish to thank especially the three institutions which have encouraged and supported this volume from its inception, American Schools of Oriental Research, Society of Biblical Literature, and The Southern Baptist Theological Seminary. Joseph A. Callaway has been deeply involved in each of these institutions for the past 30 years. Special appreciation must also be given to Gaylyn Bishop, Rachel Keeney, Tim Crawford, and Brian Jones for their help in preparing the manuscript.

Joel F. Drinkard, Jr.
Gerald L. Mattingly
J. Maxwell Miller

LIST OF FIGURES

LIST OF TABLES

ABBREVIATIONS

AASOR	*Annual of the American Schools of Oriental Research*
ADAJ	*Annual of the Department of Antiquities of Jordan*
ADPV	Abhandlungen des Deutschen Palästina-Vereins
AJA	*American Journal of Archaeology*
Am Ant	*American Antiquity*
Am Anthrop	*American Anthropologist*
Anthrop Q	*Anthropological Quarterly*
Anthrop R	*Anthropological Review*
ARA	*Annual Review of Anthropology*
ASOR	American Schools of Oriental Research
AUSS	*Andrews University Seminary Studies*
BA	*Biblical Archaeologist*
BAR	*Biblical Archaeology Review*
BASOR	*Bulletin of the American Schools of Oriental Research*
BSAJ	British School of Archaeology in Jerusalem
CA	*Current Anthropology*
CBQ	*Catholic Biblical Quarterly*
DAI	*Deutsches Archäologisches Institut*
DFG	Deutsche Forschungs-Gemeinschaft
DMG	Deutsche Morgenländische Gesellschaft
DOG	Deutsche Orient-Gesellschaft
DVzEP	Deutscher Verein zur Erforschung Palästinas
EAEHL	*Encyclopedia of Archaeological Excavations in the Holy Land*
EI	*Eretz-Israel*
HTR	*Harvard Theological Review*
HUCA	*Hebrew Union College Annual*
HUC-JIR	Hebrew Union College—Jewish Institute of Religion
IDB	*Interpreter's Dictionary of the Bible*
IDB Supp	*Interpreter's Dictionary of the Bible, Supplementary Volume*
IEJ	*Israel Exploration Journal*
JAOS	*Journal of the American Oriental Society*
JAR	*Journal of Anthropological Research*
JBL	*Journal of Biblical Literature*
JPOS	*Journal of the Palestine Oriental Society*
JSOT	*Journal for the Study of the Old Testament*
MDOG	*Mitteilungen der Deutschen Orient-Gesellschaft zu Berlin*
MuNDPV	*Mitteilungen und Nachrichten des deutschen Palästina-Vereins*

NEASB	*Near East Archaeological Society Bulletin*
PEF	Palestine Exploration Fund
PEFQS	*Palestine Exploration Fund Quarterly Statement*
PEQ	*Palestine Exploration Quarterly*
PJ	*Palästina-Jahrbuch*
QDAP	*Quarterly of the Department of Antiquities in Palestine*
RB	*Revue Biblique*
Rev Exp	*Review and Expositor*
SJA	*Southwestern Journal of Anthropology*
TA	*Tel Aviv*
UF	*Ugarit-Forschungen*
WA	*World Archaeology*
WTJ	*Westminster Theological Journal*
WVDOG	Wissenschaftliche Veröffentlichungen der Deutschen Orient-Gesellschaft
ZAW	*Zeitschrift für die Alttestamentliche Wissenschaft*
ZDMG	*Zeitschrift der Deutschen Morgenländischen Gesellschaft*
ZDPV	*Zeitschrift des Deutschen Palästina-Vereins*

PART ONE

ARCHAEOLOGISTS:
THE PRACTITIONERS

1
ANTECEDENTS TO MODERN ARCHAEOLOGY

J. Maxwell Miller
Emory University

The essays which follow in this volume focus on archaeology as practiced today in Palestine. Those in Part I review the recent history of the discipline, since approximately the turn of the century. Those in Part II discuss some of the more important techniques employed. Those in Part III explore the interpretative aspects of Palestinian archaeology, particularly as it interrelates with other disciplines. The purpose of this introductory essay, therefore, is to deal briefly with certain matters which do not represent the primary focus of the volume but which require some attention by way of background—some discussion of the designation "Palestinian Archaeology," a brief overview of the extremely long time frame and cultural variety which Palestinian archaeologists must take into account, and mention of certain pre-20th century developments which might be considered antecedent to the discipline as it is practiced today.

I. TERMINOLOGY

The term "archaeology" was used already in ancient Greek literature with general reference to "the study of earlier times." Josephus' *The Antiquities of the Jews*, for example, was entitled literally *ioudaikēs archaiologias*. Still today the term has a rather broad and ill-defined meaning for the general public. Let it be known in a conversation that you have some training or experience in archaeology and the response may have to do with anything from rocks and bones to visitors from outer space. For practicing archaeologists, however, the term pertains more specifically to artifactual evidence, material remains of the culture and civilizations of people who lived in times past, and the systematic study of these remains in an effort to learn more about the people who left them behind. Narrowly defined, therefore, archaeology is to be distinguished from other disciplines such as geology, the study of the earth's crust (rocks, rivers and the like), paleontology, the study of earlier life forms (bones), and history, the study of the human past on the basis of written records.

Yet it is one of the characteristics of archaeology, which will be apparent in every chapter of this volume, that any narrow definition is useful only as a starting point for exploring the many ramifications of the discipline. Artifactual evidence cannot be studied properly, for example, without attention to physical and historical context. In actual practice, therefore, archaeological research involves a whole host of interrelated disciplines, including geology, paleontology, history, and on and on. One of the currently debated issues is whether Palestinian archaeology has been too closely intertwined with biblical studies. It must be said in any case that much of the archaeological activity in Palestine during the present century and much of the current literature on the subject have been by people such as myself whose primary training was in biblical studies or who have particular interests in biblical history. The resulting tendency to focus on the periods relevant to biblical history will be evident in several of the essays which follow.

The term "Palestine" also requires comment, if for no other reason than to make it clear that our use of it in this volume has no intended implications regarding the current Arab-Israeli conflict. This term likewise was coined already in ancient times, at least as early as Herodotus. The whole eastern Mediterranean seaboard was generally known by his day as Syria. Thus Herodotus, wishing to refer to just the southern part of Syria, identified this portion as "Philistine Syria" *(suriā he palaistinē)*. Later we find "Palaistinei" used by itself as a proper name and then, during the second century A.D., the name "Palaestina" gained official status in connection with the Roman province system. The name remained in official use during the Byzantine period, was used by the Crusaders, and became a standard geographical term in the English language long before the establishment of the British Mandate government of Palestine following World War I. In the 1880s, for example, when Conder and Kitchener published the results of their survey between the Mediterranean Sea and the Jordan valley, they called it a *Survey of Western Palestine.* Thus, regardless of the fact that the term is sometimes used today with political (even propagandistic) overtones, "Palestine" still seems to be the most appropriate geographical designation in English for the area treated in this volume—namely, the southern part of the strip of reasonably fertile and well watered land sandwiched between the eastern shore of the Mediterranean Sea and the Arabian Desert, from approximately the southern slopes of the Lebanon and Anti-Lebanon mountains to the Gulf of ʿAqaba.

II. CHRONOLOGICAL OVERVIEW

It is difficult to say how long humans have inhabited Palestine. In fact, this is one of the issues currently debated by Palestinian archaeologists. Certainly human occupation of this area goes back more than a million years, which means that it is necessary to divide the long sweep of time into periods simply to render it comprehensible. A chronological outline of the main periods generally recognized by Palestinian archaeologists is provided on page 469. The following explanations and qualifications should be made with reference to the outline.

(1) Any periodizaton of the human past is, at least to a certain degree arbitrary. Changes in human lifestyles tend to occur gradually and there are different kinds of changes which never occur entirely in unison. Thus the dates provided in the outline are not to be understood as precise moments of transition. They are little more than convenient "handles" which indicate that some noticeable change in the human situation was occurring at approximately that time. Moreover, the earlier we go back in time the more approximate these dates should be understood.

(2) The larger the divisions, the more useful they are for broad overview. Correspondingly, the more detailed the divisions, the more useful they are for precise research. For purposes of broad overview I find it useful to divide the long sweep of archaeological time in Palestine into five major blocks. Each has its own characteristic remains which even non-specialists recognize.

Prehistoric Times: from the earliest evidences of human occupation to approximately the close of the fourth millennium B.C. Specifically, this covers the Palaeolithic, Mesolithic, Neolithic and Chalcolithic periods. Archaeological remains in Palestine from this extremely long block of time are typical of those found elsewhere in the Old World—stone tools and the like. Small village settlements began to appear in the last (Neolithic and Chalcolithic) phases, accompanied by rapid advancements in craftsmanship and some indications of overland trade.

Ancient Times: from the beginnings of urbanization in the Middle East to Alexander the Great's conquests. This covers the Bronze and Iron Ages. For some three thousand years the "Fertile Crescent," which of course included Palestine, represented center stage of human history. This was the time of the great Egyptian and Mesopotamian empires, fairly well known now as a result of archaeological explorations in Egypt and Mesopotamia, which led in turn to the recovery and decipherment of literally thousands of ancient documents. The archaeological feature most characteristic of ancient Palestine are the "tells" scattered throughout the land.

Classical Times: from Alexander's conquests to the Arab expansion. This covers the Hellenistic, Roman, and Byzantine periods. Center stage of human history shifts now from the Fertile Crescent to the Mediterranean world. Although this did not happen suddenly, Alexander's conquest does represent the main turning point. For the next thousand years, Palestine would be dominated by people who spoke Greek or Latin rather than the Semitic tongues of the indigenous population, and the major Palestinian cities were typical of those found anywhere else in the Graeco-Roman world. During the fourth century A.D., the Roman empire was Christianized and gradually split into two parts. Palestine fell within the eastern, Byzantine realm whose rulers commissioned churches at key holy places. Typical archaeological remains from this major block of time, therefore, include colonnaded streets, Roman baths, mosaic floors and walls, and churches.

Medieval and Early Modern Times: from A.D. 640, by which time Arab forces controlled the eastern Mediterranean seaboard and most of Egypt, to World War I. Actually Palestine was dominated politically by peoples other than Arabs during most of these 1200 years or so—principally the Crusaders, Mamluks and Ottoman Turks. Yet the Arabic language and what may be regarded as traditional Islamic culture dominated. Typical remains of the period are mosques, Crusader and Mamluk castles, and Turkish houses, many still in use.

Westernization: post-World War I. An archaeologist of the distant future, even if he or she were unaware of the wrenching political changes which have occurred in Palestine during the present century, would be able to recognize from the artifactual record that a new era has dawned—an era characterized by the spread of Western influence throughout the world. Characteristic artifacts which will contribute to the debris of our century and mark it as the dawning of a new era include steel reinforced buildings, asphalt roads, plastic products, and pop bottles.

(3) Theoretically, archaeological periods are divided on the basis of artifactual evidence—i.e., the divisions emerge from and correspond to typological changes in architecture, pottery, burials, etc. Beginning with the Bronze Age, however, it is clear that the archaeological periods also correlate rather closely with historical periods—i.e., divisions based on information derived from written records. Indeed, it can be argued that all of the close dates used by Palestinian archaeologists—certainly all of those figured to less than a hundred years—depend ultimately on written evidence. Carbon 14 and other chemical dating methods provide only "ballpark" figures. Pottery dating itself depends ultimately on written evidence for its dates. When the Late Bronze Age in Palestine is dated ca. 1550 to 1200 B.C., therefore, this means that the archaeological features of that period can be correlated with certain developments in Egyptian history, which in turn can be dated to ca. 1550–1200 B.C. on the basis of written records. When the Iron Age is sub-divided into Iron Age I and Iron Age II, and the Persian Period, and each of the sub-divisions dated, the dates come as much from biblical chronology as from the potsherds.

III. ANTECEDENTS TO PALESTINIAN ARCHAEOLOGY

Joshua 11:12–13 reports in connection with Joshua's campaign against the king of Hazor and other northern cities that "all the cities of those kings, and all their kings, Joshua took, and smote them with the edge of the sword, . . . but none of the cities that stood on mounds did Israel burn, except Hazor only." Deuteronomy 13:16 (v 17 in Hebrew) commands as punishment for any city which has gone after foreign gods, "You shall gather all its spoil into the midst of its open square, and burn the city and all its spoil with fire, as a whole burnt offering to the LORD your God; it shall become a heap for ever, it shall not be built again." "Mound" in the passage from Joshua and "heap" in the passage from Deuteronomy are both translations of a single Hebrew word, *tel*. This is the Hebrew form of the same word "tell" (the English spelling derived from the Arabic) which is the standard archaeological term for the ancient stratified city ruins scattered throughout Syria-Palestine. One concludes from the passages, moreover, that the biblical writers were aware that tells were ancient city ruins. This is more than can be said for modern explorers until the late 19th century. Edward Robinson observed in 1838 that a huge mound called *et-Tell* ("the tell") by local Arabs was located at what seemed to him the most likely spot for the biblical city Ai. By 1841 (vol. 2: 313), he ruled this out as a possibility because he found no evidence at et-Tell of an ancient settlement. C. R. Conder suggested as late as 1878 (vol. 2: 47) that the tells represented discard dumps of ancient brick factories. We know now, of course, that et-Tell itself was the evidence Robinson sought. In fact, one of the main points of the story in Joshua 7–8 is to explain how it happened that Ai had become "a heap of ruins as it is to this day" (see especially 8:28).

Site identification may be regarded as having to do more with historical geography than with archaeology. Yet this is another one of those situations where it is difficult to hold to a narrow definition of archaeology, since it is necessary to establish the ancient identity of a site if references to it in the ancient written records are to be taken into account for interpreting the artifactual remains. Several biblical passages reflect early attempts to deal with the problem of site identification. Consider the narrative in Genesis 14, for example, which recounts an invasion of Palestine by a coalition of kings led by Amraphel king of Shinar. We are told that

> these kings made war with Bera king of Sodom, Birsha king of Gomor-
> rah, Shinab king of Admah, Shemeber king of Zeboiim, and the king of
> Bela (that is, Zoar). And all these joined forces in the Valley of Siddim
> (that is, the Salt Sea) (vv 2–3).

The names "Sodom," "Gomorrah," "Admah," and "Zeboiim" would have
been generally familiar to the early readers of this story—i.e., about the
time of the Babylonian exile when it probably was edited in essentially its
present form. "Bela" and "the Valley of Siddim" apparently required
explanation, however, which the editor(s) supplied. Thus it was added,
correctly or incorrectly, that Bela is the same as Zoar and that the Valley
of Siddim is none other than the Salt Sea. A modern commentator might
want to explain further than the Salt Sea is what we generally refer to in
English as the Dead Sea. Among other biblical passages which reflect
ancient attempts to deal with matters of site identification are Gen 23:1–
2, 18–20 and Josh 15:8–10; 18:13–14.

The problem of site identification became more serious in classical
times when the old Semitic place names tended to be replaced with new
names based on Greek or Latin. Fortunately, writers of the day often
noted the name changes which had occurred, thus providing us with a
link between the ancient and classical names. Strabo, for example, a
Greek geographer who resided in Rome ca. 60 B.C. to A.D. 20 but
travelled widely and wrote a 17-volume *Geography*, described Palestine in
his 16th volume. Along with other such information, he notes that the
city of Ptolemais was earlier called *Akē* (16.2.25). Of particular interest in
this regard is Eusebius' *Onomasticon* (literally, "list of names"). Eusebius
was the bishop of Caesarea ca. 264–340, which makes him roughly
contemporary with Constantine, the emperor under whom Christianity
became the official religion of the Roman empire. This was the beginning of heavy Christian pilgrimage traffic, and the *Onomasticon*, which is
the surviving portion of a much more extensive work, illustrates the
increased interest in the location of biblical places. Eusebius mentions
over a thousand place names, localizes many of them in relation to the
main cities and roads of his day, and identifies many of them by their
earlier (OT) names. The *Onomasticon* was regarded as valuable enough
for Jerome to annotate and translate into Latin almost a century later; it
might have served as background for the famous mosaic map of
Medeba.

This map decorated the floor of a church which was built in the
Transjordanian town of Medeba during the sixth century A.D. Except
for the *Tabula Peutingeriana*, a Roman road map of the third century
which provides very little detail, the Medeba mosaic is the oldest map
available for Palestine. It is not a "scale" map by any means. In fact, the
mosaic artists had to distort the lay of the land considerably in order to
include both the Phoenician coast and the Nile Delta on the map and at
the same time use it to fill out the rectangular church floor. Although
much of the map was destroyed when a new church was built in the
1890s, the mosaic still provides important information. For example, its
schematic plan of sixth century Jerusalem is unique.

Christian pilgrims had begun to arrive in Jerusalem already during the second century A.D. Later, after restrictions resulting from the Jewish revolts were relaxed, they would be joined by Jewish pilgrims. Still later, in the seventh century and following, there would be Muslim pilgrims. Although the pilgrims of all three faiths were driven by piety rather than anything like scientific or academic concerns, one must admit that they were in effect the predecessors of present-day Palestinian archaeologists. They sought out the actual places where earlier events had occurred, observed what they saw (or were led to believe that they saw), and often wrote about their travels. Many of their accounts were collected, translated, and published between 1887 and 1897 by the Palestine Pilgrims' Text Society.

Early on in the Ottoman period there began to appear now and then in the Middle East a new kind of western traveler, one imbued with the spirit of the dawning age of exploration. Among those who visited Palestine and recorded their observations were Leonhard Rauchwolf and Johann Zuallart in the late 16th century, Pietro della Valle in the mid-17th century, and Henry Maundrell and Richard Pococke in the 18th century (Albright 1949: 23–4). The real turning point which initiated the modern exploration of Palestine was Napoleon's invasion of Egypt in 1798. This was an important event in the history of Palestinian archaeology for two reasons. First, Napoleon's staff prepared a trigonometrically-based, 1:100,000 scale map of Egypt and the Palestinian coast. This is the so-called Jacotin Map, the Palestinian portion of which (sheets 43–7) was prepared under the difficult circumstances of Napoleon's march up the Palestinian coast and his unsuccessful attempt to take Acre. Second, and perhaps more important in the long run, Napoleon's invasion made it clear to the other European nations, especially England, that it was politically advantageous to establish a strong presence in the Middle East. The 19th century turned out to be a time of much increased European activity in Palestine, therefore, which meant more intentional and systematical exploration of the land.

Characteristic of the first half of the century were individual travellers such as Ulrich Seetzen and Ludwig Burckhardt, the first westerners to penetrate the Transjordan since the Crusaders. Explorers of their sort increased in numbers through mid-century, an especially important figure being Edward Robinson who pioneered in the study of biblical geography and whose *Biblical Researches in Palestine, Mount Sinai, and Arabia Petraea* remains a classic. In 1865, the Palestine Exploration Fund was established in London for the purpose of fostering systematic exploration of the land. By the turn of the century, similar organizations had been established in Germany, France, and the United States.

Perhaps the most important result of this 19th century activity was the basic mapping of Palestine. Jacotin's map, which initiated the process on the eve of the century, covered only the Palestinian coast. Between 1872 and 1878, C. R. Conder and H. H. Kitchener prepared a one-inch to one-mile scale map of Western Palestine (referred to earlier in this essay). The project was sponsored by the PEF. Conder and Kitchener were particularly attentive to archaeological remains, and they published in conjunction with the map a six-volume report on their observations. The mapping and archaeological survey of other parts of Palestine proceeded more tentatively. Captain W. F. Lynch had already charted the Dead Sea in 1849, and E. H. Palmer had made a survey excursion into the Negeb in 1869. Conder did some further mapping and archaeological surveying east of the Jordan in 1881–82, which was augmented by G. Schumacher in 1885.

Some parts of Palestine remained largely unknown to westerners throughout the 19th century, however, due to geographical inaccessibility, political circumstances, or both. Such was the case with the plateau between the Wadi Mojib and the Wadi el-Ḥesa, east of the Dead Sea. Only the most daring and determined travelers entered this area. Consequently, it remained largely unexplored until 1894, when the Ottoman government took the city of Kerak by force and reasserted its authority over the local tribes. Explorations in that region between approximately 1895 and 1905, therefore, particularly the work of R. E. Brünnow and A. Musil, rounded out the basic mapping of Palestine. It is instructive in this regard to compare the map of Palestine published by the PEF in 1890 and the Fischer-Guthe map of the same year with maps published a decade or so after the turn of the century—e.g., H. Guthe's *Bibelatlas* of 1911 and G. A. Smith's 1915 *Atlas of the Historical Geography of the Holy Land*.

As the basic mapping and general archaeological survey of Palestine reached completion near the close of the 19th century, a new phase in archaeology was just getting underway—the excavation of tells. Excavations of sorts had already been conducted at Jerusalem by F. de Saulcy during the 1860s; these were followed by further excavations (i.e., tunneling) in the city by Warren during 1866–70. Gradually it became apparent, and was confirmed by Schliemann's excavations at Hissarlik (ancient Troy) during the 1870s, that many of the tells represented stratified ruins of ancient cities. In 1890, under the auspices of the PEF, Flinders Petrie began excavations at Tell el-Ḥesi. The project was continued for two more years by F. J. Bliss who, by the turn of the century, had also probed four other tells in the Shephelah.

Finally, two inscriptional discoveries deserve special mention as important 19th-century developments in the history of Palestinian archaeology. The first of these was the discovery of the Mesha inscription (sometimes called the "Moabite Stone") by F. A. Klein, a missionary from Alsace, in 1868. Unfortunately, the inscription was broken to pieces soon after its discovery. Equally important as the initial find, therefore, was C. Clermont-Ganneau's reconstruction and publication of the text in 1870. The second inscriptional discovery to be mentioned is the Siloam inscription, discovered in 1880 and also badly damaged soon after.

We turn our attention now in the essays which follow to developments in Palestinian archaeology during the present century. As we shall see, the PEF remained in the forefront for several decades, especially until the end of the Mandate period. Other national groups played an increasingly active role, however, particularly between the World Wars when archaeologists from the United States (many of them trained first in biblical studies) became actively involved. More recently, Israeli archaeologists have moved into the forefront, at least west of the Jordan where they have immediate and year-round access to the sites.

Archaeological techniques have become increasingly more sophisticated during the course of the century. The basics of pottery dating were worked out by the late 1920s, for example, and more controlled techniques of stratigraphical excavation were introduced and developed between the World Wars. The emphasis today is on the application of specialized scientific techniques, several of which are treated in Part II below. Also there seems to be a trend away from large scale excavations of major sites toward smaller scale, problem-solving projects and more intensive surveys of areas which were covered only tentatively during the 19th and early 20th centuries.

Another tendency one notices among many archaeologists currently active in Palestine is specialization within the discipline and an interest in archaeology for its own sake. Some would claim to be "dirt archaeologists," for example, which seems to mean that they wish to be totally "scientific" and remain aloof from attempts to utilize archaeological data in integrative studies (such as historical geography and biblical history). Joseph Callaway, to whom this volume is dedicated, held no such narrow perspective. He is one of the many who turned to Palestinian archaeology primarily because he regarded it as relevant to biblical studies. He demonstrated, moreover, that this kind of interest does not *necessarily* render one's field work any less scientific.

BIBLIOGRAPHY

Albright, W. F.
   1949   *The Archaeology of Palestine*. Pelican edition, revised and reprinted 1960. Baltimore: Penguin.
Abel, F. M.
   1939   Edward Robinson on the Identification of Biblical Sites. *JBL* 58:365–72.
Alt, A.
   1939   Edward Robinson and the Historical Geography of Palestine. *JBL* 58:373–77.

Ben-Arieh, Y.
1972   The Geographical Exploration of the Holy Land. *PEQ* 104: 81–
            92.
1979   *The Rediscovery of the Holy Land in the Nineteenth Century.* Jerusa-
            lem: Magnes.
Benzinger, J.
1903   *Researches in Palestine. Explorations in Bible Lands during the Nine-
            teenth Century,* ed. H. V. Hilprecht. Philadelphia: Holman.
Besant, W.
1895   *Thirty Years' Work in the Holy Land, A Record and Summary, 1865–
            1895.* London: Watt.
Bliss, F. J.
1894   *A Mound of Many Cities.* London: PEF.
1896   *The Mounds of Palestine. Recent Research in Bible Lands,* ed. H. V.
            Hilprecht. Philadelphia: Wattles.
1906   *The Development of Palestinian Exploration.* New York: Scribner's.
Bliss, F. J., and Macalister, R. A. S.
1902   *Excavations in Palestine during the Years 1898–1900.* London: PEF.
Brünnow, R. E., and Domaszewski, A. von.
1904–9   *Die Provincia Arabia. auf Grund Zweier in den Jahren 1897 und
            1898 unternommenen Reisen und der Berichte früherer Reisender.*
            Strassburg: Trübner. 3 vols.
Burckhardt, J. L.
1822   *Travels in Syria and the Holy Land.* ed. W. M. Leake for the
            Association for Promoting the Discovery of the Interior Parts of
            Africa. London: Murray.
Clermont-Ganneau, C.
1870   La Stèle de Dhiban. *Revue archéologique* 21:184–207.
Conder, C. R.
1878   *Tent Work in Palestine.* London: Bentley. 2 vols.
1882   Lieutenant Conder's Report, No. 9 *PEFQS* 12:7–15.
1883   *Heth and Moab.* London: Watt.
1889   *Palestine. The World's Great Explorers and Explorations,* ed. J. S.
            Keltie et al. London: Philip.
Conder, C. R., and Kitchener, H. H.
1881–83   *The Survey of Western Palestine.* London: PEF. 6 vols.
Elath, E.
1965   Claude Reignier Conder. In Light of His Letters to His Mother.
            PEQ 97:21–41.
Eusebius,
1966   *Das Onomastikon der biblischen Ortsnamen,* ed. E. Klostermann.
            Hildesheim: Olms.
Finnie, D.
1967   *Pioneers East. The Early American Experience in the Middle East.*
            Cambridge: Harvard University.
Fischer, H.
1890   Begleitworte zur Neuen Handkarte von Palästina. *ZDPV*
            13:44–64. (Fischer-Guthe map attached.)
1913   Referat über die moderne Topographie, Siedlungs-und Ver-
            kehrsgeographie Palästinas, besonders für die Jahre 1910–
            1912. *ZDPV* 36:136–64, 211–19.
Guthe, H.
1882   Die Siloahinschrift. *ZDMG* 36:725–50.
1911   *Bibelatlas.* Leipzig: Wagner & Debes.

Hennequin, L.
1933 Fouilles et Champs de fouilles en Palestine et en Phénicie. *Dictionnaire de la Bible.* Vol. 3, cols. 318–524.

Howell, D. R.
1965 Pilgrims to Archaeologists: A.D. 1516–1865; Palestine Exploration Fund: AD 1865–1895. *World of the Bible, Centenary Exhibition of the Palestine Exploration Fund in Co-operation with the British School of Archaeology in Jerusalem.* ed. C. B. Mortlock. London: Victoria and Albert Museum.

Josephus.
1957–65 *Antiquities of the Jews.* Trans. H. St. Thackeray in *The Loeb Classical Library.* Cambridge: Harvard.

Kallner, A. D. H.
1944 Jacotin's Map of Palestine. *PEQ* 76:157–63.

Karmon, Y.
1960 An Analysis of Jacotin's Map of Palestine. *IEJ* 10:155–73, 244–53.

King, P. J.
1975 The American Archaeological Heritage in the Near East. *BASOR* 217:55–65.

1983 *American Archaeology in the Mideast: A History of the American Schools of Oriental Research.* Philadelphia: ASOR.

Kollek, T., and Pearlman, M.
1970 *Pilgrims to the Holy Land: The Story of Pilgrimages Through The Ages.* London: Weidenfeld and Nicholson.

The Library of the Palestine Pilgrims' Text Society
1887–97 London: Palestine Pilgrims' Text Society. Reprinted in 1971. New York: AMS.

Lynch, W. F.
1849 *Narrative of the United States' Expedition to the River Jordan and the Dead Sea.* Philadelphia: Lea and Blanchard.

Macalister, R. A. S.
1925 *A Century of Excavation of Palestine and the Bible.* London: Religious Tract Society.

Musil, A.
1907–8 *Arabia Petraea.* Kaiserliche Akademie der Wissenschaften. Vienna: Hölder. 2 vols.

Palestine Exploration Fund
1873 *Our Work in Palestine, being an Account of the Different Expeditions Sent out to the Holy Land by the Committee to the Palestine Exploration Fund since the Establishment of the Fund in 1865.* London: Bentley.

Palmer, E. H.
1871 The Desert of the Tíh and the Country of Moab. *PEFQS.* 1:3–73.

1872 *The Desert of the Exodus.* New York: Harper.

Petrie, W. M. F.
1891 *Tell el Hesy (Lachish).* London: Watt.

Robinson, E.
1841 *Biblical Researches in Palestine, Mount Sinai, and Arabia Petraea.* Boston: Crocker and Brewster. 3 vols.

1856 *Later Biblical Researches in Palestine and the Adjacent Regions.* London: Murray.

de Saulcy, F.
1865   *Voyage en Terre Sainte.* Paris: Didier. 2 vols.
Schumacher, G.
1888   *The Jaulân. Surveyed for the German Society for the Exploration of the Holy Land.* London: Bentley.
1889   *Across the Jordan: Being an Exploration and Survey of Part of Hauran and Jaulan.* London: Bentley.
1890   *Northern 'Ajlūn. "Within the Decapolis."* London: Watt.
Seetzen, U. J.
1854–55   *Reisen Durch Syrien, Palästina, Phönicien, die Transjordan-länder, Arabia Petraea und Unter-Aegypten,* ed. Fr. Kruse et al. Berlin: Reimer.
Silberman, N. A.
1982   *Digging for God and Country: Exploration, Archaeology, and the Secret Struggle for the Holy Land, 1799–1917.* New York: Knopf.
Smith, G. A.
1915   *Atlas of the Historical Geography of the Holy Land.* London: Hodder and Stoughton.
Smith, W. R.
1887   Captain Conder and Modern Critics. *Contemporary Review* 51:561–69.
Strabo
1930   *The Geography of Strabo.* Trans. H. L. Jones in *The Loeb Classical Library.* New York: Putnam's.
Tufnell, O.
1965   Excavator's Progress. Letters of F. J. Bliss. *PEQ* 97:112–27.
Warren, C.
1875   *Underground Jerusalem.* London: Bentley.
Watson, C. M.
1915   *Fifty Years' Work in the Holy Land.* London: PEF.
1917   Bonaparte's Expedition to Palestine in 1799. *PEFQS* 49:17–35.
Wilkinson, J.
1977   Christian Pilgrims in Jerusalem during the Byzantine Period. *PEQ* 109:75–101.
Wilson, C. W.
1866   *The Ordnance Survey of Jerusalem.* Southampton: Ordnance Survey Office. 3 vols.
Wilson, C. W., and Palmer, H. S.
1869–72   *Ordnance Survey of the Peninsula of Sinai.* Southampton: Ordnance Survey Office. 5 vols.
Wright, G. E.
1970   The Phenomenon of American Archaeology in the Near East. Pp. 3–40 in *Near Eastern Archaeology in the Twentieth Century: Essays in Honor of Nelson Glueck,* ed. J. A. Sanders. Garden City, N.Y.: Doubleday.
Wright, T.
1848   *Early Travels in Palestine.* London: Bohn.

2
AMERICAN ARCHAEOLOGISTS*

PHILIP J. KING
Boston College

During the 19th century, few Americans distinguished themselves in the geography and archaeology of Palestine. Of those whose interest focused on that part of the world Edward Robinson, the most outstanding, deserved to be called "the founder of the scientific topography of Palestine."[1] Robinson's achievements began to have an impact on his compatriots only in the 20th century. As in the case of many Near Eastern scholars, Robinson's interest in Palestine was fostered by his training in biblical studies.

The American Schools of Oriental Research (ASOR), the primary American professional society for the archaeology of Palestine, was the brainchild of biblical scholars. Henry Thayer, professor of New Testament at Harvard University, was president of the Society of Biblical Literature in 1895. On the occasion of his presidential address that year he strongly advocated that the Society of Biblical Literature take practical steps to establish an "American School of Oriental Studies in Palestine." In the course of his remarks he (Thayer 1895:16) said:

> But I am impatient to reach a suggestion which I will frankly confess has with me for the moment vastly more interest and attraction than any other: Is it not high time that an *American School for Oriental Study and Research* should be established in Palestine? This is no new idea. Others besides myself, no doubt, have been cherishing it as a secret hope for years . . . Indeed, so alluring are enterprises of this sort at present, so great their promise of usefulness alike to Biblical learning and missionary work, that—as you are aware—a French Catholic School of Biblical Studies has established itself already in Jerusalem. . . . Shall the countrymen of Robinson and Thomson, Lynch and Merrill, Eli Smith and

---

*Adapted from his book, *American Archaeology in the Mideast: A History of the American Schools of Oriental Research* (1983).

[1] This tribute was paid by William Albright, one of the leading and most influential Near Eastern scholars in the 20th century.

Van Dyck, look on unconcerned?[2] Shall a Society, organized for the express purpose of stimulating and diffusing a scholarly knowledge of the Sacred Word, remain seated with hands folded, taking no part or lot in the matter?

The proposed American School in Palestine became a reality in 1900 as a result of the financial support of 21 American universities, colleges, and theological schools. The constitution of ASOR stated:

(1) The main object of said School shall be to enable properly qualified persons to prosecute Biblical, linguistic, archæological, historical, and other kindred studies and researches under more favorable conditions than can be secured at a distance from the Holy Land.
(2) The School shall be open to duly qualified applicants of all races and both sexes, and shall be kept wholly free from obligations or preferences as respects any religious denomination or literary institution.

Charles Torrey of Yale University traveled to Jerusalem in 1900 to establish ASOR's first overseas institute. During his year as ASOR's pioneer director, Torrey launched the School's archaeological program by excavating a series of Phoenician rock-tombs at Sidon, the ancient capital of the Phoenicians on the Mediterranean coast.

From the turn of the century to the outbreak of World War I, annual directors oversaw the activities of the School in Jerusalem. Specialists in Near Eastern studies, several of whom were biblical scholars, devoted a great deal of time to the exploration of the land. Director Nathaniel Schmidt of Cornell University was one of the more venturesome explorers. In the spirit of William Lynch and with the same indomitable courage, Schmidt made a careful study of the Jordan River and the Dead Sea. He (Schmidt 1905:29–31) described the hazardous undertaking in these words:

But I had long cherished a desire to circumnavigate the salt lake of Syria [the Dead Sea], in order to explore a part of the eastern coast never visited in modern times, and to seek fresh light on some recently discussed questions concerning the white line [a belt of foam stretching

[2] The Americans mentioned in Thayer's address knew Palestine intimately. William Thomson, a missionary who lived in Palestine for almost 50 years, accompanied Robinson on the latter part of his second journey through the Holy Land in 1852. William Lynch of the United States Navy directed an important expedition to the Dead Sea and the Jordan River. Selah Merrill participated in the exploration and mapping of Transjordan. Eli Smith was the chief traveling companion of Robinson on his journeys through the Holy Land. Henry Van Dyck served as interpreter, companion, and assistant to Merrill in his exploration of Transjordan.

across the entire lake], the currents, the bottom, and the beaches . . .
and on the 21st of February [1905] we floated down the Jordan. Our
boat, the *Dagmar*, was about 16 feet long, had four seats, a sail, a pair of
oars, and a good keel. We had supplies, consisting of bread, canned
meats and fish, potatoes, rice, oats, sugar, figs, oranges, nuts, tea, and
Jordan water, sufficient for three weeks. . . . In order to be able to
examine the coast and photograph its most characteristic features, we
did not sail or row after dark, but camped every night on the shore, each
keeping watch for two or three hours, while the others slept.

While serving as director of the School in Jerusalem in 1906–07,
David Lyon of Harvard University obtained permission from the Turkish government for Harvard to excavate ancient Samaria near the modern village of Sebasṭiyeh, which preserves the name Sebaste, the
Herodian designation of the site. Rebuilding Samaria in 30 B.C., Herod
the Great changed its name to Sebaste in honor of his patron, the
emperor Caesar Augustus. (*Sebastos* in Greek is the equivalent of *Augustus* in Latin.) Samaria was the first dig conducted in Palestine under
American auspices; in 1909–10, George Reisner, Clarence Fisher, and
David Lyon directed this project.

Reisner was a distinguished scholar who did most of his archaeological field work in Egypt, where he concentrated on the pyramids at
Gizeh, excavating there until the outbreak of World War II. Although he
spent almost his entire professional life in the field, Reisner also found
time to be professor of Egyptology at Harvard and curator of the
Egyptian collection at the Museum of Fine Arts in Boston.

Reisner played a major role in setting the standards for excavation in
Egypt, where he established a meticulous recording and classification
system. A pioneer in archaeological method, Reisner's great contribution
to the discipline was the debris-layer technique of digging which he
developed in Egypt. This technique consists of separating the occupational layers of superimposed strata of a mound, much the same way one
distinguishes the layers of a cake, while noting carefully the location of
artifacts. When Reisner introduced his excavation method, recording
system, and organizational structure at the Samaria dig, a new day had
dawned for Palestinian archaeology; it marked the beginning of systematic excavation in Palestine.

All succeeding Palestinian archaeologists profited from Reisner's
field methods and expressed admiration for his work. Albright considered him to be "the father of the field methods which revolutionized the
practice of Palestinian archaeology," while G. Ernest Wright, another
leading archaeologist, looked upon him as "one of the greatest geniuses
which field archaeology has produced in modern times." In the evaluation of field techniques before World War I, Flinders Petrie's name must

be included with Reisner's. Petrie certainly made an important contribution to archaeology, but Reisner went beyond him.

Clarence Fisher, an architect from the University of Pennsylvania, also played a key role in the development of field method for Palestinian archaeology. Before joining Reisner at the Samaria dig, Fisher had served on the American excavation at Nippur, a major Sumerian site ca. 160 km south of Baghdad in Iraq. Begun in 1888, the Nippur project was the first American dig undertaken in the Near East.

Reisner's influence on Palestinian archaeology was channeled through Fisher, who spent his entire adult life in Palestine. Reisner himself dug only at Samaria in Palestine and then returned to Egypt after World War I to continue his field work. Fisher's careful application of Reisner's technique of digging and recording resulted in the coinage of the term "Reisner-Fisher method." Between the two World Wars Fisher directed or participated in almost every American dig in Palestine; he also coordinated the results of all field projects as a first attempt to establish the chronology of ancient Palestine.

The first American excavation after World War I was initiated by Clarence Fisher when, in 1921, he undertook a large-scale dig at Tell el-Ḥuṣn. This strategic and imposing site, ca. 24 km south of the Sea of Galilee at the foot of Mt. Gilboa, is identified as Beth-shan, to whose city wall the Philistines affixed the bodies of King Saul and his sons after their ignominious defeat in battle on Mt. Gilboa. In the course of ten campaigns, the excavators distinguished 18 occupation levels, dating from ca. 3500 B.C. to the early Arab period. Among the notable discoveries at Beth-shan was a succession of Egyptian temples of the Late Bronze Age, which the Philistines later transformed to suit their own worship.

The period between the Wars was a formative time in the history of Near Eastern archaeology. Having profited from the shortcomings of earlier digs through a process of experience, evaluation, reconsideration, and learning from other people's mistakes as well as their own, archaeologists were beginning to conduct their field projects in a more systematic manner and with greater awareness of the importance of pottery as a dating tool. As excavators paid more attention to the twin principles of stratigraphy and typology, archaeology gradually developed into a systematic discipline.

In the history of American archaeology in Palestine, William F. Albright was the scholar who played the leading role. Having pursued Near Eastern studies under Paul Haupt at Johns Hopkins University, Albright later succeeded his mentor at Hopkins, where he served as the Spence Professor of Semitic Languages from 1929 to 1958. Before assuming the Spence chair, Albright was the director of the Jerusalem School from 1920 to 1929, and again from 1933 to 1936.

Albright undertook his first dig in 1922 at Tel el-Ful, ca. 5 km north of Jerusalem. Identified by Robinson as biblical Gibeah, King Saul's capital, Tel el-Ful was one of the first sites investigated in Palestine when, in 1868, British army officer Charles Warren made soundings there on behalf of the Palestine Exploration Fund. Albright concentrated on the summit of the mound where the fortress had been situated; he also excavated on the eastern side of the tell, the location of an ancient village. Because of Albright's inexperience as a field archaeologist, some of his conclusions had to be corrected later; when compared with the limited quality of digging in that period Albright's work was impressive.[3]

Between 1926 and 1932, Albright directed four seasons of excavation at Tell Beit Mirsim, situated ca. 19 km to the southwest of Hebron on the edge of the Shephelah (the foothills of the central mountain range of Judah). Albright identified this site as Debir (originally called Kiriath-sepher), the largest Canaanite city south of Hebron. Several scholars reject Albright's identification of the site; they suggest instead that Debir is to be located at Khirbet Rabud, which seems to accord better with the biblical account of Debir's history. The Bible describes Debir as the west boundary of the tribe of Judah, located in the hill country; Khirbet Rabud fits that definition, but Tell Beit Mirsim is in the Shephelah.

Tell Beit Mirsim has been referred to as the "type-site" for the chronology of Palestine because Albright, building on the results of Petrie's fieldwork at Tell el-Ḥesi, northeast of Gaza, developed and refined the ceramic index for Palestine, especially in the second millennium B.C. By classifying the stylistic changes in potsherds, Albright constructed a ceramic typology, which he then correlated with the stratigraphy of the tell. Through a combination of stratigraphy, typology, and other means, he was able to assign relative dates to the occupational levels of Tell Beit Mirsim. In the excavation of Tell Beit Mirsim, Albright was fortunate to have the valuable assistance of Fisher as archaeological adviser and coordinator.

In addition to excavating, Albright undertook extensive explorations throughout Syria-Palestine. In 1924, he made a survey of the region adjacent to the Dead Sea; during this survey, his team rediscovered the remarkable site of Bab ed-Draʿ, a Bronze Age town and a mammoth cemetery adjoining, southeast of the Dead Sea. On the basis of surface pottery, Albright dated the site to the third millennium B.C. The pres-

---

[3] In 1964, Paul Lapp excavated at Tell el-Ful in order to check some of Albright's conclusions. Scholars have voiced some skepticism about Albright's dates for "Saul's fort"; they believed it should be dated to the Hellenistic period and not the Iron Age. Confirming Albright's identification of the fortress as Saul's, Lapp was favorably impressed with Albright's work at Tell el-Ful, especially when compared with techniques of other archaeologists excavating in Palestine in the 1920s and 1930s.

ence of a group of stone pillars (called *masseboth* in the Hebrew Bible) led him to the conclusion that Bab ed-Dra͑ was a holy place, the scene of annual pilgrimages. This extraordinary site has continued to occupy the attention of American archaeologists to the present.

One of the most distinguished scholars in the history of Near Eastern studies was the American Egyptologist, James Breasted, founder in 1919 of the Oriental Institute of the University of Chicago. At Chicago, Breasted held the first chair of Egyptology established in America. A leader in the field, he compiled a record of every known Egyptian hieroglyphic inscription. As an archaeologist Breasted led expeditions to Egypt and the Sudan and later organized the dig at the ancient town of Megiddo in Palestine and at the Persian capital of Persepolis in southwestern Iran.

In 1925, work began at Tell el-Mutesellim, the site of Megiddo, which guarded the pass at the entrance to the plain of Jezreel. Breasted intended to dig the entire mound layer-by-layer to bedrock, a herculean undertaking projected over a period of 25 years. At Breasted's request, Fisher served as director of the project during the initial seasons. From 1927 to 1935, Philip Guy directed the Megiddo excavations. A pioneer in aerial photography, he suspended an electrically-controlled plywood camera from a hydrogen balloon at Megiddo. Even today, despite developments in technology, photography by balloon is not outmoded. In some ways it is superior to photography by airplane or helicopter; a plane cannot zoom in close enough to provide the desired detail, and a helicopter, by stirring up clouds of dust, may disturb the artifacts.

Gordon Loud succeeded Guy as director of the Megiddo excavations, continuing in that position until 1939, when events leading to World War II brought the ambitious project to a close. The Chicago expedition identified more than 20 strata representing occupation from ca. 3300 to 300 B.C. As a result of later study of the stratigraphy of Tell el-Mutesellim, corrections had to be made in the chronology of the site.

Between 1926 and 1935, William Badé of the Pacific School of Religion directed five campaigns at Tell en-Nasbeh, ca. 13 km north of Jerusalem. It may be the site of Mizpah of Samuel, but this identification is only tentative. Following Fisher's method, Badé established that the predominant occupation of Tell en-Nasbeh fell between 1100 and 300 B.C. He uncovered the massive fortifications of the city and dated them to ca. 900 B.C.

Between 1928 and 1933, Elihu Grant of Haverford College directed five campaigns at the site of Beth-shemesh, identified with the modest mound called Tell er-Rumeileh, or ͑Ain Shems, and situated ca. 19 km west of Jerusalem. Grant's expedition established that the occupation of Beth-shemesh had extended from the Middle Bronze Age to Byzantine times, with the town flourishing between 1500 and 918 B.C. In preparing the multivolume publication of his results at Beth-shemesh, Grant was assisted by G. Ernest Wright, who was to become one of the leaders in Palestinian archaeology.

Several other excavations took place between World War I and II, some under American auspices, others by the British, French, and Germans. In 1931, Ovid Sellers of the McCormick Theological Seminary, with Albright as scientific adviser, directed a dig at the frontier city of Beth-zur. This site, ca. 6 km north of Hebron, is identified with modern Khirbet et-Ṭubeiqah. The most important period in the history of Beth-zur was the second century B.C., the era of the Maccabees, the sons of the priest Mattathias who revolted against the Seleucid kings because they were persecuting the Jews. Here Judas Maccabeus fought a great battle against Lysias, an officer of the Seleucid King Antiochus IV Epiphanes, and defeated him.

During the first campaign, the excavators were able to trace the history of the site with the aid of the pottery they unearthed. Albright observed that "since the pottery of Beth-zur is identical in type with that of Tell Beit Mirsim, where conditions of stratification are ideal, we were seldom in any doubt as to our dating." Sellers returned to Beth-zur in 1957 for a second campaign.

In 1934 Albright, with the assistance of James L. Kelso of the Pittsburgh-Xenia Theological Seminary, undertook a full-scale campaign at Bethel, which Edward Robinson had located at the modern village of Beitin, ten miles north of Jerusalem. Bethel was an important place of cult in biblical history; it was a well-known holy place in the patriarchal era, especially in connection with Abraham and Jacob. Albright reported that the 1934 season of digging had yielded important stratigraphical results, extending in time from the end of the third millennium to A.D. 69. Through the systematic excavation of Bethel and the other sites already mentioned, Albright was inductively developing the scientific discipline of Palestinian archaeology; each of these projects was contributing to the refinement of pottery chronology for the region. After a lapse of 20 years, Kelso returned to Bethel to continue the excavation.

Between the World Wars, the British were actively engaged in digging; by reexamining sites previously dug, they were attempting to clarify some inconclusive results of earlier excavations. John Garstang, director of the Department of Antiquities in Jerusalem under the British mandate, resumed the Jericho project at Tell es-Sulṭan where Sellin and Watzinger had dug at the beginning of the century. In this same period, John Crowfoot directed a new phase of excavation at Samaria (Sebasṭiyeh), the site of the first American dig in Palestine. Clarence Fisher's acting as adviser to the Crowfoot team provided continuity between the American and British campaigns at Samaria, despite the fact that 20 years had intervened. Perhaps more important, Katheleen

Kenyon, who was to emerge as one of the most distinguished Palestinian archaeologists, also participated in the British excavation of Samaria in the 1930s.

British archaeologist James Starkey directed six seasons of excavation at Tell ed-Duweir between 1932 and 1938; Albright's identification of the site as the ancient fortress-city of Lachish is generally accepted. Strategically located on the main route from Egypt to Hebron and central Palestine, Tell ed-Duweir was occupied from the Chalcolithic to the Hellenistic period.

During this same period, the Germans excavated at Tell Balaṭa, identified as biblical Shechem. Ernst Sellin, who had dug briefly at Tell Balaṭa in 1913–14, returned to the site for another campaign in 1926. From then until 1934, Sellin, Gabriel Welter, and Hans Steckeweh directed successive excavation seasons at this important city of central Palestine. Shechem became the subject of a full-scale American field project in the 1950s and 1960s.

In the 1930s, Judith Marquet-Krause of France directed three campaigns at et-Tell, a mound situated near ancient Bethel and identified as the biblical city of Ai. She concluded that the city flourished in the third millennium but remained unoccupied from about 2200 to 1200 B.C. Marquet-Krause's death in 1936 brought this project to an abrupt end. Et-Tell required further study to clarify both its identity and chronology; in 1964, Joseph A. Callaway, in whose honor this article is presented, reopened the excavations at the site in an effort to resolve these problems.

Nelson Glueck, whose scholarly career was profoundly shaped by Albright, was an American explorer of Palestine in the tradition of Edward Robinson. Glueck undertook monumental explorations of the previously unknown lands of Transjordan, the Negeb, and adjacent areas. Between 1932 and 1947, the mapping, photographing, and surveying of Moab, Ammon, and Edom consumed most of his time; Glueck explored the Negeb from 1952 to 1964. Unlike earlier explorers, Glueck had an extensive knowledge of pottery chronology, an asset which enabled him to determine quite accurately the periods of occupation of most sites.

Although several archaeologists have conducted more recent surveys of the vast areas covered by Glueck, his comprehensive geographical, historical, and demographic studies of the ancient kingdoms of Transjordan, especially the Nabataean civilization, have not been surpassed. Of course, the use of more sophisticated techniques in the present day has occasioned some revisions in Glueck's conclusions.

Glueck supplemented his explorations with the excavation of two sites in Transjordan: the ruins of a Nabataean temple at Khirbet et-Tannur, which shed light on the religion and culture of the Nabataeans, and Tell el-Kheleifeh, which Glueck identified initially as Solomon's seaport of Ezion-geber. That proposal is no longer accepted, and the location of Ezion-geber is still debated. Glueck's excavation techniques did not match his abilities as explorer and historical geographer.

One of the most electrifying events in Near Eastern archaeology was the discovery of the Dead Sea Scrolls, also known as the Qumran Scrolls, in the wilderness of Judah. In the winter of 1947, the Taamireh Bedouin, a tribe of seminomadic Arabs dwelling in the area between Bethlehem and the Dead Sea, happened upon scrolls, which had been secreted in a cave on the western shore of the Dead Sea. This discovery impelled a zealous search for additional caves in the vicinity of Qumran with the hope of locating more manuscripts; American archaeologists participated in these systematic and productive explorations. Almost 300 caves were examined; 11 yielded scrolls and inscribed fragments. While the professional archaeologists were conducting their inspection of caves at Qumran, the bedouin carried on clandestine investigations, discovering in 1952 the famous Cave Four. The richest of all the caves, it yielded fragments from about 400 manuscripts.

Valuable manuscripts have also turned up at Wadi Murabbaʿat, Khirbet Mird, Naḥal Ḥever, and Masada, all in the region of the Dead Sea. In addition, there have been discoveries at Wadi ed-Daliyeh, ca. 14 km north of Jericho. Of all the documents recovered, the oldest manuscripts are biblical; the remaining are sectarian writings.

G. Lankester Harding, a British archaeologist, and French archaeologist Roland de Vaux excavated the ruins of a fortified monastery at Qumran, a monastery which apparently housed the Essenes. This religious community of Jews was responsible for assembling the Qumran library, whose contents date from the third century B.C. to A.D. 68.

Several excavations under various national auspices took place in the period after World War II. In the 1950s, successive directors of the American School in Jerusalem conducted four campaigns at biblical Dibon (Dhiban), the capital of ancient Moab, ca. 64 km south of Amman, Jordan. The site was the famous find-spot of the Moabite Stone, the black basalt stele with an inscription commemorating the victories of Mesha, king of Moab, over Isarael ca. 850 B.C. The discovery of this stone in 1868 by F. A. Klein, a French missionary priest from Alsace, had been a fresh stimulus to explorers of the 19th century. The American excavations established that Dibon was settled from the Early Bronze Age through the Byzantine and Arab periods, with gaps in the Middle and Late Bronze Ages.

Tell Dothan, ca. 21 km north of Shechem, preserves the ruins of biblical Dothan, a city associated with the stories of Joseph and the prophet Elisha. From 1953 to 1964, Joseph Free conducted excavations at Dothan and recovered evidence of settlement extending from the end of the Chalcolithic period to the Mamluk era (A.D. 1250–1516), although not continuously. In 1959, Robert E. Cooley excavated an unusually rich tomb at the site; in addition to some 288 bodies, it yielded 3,200 ceramic and metal vessels dating from about 1400 to 1100 B.C. As well as illustrating the prosperity of the city of Dothan, the contents of this tomb will shed light on the political, cultural, and religious history of Palestine in LB II and Iron Age I.

The most important dig of this period was Kathleen Kenyon's expedition to Tell es-Sulṭan (OT Jericho); she directed the Jericho excavations from 1952 to 1958 on behalf of the British School of Archaeology. Several Americans had the opportunity to work with Kenyon at this site where they learned her field method firsthand. The Wheeler-Kenyon method, as it is called, has influenced practically every dig in Palestine. Mortimer Wheeler, distinguished and controversial British archaeologist who was Kenyon's teacher, developed a system known as debris analysis while digging at the Romano-British town of Verulamium (England) in the 1930s. Kenyon assisted Wheeler and also helped to improve the archaeological method which bears their names. The Wheeler-Kenyon method is often contrasted with the Reisner-Fisher techniques; in fact, they are more similar than dissimilar, the latter system anticipating the former by two decades in Palestine.

In the course of excavating Jericho, Kenyon ran a deep trench, but not in the crude manner of excavators before World War I. Her procedure was characterized by stratigraphic control and careful recording, as she dug the site in stratified layers, within 5-m squares. When this grid method of excavation is used, sections automatically occur on the four sides of the 5-m square. The section is the vertical surface that is exposed in the course of excavating squares plotted on a grid. The section of earth which is left standing is also known as a balk; Kenyon paid special attention to the drawing of sections.

G. Ernest Wright must be numbered among the leading American archaeologists after World War II. Trained at Johns Hopkins by Albright, Wright was a versatile scholar who distinguished himself in both biblical theology and biblical archaeology. The convergence of these two disciplines was central to his conception of biblical studies. Holding to the basic proposition that revelation comes through event, Wright understood biblical faith as rooted in history and saw as archaeology's task the recovery of the historical foundations of the Judaeo-Christian tradition.

In 1956, Wright of Harvard University undertook a full-scale excavation of Tell Balaṭa, ancient Shechem, in central Palestine. The site had been dug earlier under German auspices, but the problems of chronology remained unsolved and the reports unpublished. Wright considered Shechem the training ground for aspiring American archaeologists in the period after World War II. He wanted younger archae-ologists to learn how to dig according to the Reisner-Fisher technique, including the refinements developed by Kenyon at Samaria and Jericho, as well as Albright's emphasis on pottery. In fact, Wright created a new school of field archaeology at Shechem; almost every subsequent American excavation came under the direct or indirect influence of the Shechem project.

The excavators at Shechem uncovered 24 strata of occupation, the oldest dating to the Chalcolithic period (ca. 4000 B.C.). The frequent references to Shechem in the Bible indicates that this city played a central role in the history of the Israelites. In addition to Shechem's place in the patriarchal narratives of Genesis, other biblical books, especially Joshua, contain references to the city. Biblical allusions to Shechem, as well as the succession of temples discovered at the site, attest to its importance as a religious center. By combining literary evidence with the results of digging, scholars are clarifying the complex history of these Shechem sanctuaries.

Tell er-Ras, the northernmost peak of Mt. Gerizim, was the site of another important temple in the Shechem region; it was excavated as a satellite of the Tell Balaṭa (Shechem) project under the direction of Robert Bull of Drew University. At Tell er-Ras, he uncovered Hellenistic and Roman remains, including the foundations of a Greek-style temple. On the basis of numismatic and literary evidence, Bull concluded that the temple, dedicated to Zeus Hypsistos, had been erected by Emperor Hadrian in the 2nd century A.D. The Roman Zeus temple was constructed over the Samaritan sanctuary, an earlier edifice dating from 335–330 B.C., which the Hasmonean ruler John Hyrcanus destroyed in 128 B.C.

James Pritchard of the University of Pennsylvania was another prominent archaeologist of this period; he directed three important excavations—el-Jib, the site of biblical Gibeon; Tell es-Saidiyeh, often identified with Zarethan; finally Sarafand, the site of ancient Zarephath (Sarepta in Greek). Located ca. 9.5 km northwest of Jerusalem, Gibeon appears frequently in the Bible; the first reference is in Joshua, when the people of Gibeon secured by ruse a covenant of peace from the invading Israelites. Pritchard undertook the excavation of Gibeon between 1956 and 1962. During five seasons he made several important discoveries, notably the spectacular water system with its huge round pool and spiral staircase, carved from solid rock and dating to the 10th century B.C. Like Jerusalem, Hazor, Megiddo, and Gezer, Gibeon had the access to its waterworks completely within the bounds of the city wall. Such a protective system was especially important at time of enemy attack. Pritchard also gained an understanding of the wine industry of Gibeon; uncovering 63 wine cellars, he estimated that Gibeon could store about 25,000 gallons of wine. It was during the 8th and 7th centuries B.C. that Gibeon flourished because of its lucrative wine industry.

In 1964, Pritchard began the excavation of Tell es-Saidiyeh, which Glueck had tentatively identified as biblical Zarethan. An impressive site, it is a double mound situated midway between the Lake of Tiberias and the Dead Sea, ca. 1.5 km east of the Jordan River. Pritchard elected to excavate Saidiyeh because so little was known about the Jordan Valley. After four seasons of digging, the Six-Day War of 1967 brought Pritchard's work to a halt. Fortunately, he had already made several important discoveries, including a cemetery dating from the 13th to the 11th century B.C. One of the spectacular burials was that of an apparent noblewoman; her skeleton, adorned with jewelry of silver, gold, and carnelian, was surrounded with bronze vessels.

The presence of bronze objects at Tell es-Saidiyeh calls to mind a verse in the book of 1 Kings, which mentions the casting of bronze vessels in the vicinity of Zarethan and Succoth for use in the temple at Jerusalem (1 Kgs 7:46). It is significant that nearby Tell Deir ʿAllah is often identified with biblical Succoth, but the excavator of the site, H. J. Franken, does not agree.

After hostilities disrupted his dig at Tell es-Saidiyeh in Jordan, James Pritchard went to Lebanon in 1969 to select a site. At the time, Lebanon's political stability provided an ideal opportunity for field archaeology. Pritchard chose to dig at the modern fishing village of Sarafand, known in the Bible as Zarephath, situated on the Mediterranean coast midway between Tyre and Sidon. The identification of the site was confirmed when the excavators found a stone inscription in Greek reading "to the holy god of Sarepta" (the Greek form of Zarephath).

Joseph Callaway, numbered among the leading Palestinian archaeologists, had the benefit of digging with G. Ernest Wright at Shechem and with Kathleen Kenyon at Jerusalem. Between 1964 and 1972, Callaway led his own expedition to et-Tell, the site of biblical Ai. His intent was to complete excavation of this site, since Marquet-Krause's work lasted only three seasons before her death in 1936.

On the basis of a survey, Albright suggested in 1924 that et-Tell was the site of Ai. Some scholars question this identification, but Callaway accepts it for lack of a satisfactory alternative. Occupied in the Early Bronze Age from ca. 3100 to 2350 B.C., et-Tell was then destroyed and abandoned. After a gap of at least 1,100 years, it was resettled for a short time in the Iron Age I period (ca. 1220 to 1050 B.C.) before being abandoned permanently. Marquet-Krause and Callaway's failure to find evidence of Late Bronze Age occupation makes it difficult to reconcile the traditional date of the Israelite settlement in the Late Bronze Age (13th century B.C.) and Joshua's capture of Ai, as recounted in the book of Joshua, with this archaeological evidence. Marquet-Krause considered the biblical account to be legendary and without historical foundation. Callaway accepts the basic historicity of the book of Joshua but suggests that the reconstruction of the settlement of Palestine, which so far as Ai is concerned may have been embellished by the biblical author, needs to be modified.

The nature of the Israelite settlement in Canaan is one of the more perplexing problems in biblical history and has generated several hypotheses. Scholars have suggested three main models for the settlement: conquest, immigration, and revolt. With their own divergent accounts, the books of Joshua and Judges prepared the way for conflicting interpretations of the Israelite occupation of Canaan. For those like Albright who champion the conquest model, understood as the decisive military assault on the principal Canaanite cities, discrepancies between the biblical data and the archaeological evidence at Jericho, Ai, and Gibeon have raised problems.

One of the promising American archaeologists of Palestine was Paul Lapp; digging at Tell Balaṭa with Wright he demonstrated his competence as a stratigrapher and a ceramicist. Before his career was cut short by a drowning accident, Lapp led archaeological expeditions to seven sites on the West Bank and in Jordan. Among the most interesting was the dig at ʿAraq el-Emir in the Wadi es-Sir between the Jordan River and Amman. Lapp decided to dig this site with the hope of unearthing evidence to illuminate the Persian and Hellenistic periods, especially the ceramic chronology of these periods. In 1961, Lapp made a sounding at ʿAraq el-Emir in his attempt to date the construction of the monumental building known as the Qasr el-Abd ("Fortress of the Servant"). A second campaign in 1961 was followed by a final season in 1962. The most exciting find of the third season was a feline, sculptured on a megalith of mottled red-and-white dolomite and situated on the lowest course of the east wall of the Qasr; the mouth of this animal functioned as a water spout.

Lapp identified the Qasr as a Hellenistic-style temple, dating to the early 2nd century B.C. If the "temple interpretation" is correct, ʿAraq el-Emir would have served as a religious center for Jews disenchanted with the Jerusalem temple. However, the archaeological data do not conclusively support a "temple interpretation."

In this same period, Lapp made soundings at Tell er-Rumeith, a small mound situated east of the Jordan in Gilead, near the modern Syrian border. He chose to dig in the Gilead region, whose archaeological history was little known, in order to learn more about the Iron Age sequence of Syrian pottery. During an earlier survey of the region, Nelson Glueck had identified Tell er-Rumeith as the site of Ramoth-gilead, mentioned several times in the OT. This site is well known as the place where King Ahab of Northern Israel (ca. 869–850 B.C.) was fatally wounded in a battle fought against Syria in his attempt to recover the city.

In addition to Tell er-Rumeith, there are at least two other sites which may have been Ramoth-gilead: Ramtha on the Syrian border and the imposing Tell el-Ḥuṣn southeast of Irbid. Lapp did not feel that his excavations at Tell er-Rumeith settled the question of Ramoth-gilead's location, although he argued in his report that "the continuity of the name, the congruence of occupational history with that of the literary record, and its geographical position fit such an identification." However, the smallness of the site does militate against such an identification. Lapp's dig demonstrated that Tell er-Rumeith had been a small fortress, occupied for about two centuries before being destroyed by Tiglath-pileser III, king of Assyria, about 733 B.C.

In the spring of 1962, the Taamireh Bedouin, famous for the discovery of the Dead Sea Scrolls, unearthed 27 papyri in a limestone cave of Wadi ed-Daliyeh, a remote and rugged site ca. 14.5 km north of Jericho. The following year Lapp made soundings there to verify the location of these papyrus scrolls; he investigated four caves and recovered abundant pottery and fragmentary papyri. These materials, written in Aramaic, date from ca. 375 to 335 B.C. These important finds cast light on the fourth century B.C., an era not well known to historians of ancient Palestine.

Almost 60 years after Ernst Sellin completed his excavation of Taanach, ca. 8 km south of Megiddo, Lapp led a new expedition to the site. During the excavation, Lapp dated the earliest occupation of Taanach to the Early Bronze Age (ca. 2700–2400 B.C.); Sellin had associated the initial occupation of the site with the 15th to the 14th centuries. Lapp also succeeded in locating the city's defense walls, which Sellin had not found despite the long trenches he dug across the mound.

As a result of illegal excavations at Bab ed-Draʿ, Early Bronze Age pottery vessels appeared for sale in Jerusalem antiquities shops in the mid-1960s. Lapp knew it was necessary to undertake systematic excavation of the site. He devoted two seasons to digging the shaft tombs and the charnel houses and one season to excavating the town proper. Bab ed-Draʿ consisted of a town of mudbrick domestic structures that was surrounded by a defense wall dating to 2700 B.C. A huge cemetery with more than 20,000 tombs was located in the adjacent area. The town was occupied from 3100 to 2300 B.C., while the massive burial ground came into use as early as 3200 B.C. and continued to serve as a cemetery for over a thousand years. There might have been as many as 500,000 individual burials at the site.

Walter Rast and Thomas Schaub have been excavating at Bab ed-Draʿ since 1975; they are especially interested in determining the settlement patterns of the region from ca. 3200 to 2200 B.C. After four seasons of digging, the excavators have arrived at the following chronological breakdown: in EB IA (ca. 3200 B.C.) nomadic pastoralists used the site to bury their dead; in EB IB (ca. 3100 B.C.) people began to settle there permanently; in EB II–III (ca. 3000–2400 B.C.) an enormous wall was built around the city; in EB IV (ca. 2200 B.C) the settlers departed from this region.

In 1963, Lapp investigated the Dhahr Mirzbaneh cemetery, situated near the modern village of Mughayir, ca. 3 km west of Wadi ed-Dalieyh. He concentrated on excavating and recording the contents of about 30 shaft tombs dating to the MB I (ca. 2050–1900 B.C.). The burials in the Dhahr Mirzbaneh cemetery have raised questions about the identity of the community that buried its dead in such a remote region and about the cultic practices associated with the burials.

During the first decade of the present century, R. A. S. Macalister, an Irish archaeologist, excavated ancient Gezer/Tell Gezer, ca. 30 km northwest of Jerusalem. Functioning as the administrator, architect, and recorder, as was customary in those days, Macalister inevitably missed much; for example, he was able to identify only nine strata of occupation on the tell. In 1964, G. Ernest Wright undertook to dig Gezer anew; for the first season he served as field director and then relinquished the position to William Dever, assisted by H. Darrell Lance. Under their joint leadership, the first phase of the new excavations continued through 1971; the second phase was directed by Joe Seger. Among American projects in the Near East, Gezer was the first to introduce the interdisciplinary approach to field archaeology. When geologist Reuben Bullard joined the Gezer staff, he was the first of a variety of specialists (e.g., physical and cultural anthropologists, paleoethnobotanists, zoologists) who eventually became an integral part of practically all digs in the Near East.

Gezer was also one of the first training grounds for student volunteers. Previously, local laborers had been hired to move dirt; at Gezer, volunteers recruited from the United States and elsewhere not only performed the tasks of the laborers, but also assumed the more technical responsibilities. Through in-service training on the tell, volunteers gained some proficiency in all aspects of a dig. With lectures and seminars at the site supplementing the fieldwork, the educational dimension of the dig evolved into a professional field school. The volunteer system, utilized by Gezer and subsequent American digs, owes much to the pioneering efforts of Israeli archaeologist, Yigael Yadin, who introduced the concept at his dig on Masada, the mountain fortress of Herod the Great. Volunteerism is an ideal way of producing the archaeologists of the future; several graduates of the Gezer program have advanced to staff positions on digs in Israel, Jordan, and elsewhere, while others are now directing their own excavations.

Through Macalister's efforts Gezer was the first Palestinian tell to be dug on a large scale; he excavated 60 percent of the 30-acre mound to bedrock. Although Dever dug less than two percent of the mound, he identified 26 separate strata ranging from Chalcolithic to post-Byzantine. Occupation at Gezer extended from late Chalcolithic to the Roman and Byzantine periods, but not continuously; in EB III–IV and MB I (ca. 2500–1900 B.C.) the site was abandoned. In MB II (ca. 1900–1550 B.C.) Gezer reached its height as a Canaanite city state; it was a time of prosperity and new construction. From this period date both the massive defense wall encircling the city and Macalister's "high place," consisting of ten pillars or standing stones, which Dever designated as an "open-air sanctuary."

Tell Ḥesban is located about ca. 24 km southwest of Amman in Jordan and is probably the Heshbon mentioned by Isaiah and Jeremiah in the oracles against Moab. Tell Ḥesban was traditionally thought to be the site of the Moabite city that Sihon, king of the Amorites, conquered and made his capital; he was defeated in turn by the invading Israelites when he opposed their proposed passage through his territory. The Andrews University team under the direction of Siegfried Horn and Lawrence Geraty excavated Ḥesban in order to answer questions about the early history of Jordan, especially the Israelite conquest and settlement, events that continue to perplex biblical historians.

Excavations at Tell Ḥesban revealed that the occupational history of the site included 26 strata, extending from the beginning of the Iron Age I period (ca. 1200 B.C.) to Mamluk times (ca. A.D. 1500). The absence of Late Bronze Age remains casts doubt on the identification of the tell with the capital city of King Sihon. The royal city may, in fact, have been located at nearby Tell Jalul, one of the largest mounds in Jordan; it had been occupied throughout the Bronze Age and in the Iron Age. In association with the excavations at Tell Ḥesban, the archaeologists conducted a regional survey, which embraced more than 125 sites within a radius of ca. 10 km of the main tell.

The Ḥesban project has been a model of interdisciplinary research. Its inquiry into questions dealing with the occupational history and the environment of central Jordan has led to an understanding of the cultural development of the region, starting in the Iron Age. Scientific archaeology in the land east of the Jordan River owes much to the pioneering efforts of the Ḥesban expedition; this was the first large-scale, interdisciplinary undertaking in Jordan. The comprehensive environmental studies at Ḥesban included work on the climate, geology, soil, hydrology, phytogeography (i.e., the biogeography of plants), and zoogeography. The Ḥesban dig also pioneered methods and procedures for processing large quantities of animal remains.

Ḥesban was the first expedition to introduce ethnoarchaeology, the ethnographic study of material and social life in the present for the purpose of aiding integration of evidence from the past. The Ḥesban team also led in the use of the computer for processing data from a dig. Ḥesban has served as the training school for many of American graduate students, a number of whom now direct their own field projects. In addition, several native Jordanian archaeologists received their initial field training at Tell Ḥesban.

The Jordanian Department of Antiquities, which was established in 1924, has played an important role in shaping the archaeology east of the Jordan. In the early days of the Department, George Horsfield and, afterward, Lankester Harding served as directors; both were active excavators. In addition to establishing the *Annual of the Department of Antiquities of Jordon,* Harding founded the Jordan Archaeological Museum in Amman. Completed in 1951, the museum is located on the ancient Citadel of Amman and incorporates the Roman, Byzantine, and Arab remains of the Citadel. The native Jordanian directors of the Department of Antiquities have not only encouraged Americans to work in Jordan, but have also been supportive of their efforts by supplying labor and equipment and in countless other ways.

Several Americans have made significant contributions to the archaeology of Jordan, but one stands above the others: James Sauer. He established a reputation as a ceramicist with his publication of Tell Ḥesban's pottery typology, extending from the Roman period to about A.D. 500. Before this study appeared, the post-NT era was the archaeologists' greatest dark age. In addition to his own survey of the East Jordan Valley, Sauer has assisted many other American archaeologists with their surveys, especially by identifying the potsherds collected during survey.

In the 1970s, American archaeologists conducted a number of regional surveys in Jordan; they were undertaken to shed light on obscure chronological periods and to provide a comprehensive view of the land east of the Jordan River. In association with the Bab ed-Draᶜ dig, the excavators conducted a survey of the isolated southeast plain of the Dead Sea, including four sites which bear resemblance to Bab ed-Draᶜ: Numeira, Safi, Feifa, and Khanazir.

Thomas Parker is carrying on a topographic and ceramic survey of the *limes arabicus,* the elaborate system of fortifications that the Romans developed along the edge of the Syrian desert. Composed of camps, forts, and watchtowers linked by the Roman road system, it served as a buffer between the nomads of the desert and the sedentary population of Syria-Palestine. This project will illuminate the history of the Roman army in Arabia and of the Arabs before the birth of Islam. David Graf surveyed Nabatean-Roman military sites in the Hisma Desert of southern Jordan to learn more about the defensive system in that era by focusing on forts, watchtowers, and caravansaries. Graf's concentration on the southern section of the defensive system complemented Parker's *limes arabicus* survey. Donald Henry is engaged in a long-term study of prehistoric sites in southern Jordan, where he is concentrating on the Ras en-Naqb Basin. It is already clear from his study that Jordan is rich in prehistoric remains.

J. Maxwell Miller of Emory University launched his survey of the Central Moab region in 1978; he has added to the evidence for occupation in Moab during the Late Bronze Age (1550–1200 B.C.). Burton MacDonald has conducted a survey in the Wadi el-Ḥesa. In biblical times, the Wadi el-Ḥesa, identified with the Valley of Zered, was the boundary between the kingdom of Moab and the kingdom of Edom. MacDonald found evidence of occupation extending from 500,000 B.C. to the end of the Ottoman Empire (A.D. 1918). David McCreery directed an archaeological survey of the southern Ghor or Rift Valley and the Arabah, moving south from the Dead Sea to the Gulf of ʿAqaba.

As these surveys continue, the archaeological outline of the land east of the Jordan will be filled in. Although much has already been done, regional surveys must continue. The archaeologists are competing with the modern development of the country; unless they complete their work soon, archaeological evidence will have been lost forever as new roads and other developments obliterate the ancient sites.

G. Ernest Wright was not content simply to conduct his own excavation at Shechem; he also prepared younger archaeologists to become dig directors. In the process he did not hesitate to point out the sites that would profit most from excavation or reexcavation. At Wright's initiative, the Tell el-Ḥesi expedition took to the field in 1970; John Worrell and Lawrence Toombs served as directors of the long-term project. Located midway between Ashdod and Beer-sheba, Ḥesi is the 37 acre mound where Flinders Petrie dug 80 years earlier, conducting there the first systematic excavation in Palestine. Although Petrie and Frederick Bliss made great progress in laying the foundations for stratigraphy and typology, questions about the history of Tell el-Ḥesi and other issues remained to be answered.

Ḥesi's occupational history extended from the Early Bronze Age to the Roman period. The Petrie-Bliss dating of the Late Bronze Age and subsequent periods was quite accurate, but their chronology for the earlier periods was too low. Their identification of Ḥesi as ancient Lachish has been disproved by Albright; his suggestion that Ḥesi is the site of ancient Eglon, a Canaanite royal city that fell to the Israelites during the conquest, is only plausible.

The Ḥesi dig is clarifying several obscure periods in the history of Palestine, notably the Persian period. In Persian times, the Ḥesi acropolis was a large grain storage area. Lawrence Stager accounted for the subterranean pits from the Persian period at Ḥesi and neighboring sites as storage facilities in seasons of bountiful harvest.

Tell el-Ḥesi is one of the largest Early Bronze sites in Palestine. In digging the lower city at Ḥesi, where they have already uncovered the massive defensive wall and glacis of EB III (2800-2400 B.C.), the excavators are shedding light on an important era in Palestinian history. This period is of special interest today in view of the recent discovery of a royal archive at Tell Mardikh, the site of ancient Ebla in northern Syria. By coordinating sites in Syria-Palestine with Early Bronze Age remains throughout the Near East, archaeologists will be able to construct a comprehensive picture of the third millennium B.C. in that part of the world.

Tell Jemmeh, located about six miles south of Gaza, resembles Tell el-Ḥesi in many ways. Separated from Ḥesi by only 32 km, Jemmeh also bears the remains of large grain storage areas of the Persian period. Gus Van Beek of the Smithsonian Institution, the excavator of Jemmeh, uncovered a well-preserved building with barrel vaults; constructed of mudbrick, it is the only example of its kind thus far found in Israel. According to Van Beek, this structure may have served as the residence of the Assyrian military governor of that district after Esarhaddon, king of Assyria and Babylonia (680-669 B.C.), conquered Arṣa (Yurza) in 679 B.C. Before his conquest of Egypt in 671 B.C., Esarhaddon probably used the site of Tell Jemmeh as a staging ground for his campaigns against Egypt.

With the encouragement of G. Ernest Wright and others, American archaeologists are excavating sites related to early Judaism, the beginnings of Christianity, and classical Graeco-Roman antiquity. A team under the direction of Eric Meyers of Duke University has been systematically investigating synagogues in Upper Galilee since 1970; they have also been conducting a survey in association with the excavations. The project began at Khirbet Shemaʿ, where the Americans uncovered the first broadhouse synagogue to come to light in Galilee. A synagogue of this type has its focal point situated on the long rather than the short wall; traditionally the short wall was the sacred wall. The scientific significance of this project lies in the fact that the synagogue at Khirbet Shemaʿ was the first to be dated through excavation, that is, on the basis of sealed pottery and coins found beneath the synagogue floor.

Meyers also excavated the Meiron synagogue, a standard basilica-type synagogue; it is rectangular in shape and has two rows of columns running the length of the room and dividing the structure into a nave and two side aisles. Gush Halav and Khirbet en-Nabratein were also the subjects of archaeological investigation. At Nabratein, the archaeologists recovered a portion of the *aedicula* or Torah shrine, dating to the third century A.D. The excavators described the Torah shrine as a pediment featuring rampant lions; it had been the uppermost part of the niche that functioned as the repository for the Torah scrolls in the synagogue.

The combination of regional survey and excavation of synagogue sites is shedding much light on several aspects of Jewish life in Galilee before the Arab conquest of A.D. 634. When the Romans destroyed the Jerusalem Temple in A.D. 70, Galilee became the center of Jewish life and scholarship in Palestine. That situation prevailed until the accession in A.D. 527 of the emperor Justinian the Great, who persecuted the Jews. With the Arab conquest, Galilee became a deprived region and the Jewish presence came to an end.

Robert Smith of the College of Wooster and J. Basil Hennessy of the University of Sydney have been digging at Pella in Jordan. Pella served as a refuge for Christians fleeing Jerusalem at the beginning of the Jewish revolt against Rome in A.D. 66. Occupation of Pella extended almost continuously from the third millennium to the late medieval period, although Pella was never rebuilt after the earthquake of A.D. 747. Its long history notwithstanding, Pella is best known as a Graeco-Roman city.

Robert Bull has been excavating at Caesarea Maritima on the Mediterranean coast. This 8,000-acre site, built by Herod the Great to honor his patron Caesar Augustus, served as the capital of Syria-Palestine for over 600 years. Bull has made important discoveries through architectural survey and excavation of the site. Having recovered the original city plan, he has been able to locate the *cardo maximus*, the main north-south road, as well as the *decumani* or side streets. The first Mithraeum ever found in Roman Palestine was unearthed in one of the barrel-vault warehouses in the vicinity of the Caesarea harbor. Roman soldiers had used this sanctuary, dating from the late third and early fourth century A.D., for the worship of Mithra, an ancient Persian warrior-deity of light and truth; the soldiers had become acquainted with this cult during their forays in the East.

In the 1980s, there has been a renewed interest in the Philistines on the part of American archaeologists. Major digs are underway at Ashkelon and Ekron, two major centers of the Philistine pentapolis. The city of Ashkelon, one of the most important seaports in the eastern Mediterranean, is being excavated by Lawrence E. Stager of Harvard University. Ekron (Tel Miqne), one of the largest Iron Age sites in Israel, is being dug under the joint directorship of of S. Gitin of the Albright Institute and Trude Dothan of The Hebrew University, Jerusalem. These long-term projects will certainly clarify the history, culture, and language of the Sea Peoples, including the Philistines.

Limitation of space does not allow for a complete survey of excavations in the Near East under American auspices. Those described in this article have been chosen as typical of fieldwork conducted by American archaeologists during the present century. Much has been accomplished, but the work has just begun.

BIBLIOGRAPHY

King, P. J.
1975   The American Archaeological Heritage in the Near East. *BASOR* 217: 55–65.

1983a   *American Archaeology in the Mideast: A History of the American Schools of Oriental Research.* Philadelphia: ASOR.

1983b   Edward Robinson: Biblical Scholar. *BA* 46: 230–32.

1984   ASOR at 85. *BA* 47: 197–205.

Schmidt, N.
1905   Report of the Director. *AJA* Second Series, Supplement 9: 29–31.

Thayer, J. H.
1895   The Historical Element in the New Testament. *JBL* 14: 1–18.

Wright, G. E.
1970   The Phenomenon of American Archaeology in the Near East. Pp. 3–40 in *Near Eastern Archaeology in the Twentieth Century: Essays in Honor of Nelson Glueck,* ed. J. A. Sanders. Garden City, NY: Doubleday.

3
BRITISH ARCHAEOLOGISTS

GRAHAM I. DAVIES
Cambridge University

It is the purpose of this essay to give a chronological outline of
British archaeological work in Palestine, particularly since 1900, and to
treat briefly some developments in archaeological method initiated by
British archaeologists there. If we discount the isolated and less than
scholarly diggings of Lady Hester Stanhope at Ashkelon in 1814
(Stanhope 1846, vol. 1:152–69), British involvement in excavations in
Palestine began with the work of Charles Warren in 1867–70. Working
under the auspices of the newly-formed Palestine Exploration Fund,
Warren and his companions had as their main task the investigation of
some problems in the topography of ancient Jerusalem, and their "shaft-
and-tunnel" method of excavation has become well known, not least
from the drawing which until recently appeared at the front of each
issue of the *Palestine Exploration Quarterly*. It was a technique borrowed
directly from the handbooks of military mining (Morrison 1871:56),
which is not surprising as the party was composed of Royal Engineers. Its
defects are now all too apparent, but it was tolerably well suited to the
limited aims of the expedition (chiefly surveying) and to the difficulties
of excavating in a built-up city and in the vicinity of holy places. Essentially the same technique was used 30 years later in Jerusalem by F. J.
Bliss and A. C. Dickie. In his 1868 excavations at Jericho, Warren used
methods at least superficially akin to those used today, with trenches and
deep probes at selected points (Conder and Kitchener 1883:224–26).

A period of 20 years elapsed before the next excavation of major
significance in the Holy Land. The PEF was preoccupied with the execu-
tion and publication of its great Survey of Western Palestine, and there
were no funds for other enterprises. But in 1890, the Fund secured the
services of W. M. Flinders Petrie, who had been surveying and excavating
in Egypt for the past decade, and in a six-week season at Tell el-Ḥesi in
the southern coastal plain of Palestine he brought to the Holy Land the
standards and methods of archaeological work which he had developed

so quickly in Egypt. His basic principles of determination of the stratigraphy, close attention to small finds, especially pottery, and prompt and detailed recording and publication opened the way to a truly historical archaeology (Petrie 1904). The work at Tell el-Ḥesi was continued (1891–93) by F. J. Bliss, an American employed by the PEF. It was established by *sondages* that the area to the west and south of the main mound had been settled in early times, contemporary with the lowest and earliest occupation on the mound itself. It is now known that this occupation belongs to the Early Bronze Age, a period in which many sites in Palestine were settled. The excavation of one quadrant of the mound to the virgin soil exposed the superimposed ruins of eight successive "cities," ranging in date from the Early Bronze Age to the Persian period, which enabled Bliss to paint an unusually vivid picture of archaeological remains in his popular account of the work (Bliss 1894).

The fruitful cooperation between the American scholar and the British organization continued for another eight years. On completion of the work at Tell el-Ḥesi, the PEF returned to the examination of Jerusalem and sent Bliss, accompanied by a Scottish architect, A. C. Dickie, to continue Warren's work south of the present Old City. A massive wall discovered by Warren (the "Ophel Wall") demonstrated that ancient Jerusalem extended beyond the Turkish walls, and further evidence of the southern fortifications had come to light in the researches of the Frenchman C. Clermont-Ganneau. Bliss and Dickie traced an artificial scarp, which apparently marked the line of an ancient wall, for 200 m to the south of the southwestern corner of the Old City, and then found that its line turned southeast for a further 110 m. From this point, one line of wall went northeast, apparently enclosing the summit of the western hill (now called Mt. Zion), while another continued to the east and eventually crossed the central valley between the western and southeastern hills in the form of a massive wall that was still quite well preserved. Bliss believed that this circuit of walls (which he thought linked up with that discovered by Warren to the north) had been built by Solomon, but his discussion is vitiated by the fact that it employs chiefly literary evidence and shows little sign of being informed by the archaeological techniques which had been applied at Tell el-Ḥesi. It is now clear that the walls in question are not earlier than the Maccabean period (second–first centuries B.C.). Like Warren, Bliss set out to map the natural rock surface in the area and showed that here too the valley between the two hills (the Tyropoeon Valley of Josephus) had once been much deeper than it is now. In the course of this work, he discovered various structures connected with the Pool of Siloam, some of which date to the NT period; he also discovered a later church, perhaps of the fifth century A.D., whose plan he drew with remarkable precision by tunneling under between 4 m and 7 m of debris. As a survey of ancient remains in Jerusalem there is no doubt that the expedition was a great success.

The next PEF excavation (1898–1900) took Bliss (with a new companion as architect, R. A. S. Macalister, a Celtic scholar) back to work on tells, this time in the low hills or Shephelah which lie between the Judaean hills and the coastal plain. Their particular aim was to locate the Philistine city of Gath. They excavated at four sites in an area south of Beth-shemesh ca. 12 km across, surveying remains visible on the surface and making, with one exception, only limited soundings in the mounds themselves. A good deal of pottery was found and recorded in their report in categories for Palestinian pottery which had been introduced by Petrie and were gradually being refined. Two of the sites produced a long sequence of finds, beginning in the Bronze Age and continuing through the Israelite period. These were Tell Zakariyeh (identified as Azekah), where the earliest remains were on the acropolis but three towers in the southwest suggested a larger settlement in the Roman or Byzantine period; and Tell eṣ-Ṣafi, which has often been identified with Gath, a conclusion which gains support from the quantity of Philistine pottery found in what Bliss called a "rubbish dump." At both sites fortification walls were traced which were thought to be those of Rehoboam's fortification of border cities (cf. 2 Chr 11:8–9). Recent studies have tended to date them a little later but still in the Iron Age. Numerous stamped jar-handles were also found bearing the Hebrew letters *lmlk* ("for the king") and a place-name. These occur at many sites in Judah and appear to reflect either a system of taxation or one for supplying outlying garrisons, from the time of Hezekiah.

At the other two sites some early remains were found, but the main finds were later. At Tell el-Judeideh an irregular wall with four gates at the cardinal points of the compass was found with a pair of square buildings of typical Hellenistic or Roman plan at the center; they looked as though they might be the headquarters of a local official. Tell Sandaḥannah is the site of ancient Mareshah/Marisa, which is mentioned a few times in the OT but was most important in the Hellenistic period as a (or even *the*) leading city of Idumaea. Bliss and Macalister cleared the whole summit to expose the final city, whose orderly street-plan is most interesting and reflects, as do several Greek inscriptions and other finds, the strongly Hellenized character of this city. Caves underneath the mound, some of which the expedition explored, had been used for a variety of purposes.

The relationship between Bliss and Macalister was in fact far from harmonious and there seem to have been complaints from London that Bliss did not produce results quickly enough (Silberman 1982:163–4; Tufnell 1965:126–7). As a result and much to the detriment of archaeological work in Palestine (Albright 1958:44), Bliss's services were not retained by the Fund, and Macalister alone was entrusted with the PEF's next excavation; this excavation was the larger and important site of Gezer (Tell Gezer), where Macalister worked from 1902 to 1909, with a break in 1906. It was the biggest excavation which the Fund (or anyone else in Palestine) had undertaken up to that time. Macalister's plan was grand in the extreme; he intended to work from one end of the tell to the other by excavating trenches across the whole breadth of the mound, disposing of the debris from each trench into the one previously excavated. Despite the scale on which he worked—he had up to 200 workers at any one time—he had only himself and an Egyptian foreman in charge; this led to imprecision in recording, a weakness all the more serious when the ancient levels were being explored a strip at a time. If good records are kept, it is possible to piece together the whole picture at the end, but Macalister's six plans are an unreliable hodgepodge of walls that are in some cases centuries apart. He was particularly bad at recording heights, and objects are not generally related to the places where they are found. In fact, he actually wrote that "the exact spot in the mound where any object chanced to lie is not generally of great importance" (cited in Dever 1976:434). In this he fell far below the standards set by Petrie. As a catalog of objects his reports retain some interest, but they are almost valueless for historical purposes.

Fortunately, Macalister did not excavate the whole mound—the presence of a cemetery and a Muslim shrine saved one area—and it has been possible more recently (1964–73) for an American expedition to salvage some evidence of the real history of the site. As a result, two of Macalister's finds can now be fitted into their proper historical context. The first is a row of eight standing stones (remains of two more were found), which are in a line running north-south. Macalister called it a "High Place" (i.e., an open-air Canaanite shrine) and suggested that the stones were examples of the "pillars" often condemned in prophetic and Deuteronomic passages in the OT. There is little doubt that he was correct about this, and the recent excavations have indicated a date for its construction at the end of the Middle Bronze Age. The other is a structure on the south side of the mound which Macalister called "the Maccabean castle." A Greek inscription found at the site mentions "the palace of Simon," probably Simon Maccabeus, who reigned from 142–134 B.C. (cf. 1 Macc 13:48). But in a brilliant conjecture based on a comparison with the Solomonic gates at Hazor and Megiddo, Y. Yadin proposed that it was one half of a city gate from the reign of Solomon (1958:80–86), and his reasoning was confirmed when the American expedition uncovered the other half of the gate, which Macalister had not touched, and showed that it had indeed been constructed in the tenth century B.C.

A return to a more disciplined method of excavation can be seen in the work of D. Mackenzie, who after initial work in Transjordan conducted three seasons of excavation at Tell er-Rumeileh/Beth-shemesh in 1911 and 1912. He traced the plan of what he called a Byzantine convent but was unable to find the expected adjacent church. He also followed fortification walls around the summit and found a city gate in the south. One of his most important discoveries was a large quantity of Philistine pottery, which was still poorly attested at that time. Much more extensive excavations were later carried out at this site by an American expedition in 1928–31 and 1933.

During the years 1909–11 a much less reputable, though very well financed, expedition was also in the field; its leader was Montague Parker. It appears to have been inspired by the hope of discovering treasure from Solomon's temple, but this aim was kept a secret at the time. In two seasons of work, tunnels explored by Warren in the Ophel ridge of Jerusalem, along with some other tunnels, were cleared of debris; in the closing stages, excavations were even begun—under cover of darkness—on the Temple Mount itself. When this sacrilege became known, Parker and his men made a hasty retreat and were lucky to escape with their lives. The episode is of lasting importance for only two reasons: (1) it was at this time that the Siloam tunnel was finally cleared of silt, a convenience for the local inhabitants and visitors alike; and (2) the work underground was observed by the noted French archaeologist, L. H. Vincent, who was able to make plans of the various water installations and to arrive at a reconstruction of their history (Silberman 1982:180–88; Vincent 1911).

The PEF did not undertake any further excavation between 1912 and the outbreak of World War I, but it did participate in a survey of the far south of Palestine (i.e., the Negeb) which rounded off what had been achieved in the great Survey of the 1870s. Its representatives were Leonard Woolley and T. E. Lawrence, and they explored and recorded the ruins of the Nabataean cities such as Subeita and Nessana, as well as an Iron Age fortress at ʿAin Qudeirat, further south still, which has been thought to be the site of Kadesh-barnea (Woolley and Lawrence 1914).

After the War, when Palestine passed from Turkish rule into the control of a British Mandatory Government, even greater opportunities than before were opened up for British participation in archaeological work there, and indeed the period from 1920 to 1939 can be regarded as the high point of British activity in this field, at least as far as the area west of the Jordan is concerned. In 1919, a British School of Archaeology was established in Jerusalem on the model of the older Schools in Athens and Rome, largely through the generosity of Mr. (later Sir) Robert Mond, and a year later, with the help of the School, a Department of Antiquities was set up by the Government of Palestine (Myers

1939; Garstang 1922). Initially, these two institutions shared a common leadership (Professor J. Garstang, seconded by the University of Liverpool [1920–26], and W. J. T. Phythian-Adams [1920–24]), and important work was undertaken in conservation of ancient remains, the establishment of museums, and the maintenance of records. At this time, the PEF retained a strong hold on the planning of excavations, as can be seen in the work of Garstang and Phythian-Adams at Ashkelon and neighboring sites (1920–22) and in that of Macalister, J. G. Duncan, and J. W. Crowfoot in Jerusalem (Ophel) (1923–25, 1927–28). But gradually, as the new institutions became established, the PEF's active role in the field was diminished, although it has continued to the present day to be a financial sponsor and supporter of excavations, and it has provided in its public lectures a forum in which the results of archaeological expeditions can be made known and discussed.

A very important excavation of prehistoric remains was carried out under the auspices of the British School between 1925 and 1934 in three caves on the western side of Mt. Carmel, by F. Turville-Petre and Dorothy Garrod. The finds are from the palaeolithic period and, according to E. Wreschner, "give a most detailed conception of the world of prehistoric man, enabling us to draw numerous conclusions regarding the development of man—his material, religious and artistic culture—as well as the flora and fauna of the period and the modifications of them through climatic changes" (1975:290).

In 1926, Flinders Petrie, now 73 years of age, returned to Palestine to work for the British School of Archaeology in Egypt. He was encountering difficulties with the French authorities in Egypt but also wanted to widen his historical understanding of Egypt, especially of the 17th and 16th centuries B.C. when Egypt was ruled by the Hyksos, who were thought to have come from Palestine. He excavated at three sites in the southwestern corner of the country, probably getting the identification wrong in all three cases: Tell Jemmeh/"Gerar" (1926–27), Tell el-Far ʿah/"Beth-pelet" (1927–29) and Tell el-ʿAjjul/"Gaza" (1930–34). One of his most important contributions here was the training of some assistants who were to be very influential in the next generation of British archaeologists in Palestine, the so-called "Petrie's pups:" G. L. Harding, J. L. Starkey and Olga Tufnell (James 1979; Tufnell 1982).

Crowfoot had meanwhile become the Director of the British School (in 1927) after a career in Egypt and the Sudan, and in 1928 he began work at the Hellenistic and Roman-Byzantine site of Jerash, where remains of a splendor unusual for the Holy Land and more typical of the Aegean are now visible. Also in 1928, Garstang identified the site of Hazor and did some small-scale excavations, details of which were only published in Y. Yadin's account of his own much more extensive work at the site (1972:18–22).

In the early 1930s British archaeological research was progressing at a pace that has been unequalled before or since in the Holy Land. In addition to Petrie's last dig at Tell el-ʿAjjul, there were three major expeditions in the field at one and the same time, as well as others on a smaller scale. The sites were all of major importance and, while two had been excavated before, one was quite new. Garstang excavated from 1930 to 1936 at Tell es-Sulṭan/Jericho. The site had already been the object of a major excavation in 1907–9 by Austrian and German archaeologists, who had found two fortification systems, about whose date they disagreed, and some houses which they dated to the Late Bronze Age and the Israelite period. The problem of the city walls was one to which Garstang gave a lot of attention and, to his credit, he realized that trenches and vertical sections had an important part to play in solving it. But first we must note his discovery that the history of Jericho began much earlier than his predecessors had suspected, in the Neolithic period. Particularly in the northeast corner of the mound he found deep deposits of this early period of settled life, including houses, flint tools and weapons and, in the later levels, pottery; the stages by which this craft originated and developed could be traced through the Neolithic levels. Garstang thought that these remains were from between 4000 and 3000 B.C. Thereafter, Garstang identified two Early Bronze Age cities, one above the other; the earlier city had its own wall, and the later city had two parallel walls. In the Middle Bronze Age, a great earth rampart was thrown around the site, enlarging its area considerably; this was done at other sites in the same period, and Garstang thought these ramparts were the work of the Hyksos rulers of Egypt. Garstang recovered considerable evidence from Jericho's Middle Bronze Age tombs to indicate that this was a period of prosperity. After the destruction of this "Third City" ca. 1600 B.C., by the Egyptians according to Garstang, the city was rebuilt on a smaller scale; he identified buildings on the mound and pottery in some of the tombs belonging to the Late Bronze Age "Fourth City." More significantly, he attributed to this period two walls, which he took to be a double wall, at the edge of the mound. This city, he argued strongly, must have been destroyed soon after 1400 B.C. because no remains of a later date than Amenophis III were found in it, and Jericho was not mentioned in the extensive Amarna correspondence. After a minor settlement in the Late Bronze Age, there followed a gap in occupation of some 500 years before an Israelite settlement was established under Ahab (1 Kgs 16:34). All this appeared to tally well with the biblical references to Jericho, especially in the book of Joshua; the very walls that collapsed before Joshua appeared to have been found. Their collapse could be attributed to an earthquake, one of a series of seismic disturbances which could be cited as the cause of a succession of events described in the Bible, most particularly the drying up of the

Jordan (Joshua 3–4). These findings figured prominently in books about the OT and its reliability for a generation. Unfortunately, it is a construction largely founded on sand, and very little of it remains intact today (Bartlett 1982: 32–34; and below, p. 51).

The Joint Expedition to Samaria (1930–35) was directed by Crowfoot for the British School in Jerusalem and was the first Palestinian excavation in which Kathleen Kenyon took part. Like Jericho, it had been excavated before, in this case by an expedition from Harvard University (1908–10), who collaborated with the British School and the Hebrew University of Jerusalem in staging the new excavations. The Harvard expedition had found parts of the palaces of the Israelite kings—Samaria being the capital of the northern kingdom for most of its history—an important series of Hebrew inscriptions, probably tax receipts, known as the Samaria ostraca, and large later structures from the Hellenistic, Herodian and Roman periods (e.g., a theater and a temple to Augustus which was erected by Herod the Great). In Herod's time the city was given the title *Sebaste,* the "august" city, after the Greek form of the name Augustus, and this name still survives in the name of the adjacent Arab village of Sebastiyeh. The Joint Expedition uncovered further areas of the acropolis and paid especially careful attention to the distinction of strata, a task which was unusually difficult because of numerous robber trenches. It was, however, by this means possible to establish with greater certainty the succession into which the various fortification systems were to be fitted. Omri and Ahab, who built most of this acropolis, seem likely to have employed masons from Phoenicia, with which they enjoyed close relations. This is probably also the origin of a large number of ivory plaques found by the Joint Expedition (a few had been found by the Harvard expedition); ivory was used to decorate furniture and can be related to the biblical references to Ahab's "ivory palace" (1 Kgs 22:39) and the "beds of ivory" of the nobility in general (Amos 6:4). The plaques depict a variety of motifs from Near Eastern mythology and art, including a winged sphinx, the Egyptian goddesses Isis and Nephthys and the god Horus (Crowfoot and Crowfoot 1938). Quite apart from transgression of the second commandment, these carvings showed how cosmopolitan in culture, if not also in religion, the royal court at Samaria had become.

The third of this group of excavations was on a new site, Tell ed-Duweir in the Shephelah hills, which had in 1929 been proposed as the location of ancient Lachish by W. F. Albright. This identification was not at first universally accepted, at least in Germany, but in the light of the British excavations and those sponsored more recently by Tel Aviv University there is no real basis for doubt (Davies 1982:25–28; Davies 1985). The British excavations (1932–38) were directed by J. L. Starkey until he was brutally murdered in an ambush while on his way to Jerusalem in 1938; Starkey had worked with Petrie at Tell Jemmeh and Tell el-Far‘ah. The final stages of the work were supervised by C. H. Inge and G. L. Harding, who with Olga Tufnell took responsibility for the publication of the results. The expedition was independent of the usual British sponsors of excavations in Palestine and was financed by a group of private benefactors, including Sir Charles Marston, who also assisted Garstang's work at Jericho. Starkey's special interest was to discover the foreign contacts which had been most influential on Palestinian culture in the period before Greek influence became pronounced. Recognizing the need first to examine areas that could later be used for the dumping of debris, he began with the areas surrounding the mound, where a very large number of tombs were found; these tombs dated from the Early Bronze Age to the Iron Age, and from these much pottery and other evidence of daily life was extracted. The clearance of these cemeteries was one of the few things that Starkey completed and probably represents, for its time, the largest investigation of its kind in Palestine. In the first season, he also had two trenches ("sections") dug, which between them gave a clear indication of the history of the mound. The expedition concentrated its attention on the defenses, chiefly the walls and gates of the Iron Age, though it was realized that the mound owed its shape to a typical rampart-and-fosse construction from the Middle Bronze Age. Inside the city a massive stone structure was visible even before excavation began, and on it were found the remains of an official residence from the period of Persian domination. The base or podium itself proved to have been constructed in three stages by the kings of Judah, no doubt for palace buildings of their own.

Two further discoveries are of particular importance. First, in the defensive ditch at the foot of the mound, near the northwest corner, were found three superimposed temples of the Late Bronze Age, the so-called "Fosse Temples." The importance of these structures is twofold: (1) they provide evidence of Canaanite religion, perhaps of a sectarian or unofficial kind, in view of their position; and (2) they contained large quantities of pottery from three successive phases of the Late Bronze Age, the dating of which was approximately fixed by Egyptian scarabs also found there. The publication of this find (Tufnell, Inge, and Harding 1940) remains to this day a key work of reference for the development of Palestinian pottery in the Late Bronze Age. Second, in January of 1935, while working on a guardroom in the gate area, the excavators found a group of 18 inscribed potsherds or ostraca which proved, so far as they were legible, to be letters or lists of names in the ancient Hebrew script from the time of Jeremiah. Three more ostraca were found in 1937–38. The letters are apparently from a military outpost of Lachish and are addressed to a certain Ya'-ush, who was probably the commander of Lachish. They reflect the critical situation in Judah just before the final Babylonian attack in 588 B.C.

The excavations on the tell gave rise to a fierce controversy which has only recently been settled. Indeed, some would say that it has not been settled yet! While the stratum in which the main cache of inscriptions was found (Stratum II) is agreed to have been destroyed by the Babylonians, evidence was found of an earlier stratum (Stratum III) which had suffered an even more catastrophic destruction. The date of this was clearly in the later part of the Iron Age, and from about 1935 Starkey believed that it has fallen to the Babylonians in an earlier attack on the city in 597 B.C. This was also the view of Inge, who wrote the report on the final season's work, and later of Kenyon. But Tufnell (1953:55–56; 1959:90–105) dated this earlier destruction ca. 700 B.C., so that it could be connected with the Assyrian attack under Sennacherib, whose encampment at Lachish is mentioned in the Bible (2 Kgs 18:14–15) and who recorded his siege and capture of the city on reliefs in his palace at Nineveh. The recent excavations at the site by Tel Aviv University have made it practically certain that Tufnell is right, and this has become an important fixed point in the history of pottery styles in Judah in the period of the monarchy (Ussishkin 1977:28–60; compare Rainey 1975:47–60).

It is at this point appropriate to mention the excavations carried out by the Department of Antiquities of Palestine, which had an independent staff from 1927 and gradually increased the scope of its work, as is particularly indicated by the inauguration in 1931 of its own *Quarterly*. The senior officials were E. T. Richmond (Director 1927–37) and R. W. Hamilton (Chief Inspector 1931–38, Director 1938-48). Between 1930 and 1933, the Department's Field Archaeologist, C. N. Johns, directed excavations at the Crusader site of 'Athlit ("Pilgrims' Castle"), south of Haifa on the coast; the castle was begun in 1218 and survived until 1291, when the Latin Kingdom collapsed. The excavations concentrated on various areas of the town adjacent to the castle and identified fortifications, a church, stables, a bathhouse and a cemetery. There were signs of earlier occupation stretching back into the second millennium B.C. Not far away, on the other side of Haifa, Hamilton spent two seasons on the excavation of Tell Abu Hawam (1932–33). The site lies near the mouth of the river Kishon and seems to have been actually on the coast in antiquity, before the shoreline changed. This was a full-scale excavation, which shows an awareness of both the importance and the limitations of stratigraphical excavation (Hamilton 1935:1–2). Hamilton distinguished five main strata from the Late Bronze Age to the Hellenistic period. The prompt publication of reports on these extensive excavations is notable. In the following year, Johns began a series of excavations in Jerusalem, where the Department was naturally often engaged in relatively small-scale work. Johns was put to work in the medieval castle of Jerusalem, the Citadel, and he found, under the courtyard of the medieval building, a much older city wall and remnants of towers. Subsequent refinement of the work made it possible to assign the various phases of its construction to the Maccabean and Herodian periods, and it became an important piece of the complicated jigsaw puzzle of the history of Jerusalem's walls. Finally, we should mention that in 1935 one of the Department's Inspectors, D. C. Baramki, began the investigation of a ruin just north of Jericho known as Khirbet el-Mafjar; this work continued until 1948. The ruin turned out to be that of a desert palace of one of the Umayyad Caliphs, probably al-Walid (A.D. 743–44), though it is popularly known as "Hisham's Palace." The buildings on the site comprise the palace itself, arranged around a central courtyard, an open enclosure with an ornamental pool and fountain at the centre, a mosque and a splendid bathhouse, exquisitely decorated with mosaic floors, statues, and moldings of carved plaster.

In Transjordan, British officials also played an important role in the excavation and preservation of archaeological remains. The antiquities were in the charge of G. Horsfield (1924–36) and, subsequently, of G. L. Harding (1936–56). A small museum was established at Amman, and Horsfield was involved in repair work and excavations at Jerash, Petra and Jebel er-Ram. Harding, who had worked with Petrie and Starkey in Palestine, undertook many small investigations in Transjordan during his time as Director of Antiquities and developed a special interest in the pre-Islamic Arabian inscriptions of the country. But his hour of greatest glory came in the aftermath of the discovery of the Dead Sea Scrolls when, with R. de Vaux, he led the archaeological expedition to Khirbet Qumran; they excavated the buildings which were occupied by the community who wrote and studied the Scrolls, and it was conclusively shown that the documents originated in the centuries immediately preceding the birth of Christ and the first century A.D.

Before proceeding further with an account of British excavations in Palestine and Transjordan after World War I, it is necessary to go back to the years immediately preceding World War II to note the beginnings of a new institution which has come to stand alongside the Palestine Exploration Fund and the British School of Archaeology in Jerusalem. The Institute of Archaeology at London University was the brainchild of Mortimer Wheeler, in whose mind it had already taken shape as early as 1926 (Wheeler 1955:83–94; Hawkes 1982:122–43). Palestine actually played an important part in bringing his dream to fruition; he discovered about 1929 that the aging Flinders Petrie had similar, though less realistic, hopes of his own about a permanent home for the finds from Petrie's Palestinian digs. When Wheeler's first wife, Tessa, suddenly died in 1936, it was Kathleen Kenyon who took up the day-to-day administration of the embryonic Institute and, perhaps, did more than anyone to keep it alive during the first eleven years of its life (1937–48). Subsequently, she held the post of Lecturer in Palestinian Archaeology at the Institute (1948–62). One of her tasks was the cataloging of the Petrie collection, and in 1953 she arranged and wrote the catalog for a special exhibition at the Institute to commemorate the centenary of Petrie's birth.

In the late 1930s, following the conclusion of the work at Samaria, the British School of Archaeology in Jerusalem had plans for a new Archaeological Survey of Palestine; these plans were partly accomplished by P. L. O. Guy who became Director on Crowfoot's retirement in 1935. But the political problems of the time prevented extensive fieldwork, and the School also suffered serious financial problems in the mid-1930s. After World War II, the affairs of the School had virtually come to a standstill, but were revived in 1951 thanks to the securing of some Government funds by Mortimer Wheeler, who was then Secretary of the British Academy, and the interest of Kathleen Kenyon, who was appointed its Director, a post which she held until 1966 (Wheeler 1970:18–21; Hawkes 1982:284–85). The revival of the School was intimately connected with a proposal for renewed excavations and, after an investigation on the spot, it was decided to undertake a new campaign at Jericho. Garstang's work had made it plain that there was much to be learned there about the beginnings of settled occupation in the Middle East, but at the same time his conclusions about the date and manner of the Israelite capture of Jericho had been the subject of much discussion, particularly as more precision about the dating of Late Bronze Age pottery became possible (Kenyon 1951:101–38).

This is a suitable place to consider the contribution of Kathleen Kenyon to archaeological method, which was at least as important as any particular results of her excavations (Moorey 1979; 1982:20–35). To a certain degree, it was not an original contribution, but the transference to Palestine of a method that had already been developed in Europe. Kenyon was an early associate of Mortimer Wheeler; in fact, she learned her excavation technique from him at St. Alban's/Verulamium in England (1930–35), and it is common to speak of the "Wheeler-Kenyon" method of excavation. They were both trenchant in their criticism of the methods employed by Petrie, although they both recognized his pioneering achievement. For example, Wheeler wrote in 1954 (15–16):

> It is abundantly apparent that, between the technical standards of Petrie and those of his older contemporary Pitt Rivers [for whom Wheeler had immense admiration] there yawned a gulf into which two generations of

near Eastern archaeologists have in fact plunged to destruction. . . .
Those who have witnessed Palestinian excavation with a critical eye know
all too well how widespread and enduring has been the technical irre-
sponsibility of much of its direction throughout an active half-century.

Three particular criticisms of Petrie's work can be discerned:

1. His *conception of strata* was over-schematic and undifferentiated.
He seems to have believed that a tell was formed in tidy horizontal layers
with the later objects always lying above the earlier ones, so that a scale
could be drawn and calibrated to correlate elevation above sea-level with
specific dates. At the same time, as Kenyon pointed out, one of his strata
extended from the foundations of a building (with objects dating from
the time of its construction and before) to the debris formed by the
collapse or destruction of the building decades and perhaps centuries
later. His failure to distinguish between these phases of a stratum led to
great imprecision in interpretation. Kenyon also identified (1939:29–40;
1953:98–107) a number of factors which would disturb the simple
scheme of one layer lying on top of another: ground slope, pits, fills,
foundation trenches, and robber trenches.

2. There was inadequate *supervision* of the work of digging, which
was in the hands of an often very large force of workers who had no
appreciation of what scientific archaeology was about. Consequently,
much important information was never observed or recorded.

3. The weakness in recording was especially evident in the drawings
of *vertical sections,* which constitute a vital record of the way in which
various structures and surfaces are related. Wheeler wrote that Petrie's
sections "belong technically to the infancy of archaeology and were, in
fact, obsolete more than a century ago" (1954:16). This resulted from
Petrie's failure to link the strata of a site in a meaningful way. A section
should show "how all the various levels can be associated with the
contemporary walls, which thus can be dated from the contents of the
levels, even when structural evidence is lacking. Further, by linking up of
a whole series of sections, the plan and history of the whole site can
gradually be built up" (Kenyon 1939:34).

Clearly, if importance is attached to the drawing of such sections,
there must be skilled supervisors in each area and this is now generally
recognized. Extensive horizontal exposure is also excluded, since this will
leave vertical surfaces for drawing only at the edge of the area and not
where they are needed for the interpretation of the succession of strata
in and around each building. Great emphasis was therefore laid by
Kenyon, in practice as well as theory, on the digging of narrow trenches
across a mound, simply to gain two deep vertical surfaces where the
succession of strata could be observed and chronology accurately determined. Broader areas could be opened up by the use of a "grid" of

squares, with strips ("balks") left unexcavated between them, so that the stratification could be constantly observed.

Kenyon also wished to correlate small finds with structures in a way that has produced some criticism. For her, especially in her work at Samaria, the decisive deposits were those belonging to the period of construction of a building, the constructional fills and the foundation trenches. The latest objects in these deposits normally indicate the time when the building was erected. Others have laid greater stress on the objects found above the floors of buildings, which of course date from their destruction or abandonment and thus indicate the opposite limit of a building's lifetime. The result has been a heated controversy about the development of pottery and the history of certain sites in the Iron Age (Kenyon 1964:143–56). As far as excavation method is concerned (and that is all that we are dealing with here), there can be no right or wrong in this dispute, as both types of evidence have their own value, provided they are identified and interpreted correctly. Kenyon appears to have been more aware of this than her opponents.

The excavations at Jericho lasted for seven seasons (1952–58). Full reports on the excavated tombs were published by Kenyon (1960; 1965), and the stratigraphy of the tell is described by her in a volume completed after her death in 1978 by T. A. Holland, who was her assistant for a number of years (Kenyon 1981). The two final volumes of the report, containing the pottery type series, the pottery phases on the tell and various specialist reports, have also now been published (Kenyon and Holland 1982; 1983). The excavated areas can be divided into three main groups: (1) the tombs north and northwest of the tell; (2) three trenches through the slopes of the mound, in the north, west and south; and (3) areas of wider exposure, among which Area E in the north, where very early levels were reached, is of special importance. The excavations greatly increased the knowledge of Jericho's Neolithic inhabitants gained from Garstang's work. It was shown that Jericho had been surrounded by a city wall 1.8 m thick with at least one defensive tower at a time when pottery had not yet been invented (Pre-Pottery Neolithic A), a remarkable indication of the social organization and architectural skills which had been achieved. Kenyon was able to show that the beginnings of Neolithic Jericho were much older than Garstang had suspected; carbon-14 dates point to ca. 8300 B.C. for the first phase. The careful distinction of four separate stages of the Neolithic in a stratigraphical relationship has provided a rare key to the succession of cultural developments in these early times.

Kenyon's work also added much to knowledge of the Chalcolithic, Early Bronze and Middle Bronze cultures of Palestine. But it is for her clear identification and description of a culture, that seemed to her to fall outside these well-known categories that she will particularly be remembered. This is what she liked to call (taking up a term coined by J. H. Iliffe of the Palestine Department of Antiquities) the "Intermediate Early Bronze-Middle Bronze period," a culture which was chiefly evident at Jericho in tombs but which was also attested on the tell itself, between deposits of the Early Bronze Age and the Middle Bronze Age proper. As against the common tendency to refer to this period as "MB I" (or, in certain instances, EB IV) she insisted on its distinctiveness from the urban civilizations that preceded and followed it, in its pottery, burial customs and social organization, and she accepted the view that it was at this time that the Amorites settled in Palestine (1966:6–52; 1979: 119–147).[1]

Of especial interest to biblical scholars are the implications of Kenyon's work for the history of Jericho in the Late Bronze Age, the time when the arrival of the Israelites is to be placed and in which any archaeological evidence relating to Joshua's conquest must be sought. Negatively, her trenches showed that the walls of Garstang's "Fourth City," supposedly of the Late Bronze Age, were in fact overlaid by the Early Bronze-Middle Bronze strata, and must therefore be from the Early Bronze Age. Her work in Area H on the east side confirmed what she had written about Garstang's interpretation of the "Palace" before her excavations began (1951:101-38). She found only the slightest trace of Late Bronze occupation above the Middle Bronze destruction levels— some walls, a small area of floor, and the remains of an oven and a juglet on it. It was clear that most of the Late Bronze remains had been removed by weather erosion in antiquity, but even the pottery from tombs unearthed by the various expeditions gave no reason to think that Late Bronze Age Jericho existed outside the limits of the 14th century B.C., and no evidence at all existed to show that it was a walled city.

Two final points deserve to be made about this massive undertaking. The first is that it was, like other major expeditions of recent times (Hazor, Shechem, Gezer), a school of excavation technique as well as a research project, and several of those whose own excavations will be referred to later gained their first experience of excavation in Palestine on it. Secondly, the report represents the mature putting into practice of the principles of archaeological method for which Kenyon is famous, and provides as it were a test-bed on which they can be judged. No doubt one might look for further refinements in the Jerusalem report when it

---

[1] A greater degree of continuity with the earlier and later civilizations is affirmed by Prag (1974:69–116) and Tubb (1983:49–62). The excavations of Prag (a pupil of Kenyon) at Tell Iktanu in Jordan in 1966 provided an important range of stratified pottery from domestic areas which has been one of the key factors in the recent new appreciation of the character of this period and in particular of its links with the Early Bronze Age (Prag 1974:77–83, 97–9). The full report is expected to appear as a monograph of the British School of Archaeology in Jerusalem.

is published, but it will not take us so directly to the mind of the "great Sitt" herself, since her part in the writing of it will be minimal. In view of the mass of detail and drawings, particularly in *Jericho III*, it is the more important to note some remarks in the introduction to that volume. She refers to the "very minute examination of all excavated soil" in connection with the increased importance of ecologial studies, and the use of flotation apparatus and continues (Kenyon 1981:5):

> The use of this method should certainly be used [sic] in any future excavations, but one would hope only in a selective and commonsense way. There is so much in the way of basic history to be established in Palestine, and until this is much further advanced it would be a pity to get too bogged down in details.

There is a sense of proportion here, and an appetite for history, which should belie any suggestion that Kenyon was interested only in "dirt."

From 1961 to 1967 she was back in the field, with the excavations in Jerusalem. This undertaking was again sponsored by the British School in Jerusalem, but this time in conjunction with, for the first three years, the Ecole Biblique in Jerusalem, and from 1962 the Royal Ontario Museum. Numerous other institutions also contributed to the costs. Kenyon was joined in the direction of the work by R. de Vaux and A.D. Tushingham, and the large team of site supervisors again included several who have since become well-known archaeologists in their own right.[2] Excavation was carried out in a large number of separate areas, some of which were quite small, since they were located in between existing houses. It should also be remembered that the work was confined to areas then under Jordanian control. The main effort was concentrated in Area A on the eastern slope of Ophel, where a trench 53 m × 11 m was excavated from the crest of the hill down a slope of ca. 45°. The main purpose in opening this trench was to determine the line of the earliest walls of Jerusalem in this area. Fortifications already known on the crest of the slope had been dubbed Jebusite and Davidic by their excavator, Macalister. But there was a problem: the protected route of access to the spring known as Warren's Shaft was entered halfway down the slope. What was the point of digging a tunnel that did not provide access from inside the walls? Kenyon established that the fortifications at the top of the slope were not the earliest defenses of Jerusalem but date most probably from the Maccabean period. Almost at the bottom of the trench successive lines of fortifications were found, which were in use between the Middle Bronze Age and the end of the Israelite monarchy.

---

[2] Professor Callaway was a site supervisor in 1961 and 1962.

Since these walls lay below, and therefore outside, the upper entrance to the tunnel, the problem about the location of the latter was nicely solved. The trench also provided important information about a series of artificial terraces on the slope which were first constructed in the Late Bronze Age. These may be the "Millo" mentioned several times in the OT (e.g., 2 Sam 5:9). Apart from this, the main discovery of interest in Area A was a complex of walls associated with a cave, which Kenyon tentatively suggested might be an unofficial (and probably non-Yahwistic) cultplace of the Israelite period (Holland 1977:121–55).

The work in the other areas produced little in the way of structures and is chiefly important for the conclusions to which it led Kenyon about the extent of the walled city of Jerusalem at various stages of its history. In particular, it was her hope that careful stratigraphic excavation in small but well-chosen areas would resolve the longstanding "maximalist-minimalist" controversy about the extent of Jerusalem in OT times (Simons 1952:226–81). Kenyon's initial conclusions were as follows. Jebusite Jerusalem was limited to the southeastern hill and these limits remained unchanged under David. Solomon extended the city to the north to incorporate the site of the new temple and a space for his royal buildings. An additional strip on the eastern slopes was enclosed during the later monarchy, but the western hill remained unoccupied; soundings on its eastern slopes and in the central valley revealed no evidence of occupation until the first century A.D. In early postexilic times the eastern wall was withdrawn to the summit of the slope, but the Maccabees extended the city area by adding an artificial platform on the west of the southeastern hill and (as Johns' excavations in the Citadel had shown) by enclosing the northern part of the western hill. The "Second Wall" built by Herod the Great incorporated an area to the west of the temple area, and it was only under Herod Agrippa in the mid-first century A.D. that the whole of the western hill was included by the building of a wall in the far south, a wall traced by Bliss and Dickie. Aelia Capitolina, the new city of Hadrian, corresponded in extent almost exactly to the present Old City, but in the Byzantine period the southern limit was pushed out again to the "Bliss and Dickie" wall (Kenyon 1967:passim). This was, for the earlier periods at least, "minimalism" with a vengeance. Subsequently, in the light of Avigad's excavations in the Jewish Quarter and further study of strategic factors and evidence uncovered by Kenyon's predecessors, she modified her views about the extent of Jerusalem in the late monarchy and Maccabean periods (Kenyon 1974:148, 195–204). Even so, her position on both these issues remains distinctive. A major reason for this is her interpretation of the absence of building remains and occupation debris as an indication that the area in question was outside the contemporary city walls, an axiom which by no means all investigators have been willing to share. She was forced by it into a bold hypothesis that the pool of Siloam, which on her view would curiously lie outside the walls of the time when it was formed, was originally intended as an enclosed cistern within the natural rock (1967:71, 77; 1974:159). It is possible that this was the case, but it remains a conjecture. Kenyon's views about the lines of the "second" and "third" walls mentioned by Josephus (*JW* 5.4.2 §§146–155) are also controversial (and in the latter case difficult to reconcile with what Josephus says) but are based on precise archaeological evidence gained in her own excavations and those of Mrs. C. M. Bennett and J. B. Hennessy (Kenyon 1974:238–43, 251–54; Hennessy 1970:22–27; Hamrick, 1981:262–66). At the time of writing, no evidence has been found to show that Kenyon's modified position is wrong and that other hypotheses are correct. But much is based on inference and conjecture, and future excavations may, of course, produce new and decisive evidence.

The British School, the promoter of the excavations at Jericho and Jerusalem, was by these and other activities in the field firmly re-established as the major organ of British archaeological research in Palestine. In 1956 (with the help of an increased grant from the British Academy), it once again acquired its own building in Jerusalem, for the first time since 1926 (Kenyon 1957:97–100), and P. J. Parr (1956–62) and Mrs. Bennett (1962–65) became permanent, resident officers of the School, combining the duties of Secretary and Librarian. With the help of further increases in the Academy grant, this post was upgraded first to Deputy Director and then, in 1966, to Resident Director. It was held from 1965 to 1970 by J. B. Hennessy, an Australian. In 1967, the School moved to new premises in Sheikh Jarrah, and from 1969 younger scholars have been resident as Assistant Director.

In addition to his work at the Damascus Gate in Jerusalem, Hennessy directed three other excavations during his time at the School, each of quite short duration. In 1966, he made a fresh examination of the Late Bronze Age temple at Amman Airport, which had first been examined by Harding in 1955. Three stages of construction were distinguished, and its isolation from any settlement was confirmed. In the early part of the following year, Hennessy turned to Tuleilat et-Ghassul, the Chalcolithic site ca. 5 km north of the Dead Sea, where the Pontifical Biblical Institute had excavated in 1929–38 and 1960. Hennessy's primary purpose was to check the stratification of this important site, a task which proved exceptionally difficult because of earthquake damage. Nevertheless, he was able to distinguish nine strata in the area which he excavated. Further work in more recent years has produced pottery from the lowest levels, pottery which is similar to that of the Pottery Neolithic B period at Jericho and raises the possibility that the Ghassulian culture is a direct development from it (Kenyon 1979:55–57, 328). It also now seems that the small mounds which make up the site (the *tuleilat*) were originally a single mound, which was divided by erosion. Hennessy's final excavation for the School was at Samaria in 1968. His aim was to uncover some of the almost unknown lower city below the acropolis. Although the results were disappointing in four out of the five trenches which he opened, in one trench substantial remains were found close to the surface. The main periods of occupation attested were the Hellenistic and Early Roman, so that the existence (or at any rate the location) of an Iron Age lower city remains an unsolved enigma.

While Harding was still Director of Antiquities in Jordan, Parr and Miss D. Kirkbride (Mrs. Helbaek) had participated in conservation work initiated by the Jordanian Government at Petra and Jerash. In 1955–56, Miss Kirkbride undertook an excavation in the area of the Roman *cardo* at Petra, while Parr excavated at the Early Bronze site of Khirbet Iskander, a site located in the hills that rise above the eastern shore of the Dead Sea. Each then took charge of a major series of excavations in Transjordan which were, in fact, within a few miles of each other. In 1956, Miss Kirkbride discovered a low mound in Seyl Aqlats (Beidha) near Petra, and she directed excavations there for seven seasons (1958–67). Apart from Nabataean terrace walls, the remains are from the Mesolithic and Neolithic periods. The Neolithic remains correspond largely to those of the Pre-Pottery Neolithic B period at Jericho and provide important additions to our knowledge of these people, especially of the development of their architecture. In the final season, a retaining wall that may also have served a defensive purpose and a possible sanctuary were located. Mesolithic levels of the Lower Natufian culture were recorded in several areas.

Miss Kirkbride also contributed to Nabataean studies by her excavation of a first century A.D. temple at er-Ram in southern Jordan in 1959, but the major British effort in this area of research was Parr's series of excavations and other studies at Petra (1958–68). They were undertaken with the primary aim of establishing a dated sequence of stratified Nabataean pottery. The brightly-painted wares of the Nabataeans had been known since the years between the Wars, when they played a key role in Nelson Glueck's surveys. But little was known of the inner development and chronology of this pottery, and a careful excavation at Petra, the Nabataean capital, was the obvious way to seek this information. Moreover, the clearance and conservation work of earlier years had indicated that there were promising deposits in the vicinity of the main colonnaded street of the Roman period. Other aims were to find evidence of the earliest Nabataean settlement at Petra and to study the development of architecture in a particular area. All these aims were satisfactorily fulfilled in a trench dug at right angles to the main street (Parr 1968:348–81). The earliest settlement was shown to belong to the third (or possibly the fourth) century B.C., and a succession of levels and structures culminating in the (possibly late Nabataean rather than Roman) colonnaded street was identified. In addition, in the south a large Nabataean building of the first century A.D. was partly uncovered and provided further evidence of the development of pottery styles. Excavations in and around Qasr el-Bint, a Nabataean temple of the first century A.D., revealed important architectural features and provided new evidence for its history of construction. In the north, it was shown that the so-called "Conway High Place" was not a sacred site but a circular tower belonging to the early fortifications of Petra. Between 1964 and 1969 a new topographical map of the site was drawn by means of aerial photography and photogrammetric equipment made available by University College, London.

During the Petra excavations, Mrs. Bennett made a special study of Umm el-Biyyara, the flat-topped mountain which overlooks central Petra from the west and had been identified as the site of Edomite Sela (2 Kgs 14:7). In excavations conducted in 1960, 1963 and 1965, a number of rooms were uncovered, with no apparent break in occupation. They were built largely of flat stones of the local sandstone and contained evidence of weaving and other domestic activities. The small finds were of the late eighth and seventh centuries B.C., and this dating for the settlement was confirmed by the discovery of a seal-impression inscribed *lqwsg[br] // mlk ʾ[dm]*, "Of Qaws-gabri king of Edom," who is mentioned in inscriptions of Esarhaddon and Ashurbanipal of Assyria.

Mrs. Bennett later returned to the study of another Edomite site, in this case at Ṭawilan, located ca. 5 km east of Petra. Excavation in three main areas between 1968 and 1970 (and again in 1982) has shown that the Edomite occupation was limited to the eighth-sixth centuries B.C. Houses of this period, some more strongly built than others, were found in all three areas, and further additions were made to the corpus of Edomite pottery and other small finds. No fortifications were found, and the impression left is of a well-to-do agricultural settlement rather than a major capital city. The proposed identification with Teman has now been given up on other grounds (de Vaux 1969:379–85).

After taking over from Hennessy as Director of the British School in 1970, Mrs. Bennett turned to the excavation of what is very probably the site of the ancient Edomite capital city of Bozrah, at Buṣeirah in southern Jordan (1971–74). Even though the work was on a comparatively small scale, important conclusions about the layout of the site and its periods of occupation have been reached. In Iron Age II, the site, a spur which is naturally well-protected by steep slopes on three sides, was strongly fortified with a glacis and a defensive wall 3–4 m thick, which was traced round most of the perimeter. Near the southeastern end of this enclosure was an acropolis containing buildings of monumental proportions; some of the structures resemble the Assyrian "open court" buildings, and it was possible to assign them to two distinct phases. These buildings are of a kind previously unattested in Iron Age Transjordan.

On either side of these presumably public buildings, below the acropolis, were smaller, less well-built, complexes of houses which (it is presumed) were for the ordinary Edomite citizens. Some of this poorer occupation may go back to the end of the ninth century. Corresponding to the difference between the (royal?) buildings on the acropolis and the humbler dwellings below, there are two distinct traditions of pottery, one very finely painted and the other coarser and unpainted, and considerable quantities of both were found in the excavations.

It is not too much to say that Mrs. Bennett's three excavations at central Edomite sites have inaugurated a new stage in the archaeology of Edom, which had previously been based on surface surveys and Glueck's excavations at the important, but probably untypical, site of Tell el-Kheleifeh. Both Edomite history and Edomite culture have begun to be clarified by her work (Bartlett 1973:229–58). In particular, it appears from all three sites that settled occupation in Edom flourished only rather late in the Iron Age and that Glueck's statements about "Early Iron Age I–II pottery" Edom need to be treated with great caution, although at certain sites, mainly in northern Edom, occupation in Iron Age I is attested (Weippert 1979:29–30).

Meanwhile, the Jerusalem School was also involved as a sponsor in the very important excavations of S. Helms at Jawa in the "Black Desert" of Jordan (1973–75); his research has brought to light a short-lived but, for its age and position, remarkably large urban settlement of the fourth millennium B.C. Between 1975 and 1978, Mrs. Bennett took charge of rescue excavations on the Citadel at Amman; this work added significantly to knowledge of the Byzantine and early Islamic occupation of the city. These excavations were promoted and financed by the Jordanian Department of Antiquities. In 1978, she resigned from the Directorship of the Jerusalem School in order to take charge of the newly established British Institute at Amman for Archaeology and History. For some years the Jerusalem School had at her instigation maintained an office in Amman. The decision to upgrade this into a full-fledged Institute, which now has an entirely independent status, was a natural one in view of the current scope of British archaeological activity east of the Jordan. During Mrs. Bennett's brief tenure of the Directorship (she resigned at the end of 1982), it became a flourishing part of the archaeological community in Amman. In addition to her own continuing work, there have been a number of projects carried out with her help and guidance by younger scholars, especially from the Institute of Archaeology at London University.

West of the Jordan, the Jerusalem School (of which John Wilkinson became Director in 1979) has been occupied with a series of architectural surveys throughout the 1970s and work on these continues. A survey of medieval Islamic buildings in the Old City of Jerusalem was begun in 1968 (Walls 1974:25–50; 1975:39–76; 1977:168–73; Burgoyne 1971:1– 30; 1973:12–35; 1974:51–64). Since 1979, further projects on Byzantine and Crusader churches have been in progress (Wilkinson 1981:156–72; Pringle 1981:173–99; 1983:141–77). Another important development has been the founding of *Levant* in 1969, first as the journal of the Jerusalem School alone but since volume XII (1980), jointly sponsored by it and the British Institute at Amman.

This survey has revealed the important part played in British archaeological work in Palestine not only by some very distinguished individual archaeologists, among whom the names of Petrie and Kenyon stand out, but by the institutions which have provided the context of interest, continuity, and resources without which little could have been achieved. In the early years, the Palestine Exploration Fund alone carried this responsibility, but the years between the World Wars saw the birth of the British School in Jerusalem, the Department of Antiquities of Palestine, and the Institute of Archaeology at London University, as well as the involvement of the British School of Archaeology in Egypt in several projects in Palestine. Most recently, the British Institute in Amman has been founded. The contribution of each of these bodies and their respective officers could (and should) be much more thoroughly chronicled than has been possible here.

It is also possible to distinguish broadly three phases of British work in Palestine, which no doubt correspond at least partly to phases in the work carried out by other countries. The first and longest is what might be called the pioneering stage, in which many tells were opened up for the first time. Work of this kind was still continuing during the 1930s. But already then a second phase had begun, a phase dominated by Kenyon, in which the emphasis fell not so much on new discoveries as on the solving of problems raised by earlier excavations and the establishment of an accurate chronological framework. The discipline needed a phase of this kind and its indispensable companion, a highly refined stratigraphical method, if it was not to dissolve into a mere accumulation of finds and disparate interpretations. Kenyon's work, first under Crowfoot at Samaria and then in her own excavations at Jericho and Jerusalem, both established the need for such an approach and carried it through, and it has been continued by two of her close associates, Parr and Hennessy. But since about 1970, a new phase is discernible, a phase which represents a return to the pioneering approach of the first phase in the particular case of Jordan, where much new work remains to be done. A major impulse to this "new beginning" has been given by Mrs. Bennett, but it may be significant that most of those now involved represent a new generation of archaeologists who are too young to have worked on either of the great Kenyon excavations, and it is perhaps fitting that this work should be channeled through an Institute that is itself still less than five years old.

BIBLIOGRAPHY

Albright, W. F.
1958   Bliss, Frederick Jones. Pp. 44–45 in *Dictionary of American Biography*, eds. R. L. Schuyler and E. T. James, Vol. 22 (Supplement Two). London: Oxford University Press.

Avi-Yonah, M., and Stern, E., eds.
1975–78   *EAEHL*, vols. 1–4. Englewood Cliffs, NJ: Prentice-Hall.

Bartlett, J. R.
1973   The Moabites and the Edomites. Pp. 229–258 in *Peoples of Old Testament Times*. ed. D. J. Wiseman. Oxford: Clarendon.
1982   *Jericho*. Cities of the Biblical World. Grand Rapids: Eerdmans.

Besant, W.
1886   *Twenty-One Years' Work in the Holy Land*. London: PEF.
1895   *Thirty Years' Work in the Holy Land*. London: PEF.

Bliss, F. J.
1894   *A Mound of Many Cities or Tell el Hesy Excavated*. London: PEF.

Burgoyne, M. H.
1971   Some Mamelūke Doorways in the Old City of Jerusalem. *Levant* 3: 1–30.
1973   Ṭarīq Bāb al-Ḥadīd—a Mamlūk Street in the Old City of Jerusalem. *Levant* 5: 12–35.
1974   The Continued Survey of the Ribāṭ Kurd/Madrasa Jawhariyya Complex in Ṭarīq Bāb al-Ḥadīd. *Levant* 6:51–64.

Callaway, J. A.
     Sir Flinders Petrie: Father of Palestinian Archaeology. *BAR* 6/6: 44–55.

Conder, C. R., and Kitchener, H. H.
1883   *The Survey of Western Palestine. Memoirs of the Topography, Orography, Hydrography and Archaeology*. Vol. 3 Judaea. London: PEF.

Crowfoot, J. W., and Crowfoot, G. M.
1938   *Samaria-Sebaste 2. Early Ivories from Samaria*. London: PEF.

Davies, G. I.
1982   Tell ed-Duweir = Ancient Lachish: A Responnse to G. W. Ahlstrom. *PEQ* 114: 25–28.
1985   Tell ed-Duweir: Not Libnah but Lachish. *PEQ* 117: 92–96.

Dever, W. G.
1976   Gezer. Pp. 428–443 in *EAEHL*, Vol. 2, eds. M. Avi-Yonah and E. Stern. Englewood Cliffs, N.J.: Prentice-Hall.

Garstang, J.
1922   Eighteen Months' Work of the Department of Antiquities for Palestine. *PEFQS* 54: 57–62.

Hamilton, R. W.
1935   Excavations at Tell Abu Hawām. *QDAP* 4: 1–69.

Hamrick, E. W.
1981   The Fourth North Wall of Jerusalem: "A Barrier Wall" of the First Century A.D. *Levant* 13: 262–66.
Hawkes, J.
1982   *Mortimer Wheeler. Adventurer in Archaeology.* London: Weidenfeld and Nicolson.
Hennessy, J. B.
1970   Preliminary Report on Excavations at the Damascus Gate, 1964–6. *Levant* 2: 22–27.
Holland, T. A.
1977   A Study of Palestinian Iron Age Baked Clay Figurines, with special reference to Jerusalem: Cave 1. *Levant* 9: 121–155.
James, F. W.
1979   Petrie in the Wadi Ghazzeh and at Gaza: Harris Colt's "Candid Camera." *PEQ* 111: 75–77.
Kenyon, K. M.
1939   Excavation Methods in Palestine. *PEQ:* 29–40.
1951   Some Notes on the History of Jericho in the Second Millennium B.C. *PEQ:* 101–38.
1953   *Beginning in Archaeology.* 2nd rev. ed. New York: Praeger.
1957   The British School of Archaeology in Jerusalem: The New School Building. *PEQ* 89: 97–101.
1960   *Excavations at Jericho*, Vol. 1. The Tombs Excavated in 1952–4. London: BSAJ.
1964   Megiddo, Hazor, Samaria and Chronology. *Bulletin of the Institute of Archaeology, University of London* 4: 143–56.
1965   *Excavations at Jericho*, Vol. 2. The Tombs Excavated in 1955–8. London: BSAJ.
1966   *Amorites and Canaanites.* The Schweich Lectures 1963. London: British Academy.
1967   *Jerusalem. Excavating 3000 Years of History.* London: Thames and Hudson.
1974   *Digging up Jerusalem.* London: Benn.
1979   *Archeology in the Holy Land,* 4th edition. New York: Norton
1981   *Excavations at Jericho*, Vol. 3. The Architecture and Stratigraphy of the Tell. Text edited by T. A. Holland. London: BSAJ.
Kenyon, K. M., and Holland, T. A.
1982   *Excavations at Jericho*, Vol. 4. The Pottery Type Series and Other Finds. London: BSAJ.
1983   *Excavations at Jericho*, Vol. 5. The Pottery Phases on the Tell and Other Finds. London: BSAJ.
Macalister, R. A. S.
1926   *A Century of Excavation in Palestine.* London: Religious Tract Society.
Moorey, P. R. S.
1979   Kathleen Kenyon and Palestinian Archaeology. *PEQ* 111: 3–10.
1983   *Excavation in Palestine.* Cities of the Biblical World. Grand Rapids: Eerdmans.
Morrison, W., ed.
1871   *The Recovery of Jerusalem.* London: Bentley.
Myres, J. L.
1939   Sir Robert Mond and the British School of Archaeology in Jerusalem. *PEQ* 71: 44–46.

Palestine Exploration Fund
    1965   *World of the Bible*. Catalogue of the Centenary Exhibition of the Palestine Exploration Fund. London: PEF.
Parr, P. J.
    1968   A Sequence of Pottery from Petra. Pp. 348-381 in *Near Eastern Archaeology in the Twentieth Century: Essays in Honor of Nelson Glueck*, ed. J. A. Sanders. Garden City, NY: Doubleday.
Petrie, W. M. F.
    1904   *Methods and Aims in Archaeology*. New York: Macmillan.
Prag, K.
    1974   The Intermediate Early Bronze-Middle Bronze Age: An Interpretation of the Evidence from Transjordan, Syria and Lebanon. *Levant* 6: 69–116.
Pringle, R. D.
    1981   Some Approaches to the Study of Crusader Masonry Marks in Palestine. *Levant* 13: 173–99.
    1983   Two Medieval Villages North of Jerusalem: Archaeological Investigations in Al-Jib and Ar-Ram. *Levant* 15: 141–77.
Rainey, A. F.
    1975   The Fate of Lachish during the Campaigns of Sennacherib and Nebuchadrezzar. Pp. 47–60 in *Investigations at Lachish. The Sanctuary and the Residency (Lachish V)*, ed. Y. Aharoni *et al.* Institute of Archaeology Publications, 4. Tel Aviv: Tel Aviv University.
Silberman, N. A.
    1982   *Digging for God and Country. Exploration, Archaeology and the Secret Struggle for the Holy Land 1799–1917*. New York: Knopf.
Simons, J. J.
    1952   *Jerusalem in the Old Testament*. Researches and Theories. Leiden: Brill.
Stanhope, H.
    1846   *Travels of Lady Hester Stanhope, forming the completion of her memoirs*. Narrated by her Physician. Vols. 1–3. London: Colburn.
Tubb, J. N.
    1983   The MB IIA Period in Palestine: Its Relationship with Syria and its Origin. *Levant* 15: 49–62.
Tufnell, O.
    1953   *Lachish III. The Iron Age*. Text. London: Oxford University Press.
    1959   Hazor, Samaria and Lachish. *PEQ* 91: 90–105.
    1965   Excavator's Progress. Letters of F. J. Bliss, 1889–1900. *PEQ* 97: 112–27.
    1982   Reminiscences of a "Petrie Pup" *PEQ* 114: 81–86.
Tufnell, O; Inge, C. H.; and Harding, G. L.
    1940   *Lachish II. The Fosse Temple*. London: Oxford University Press.
Ussishkin, D.
    1977   The Destruction of Lachish by Sennacherib and the Dating of the Royal Judean Storage Jars. *TA* 4: 28–60.
Vaux, R. de
    1969   Teman, Ville ou Region d'Edom? *RB* 76: 379–85.
Vincent, L. H.
    1911   *Underground Jerusalem. Discoveries in the Hill of Ophel (1909–11)*. By H. V. Translated from the French. London: Horace Cox.

Vogel, E. K.
    1971   Bibliography of Holy Land Sites. *HUCA* 42: 1–96.
Vogel, E. K., and Holtzclaw, B.
    1981   Bibliography of Holy Land Sites, Part II. *HUCA* 52: 1–92.
Walls, A. G.
    1974   The Turbat Barakat Khān or Khalidi Library. *Levant* 6: 25–50.
    1975   The Mausoleum of the Amir Kīlānī, Jerusalem. *Levant* 7: 39–
                  76.
    1977   The Mausoleum of the Amir Kīlānī: Restored Elevations. *Levant*
                  9: 168–73.
Watson, C. M.
    1915   *Fifty Years' Work in the Holy Land.* London: PEF.
Weippert, M.
    1979   The Israelite "Conquest" and the Evidence from Transjordan.
                  Pp. 15–34 in *Symposia Celebrating the Seventy-Fifth Anniversary of
                  the Founding of the American Schools of Oriental Research,* ed. F. M.
                  Cross, Cambridge: ASOR.
Wheeler, R. E. M.
    1954   *Archaeology from the Earth.* Oxford: Clarendon.
    1955   *Still Digging.* London: Joseph.
    1970   *The British Academy 1949–1968.* London: British Academy.
Wilkinson, J.
    1981   Architectural Procedures in Byzantine Palestine. *Levant* 13:
                  156–72.
Woolley, C. L., and Lawrence, T. E.
    1915   *The Wilderness of Zin.* Annual of the Palestine Exploration Fund
                  3 (1914–15). London: PEF.
Wreschner, E.
    1975   Carmel Caves. Pp. 290–98 in *EAEHL,* Vol. 1, eds. M. Avi-Yonah
                  and E. Stern. Englewood Cliffs, NJ: Prentice-Hall.
Yadin, Y.
    1958   Solomon's City Wall and Gate at Gezer. *IEJ* 8: 80–86.
    1972   *Hazor.* The Schweich Lectures 1970. London: British Academy.

4
FRENCH ARCHAEOLOGISTS

PIERRE BENOIT, O.P.
École Biblique

From the other essays in this section the reader will note that French researchers have participated in the archaeological investigation of Palestine since the 19th century. Among the early French scholars were Albert de Luynes (1802–1867), Léon de Laborde (1807–1869), Félicien de Saulcy (1807–1880), Victor Guérin (1821–1890), Melchior de Vogüé (1829–1916), and Charles Clermont-Ganneau (1846–1923). These men primarily conducted surface explorations rather than excavations.

I. EXPLORATION AND RESEARCH SPONSORED BY ÉCOLE BIBLIQUE

The first permanent French institution for archaeological research in Palestine was the École Biblique (Bible School) of the Dominican Fathers, founded in 1890. Its founder, Father Marie-Joseph Lagrange, O.P., only 35 years old at the time, intended to illuminate the study of the Bible with a thorough knowledge of the human environment where biblical events were lived, spoken, and written. The purpose of the institute, therefore, was to study the geography of the Holy Land, the ancient history of the Near East, oriental languages, archaeology, epigraphy, and culture. Accordingly, Fr. Lagrange called it "École *pratique* d'Études bibliques" (a *practical* school of biblical studies).

Fr. Lagrange had studied in France, Spain, and at the University of Vienna, but in Palestine he was obliged to create his school from scratch. He was soon successful in forming a team of young Dominican co-workers, each assigned a specialty. Devoting himself mainly to exegesis and biblical theology, he launched Fr. Hughes Vincent in archaeology, Fr. Félix Abel in history and geography, Fr. Antonin Jaussen in the Arabic language, Fr. Raphaël Savignac in Syriac and epigraphy, and Fr. Paul Dhorme in Akkadian language and culture, to list only the principal scholars.

Course work began on 15 November, 1890. Publications soon followed: the *Revue Biblique*, a quarterly publication began in 1892, and the *Études Bibliques*, a collection of commentaries and other works concerning the Bible, began in 1900. The École was housed in the Dominican priory which had been established in 1882.

From the beginning, teaching and publishing were accompanied by archaeological research. The first dig was conducted on the grounds of the Dominican priory. Uncovered were the remains of a basilica erected in the mid-fifth century by the empress Eudocia on the traditional site of the martyrdom of Saint Stephen (Acts 6 and 7). The basilica had three naves and was large for the period, 40 m long and 20 m wide. In front of the basilica was an atrium. Beneath the atrium were large cisterns and some Byzantine-age tombs. Lagrange reported the results of this dig in 1894 in his first work, *Saint Étienne et son sanctuaire à Jérusalem*. He also described some related finds, notably a hypogeum (burial complex) located in the garden to the south of the basilica. Parallels offered by recent discoveries in Judea suggest a date in the seventh century B.C. for the hypogeum.

Apart from this dig on its own grounds, the École devoted its efforts to surface exploration. Professors and students alike covered the country systematically in excursions. They studied its geography and place names, retraced the ancient routes, deciphered the Roman milestones, and gathered the fragments of inscriptions, architecture, and sculpture left by the destructions of past centuries. Travel was by horse or by camel. "You saw less, but you saw better," Fr. Abel liked to say.

One can page through the early volumes of *Revue Biblique* to find accounts of the excursions directed at first by Fr. Lagrange or Fr. Séjourné, and then by Frs. Jaussen, Vincent, Savignac or Abel: Masada (1894:236–76), Transjordan and Southern Lebanon (1894:615–27), Jordan Valley (1895:611–19), Hauran (1898:596–611), Philistia (1900:112–17), etc. These trips always resulted in new discoveries, especially those of Fr. Lagrange and his young team to Sinai and southern Transjordan. Lagrange travelled to Sinai first in 1893, and again in 1896. The 1896 trip took more than a month (*RB* 1896:618–41; 1897:107–30, 605–25), and the data gathered enabled the faculty and students to advance the discussion of problems such as the location of the biblical Mt. Sinai (*RB* 1899:369–92) and the route of the Exodus (*RB* 1900:63–86, 273–87, 443–49). The site of Punon (Numbers 32:42) was discovered by the École (*RB* 1898:112–15).

Lagrange was asked by the Académie des Inscriptions et Belles-Lettres (Paris) to locate at Petra a lost Nabataean inscription. Thanks to Vincent's dogged search, this inscription was recovered in October 1896 (*RB* 1897:208–38), and Lagrange was able to send a squeeze and an excellent copy to Marquis Melchior de Vogüé who was in charge of the Aramaic section of the Corpus of Semitic Inscriptions project. Other

Petra inscriptions followed (*RB* 1898:165–82, etc.), along with many from other places and in other languages. Epigraphic research was always a major concern of the École professors, especially Savignac and Abel. In the Alphabetic Index of the *Revue Biblique*, 1892–1968, published by Fr. J. Rousée in 1976, there are over 15 pages (pp. 280–95) of references to notes or articles dealing with inscriptions in Akkadian, Arabic, Aramaic, Ethiopic, Greek, Hebrew, Egyptian Hieroglyphics, Latin, Nabataean, Palmyrene, Phoenician, Proto-Sinaitic, Samaritan, South Arabic, Syriac, and Thamudic.

In 1899, again at the request of the Académie des Inscriptions et Belles-Lettres, Lagrange and his team defined the limits and orientation of Tell Jezer/Gezer (*RB* 1899:422–27). In 1904, in the course of a mission to the Negeb assigned to the École by the same Académie, Jaussen, Savignac, and Vincent undertook the first serious exploration of the famous Nabataean and Byzantine site of ʿAbdeh (*RB* 1904:403–24; 1905:74–89, 235–44).

From the start, the École was interested in Transjordan, especially the village of Medeba. In the *RB* of 1892 Séjourné reported on the first archaeological and epigraphic finds at Medeba (617–44), and many more such reports were to follow (1897:648–56, etc.). The explorations gradually revealed the importance of the mosaic art form at Medeba which made the town famous as a representative of the Byzantine period. In the *RB* of 1897 Lagrange described and analyzed the mosaic map for which Medeba is especially well known (165–84, 450–58).

Medeba is also well suited for the study of the customs of the Arabs, whose age-old traditions shed much light on the ancient Near East, and, consequently, on the biblical environment. A specialist in Arabic, Jaussen chose Medeba as a base for cultural studies. As a result of these studies he produced several important articles in the *Revue Biblique* (1901, 1902, 1903, 1906, 1910) and then a book: *Coutumes des Arabes au pays de Moab* (1908; repr. 1948).

Jaussen and his associate Savignac combined archaeology, epigraphy and ethnography in their exploration of northern Arabia conducted in 1907, 1909, and 1910–12. The results were recorded in a major work in three volumes under the general title *Mission archaéologique en Arabie:* I. *De Jérusalem au Hedjaz. Médain-Saleh* (1909); II. *El-ʿEla, d'Hégra à Teima, Harrah de Tebouk* (1914; Text and Atlas); III. *Les châteaux arabes de Qeṣeir ʿAmra, Harâneh et Ṭûba* (1922). This mission, funded by the Société française des fouilles archéologiques and later by the Académie des Inscriptions et Belles-Lettres, required courage and endurance on the part of the explorers. There was no convenient transportation; the railroad of the Hejaz was only then under construction, and camels were not always available. The climate was harsh with temperatures under the tent reaching as high as 42° C = 108°F. Often the local authorities would not cooperate fully. The bedouin at times were hostile or involved in internal wars which created delays. Nevertheless, the two explorers brought back a rich harvest of new information. They provided detailed topographic statements of their itineraries and descriptions of monuments. They made copies of many inscriptions: Nabataean inscriptions from the large necropolis of Medain-Saleh (ancient Hegra), Minean inscriptions of el-ʿUla (ancient Dedan), Liḥyanite inscriptions from the neighboring site, Hereibeh, as well as Thamudic graffiti from the vicinity of Teima and Tebuk. Jaussen and Savignac also made new inquiries into bedouin customs and examined anew the Umayyad castles in the desert to the southeast of Amman.

The pioneer explorations which we have just mentioned were followed by many others and remain a tradition at the École. Among the most important before the first World War were those of Abel: *Une croisière autour de la Mer morte* (four articles in *RB* 1909–10; published as a single volume in 1911); *Exploration de la vallée du Jourdain* (four articles in the *RB* 1910–13); *Le littoral palestinien et ses ports* (*RB* 1914). In July 1914 Jaussen and Savignac set out again, this time for an epigraphic mission to Palmayra which was entrusted to them by the Académie des Inscriptions et Belles-Lettres (1920:359–419).

Even though the École could not yet undertake major excavations, it was interested in those led by more fortunate institutions. Thus the École professors (especially Vincent) maintained steady contact with other archæologists and reported on their operations in the "Chroniques" of the *Revue Biblique*. Gradually, Vincent developed a synthesis of archæological findings throughout Palestine which he published under the title *Canaan d'après l'exploration récente* (1907). The visits to sites were usually most friendly and sometimes led to real collaboration, as in the case of the excavations at Jerusalem directed by Parker in 1909–11. The École was deeply involved in this project, and the English explorers asked Vincent to edit the final report: *Jérusalem sous terre. Les récentes fouilles d'Ophel* (1911).

The Holy City, where the École was located, remained the privileged place for research. From the first issue of the *Revue Biblique*, Lagrange firmly held that the little eastern hill between the Kidron and the Tyropoeon valleys ("Ophel"), rather than the western hill as had been thought for centuries, was the site of Jebusite and Davidic Zion (1892:17–38). This identification is now generally accepted by scholars. Soon a full-scale investigation of Jerusalem's history and of its monuments was undertaken. Vincent was responsible for the archæology, Abel for the history. In terms of archæology, there was no excavation, but rather an examination and interpretation of all visible traces of the past: walls and gateways, pools, civil monuments, and religious shrines. The suspicion, and often intolerance, of the inhabitants, clergy as well as laity, raised many difficulties. It took all of Vincent's determination to proceed with the research. As for the history of the city and the texts which record it, no one was better qualified to treat them than Abel, whose vast learning and keen memory were controlled by a fine and demanding critical spirit. From this collaboration a major work resulted which, despite corrections due to recent discoveries, remains an indispensible classic.

Vincent and Abel naturally began with the ancient periods, and in 1912 the first fascicle of volume I appeared: *Jérusalem Antique. Topographie*. But the First World War interrupted this publication, and it was not resumed until 1954–56. In the meantime, Vincent and Abel presented the results of another fruitful collaboration—the examination of the architecture of the Bethlehem basilica which had been undertaken in 1911 at the request of the Marquis M. de Vogüé. This project led to a fresh interpretation of the whole edifice and became the subject of a substantial monograph: *Bethléem. Le sanctuaire de la Nativité* (1914).

The War of 1914–18 interrupted the activity of the École Biblique. All the French priests had to depart from Jerusalem and leave the house under the protection of Swiss Dominican friars. With the exception of Lagrange who spent the War in Paris, all the scholars of the École Biblique were young enough to be drafted and to serve in different capacities in the army or navy. Archaeology had become such a part of Savignac that he used his enlistment on a ship in the Mediterranean to explore the islands of Ruad (*RB* 1916:565–92) and of Castellorizo (*RB* 1917:520–36).

After the War, the French priests resumed their work, and archaeology remained one of their key concerns. From 1920 on, the École was affiliated with the Académie des Inscriptions et Belles-Lettres. This affiliation led to the addition to the name "École Biblique" the words "et Archéologique Française." Its director, appointed by the Master General of the Dominicans, is approved by the Académie. The Académie sends annual fellows who participate in the activities of the École and use its library. The fellows write a "Mémoire" (a long technical paper) at the end of their term which is submitted to the Académie. This affiliation has enabled the École to collaborate in the training of a number of French archaeologists for the Near East.

Vincent and Abel's Jerusalem project was taken up again but with attention now to the Jerusalem of the Christian era. (As noted above, the study of the O.T. city was not published until 1954–56). All the holy places, beginning with the Church of the Holy Sepulcher, were studied both architecturally and historically from the date of their construction to the modern period. The result was "Tome II" entitled *Jérusalem Nouvelle*, in four fascicles: I and II. *Aelia Capitolina, le Saint-Sépulcre et le mont des Oliviers;* III. *La Sainte-Sion et les santuaries de second ordre.* IV.

Sainte-Anne et les sancuaires hors de la ville. Histoire monumentale de Jérusalem Nouvelle (1914, 1922, and 1926).

In the same period there appeared another large work, this one devoted to the famous Haram of Hebron, correctly judged to be of Herodian origin. It covered over the cave of Machpelah, the burial place of the Patriarchs according to the Bible. From the start of the British occupation, the Mandate government decided to promote an archaeological examination of this outstanding monument, till then practically inaccessible. The task was entrusted to Captain Mackay who was willing to have Vincent as an associate in his investigation. A week of minute work, confirmed by some further checks, was enough to draw up a complete inventory of the monument. The cave was not included because it was always strictly off-limits. The results of this inquiry, conducted in 1920, were published in a beautiful folio volume under the title: *Hébron. Le haram el Khalil. Sépulture des Patriarches* (1923). Mackay and Vincent prepared the archaeological section, with detailed descriptions, plans, and photographs, while Abel edited the historical part from the original construction to the present. (See also Vincent's related article in the *RB* 1920:507–39).

Topographical and archaeological explorations resumed, facilitated by a rapidly expanding network of roads. The camel era faded with the advent of the automobile. Savignac studied the region of ʿAin Qedeis in 1921 (*RB* 1922:55–81) and again in 1937, accompanied the second time by Frs. de Vaux and Benoit (*RB* 1938:89–100). During an expedition in southern Transjordan in 1935 (*RB* 1936:235–62), he was able to visit and photograph the Muslim holy place of Jebel Harun near Petra, normally strictly prohibited.

From 1923 to 1926 Abel published in the *Revue Biblique* six articles on "the topography of the Maccabean campaigns," in 1923 two articles on "a trip around Transjordan," in 1929 some "supplementary notes on the Dead Sea," and in 1931–32 four articles on an "exploration of the southeast of the Jordan Valley." In 1935 he successfully identified the biblical site of Tappuah (*RB* 1936:103–12). Abel's exploration was sometimes limited to a particular monument: the church of the Well of the Samaritan Woman (surveyed in 1919, published in *RB* 1958:547–67), the mosque-church of Nebi-Samwil (*RB* 1922:360–402; cf. already 1912:267–79), the monuments of Qubeiba (surveys of 1896–1902, published in the *RB* 1931:72–80).

New faculty members replaced senior members at the École. Among these were Fr. Tonneau who explored the Negeb once again (*RB* 1926, 583–604; 1927:93–98) and the land of Samson (*RB* 1929:421–31), Fr. Barrois who took part in the American expedition to the desert mines in the Sinai at Serabit el-Khadim (*RB* 1930:578–98), and, a little later, de Vaux and Benoit who explored the Salt region in Transjordan (*RB*

1938:398–425; 1941:16–47) and the Mt. Ephraim (*RB* 1946:260–74). Excavations by various foreign institutions were increased under the British Mandate. The École followed with interest the undertakings of the English, Americans, and Germans, and planned for the day when it would have its own excavations.

These began on a modest scale and partly by chance. In September 1918, a German-Turkish artillery shell uncovered upon impact some mosaic fragments near ʿAin ed-Duyuk, to the northwest of Jericho. A passing Australian regiment cleared away more of this mosaic pavement. As soon as peace was restored, the Mandate government tried to save the endangered artwork. Two English officers, Captain Engelbach and Lieutenant Mackay, who were in charge of the task, asked the École for assistance. Clearing began in June 1919 and continued until 1921. It revealed the plan of a synagogue with Hebrew-Aramaic inscriptions and a beautifully ornamented mosaic floor with a zodiac in the center. This was a unique find at the time (*RB* 1919:532–63; 1921:442–43; 579–601; 1961:163–77).

The accidental discovery of an ancient burial complex at Nablus, on the slope of Mt. Ebal, led to another clearing project by the École in 1919 (*RB* 1920:126–35) and in 1921 (*RB* 1922:89–99). The site had been pillaged by the army of occupation as well as by private treasure hunters. The École team studied and interpreted what remained after these ravages. They determined that the site had been a Jewish-Samaritan burial complex. It dated from the beginning of the present era and was embellished around A.D. 135–150. The excavators salvaged two beautiful, intact sarcophagi, fragments of two others, and various small objects which had escaped the pillage: lamps, coins, broken pottery, and glass.

Shortly thereafter, in December 1921 (*RB* 1922:259–81) and again in May 1924 (*RB* 1924:583–604), at the request of the British Department of Antiquities, the École dug at Beit Jibrin and discovered a beautiful villa of the Roman period. This villa was begun in the early third century A.D. and later enhanced by a beautiful mosaic with figures of the seasons, fawns, and hunting scenes. The excavators also found a courtyard surrounded by a portico paved with marble inlay. Destroyed in the fourth century, perhaps by the earthquake of A.D. 362, this rich villa became the home of the bishop (?) Obodian around A.D. 500. He added a chapel, paved with a lovely "bird mosaic" and marked with a dedicatory inscription. After another destruction in A.D. 634 (the Arab invasion), the edifice was restored in about A.D. 638 as a modest church. The raising of the floor level by this latter structure happily preserved the Roman and Byzantine levels. It is a pity that these levels, restored by the dig and carefully protected, were then irremediably damaged by soldiers' boots during the Second World War. In connection with the

Beit Jibrin dig, three tombs of the nearby site Tell Sandaḥannah (Marisa), of the type published by Peters and Thiersch in 1905, were also studied (restudied in one case). This resulted in the decipherment of the tomb inscriptions.

Also in 1924, a Byzantine church with a mosaic and tomb (of a certain Claudianus) was cleared at Khirbet el-Hubeileh (*RB* 1925:279–82; cf. 1939:87–90). A large project followed, this time concentrating on the basilica of ʿImwas. An inventory of what became visible of this building after the clearances by Captain Guillemot (1876–82) had already been published by Vincent (*RB* 1903:575–94). But a further, more extensive dig was deemed useful and took place with the agreement of the British Department of Antiquities at the end of 1924 and during the spring of 1925. A first brief presentation of the results appeared in *RB* (1926:117–21), but the complete publication of the final report was the object of a large, richly illustrated volume: *Emmaüs: Sa basilique et son histoire* (1932). Vincent and Abel collaborated on this as usual, one doing the archaeology, the other the history. While Abel concluded from his historical investigation that ʿImwas was in fact the Emmaus of the gospel—a view which remains debatable—Vincent thought he could affirm that the first basilica had been built originally in the first quarter of the third century on the site of a Roman villa of the Severan era. Vincent's bold thesis was also challenged, and a further dig in 1935 gave him the chance to defend his position (*RB* 1936:403–15; see also *RB* 1948:348–75).

These developing archaeological investigations extended to neighboring countries as well. In 1926 the Académie des Inscriptions et Belles-Lettres commissioned the French Archaeological School of Jerusalem to undertake methodical research on Tell Nerab, 7 km to the southeast of Aleppo in Syria. This site had been made famous through the discovery, in 1891, of two Aramaic steles. Two separate digs were conducted in the autumn of 1926–27. The first was directed by Carrière and Barrois and the second by Abel and Barrois, assisted each time by André Parrot, then a fellow of the Academy at the École. (Parrot later became the excavator of Mari and still later Director General of the Louvre Museum.) "A complete destruction from the distant past" which left largely incoherent ruins, plus the presence of a modern village on the main location of the site, permitted only limited results, but nonetheless important ones. The exploration of a necropolis dating from the end of the Neo-Babylonian empire and from the earliest part of the Persian era attested to the presence, in the seventh century B.C., of an Aramaic population whose culture disclosed strong Babylonian and Hittite influences. The excavators collected important information about ancient burial methods as well as numerous objects: funerary jars, figurines, seals, scarabs, jewelry, arrowheads, etc., and a prize of 25 cuneiform tablets which are for the most part contracts (See *Syria* VIII 1927:126–42, 201–15; IX 1928:187–206, 303–19; *RB* 1927:257–65; 1928:263–75; Dhorme, *Revue d'Assyriologie,* XXV 1928:53–82).

In the spring of 1932, Fr. Savignac was invited by G. Horsfield, Director of the Transjordanian Department of Antiquities, to participate in the study of a Nabataean site which he had just discovered in the region of Jebel er-Ram, to the northeast of Aqaba. At the foot of an imposing rocky chain of mountains with a high point of 1750 m, numerous springs made possible the establishment of a Nabataean village. One of the springs, ʿAin Shellaleh, was nestled in a picturesque wadi and had been encircled by a rupestral sanctuary, that is, a circle of sacred stones. The stones bore Greek and Nabataean inscriptions including the names Allat of Boṣra and el-ʿUzza, "Lord of the Temple." Also there were traces of a monument dedicated to the Nabataean king Rabbel II. All of these materials were analyzed and deciphered during 1932–34 by commission of the Académie des Inscriptions et Belles-Lettres in collaboration with Barrois (*RB* 1932:581–97; 1933:405–22; 1934:572–91). The exploration also brought to light a small Nabataean temple situated at the site of the ancient village with additional inscriptions and graffiti in Greek, Nabataean, and Latin (*RB* 1935:245–278). Since this dig could not be completed, a later expedition by the British School of Archeology of Jerusalem, directed by Diana Kirkbride, helped revise and complete the findings (*RB* 1960:65–92).

At Maʿin, a large village 8 km to the southwest of Medeba, the accidental discovery of a mosaic led Savignac and de Vaux to undertake in October 1937, with the authorization of the Transjordanian Department of Antiquities, the clearing of a Byzantine church (*RB* 1938:227–58). The building was almost totally destroyed, but what remains of its mosaic floor is especially interesting. The floor is surrounded by a topographical border which depicts certain cities in Palestine. The cities are represented by churches whose clumsy and rather conventional designs seem to represent real buildings of the day. Each mosaic church is accompanied by the name of the city which it represents. Eleven of the names can still be read: Nicopolis, [Georgiou or Eleuthero]polis, Ascalon, Maioumas, [Ga]za, Od[roh], [Karakmo]uba, Areopolis, Gadoron, Belemounim. This mosaic floor was built during the last part of the sixth or the first part of the seventh century A.D. Its animated figures were destroyed by iconoclasts, probably under Omar II around the year A.D. 717, and restored in A.D. 719/720 as an inscription indicates. This exploration also produced other "archaeological gleanings at Maʿin" (*RB* 1939:78–86).

The Second World War again disrupted the activities of the École. Since Palestine was in the Western allies' camp, the eligible priests were mobilized in Palestine. Thus, while working at the General Consulate of

France in Jerusalem, de Vaux undertook, in 1944, an archaeological exploration of the church of Abu Ghosh, thanks to a subsidy of the provisional government of the French Republic (*RB* 1946: 125–34; see also de Vaux and Steve, 1950). The evolution of the site, as reconstructed by de Vaux, is as follows: (1) In the second and third centuries of the present era, the site had a reservoir collecting the waters of a spring and feeding the *mutatio,* probably at the ninth milestone of a Roman road leading from Jerusalem to Nicopolis. (2) An Arab caravanserai, serving the same ancient road, was built in the ninth century A.D. This became the road of the Califs from Jerusalem to Ramleh, their new capital. (3) The caravanserai was reworked by the Knights Hospitalers in the 12th century. The Hospitalers also constructed a church above the ancient reservoir, and the reservoir itself was transformed into a crypt. The site became for the Crusaders the "Fountain of the Enamels," by identification with the gospel site Emmaus. (4) After the victory of Saladin and the partial destruction of the site, there was a Mamluk restoration of the caravanserai. The site was finally abandoned at the end of the 15th century A.D. In addition to clarifying the evolution of the site, this well-conducted investigation produced new information on Muslim ceramics of the 10th–11th centuries A.D.

In 1945–46, de Vaux, assisted by Steve and other members of the École, undertook an excavation at ʿAin el-Maʿmudiyeh near the village of Taffuḥ, 8 km to the west of Hebron. Dr. Clemens Kopp, an expert in ancient pilgrimages, had identified ʿAin el-Maʿmudiyeh as the site venerated by pilgrims of the Middle Ages in connection with the baptism of John the Baptist (*RB* 1946: 547–58). De Vaux and his team cleared a small chapel whose baptismal character was clearly indicated by the discovery of a large basin in its center and a tunnel which brought water from a nearby spring. A large lintel with a Greek inscription was discovered in the vicinity, apparently the remains of a monastery which had been built to welcome pilgrims. On the hill which overlooks the chapel and the monastery-hospice are the ruins of a fort which protected this place of pilgrimage. The fortress gate is still standing, and carved on its lintel is a cross with the letters, α, ω and IC XC (an inscription which has become the emblem of the Jerusalem Bible). The whole complex probably dates back to the period of the Emperor Justinian. A living tradition to this effect remained up to the Middle Ages, as the pilgrims bear witness, and it is still alive in the memory of the present inhabitants of the region.

These various excavations, while relatively modest, prepared the École little by little to undertake projects on a grander scale. Thus Fr. de Vaux, who became Director of the École after the Second World War, conducted excavations at Tell el-Farʿah (north, to distinguish it from the site of the same name in southern Palestine). Tell el-Farʿah is a large tell,

600 m long and 300 m wide, located 11 km northeast of Nablus and situated between two springs. The most important of these, ʿAin Farʿah, is the source of a perennial stream of water descending through the Wadi Farʿah towards the Jordan valley. Fr. de Vaux, assisted at first by Fr. Steve, then by Frs. Boismard, Coüasnon, Rousée, and other professors and students of the École, conducted nine campaigns of excavations from 1946 to 1960 and reported the results each year in the *Revue Biblique*.

Above Neolithic and Chalcolithic remains at Tell el-Farʿah, de Vaux isolated five levels of a flourishing Early Bronze Age city. After an interruption at the end of the Early Bronze Age, a new city was founded during MB II which would continue without another major occupational break into the Iron Age. Numerous houses dating from the Iron Age were found, their floor plans quite clear. Some are large, presumably houses of the wealthy; others are small, humble dwellings. One is reminded of the reproaches of the prophets regarding the wealthy and the poor during Old Testament times (Amos 5:11; Isaiah 9:8–9). One especially large, costly building, still unfinished, was interpreted by de Vaux as King Omri's palace. The palace would have been under construction, according to de Vaux's interpretation, when Omri decided to transfer his capital to Samaria in approximately 885 B.C. (1 Kings 16:23–24). De Vaux was convinced, in other words, that Tell el-Farʿah was none other than Tirzah, first capital of the Kingdom of Israel, an identification already suggested by W. F. Albright. The Iron Age city was completely devastated during the eighth century B.C., presumably by the Assyrians. It survived for some time under Assyrian occupation, but died out finally around the year 600 B.C.

In addition to architectural finds, the excavators turned up objects of all sorts: flint, bones, and above all abundant pottery. Much of the pottery came from a cemetery used during the Chalcolithic, Middle Bronze II, and Late Bronze ages.

The dig at Tell el-Farʿah was interrupted by the involvement of the École at Khirbet Qumran. Exploration of Khirbet Qumran and vicinity, the site of the discovery of the so-called Dead Sea Scrolls, was undertaken as a joint project by the Department of Antiquities of Jordan whose director was Mr. Lankaster Harding, the Palestine Archaeological Museum (or Rockefeller Museum) with de Vaux as President of the Board of Trustees, and by the French Archaeological School of which de Vaux was Director. Because of his double connection, and because Mr. Harding was often detained at Amman by the duties of his office, de Vaux became the principal person responsible for the operations. Work began in 1951 with examination of cave I. Excavation of the ruin (the khirbet) took four campaigns from 1953 to 1956. ʿAin Feshkha, a neighboring and connected site, was explored in 1958. The American School of Oriental Research in Jerusalem assisted in exploration of the rocky bluff in search of other caves. Two hundred and thirty caves were found sterile; forty yielded pottery and other objects; the pottery of twenty-six of the caves was identical to that of cave I. Eleven caves furnished manuscripts in varying quantities.

De Vaux reported on the work at Khirbet Qumran in *RB* 1949, 1953, 1954, 1956, 1959, and in the Schweich Lectures of the British Academy for 1959. The latter appeared in a volume under the title *L'archéologie et les manuscrits de la Mer Morte* (1961; English edition 1973: *Archaeology and the Dead Sea Scrolls*). Final publication of the excavation results and edited manuscripts was reserved for a monograph series entitled *Discoveries in the Judaean Desert*. De Vaux served as editor-in-chief of the series until his death, at which time the responsibility was passed to Fr. Benoit. This series was begun in 1955; seven volumes had appeared by 1982, and it is not yet completed. The important results of the Qumran project are too well known to warrant description here. We note only that the competence and authority of de Vaux provided a firm basis for all future study of these famous manuscripts.

The exploration of Qumran was accompanied in 1952 by an expedition in the Wadi Murabbaʿat, about 20 km further south, where bedouins had discovered other caves with manuscripts. This led to the recovery of manuscript fragments (of the Bible and various other documents in Hebrew, Aramaic, Greek, and Latin) from a different epoch, that of the second Jewish revolt under the Emperor Hadrian. The finds were published in volume II of *Discoveries in the Judean Desert* (1961) and in a work by D. Barthélemy (a member of the École who participated in the project): *Les devanciers d'Aquila. Première publication intégrale du texte des fragments du Dodécapropheton trouvés dans le désert de Juda* (1963).

In 1950 a cave was discovered accidently near Bethany on the property of the Sisters of St. Vincent de Paul. It was almost full of earth, but a cross painted near its roof invited investigation. Clearance by de Vaux revealed that its walls were covered with carved or painted inscriptions and numerous crosses. Fr. Benoit, assisted by Fr. Boismard, deciphered the inscriptions which include proper names and proscynems (statements of devotion) in Greek, Latin, Syriac, and Arabic (*RB* 1951:200–51). Apparently, pilgrims from Jerusalem to Bethany during the fourth to the seventh centuries left these markings to commemorate their visit.

De Vaux was also involved in Dame Kathleen M. Kenyon's archaeological excavations in Jerusalem in 1956 and from 1961 to 1963. These digs, both south of the Temple mount, were interrupted each time by political disturbances. About this same time Vincent, assisted by Fr. A. M. Steve as draftsman, succeeded in publishing *Jérusalem de l'Ancien Testament* (3 vols. in 2, 1954–56). The first volume treats the ramparts, the fortresses Acra and Antonia, the palaces, the hydraulic installations, and the cemeteries. The second volume is devoted essentially to the Temple and concludes with a synthesis of the whole work.

An agreement was concluded in 1959 for the restoration of the entire basilica of the Holy Sepulcher. Fr. Charles Coüasnon, an architect certified by the French Government and attached to the École in order to participate in de Vaux's excavations, was put in charge of the works for the Latin community by the Franciscan Custody of the Holy Land. He worked with a tireless zeal until his death in 1976 and made important archaeological observations. These he summarized in his 1972 Schweich Lectures published under the title *The Church of the Holy Sepulchre, Jerusalem* (1974).

In 1963, Fr. Prignaud, assisted by other young members of the School, conducted soundings at the Khan Ṣaliba near the road that descends from Jerusalem to Jericho. These soundings revealed mosaic pieces with an inscription of a "priest and higoumenos [abbot] Paul" (*RB* 1963:243–54). Probably this was part of a monastic building constructed toward the beginning of the sixth century A.D. to shelter Christian pilgrims. This Christian "khan" suffered damage at the start of the seventh century A.D. (incursion of Khosroe II?) and was violently destroyed in the eighth century.

In February 1971, de Vaux, already weak from an illness that would cause his death in September of that year, proposed a new dig to be conducted by younger members of the École faculty. The exploration of Qumran was completed, and the one of Tell el-Farʿah could not be continued because of political circumstances, so he chose Tell Keisan and obtained authorization to dig from the Israeli Department of Antiquities. Keisan is a beautiful tell that rises in the middle of a vast plain, some 10 km southeast of Akko. This geographical location promised interesting information on cultural relations between Cyprus, Crete, Phoenicia, and Palestine. Six campaigns were conducted in 1971–76, directed first by Fr. Prignaud, then by Abbe Jacques Briend, and finally by Fr. J. B. Humbert with the assistance Fr. E. Nodet. The major results have been published in *Tell Keisan (1971–76), une cité phénicienne en Galilée* (1980). Underneath a Byzantine church found on the surface, the excavators reached Hellenistic, Persian, Iron II, Iron I, and Late Bronze levels.

Fr. J. B. Humbert and Abbe A. Desreumaux, assisted by Fr. J.-M. de Tarragon, also excavated at Khirbet es-Samra, 33 km northeast of Amman, a site already noted by Savignac (*RB* 1925:115–31). Two campaigns, in 1978 and 1981, revealed a small settlement with four churches of the fifth and sixth century A.D. Preceded by two occupations that could go back to Nabataean times, the town itself (perhaps Hanita, a stopover on the Via Nova between Philadelphia and Boṣra) had its peak in the sixth and seventh centuries A.D. and was abandoned in the eighth century.

II. OTHER EXPLORATION AND RESEARCH BY FRENCH ARCHAEOLOGISTS

In addition to the extensive archaeological activities of the École Biblique reviewed above, research conducted by French archaeologists under other auspices requires attention.

We have already spoken of Fr. J. Germer-Durand, the distinguished epigraphist who published numerous Greek inscriptions from Jerusalem in the *Revue Biblique* (1914:71–94; 222–46). He and his Assumptionist confreres conducted their investigations from 1889 to 1912 in the vast area that they had acquired on the eastern slope of the western hill of Jerusalem. They discerned the following features: a burial complex cut out prior to the time of Herod; a rich Jewish residence with agricultural installations dating from the first century of the current era; a Byzantine church of the fifth century A.D. built over a deep grotto; and a Muslim residence. Fr. Germer-Durand traced the following evolution of the site: The original tomb was transformed into a grotto by further digging which doubled its depth; this grotto eventually became the object of Christian veneration (judging from painted and engraved crosses on the inner walls). Still later, the grotto was replastered and utilized as a cistern. No doubt this is the grotto which Christian pilgrims of the Middle Ages associated with St. Peter's denial: Saint Peter in Gallicantu. But Fr. Germer-Durand believed he could reconstruct even more of its history. Analyzing ancient pilgrim texts and objects discovered on the spot (numerous Jewish weights and measures and a lintel with the Hebrew inscription including the word "Qorban"), he concluded that the first century Jewish residence was none other than the house of the high priest Caiaphas. The grotto would be the prison where Jesus spent the night from Holy Thursday to Good Friday. Naturally these conclusions are controversial. (See the articles of Vincent in *RB* 1927:633–6; 1929:155–9; 1930:226–56, and the remarks of Barrois on the alleged standards of weights and measures, *RB* 1931:210.)

While not claiming to be an archaeologist, Fr. Prosper Viaud, the Guardian of the Franciscan Convent of the Annunciation at Nazareth, conducted fruitful excavations in this monastery from 1890 on, with a concerted effort in the years 1907–09, and published the results under the title: *Nazareth et ses deux églises de l'Annonciation et de Saint-Joseph d'apprès les fouills recéntes* (1910). Specifically, he rediscovered the cathedral of the Crusader period, a church 75 m long with three apses whose walls still rise to a height of almost 3 m. He also found, buried in a convent room, five well preserved capitals dating from the end of the 12th century A.D. Another Crusader church which probably served for parish worship was uncovered to the north of the cathedral. More recently, from 1955 to 1966, continued excavations at the site by Fr. Bagatti, O.F.M., revealed ruins which go back to the Byzantine and Roman eras. A new basilica has been erected which retains some of the plan of the medieval cathedral and preserves the vestiges of the earlier periods.

Toward the summit of the Mt. of Olives lies a piece of ground where tradition places the Eleona, a church constructed by Helen, the mother of Constantine the Great. The Princess of La Tour d'Auvergne purchased this land for France, and the White Fathers (the "missionaries of Africa" of Cardinal Lavigerie) were given custody of it. Frs. Jean-Louis Féderlin and Léon Cré excavated at the site in 1910 and 1911 and found remains of a Byzantine church and grotto. Fr. Vincent, followed the work very closely and published a description and an interpretation of the findings (*RB* 1911:219–65).

In 1913–14 Captain Raymond Weill excavated an area purchased by Baron Edmond de Rothschild on the eastern slope of Ophel, about 200 m south of the Gihon spring (Weill, 1920; see the analyses by Fr. Vincent in *RB* 1921:410–33; 541–69). Weill dug again on Ophel in 1923–24 and thought he had found a Canaanite fortress and dungeon, but his interpretation was entirely mistaken (Weill, 1947; see Vincent, *RB* 1949:614–617). An important result of this second campaign was the discovery of a diversion of the channel which brought water from the Gihon spring toward a large pool at the southern end of Ophel (the present day Birket el-Hamra).

Teleilat el-Ghassul is the name of three small knolls situated about 5 km east of the Jordan and north of the Dead Sea. Fr. Alexis Mallon, S.J., then Rector of the Pontifical Biblical Institute of Jerusalem, conducted excavations there in 1929–32. In spite of some misadventures (some engraved stones which proved to be fakes) and mistakes (identification of the site and of its region with Sodom and the Pentapolis, a theory which has since been abandoned), this exploration revealed a culture of the Neolithic and Chalcolithic eras (around 4000–3500 B.C.) typical enough to warrant a new term of archaeological reference: "Ghassulian" (cf. *RB* 1931:388–400; 1932:489–514; Mallon, 1934). After the death of Fr. Mallon in 1934, the excavation was continued by non-French members of the Pontifical Biblical Institute: Robert Köppel to 1938, Robert North in 1959–60, and finally, from 1967 on, Dr. Basil Hennessy of the British School of Archaeololgy at Jerusalem.

The lithic industry discovered at Teleilat el-Ghassul was studied by René Neuville who was attached to the Consulate General of France in Jerusalem from 1926 to his death in 1952 (at first in the office of

Chancellor, then in the office of Vice-Consul, and finally, from 1946 to 1952, as Consul General). Combining his diplomatic obligations with a rich career as a prehistorian, Neuville also made surface explorations and excavated numerous caves in the Judaean hills south of Bethlehem. The cave of Umm Qaṭafa in the Wadi Khareitun (explored in 1928, 1932, and 1949) is probably the best known. The results of his research were the object of numerous publications. For example, a first summary essay on "the pre-history of Palestine" appeared in the *Revue Biblique* 1934:237–59; and shortly before his death a work entitled *Le Paléolithique et le Mésolithique du désert de Judée* (1951) presented a more extensive summary of his work and conclusions. With assiduous research and penetrating intuitions, René Neuville was one of the pioneers who brought the discipline of Palestinian pre-history from infancy to early maturity.

It is appropriate to mention next, following a chronological order, the excavations begun in 1931 in the Convent of the Sisters of Notre-Dame de Sion in Jerusalem (known as "Ecce Homo"). These excavations were led by Mother Marie Godeleine, Superior of the institution, and later by Mother Marie-Aline de Sion, who succeeded her. The latter published the results under the title *La forteresse Antonia à Jérusalem et la question du Prétoria* (1955). Meanwhile, Fr. Vincent, who followed the excavations closely and served as consultant, published several articles related to the project (*RB* 1933:83–113; 1937:563–70; 1952:513–30; 1954:87–107). Two issues associated with the "Ecce Homo" site remained unresolved: 1) the accuracy of the plan of the Antonia fortress as reconstructed by the excavators, and 2) whether or not the Antioch fortress is to be identified with the Praetorium where Jesus was judged by Pilate (see Benoit, 1952:531–50 [Eng. 1973:167–88]; 1971:135–67).

In 1933 Madame Judith Marquet-Krause undertook excavations, under the patronage of Baron Edmund de Rothschild, at et-Tell (biblical 'Ai). Unfortunately she was able to complete only three seasons of field work before her premature death in 1935. But these were three very fruitful seasons. Et-Tell turned out to be primarily an Early Bronze Age site, with occupation interrupted in the Middle and Late Bronze Ages and resumed briefly in the Early Iron Age (see Vincent, *RB* 1937:231–66). The death of the excavator prevented her from confirming or revising her initial conclusions. In fact some of these would have required revision, as can be seen from de Vaux's review of *Les fouilles de 'Ay (Et-Tell) 1933–35. La résurrection d'une grand cité biblique* (1949) in *RB* 1950:621–24. More extensive excavations have since been conducted at the site, notably those in 1964–70 under the direction of Professor Joseph A. Callaway, to whom this work is dedicated.

The property of the Church of St. Anne in Jerusalem is situated at the site of the pool of Bethesda which, according to John 5:2, had five porticos. Turkey ceded this medieval church to France in 1873, and C. Mauss, an architect, was commissioned to restore it. Mauss had the good luck to discover a little basin which belonged to the ancient pool. Starting in 1878, therefore, the White Fathers, who had become guardians of the church, made numerous soundings in an effort to discover the original dimensions of the pool. Fr. L. Cré directed these excavations, and the results are reported in a volume by N. van der Vliet, "*Sainte Marie où elle est née" et la Piscine Probatique* (1938). In 1956 new excavations were undertaken by the White Fathers, in particular by Frs. Blondeel and Pochet, in close cooperation with the École Biblique, represented by de Vaux and Rousée. The results gained by earlier research were in part confirmed and in part corrected and completed. Columns were unearthed which belonged to a Byzantine church, but none which could be construed as part of the "porticos" of which the gospel speaks. Perhaps the most important discovery was that the eastern half of the Byzantine church covered—and obliterated—an earlier healing shrine. Only preliminary publications of the findings have appeared thus far (*RB* 1957:226–28; 1962:107–109; J. M. Rousée, 1965:169–76; Benoit, 1968:48–57; A. Duprez, 1970).

III. The French Mission

Monsieur Jean Perrot, who was a student at the École Biblique et Archéologique Française in 1945–46, has kindly provided the following report on the activities of the French Mission which he directs:

In 1950 the Centre National Français de la Recherche Scientifique (CNRS) and the Direction générals des Relations culturelles, scientifiques et techniques of the Ministère des Relations extérieures assigned to M. Jean Perrot an archaeological mission in Israel. Perrot began work under the auspices of the mission with explorations in the Beer-sheba area where he identified fourth millennium remains comparable to those of Teleilat el-Ghassul. From 1952 to 1962, the French Mission explored successively the sites Zumeili (1951–52), Tell Abu Maṭar (1952–54), Safadi (1954–60), Nahal Besor (1961), and Wadi Zeita (1962). These excavations led to the discovery of subterranean villages in the region of Beer-sheba and of a technologically advanced pastoral civilization (copper metallurgy, work in hard stones and in ivory, etc.) characterized by a high degree of adaptation to the semi-desert environment and by a very developed economy of production in which hunting and food gathering no longer played more than a negligible role.

Meanwhile, starting in 1955, the French Mission joined with the Israel Department of Antiquities in exploration of the vast Natufian layer of Mallaha (Eynan) alongside the former Lake Huleh in the upper Jordan valley. Apart from the caves of Carmel excavated by D. Garrod, those of Judea excavated by Neuville, and a few small seasonal encampments, scarcely anything was known then of the Natufian culture. The discovery at Mallaha of a Natufian settlement which covered several thousand square meters and included great circular habitations of stone overturned previously held perceptions. The absence, or the extreme rarity, of domesticated animals led the French Paleoethnozoologist, Fr. Ducos, to pose anew the problem of domestication. At the same time, the English excavations of Jericho, with their spectacular results, led to an earlier dating of the Natufian culture.

From 1959 to 1962, with the aid of the CNRS, the French Archaeological Mission in Israel undertook a systematic survey of southern Turkey, from Adana to the Euphrates, and the excavation of a Halafian and pre-Halafian site at Turlu, near Gaziantep. There was close collaboration with other foreign researchers, notably with Professor R. J. Braidwood of the Oriental Institute of Chicago. After 1963 the Archaeological Mission in Israel was reinforced by the addition of new teams and by a new administrative structure—the Cooperative Research Programs (RCP) established by the CNRS. Directed by J. Perrot, RCP 50, entitled "Prehistoric and Protohistoric Civilizations of the Asiatic Near East," had as themes: (1) the origins of modern man in the Levant; (2) the beginnings of settlements in the Mediterranean Near East; and (3) the process of urbanization (in southern Mesopotamia and in the southwest of Iran).

In Israel, where several different teams worked under the auspices of "The Center of French Prehistoric Research of Jerusalem," research focused on the first two of the themes indicated above. The cave of Qafzeh near Nazareth was excavated under the direction of B. Vandermeersch of the Laboratory of Vertebrate Paleontology and of Human Paleontology of the Pierre and Marie Curie University (Paris). Also, from 1962 to 1967, J. Perrot directed excavations at the Munhata settlement in the Jordan valley south of the Sea of Galilee. Other excavations were conducted at Beisamun and at Abu Ghosh by M. Lechevallier and at Mallaha by Monique Lechevallier and François Valla assisted by researchers of the CNRS.

The cave of Qafzeh, first explored by R. Neuville and M. Stekelis, yielded a remarkable series of skeletons of Homo Sapiens in a Mousterian context dated to about 50,000 B.C. (long before Neanderthal man was replaced by Cro-Magnon man in western Europe). The excavations of Mallaha, Munhata, Beisamun, etc., showed that the process of pre-historic settlement did not have as a necessary precondition the acquisition of techniques of production such as the domestication of plants and animals. Instead, in favorable natural conditions, groups living from hunting, fishing, and food gathering were able to settle down and to lead a quasi-sedentary existence. This new way of life in Palestine resulted in the development of techniques of house construction as well as of conservation (silos) and of preparation of foods (mills, pestles, grinders, and stone vases). One long term consequence appears to have been the rapid increase in population (if one can judge by the number and increasing importance of urban centers). Some groups found themselves pushed to the limit of the natural climate and, pressured by their needs and by their food habits, began the first cultivation of cereals. In other words, the development of agriculture in the Mediterranean Near East could have been a consequence of the sedentary life rather than one of its pre-conditions.

In 1973, when RCP 50 completed its ten-year term, an administrative restructuring took place. The Center of French Prehistoric Research of Jerusalem (CRPFJ) became a permanent Mission—i.e., an official laboratory of the CNRS, with the support of the Direction générals des Relations cuturelles, scientifiques et techniques of the Ministere des Relations extérieures. At the same time the need for better information and for a closer coordination of research in the Near East led the researchers of the CRPFJ to initiate a specialized periodical which facilitates the exchange of ideas. Thus, in 1973, the first issue of *Paléorient* was published. This journal provides a multidisciplinary review of exploration and research pertaining to the pre-history and proto-history of the Asiatic Southwest. *Paléorient* continues publication under the sponsorship of CNRS.

Since 1979, with the transfer of the laboratories at the CRPF from Jerusalem to Emmaus, the activities of the center have been expanded considerably. The programs have been notably extended in the domains of geology, anthropology, and animal and human paleontology. Twenty-six French and fourteen Israeli researchers work together on themes which have as their common denominator the biological evolution of man, his environment, and his activities, from the origins to the second millennium B.C. This research attracts exceptional interest because of the abundance of data and because of the geographic position of Palestine at the point of contact between Africa, Asia, and Europe.

Jerusalem
23 May 1982

Translated by B. T. Viviano, O.P., with the assistance of O. Chiapetta, E. Miller, D. Culbertson, and N. Hardesty. Abbreviated by the editors.

BIBLIOGRAPHY

Abel, F. -M.
    1909–10   Une croisière à la Mer morte. *RB* 18: 213–42, 386–411, 592–
               605; 19: 92–112, 217–33.

1910–13   Exploration de la vallée du Jourdain. *RB* 19: 532–56; 20: 408–36; 21: 402–23; 22: 218–43.
1911   *Une croisière autour de la Mer morte.* Paris: Gabalda
1914   La littoral palestinien et ses ports. *RB* 23: 556–90.
1921   Les fouilles d'Ascalon. *RB* 30: 102–06.
1922   Notre exploration à Naplouse. *RB* 31: 89–99.
1923–26   Topographie des campagnes machabéennes. *RB* 32: 495–521; 33:201–17, 371–87; 34: 194–216; 35: 206–22, 510–33.
1924   Découvertes récentes à Beit-Djebrin. *RB* 33: 583–604.
1925   Église byzantine au Khirbet Hebeileh. *RB* 34: 279–82.
1928   La circuit de Transjordanie. *RB* 37: 425–33, 590–604.
1929   Notes complémentaires sur la Mer morte. *RB* 38: 237–60.
1931–32   Exploration du sud-est de la vallée du Jourdain. *RB* 40:214–26, 375–400; 41: 77–88, 237–57.
1936   Tappouah. *RB* 45: 103–112

Abel, F. -M., and Barrois, A.
1928   Fouilles de l'École archéologique française de Jérusalem. *Syria* 9: 187–206, 303–19.

Barrois, A.
1927   Fouilles à Neirab Septembre–Novembre 1926. *RB* 36: 257–65.
1928   Fouilles de l'École à Neirab. *RB* 37: 263–75.
1930a   Découverte d'une synagogue à Beit Alpha. *RB* 39: 265–72.
1930b   Aux mines du Sinaï. *RB* 39: 578–98.
1931   La Métrologie dans la Bible. *RB* 40: 185–213.

Barthelemy, D.
1963   *Les devanciers d'Aquila. Première publication intégrale du texte des fragments du Dodécapropheton trouvés dans le désert de Juda.* Leiden: Brill.

Benoit, P.
1951   Un ancien Sanctuaire crétien a Béthanie. *RB* 58: 200–51.
1952   Prétoire, Lithostroton et Gabbatha. *RB* 59: 531–50.
1968   Découvertes archéologiques autour de la piscine de Bethesda. Pp. 48–57 in *Jerusalem Through the Ages,* ed. Y. Yadin. Jerusalem: Israel Exploration Society.
1971   *"L'Antonia d'Hérode le Grand et le Forum oriental d'Aelia Capitolina."* HTR 64: 135–167.
1973   *Jesus and the Gospel.* N. Y.: Crossroads.

Benoit, P., et al.
1961   *Le grottes de Murrabba'ât. Discoveries in the Judean Desert,* vol. 2, Oxford: Clarendon.

Blomme, Y.
1980   Inscriptions gregues a Kursi et Amwas. *RB* 87: 404–07.

Briend, J. et al.
1980   *Tell Keisan (1971–1976) une cité phénicienne en Galilée.* Paris: Gabalda.

Carriere, B. and Barrois, A.
1927   Fouilles de l'École archéologique française de Jérusalem *Syria* 8: 126–42, 201–15.

Coüasnon, C.
1974   *The Church of the Holy Sepulchre, Jerusalem.* London: British Academy.

Dhorme, E.
1928   Les tablettes babyloniennes de Neirab. *Revue d'Assyriologie* 25: 53–82.
Duprez, A.
1970   *Jésus et les dieux guérisseurs. A propos de Jean v.* Paris: Gabalda.
Germer-Durand, J.
1914   La Maison de Caïphe et l'Église Saint-Pierre a Jérusalem. *RB* 23: 71–94, 222–46.
Jaussen, A.
1901   Coutumes arabes aux environs de Mâdaba. *RB* 10: 592–608.
1902   Les tribus arabes à l'est du Jourdain. *RB* 11: 87–93, 419–25.
1903   Coutumes arabes. *RB* 12: 93–99, 244–46.
1906   L'immolation chez les nomades à l'est de la Mer morte. *RB* 15: 91–114.
1908   *Coutumes des Arabes au pays de Moab.* Paris: Gabalda.
1910   Coutumes des arabes. *RB* 19: 237–49, 391–98.
Jaussen, A., and Savignac, R.
1909–22   *Mission archéologique en Arabie.* 3 vols. Paris: Leroux and Geuthner
Jaussen, A., Savignac, R. and Vincent, L. -H.
1904–05   'Abdeh. *RB* 13: 403–24; 14: 74–89, 235–57.
Kirkbridge, D.
1960   Le Temple nabatéen de Ramm: son evolution architecturale. *RB* 67: 65–92.
Kopp, C.
1946   Le désert de Saint Jean près d'Hébron. *RB* 53: 547–58.
Lagrange, M. -J.
1892   Topographie de Jérusalem. *RB* 1: 17–38.
1894a   Excursion à Sebbé. *RB* 3: 263–66.
1894b   *Saint Étienne et son sanctuaire à Jérusalem.* Paris: Picard.
1895   Chronique de Jérusalem. *RB* 4: 611–19.
1896   De Suez à Jérusalem par le Sinaï. *RB* 5: 618–43.
1897a   Du Sinaï à Naḥel. *RB* 6: 107–30, 605–25.
1897b   Mâdaba. *RB* 6: 165–84.
1897c   Notre exploration de Pétra. *RB* 6: 208–38.
1897d   Jérusalem d'après la mosaïque de Mâdaba. *RB* 6: 450–58.
1898a   Phounon. *RB* 7:112–25.
1898b   Recherches épigraphiques à Petra. *RB* 7: 165–82.
1898c   A travers le Hauran. *RB* 7: 596–611.
1899a   La Sinaï biblique. *RB* 8: 369–92.
1899b   Gézer. *RB* 8: 422–27.
1900   L'itinéraire des Israélites. *RB* 9: 63–86, 273–87, 443–49.
1932   Le site de Sodome d'après les textes. *RB* 41: 489–514.
Mallon, A.
1934   *Teleilat Ghassul, I.* Rome: Pontifical Biblical Institute.
Marie-Aline de Sion, M.
1955   *La forteresse Antonia à Jérusalem et la question du Prétoire.* Jerusalem: Franciscan.
Marquet-Krause, J.
1949   *Les fouilles de 'Ay (Et-Tell) 1933–1935. La resurection d'une grande cité biblique.* Paris: Geuthner.

Neuville, R.
1934　　　La préhistorique de Palestine. *RB* 43: 237–59.
1951　　　*Le Paléolothique et le Mésolithique de désert de Judée.* Paris: Masson.
Prignaud, J.
1963　　　Une Installation monastique byzantine au Khan Ṣaliba. *RB* 70: 243–54.
Rousée, J. M.
1962　　　Jérusalem. *RB* 69: 107–09.
1965　　　L'église Sainte-Marie de la Probatique. Chronologie des sanctuaries à Sainte-Anne de Jérusalem d'après les fouilles récentes. Pp. 169–76 in *Atti del VI Congresso Internazionale di Archeologia Cristinana. Ravenna 23–30 settembre 1962,* ed. by Vatican City.
1976　　　*Table Alphabétique des Tomes I–LXXV, 1892–1968, Revue Biblique.* Paris: Gabalda.
Ryckmans, G.
1934　　　Le Sanctuaire d'Allat à Iram. *RB* 43: 572–91.
Savignac, M. R.
1916　　　Une visite à l'ile de Rouad. *RB* 25: 565–92.
1917　　　Monuments funéraires et religieux de Castelorizo. *RB* 26: 520–36.
1920　　　Mission épigraphique à Palmyre. *RB* 29: 359–73.
1922　　　La region de ʿAïn Qedeis. *RB* 31: 55–81.
1925　　　Excursion en Transjordanie et au Kh. es-Samrâ. *RB* 34: 110–31.
1932　　　Notes de voyage. Le Sanctuaire d'Allat à Iram. *RB* 41: 581–97.
1933　　　Le Sanctuaire d'Allat à Iram. *RB* 42: 405–22.
1936　　　Sur les pistes de Transjordanie méridionale. *RB* 45: 235–62.
Savignac, M. R., and Abel F. -M.
1912　　　Neby Samouil. *RB* 21: 267–79.
Savignac, M. R., and Horsfield, G.
1935　　　Le Temple de Ramm. *RB* 44: 245–78.
Séjourné, P. -M.
1892　　　Médeba. Coup d'oeil historique, topographique et archéologique. *RB* 1: 617–44.
1894　　　Chronique palestinienne. *RB* 3: 615–28.
1897　　　L'Élianée à Madaba. *RB* 6: 648–56.
1900　　　Excursion en Philistie. *RB* 9: 112–17.
Tonneau, R.
1926　　　Excursion biblique au Négeb. *RB* 35: 583–604.
1927　　　Épigraphie grecque du Négeb. *RB* 36: 93–98.
1929　　　Caravane biblique au pays de Samson. *RB* 38: 421–31.
Vaux, R. de
1938a　　Nouvelles recherches dans la région de Cadès. *RB* 47: 89–97.
1938b　　Une mosaïque byzantine à Maʿin (Transjordanie). *RB* 47: 227–58.
1938c　　Exploration de la région de Salṭ. *RB* 47: 398–425.
1939　　　Glanes archéologiques à Maʿin (Transjordanie). *RB* 48: 78–86.
1941　　　Notes d'historie et de topographie Transjordaniennes. *RB* 50: 16–47.
1946a　　Fouilles autour de l'Église médiévale d'Abou Gosh. *RB* 53: 125–34.
1946b　　Notes archéologiques et topographiques. *RB* 53: 260–74.
1950　　　Les fouilles de ʿAy (et-Tell). *RB* 57: 621–24.
1957　　　Jérusalem. *RB* 64: 226–28.

Vaux, R. de, et al.
1947 La première campagne de fouilles à Tell Fâr'ah, pres Naplouse. *RB* 54: 394–433, 573–89.
1948 La seconde campagne de fouilles à Tell Fâh'ah, pres Naplouse. *RB* 55: 544–80.
1951 La troisième campagne de fouilles à Tell Fâr'ah, pres Naplouse. *RB* 58: 393–430, 566–90.
1952 La quatrieme campagne de fouilles à Tell Fâr'ah, pres Naplouse. *RB* 59: 551–83.
1955 Les fouilles de Tell el-Fâ'ah, pres Naplouse. Cinquieme campagne. *RB* 62: 541–89.
1957 Les fouilles de Tell el-Fâr'ah, pres Naplouse. Sixtieme campagne. *RB* 64: 552–80.
1961a *L'archéologie et les manuscrits de la Mer Morte.* London: British Academy. (English version: *Archaeology and the Dead Sea Scrolls,* 1973.)
1961b Les fouilles de Tell el-Fâr'ah, pres Naplouse. Rapport préliminaire sur les 7e, 8e, 9e campagnes, 1958–1960. *RB* 68: 557–92.

Vaux, R. de and Steve, A. M.
1950 *Fouilles a Qàryet el-'Enab, Abū Gôsh, Palestine.* Paris: Gabalda.

Viand, P.
1910 *Nazareth et ses deux églises de l'Annonciation et de St. Joseph d'après les fouilles recentes.* Paris: Picard.

Vincent, L. -H.
1898 Notes de voyage. *RB* 7: 424–51.
1903 Les ruines d"Amwâs. *RB* 12: 571–99.
1907 *Canaan d'après l'exploration récente.* Paris: Gabalda
1911a L'Église de l'Éléona. *RB* 20: 219–65.
1911b *Jérusalem sous terre. Les récentes fouilles de'Ophel.* London: Cox.
1919–21 Le Sanctuaire juif d"Aïn Douq. *RB* 28: 532–63; 30: 442–43.
1920a Un Hypogée antique a Naplouse. *RB* 29: 126–36.
1920b La Sépulture des Patriarchs. *RB* 29: 507–39.
1921a Découverte de la "Synagogue des Affranchais" à Jérusalem. *RB* 30: 247–77.
1921b La Cité de David. *RB* 30: 410–33, 541–69.
1922a Les fouilles américaines de Beisan. *RB* 31: 111–15.
1922b Une villa gréco-romaine à Beit Djebrin. *RB* 31: 259–81.
1922c Néby Samouil. *RB* 31: 360–402.
1923 Fouilles américaines à Tell el-Foul. *RB* 32: 426–30.
1924 Explorations et fouilles de l'École anglaise. *RB* 33: 422–23.
1926 Fouilles de l'École à la Basilique d"Amwas. *RB* 35: 117–21.
1927a Fouilles de l'École américaine à Beit Mirsim. *RB* 36: 408–13.
1927b Fouilles allemandes au Ramet el-Kahlîl. *RB* 36: 413–14.
1927c Fouilles américaines à Tell en-Nasbeh. *RB* 36: 414–18.
1927d Fouilles danoises à Seiloun. *RB* 36: 418–19.
1927e Fouilles allemandes à Balata-Sichem. *RB* 36: 419–25.
1927f Palestine. *RB* 36: 633–38.
1929a Fouilles de l'École anglaise à Tell Djemmeh. *RB* 38: 92–99.
1929b Fouilles anglaises à Tell Far'a. *RB* 38: 99–103.
1929c Fouilles américaines à Beth šémèš. *RB* 38: 110–13.
1929d Fouilles de l'université hébraique à Tell Djérišeh. *RB* 38: 113–14.

1929e   Palestine. *RB* 38: 155–60.
1930   Saint-Pierre en Gallicante. *RB* 39: 226–56.
1931   Les Monuments de Qoubeibeh. *RB* 40: 57–91.
1933   L'Antonia et le Prétoire. *RB* 42: 83–113.
1935a   Tell Abou Hawam. Origines de Haifa. *RB* 44: 416–37.
1935b   Jericho et sa chronologie. *RB* 44: 583–605.
1936a   Autour du groupe monumental d'ʿAmwas. *RB* 45: 403–15.
1936b   Bethléem. Le sanctuaire de la navitité d'après les fouilles récentes. *RB* 45: 544–74.
1937a   Fouilles Krause-Marquet. *RB* 46: 231–66.
1937b   Autour du prétoire. *RB* 46: 563–70.
1939a   L'Église byzantine de Hebeileh. *RB* 48: 87–90.
1939b   Les fouilles de Tell ed-Douweir = Lachish. *RB* 48: 250–77.
1948   La Chronologie du groupe monumental d'ʿAmwas. *RB* 55: 348–75.
1949   La Cité de David. *RB* 56: 614–17.
1952   Le Lithostrotos évangélique. *RB* 59: 513–30.
1954   L'Antonia, Palais primitif d'Herode. *RB* 61: 87–107.
1954–56   *Jerusalem de l'Ancien Testament, recherches d'archéologie et d'histoire.* 3 vols. in 2. Paris: Gabalda.
1958   Puits de Jacob ou de la Samaritaine. *RB* 65: 547–67.
1961   Un Sanctuaire dans la région de Jéricho. La Synagogue de Naʿarah. *RB* 68: 160–73.

Vincent, L. -H. and Abel, F. -M.
1912   *Jérusalem Antique. Topographie.* Paris: Gabalda.
1914   *Bethléem. Le Sanctuaire de la Nativité.* Paris: Gabalda.
1914–26   *Jérusalem Nouvelle. Recherches de topographie, d'archéologie et d'histoire.* Paris: Gabalda.
1932   *Emmaüs: Sa basilique et son histoire.* Paris: Leroux.

Vincent, L. -H. and Mackay, E. J. H.
1923   *Hebron. Le Haram el-Khalil. Sépulture des Patriarches.* Paris: Leroux.

Vliet, W. van der
1938   *"Sainte Marie où elle est née" et la piscine probatique.* Jerusalem: Franciscan Press/Paris: Gabalda.

Weill,R.
1920   *La Cité de David; Compte rendu des fouilles exécutées à Jérusalem, sur le site de la ville primitive. Campagne de 1913–14,* 2 vols. Paris: Geuthner.
1947   *La Cité de David. II. Campagne de 1923–24.* Paris: Geuthner.

5
GERMAN ARCHAEOLOGISTS

MANFRED AND HELGA WEIPPERT*
University of Heidelberg

I. BACKGROUND

The development of biblical archaeology in Germany during the 20th century was disrupted for a number of reasons. Two World Wars (1914–18 and 1939–45) and the post-1929 global economic depression took its toll on scholarship. The "spring" of biblical archaeology, which began to blossom at the turn of the century, was abruptly cut short by World War I. Just as Germany started to recover from the aftermath of World War I, it began to feel the effects of the depression. For more than a decade, the study of the past and present of Palestine in Germany and by Germans in Palestine was seriously handicapped both extrinsically and intrinsically by antisemitism, the official ideology of Nazi Germany under Hitler (1933–45), and the subsequent systematic extermination of the European Jews (i.e., holocaust). German-based biblical archaeology still bears the burden of this heritage.

One additional factor also influenced the trend of biblical archaeology. Traditionally, Germany, as the rest of the world, was more interested in the "biblical" archaeology of Palestine than in Palestinian archaeology in general. During the 20th century, Palestinian archaeology has developed into an independent discipline, a fact that is acknowledged in the German-speaking countries as well as the rest of the world. Although Palestinian archaeology is no longer dominated by biblical questions, its institutional relationship to church-sponsored organizations in Germany and German-speaking countries remains intact. All current university institutes for biblical archaeology in German-speaking countries, for example, are affiliated with departments of Protestant (Tübingen, Kiel, Göttingen, and Mainz in the Federal Republic of Germany; Greifswald in the German Democratic Republic; Vienna in Austria) or Roman Catholic (Münster in the Federal Republic of Germany; Freiburg in Switzerland) theology.

---

*Translation from the German by Margaret M. Clarkson (Tübingen).

A similar situation exists in regard to German professional associations for Palestinian research and for German institutes in Palestine. The Protestant Church has sponsored the "Deutsches evangelisches Institut für Altertumswissenschaft des Heiligen Landes" (German Institute for the Archaeology of the Holy Land) in Jerusalem since 1900 and an affiliated institute in Amman since 1978. Between 1905 and 1941, the *Palästina-Jahrbuch (PJ)* was the official journal of this institute. Many studies done under the auspices of this institute, however, were also published in the *Zeitschrift des Deutschen Palästina-Vereins (ZDPV)*, the official journal of the "Deutscher Verein zur Erforschung Palästinas" (DVzEP) (German Society for the Study of Palestine), which was founded in 1877. This nondenominational society, which also published *Mitteilungen und Nachrichten des Deutschen Palästina-Vereins* (MuNDPV), inaugurated a monograph series "Abhandlungen des Deutschen Palästina-Vereins" (ADPV) in 1969. The "Deutsche Verein vom Heiligen Lande" (Germany Society of the Holy Land) was founded by the German Roman Catholic Church in 1877. Together with the "Görres-Gesellschaft" (Görres-Society), it sponsors archaeological projects and regularly publishes short excavation reports in its journal *Das Heilige Land* and larger archaeological studies in its monograph series "Palästina-Hefte."

Another influential nondenominational organization active in Palestine itself is the "Deutsche Orient-Gesellschaft" (DOG) (German Middle Eastern Society). This society, which was founded in 1898, sponsored excavations and surveys. Relevant studies are published in its journal *Mitteilungen der Deutschen Orient-Gesellschaft (MDOG)* and a monograph series "Wissenschaftliche Veröffentlichungen der Deutschen Orient-Gesellschaft" (WVDOG). As its name indicates, its interest extends to the entire Levant; Palestine, therefore, is just one of its aims.

The same holds true for the "Deutsche Morgenländische Gesellschaft" (DMG) (German Middle-East Society), the affiliating Institutes of the "Deutsches Archäologisches Institut" (DAI) (German Archaeological Institute), and the "Vorderasiatisch-Ägyptische Gesellschaft" (Near Eastern-Egyptian Society), which was not reinstituted after 1945. These groups therefore have undertaken little, if any, fieldwork in Palestine.

Church and secular organizations received funds from the State (German or Austrian monarchy) until 1918 and then the "Notgemeinschaft der Deutschen Wissenschaft" and its successor, the "Deutschen Forschungs-Gemeinschaft" (DFG); business circles (e.g., Fritz Thyssen and Volkswagen foundations); and private sources (e.g., Hugo Gressmann Endowment).

The gaps in biblical archaeology during the 20th century can be explained by Germany's political history. Excavations and surveys were repeatedly shut down and then slowly (and hesitantly) resumed after 1945. The political events were also responsible for the interruptions in the work of the Jerusalem institute and the somewhat erratic publication of the journals. Due to the economic crises as well as the cultural poverty, death, emigration, and extermination of ethnic and political minorities under Hitler, the membership of the various societies declined sharply between 1914 and 1945; the current membership of many of these societies is still not as high as it was at the time of their constitution.

The way in which Palestinian archaeology was carried out in German-speaking countries, in spite of the many politically and economically related obstacles and setbacks during the first half of the 20th century, was influenced primarily by its institutional relationship to church-supported organizations. Biblical archaeology is still treated as an *ancilla theologiae*, i.e., an auxiliary discipline for OT and NT exegesis and early church history. This relationship is both advantageous and disadvantageous for biblical archaeology in German-speaking countries. The incorporation of biblical archaeology in theological studies, which hinders its independent development, is unquestionably a major disadvantage. There were and are no pure biblical archaeologists in German-speaking countries, but rather OT and NT scholars and church historians, as well as classical and ancient Near Eastern archaeologists, who are *also* biblical archaeologists. On the other hand, such biblical archaeologists are certainly also a distinct advantage; their education and research enables them to deal with both literary and archaeological sources, a combination which is absolutely mandatory for a valid reconstruction of political and cultural history. Biblical archaeology in German-speaking countries, therefore, is integrated into the historical disciplines and thus into the humanities. This then also accounts for the unusually high number of publications in German-speaking countries that incorporate both the systematic compilation and the evaluation of individual findings.

Not all characteristic aspects of biblical archaeology in German-speaking countries, however, are the direct result of political events and institutional relationships. Many committed scholars have helped shape the orientation of biblical archaeology. Three such scholars were past directors of the Jerusalem institute: G. Dalman (1902–17), who integrated ethnographical research into biblical archaeology; and A. Alt (1921–33) and M. Noth (1964–68), who both emphasized historical topography.

II. EXCAVATIONS

The prospects for German excavation projects in Palestine looked very promising at the beginning of the 20th century. Three excavations on large ruin mounds, which were begun in rapid succession, were all published before the outbreak of World War I. The first excavation was carried out between 1902 and 1903 on Tell Taʿannak (Taanach) under the direction of the OT scholar E. Sellin and the architect G. Schumacher. Most of the financial support for this excavation was provided by the Imperial Academy of Sciences in Vienna. Immediately after completing the Tell Taʿannak excavation, between 1903 and 1905, G. Schumacher began sounding the neighboring Tell el-Mutesellim (Megiddo). This excavation was supported by funds from the German Emperor Wilhelm II, DVzEP, and DOG. The cataloging and publication of the small finds was undertaken by the classical archaeologist C. Watzinger, who, together with E. Sellin, excavated on Tell es-Sulṭan (Jericho) between 1907 and 1909. This excavation was supported by funds provided by DOG. Architects F. Langenegger, A. Nöldeke and G. Schultze also participated in this excavation; they were responsible for drawing the maps and ground plans.

The constellation of excavators in these three early projects was typical of 20th century German scholarship; excavations and their publication were in the hands of OT scholars, classical archaeologists, and architects. Because architects participated, German-language publications of excavations were always characterized by exact maps, ground plans, and sectional drawings.

During his excavations at Tell Taʿannak, E. Sellin benefited from the methodological developments and results of W. M. F. Petrie's work at Tell el-Ḥesi in 1890. Petrie's Tell el-Ḥesi excavation had clearly indicated that the key to understanding the archaeology of Palestine is pottery, and Sellin incorporated this emphasis into his first excavation. Obviously, his excavation on Tell Taʿannak was a "protostratigraphical" excavation, i.e., he used pottery sherds to determine subsequently the "cultural strata" (*Kulturschichten*) instead of dating the strata according to the sherds found in them, as was the case with excavations carried out after the development of the stratigraphical method. The archaeologist at the beginning of the 20th century, however, was still a long way from such a method. Sellin's stratigraphical classification, therefore, was correspondingly simple: he reported four cultural strata for the settlement history of Tell Taʿannak (we now know that settlement there extended from the Early Bronze Age into the Islamic period) and therefore assigned widely divergent material from the Early Bronze to the Late Bronze ages to the earliest "stratum."

There are probably two reasons why G. Schumacher had a more differentiated view of the stratigraphical sequence in his excavation of Tell el-Mutesellim: (1) he was able to draw on the experiences of R. A. S. Macalister, who began excavating at Gezer in 1902, and (2) he was an architect, which means that he was more concerned with using architectural finds to differentiate the strata. In view of the many sectional drawings in the volume of plates of the excavation report and the occasional remarks in the text, which show that Schumacher thoroughly considered the different composition of the individual strata, it is obvious that he was well on the way to a stratigraphical excavation. If Schumacher's "earliest stratum of the *Mittelburg*" (Central Palace) is equated with stratum XII of the American excavations, a limited correlation is possible between Schumacher's strata of sequence and that established later by American archaeologists.

When E. Sellin and C. Watzinger then excavated together on Tell es-Sulṭan, their stratigraphical differentiation was based even more on the interrelationships between different walls and foundations. Since the excavation was carried out, recorded, and published with true "German thoroughness," the final excavation report was a respectable piece of work for the time. According to W. F. Albright, it is "in many respects the best publication of the results of Palestinian excavation yet issued." (1924:24, n.2) Unfortunately, because of inadequate reflection on the combination of excavation results and biblical statements on Jericho, the absolute dating of the strata was incorrect. As has often been the case in the history of the excavation of Tell es-Sulṭan, the legendary walls of Jericho cast a shadow on the archaeological findings. C. Watzinger, recognizing this problem, corrected the dating in a study published in 1926. The influence of the alleged "biblical dating" on the excavation results from Tell es-Sulṭan was perhaps not completely negative: it also forced German-speaking biblical archaeologists at an early date to develop an appropriate way of combining textual evidence and archaeological data.

Apart from the general knowledge of the political and cultural history of Palestine contributed by these three excavations, each was also extremely productive in its own right. On Tell Taʿannak, archaeologists found a group of twelve cuneiform texts, mostly letters, from the Late Bronze Age, a cylinder seal with an Old Babylonian legend, and restorable fragments of a 90 cm high clay incense burner that was adorned with 36 sculptured human and animal heads. With the so-called *Westburg* (Western Palace), Sellin excavated what we know today is a Canaanite palace from MB II. G. Schumacher also excavated two palaces from this period on Tell el-Mutesellim: the so-called *Nordburg* (Northern Palace) and the *Mittelburg* (Central Palace), along with their underground vaulted tombs. The first voluted (proto-Aeolic) capital ever reported from Palestine was found in secondary use by the excavators in the Israelite pillared building, which was referred to as the *Templeburg* (Temple Palace). Among the small finds, two inscribed seals, that of "Shemaʿ, servant of Jeroboam" and that of "Asaph," are particularly important. Although Schumacher was not as successful in his excavation of the northwest terrace of the tell, it should not be forgotten that he had already dug two probe trenches in the lower city. The excavations on Tell es-Sulṭan provided the first important information about the course of the various fortification systems of the city. The finds from MB I, Iron Age I, and the Persian period are especially interesting, since later British excavations on the tell were able to uncover very little from these periods.

Shortly before the outbreak of World War I (1913–14), E. Sellin began his third excavation on Tell Balaṭa (Shechem). The project was interrupted by the War and could not be resumed until 1926, at which time excavation was hampered by personnel, financial, and political conditions. The excavation was finally discontinued in 1934. All hope that E. Sellin would publish a final excavation report was shattered after many small finds, the excavation notes, and most of the sketches were destroyed in a bombing raid on Berlin during World War II.

Scholars supported by Roman Catholic organizations fared somewhat better in the difficult time between World Wars I and II when funds were scarce. They carried out several excavations, predominantly of sites with post-biblical occupation, most of which were situated on church-owned property. A. E. Mader (1926–28) uncovered the Roman-Byzantine complex on Ramat el-Khalil close to Hebron. In 1928, A. M. Schneider began to excavate the octagonal Theotokos Church built by the emperor Zeno on Mt. Gerizim. Although work was begun by P. Karge in 1911, it was not until 1932 that Mader completed the excavation of the Byzantine church at Ṭabghah. The famous mosaics with their impressive Nile landscape, which were recently endangered by shifting soil, were successfully preserved by a restoration project completed in 1982. In 1934, A. E. Mader began excavating the Omayyad palace on Khirbet el-Minyeh near Ṭabghah, a project which was continued during 1937–39 by O. Puttrich-Reignard. In 1932, R. Köppel conducted soundings on the adjacent Tell el-ʿOreimeh, and he directed his first major campaign at this site in 1939; the preliminary report was published by G. Darsow. The outbreak of World War II marked the end of German excavations in Palestine.

On the whole, the contribution to biblical archaeology made by German-speaking scholars during this second period of excavations was not so great as that of the first period. Most excavations were carried out on sites from the Roman Period or later; the promising excavation of Tell el-ʿOreimeh had to be prematurely discontinued; some of the important finds from Tell Balaṭa were published only in rough preliminary reports.

War and the postwar period imposed a 25-year intermission on German excavations. It was not until 1966 and 1967 that Ute Wagner-Lux, a classical archaeologist and later director of the Jerusalem institute, resumed excavation activity, clearing two Byzantine churches with mosaic floors in Transjordanian Medeba. During the restoration of the German Lutheran Church of the Redeemer in the Old City of Jerusalem in 1970, she carried out deep soundings under the church floor. The excavation was completed in 1974 by K. H. J. Vriezen, her assistant. This small-scale project, which was intended to determine the course of the much discussed "second" north wall of Herodian Jerusalem, was successful: it showed that the wall under the Lutheran Church of the Redeemer could not have been built before 67/68 A.D. and that it, therefore, is not a candidate for the "second wall" of Josephus. Before the excavation under the Lutheran Church of the Redeemer was completed, a German-Israeli project was begun on Khirbet el-Meshash in the Negeb; the excavators were Israeli archaeologists Y. Aharoni and A. Kempinski and the German OT scholar V. Fritz. Three campaigns at this site in 1972, 1974, and 1975 uncovered important information about the transition period between the Late Bronze and Iron Ages. Since 1978, German biblical archaeology has also been represented at the Israeli excavations on Tell el-Fukhkhar (Acco) by the OT scholar D. Conrad. In 1976, U. Wagner-Lux, K. H. J. Vriezen, and E. W. Krueger, an architect, began to excavate and restore the large ancient city of Umm Qeis (Gadara) in Transjordan; this site is well known for its monumental Roman and Byzantine structures. A partial goal of the project was accomplished with the excavation and restoration of an octagonal memorial church. The most recent German excavation, directed by V. Fritz in 1982, was the resumption of the Tell el-ʿOreimeh project, which had been started in 1939, but discontinued after just one campaign.

The importance of the German excavations resumed since 1966 cannot be estimated until the final excavation reports have been published.

III. SURFACE EXPLORATION

Surface explorations undertaken by German-speaking scholars at the beginning of the 20th century continued in the tradition of the 19th century travelers and, to a certain extent, carried on the projects which had been started before the turn of the century. The expeditions undertaken by A. Musil in southern Transjordan and Palestine between 1896 and 1902 are one example of such projects, the primary purpose of which was to obtain geographical and ethnographical information. G. Schumacher, an architect residing in Haifa, also carried out a large-scale survey of Jaulan and Ajlun in northern Transjordan between 1885 and 1914. This project was funded by PEF, railroad companies, and DVzEP. The resulting maps, which included the region between the Hermon and the Jabbok (Nahr ez-Zerqa), the Jordan, and the Hejaz railway, were published between 1908 and 1924 as the *Karte des Ostjor-*

danlandes (Map of Transjordan) (Ten Sheets in a scale of 1:63360). This set of maps supplements those of Western Palestine published in the 19th century by the PEF. Schumacher's expedition notes, part of which were published by Schumacher himself and part by C. Steuernagel, are also important. These notes included a geographic description of the region and its settlements, information about local and regional names, and a description of monuments which could be seen on the surface at that time. The Deutsch-Turkisches Denkmalschutz-Kommando (German-Turkish Command for the Preservation of Historical Monuments), under the direction of Th. Wiegand, was active in the Negeb and the northern part of the Sinai peninsula from 1914 until the conquest of this region by the British in 1916. Wiegand's descriptions of the Nabataean-Byzantine city ruins in the Negeb both duplicate and supplement the reports of C. L. Woolley, T. E. Lawrence, and S. F. Newcombe, which were not available in Germany until after World War I. On two trips during the winters of 1932/3 and 1933/4, F. Frank, a Palestinian-German who covered most of these regions on foot, compiled important information on the Arabah, the eastern Negeb, and the southernmost part of Transjordan. The publication of his reports, in 1934, resulted in an historical evaluation by A. Alt (1935) and coincided with the appearance of the first volume of N. Glueck's *Explorations in Eastern Palestine* (1934).

More characteristic of the "German style" than these expeditions are the training courses *(Lehrkurse)* sponsored by the Deutsches Evangelisches Institut für Altertumswissenschaft des Heiligen Landes (German Protestant Institute for the Archaeology of the Holy Land) in Jerusalem. Initially, the courses, which were inaugurated by G. Dalman, were held every six months, but they soon became an annual event. They were conducted by Dalman between 1903 and 1914 and then, after an interruption necessitated by the political events, by A. Alt between 1924 and 1931. Since 1953, the courses have been taught alternately by H. Donner, K. Galling, A. Kuschke, M. Noth, H. J. Stoebe, U. Wagner-Lux, and M. Weippert. The participants in the course are qualified Fellows sent by the German Protestant churches. These Fellows, generally younger scholars or pastors, receive a detailed on-the-spot introduction to the geography and archaeology of Palestine and some of the neighboring countries in a combined lecture-and-excursion program extending over a two- to three-month period. Prior to World War II, most excursions were made on horseback; now a small van is used. Frequently, the course motivates the Fellows to do scientific studies in this field. Observations and evaluations from the study tour are contained in reports of the director and in articles published by the Fellows in the *Palästina-Jahrbuch* (prior to 1941) and *ZDPV*. Characteristic of the method used in these courses is the close relationship between a critical treatment of the entire literary tradition regarding sites, roads, regions, and territories, and the empirically acquired geographical and archaeological data.

To appreciate fully Dalman's contributions in this field, it should not be forgotten that the currently accepted method of dating with surface pottery was very limited at the time of Dalman's activities. Alt, the first to use this method consistently, was most certainly influenced by W. F. Albright, who undertook similar field trips while director of the American School of Oriental Research (ASOR) in Jerusalem in the 1920s. Several successive training courses between 1953 and 1967 occasionally dealt with larger regional projects: the so-called Ammonite watch towers, the topography of the Kingdom of Moab, and the settlement history of areas around Tell Balaṭa (Shechem), Wadi Far'ah, and Wadi Kufrinjeh.

In addition to the training courses, two post-World War II regional surveys in Transjordan, in which the use of surface pottery as a means of dating played an important role, are deserving of mention. First, S. Mittmann conducted a survey of the northern Transjordanian region between the Yarmuk and the Jabbok. This research was carried out from 1963 until 1966 under the sponsorship of the Fritz Thyssen Endowment and in association with the Jerusalem institute. Second, M. Weippert conducted a survey of the former Edomite territory between Wadi el-Ḥesa and Ras en-Naqb in 1974, 1978, and 1983; this survey has not yet been concluded. As a result of the information uncovered by these two projects, Glueck's view of the early settlement history of Transjordan had to be substantially revised.

In addition to the regional surveys, local surveys were also carried out; these surveys concentrated primarily on the topographical and archaeological mapping of one single site and its immediate surroundings. During the time Dalman was director of the Jerusalem institute (1902–14), he recorded many topographical details of Jerusalem and its surroundings, which were published in 1930 under the title *Jerusalem und sein Gelände* (Jerusalem and its Terrain). This volume has become a standard reference work for Arabic place and field names and their exact location, particularly since many of these names were lost after 1948. One of Dalman's special projects was his investigation of the cemeteries of ancient Jerusalem (1907–11). This project was concluded, for the time being, by K. Galling in 1935. In 1905 and 1907, H. Kohl and C. Watzinger, sponsored by the DOG, surveyed the ruins of ancient Galilean synagogues. G. Dalman, who was in Petra several times between 1904 and 1910, concentrated primarily on the many Nabataean cultic installations there. In 1916, the actual city area and en-Nebi Harun (Aaron), a sanctuary with Byzantine foundations on Jebel Harun, was surveyed by the German-Turkish Command for the Preservation of Historical Monuments under the direction of Th. Wiegand, who was

assisted by W. Bachmann, C. Watzinger, and K. Wulzinger. Between
1917 and 1918, C. Watzinger and K. Wulzinger, on behalf of this
organization, also studied ancient and Islamic monuments in Damascus.
Even after Y. Yadin's excavations, A. Schulten's description of the ruins of
the Herodian fortress of Masada, which was made during the period
between the two World Wars (1932), has still remained a valuable contribution. In this connection, Schulten, an archaeologist well known for his
excavations in Numantia (Spain), also undertook an exact survey of the
Roman circumvallation of Masada, which dates from the first Jewish
War, and then studied the circumvallation of Khirbet el-Yehud near
Bittir (Beth-Ter), which dates from the second Jewish (Bar-Kochba) War.
A. Strobel became part of this tradition in 1973 when he surveyed and
published the Roman siege wall (discovered by the 1965 training course
of the Jerusalem institute during a field trip) surrounding the Herodian
fortress of Machaerus (Khirbet Mukawer) in Transjordan.

IV. ETHNOARCHAEOLOGY

Since biblical and modern everyday life are so very different, there
are no direct points of contact between Palestinian ethnography and
biblical archaeology. The recognition and differentiation between the
"old" and the "new" in the here-and-now is imperative before preserved
elements in work and customs can be compared with those mentioned or
presupposed in biblical texts or with those ascertainable through excavations. Therefore, these elements must be seen and understood in terms
of their contemporary and local context before any attempt can be made
to relate the present with the past.

Basically, these are the principles that guided G. Dalman in his study
of the life of the Palestinian people. Dalman's life and work are closely
intertwined: his acquaintance with Palestine began with two long trips, in
1899 and 1900, when he was almost 50 years old. His first trip took him
to Aleppo, the second, to Balat, between southern Lebanon and the
Hermon. Here he was introduced to local forms of rural life. The route
of the trip, which took him southward as far as Hebron and En-gedi and
then northward to Damascus through Transjordan, gave him ample
opportunity to stop for the night at farmhouses and nomad tents so that
he could observe the people and their customs. The information he
compiled on these trips formed the basis of his study of the life of the
Palestinian people. As director of the institute in Jerusalem (1902–14),
he dealt mainly with the history of Palestine. He also used every excursion, whether on foot or horseback, to study and document daily life in
rural Palestine. In addition to archaeological and scientific collections,
G. Dalman started an ethnological collection including originals and
models of farmhouses, agricultural implements, craftsmen's tools, and

musical instruments. This collection is housed in the Jerusalem institute. Dalman's students, who participated temporarily in the work of the institute as staff members or fellows, also carried out ethnological studies in addition to their study of the history of Palestine.

The fruits which this secondary compilation bore are amazing. The early volumes of the *Palästina-Jahrbuch* and the *ZDVP* contain many ethnological studies from Dalman and his students. The principle that each individual phenomenon can only be understood in its own context meant that no aspect of rural life and work could be overlooked. As a result, the different articles deal with broad subjects: farmhouse, agriculture and the market, forms of hospitality, marriage and burial customs, education, and law. The studies related to religion included descriptions of Islamic sanctuaries and graves of saints; many deal with the Passover celebration of the Samaritans on Mt. Gerizim. Oral folk traditions, songs, folktales, proverbs, and expressions, which, in turn, formed the basis for dialect research, were also compiled.

Even though some of the articles were not published until after World War I, their roots went back to the time between 1902 and 1914, when Dalman was director of the Jerusalem institute. His most important ethnological study appeared long after the first "spring" of the institute. In 1917, Dalman resigned as director of the institute and accepted a call to the University of Greifswald. He returned to Palestine in 1921 and 1925 to complete his ethnological research. The fruits of his long years of compilation appeared between 1928 and 1942 in *Arbeit und Sitte in Palästina* (Work and Customs in Palestine), a 7-volume study that documented many aspects of rural life. Daily and yearly patterns influencing the rhythm of life in Palestine are treated first, followed by subjects such as agriculture, harvest, and preparation of foodstuffs. Chapters on textile techniques and products, tent life, animal husbandry and milk production, hunting, and fishing are also included. After the section dealing with farmhouses, chicken and pigeon raising, and beekeeping, Dalman had planned to treat domestic life, i.e., music and customs related to birth, marriage, and death. Dalman completed the compilation of this material at the age of 87; unfortunately, he died (1941) before it could be prepared for publication.

Arbeit und Sitte is a well organized study. The illustrated section of each volume contains photographs and drawings that complement the detailed descriptions of each technique and the corresponding tools. Every chapter in the text is divided into two parts: the first part records the modern objects and techniques and the related terminology with their local variants; the second part deals with the same object or technique in ancient times, insofar as this can be reconstructed from biblical sources, other texts from the biblical period, and post-biblical Jewish texts. These thorough studies of past and present conditions were necessary to show where and how the past is still reflected in the present and to show how the latter can shed light on the early cultural history of Palestine.

While Dalman had many students, no one truly succeeded him. A. Alt, who followed him in 1921 as director of the Jerusalem institute, was interested mainly in the political history of Palestine and less in its cultural history. While Dalman was always looking for what remained the same through the ages, Alt sought what changed in the course of time. Therefore, the study of specific items and customs reflecting the past in the present receded into the background.

V. REFERENCE WORKS AND SYSTEMATIC STUDIES

The *ancilla theologiae* role of biblical archaeology in German-speaking countries continuously forced archaeologists to present their results in a form that could be utilized by related disciplines and by laypersons. The many reference works and systematic studies (i.e., bibliographies, lexicons, atlases, monographs, comprehensive studies of cultural history, pictorial volumes, slide series illustrating biblical texts, and travel guides that point out existing traces and remains of the past for the interested tourist) are examples of how biblical archaeology has attempted to fill this role.

Reflection on the way in which archaeological discoveries, the silent witnesses of the past, are to be combined with statements found in texts from the same period, primarily biblical texts, is absolutely necessary before the results of research can be compiled and evaluated. That finds and texts cannot simply be added together had been undisputed in German-speaking countries since the beginning of the 20th century: before a comprehensive picture can be drawn, the archaeological data and texts must be interpreted in their context. This theory, which is rooted in German Idealism, strongly influenced the kinds of questions and the subsequent answers found in the early works of G. Dalman, A. Alt, and their students. In three systematic studies (1938, 1957, 1960), M. Noth provided a detailed presentation and substantiation of this position, which is so characteristic of German-speaking biblical archaeology.

It was the fieldwork of German scholars, not their theoretical work, that was hampered by political and economic conditions. One example of this continuity is P. Thomsen's monumental survey of literature on Palestine work, covering the period between 1878 and 1945; the first volume of this work appeared in 1908, with the last appearing in 1972. Apart from journals, series, and training courses of the Jerusalem institute, this bibliography is the longest continuous German biblical archaeology project in the 20th century. Its success is due not only to the

untiring efforts of Thomsen, but also to F. Maass, L. Rost, and
O. Eissfeldt, who completed the work started by Thomsen.

Palestinian archaeology in German-speaking countries during the
20th century clearly served the exegetical disciplines. Its role as an
"auxiliary discipline" to biblical studies is best exemplified by the lexicons, atlases, and cultural-historical monographs, the titles of which
already indicate that the intention was not simply to present the political
cultural history of Palestine but rather to portray the world out of which
the Bible came. These publications often appeared in series on biblical
studies, as supplements to commentary series, or in connection with
introductions to various aspects of biblical studies. The many standard
works bear witness to the fact that this orientation did not result in a
suppression of those archaeological findings critically related to biblical
tradition. The most important lexicons were H. Guthe's *Kurzes Bibelwörterbuch* (Short Bible Dictionary) from 1903 and K. Galling's *Biblisches
Reallexikon* (Biblical Encyclopedia), the first edition of which was published in 1937 and the second, in 1977. The most important atlas is
H. Guthe's *Bibelatlas* (Atlas of the Bible), which was published in 1911
with a second edition in 1926. The first comparable successor to this atlas
was the Palestine map prepared by E. Höhne for the *Biblisch-historisches
Handwörterbuch* (Handbook of Biblical History), edited by B. Reicke and
K. Rost, also published separately under the title *Palästina: Historisch-
archäologische Karte* (1981). Many geographical and historical maps of
Palestine are currently being drawn for the interdisciplinary research
project, *Tübinger Atlas des Vorderan Orients* (Tübingen Atlas of the Near
East). The differences between the many comprehensive 20th century
German-language publications on cultural history, most of which appeared in several editions, and their 19th century predecessors are
obvious: the reconstruction of the biblical world in the 19th century was
based predominantly on the Bible as primary source, while 20th century
cultural histories based their reconstruction on the results of archaeological research.

The number of monographs dealing with individual categories of
finds or certain periods of history is relatively small. This is surprising
because such studies form the necessary links between the various lexicons and comprehensive cultural histories; these narrowly focused
monographs document and discuss the concise headings found in reference works and thereby lay the foundation for surveys of cultural history. The distinct lack in this area is probably related to the role of
biblical archaeology as an auxiliary discipline, for it best fills this role
when the results are presented in lexicon-like or a similar summarizing
form. There is no current history of architecture which compares with
C. Watzinger's *Denkmäler Palästinas* (Monuments in Palestine) published
between 1933 and 1935. Few modern studies can be compared with

K. Galling's works on lamps, altars, and pictorial seals with legends. However, the monographs on royal stamps by P. Welton (a Galling student), on the temple in Israel by V. Fritz, and on metal figurines of gods by H. Seeden are well worth mentioning. A study of Greek imported ware from the Persian period is being prepared in Münster with the support of the Volkswagen Foundation; a preliminary report has already been published by R. Wenning.

Since archaeology provides material suitable for illustrating objects and procedures described in texts, the archaeological heritage of a country such as Palestine is also used to illustrate biblical texts. One of the best volumes on this subject was H. Gressman's *Altorientalische Bilder zum Alten Testament* (The Ancient Near East in Pictures Related to the Old Testament), published in 1909; especially valuable is the second edition of 1927, which has never found an adequate successor in German literature. A comparable volume, however, has been published in the United States: J. B. Pritchard's *The Ancient Near East in Pictures Relating to the Old Testament* (Princeton 1954, 1969²). H. Th. Bossert's volume of pictures entitled *Altsyrien* (Ancient Syria) (1951) stresses the arts and crafts. Most of the other volumes of pictures portray the country, its people, its culture, and its past, insofar as this is still discernible in structures, ruins, and customs. All volumes of pictures mentioned, however, remain on the surface, i.e., they do not go beyond the objective world. O. Keel has made numerous attempts to penetrate beyond the objective world in order to understand the symbolic meaning of objects. His work *Die Welt der altorientalischen Bildsymbolik und das Alte Testament* was particularly well received; the German version is already in its third edition (English edition: *The Symbolism of the Biblical World: Ancient Near Eastern Iconography and the Book of Pslams,* New York, 1978).

The illustrative material made available by archaeology is particularly well suited for educational purposes, a possibility which was utilized early in German-speaking countries. A series of 108 slides with text was available from I. Benzinger for classroom use as early as 1921. While this series lacks the technical perfection and scope of J. Zink's series, it compares well in terms of content and method.

Biblical archaeology in German-speaking lands has served more than scientific and educational purposes. The more popular publications such as tourist guides are also extremely good. One classic example is the travel guide from K. Baedeker, published at the end of the 19th century. The first two editions were prepared by A. Socin, with later editions by I. Benzinger. By the beginning of World War I, this travel guide was available in several editions and languages. The tourist guide *Orte und Landschaften der Bibel* (Places and Regions of the Bible), which is being produced by O. Keel and M. Küchler, promises to be a worthy successor to the Baedeker guide. The first two volumes of this three-volume work have been published.

BIBLIOGRAPHY

Aharoni, Y.; Fritz, V.; and Kempinski, A.
1973   Vorbericht über die Ausgrabungen auf der Hirbet el-Mšāš (Tēl Maśôś), 1. Kampagne 1972. ZDPV 89: 197–210.
1975   Vorbericht über die Ausgrabungen auf der Hirbet el-Mšāš (Tel Maśôś), 2. Kampagne 1974. ZDPV 91: 109–30.
Alt, A.
1921   Die griechischen Inschriften der Palaestina Tertia westlich der ʿAraba. Wissenschaftliche Veröffentlichungen des deutsch-türkischen Denkmalschutz-Kommandos 2. Berlin: Vereinigung Wissenschaftlicher Verleger.
1941   Gustaf Dalman. PJ 37: 5–18.
Bachmann, W.; Watzinger, C.; and Wiegand, Th.
1921   Petra. Mit einem Beitrage von K. Wulzinger. Wissenschaftliche Veröffentlichungen des deutsch-türkischen Denkmalschutz-Kommandos 3. Berlin: Vereinigung Wissenschaftlicher Verleger.
Baedeker, K., ed.
1910   Palästina und Syrien. Handbuch für Reisende, 7th ed. Leipzig: Baedeker.
Benzinger, I.
1907   Hebräische Archäologie, 2nd ed. Grundriss der Theologischen Wissenschaften 2/1. Tübingen: Mohr.
1913   Bilderatlas zur Bibelkunde. Stuttgart: Steinkopf.
1924   Erläuterungen zu 108 ausgewählten Lichtbildern für den Religionsunterricht, 2nd ed. Stuttgart: Steinkopf.
1927   Hebräische Archäologie, 3rd ed. Angelos-Lehrbücher 1. Leipzig: Pfeiffer.
Bergsträsser, G.
1915   Sprachatlas von Syrien und Palästina. ZDPV 38: 169–222.
Bertholet, A.
1919   Kulturgeschichte Israels. Göttingen: Vandenhoeck & Ruprecht.
Bossert, H. Th.
1951   Altsyrien: Kunst und Handwerk in Cypern, Syrien, Palästina, Transjordanien und Arabien von den Anfängen bis zum völligen Aufgehen in der Griechisch-römischen Kultur. Tübingen: Wasmuth.
Brünnow, R. E., and von Domaszewski, A.
1904–09   Die Provincia Arabia, auf Grund Zweier in den jahren 1897 und 1898 unternommenen Reisen und Berichte früherer Reisender, 3 vols. Strassburg: Trübner.
Dalman, G.
1908   Petra und seine Felscheiligtümer. Leipzig: Hinrich.
1910   Einst und Jetzt in Palästina. PJ 6: 27–37.
1912   Neue Petra-Forschungen und der heilige Felsen von Jerusalem. Palästinische Forschungen zur Archäologie und Topographie 2. Leipzig: Hinrich.

1924   Dass und wie wir Palästinaforschung treiben müssen. *PJ* 20: 5–22.

1928–42   *Arbeit und Sitte in Palästina*, 7 vols. Schriften des Deutschen Palästina-Instituts 3–10. Gütersloh: Bertelsmann.

1930   *Jerusalem und sein Gelände.* Schriften des Deutschen Palästina-Instituts 4. Gütersloh. Bertelsmann.

Darsow, W.

1940   Tell el-ʿOrēme am See Genezareth: Vorläufiger Bericht über die erste Grabung im März und April 1939. *Mitteilungen des Deutschen Archäologischen Instituts* 9: 132–45.

Donner, H.

1976   *Einführung in die biblische Landes- und Altertumskunde.* Darmstadt: Wissenschaftliche Buchgesellschaft.

Dothan, M. and Conrad, D.

1978   Notes and News: ʿAkko, 1978. *IEJ* 28: 264–66.

1979   Notes and News: ʿAkko, 1979. *IEJ* 29: 227–28.

Frank, F., and Alt, A.

1934   Aus der ʿAraba. *ZDPV* 57: 191–280.

1935   Aus der ʿAraba. *ZDPV* 58: 1–78.

Fritz, V.

1977   *Tempel und Zelt. Studien zum Tempelbau in Israel und zu dem Zeltheiligtum der Priesterschrift.* Wissenschaftliche Monographien zum Alten und Neuen Testament 47. Neukirchen-Vluyn: Neukirchener.

1978   Kinneret und Ginnosar: Voruntersuchung für eine Ausgrabung auf dem *Tell el-ʿOreme* am See Genezareth. *ZDPV* 94: 32–45.

1980   Biblische Archäologie. *Mitteilungen des Deutschen Archäologen-Verbandes* e.V. 11: 9–12.

Fritz, V., and Kempinski, A.

1976   Vorbericht über die Ausgrabungen auf der Ḫirbet el-Mšāš (*Tēl Māśōś*, 3. Kampagne 1975.) *ZDPV* 92: 83–104.

Fritz, V., et al.

1983   *Ergebnisse der Ausgrabungen auf der Ḫirbet el-Mšāš (Tēl Māśōś) 1972–1975.* Wiesbaden: Harrassowitz. 3 volumes.

Galling, K.

1923   Die Beleuchtungsgeräte im israelitisch-jüdischen Kulturgebiet. *ZDPV* 46: 1–50.

1925   *Der Altar in den Kulturen des alten Orients. Eine archäologische Studie.* Berlin: Curtius.

1936a   Die Nekropole von Jerusalem. *PJ* 32: 73–101.

1936b   Ein Etagen-Pilastergrab im Norden von Jerusalem. *ZDPV* 59: 111–23.

1937   *Biblisches Reallexikon. Handbuch zum Alten Testament* I/1. Tübingen: Mohr.

1941   Beschriftete Bildsiegel des Ersten Jahrtausends v. Chr. vornehmlich aus Syrien und Palästina. *ZDPV* 64: 121–202.

Galling, K., ed.

1977   *Biblisches Reallexikon. Handbuch zum Alten Testament* I/1, 2nd ed. Tübingen: Mohr.

Gressmann, H.

1927   *Altorientalische Bilder zum Alten Testament,* 2nd ed. Berlin: de Gruyter.

Gröber, K.
1925   *Palästina, Arabien und Syrien: Baukunst, Landschaft, Volksleben.*
        Berlin: Wasmuth.
Guthe, H.
1926   *Bibelatlas in 20 Haupt- und 28 Nebenkarten. Mit einem Verzeichnis
        der alten und neuen Ortsnamen,* 2nd ed. Leipzig: Wagner & Debes.
1927   *Palästina,* 2nd ed. Monographien zur Erdkunde 21. Bielefeld:
        Velhagen & Klasing.
Guthe, H., ed.
1903   *Kurzes Bibelwörterbuch.* Tübingen: Mohr.
Haag, H., ed.
1968   *Bibel-Lexikon,* 2nd ed. Einsideln: Benziger.
Höhne, E., ed.
1981   *Palästina. Historisch-Archäologische Karte. Zwei vierzehnfarbige Blät-
        ter 1:300,000. Mit Einführung und Register.* Göttingen:
        Vandenhoeck & Ruprecht.
Jäger, K.
1912   *Das Bauernhaus in Palästina mit Rücksicht auf das biblische
        Wohnhaus.* Göttingen: Vandenhoeck & Ruprecht.
Jaroš, K.
1976   *Sichem: Eine archäologische und religionsgeschichtliche Studie mit
        besonderer Berücksichtigung von Jos 24.* Orbis Biblicus et Orientalis
        11. Freiburg: Universitätsverlag.
Jeremias, J.
1932   *Die Passahfeier der Samaritaner und ihre Bedeutung für das Ver-
        ständnis der alttestamentlichen Passahüberlieferung.* BZAW 59.
        Giessen: Topelmann.
Kalt, E.
1931   *Biblisches Reallexikon.* 2 vols. Paderborn: Schöningh.
Keel, O.
1978   *The Symbolism of the Biblical World: Ancient Near Eastern Iconogra-
        phy and the Book of Psalms.* Trans. T. J. Hallet from 2nd German
        ed. New York: Seabury.
Keel, O., and Küchler, M.
1982   *Orte und Landschaften der Bibel. Ein Handbuch und Stu-
        dienreiseführer zum Heiligen Land, 2: Der Süden.* Göttingen:
        Vandenhoeck & Ruprecht.
Keel, O.; Küchler, M.; and Uehlinger, C.
1984   *Orte und Landschaften der Bibel. Ein Handbuch und Stu-
        dienreiseführer zum Heiligen Land, 1: Geographisch-geschichtliche
        Landeskunde.* Göttingen: Vandenhoeck & Ruprecht.
Kellermann, M. et al.
1982   *Welt aus der die Bibel kommt.* Biblische Basis Bücher 2. Kevelaer:
        Butzon & Bercker.
Köppel, R.
1930   *Palästina: Die Landschaft in karten und Bildern.* Tübingen: Mohr.
1932   *Der tell el 'Orēme und die Ebene Genesareth. Biblica* 13: 298–
        308.
Kohl, H., and Watzinger C.
1916   *Antike Synagogen in Galiläa.* WVDOG 29. Leipzig: Hinrich
Kroll, G.
1975   *Auf den Spuren Jesu,* 5th ed. Leipzig: St.-Benno-Verlag.

Lamer, H.
1923   *Altorientalische Kulter im Bilde.* Wissenschaft und Bildung 103.
            Leipzig: Quelle & Meyer.
Landauer, G., ed.
1925   *Palästina: 300 Bilder.* Munich: Meyer & Jessen.
Lux, U.
1967   Eine Altchristliche Kirche in Mādeba. *ZDPV* 83: 165–82.
1968   *Die Apostelkirche in Mādeba. ZDPV* 84: 106–29.
1972   Vorläufiger Bericht über die Ausgrabung unter der
            Erlöserkirche im Muristan in der Altstadt von Jerusalem in den
            Jahren 1970 und 1971. *ZDPV* 88: 185–201.
Mader, A. E.
1933a   Die Ausgrabung der Kirche der Brotvermehrung durch die
            Görresgesellschaft. *Theologie und Glaube* 25: 669–77.
1933b   Die Ausgrabung eines römischen Kastells auf *chirbet el-minje* an
            der Via Maris bei eṭ-ṭābgha am See Gennesareth. *JPOS* 13: 209–
            220.
Mader, E.
1957   *Mambre. Die Ergebnisse der Ausgrabungen im heiligen Bezirk Râmet
            el-Halîl in Südpalästina, 1926–1928, I. II.* Freiburg: Wewel.
Mittmann, S.
1970   *Beiträge zur Siedlungs- und Territorialgeschichte des nördlichen Ost-
            jordanlandes.* ADPV 2. Wiesbaden: Harrassowitz.
Musil, A.
1907–08   *Arabia Petraea.* 2 vols. Wien: Hölder.
Noth, M.
1938   Grundsätzliches zur geschichtlichen Deutung archäologischer
            Befunde auf dem Boden Palästinas. *PJ* 34: 7–22.
1957   Hat die Bibel doch recht? Pp. 7–22 in *Festschrift für G. Dehn,* ed.
            W. Schneemelcher. Neukirchen: Kreis Moers.
1960   Der Beitrage der Archäologie zur Geschichte Israels. *Vetus Tes-
            tamentum Supplements* 7: 262–82.
1966   *The Old Testament World.* Trans. V. I. Gruhn from 4th German
            ed. Philadelphia: Fortress.
Nötscher, F.
1940   *Biblische Altertumskunde. Die Heilige Schrift des Alten Testamentes,
            Ergänzungsband 3.* Bonn: Hanstein.
Preiss, L.; Dalman, G.; and Volz, P.
n.d.   *64 Bilder aus dem Heiligen Land.* Stuttgart: Württembergische
            Bibelanstalt.
Preiss, L., and Rohrbach, P.
1925   *Palästina und das Ostjordanland.* Stuttgart: Hoffmann.
Puttrich-Reignard, O.
1938   Excavations in Palestine and Trans-jordan: Khirbet Minya.
            QDAP 7: 49–51.
1939   Excavations in Palestine and Trans-jordan: Khirbet Minya.
            QDAP 8: 159–60.
1942   Excavations in Palestine and Trans-jordan: Khirbet Minya.
            QDAP 9: 209–10.
Puttrich-Reignard, O., and Schneider, A. M.
1939   *Die Fünfte Grabungskampagne auf Chirbet el-Minje. Palästina-Hefte*
            17–20. Köln: J.P. Bachem.

Reicke, B., and Rost, L., eds.
1962–79   *Biblische-historisches Handwörterbuch.* 4 vols. Göttingen: Vandenhoeck & Ruprecht.

Schmidt, H., and Kahle, P.
1930   *Volkserzählungen aus Palästina Gesammelt bei den Bauern von Bir-Zet und in Verbindung mit Dschirius Jusif herausgegeben.* Forschungen zur Religion und Literatur des Alten und Neuen Testaments 17. Göttingen: Vandenhoeck & Ruprecht.

Schneider, A. M.
1933   Excavations in Palestine in 1931–32: Khirbet Minya. *QDAP* 2: 188–89.
1934   *Die Brotvermehrungskirche von eṭ-ṭâbǧa* am Genesarethsee und ihre Mosaiken. Collectanea Hierosolymitana: Veröffentlichungen des Orientalischen Instituts der Görresgesellschaft in Jerusalem 4. Paderborn: Schoningh.
1937   Excavations in Palestine, 1935–36: Khirbet Minya. *QDAP* 6: 215–17.
1946–51   Römische und byzantinische Bauten auf dem Garizim. *ZDPV* 68: 217–34.
1952   Hirbet el-Minje am See Genezareth. *Annales archéologiques de Syrie* 2: 23–45.

Schneider, A. M., and Puttrich-Reignard, O.
1937   *Ein Frühislamischer Bau am See Genesareth: Zwei Berichte über die Grabungen auf Chirbet el-Minje.* Palästina-Hefte 15. Köln: J.P. Bachem.

von Schuler, E.
1968   Siebzig Jahre Deutsche Orient-Gesellschaft. *MDOG* 100: 6–21.

Schulten, A., et al.
1933   Masada, die Burg des Herodes und die römischen Lager, mit einem Anhang: Beth-Ter. *ZDPV* 56: 1–185.

Schumacher, G.
1908   *Tell el-Mutessellim: Bericht über die 1903 bis 1905 mit Unterstützung Sr. Majestät des Deutschen Kaisers und der Deutschen Orient-Gesellschaft vom Deutschen Verein zur Enforschung Palästinas veranstalteten Ausgrabungen I: Fundbericht: A. Test, B. Tafeln.* Leipzig. Rudolph Haupt.
1913   El-Maḳārin und der Tell ed-Dschamīd. *ZDPV* 36: 114–23.
1913–17   Unsere Arbeiten im Ostjordanland. *ZDPV* 36: 123–29; 37: 45–54, 123–34, 260–66; 38: 136–49; 40: 143–70.

Seeden, H.
1980   *The Standing Armed Figurines in the Levant.* Prahistorische Bronzefunde 11. Munich: Beck.

Sellin, E.
1904   *Tell Taʿannek: Bericht über eine mit Unterstützung der kaiserlichen Akademie der Wissenschaften und des k. k. Ministeriums für Kultus und Unterricht unternommene Ausgrabung in Palästina, nebst einem Anhange von Fr. Hrozný: "Die Keilschrifttexte von Taʿannek."* Denkschriften des Kaiserlichen Akademie der Wissenschaften in Wien. Wien: Carl Gerold's Sohn.
1905   *Eine Nachlese auf dem Tell Taʿannek in Palästina, nebst einem Anhange von Fr. Hrozný: "Die neugefundenen Keilschrifttexte von Ta ʿannek."* Denkschriften Kaiserlichen Akademie der Wissenschaften in Wien. Wien: Hölder.

1914   Tell Balāṭah-Sichem. Pp. 35–40, 204–07 in *Anzeiger der Kai-serlichen Akademie der Wissenschaften* 51. Wien: Akademie.

1926a   Die Ausgrabung von Sichem: Kurze vorläufige Mitteilung über die Arbeit im Frühjahr 1926. *ZDPV* 49: 229–236.

1926b   Die Ausgrabung von Sichem: Kurze vorläufige Mitteilung über die Arbeit im Sommer 1926. *ZDPV* 49: 304–19.

1927a   Die Ausgrabung von Sichem: Kurze vorläufige Mitteilung über die Arbeit im Frühjahr 1927. *ZDPV* 50: 205–11.

1927b   Die Ausgrabung von Sichem: Kurze vorläufige Mitteilung über die Arbeit im Sommer 1927. *ZDPV* 50: 265–74.

1932   Der Gegenwärtige Stand der Ausgrabungen von Sichem und ihre Zukunft. *ZAW* 50: 303–08.

Sellin, E., and Steckeweh, H.
1941   Kurzer vorläufiger Bericht über die Ausgrabungen von Balâṭa (Sichem) im Herbst 1934. *ZDPV* 64: 1–20.

Sellin, E., and Watzinger, C.
1913   *Jericho: Die Ergebnisse der Ausgrabungen.* WVDOG 22. Leipzig: Hinrich.

Steuernagel, C.
1924–26   Der ʿAdschlūn. Nach den Aufzeichnungen von Dr. G. Schumacher, Baurat, Schwäbisch-Gemünd. *ZDPV* 47: 191–240; 48: 1–144; 49: 1–167, 273–303.

Strobel, A.
1968   Machärus—Geschichte und Ende einer Festung im Lichte arch-äologisch-topographischer Beobachtungen. Pp. 198–225 in *Bibel und Qumran: Beiträge zur Erforschung der Beziehungen zwischen Bible- und Qumranwissenschaft.* Berlin: Evangelische Haupt-Bibelgesellschaft.

1974   Das Römische Belagerungswerk um Machärus: To-pographische Untersuchungen. *ZDPV* 90: 128–184.

TAVO (Tübinger Atlas des Vorderen Orients)
1975   Sonderforschungsbereich 19: Tübinger Atlas des Vorderen Orients. Arbeitscheft 1: Gesamtplan. Tübingen: Sonder-forschungsbereich.

Thomsen, P.
1917   *Palästina und seine Kultur in fünf Jahrtausenden.* 2nd ed. Aus Natur und Gesteswelt 260. Leipzig: Teubner.

1925   *Die neueren Forschungen in Palästina-Syrien und ihre Bedeutung für den Religionsunterricht.* Sammlung gemeinverständlicher Vorträge und Schriften aus dem Gebiet der Theologie und Religionsgeschichte 114. Tübingen: Mohr.

1931   *Palästina und seine Kultur in fünf Jahrtausenden.* 3rd ed. Der Alte Orient 30. Leipzig: Hinrich.

Thomsen, P., ed.
1908–72   *Die Palästina-Literatur: Eine Internationale Bibliographie in sys-tematischer Ordnung mit Autoren- und Sachregister, I–VII* (Die Literatur der Jahre 1895–1945), I–V. Leipzig. VI–VII. Berlin. (From vol. 6, the bibliography was produced in cooperation with F. Maass, L. Rost, and O. Eissfeldt.)

1957–60   *Ergänzungsband A.: Die Literatur der Jahre 1878–1894.* Berlin. (This section of the bibliography was produced in cooperation with L. Rost and O. Eissfeldt.)

Volz, P.
1925   *Die biblischen Altertümer,* 2nd ed. Stuttgart: Calwer Ver-
            einsbuchhandlung.
Vriezen, K. J. H.
1978   Zweiter vorläufiger Bericht über die Ausgrabung unter der
            Erlöserkirche im Muristan in der Altstadt von Jerusalem
            (1972–1974). *ZDPV* 94: 76–81.
Wagner-Lux, U., et al.
1978   Bericht über die Oberflächenforschung in Gadara (Umm Qēs)
            in Jordanien im Jahre 1974. *ZDPV* 94: 135–44.
Wagner-Lux, U., and Vriezen, K. J. H.
1980a   Vorläufiger Bericht über die Ausgrabungen in Gadara (Umm
            Qēs) in Jordanien in den Jahren 1976–1978. *ZDPV* 96: 48–58.
1980b   Vorläufiger Bericht über die Ausgrabungen in Gadara (Umm
            Qēs) in Jordanien im Jahre 1979. *ZDPV* 96: 158–62.
1982   Vorläufiger Bericht über die Ausgrabungen in Gadara (Umm
            Qēs) in Jordanien im Jahre 1980. *ZDPV* 98: 153–62.
Watzinger, C.
1926   Zur Chronologie der Schichten von Jericho. *ZDMG* 80: 131–36.
1928   *Tell el-Mutesellim: Bericht über die 1903 bis 1905 mit Unterstützung
            Sr. Majestät des Deutschen Kaisers und der Deutschen Orient-
            Gesellschaft vom Deutschen Verein zur Erforschung Palästinas ver-
            anstalteten Ausgrabungen II: Fundbericht.* Leipzig: Rudolph
            Haupt.
1933–35   *Denkmäler Palästinas: Eine Einführung in die Archäologie des
            Heiligen Landes,* 2 vols. Leipzig: Hinrichs'sche Buchhandlung.
1939   Phönikien und Palästina—Kypros. Pp. 797–848 in *Handbuch der
            Archäologie,* ed. W. Otto. Munich: Beck.
Watzinger, C., and Wulzinger, K.
1921   *Damaskus: Die Antike Stadt.* Wissenschaftliche Veröf-
            fentlichungen des deutsch-türkischen Denkmalschutz-Kom-
            mandos 4. Berlin: Vereinigung Wissenschaftlicher Verleger.
1924   *Damaskus: Die islamische Stadt.* Wissenschaftliche Veröf-
            fentlichungen des deutsch-türkischen Denkmalschutz-Kom-
            mandos 5. Berlin: de Gruyter.
Weippert, H., and Weippert, M.
1976   Jericho in der Eisenzeit. *ZDPV* 92: 105–48.
Weippert, M.
1979a   The Israelite Conquest and the Evidence from Transjordan.
            Pp. 15–35 in *Symposia Celebrating the Seventy-fifth Anniversary of
            the Founding of the American Schools of Oriental Research (1900–
            1975),* ed. F. M. Cross. Cambridge: ASOR.
1979b   Nabatäisch-römische Keramik aus *Hirbet Ḏōr* im Südlichen Jor-
            danien. *ZDPV* 95: 87–110.
1983   Remarks on the History of Settlement in Southern Jordan dur-
            ing the Early Iron Age. Pp. 153–62 in *Studies in the History and
            Archaeology of Jordan, I,* ed. A. Hadidi. Amman: Department of
            Antiquities.
Weissbach, F. H.
1922   *Die Denkmäler und Inschriften an der Mündung des Nahr el-Kelb.*
            Wissenschaftliche Veröffentlichungen des deutsch-türkischen
            Denkmalschutz-Kommandos 6. Berlin: de Gruyter.

Welten, P.
1969   *Die Königs-Stempel: Ein Beitrag zur Militärpolitik Judas unter Hiskia
            und Josia* ADPV 1. Wiesbaden: Harrassowitz.
Welter, G.
1928   Deutsche Ausgrabungen in Palästina I. *Forschungen und Fort-
            schritte* 4: 317–18.
1932   Stand der Ausgrabungen in Sichem. *Archäologischer Anzeiger* 47:
            289–316.
Wenning, R.
1981   Griechische Importe aus der Zeit vor Alexander d. Gr. *Boreas* 4:
            29–46.
Wiegand, Th., et al.
1920   *Sinai.* Wissenschaftliche Veröffentlichungen des deutsch-türk-
            ischen Denkmalschutz-Kommandos 1. Berlin: Vereinigung
            Wissenschaftlicher Verleger.
Zink, J.
1980–1983   *Bildwerk zur Bibel, I–IV and Ergänzungsband.* Stuttgart: Kreuz-
            Verlag.
Zobel, H.-J.
1981   Geschichte des Deutschen Evangelischen Instituts für Alter-
            tumswissenschaft des Heiligen Landes von den Anfängen bis
            zum Zweiten Weltkrieg. *ZDPV* 97: 1–11.

6
ISRAELI ARCHAEOLOGISTS

AMIHAI MAZAR
The Hebrew University, Jerusalem

This essay reviews some current trends in Israeli archaeology. The survey will be limited to the activity of Israeli archaeologists involved in research related to the Bronze and Iron Ages, and special emphasis will be given to methodological questions.

I. HISTORICAL BACKGROUND

A small group of archaeologists grew out of the academic community of the Jewish population in Palestine during the British Mandate (1918–48). Most of these scholars, who may be identified as the "founding fathers" of Israeli archaeology, became involved in fieldwork in a secondary phase of their careers, after having had their basic training in other fields like Judaic studies, Egyptology, Assyriology, Islamic studies, Classics, etc. Only a few of them were involved in continuous archaeological activity. The most prominent was E. L. Sukenik, who founded the Institute of Archaeology of The Hebrew University of Jerusalem, which for many years was the only center for training archaeologists in Israel; others included B. Mazar, S. Yeivin, M. Stekelis, M. Avi-Yonah, N. Avigad, and I. Ben-dor. However, research in the Bronze and Iron Ages was very limited during this early period. Sukenik participated in the expedition to Samaria-Sebaste, in cooperation with British archaeologists such as Crowfoot and Kenyon, but began his own independent research of Bronze Age sites at Tell el-Jerisheh and ʿAffulah. Also during the Mandate period, the Israel Exploration Society conducted an expedition to Beth-yeraḥ, directed by Mazar, Avi-Yonah and Stekelis. This resulted in the excavation of the famous Early Bronze Age granary at this site.

A most important factor in this early phase of research was the exposure of Jewish scholars to the wide range of foreign archaeological activity taking place in the country. Scholars such as W. F. Albright, W. M. F. Petrie, J. W. Crowfoot and others had great influence on later developments through their relations with the first Jewish scholars who in turn trained the next generation of Israeli archaeologists. Albright in particular left his mark on the thinking of a number of Jewish scholars—specifically in the wide-scale integration of ancient Near Eastern studies, biblical studies, philology, historical geography and archaeology—and was followed especially by B. Mazar.

Shortly after the foundation of the State of Israel in May 1948, archaeological activity was resumed by Israeli nationals. The first organized excavations were those of B. Mazar at Tell el-Qasileh near Tel Aviv, soon followed by other excavations, particularly by the Department of Antiquities, like those of I. Ben-Dor and M. Dothan at Nahariah and M. Dothan at 'Affulah.

A great step forward was made with the large-scale excavations at Hazor, carried out between 1954–58. Y. Yadin, son of E. L. Sukenik, directed this excavation with the help of some who were to be the most prominent Israeli archaeologists in the years to come: Y. Aharoni, Ruth Amiran, M. Dothan, Trude Dothan, and the French scholar Jean Perrot. By reason of his unique natural talent, the architect I. Dunayevsky played an important role not only in recording the architectural remains but also in the analysis of the stratigraphic evidence. The junior staff at Hazor, composed of students in the Department of Archaeology of The Hebrew University, became the core of the younger generation of Israeli archaeologists which today carries the main burden of the profession. In the 1958 season at Hazor Yadin was assisted by some of these younger archaeologists: A. Ben-Tor, Y. Shiloh, A. Eitan, Malka Hershkovitz, and the author. In many respects Hazor served as the main field school for many Israeli archaeologists. The fast and prompt publication of the first two seasons served as a model for the publication of field results. The methods used at Hazor were, to a large degree, a direct continuation of excavation methods used during the 1930s all over the Middle East and employed in Israel at sites such as Megiddo and Lachish. The underlying principle was to try to understand main features in the development of the site and its fortifications by digging large areas and exposing complete architectural units. The grid system with 5 m by 5 m squares separated by earth balks was not yet known, though Jean Perrot had introduced a similar method at another Bronze Age site. The recording technique was also based on methods used in the past, though experiments were made in the use of field notebooks with daily graphs and basket lists. When one considers the conditions and timing of the Hazor excavations, it becomes apparent that the achievements were enormous, both in the actual results in the field and in the experimental field school.

The 1960s and early 1970s were very fruitful years for members of the Hazor team and others who began initiating their own projects. A still younger generation was yet to follow, and together there are now several dozen active archaeologists directing projects of various sizes and types throughout the country relating to the periods under survey here.

The list of these excavations and projects includes large-scale operations which extended over a period of more than ten years as well as smaller projects which lasted only a few seasons. The following table (Table 1) includes some of the major excavations which have been conducted since 1960 by Israeli archaeologists working either alone or in collaboration with foreign scholars. The table does not include dozens of additional small salvage excavations carried out mainly by the Department of Antiquities. A bibliography relating to these excavations, updated to 1980, can be found in Vogel 1971 and 1981.

The overall picture gained is that of widespread activity, which has led to the recovery of a large amount of archaeological material related to the periods of our interest.

II. INSTITUTIONS AND PERSONNEL

The current activity in Israeli archaeology is organized by various institutions and organizations.

The Department of Antiquities of the State of Israel, headed by Mr. A. Eitan, is responsible for issuing permits for excavations and supervising them. The Department itself conducts dozens of small salvage excavations which are directed by a staff of field archaeologists and sometimes by archaeologists from outside the Department. The Department is advised by the Archaeological Council of Israel, a public council appointed by the government to supervise archaeological activity. The Israel Exploration Society, a most important body in organizing excavations and publication, is a voluntary association of which most Israeli archaeologists are members. The society helps in various ways with organization, fund-raising and technical assistance. The universities are the main initiators of large-scale excavation, mostly in collaboration with the Israel Exploration Society. The Institute of Archaeology of The Hebrew University and that of the Tel Aviv University are the largest and most active bodies, yet the smaller universities of Israel, in Haifa and Beer-sheba, and the Bar Ilan University also sponsor archaeological activity, mostly in their own regions. The Israel Museum, Museum Haaretz in Tel Aviv, and other local museums are responsible for important excavations carried out by archaeologists who are usually their staff members.

Many of the excavations have been made possible through international cooperation, and more and more projects in Israel are the result of such cooperation between Israeli archaeologists and scholars from abroad. Programs vary from project to project, though all result in the involvement of hundreds of foreign student volunteers each summer. In most cases, an expedition organizes an educational program, and thus

TABLE OF ISRAELI ARCHAEOLOGICAL EXCAVATIONS
SINCE 1960*

Site	Director	Years	Main Sponsoring Institution
Tel Dan	A. Biran	1966–	Department of Antiquities and Hebrew Union College
Hazor	Y. Yadin	1968	The Hebrew University
Achzib	M. Prausnitz	1958–64	Department of Antiquities and University of Rome
Acco	M. Dothan	1973–	Haifa University
Shiqmona	Y. Elgavish	1962–79	Haifa Museum
Golan Heights	C. Epstein	1974–	Department of Antiquities
Beth-yeraḥ	D. Ussishkin, D. Bahat, E. Eisenberg	various	Department of Antiquities
Tell Qiri	A. Ben Tor	1975–78	The Hebrew University
Yoqneam	A. Ben Tor	1977–	The Hebrew University**
Tell Qasis	A. Ben Tor	1979–	The Hebrew University
Megiddo	Y. Yadin	1960, 1965–67, 1971	The Hebrew University
Beth-shan	Y. Yadin	1983	The Hebrew University
Tell Kitan	E. Eisenberg	1975–77	Department of Antiquities
Tell Dor	E. Stern	1980–	The Hebrew University**
Tell Mevorakh	E. Stern	1973–76	The Hebrew University
Tell Zeror	K. Ohata	1964–66 1974	Society for Near Eastern Studies in Japan
	M. Kochavi (field director)	1964–66	
Tell Hefer	S. Palei, Y. Porat	1979–	Department of Antiquities and State University of N.Y., Buffalo
Tell Poleg	R. Gophna	1959, 1962	Department of Antiquities
Tell Michal	J. Muhly, Z. Herzog	1977–80	Tel Aviv University
Tell el-Qasileh	A. Mazar	1972–74, 1982	Hebrew University and Museum Haaretz**
Jaffa	Y. and H. Kaplan	1970–74	Museum Haaretz
Tell Gerisa	J. Muhly, Z. Herzog	1981–	Tel Aviv University
Aphek	M. Kochavi, P. Beck	1972–	Tel Aviv University
ʿIzbet Ṣarṭah	M. Kochavi, I. Finkelstein	1976–78	Tel Aviv and Bar Ilan Universities
Tell Dalit	B. Cresson, R. Gophna	1978–80	Tel Aviv University and Baylor University
Shiloh	I. Finkelstein	1981–	Bar Ilan University

Site	Director	Years	Main Sponsoring Institution
Jerusalem			
Temple Mount	B. Mazar	1968–79	The Hebrew University
Jewish Quarter	N. Avigad	1969–82	The Hebrew University
Citadel	R. Amiran, A. Eitan, H. Geva	various	Israel Museum, Jerusalem City Museum
City of David	Y. Shiloh	1979–	Hebrew University
Hinnom Cemeteries	G. Barkay	1979–80	Tel Aviv University
Giloh Suburb	A. Mazar	1977–81	The Hebrew University and Department of Antiquities
Ramat Raḥel	Y. Aharoni	1959–62	The Hebrew University
Tel Baṭash (Timnah)	G. L. Kelm, A Mazar	1977–	Southwestern Baptist Theological Seminary and The Hebrew University
Tel Miqne (Ekron)	S. Gitin, T. Dothan	1981–	W. F. Albright Institute of Archaeological Research and The Hebrew University
Beth-shemesh (MB)	C. Epstein, D. Bahat		Department of Antiquities
Yavneh Yam	Y. Kaplan	1966–69	Museum Haaretz
Ashdod	M. Dothan, D. N. Freedman, J. L. Swauger	1962–72	Department of Antiquities
Lachish	Y. Aharoni, D. Ussishkin	1966, 1973–	The Hebrew University and Tel Aviv University**
Tell Nagila	R. Amiran, A. Eitan, R. A. Mitchell	1962–63	Institute for Mediterranean Studies**
Tell Sera	E. D. Oren	1972–	Ben Gurion University
Tel Haror	E. D. Oren	1982–	Ben Gurion University
En-gedi	B. Mazar	1961–65	The Hebrew University
Deir El-Balaḥ	T. Dothan	1972–81	The Hebrew University
Arad			
Iron Age	Y. Aharoni	1962–67	The Hebrew University
Early Bronze Age	R. Amiran	1964–	Israel Museum
Beer-sheba	Y. Aharoni	1969–74	Tel Aviv University
Tel Malḥata	M. Kochavi	1967, 1971	The Hebrew University Tel Aviv University
Tel Masos	Y. Aharoni, F. Fritz, A. Kempinski	1972–75	Tel Aviv University and University of Mainz

Site	Director	Years	Main Sponsoring Institution
Tel ʿIra	Y. Beit Arieh A. Biran	1977–81 1977	Tel Aviv University Hebrew Union College
Aroer (in the Negeb)	A. Biran, R. Cohen	1976–	Department of Antiquities and Hebrew Union College
Tell Esdar	M. Kochavi	1963–64	Department of Antiquities
Ḥorvat ʿUza	B. Cresson, I. Beit-Arieh	1982–	Tel Aviv University and Baylor University
Kadesh-barnea	R. Cohen	1975–82	Department of Antiquities
Negeb Heights Iron Age Sites	R. Cohen Z. Meshel	various	Department of Antiquities Tel Aviv University
Kuntillet ʿAjrud	Z. Meshel	1975–76	Tel Aviv University and Department of Antiquities
Timnaʿ	B. Rothenberg	1964–	Museum Haaretz
Har Yeruḥam	M. Kochavi, R. Cohen	1963, 1973	Department of Antiquities
Beer-resisim	W. G. Dever, R. Cohen	1978–80	Department of Antiquities and University of Arizona

*Sites are arranged from north to south
**Sponsored also by the Israel Exploration Society

the archaeological project achieves goals which extend beyond mere archaeological research. Perhaps this international participation is one of the most important phenomena in the annual activity of Israeli archaeology.

While the directors of Israeli expeditions are usually permanent staff members of the various institutions, their junior staff includes mainly graduate students from the local universities as well as students from abroad who gained experience in previous years. Many of these junior staff members are dedicated to fieldwork and spend many months in the field, thus gaining firsthand experience which, in addition to the theoretical study in the classroom, is essential training for their future careers. This extensive field experience at various excavations, combined with study tours of many other excavations, is characteristic of the background of the young Israeli archaeologist.

III. TYPES OF PROJECTS

Choosing the site for a future archaeological enterprise is one of the major factors in the success of the project. The interest of individual archaeologists in a particular region, culture or period is the main factor in selecting a site for excavation. Some of the major projects in Israel are dedicated to the systematic excavation of one particular site. These projects may continue for more than a decade; the longest thus far has completed its fourteenth year. Examples are the excavations at Dan, Acco, Dor, Aphek (fig. 1), Tel Batash (fig. 2), Lachish, Tell Sera, Early Bronze Arad, etc. Other projects emphasize the regional aspect where the archaeologist investigates a whole region by systematic surveys and selective excavations at a series of sites. The long-term project which Aharoni and his colleagues conducted in the Arad/Beer-sheba basin was a pioneering example of this approach. Other examples are the regional project in the western Esdraelon Valley conducted by Ben Tor, the Yarkon Basin project conducted by Tel Aviv University scholars, and the extensive research of the central Negeb carried out over many years by Meshel and Cohen.

Another class of excavations are those devoted to a particular period or subject. Examples are the digs at Deir el-Balaḥ where an Egyptian fortress and cemetery were uncovered (fig. 3), the excavation at Tell el-Qasileh where emphasis was placed on the study of the Philistine culture (fig. 4), and the excavations at Megiddo which were intended to solve particular problems at the site. The archaeology of Jerusalem is a unique project in itself, to which great effort has been dedicated in recent years by several archaeologists.

In addition to the excavations of main sites, important work is done in what may be defined as "rural archaeology" which is concerned with the country's ancient villages, hamlets, forts, agricultural installations, irrigation systems, terraces, etc. Part of this work is related to widespread archaeological surveys which have been conducted throughout the country (see A. Rainey's article in this volume). Another aspect—salvage excavations—is carried out by the Department of Antiquities. The rich data accumulated from this activity, involving many young archaeologists, have contributed much to the knowledge of rural life in the country throughout the ages. One cannot begin to understand the reconstruction of society and economic life during ancient times without the integration of this vast material into a comprehensive picture. Examples of this work are plentiful; we may mention the Middle Bronze II rural settlement excavated near Beth-shemesh, the Iron Age I settlements excavated in the Upper Galilee and the Central Hills, forts and fortresses dated to the period of the Monarchy excavated in the Judaean Hills and the Judaean Desert, the Iron Age II agricultural hamlets and small settlements excavated in the Judaean Desert, around Jerusalem and in the Shephelah, and the agricultural terraces explored in the Judaean Hills.

FIG. 1 *Aphek: Excavations of Middle Bronze and Late Bronze buildings (directed by M. Kochavi)*

FIG. 2 *Deir el-Balaḥ: Excavation of Late Bronze Age Egyptian settlement discovered below high sand dunes (directed by T. Dothan)*

FIG. 3   *Tel Baṭash: Exposure of Iron Age city gates (directed by G. L. Kelm and A. Mazar)*

FIG. 4 *Tell el-Qasileh: Philistine temple fully exposed after removal of balks (directed by A. Mazar)*

IV. FIELD STRATEGY AND METHODS USED

A general characteristic of Israeli activity in the field is the desire to excavate areas as large as possible in order to uncover complete architectural units and to get a general idea about town planning, plans of individual buildings, etc. This "architectural" approach—in contrast to the "trenching" approach used by some foreign expeditions working in the Holy Land, particularly that used by Kenyon in her excavations at Jericho and Jerusalem—tends to be a continuation of a more general tradition of Near Eastern archaeology as seen especially in the large archaeological enterprises conducted in the Levant during the 1930s. The work at Hazor was inspired by this tradition and consequently dictated the basic approach adopted by many Israeli archaeologists. Extreme examples of the use of this approach may be seen in Aharoni's work at Arad and Beer-sheba where almost the whole site was exposed, or in Amiran's work in the Early Bronze city of Arad where a major part of the city was excavated because of easy access to remains found close to the surface. However, the tendency to excavate large areas is always motivated by the desire to study different areas and different subjects at the same site; it results in the simultaneous exposure of several excavation areas. This strategy was used at Hazor and has been maintained in most Israeli excavations. It has made possible an understanding of the development of various parts of a tell in different periods and often has led to important conclusions regarding such things as the size of the settlement, general town planning, the specific structural development of various quarters, etc.

There are many advantages to excavating a large area of the same stratum over the course of several seasons. An important factor is the greater possibility of understanding stratigraphic development in each of the main strata. Subphasing of one major stratum may differ from one square to the next. Erosion and leveling activities in antiquity sometimes may be responsible for the destruction of certain phases of a particular area. A limited excavation area may thus give misleading information, whereas a wide-scale excavation area and its correlation to other areas may provide a better understanding of the stratigraphic and architectural history of a site.

The gains of this "architectural" approach become apparent when one considers some of the sites excavated in the past with other methods. The best example is Jerusalem, where excavations were carried out by Kathleen Kenyon using the trenching and probing method. The results of the Israeli excavations in four different areas of Jerusalem (south of the Temple Mount, in the Jewish Quarter, in the Armenian Garden and recently in the City of David) have proved many of Kenyon's conclusions wrong because these conclusions were based on sophisticated sections of debris layers in restricted areas. The mistakes in dating buildings by this method, not to speak of the impossibility of learning their plans, point to the problems inherent in the method. The Israeli excavations of broader areas have revealed much more secure data concerning the dates and plans of buildings and have enabled reconstruction of various aspects in the topographical history and daily life of the city during various periods.

While the "architectural" approach emphasizes the exposure of architectural units and the understanding of the relationships between them, it does not necessarily overlook other features in the field. The careful study of the process of accumulation of earth layers is usually done in detail, and features like robber trenches, foundation trenches and pits are defined with the aid of vertical sections and the careful cleaning and investigation of each exposed surface. Yet the amount of work invested and the speed of the excavation may differ from one excavation to another, according to the approach of each archaeologist and the problems encountered in the field. Naturally, a slow, more careful process of digging is needed at coastal sites where construction is predominatly mudbrick, in contrast to inland sites where stone architecture is dominant. The different problems raised by these two types of sites are solved by *ad hoc* accommodation of work methods to the conditions in the field. Flexibility, freedom from dogmatism, and common sense are typical features of fieldwork by Israeli archaeologists. Sometimes these tendencies lead to extreme actions, such as using a bulldozer to cut through massive earth works, especially Middle Bronze earthen ramparts. Such deep and rapidly prepared sections have made possible the understanding of the inner structure of ramparts at sites like Tel Dan, Acco, Tel Zeror, and Shiloh. On the other hand, there were many cases in which fortifications on slopes of tells were excavated with a minute trenching method, not very different from that used by Kenyon in her excavations. This combination of two extreme methods seems paradoxical, yet it reflects the flexibility in Israeli field methodology.

Since the early 1960s, the basic technical procedures of the Wheeler-Kenyon method have been introduced on a wide scale in Israeli archaeology. Five-meter squares and the preservation and study of earth balks left between them are now standard features in every excavation (fig. 1). Yet there are disputes concerning the amount of work that should be invested in shaving, recording and preserving these balks. This issue has been a subject of debate between some Israeli and American archaeologists (Dever 1973; Aharoni 1973b). Today one can find various solutions to the problem; some excavators simply photograph their balks, some draw all of them, while others decide arbitrarily to draw only those balks which are of special interest for observing stratigraphy.

The method of recording architectural features has not changed since the Hazor excavations. Special emphasis is given to drawing exact plans and finding the top and bottom levels of each wall, thereby relating each wall to floor levels and adjoining walls. In looking for these architectural relationships, however, Israeli archaeologists usually do not hesitate to remove balks after their contents are studied and recorded. In many cases, the result is the complete exposure of large parts of buildings of the same stratum (fig. 4). Only after studying a comparatively large area of one stratum in this "architectural" approach will the excavators proceed to the lower stratum, usually by reestablishing the balks either on their original grid pattern or according to a fresh layout fitting the new situation in the field. Extensive dismantling of buildings from the upper strata, after proper drawing and photographing, is also a common procedure on Israeli excavations, for it enables wide-scale excavation of deeper strata.

The process of documentation of fieldwork common to most Israeli expeditions was described in detail by Aharoni (Aharoni 1973a: 119–132). Improvement of this method has been made recently by introducing the computer as a technical aid in recording field results; experiments are being made at the Yoqneam (fig. 5), Aphek, Tel Baṭash and Tel Haror excavations. The older recording methods have been replaced by new ones geared to computer processing. This relatively recent innovation promises easier and faster processing of finds for publication.

A widely debated issue is to what extent methods of the "New Archaeology" should be used in Israeli archaeology. In fact, the historical development of Israeli archaeology has been such that archaeological activity has always been related to biblical and historical research and in general has been part of the humanities. The New Archaeology which emanated from American anthropological research has remained alien to traditional thinking in Israeli archaeology. Modern research methods such as the use of statistics and quantitative analyses have been introduced by Israeli scholars in prehistoric research but almost not at all by those who deal with the historical periods. More and more archaeologists in Israel are aware that the traditional methods are inadequate for producing a breakthrough in certain aspects of research. It is probable that future research on pottery will utilize more sophisticated methods, including more extensive use of computers.

V. INTERDISCIPLINARY STUDIES

The cooperation between archaeologists and scientists from various branches of research is relatively easy in Israel, because of the availability of scholars from various fields of research. The small size of the country permits extensive cooperation without the need of enlisting these scientists as full time staff members of expeditions. Thus the services of

FIG. 5   *Yoqneam: Exposure of Iron Age and Turkish fortifications (directed by A. Ben-Tor)*

geologists, paleobotanists, osteologists, physical anthropologists, and chemists are readily available. The Hebrew University maintains an archeometry laboratory which, for the time being, specializes mainly in neutron-activation analysis of pottery and certain other materials, such as obsidian. This laboratory enables neturon-activation analysis of a wide range of pottery samples, and some important conclusions have already been drawn as a result. Petrographic analysis of pottery with the aid of thin sections, a simpler method of analyzing pottery, also is being used by several archaeologists in Israel. Pollen analysis has been very restricted on the other hand; it has been done mainly with cores taken from lakes (like the Huleh and the Sea of Galilee), since results from occupational strata have proven disappointing. Nevertheless, the lake core samples have recently provided important data concerning ancient vegetation in the country during various periods and consequently have contributed to our understanding of the ancient climatic changes. Other botanical research has been dedicated to dendro-archaeology and to the analysis of ancient grain and seeds. In the latter fields, much data was collected in recent years which contributes to our knowledge of food, agriculture, and landscape prevalent in Israel in various periods.

VI. THE PROCESSING OF FINDS

Naturally, the bulk of the archaeological material recovered on the excavations is pottery sherds. The methods of treating this material vary greatly. One of the main advantages of the architectural approach is the recovery of abundant pottery assemblages in well-defined loci, e.g., rooms and pits, which provide a good amount of restorable material. Consequently, one of the characteristics of the Israeli method is its emphasis on restoration of pottery vessels. The investment of time and effort in the restoration of complete assemblages is worthwhile because it affords the opportunity for studying large, complete, homogeneous pottery groups. It also aids in establishing stratigraphy, since a connection between pottery sherds found in different loci may demonstrate the stratigraphic relationship of the loci and may contribute to an understanding of related chronological and architectural features. On the other hand, small sherds may be misleading; even if they are found in clear stratigraphic context, their deposition may have been the result of various past activities, like digging earth from a lower level for a fill. Aharoni has presented an extreme view which denies the importance of using small sherds for dating (Aharoni 1973:50). When there is no available restorable material, small sherds are the only other possible source for dating, but they should be used with caution.

The pottery is usually published in section drawing on a scale of 1:5. The method of presentation varies from one excavation to the next, according to the objective character of the material and the archaeologist's subjective judgment. In most cases, homogeneous loci are drawn and presented in the publication as completely as possible. When such assemblages are not available, a sherd collection which represents the various types from a certain level is published. In most excavation reports, the pottery is discussed in detail on a comparative basis; typology within the site and comparisons to finds in other sites are discussed, and chronological and cultural conclusions are drawn. Most excavation reports do not include, however, a quantitative analysis and systematic type-series, and there is as yet no general type-series developed for Israeli archaeology. This is a desirable goal for the future.

Other finds such as metals, beads, glyptic material, and written material, are usually submitted to experts in the particular fields for investigation. Laboratory work in cleaning and preserving finds is available in most of the larger archaeological institutions, and experts process these materials for publication.

In recent years the computer has become an important tool in processing archaeological material. Several expeditions have already adjusted their registration forms to allow for computerized processing, and programs have been written to enable immediate processing. Since this is a rather new feature, one cannot yet evaluate the results. In processing the finds from Tell el-Qasileh and Tel Baṭash, the author uses a computer program based on typological classification of the pottery. Each significant sherd is registered on a special form and the material is then processed by the computer. The immediate result is a fast and easily retrievable catalog of the finds according to locus and type. The next phase is gathering quantitative data about the appearance of types in the various stratigraphic phases and the analysis of specific features such as slip burnish and decoration in relation to the typological-morphological subdivision. This method has great advantages and provides a more precise analysis of features which heretofore were investigated only in a cursory fashion. This method should enable more accurate classification, dating and correlation with other sites in the future when similar methods will have gained wider usage.

VII. PUBLICATION OF FIELD REPORTS

As in many other branches of archaeology today, Israeli archaeology suffers from a great delay in publication of raw material. Too often interpretations and conclusions are submitted before the full publication of the material itself. Preparing the material for publication and actual publication are long and expensive undertakings; often the process is delayed or brought to a halt altogether. Only a few excavations have been fully published, and even these often more than a decade after the actual dig took place. In many cases, there is already a gap of 10 to 20 years since the final season of excavation, and the publication is still far from imminent. The large number of excavations conducted each year makes it impossible to control all the data. At the same time, it is frustrating for the researcher to know that there is much unpublished material which may justify changing conclusions of any general study. Therefore, in recent years there has been a consensus that this situation must be changed, and many archaeologists have committed themselves to publishing their material as soon as possible.

Series of publications, like those of the Israel Exploration Society, *Qedem* (published by the Institute of Archaeology of The Hebrew University), occasional publications of Tel Aviv University, and *ʿAtiqot* (published by the Department of Antiquities) provide space for final publication reports, though some archaeologists face a serious problem of finding a publisher even after their report is written. Preliminary reports are much more regularly published. The Hebrew *Ḥadashot Arkheologiyot* (which is also published in an English edition) and the English *Notes and News* in the *Israel Exploration Journal* provide the most immediate updated survey of each year's finds. More detailed reports are published in the various periodicals, especially the *Israel Exploration Journal, Tel Aviv* and *Eretz Israel. Qadmoniot*, the popular Hebrew archaeological quarterly published by the Israel Exploration Society, provides firsthand archaeological news and more general discussions.

VIII. THEORETICAL RESEARCH

In addition to field activity, which is the main subject of this survey, there is also a wide range of theoretical research being done by field archaeologists and by other specialists both in analysis of various finds and in syntheses of a wide range of subjects. There is a great variety of subject matter: correlation between archaeological finds and historical documentation; epigraphic and palaeographic research; various aspects of art history, such as the development of architectural styles and planning, glyptic art, ivory carvings, iconography and metal objects. This "armchair" archaeological activity complements fieldwork and is an important step towards a general synthesis.

We do not have at our disposal an updated general synthesis for most of the archaeological periods. The *Encyclopaedia of Archaeological Excavations In the Holy Land* contains the most recent general summaries on archaeological finds in the Holy Land, though it does not contain a general synthesis of the various periods. Aharoni's recently published *The Archaeology of the Land of Israel* (1982) is the only available general discussion of the subject written by an Israeli scholar, yet to a large extent it reflects only the author's views on many subjects. General syntheses of various periods and cultures are available only in a limited way and include mainly E. Stern's discussion of the Persian period and Trude Dothan's volume on the Philistine culture. Such general summaries will be needed more and more in the future, in light of the vast amount of raw material uncovered in recent years.

IX. *THE POSITION OF ISRAELI ARCHAEOLOGY*

In recent years there has been much discussion about the position of archaeology in Israel in relation to other fields of research. There is still a dispute as to whether archaeology of a certain period and region is a discipline in itself, or whether it should be integrated academically with the study of the culture to which it is related. This dispute is reflected in the academic organization of the study of archaeology. At The Hebrew University, archaeology is studied in the framework of an independent department, while at the Tel Aviv University it is part of an Institute for Ancient Near Eastern Studies. These differing organizational structures reflect the general tendency of the founders of these institutions.

The term "Biblical Archaeology," which recently has been an object of attack by some scholars (Dever 1981, 1982), is not used officially, but biblical sources have always been considered important background for the archaeological process, even if a critical approach to the study of biblical text is used. Quite naturally, every opportunity is taken to relate archaeological evidence to the biblical text. In Israel, this process has been developed mainly by scholars like B. Mazar, S. Yeivin, Y. Yadin, and Y. Aharoni. The term "Syro-Palestinian Archaeology" has been suggested by Dever and does not necessarily contradict the term Biblical Archaeology; it merely emphasizes the unity of the material culture in the geographical region of the Levant in certain periods, a fact of which all are well aware. The term Biblical Archaeology, however, fits more precisely the nature of the activity in this field, which involves all aspects of material culture of the biblical world.

The general popularity of and impetus to archaeological research in Israel must be understood against the background of the establishment of the modern State of Israel. Sometimes Israeli archaeology is accused of serving nationalistic tendencies when, in fact, many of the Israeli archeologists came to this field through their deep love of and emotional connection to the land itself and to its history. Though this factor would be denied by most Israeli archaeologists who define themselves as pure scientists, there is probably a subconscious motivation to relate modern Israeli culture to its ancient roots. This identity has provided archaeological activity with broad support from the general public and has enhanced its popularity. Under such circumstances it would be easy to turn archaeology into a tool of complex current national or political discussion. Fortunately, however, this has not happened, even though archaeology naturally has an important role in modern Israeli culture.

BIBLIOGRAPHY

Aharoni, Y.
  1973   Remarks on the 'Israeli' Method of Excavation. *EI* II:48*–53*.
  1973a   *Beer Sheba I*. Excavations at Tell Beer Sheba, 1969–71 Seasons. Tel Aviv.
  1982   *The Archaeology of the Land of Israel*. Translated by Anson F. Rainey. Philadelphia: Westminster.
Dever, W. G.
  1973   Two Approaches to Archaeological Method—the Architectural and the Stratigraphic. *EI* 11:1*-8*.
  1980   Archaeological Method in Israel: A Continuing Revolution. *BA* 43:40–48.
  1981   Should the Term 'Biblical Archaeology' Be Abandoned? *BAR* 7, no. 3:54–57.
  1982   Retrospects and Prospects in Biblical and Syro-Palestinian Archaeology. *BA* 45:103–107.
Fogel, E. K.
  1971   Bibliography of Holy Land Sites. *HUCA*, XLII, 1–96.
  1981   Bibliography of Holy Land Sites, Part II. *HUCA*, LII, 1–92.

For Further Reading:

Encyclopaedia of Archaeological Excavations in the Holy Land (eds., M. Avi-Yonah and E. Stern), Tel Aviv, 1975–78, as well as numerous articles in the following periodicals: ʿAtiqot, Biblical Archaeologist, Biblical Archaeology Review, Israel Exploration Journal, Qedem, Tel Aviv.

PART TWO

ARCHAEOLOGICAL METHODOLOGY: THE TECHNIQUES

7
EXCAVATION OF TELLS

GUS W. VAN BEEK
Smithsonian Institution

For the reconstruction of human history, the primary sources available are written records and archaeological sites that have survived the ravages of time. Written records—whether in the form of manuscripts on papyrus or skins, inscriptions on stone, metal, clay, or wood—have distinct limitations in quantity, quality, subject matter, and time range. Such records are non-existent in some cultures either because they were not kept at all, or because they were written on organic materials that have disappeared through decay in all but the driest climates. Where they exist, they are often narrow in scope or not sufficiently factual, having been designed to show the ruler and his people only in a favorable light, somewhat like much of modern advertising. Moreover, they seldom describe the environments in which ancient man lived and which he utilized in his quest for survival, and they rarely supply information on daily life. Written records go back no earlier than about 3000 B.C. in Egypt and Mesopotamia, and they make their appearance somewhat later in other Near Eastern and Mediterranean cultures, so that the important prehistoric and formative periods of all cultures would remain entirely unknown if they were our sole source.

Archaeological sites, on the other hand, address all of these lacunae in the written record, and largely account for the present state of knowledge of the ancient world, however provisional and imperfect it may be. Of the various types of archaeological sites, none provides as many data for the reconstruction of antiquity as the tell. The word *tell* is an ancient word occurring in both Hebrew and Arabic, derived from Akkadian *tillu* and meaning "ruin heap" in all languages. Thus a tell is an artificial mound—as distinct from a natural geological formation—consisting of the successive remains of an ancient settlement. Generally, but not always, it has the form of a flat-top hill whose sides seldom slope more than about 40° (fig. 1). On plains and relatively flat land, tells stand out as unexpected hills on the landscape and are easy to see; in hilly country, they tend to blend into the terrain and are often more difficult to recognize. In the Levant, the surface area on top of a site is surprisingly

FIG. 1   *Aerial view of Tell Jemmeh, a typical Near Eastern tell (except that it is more eroded than most), looking west. The area of new excavations (as of 1971) can be seen near the northwest corner, with Petrie's 1927 area of excavation adjacent on the left. Virgin soil extends to the top of the light band of soil on the near (east) side, and the 14-m deposit of darker debris above represents 1600 years of occupation.*

small, commonly ranging from ca. 2.5 to 15 acres, although a few are larger; Hazor, for example, covers about 15 acres in the upper city and 200 acres in the lower city. Depending on the vegetation cover and extent of erosion, artifacts—especially potsherds and, occasionally, remnants of walls—appear on the surface and slopes which show that the mound is an ancient site.

An analogy has frequently been drawn between a tell and a layer cake, in which the occupation periods or strata in a site resemble the layers in a cake, with the earliest deposited stratum at the bottom, followed by other strata laid down successively in time, and with the latest stratum at the top. The analogy is apt, but it cannot be pressed too far. Generally, constructions of a later stratum intrude into earlier strata, and instances are known in which later fortification systems were constructed at levels below earlier systems farther out around the base of the site. Moreover, strata in most tells are not nearly as horizontal and level as the layers in a cake. They generally conform to the debris of the stratum below, and sometimes thin or thicken, slope upwards or downwards, depending on the uses and building phases of structures within it. Occasionally, strata disappear altogether over a substantial part of the tell, indicating that the settlements of those periods did not occupy the entire site.

A tell contains materials that enable us to define its ancient environment and to describe human manipulation of that environment through the exploitation of natural resources by hunting and gathering, agriculture, animal husbandry, quarrying and mining, and the imaginative combining of natural substances to create new materials. A tell also preserves material remains that shed light on most facets of ancient cultures, e.g., social organization, political events and economic activities, technological processes and industries, aspects of daily life—including types of dwellings, security devices such as fortifications and gateways, religious structures and cult paraphernalia, cooking facilities and pots and pans, diet, jewelry and personal adornments, toys and games—so that it is possible to understand a culture and the interaction between different cultures. Indeed, *everything* in a tell is potentially significant for the reconstruction of the past, and the only limitations on the utilization of this vast and diverse array of materials are imposed by our own deficiencies in curiosity and imagination, and by the state of the arts of archaeological excavation, analysis, and interpretation.

All excavation involves destroying a portion or portions of a site, and once dug, the excavated areas cannot be restored to their original state. Therefore, archaeology—unlike most other disciplines in the humanities and sciences—is one in which an experiment (i.e., the excavation) cannot be exactly duplicated; one can dig an adjoining area in the same tell, but the stratigraphy and structures found will not be identical with those previously excavated. The only means available for reconstructing the excavation of a tell is the report or publication. Therefore, it behooves all archaeologists to excavate as carefully as possible, to record the excavations completely, and to publish full data and the most reasoned interpretations of those data as their knowledge and imaginations allow.

Tells are also finite in number and are not, therefore, an inexhaustible resource. It is imperative that we dig only small areas of a site, with the areas so arranged that they do not spread all over the tell, except in instances involving salvage archaeology when the tell itself is threatened with imminent destruction due to natural phenomena or to 20th century demands for expansion, industrialization, etc. Archaeology is a constantly developing discipline with new questions asked of sites and new methodologies employed. Today's archaeologists are far more skilled than those of the last generation, and we can expect those of the next generation to be better than we are. It is incumbent on us to confine our excavations to discrete areas so that most of the tell is left untouched for archaeologists of the future. At Megiddo, one of the most important sites in Israel, the excavators, with the best of intentions, stripped the uppermost four strata from the entire tell. By today's standards, their techniques in fieldwork and their method of publication were primitive and did not yield full and conclusive data. Having removed all of those strata, there is no possibility for anyone now or in the future to reexcavate them and to refine the data and interpretations. What a loss that is for reconstructing the full cultural history of that great site! Similarly, to excavate many large areas spread over a site is to leave it not only unattractive, but also without sufficiently large areas to make later excavation meaningful.

It was mentioned above that everything in a tell is potentially significant for the reconstruction of the past. "Everything" obviously includes all man-made artifacts: every potsherd, fragment of glass, worked stone and bone, piece of plaster, slag, and metal fragment. "Everything" also includes materials or artifacts, characteristic of the site environment and relating to mankind's use of the environment: rocks, soils, native and cultivated plants, wild and domesticated animals, and materials employed in construction as well as in the manufacture of objects. All artifacts in a tell may be useful sooner or later for defining natural resources and human activities in the various periods of occupation. It follows, then, that every portable thing found in a tell should be saved for present and future research involving identification, reconstruction, analysis, interpretation and, sometimes, experimentation, even if the excavator cannot fully utilize all of the artifacts in the processes of research and publication. If everything is saved with full provenience data, future generations of archaeologists will be able to conduct research on the artifacts, secure in the knowledge that no biases governed the collection and retention procedures of the excavator.

In earlier tell excavations, highly selective and biased procedures determined which artifacts were normally saved. All obviously important man-made objects were retained, such as written documents, art objects, architectural fragments, whole or easily reconstructible pots, etc. Of the vast number of other artifacts, only "representative" collections were saved, while the remainder were discarded. Sample collections of potsherds including rims, handles, bases, decorated and imported fragments were retained, while the remaining sherds, which constitute the bulk of finds in any tell excavation, were tossed on the pottery dump. Exceptional animal bones and large deposits of burned seeds were sometimes kept, but most of the bones were also thrown out, and no attempt was made to recover other less obvious seeds. Thus, the vast majority of artifacts ended up in the soil and pottery dumps and were forever lost for future research, in spite of the heavy investment of time, hard work, and money in excavating them in the first place. The act of discarding artifacts represents a kind of arrogance on the part of the archaeologist, since it rests on an implicit assumption that the archaeologist knows all that is important for cultural research both now and in the future. Obviously, no one can legitimately claim to possess such knowledge.

It is now unthinkable that any artifact, either man-made or natural, should be discarded, because new questions are being asked about climatic change, animal herd culling and butchering practices, artifact repertories, ancient technologies, intraregional as well as international trade, social organization, etc. Moreover, new techniques and strategies for answering these questions are being rapidly developed. For example, pottery repertories can no longer be based on the chance finds of whole or easily reconstructible pots. We now know that from the masses of sherds recovered, it is possible to reconstruct additional pots that not only add new forms to the repertory, but also yield a better index of functions, standardization of sizes and permissible variation, and household population densities, that can only be obtained from a maximum number of reconstructed vessels. Thus, the failure to save everything precludes the possibility of addressing many questions for which the tell has potential answers; the tell is not only less informative than it might be, but also much possible research on the artifacts by future generations of archaeologists is thereby foreclosed.

A tell is excavated in the inverse order of deposition, i.e., the latest occupation period or stratum is removed first, followed by the next earlier stratum, and so on through the earliest stratum until virgin soil or bedrock is reached. Before World War II, most archaeologists excavated in arbitrary levels, for example, stripping off 30-cm thick layers of debris across the area with large picks and hoes. When walls appeared, excavators usually trenched along one or both faces with a pick to define the wall more clearly, and they assumed that walls at about the same level were contemporary. They separated artifacts by discrete areas, such as rooms or open spaces, and if the artifacts were similar, they assumed that the areas belonged to the same occupation. While these techniques enabled the archaeologists to excavate large areas quickly, precise relationships of layers and walls and all but the most obvious intrusive features were often missed, resulting in serious stratigraphic errors. Consequently, many older excavation reports are unreliable and can only be used with the greatest caution in redefining the various periods of occupation.

Following the work of Kathleen Kenyon at Jericho, which began in 1952, excavation techniques changed considerably. Now virtually all archaeologists excavate tells by following the natural stratigraphy, defining and stripping each soil layer, precisely associating walls with construction and occupation layers, identifying intrusive features, and keeping artifacts separated by soil layers and features. While large picks and hoes are still used for some applications, nearly all excavation is done with small hand picks, masons' pointing trowels, spatulas, dental tools, and an assortment of brushes. Modern recording methods reflect these stratigraphic techniques and make it possible to reconstruct the natural stratigraphy and the associated sequence of structures and artifacts. Such painstaking procedures inevitably slow the pace of excavation so that we do not excavate nearly as large horizontal and vertical areas as in earlier times. But if the areas are smaller, they are better excavated, and the data recovered are far more reliable for cultural and historical interpretation.

I. PREPARATION FOR TELL EXCAVATIONS

A considerable amount of organization and a number of preliminary steps precede the excavation of a tell in the Levant and elsewhere, including selection of a site, of areas within the site for excavation, of staff, and the financing of the project.

Selection of Site

As with all proposed archaeological activities abroad, the selection of the site begins with discussing the proposed project with the Department of Antiquities of the nation in which the research is to be conducted. If the Department expresses an interest, one or more visits to the chosen site follows; several sites will be visited, if the choice is yet to be made. A tell is selected not because of its pristine condition or beauty, although all archaeologists are impressed by a fine site, but because of its promise for solving one or more specific cultural problems. In former times, these problems focused primarily on historical and chronological questions, but today's archaeologists ask a much wider range of questions. Because of an increasingly holistic approach to the study of culture, questions are asked concerning such issues as environment, subsistence, economy, and technology. For example, archaeologists are not only concerned with defining and dating occupation periods in a site, but they are also interested in recovering floral and faunal specimens that enable them to describe the ancient environment and its resources (e.g., plants gathered and cultivated, animals hunted or raised for food). Logistical considerations also enter into the selection of a tell, not only because of intermittent warfare and security concerns, but also because of such practical aspects of digging and camp management as remoteness from sources of water, supplies, and workers.

Selection of Areas for Excavation

The choice of areas for excavation depends on the excavator's immediate and long-range interests and plans. If the site was previously excavated, the archaeologist may wish to correlate areas of excavation with those dug earlier and will select an area adjacent to the earlier excavations. If information about fortifications and their relationship to the buildings of the various periods of occupation is sought, the excavator will choose an area along the perimeter and extending a short distance into the site, possibly including a saddle-like depression along the perimeter where a gateway might have been situated. If data on important buildings are sought, the archaeologist may choose the acropolis—the most elevated area of the site—or an area immediately inside the perimeter on the side facing the prevailing wind, as Petrie (1928: 2) did at Tell Jemmeh; Petrie reasoned that ancient builders chose locations where they could enjoy the fresh unrestricted breeze, and both the royalty and wealthy would insist on the choicest building plots. If the excavator wants to investigate the domestic area of the settlement where the common people lived, an area on the opposite side of the site from the royal-wealthy area will be selected. Normally, an archaeologist will plan to explore several such areas as part of the overall research design, and may schedule the opening of the various areas for different field seasons. Such long-range research designs are often modified in the course of excavations as new questions arise and as unexpected finds are made.

Having selected the site and area(s) to be excavated, the archaeologists discusses these plans with the Department of Antiquities, meets whatever requirements the Department imposes with respect to assurances of continuity, funding, and inspection, and formally applies for a license or permit to conduct excavation. When the license is issued, or assured of issue, the archaeologist begins serious planning.

Selection of Staff

A staff must be assembled to undertake the excavations and to conduct research in diverse disciplines such as geology, botany, and zoology, as well as physical anthropology and possibly epigraphy. Ideally, the same staff participates in all field seasons of the excavations to provide maximum continuity. A fully-staffed expedition consists of the director, an archaeological architect, a photographer, a cataloger, a conservator, a group of digging supervisors whose number depends on the number of squares to be opened, a field camp manager, and specialists in the above-mentioned ancillary disciplines. Not all of the latter need to be in the field every season; at Tell Jemmeh, for example, the geologist spent only two of the eleven seasons on the site but has always been available for consultation and continuing research in the laboratory. In field projects with smaller staffs, the diverse activities are combined in various ways with members having more than one task, e.g., the director may also serve as architect, photographer as cataloger, zooarchaeologist as a square supervisor, a square supervisor as cataloger, etc. In most Near Eastern countries, the dig will hire local workers who excavate under the direction of the square supervisor, but in some, notably Israel, student-volunteers who must be recruited each field season are used for excavation.

Funding the Project

Funding is commonly sought from foundations and organizations whose function it is to make research grants, such as the National Science Foundation or the National Endowment for the Humanities, from university and museum research funds, and from private sources. The proposals submitted to granting agencies and other funding sources describe the problems to be solved, the site and areas selected where these problems will be addressed, and the immediate and long-range research design, including methodology, staffing, and a detailed budget for the multiseason effort broken down by years. Increasingly, archaeological expeditions are team projects which involve the formation of a consortium consisting of a group of universities and their faculties, many of which pledge a sum toward the cost of each field season, subsequent laboratory research, and publication.

II. TELL STRATIFICATION

As alluded to above, all tells are stratigraphically complex. The stratification, however, becomes comprehensible when the basic components and their relationships are understood. All tells are composed of layers, walls, and features, and each must be isolated and defined as to relationship and function whenever possible.

Layers

A layer consists of a band of soil that is uniform in color and texture and can be distinguished or segregated from bands of soil above and below; it can often be ascribed to a particular activity or event so that its nature and reason for deposition can be defined. A construction layer, especially in a site with stone buildings, may contain chips from the dressing of ashlar blocks *in situ* or small stones left over from chinking rubble walls. A floor may be of packed pebbles, cobblestones, flagstones, plaster, mudbrick, or more commonly packed earth. An occupation layer which represents the debris left on the floor by the inhabitants, may be composed of fine-grain soil like that which we find in our buildings today but includes potsherds, animal bones, and other artifacts. Hearth and oven debris layers contain ash that extends on one or more sides of the structure; such layers, which frequently contain potsherds, animal bones, and burned seeds, result from cleaning out the burned material from inside the structure. Destruction layers resulting from whatever cause—warfare, earthquake, accidental fires—consist of more grainy soil and fragments of stone, mudbrick, and roofing materials (e.g., packed mud with reed impressions and large pieces of charcoal from burned wooden roofing beams) and may contain comparatively little pottery and artifacts. Wash layers derive from the gradual erosion of walls, especially in sites with mudbrick construction, and roofing materials, chiefly after the destruction or abandonment of the buildings; but wash layers also result from the erosion of uneven places in the site during rains. These layers normally contain relatively few artifacts. Ponding layers consist of the finest grain soil and are found in what were once low places in which water collected during rains; these layers generally contain few or no artifacts.

These layers are stripped off one-by-one, with careful attention to their extent, varying thicknesses, and inclines. Their precise relationships to walls are determined. All layers that continue over some distance and abut against the face of the wall are layers that accumulated after the wall was erected. Continuous layers that run beneath a wall obviously predate the construction of the wall, while layers that run over the top of a wall postdate it. By carefully studying the relationship of layers between a number of walls, as well as the relationship of the walls themselves, one can ascertain which walls were contemporary and which represent earlier or later building phases. All layers and structures that are contemporary belong to a stratum or an occupation period, although one or more building phases may be represented.

Intrusive Features

In all tells a number of different intrusive features are found which disturb the stratification by cutting through existing layers and, if not recognized, result in an inevitable mixing of earlier and later artifacts. Such features must be identified as soon as possible and excavated as units, and the layers from which they are cut must be precisely determined. The artifacts from intrusive features must be kept separate from those recovered from the layers. If the artifacts from intrusions are mixed with those from existing layers, it becomes almost impossible to date the layers precisely, because all layers are dated by the latest artifacts in them.

The most common intrusive features are the following: (1) The Foundation Trench. Some, but by no means all, buildings were constructed with foundations that go below the existing surface, and thus required foundation trenches to be dug before construction. Such trenches cut into earlier debris layers, and the soil from these layers with earlier artifacts was normally used to backfill the trench following construction, with the remaining soil left on the surface. The top of the foundation trench marks ground level at the time the building was built. (2) Partially Subterranean Structures. Occasionally, buildings were set deep in the ground, requiring the excavation of a large hole, as in modern construction. The digging of such holes penetrated earlier strata, and, since the soil removed from these holes was distributed on the site's surface or used in some aspect of construction, vast quantities of early artifacts were introduced into later cultural deposits. At Tell Jemmeh, two large granaries or silos were found, belonging to the late fourth-early third centuries B.C. Both were partially subterranean structures built of mudbrick; for one, the construction hole cut through all earlier debris into the layers of the seventh century B.C.; for the other, the hole cut through all debris into the Philistine stratum of the 12th century B.C. (3) The Robber Trench. In sites with stone construction, especially those in which ashlar masonry was employed, stones from an abandoned or destroyed building were often removed and reused in later buildings. Such activity frequently leaves a trench, either the original foundation trench or the cutting made by the stone robbers, which fills with material dating to the period of the robbing or a little later, thus introducing later artifacts into the level of an earlier stratum. (4) Access Shafts and Passages to Springs or Ground Water. To make water available to the inhabitants in time of siege, large shafts were sometimes excavated through all layers of a site into bedrock or virgin soil; these shafts normally contained a stairway leading to the water source. Tremendous quantities of material from all earlier periods were brought to the surface by such operations. At Megiddo, the debris from the water-system shaft was used to fill a nearby sloping area to level a large walled courtyard of the early ninth century B.C. (5) Minor Graded Areas. High spots were occasionally graded to make an area more level, and the earlier debris and artifacts were spread over the surface or used to fill low places, pits, etc. (6) Pits. All sites have a variety of pits with diverse functions (e.g., for burials, rubbish, storage, sumps), the cuttings of which bring earlier material to the surface and leave cavities to be filled with later material. In sites with mudbrick construction, builders often dug vast pits on the site itself to obtain soil for making bricks; this practice saved considerable time and labor over the alternative method of quarrying soil from the land around the tell and transporting it up the tell to the building site. Such pits may be several meters in diameter and two or three meters deep.

The process of analyzing the stratigraphy continues throughout the excavation. Ideally, archaeologists recognize all layers and intrusions when they first appear, but this seldom happens in the course of a field season. Sometimes intrusions are missed, only to be identified a little later; buckets of artifacts from all layers below the one from which the intrusion was cut are labeled "contaminated." While contaminated artifacts are kept and may be useful for reassembling vessels, they are not used for stratigraphic analysis and dating.

III. TECHNIQUE OF TELL EXCAVATION

The methodology employed in modern stratigraphic excavation of tells has been the subject of a number of good handbooks and review articles, especially Kenyon (1952), Wheeler (1954), Dever and Lance, (1978), Conlon (1973), and Van Beek (1981). These books deal with the actual mechanics of an excavation, including preparation of contour and top plans, architectural and balk (or section) drawings, selection of tools, notebook recording systems, cataloging, photography, and drawing of artifacts. The reader is referred to these books for detailed instructions and "how-to" procedures. Here the discussion will be confined to a summary of basic principles involved and techniques employed.

Contour Plan and Grid

At the beginning of tell excavations, a plan of the entire site is made showing contours at 1-m or 2-m intervals (fig. 2). Such a plan is an extremely useful record of the shape, extent, and slopes of the site at a given point in time. When accurately done, features such as perimeter ridges may show lines of fortifications, depressions in a ridge line may point to a gateway, and various other structures may be similarly indicated. A grid of squares is laid out on this plan with symbols—usually letters of the alphabet assigned to one direction, and numbers to the other direction—so that each square is readily identified by a letter and

FIG. 2   *The contour plan of Tell Jemmeh. Light lines represent 1-m contours above sea level. This plan is more complex than most owing to the extensive erosion on the north and south sides. Petrie's area of excavation appears to the right of survey point E.*

number. All areas of excavation are shown on this plan, not only for immediate reference but also for use by future archaeologists who will need to locate previous excavated areas precisely in spite of subsequent alterations to the tell by erosion and human activity. The size of the squares in the grid is normally 5 m, but it may be somewhat smaller or larger; the dimensions selected are determined by the nature and size of the site, the aims of the project, and the amount of laborers available for digging. In no case should the size of the square be larger than can be adequately controlled by the supervisor while digging and recording. The preparation of the contour plan and grid is the task of the architect, who employs surveying instruments, such as a theodolite, dumpy level, meter staff, and one or two helpers. At Tell Jemmeh, which is a deeply eroded site, the one-meter contour plan required about 10,000 instrument readings; these readings were cross-checked by walking over and studying each area of the site, an assignment that formed the principal task of the architect for two field seasons.

In the area(s) to be excavated, permanent markers are set in concrete at the intersection of grid lines that form each square; these markers serve as points from which measurements are taken in triangulating walls and features within the square. The cutting line of the square is normally set 0.5 m inside the grid pins; in other words, in a 5-m grid, a 4-m square is actually excavated. The unexcavated 0.5-m area on all sides becomes half of a balk which, together with the 0.5-m unexcavated area in an adjacent square, forms a 1-m wide balk. The balk serves as the reference library for the stratification of the square as digging proceeds downward. To protect the edge of the balk, many excavators place a line of stones between the grid and cutting lines to remind personnel of the excavating team and visitors not to step too near the edge which might collapse a portion of the balk.

Test Trenches and Test Pits

All soils, including those that compose tells, are slightly damp when excavated; this dampness obscures the subtle differences in color and texture that distinguish layers and even the vertical cuttings of intrusive features. Thus, layers are extremely difficult and often impossible to isolate when dug from the surface downward, and only the most experienced excavator who has gained familiarity with the soils from previous work at the site should ever try to strip layers over an entire square from the surface. But when layers are seen in cross section, characteristic colors and textures, vertical thickness, tilt, and extent can be more easily identified. For this reason, it is always important to get a preview of the layering in cross section before trying to strip the layers of a square. This is accomplished by employing a Test Trench or Test Pit (fig. 3), in which a small area, perhaps 1 m wide along one side of the square, is excavated

FIG. 3   *Test trenches being excavated along the west side of two squares at Tell Jemmeh during the first field season (1970).*

from the surface downward to a depth of no more than 1 m. The sides of this trench or pit are cut vertically, smoothed, and the layering is studied. All artifacts from the test trench are so marked; these artifacts are kept separate from those of the remainder of the area, since the stratification of the test trench as dug almost never fully corresponds to the actual layering in the remainder of the square. Such artifacts may be useful for reconstruction, but they are seldom of value for dating, unless a find spot can be assigned with certainty to one of the natural layers seen in the profile of the unexcavated area. Frequently, one or more of the layers will disappear as they are stripped off, and it often becomes necessary to excavate more than one test trench or test pit to control the layering precisely. The rule is: vertical digging first; horizontal digging afterwards (Wheeler 1954: 85).

When a wall appears, a test pit should be excavated against each face of the wall to ascertain the relationship of the layers to the wall on both of its sides (fig. 4). On the outside of the wall, a foundation trench can often be seen as a straight or ragged vertical line cutting through the built-up layers before they reach the wall face, and the debris between that line and the wall—representing backfill following construction of the wall—will have entirely different layering (fig. 5). On the inside of the wall, the layering will be different, representing the floor and the accumulation of occupation and collapse debris (fig. 6). Ancillary to the rule stated above: When in doubt about the layering, excavate a test trench. It provides the surest means available for controlling the stratigraphic excavation of an area.

Excavating Layers

Based on the cross section of layers disclosed by the test trench, the layers are systematically stripped off one-by-one over the square, and all artifacts from each layer are kept separate as the layer is removed. If, when excavating a layer, the dividing line between it and the layer below is not easily defined, it is better to cut into the layer below than to leave unexcavated a part of the layer being removed. This is because a layer is dated by the latest artifacts contained in it. It must be remembered that layers containing material of the same date can always be grouped or combined later, but layers with material of different dates cannot be separated into individual components at a later time if they have been excavated as a unit. When the stripping of a layer reaches the balks, a tag bearing the square and layer number is attached to the balk with a nail, and the lines defining the layer are scored on the balk with the point of a trowel or other sharp instrument. Vertical lines of any feature that extend from the square into the balk—such as a pit or foundation trench—are similarly scored on the balk. The tags and scoring provide a quick and easy-to-read reference when later studying the stratigraphy

FIG. 4   *A test pit being excavated inside a granary at Tell Jemmeh to locate the floor of the structure. Note the fallen brick fragments of the superstructure, which have been cleaned to illustrate the typical concentration of brick in the debris.*

FIG. 4   *A test pit being excavated inside a granary at Tell Jemmeh to locate the floor of the structure. Note the fallen brick fragments of the superstructure, which have been cleaned to illustrate the typical concentration of brick in the debris.*

FIG. 5   *A backfilled foundation trench (beneath the 50-cm scale directional arrow) against the outer wall of the seventh century B.C. vaulted building with basement rooms at Tell Jemmeh. The surface of the light colored layers in the foreground represents ground level when the building was begun, and the series of these layers predate the construction of the mudbrick building, even though they are considerably higher than the base of the wall.*

FIG. 6   *A section of debris filling a room of the vaulted building at Tell Jemmeh. Coarser debris with fallen vault brick fragments rests in the lower layer, with a layer of disintegrated lime plaster and finer grained debris above.*

and when recording the balk. After several layers have been removed, the balk is dressed vertically with a plumb bob and smoothed; tags are reset and layer lines are rescored. The vertical dressing of balks is absolutely essential to maintain the original size of the excavated area as digging proceeds downward; otherwise, what began as a 4-m square may be reduced to a 3.5- or 3-m square by the time the excavation has reached a depth of 2 or 3 m.

Excavating Features

The various types of intrusive features described above must be isolated and excavated separately, because they introduce later artifacts into the lower levels of the square. The edge line of pits, foundation trenches, and robber trenches are often recognizable when the surface is scraped with a trowel (fig. 7). There are many instances, however, in which an excavator cannot pick up the cutting line of such a feature, especially if the line happens to be hidden in a balk, or if the pit is unusually large and occupies most of the square. In such instances, the feature is identified only sometime later, a situation requiring reassessment of the stratigraphy and corresponding corrections of the records. If the feature is a small pit or a relatively shallow robber trench, and the surrounding layers provide readily distinguishable contrasts in color and texture, it is sometimes possible to excavate it from above; in such instances, it is preferable to cut into the surrounding layers slightly as the feature is cleared to make certain that it and all associated pockets of debris are completely removed. Larger pits, foundation trenches, and robber trenches are normally left in place while the excavation of the layers around them proceeds leaving a few centimeters-thick "skin" of the layers around the features to isolate them (fig. 5). The earlier artifacts contained in the "skin" will not adversely affect the dating of the material within the feature. Large pits should be excavated by quadrants whenever possible to obtain the stratigraphy within the pit. For example, the northwest quadrant might be excavated first followed by the southeast quadrant; the four sections of debris layers thus exposed provide complete north-south and east-west sections of pit layering for recording by photographs and section drawings. Afterwards, the northeast and southwest quadrants can be removed layer by layer.

Excavating Walls

The common building materials of the ancient Near East are stone and soil. The most common types of construction in stone are rubble (stones of irregular shape and size with little or no dressing), and ashlar (stones dressed square or rectangular); in soil, sun dried mudbrick (a mixture of soil, straw, and water molded either by hand or in a square or rectangular form) (fig. 8), and pisé (soil rammed or packed down,

FIG. 7   *An easily defined circular pit cutting into an earlier eighth century B.C. mudbrick fortification wall at Tell Jemmeh.*

FIG. 8   *An unusually well preserved mudbrick wall, the east wall of the vaulted building at Tell Jemmeh.*

frequently utilizing forms as in poured concrete construction) (fig. 9). As noted above, it is important to establish the specific layers associated with the construction of the walls so that they can be assigned to a specific period of occupation, a task normally requiring the excavating of test pits at right angles to the lines of the walls. The layers enclosed by the walls are excavated separately as a unit, isolating them from the layers outside the walls, and their artifacts are kept separate by layer.

When exposed, all walls must be meticulously cleaned, stone walls brushed, and mudbrick walls dressed gently with a trowel to disclose all mortar joints and the corners of each brick. In rubble walls of late periods, distinctive architectural fragments of earlier buildings were sometimes reused, and the careful examination of each stone may bring such fragments to light. Care must also be used in cleaning mudbrick walls, since portions of the original mud plaster that normally covered and protected the brick occasionally survive (fig. 10).

In both ashlar and mudbrick walls, blocks and bricks are measured (length, width, and thickness), and the bonding pattern is described. These characteristics tend to vary from period to period and represent different styles of block and brick manufacture and construction. Where walls join other walls—as at corners, interior partition walls, and party walls—joints must be examined to ascertain if they are bonded or straight. Bonded walls were constructed simultaneously, while abutting walls—those with straight joints—may have been built at the same time or, more typically, at different times with one wall having been finished before the other was erected. When this evidence is coupled with the stratigraphic relationship of layers to the walls, contemporaneousness or construction phase differences of the walls can be determined. Walls must also be examined for repairs or for evidence of later reconstruction which will also indicate one or more building phases.

When walls are removed, they must be searched for artifacts, virtually all of which predate the construction of the wall. In stone walls, reused architectural elements and artifacts may appear; in mudbrick walls, artifacts may be found in the bricks themselves—when soil for brick-making was quarried on the site—and in mud mortar joints. All mudbricks encountered in excavation should be broken up and sifted for such artifacts.

Removal of Balks

Interior balks between squares must be removed (1) when they obscure buildings and structures making the drawing and interpretation difficult, and (2) when the excavated depth of the square is approximately the same as the length of a side of the square (e.g., a 4-m square can be dug to a depth of about 4 m), since at the depth the amount of light falls off rapidly, which makes it difficult to dig deeper. Before

FIG. 9 *A pisé wall (right center) with accumulated debris layers on left. Note the absence of bedding and joints in the cross section of the wall, which are usually present in a mudbrick wall.*

FIG. 10   *Original mud plaster substantially intact on the interior surface of a mudbrick wall of the vaulted building at Tell Jemmeh. The angled bricks above are surviving remnants of the mudbrick barrel vault of the room.*

removing a balk, both faces must be dressed vertically, lightly scraped to freshen the layering, scored along layer, building, and feature lines, retagged if necessary, and fully recorded. When the balk is prepared for recording, the director and the supervisors of the squares on either side of the balk should study it together, correlating stratigraphy on both faces until they agree on all stratigraphic details, since this is the last opportunity they will have. The director and both supervisors normally share the task of drawing both sides of the balk in scale (fig. 11), after which both sides are photographed in black-and-white and color (fig. 12).

The balk is excavated layer-by-layer from the top downward and, since stratigraphy can be seen on both sides, it provides a precise stratigraphic record. Artifacts are designated as balk material and marked by stratigraphic unit. A sheet of plastic should be spread on the surface below the balk on both sides to catch artifacts that may fall during excavation, and the plastic should be cleaned when each layer or other unit is removed to prevent contamination with other artifacts. The lowest layer or two of the balk above the surfaces previously reached in both squares should be left in place to establish continuity with the new balk as excavation of the squares resumes.

IV. RECORDING THE EXCAVATION

The aim in recording is to preserve sufficiently detailed information about the excavation to permit its reconstruction in a publication. Records are required which accurately describe each layer, feature, wall, and associated artifacts and show their relationships to one another in the cultural sequence. Any recording system that fulfills these requirements is suitable. In the Near East today, there are two basic recording systems employed: (1) the Locus System, and (2) the Descriptive System; the former is probably more widely used than the latter, though both provide adequate control and have advantages and disadvantages. In the Locus System, every distinguishable unit in the stratigraphy—e.g., a layer, surface, wall, feature, etc.—is assigned a locus number at the moment it is recognized during the excavation. A locus number is used only once in an excavation, and a distinctive block of numbers is employed by a given square through all field seasons. In instances where subsequent digging or study shows that units, (e.g., layers or walls) in different parts of the square, which were originally assigned different locus numbers, are actually one and the same, one of the locus numbers is subsequently cancelled. In some excavations, the pottery basket forms a necessary corollary; it is the smallest unit of excavation and represents all artifacts from all or part of a given locus. The pottery basket is designated by site, date, field, area, basket number, and locus number.

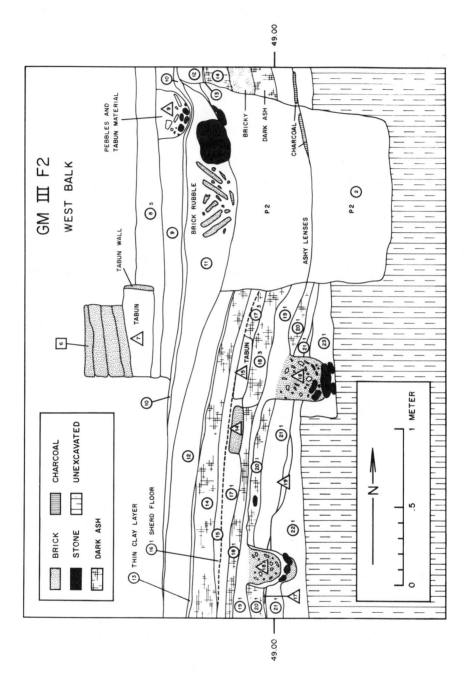

FIG. 11   *Balk drawing from Tell Jemmeh.*

FIG. 12   *Photograph of the balk drawn in fig. 11. The photograph does not show the entire balk.*

Individual artifacts are marked to show field season, field, area, basket, and these artificates are assigned numbers from a special sequence.

In the Descriptive System, all data—site, field, square, layer number, wall, feature—are recorded directly, utilizing a code which contains all information in an abbreviated form to mark tags and each artifact or artifact container. Any subsequent equations or corrections are entered in the square notebook for future reference. The locus number is therefore not employed to represent a stratigraphic unit, since the unit itself is used as the basis of the recording system. The term "locus" may or may not be used. At Tell Jemmeh, it is employed to indicate a horizontal division within a square as, for example, the layering on either side of a wall, which is assigned a different locus number while the sequence of layer numbers is continued. The most obvious advantage of this system is that exact locations are recorded on the artifacts without having to refer to a separate list of locus numbers, as in the Locus System. The major disadvantage is the greater number of symbols that must be recorded on each artifact, which may require as many as eight or nine letters and numbers.

The principal records are: the square notebook; the drawings of the site plan, top plans, balks, elevations of structures and sections and, occasionally, reconstructions; the photographs; and the catalog of artifacts. All are essential for an understanding of what has taken place in the course of the excavation and for publication.

The Square Notebook

The notebook consists of alternate pages of centimeter graph paper and ruled pages, and may be either a loose-leaf notebook with the ring holes of the pages reinforced, or a bound notebook. Normally in the Near East, a separate notebook is used for each square and is continued for as long as the square is excavated. If bound notebooks are used, a new notebook is generally required for each square each field season. Sketches, measured top plans, and balks are drawn on the centimeter graph paper, and descriptions of layers, walls, features, and registers of pottery buckets, small finds, and photographs are kept on the ruled pages (fig. 13). Some excavations, especially those employing the Locus System, utilize preprinted forms in the loose-leaf format, which are filled in daily by the square supervisor. For details on keeping the notebook and preparing top plans and section drawings, see the handbooks cited above.

The notebook is not a diary, but a concise description of layering, walls, and features found in the course of excavation. Each layer is numbered, described as to texture, color (using the Munsell Color System), type (i.e., hearth ash, floor destruction debris, fill), and significant finds. Walls are described as to type, stone or brick sizes, color if relevant,

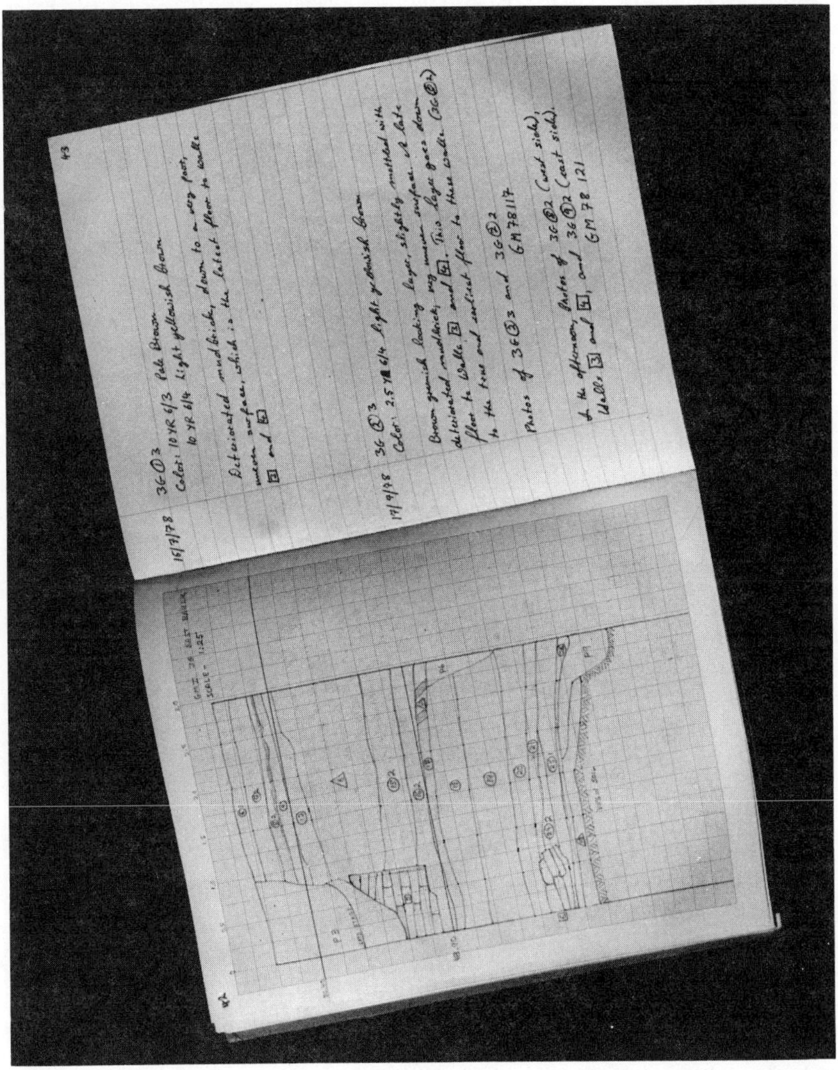

FIG. 13 *Typical pages of a square notebook, with balk drawing on graph page on left, and description of layers on right.*

and association with layers and with other walls. Features are defined as to type, stratigraphic relationships, function, size, colors, and noteworthy artifacts. Ample space is left between all unit descriptions for adding later observations, equations and correlations, later decisions on relationships between layers, walls, and features, and dating information.

All drawings including top plans and balk drawings of the four balks, as well as sections of test trenches and test pits, walls and features are drawn on the accompanying graph pages. Some excavations require daily top plans, while others demand top plans only when new layers, walls, or features appear in the square. In addition to measured scale drawings, quick but informative sketches to clarify specific points are also made on the graph pages.

A serial register of each pottery and bone bucket and small find box is also kept; this register contains bucket number, provenience, date excavated, and any identifying information. Special instructions for handling (e.g., reconstructible pot, don't wash) are included in the square notebook. Included also is a serial register of photographs taken in the square; this register contains negative number, date photographed, a full explanation of details seen in the photograph (layers, walls, features, relationships, and direction from which taken), and photographer's name, if more than one person is taking photographs of the square. At the end of the season, it is worthwhile for the supervisor to describe the interpretations and conclusions which he and the field supervisor or director have reached regarding the stratification of the square and to recommend specific operations in chronological order for continuing the excavation of the square in the next field season. Naturally, this kind of planning depends upon the availability of accurate records.

The Drawings

The drawings, which include not only those drawn by the supervisor in the square notebook, but also those prepared by the architect, form the visual base for the schematic illustration of stratigraphy and features in publications. The architect's drawings comprise the contour plan, comprehensive drawings of all top plans, features, and building walls, including elevations and architectural details, of each stratum in all squares. The comprehensive plans are replete with details, such as wall and room numbers, levels of walls, features, and layers, and with lines showing where cross sections of buildings or walls have been made. With the points of the square pins and other permanent benchmarks shown, it is possible to superimpose plans of successive strata to show the changing alignments of buildings in the different occupation periods. Isometric and reconstruction drawings of all buildings and features that are sufficiently preserved and are of enough significance to warrant detailed presentation are also the responsibility of the architect.

For the architect to draw accurately, all walls and features must be meticulously clean and all points, such as the four corners of each ashlar block or mudbrick, must be clearly visible (e.g., fig. 8). In the case of mudbrick walls whose top surfaces may be irregular and uneven due to erosion, it is often necessary to remove one or more courses to obtain a continuous clean surface so that the bonding pattern will be clear in the drawing. For making the final comprehensive plans, the architect uses surveying instruments or triangulation from the square pins or, more commonly, a combination of both.

Photography

It is impossible to take too many photographs of excavation. Every subject should be photographed in color and black-and-white; the former is useful for lectures and for subsequent study of stratigraphy, because of the superior rendering of soil colors; the latter is required for publication. Owing to the increasingly fine quality and wide range of lenses and photographic emulsions, the lightweight and versatile 35 mm cameras are becoming the standard, although many excavators prefer using a larger format camera, such as a 2¼ × 2¼ or 4 × 5, for black-and-white photography which permits greater enlargements. On virtually all tell excavations with permanent base camps, black-and-white negatives are developed immediately at the site before the photographed feature is removed; this guarantees that all details are shown and the photograph is of printable quality. Wherever possible, it is also highly desirable to process color film—such as Ektachrome or similar emulsions—in the camp darkroom at the earliest moment.

The square supervisor must think photographically in determining the exact area to be covered by the camera, the best angle(s), and the most favorable time of day in terms of lighting to show details. The supervisor's responsibilities also include preparing the area for photography by brushing and pointing up details, removing footprints and all digging paraphernalia, arranging the scale staff or arrow and the letters indicating the square and feature number, and providing full details for the square notebook and the photographer's record. As a final check, it is important for the supervisor to view the scene through the camera viewer before the photograph is taken, because the angle might be improved and frequently extraneous items overlooked in preparing the square will be seen. In addition to the list of photographs kept by each square supervisor, the photographer maintains a full record of all photographs taken for the entire excavation; this assures a duplicate record and provides a convenient list for sorting the photographs later.

The Catalog

The catalog is the permanent record of artifacts found in an excavation. Artifacts can be assigned to one of two categories: Category 1 includes the "small finds," the obviously significant objects, and Category 2 comprises the remainder of the objects, including potsherds, glass sherds, whole or fragmentary worked-stone artifacts and unworked-stone pieces, metal fragments, fauna, flora, and soil samples, lime plaster, vitrified soil and slag, wood, and pigments. Because of the overwhelming number of artifacts as defined here, the director and staff determine which ones should be assigned to these categories so that the artifacts receive either full or partial cataloging.

The cataloging of small finds includes the following data: (1) full provenience, (2) date excavated, (3) basket number, (4) material, (5) type of object, (6) measurements, (7) color(s), (8) detailed description, (9) full description of conservation treatment, (10) negative numbers of all photographs, (11) drawing number(s) and (12) disposition of the object (i.e., held by the Department of Antiquities or retained by the expedition). In a typical field season, this group may not number more than 100–200 items, although hoards of pottery, coins, jewelry, architectural fragments, tablets, etc. may appear and increase the size of the small finds catalog. Such a catalog must be open-ended in order to receive additional pieces that are later restored in the laboratory or transferred from Catagory 2.

Those in Category 2, forming the bulk of the finds, may be separately and partially cataloged in materials registers, i.e., ceramics, metals, stones, etc., or not cataloged at all. At the very least, all such items must have full provenience data, date found, and basket number appended to them. Sometimes, following laboratory analysis and cleaning, a piece in this category proves to be of sufficient interest to be cataloged as a small find, as for example, an undistinguished fragment of what appeared to be a broken bronze ring from Tell Jemmeh. Upon x-raying this piece, it was discovered that it was actually a portion of a decorated silver earring; the piece was then shifted to Category 1 and fully cataloged as a small find for that field season.

The format of catalogs employed by different excavations varies considerably. Some expeditions use loose-leaf notebooks, others bound notebooks, and still others a card system consisting of either a punched card or sheet for data processing, or a plain card on which all information is recorded, preferably by a typewriter (fig. 14). Many expeditions routinely attach a small black-and-white photographic print of the object to the catalog entry for ready identification. All objects—or their containers—are marked with catalog number, provenience data, etc. by using a non-fading, water-resistant ink and pen, or certain felt-tip markers. All containers must be rigid in construction and securely fastened to prevent damage to artifacts or loss while in storage and transit.

V. INTERPRETING THE EXCAVATION

While it is obviously necessary to publish the data generated by an excavation and to synthesize those data for a chronological ordering of

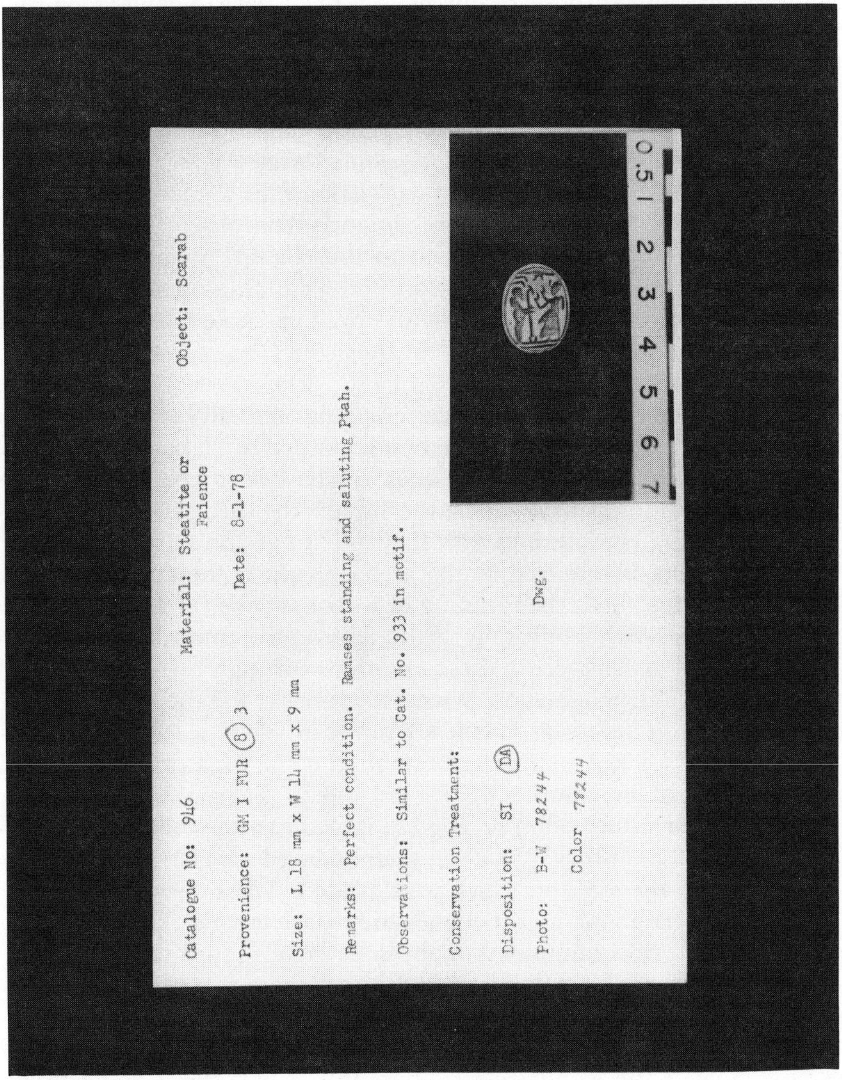

Catalogue No: 946 Material: Steatite or Faience Object: Scarab

Provenience: GM I FUR (8) 3 Date: 8-1-78

Size: L 18 mm x W 14 mm x 9 mm

Remarks: Perfect condition. Ramses standing and saluting Ptah.

Observations: Similar to Cat. No. 933 in motif.

Conservation Treatment:

Disposition: SI (DA)

Photo: B-W 78244 Dwg.

Color 78244

FIG. 14 *A typical category 1 "small find" catalogue card at Tell Jemmeh.*

the site, it is also the responsibility of the archaeologist to interpret those data with respect to their larger environmental, cultural, and historical meaning. More specifically, what light did the excavation shed on the natural resources and climate of the site and their interaction, on mankind's utilization of those resources to achieve a reasonably good and comfortable life in terms of subsistence through agricultural activities and animal husbandry, and of product surpluses to guarantee security and provide a margin for commerce? What information was provided on technological processes, on the level of craftsmanship, and the variety of crafts that produced things useful to people? What was learned about the organization of the community, of its relationships to neighboring communities as well as to those more distant? What discoveries relate to historical events that occurred and to the changes wrought by those events? What can be inferred for an understanding of social and religious customs? A relatively simple and brief example may be found in the chapter entitled "Conclusions" in *Hajar Bin Humeid* (Van Beek 1969: 367–71).

Such interpretations, however imperfect, tentative, and subject to correction, *must* be made by those best equipped to make them, namely the excavation team. They are the ones who have lived and worked at the site for months and years, who know the soil, the successive occupations in their varying complexities with their buildings and paraphernalia of daily life. What is required of the archaeologist is the curiosity to ask broad questions about the meaning of what has been found, to view the sweep of the work holistically with rigorous common sense, and to conceive ways of answering these questions through the detached and patient use of the imagination. What, for example, was the function of an unusually large building? Was it a temple, a palace, a wealthy family's residence, or a large commercial establishment? What does the overall organization of its complex of rooms and its internal traffic pattern suggest? What information do the layers within and without the structure tell us of its history? What did the building look like? Which rooms were open to the sky and which were roofed? What does the range of artifacts tell us about its function and socioeconomic status? Do they include what are commonly thought to be cultic vessels? How does the range of artifacts from it compare with those of other contemporary structures of that particular occupation in the site? Are they more specialized, finer in quality, and do they include a higher ratio of imported items? How do they compare with those from similar large and contemporary buildings at other sites in the region? What do the animal bones recovered from the building suggest? Do they include more younger domestic animals than those collected from other buildings of the same occupation period, or more wild hunted animals? Do they include fish and bird bones and in what quantities? Household pests? If the archaeologist decides that it is a residence, is it possible to estimate the number of inhabitants who lived in the building from such evidence as the number of rooms, courtyards, bread ovens, number and size of cooking pots? Do these data suggest that it was inhabited by a nuclear or extended family? The answers to these and similar questions will at the very least enable the excavators to speculate on the function of the building with reasonable probability. The results of the inquiry or thought process must be described in the interpretations to form a reasoned basis for the suggested function. It is not enough for the excavator to conclude that because it is an unusually large building, it must be a palace.

At the same time, archaeologists must beware of overdrawing their evidence in framing their conclusions. For example, a single room, house, or even several houses with evidence of burning do not necessarily indicate a destruction by warfare, even if historical records describe the conquest of the site in the time frame of the burning. Nor, for that matter, does the lack of evidence of destruction in an excavation justify the questioning of the validity of historical accounts of the conquest of the site in a given period. In both instances, the amount of the site actually excavated is usually a small fraction of the whole site, and the evidence, or lack of evidence, must be weighed against the probability of finding conclusive evidence in the tiny fraction of the site excavated. At Tell Jemmeh, the best represented occupation period in terms of the number of square meters excavated, is the LB II; while the area seemed large to the excavators, it actually represented only 1.65 percent of the surface area of the tell in that period. No evidence of destruction was found, but it is impossible to argue from such a small sample that the settlement of that period was not destroyed in war.

Even if there are clear indicators of destruction, there are many possible agents of destruction apart from invading and conquering armies. Earthquakes, which are common in the Levant, accidental fires, deliberate fires set by someone in the town in the course of a vendetta, or by a householder seeking to destroy quickly all or part of a building, and numerous other possibilities may be the agents of burning. To be on firm ground in attributing a burning to destruction by warfare, one must have some solid evidence of warfare—a hole punched into the fortification, the remains of a sapper's tunnel beneath the walls, a portion of a ramp for siege engines, accouterments of warfare such as stone missles, a higher frequency of arrow and spear points, fragments of armor, or at least something apart from fire to suggest military action. Lachish and Masada provide sufficiently convincing evidence to serve as examples. Since the excavated areas of most sites are so small, it would be extraordinary good fortune to find such unequivocal evidence of warfare. It is moreover, highly unlikely that ancient conquerors intent on stabilizing a region to obtain tribute would destroy entire settlements—and thereby reduce the economic productivity of a region which made the payment of tribute possible—except in instances of uncontrollable anger. Their major objective was the peaceful surrender of the inhabitants, which was usually accomplished by the presence of an overwhelming force or, failing that, by a small demonstration of power, such as in destroying a gateway, a small section of the defense wall, or burning a building or two. Even a substantial fire does not necessarily indicate a destruction by warfare, and to interpret it in this manner in the absence of solid evidence of military activity is to misuse the data.

Archaeologists must walk a thin line in framing conclusions about what happened at the site, balancing imagination with rigorous criticism and intuition with common sense. But the interpretation of the evidence and the framing of conclusions must be done, if archaeologists are not to merit the reproach that they are concerned only with potsherds. As Wheeler (1954: 228–229) has emphasized,

> ". . . an archaeologist who is not more that a potsherd-catcher is unworthy of his *logos*. He is primarily a fact-finder, but his facts are the material records of human achievement; he is also, by that token, a humanist, and his secondary task is that of revivifying or humanizing his materials with a controlled imagination that inevitably partakes of the qualities of art and even of philosophy."

Someone once said in reviewing an archaeological research proposal for funding that the site was better than the archaeologist. In a real sense, this applies to every site and to every archaeologist. The site is always far more important than the archaeologist because it contains a unique but fragile segment of cultural history, the fullest existing record of what an ancient population did and how it lived. An archaeological site is primarily the patrimony of mankind; secondly, it is the patrimony of the nation in whose territory it is presently situated; thirdly—and only thirdly—it is the patrimony of archaeologists engaged in cultural reconstruction. It deserves the best that one can give, and second best is not good enough.

BIBLIOGRAPHY

Callaway, J. A.
　　1972　　*The Early Bronze Age Sanctuary at Ai (et-Tell).* London: Quaritch.
Conlon, V. M.
　　1973　　*Camera Techniques in Archaeology.* New York: St. Martins.
Dever, W. G., and Lance, H. D., eds.
　　1978　　*A Manual of Field Excavation: Handbook for Field Archaeologists.* New York: HUC-JIR.

Kenyon, K. M.
1952   *Beginning in Archaeology.* Aldine Paperback No. 28. London: Dent.
Munsell, A. H.
1954   *Munsell Soil Color Charts.* Baltimore: Munsell.
Petrie, W. M. F.
1928   *Gerar.* London: Quaritch.
Van Beek, G. W.
1969   *Hajar Bin Humeid: Investigations at a Pre-Islamic Site in South Arabia.* Baltimore: American Foundation of the Study of Man.
1981   Review of Dever, W. G., and Lance, H. D., eds., *A Manual of Field Excavation: Handbook for Field Archaeologists.* BASOR 242: 83–86.
1984   Archaeological Investigations at Tell Jemmeh, Israel. Pp. 675–96 in *National Geographic Research Reports: 1975 Projects.* Washington, D.C.: National Geographic Society.
Wheeler, M.
1954   *Archaeology from the Earth.* Baltimore: Penguin.

8
EXCAVATION OF LOW-LEVEL SETTLEMENT SITES

JOHN MCRAY
Wheaton Graduate School

Perhaps the proper way to begin this contribution to the *Festschrift* honoring Professor Callaway is by explaining what is meant by the title of the paper, since it will probably appear as an oddity to those who have been working in field archaeology or reading manuals on the subject. The writer was asked to contribute this essay because of his work at Caesarea Maritima since 1972. Caesarea, an 8000-acre site situated on the coast of Israel midway between Haifa and Tel Aviv and standing virtually at sea level, would be indisputably regarded as a "low-level settlement site" (Moorey 1981: 55) or in better known but less descriptive terms a "non-tell site." Since most works dealing with Middle Eastern archaeology discuss the excavation of tells, one rarely reads of any thing else and understands why Nelson Glueck spoke of "other antiquity sites" (Glueck 1970: 37) when categorizing sites other than tells. Glueck (1959: 6) describes Transjordan and the Negeb as "countries where these multi-layered mounds of former civilizations are rare."

However, Glueck dealt primarily with sites which are briefly oc-cupied by bedouin or other nomadic peoples who lived in tents and never stayed long enough in one place to construct permanent build-ings. His work in surveying such sites is well known and has been mentioned in other essays in this volume. The present paper will not, therefore, deal with this type of low-level settlement. Nor will it be profitable to discuss the details of normal excavation procedure which are treated extensively in the Van Beek article. These procedures are standard in any kind of excavation and are discussed in the basic man-uals (Kenyon 1952; Dever and Lance, 1978; Moorey 1981; Albright 1949; Wheeler 1954; Parrot 1955; Fagan 1983; etc.). Current meth-odology used in surveys more recent than Glueck's may be found in reports such as J. Maxwell Miller's on Moab (1979: 43) and Cohen and Dever's article on the Negeb (1978: 29). Reference may also be made to the article by James Kautz in this volume for further discussion of such surveys.

What remains to be discussed here, then, are those sites that require excavation but do not constitute tells. As a matter of interest, before beginning to write, the writer consulted approximately 25 volumes on the archaeology of the Middle East, the Mediterranean, and Europe that contain discussions on the methodology of excavation. None dealt specifically with "non-tell" sites. At first I was perplexed by this because of the fact that so many sites of classical antiquity are not tells, e.g., Rome, Ostia, Pompeii, Herculaneum, Corinth, Philippi, Ephesus, Sardis, Pergamum, and Hierapolis. And in Palestine one thinks of Capernaum, Caesarea, Magdala, Chorazin, Jerash, Baalbek, and Petra, among others. After careful reflection, however, the reason for this omission became evident: the basic procedures for digging are the same for all sites. The techniques of excavation discussed in the handbooks have to do almost exclusively with stratified sites, and most low-level sites are also stratified. The excavation handbooks discuss two fundamental types of excavation—vertical and horizontal. The former has to do with digging trenches, the method used effectively by Wheeler in his early work (1954: 81), but less effectively by Macalister at Gezer and Garstang at Jericho. The latter has to do with the systematic removal of strata by a grid system that was developed by Kenyon at Jericho and Jerusalem and was refined by Wright at Shechem and by Dever at Gezer. Even though common sense dictates that excavation can only be done vertically and/or horizontally, the handbooks presuppose the excavation of tells when discussing these techniques.

I have been asked to make some observations on the unique aspects of digging sites which are not tells, but this does not mean sites with only one occupational level. Such would be an unwarranted narrowness in the conception of low-level sites. Indeed, it is extremely rare to find a site like Tell el-Amarna in Egypt which was occupied only during the reign of Amenhotep IV (Akhenaton). Such a site does simplify the problem of chronology and the identification of pottery types, as well as the evaluation of cultural remains, but such a site is also as rare as the unique historical circumstances which contributed to its rapid rise and equally rapid decline. We cannot hope to treat it as more than an anomaly in the pattern of settlement in the ancient world.

I. THE FORMATION OF LOW-LEVEL SITES

We have reached the point, ironically, in treatments of Palestinian archaeology where it seems necessary to provide some explanation for the existence of "low-level sites." Since Schliemann's discovery of the principle of tell stratification in 1870, every book on Middle Eastern archaeology necessarily explains how tells developed. Beek's *Atlas of Mesopotamia* showed in 1962 there were more than 5000 of these mounds in Mesopotamia, and Paul Lapp estimated in 1963 that there were 5000 sites in Palestine, a large percentage of which are tells. So, since Schliemann's discovery a hundred years ago, we have now reached the point that a non-tell site, rather than a tell site, is the oddity, and we are compelled to explain why sites have not become tells.

We have learned since the work at Troy in 1870 that tells are created by the repeated accumulation of destruction debris where destroyed cities are rebuilt over existing ruins without first clearing the ruins. The accumulation of debris at particular locations resulted from the limited number of places where settlement could occur. These limitations may be due to the need for a high hill on which to place the city for defensive purposes, the need for access to a nearby water supply, the need to use every foot of surrounding land for agricultural purposes, the rugged terrain adjacent to the tell, the availability of earlier usable structures on the site, or a number of other reasons. On the other hand, sites that do not become tells were not restricted by such factors. A city like Caesarea Maritima, for example, was situated in the midst of the extremely fertile Plain of Sharon and did not lack for cultivable land around it. It had no high point on which to build from the beginning, and water had to be brought in by aqueduct from Mt. Carmel ca. 10 km to the east. Consequently, without such built-in restrictions, Caesarea spread over 8000 acres, reaching its apex in the Byzantine period. It never developed a tell, though its history spans about 1200 years.

Closely associated with the environmental constraints that cause a site to build up in a rather limited area is the site's history of destruction. Sites which were continually inhabited over long periods of time did not necessarily build up into mounds with deep debris. The continued use of a site frequently required the reuse of structures that were damaged or destroyed. This results in multiphasing in some buildings, such as the well-known stone structure on top of Sepphoris (a Hellenistic-Roman period site in Lower Galilee). When this site was excavated in 1983, it was determined to have been built in the Byzantine period, added to and modified in the Crusader period, and repaired until the 20th century, being used most recently as a school building. Jerusalem is filled with examples of this phenomenon.

Some low-level sites are probably non-tells because they simply were not occupied long enough to become such. Sites like Capernaum, Magdala, and Chorazin, may well fit this pattern. However, it is not merely the length of time a site was occupied, but the frequency of times it was destroyed and followed by periods of disuse, that produces tells. And yet it must be observed that a close correlation exists between the two; i.e., in that part of the ancient world, longer occupational history normally includes larger numbers of destructions.

It should also be observed that the occupation of some tell sites is largely, though not exclusively, limited to the top or upper slopes of the tell itself (e.g., Megiddo, Gezer, and Shechem). Far more often, however, the tell will only be a part of a much greater complex, including low-level settlement, as at Hazor, Arad, Herodian Jericho, and Herodium. Other sites might have been basically tell sites in their older history and then expanded to include larger low-level areas in later periods of occupation, such as Samaria and Beth-shan.

The existence of non-tell sites in Transjordan and the Negeb is explained in the following way by Nelson Glueck (1959: 6):

> The extreme desolation created repeatedly by merciless invaders resulted often in the total disappearance of civilizations. "And he took the city, and slew the people that were therein; and he beat down the city and sowed it with salt" (Judges 9:45).
>
> In the fallow periods that followed, there was no law nor order, and Bedouins roamed the countryside. Their depredations, along with the forces of natural deterioration, resulted frequently in the remaining ruins being leveled to the ground. When new settlers arrived, sometimes after prolonged intervals of time, they would neither know nor be able to recognize the locations of the previous town sites and would build their houses of stone or of mud brick on virgin soil. No firmly rooted people of the land would be left who had retained and could transmit from historical memory the heritage of unbroken tradition. Only by chance would they build exactly where perhaps a thousand years earlier another village had once stood.

Glueck was convinced that it was not a major change in the climate in these areas that contributed to this situation but what he calls "the vagaries of human character" (1959: 11).

Cohen, working on non-tell sites in the Negeb, primarily fortresses which appear to have been constructed in the Iron Age and then disappeared, is of the opinion that these low-level sites were destroyed by Pharaoh Shishak; Meshel, on the other hand, argues that "the sites were abandoned when the 'local inhabitants' recognized the permanency of the central authority and hence determined that there was no longer any need for fortresses" (Herzog 1983: 43).

Some of the most impressive work done recently on low-level sites is that of Cohen and Dever, also in the Negeb. In this "moundless" region of Palestine, to use Glueck's term, we have a good concentration of one-period sites, unlike most of the area to the north. Cohen and Dever (1978:29) describe the region in this way: "The MB I settlements are mostly small, one-period sites, with well preserved remains visible on the surface." The reasons for such limited occupation on these sites, according to Cohen and Dever, lie in the remoteness of the area, the ruggedness of the terrain, the poor soils and small amounts of annual rainfall.

They write that ". . . within the entire historical period the Central Negeb highlands have never been extensively or permanently settled" (Cohen and Dever, 1978: 29).

Archaeologists would welcome a discussion by Cohen and Dever on the most effective methodology of dealing with these one-level sites. For now we may refer to their three reports on the Central Negeb Highlands Project (1978; 1979; 1981) and to Aileen Baron's important essay, "Adaptive Strategies in the Archaeology of the Negeb" (1981). A selection from Cohen and Dever's second report regarding their methodology will, therefore, be helpful at this point:

> Our excavation technique was again relatively simple, since architecturally Beer Resisim is a one-period site. We cleared collapsed stones until we could discern the outline of the architecture on the surface and then laid out section-lines which would both bisect the individual structures and would later connect them as conveniently as possible. Since all were small, circular independent units with rather elementary stratification, we developed an expeditious method for clearing these structures. We dug one-half rather rapidly (in effect as a "probe trench"), putting aside all the collapsed stone in the upper levels for possible reconstruction and seiving [sic] the material down toward the surface and/or bedrock. We drew the section and then removed the other half of the material similarly but more slowly to check our stratigraphy. In addition to sieving all the debris related to living-surfaces, we attempted flotation of some 10% of this material. . . . Frequent soil samples and palynological samples were taken. All sections were analyzed and sampled by the geomorphologist before being drawn, and all loci were described. . . . Because the material was scant, we attempted "total retrieval" as far as was compatible with the salvage nature of the project (1979: 46–47).

II. CHARACTERISTIC FEATURES OF LOW-LEVEL SITES

The excavation of low-level sites, although done according to the basic techniques used on any reputable dig today, calls for the recognition of problems characteristic of this type of site. In the first place it should be observed that a majority of low-level sites are stratified to some extent and have a history of more than one occupational period. Thus, stratigraphic excavation must be employed, just as on a tell. However, low-level sites will more likely have expanded horizontally than tell sites, and special attention must be given to surveying the immediately surrounding area for evidence of a large occupational surface. One-level sites, like those of the MB I period in the Negeb will have little or no stratification because they were not inhabited over long periods of time. Thus, their horizontal element will be limited. Although Caesarea Maritima is spread out over thousands of acres and exhibits a relatively small number of major cultural resettlements (Roman, Byzantine, Arab, Crusader), it has nine phases of occupation discernible at the present time. Material from the Hellenistic period is sparse, and the Crusader occupation was brief. The greater part of the history of the site is found in phases from the Roman, Byzantine, and Arab periods, each of which has subphases. This, together with the obvious material from the modern period, would suggest a sizeable tell upon the first encounter with the evidence, but a visit to the site impresses one with the fact that we are looking at a site which is virtually at sea level. The reason is that one rarely encounters all these nine phases in any one area of the huge site. Such a low-level stratified site will of necessity require different procedures of excavation than a strictly one-level site. Indeed, excavation of this kind of site will require techniques more like those used on a tell. One difference, more in degree than in kind, that immediately becomes evident is that the task of selecting areas of such a large site in which to place squares becomes more complex and perhaps even more crucial than on a tell. The reason is that the probability of one square or trench providing information directly relevant to another is much more unlikely due to the large distances between the squares. Several seasons were required to determine the details of Caesarea's road system because it took a long time to find the roads; one portion of the road found in the northern part of the city was 0.4 km from the other portions found further south. The sheer magnitude of the site presents such problems in laying out areas for excavation.

This problem led Wheeler to advocate going directly to the center of the ancient town, if it is readily discernible, and zeroing in on the civic center (Wheeler 1954: 106). Some of his thinking is not acceptable by today's standards of excavation, since we demand a full stratigraphical history of the site with equal attention to each succeeding stratum. Wheeler, however, in commenting on the excavation of "flat sites" (1954: 104) in Pakistan and Afghanistan, criticized the excavators for not exercising enough care in choosing the areas which had less stratification above the layers representing the most important historical periods of these cities. To be sure, these areas are not always, or even often, easily located, but constraints of time and money, he felt, necessitate that on large sites one should concentrate on the most important historical periods (Wheeler 1954:110). Wheeler (1954: 110–11) advocated picking the lower areas of sites, where human and natural forces have removed the higher strata containing Sikh and Muslim phases. Thus, where "the familiar top-stuff is absent," one may "penetrate to the earlier levels;" according to Wheeler, these are the strata that justify the time and expense of excavating a site.

While there are pros and cons to what Wheeler advocates, one notices the trend today in choosing excavation sites that are small and capable of both excavation and publication within the time and resources available to the expedition. Most sites will never be fully dug, or perhaps even adequately dug. Yigael Yadin estimated that at the normal rate of digging at Hazor in Galilee it would take 8000 years to excavate the site thoroughly. Hazor covers about 200 acres in its upper and lower levels. How long would it take to excavate thoroughly the 8000 acres of Caesarea Maritima?

Another difference between large low-level sites and tells is that the standard 5-m square will normally not be large enough to be effective. Excavators at Caesarea used 10-m squares and, in 1978, the writer had the task of dealing with a 10m × 40m square. The justification was that it lay above the intersection of major streets, and a broad exposure was necessary. On horizontally expanded sites, this is the only way to get more results in less time. Otherwise, archaeologists are engaged merely in what Fagan calls "stratified sampling" (1975: 152). He says "sampling technique is new to archaeology, and as this methodology is developed and applied more widely, excavation methods will change, especially in sites which lend themselves to quantitative investigation, such as . . . town sites" (1975: 153). In context, Fagan is dealing both with sampling of excavated data and selection of excavation areas on a site.

While one may usually assume that the high point of a tell contains the palace or fortress of the city, and a depression (as at Hazor, Gezer, and Megiddo) indicates the water source, it is generally more difficult to locate these places on a low-level site. Woolley wrestled with such problems in his work in Mesopotamia and Britain and found ingenious ways to determine what lay beneath the surface; for example, he imagined that he could see the entire plan of an unexcavated Roman villa laid out before him simply because "in the dry summer the grass withers more quickly where the soil lies thin over the buried tops of stone walls" (Woolley 1930: 28). At Caesarea, an amphitheater that is not visible above ground was located by means of aerial infrared photography; this technique records concentrations of heat that emanate from subsurface rocks differently than where no rocks exist. Such a technique is valuable for low-level sites, but of little value on tells, where the superimposed strata insulate the lower levels and prevent heat loss.

Methods of this kind are becoming increasingly necessary as we deal with the larger and more complex sites. Stephen Dyson laments the fact that "new archaeologists" have often ignored large sites because their size and massive amounts of material culture "tend to compound their already complex problems." He argues that "new methods have to be developed . . . to deal with large areas, massive data, and our own mortality" (Dyson 1981:11).

Other difficulties are encountered in low-level excavation when different projects divide a site for their own investigations. This rarely happens on a tell, which is usually considered the preserve of one expedition. At Caesarea, for example, the Italians dug the theater, the Israelis dug the synagogue, the Joint Expedition to Caesarea is digging a number of areas along the coast and inland, while the harbor is simultaneously being dug by the Universities of Haifa, Colorado, and Maryland. In recent years, two totally independent expeditions have been working in close proximity at Capernaum. Jerusalem is an obvious example of this condition; at this site, numerous teams are currently at work, although they are not operating in total isolation of each other.

There is one aspect of low-level digging that tends to have the advantage over heavily stratified sites—the capability of effective and permanent reconstructions. Obviously, sites with complex stratigraphy must be dismantled as work progresses, and this procedure hampers, at least temporarily, the possibilities of large-scale reconstruction. Low-level sites, and especially one-level sites, are much more likely to be suitable for permanent reconstruction. The kind of reconstruction done in the Negeb project by Cohen and Dever (Cohen and Dever 1978) is a model for work elsewhere. With the Department of Antiquities of Israel requiring reconstruction as a part of every excavation, a new impetus has been given to a neglected aspect of archaeology in this part of the Middle East.

The trend in archaeological reconstruction illustrates another important element in fieldwork in general, but especially in low-level sites, that is, the formulation of an overall design for the excavation; project designs should include finances for restoration and details on day-to-day tactics. Fagan has summarized a great deal by observing that "excavation costs are such that problem-oriented digging is now the rule rather than the exception . . ." (1975: 144). We will not again see large sites approached in the way Megiddo and Samaria were dug. Financial considerations have transformed labor arrangements in field archaeology; one obvious difference is the gradual replacement of paid labor with volunteer help, usually chosen from college students (Kenyon 1952: 55–56). The consortium (i.e., a cooperative program in which several institutions pool their resources) has largely replaced the individual person or school in Middle Eastern archaeology today. For example, the Joint Expedition to Caesarea Maritama has included up to 20 institutions. This trend will probably become the norm in the excavation of both tells and low-level settlement sites.

BIBLIOGRAPHY

Albright, W. F.
    1949   *The Archeology of Palestine.* Baltimore: Penguin.
Baron, A. G.
    1981   Adaptive Strategies in the Archaeology of the Negev. *BASOR* 242: 51–81.

Beek, M. A.
   1962   *Atlas of Mesopotamia.* New York: Nelson.
Cohen, R., and Dever, W. G.
   1978   Preliminary Report of the Pilot Season of the "Central Negev
               Highlands Project." *BASOR* 232: 29–46.
   1979   Preliminary Report of the Second Season of the "Central Negev
               Highlands Project." *BASOR* 236: 41–60.
   1981   Preliminary Report of the Third and Final Season of the "Cen-
               tral Negev Highlands Project." *BASOR* 243: 57–77.
Dever, W. G., and Lance, H. D., eds.
   1978   *A Manual of Field Excavation: Handbook for Field Archaeologists.*
               New York: HUC-JIR.
Dyson, S. L.
   1981   A Classical Archeologist's Response to the "New Archeology."
               BASOR 242: 7–13.
Fagan, B. M.
   1975   *In the Beginning: An Introduction to Archeology.* Boston: Little,
               Brown.
   1983   *Archeology: A Brief Introduction.* Boston: Little, Brown.
Glueck, N.
   1959   *Rivers in the Desert: A History of the Negev.* New York: Farrar,
               Straus and Cudahy.
   1970   *The Other Side of the Jordan.* Cambridge: ASOR.
Herzog, Z.
   1983   Enclosed Settlements in the Negev. *BASOR* 250: 41–50.
Kenyon, K. M.
   1952   *Beginning in Archeology.* New York: Praeger.
Miller, J. M.
   1979   Archaeological Survey of Central Moab: 1978. *BASOR* 234: 43–
               52.
Moorey, R.
   1981   *Excavation in Palestine.* Grand Rapids: Eerdmans.
Parrot, A.
   1955   *Discovering Buried Worlds.* Chicago: SCM Book Club.
Wheeler, M.
   1956   *Archeology from the Earth.* Baltimore: Penguin.
Woolley, L.
   1937   *Digging Up the Past.* Baltimore: Penguin.

9
EXCAVATION OF BURIALS

JOHN J. DAVIS
Grace Theological Seminary

Ancient burials and the materials placed with them have long been a source of fascination for pilgrims and archaeologists in the Near East. Unfortunately, the pursuit of burial materials has not always been executed with scientific discipline and ethical sensitivity.

Early explorers employed a variety of very dubious techniques to recover tomb materials. Typical of the brutal methods utilized was the work of Giovanni Battista Belzoni in Egypt. Having located the entrance to a royal tomb in the western Valley of the Kings, he proceeded to open it with a battering-ram made of two palm logs (Baikie n.d.:12). Belzoni's own account of his work is enough to send chills up the spine of the modern excavator. Elaborating on his experience inside the tomb he states; "Every step I took I crushed a mummy in some part or other" (Belzoni 1966:141). Elsewhere he relates that the tomb ". . . was choked with mummies, and I could not pass without putting my face in contact with that of some decayed Egyptian; but as the passage inclined downward, my own weight helped me on; however, I could not avoid being covered with bones, legs, arms, and heads rolling from above" (Belzoni 1966:141).

In one European archaeological report, the observation is made that "where necessary, the dolmens were blasted, the circles of stones removed . . ." (Wheeler 1954:113). In Italy, the pursuit of buried treasure both in and out of tombs was carried on with use of tunnels which often destroyed as much artifactual material as was recovered (Deiss 1966:22–28).

There are at least two reasons why such crude methodology was employed in these early expeditions. First, this was a period of exploration when historical, cultural, and anthropological concerns were minimal, if not absent entirely. The principal goal of many tomb excavations from the 18th through the early 20th centuries was largely to recover valuable objects for European collectors. Second, many tombs were located and dug for the sole purpose of recovering artifactual materials suitable for display in museums or to satisfy the demands of a heavily financed expedition. The primary motivation for these excavations was clearly object retrieval as opposed to data retrieval.

It is evident, therefore, that the goals of tomb excavation always determine the qualitative factors for field methodology.

I. THE GOALS OF BURIAL EXCAVATION

No feature of an ancient site is more common than human burials. It is therefore critical that a philosophy of excavation be established which produces highly disciplined methods of excavation and observation.

Early excavators approached human burial analysis with rather restricted goals. One of their primary interests was to establish the kind of data base that would provide information on "primitive religions." Others focused on the social character of the individual and the society (Hertz 1960:82). A dominating philosophy of excavators was to recover any material that would assist in historical reconstruction (Mason 1893:40; Kroeber 1937:163). The goals mentioned above are legitimate in themselves, but are very incomplete. The pursuit of only one line of information will invariably lead to poor field discipline. The responsibility of the excavator is to recover all information possible at a burial site, whether or not it can be directly linked to religion, history, or social institutions.

Mortuary rituals generally consist of two basic phenomena. The first relates to the mechanical or technical aspects of burial practice involving the physical preparation of the burial site and its architectural features. The other dimension relates to the ritual acts which accompanied the burial process. It is this latter feature which has often been ignored by the archaeologist. It is far easier to adopt a purely descriptive approach to burial practice while ignoring an analysis of the ritual of religious acts which accompanied the whole process. Of course, it must be acknowledged that ritual acts can often be complex if not conflicting in interpretation. It has been properly pointed out that ". . . groups may share the same set of mortuary symbols but employ them antagonistically, e.g., one group cremates its chiefs and the other cremates its criminals" (Binford 1972:224). The extent to which one can effectively address oneself to the matter of ritual and religion in mortuary practices will depend on the quality of the burial setting or site. Where tomb robbery has been extensive, as is often the case in Near Eastern sites, the data base may be minimal and distorted. Fortunately, however, some of the more significant items that relate to mortuary rituals are often overlooked in favor of gold or other valuable objects which are more easily passed on to the antiquities market. Even when the burial site has been disturbed, it is often possible to recover the kind of material which can be correlated and compared with similar data at other sites for the reconstruction of social or religious funeral practices.

The principal goal of tomb excavation, therefore, should be to recover all information related to a burial setting for the purpose of establishing that kind of cultural model which will include historical, anthropological, geological, architectural, social, and religious concerns.

II. BURIAL SITES

Graves

The most common form of burial in the ancient Near East was the simple grave designed for primary inhumation (McKenzie 1965:168; fig. 1). Trenches or shafts were dug and lined with mats, wood, brick work, or stone slabs. That the grave-type burial was the most common has been statistically confirmed by the fact that the vast numbers of tombs discovered in the vicinity of Jerusalem account for only five percent of the population of that area (Goodenough 1953:53). Such simple grave burials are also well attested at Qumran (De Vaux 1961:37).

Earth-cut graves that were lined and covered with slabs of stone or brick are normally designated cists because of their box-like shape. Some of the cists were short and designed for a single contracted inhumation, while others were longer and designed to take a corpse laid in an extended position (Childe 1956:68). Single inhumation in a lined pit of this type was the standard grave throughout the Middle Bronze Age in Greece (Kurtz and Boardman 1971:24) and in the British Isles (Childe 1956:68).

In Palestine, cist graves show considerable variation in construction. The sides of the grave were often lined with stone or, in some cases, mudbrick. These burial settings normally have an earthen floor, although a few have been discovered with stone-paved floors (Abercrombie 1979:46).

Graves cut into solid rock were common in the Byzantine period and were sealed with three to five flat stones placed in carefully prepared ledges. These usually accommodated one fully extended burial only, but there are examples where two were placed in such a grave. At ancient Abila in Jordan, one such grave contained the burial of two females, one between 10–14 years of age and the other approximately 45 (Davis 1985; and fig. 2).

Pits

While shallow earthen pits were utilized for burials in Palestine, they were not numerous. Some were designed for a single contracted burial while others were large enough to accommodate several cinerary urns or

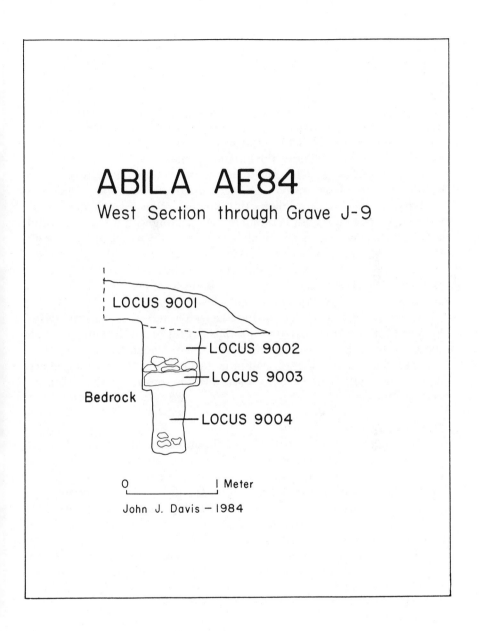

FIG. 1   *Simple grave burial with body in an extended position (courtesy of Heshbon Archaeological Expedition)*

FIG. 2   *Section through Grave J-9 at Abila*

storage jars. In most cases, these pits were simply holes dug into the ground and display no other special treatment. One exception appears to be a stone-encased pit (D 63) which was discovered at Azor (Abercrombie 1979:44–45).

Pyres

The simplest of Palestinian burial settings was the pyre. Those discovered thus far usually consist of burnt timbers on top of which were partially incinerated skeletons and whole vessels. These materials were covered by sand or soil after the burning (Abercrombie 1979:44).

The pyre was used in the Roman world for the cremation of the corpse and usually consisted of a rectangular pile of wood, sometimes mixed with papyrus to facilitate the burning. "The eyes of the corpse were opened when it was placed on the pyre, along with various gifts and some of the deceased's personal possessions. Even pet animals were killed round the pyre to accompany the soul into afterlife" (Toynbee 1971:49–50). In these burial rites, the pyre was ultimately left behind and the burnt bones and ashes of the body were collected by relatives and placed in various types of receptacles.

In Palestine, pyre burials included a wide range of ages from infants to adults. In a number of these burials dating to the seventh through sixth centuries B.C., the bodies appear to have been laid in a fetal or contracted position. Funerary equipment usually included bowls, juglets, jugs, storage jars, and other artifacts such as beads, earrings, scarabs, and weapons.

Tombs

Rock-cut tombs constitute one of the most well documented burial types in Palestine and display a wide variety of geotectural features. (The term "geotecture" more accurately describes subterranean rock-cut tombs, while "architecture" is best used for block or brick constructed tombs above or below ground.) One of the simplest types was the vertical shaft tomb which could have an enlarged pit, small domed chamber, or arcosolia at the bottom. These were utilized as early as the Early Bronze Age and continued in use through the Byzantine period. Such tombs were often sealed at the base with a single slab of stone where a horizontal chamber had been dug, such as those found at Jericho (Kenyon 1957:196). Similar tombs at Bab ed-Dra' were sealed with a pile of stones (Lapp 1968:14–17).

In the Byzantine period, vertical shaft tombs were also common with single or double arcosolia at the bottom. These were characteristically sealed near the top of the shaft with the use of flat stones placed on a ledge prepared for that purpose (Davis 1977:62).

The single chamber tomb was one of the more common tomb forms utilized in Palestine with a variety of geotectural features and were normally entered on a horizontal level. Some chambers were small and accommodated only a single interment, while others were massive in size and obviously designed for multiple burials. Modifications of the single chamber tomb included benches cut around the sides, typical of the Iron Age period, along with shafts radiating from the sides commonly utilized in the Iron Age II period. These tombs have been categorized into five types by Stanislao Loffreda (1968:200–287). They are: type "C" (circular chambered with recesses), type "CC" (circular chambered with divans), type "R" (rectangular single chambered), type "RR" (rectangular multiple chambered), type "S" (single square chambered), type "T" (trapezoidal single chambered), and type "TT" (trapezoidal chambered with subsidiary chambers). Some refinement of this typological analysis has been provided by Abercrombie on the basis of more recent discoveries (Abercrombie 1979:49–53).

Provision was often made in these tombs for secondary burials as evidenced by the numerous repository pits which appeared either in the main chamber or at the end of the shafts or sub-chambers which radiated from the principal chamber (Davis 1970:28; see fig. 3 and fig. 4).

During the Greek and Roman periods in Palestine, chambered tombs characteristically had a series of loculi or kokhim radiating from the sides (see fig. 5). These were normally rectangular shafts designed for a single inhumation (fig. 6), but many times bones were pushed to the back and subsequent burials were placed in the loculus (Davis 1978:28). Some chambers would have upper and lower rows numbering to 45 loculi.

The early Roman period also provided very simple burials normally designated as a single loculus type. Such tombs were common at Jericho (Bennett 1965:521) and to a lesser degree at Heshbon (Waterhouse 1973:120).

One other type of tomb complex might be designated a multiple chamber type. These tombs often have a series of chambers connected by small passageways and may feature benches around the sides or loculi radiating from the walls. Examples of such multiple chamber burial sites are the tombs of James and Zechariah located in the Kidron Valley. The tomb of James, for example, contains four chambers with both loculi and arcosolia.

Monumental

This type of burial site is characterized by a stone or brick structure built above the ground. The most famous examples of this type are the great pyramids of Egypt. These structures, however, present a two dimensional feature including subterranean passages for the burial, but with a monumental structure above ground.

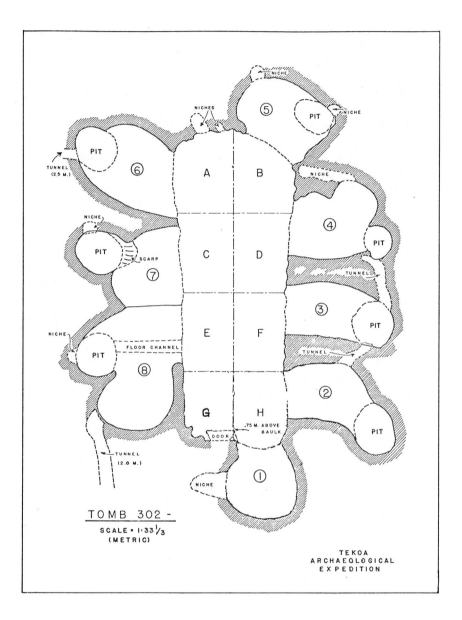

FIG. 3   *Tomb 302 at Tekoa*

FIG. 4   *A partially excavated repository pit in Tomb 302 at Tekoa (photo by J. Davis)*

FIG. 5 *Early Roman tomb at Heshbon with loculi (photo by J. Davis)*

FIG. 6   *Single disarticulated burial in a loculus, Tomb F.31, Heshbon (photo by J. Davis)*

In Palestine, one of the better documented monumental burial structures is the dolmens. These are rectangular in shape with four upright stones supporting a single large capstone. Large megaliths seal off each end of the structure with one end providing a small door or opening (fig. 7). There are, of course, a number of variations in the architectural features of these monuments. Some have more than one roof slab while others employ several stones to form a wall. There are several thousand individual dolmens in Palestine spread from the Syrian and Lebanon borders south to about the latitude of Kerak, from the Mediterranean foothills of the central mountain range of Palestine east to the desert regions (Swauger 1966:107–8). Dating these megalithic structures has been most difficult for archaeologists. Estimates have ranged from the pre-pottery Neolithic (Anati 1963:278–283) through the EB IV/MB I periods (Waterhouse and Ibach 1975:230). The absence of artifactual materials makes dating these structures nearly impossible. Current evidence points to a late Chalcolithic or EB I time frame for their construction.

Another type of monumental burial site is the mausoleum. Like the dolmen, this is a megalithon constructed of cut-blocks of stone forming a small "house" for the dead. The term mausoleum is derived from the elaborate monument built at Halicarnassus in Asia Minor for King Mausoluss in the fourth century B.C. This type of burial structure is not common in Palestine but is represented at Khirbet Shemaʿ (Meyers, Kraabel, and Strange 1972:20–21).

Caves

From the earliest times caves provided a very convenient burial site and were utilized in every archaeological period. In most cases, they were used over a lengthy period of time for many burials. Some of the earliest cave burials are found along the Carmel range (Anati 1962:99–109).

Some caves were left intact for simple grave type burials, as for example, cave F.38 at Heshbon (Davis 1978:143–45). Other caves were altered to provide a more sophisticated setting for the burials. Special treatment of the walls and the entrance was common. Some caves received a stone-block floor and contained sarcophagi burials. An example of this type of cave is Heshbon F.37 (Davis 1978:142–43; fig. 8).

Accidental Burials

One other type of burial setting worth mentioning is that of accidental character. Volcanic eruptions such as that of Mt. Vesuvius which covered Pompeii and Herculaneum on August 24, A.D. 79, would be one example. Because of the geographical position of Herculaneum, few people lost their lives, but an estimated 2000 died at Pompeii. In Pal-

FIG. 7   *Palestinian Dolmen (photo by J. Davis)*

FIG. 8   *Sarcophagi inside cave F.37 at Heshbon (photo by J. Davis)*

estine, accidental burials are usually the result of earthquake or military activity.

III. BURIAL CUSTOMS

Tomb excavation not only involves a descriptive analysis of the burial setting, but the mortuary customs which accompanied that burial are of particular importance to archaeologists. As noted above, without written materials the process of determining the character of burial rituals can be quite complex and at times even impossible. Mortuary practices include both technical and ritual acts (Binford 1972:223). The technical aspect of mortuary rites has to do with all those physical activities relating to the preparation of the burial site and of the body for proper disposal. The ritual aspect of mortuary customs refers to that number of symbolic acts which accompanied the entire funerary procession.

Generally speaking, the technical aspects of mortuary practice may be determined on the basis of three categories of data. First, there are the character, location, and dimensions of the burial site; secondly, the physical preparation of the corpse for burial; finally, the artifactual assemblage accompanying the burial.

In Palestine, there were three basic treatments accorded the dead. The first was simple inhumation in which the body was placed in a tomb, grave, pit, or shaft, either in a contracted (fetal) or an extended position. A sarcophagus or a coffin might also have been employed for the burial. The Philistines often utilized clay anthropoid coffins while the Romans later made some coffins of lead.

Clay jars were often employed for the burial of infants and several of these were discovered at Dothan (Free 1960:9–10); these clay jars were frequently utilized for foundation burials (Free 1956:46–47). Some earlier writers suggested that these burials were "foundation sacrifices," but this assumption has been questioned recently.

The second type of body treatment was cremation. The origin of this practice in the ancient Near East is shrouded in obscurity. E. O. James proposes that the earliest cremations may well have been accidental. Evidence from prehistoric times indicates that there were already recognizable cults of the dead and that fire was associated with certain funerary rituals (James 1957:99). It is conjectured that the use of fire in funerals probably existed before the adoption of cremation (Irion 1968:3).

Indications are that cremation originated on a formal basis during the Stone Age in both eastern Europe and the Middle East. Early Bronze Age evidence of the practice is found at the so-called Troglodyte Crematorium of Gezer. Ashes from the cremations reached a depth of about one foot inside the stepped entrance to the tomb at Gezer. Tomb A94 at

Jericho also displays evidence of this practice from about the same period (Callaway 1963:82). Commenting on the data of Jericho's Tomb A94 Callaway suggests that ". . . cremation was a method of disposing of accumulated skeletal remains to make room for more burials . . ." (Callaway 1963:83). The practice of cremation continued to a greater or lesser degree through most Palestinian archæological periods, reaching a peak during the Roman occupation of that territory (fig. 9). Examples of this practice are abundant especially during the Early Roman period (Davis 1978:138–139).

Equally important for the study of mortuary customs is the common practice of secondary burial or ossilegium. "Such a practice is characterized by the collection of skeletalized remains at some point after the flesh had wasted away and by their deposition in a new place of repose" (Meyers 1970:2). The plastered skulls found at Neolithic Jericho probably represent one of the earliest phases in the development of secondary burials in Palestine (Kenyon 1957:60–64). During the Early and Middle Bronze Ages bones were often collected in piles and then pushed to the back of the chambers or otherwise redeposited. Skulls and long bones were collected and placed at different places within the burial site.

Iron Age tombs often had special repository pits designed for the relocation of bone materials and artifacts. A classic example of this type of tomb dating to the Iron Age II period was found at Tekoa (Davis 1974:29–36; see fig. 3). Ossilegium was also widely practiced during the Hellenistic and Roman periods (fig. 10). Bones were commonly collected and deposited in loculi or kokhim, baskets (Bar-Kokhba Cave), or ossuaries.

The third body of information vitally important for the excavator in determining mortuary ritual involves the funerary assemblage at the burial site. The presence or absence of grave goods can help to determine specific mortuary traditions or social rank of individuals. Matters of concern to the excavator include the form, quality, and placement of materials within the burial context. The functional qualities of funerary equipment are also important in analyzing the burial tradition. Some materials had a simple practical use in the funerary process, while other objects clearly had symbolic or religious value. Of course, the most complete reconstruction of mortuary tradition can occur when written materials are present to complement the artifactual assemblage at a given site.

IV. LOCATING TOMBS

Often tombs or burial sites are located by sheer chance or accident. Many tombs are discovered by road work or general construction and are excavated on a salvage basis. Tombs are also located by agricultural

FIG. 9 *Cremated remains of an Early Roman burial at Heshbon (photo by J. Davis)*

FIG. 10 *Disarticulated bones of secondary burials in a Roman tomb at Abila*
(photo by J. Davis)

activity or by a ceiling collapse which leaves a noticeable depression in the ground.

Locating ancient cemeteries can be, on the one hand, a rewarding task and, on the other, frustrating. Some of the most significant urban archaeological sites in Palestine have yet to reveal the location of their cemeteries. The archaeologist does have several means by which to locate burial sites associated with a city or town.

Written Sources

An important source of information in determining burial customs and sites for a given city is ancient written material. For example, significant information regarding Hebrew burial rites can be gleaned from the OT. While such information can aid the excavator in excluding certain locations for burials, it will rarely lead him to the exact site of the cemetery. For example, beliefs concerning both the physical and ceremonial uncleanness of the corpse led many societies to establish cemeteries or communities of the dead outside the city walls. Ancient literature also provides specific information on funerary preparations and processions. Tomb specifications are sometimes revealed, but rarely are cemeteries located on the basis of detailed geographical information.

The death and burial of Alexander the Great, for example, is one of the best documented events of that period. Details provided by Diodorus and others describe his death, funeral procession, burial chamber, temple building above the site, and many other details; yet the royal cemetery in which Alexander was buried has yet to be discovered.

Topographical and Geological Features

The geological features of Palestine are quite diverse, and not all rock formations were suitable for the digging or cutting of tombs. Cemeteries were often located at a given place simply because the rock formation permitted easy tomb preparation. Tombs in Palestine are carved out of a soft chalky limestone which is common to most mountain areas. The geological character of a given region can quickly aid the excavator in eliminating certain areas as a probable tomb field. A careful geological survey of a region, therefore, is vital to productive tomb exploration.

In addition to geological analysis, a topographic survey is also necessary in determining significant coutour changes in the region. Unusual surface contours and soil changes often provide clues as to the location of tomb entrances. With time, the soil and rocks utilized to fill the entrance of tombs settle and leave discernible depressions in the ground. Examination of such areas while the sun is low can often provide clear indications of these depressions by a shadowing effect.

Aerial Photography

One of the most effective ways of determining subterranean burial sites is aerial photography during all seasons of the year and at various sun levels. A classic example of this procedure is seen in Crawford's photograph of an Etruscan necropolis (1966:393). Soil discoloration from backfilling is easily discernible from the air after an area has been dampened by a rainstorm. Needless to say, such observation would have to occur rather quickly after the rain due to the rapid drying of the ground's surface. In much of Palestine, the presence of heavy accumulations of lime and lime byproducts cause the surface of the ground to take on a uniform white or light tan appearance when dry.

The use of colored, black-and-white, and heat sensitive films are also recommended for aerial photography. Photographs taken of the same site under different light conditions can be very revealing. Where aerial photography cannot be carried out by the use of an airplane, balloons may also be employed for the same purpose and may be preferable in militarily sensitive areas.

Magnetic and Resistivity Survey

The earth's magnetism has been for many centuries crucial to geological prospecting. One of the important developments in this field is the use of the proton magnetometer which was first utilized experimentally in 1954. On a local level the earth's magnetic field is disturbed by the presence of metals such as iron. Such effects are called anomalies or deviations from the normal magnetic intensity of the earth which is usually measured in gamma units. The proton magnetometer is a very sensitive instrument, recording anomalies of less than one gamma. This instrument is effective in detecting iron objects, fired structures such as kilns, furnaces, ovens and bricks, pits and ditches filled with top soil or rubbage, walls, foundations, roads and tombs (Aitken 1963:555). Depending on field conditions, an acre of land can be surveyed in about four hours (Thompson 1966:117).

Subsurface investigations have also been successfully conducted by means of resistivity surveying for the past twenty years. Soil resistivity measurement has long been employed by geologists and civil engineers, but its specific archaeological application first came in 1946 when R. J. C. Atkinson used the method in excavating a group of Neolithic henge monuments at Dorchester, Oxfordshire (Clark 1963:569). This survey method has been used with varying degrees of success at Petra (Hammond 1974:39) and Heshbon (Davis 1978:134).

Soil is able to conduct electricity but in varying degrees. This variation is due to the amount of moisture and dissolved minerals in the soil. Subterranean archaeological features also cause the normal conductivity of soil to vary. This variation can be accurately measured with several types of probes and meters. Resistivity surveys can be especially useful in locating tombs where subsoil disturbance has been minimal.

Steel Rod Probes

Tombs can also be located by the use of a series of steel rod probes to bedrock. This is not an efficient way to locate a cemetery area generally, but it is very effective in pinpointing tomb entrance once the cematary has been found. Resistivity and proton magnetometer surveys can locate the probable site of a tomb, but steel rod probes will provide specific information about the location of its entrance.

These probes are conducted by driving a short steel rod in the ground to bedrock at intervals of ca. 0.3 m. When the tomb entrance is reached, the rod will penetrate much deeper than the previous bedrock layers. It should be noted that many times these probes will produce as many ancient stone quarries as they will tomb entrances!

V. THE EXCAVATION OF TOMBS

The excavation of rock-cut Palestinian tombs involves four basic responsibilities. The first of these is stratigraphic in nature. In keeping with the Kenyon-Wheeler technique of digging, the tomb entrance and interior should be approached at right angles so a clear stratigraphic profile might be observed. The stratigraphy of a tomb's exterior can help determine its range of use, the time when it may have been robbed, or the last sealing of the tomb (fig. 11).

Soil deposition inside the tomb can be quite substantial, depending on the location and mortuary customs practiced in a particular region. A tight grid of 1-m squares or less should be laid on the floor of the tomb and each unit dug stratigraphically in order that periodization and phasing of the tomb's use can be accomplished. Right angle sections should always be maintained against geotectural features such as loculi or objects.

Soil was often brought into the tomb to cover a burial; this process took place over a long period of time, thus providing a substantial stratigraphic record. Special attention should be given to silt and water compacted layers on the tomb's floor (fig. 12). Ceramic materials embedded in these loci can provide vital information about the tomb's earliest use. The artifactual assemblages in relation to these stratigraphic features provide the necessary data base for historical and cultural interpretation.

The archaeologist's second concern relates to the tomb's geotectural characteristics. These are normally best studied after the tomb has been completely excavated. Matters of importance are the tomb's overall design, unusual features, and the method of tomb construction. Special

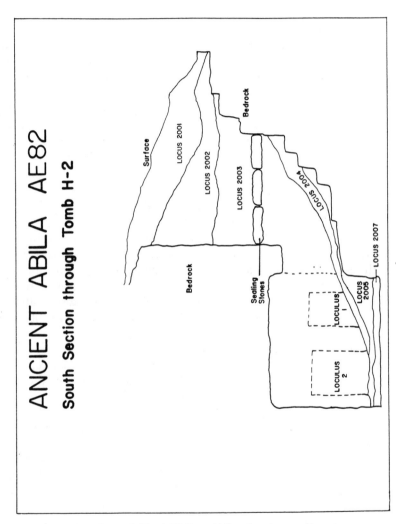

FIG. 11   *Section through Tomb H-2 at Abila, showing sealing stones*

FIG. 12   *Separated silt and soil layers on the floor of Tomb F.31 at Heshbon (photo by J. Davis)*

attention to such detail as the tool technology employed to dig the tomb can be very useful in phasing its construction.

The value of analyzing tool marks inside rock-cut tombs was recognized some years ago by R. A. S. Macalister:

> The tool marks are always instructive. They show the process followed in excavating the chambers; sometimes also the order in which chambers were cut out; and give much valuable information on the nature of the tools employed. It is just possible that wooden tools were used in some of the caves, but the great majority of the tool marks to be observed can not have been made except by metal chisels (1902:211).

While the importance of tool analysis has been occasionally recognized, few have systematized the analysis and reported the results with any regularity. Such analysis should include three basic goals. The first goal is to determine the number of tools employed in the preparation of the tomb. This is normally accomplished by measuring the blade impressions in the stone with the use of calipers (fig. 13). The end of the blade is most accurately measured and its character is best represented in the soft limestone. Such tools often have rounded edges as well as square.

The second goal of tool analysis is to determine the number of masons who worked in the tomb. Since each mason had his own peculiar method of tomb digging, it is normally not difficult to analyze stroke patterns and quickly detect when a different hand was doing the work. Stroke patterns are consistent when a particular mason uses one type of tool, but will differ significantly when another mason uses that same instrument.

The third feature of concern to the archaeologist is the actual penetration of the tools in the stone. With varying strengths of working masons, there are significant differences in penetration patterns in the soft limestone. When these data are combined, one is able to determine whether a tomb was cut by one mason or many, or whether it was prepared in phases or completed all at once.

In Heshbon tomb F.27, we were able to determine (on the basis of geotectural features of the tomb, along with tool technology) that several masons had done the work with the use of no less than four different tools (Davis 1978:132). A Late Roman tomb at ancient Abila (Tomb H-1) was determined to have had several construction phases as exhibited in masonary work, geotectural variation, and ceramic analysis (Davis 1983:42–43). Furthermore, comparisons between the tool technology of the cemetery with that of the adjacent city can provide additional clues as to whether the masons were tomb specialists or also applied their craft to urban construction as well.

The geotectural sophistication of a tomb can also provide eloquent testimony to the social or political status of the individual(s) who was

FIG. 13 *J. Davis taking calibrated measurements inside Abila Tomb H-2*

buried there. In recent years there has been a greater emphasis on the importance of social organization and the dynamics of cultural systems (Binford 1974:6–29).

The third area of concern in tomb excavation is the information supplied by the bone materials and their position in the earth matrix. Since burials are generally evidence of human ritual, careful observation of the position of the body and the grave goods aids the archaeologist in distinguishing between fixed traditions at a site and the introduction of new customs.

The excavation of a human burial is one of the most exacting processes in archaeology; it requires the use of small tools such as a pointed trowel, brush, spatula, bulb syringe, teaspoon, camel-hair brush, and dental picks (fig. 14).

The excavator must determine whether or not the burial is articulated or unarticulated. Normally the excavator should expose the central areas of the skeleton first, particularly the rib cage, abdominal cavity, and pelvis. Afterward, the long bones of the arms and legs should be cleared. The best procedure is to start at one end of the bone and follow the length of it with a small dental pick and brush. The small bones of the feet and hands should be left until last so as to prevent accidental disturbance. All objects associated with the burial should remain *in situ* until complete exposure of the burial. The skeletal material should then be examined by a physical anthropologist before removal. Soil from the tomb entrance and interior must be carefully shifted by locus for small objects such as beads and jewelry. Soil samples from each layer should be subjected to flotation analysis for the recovery of botanical samples.

Detailed drawings and photographs of the burial are also required before any materials are removed for further processing. All human bone materials should be analyzed for sex, age, pathology, and other important characteristics which might shed light on the relationship of individuals within a burial.

The final aspect of tomb excavation relates to historical and cultural concerns. Older archaeological reports tend to include only the most meager description of the tomb itself and often provide no detailed analysis of the associated artifactual materials. Such procedures reflected only broad historical concerns about the burial site itself. If tombs are to make a significant contribution to the study of social organizations, religious practices, and population analysis, data must be recovered with the greatest care. This means that every feature outside and inside a tomb needs to be diligently observed, recorded, and analyzed.

VI. CORRELATION OF DATA

The final steps in tomb excavation (other than publication) are correlation and interpretation of the recovered data. Tomb assemblages

FIG. 14   *Clearing skeletal remains in a Roman tomb at Heshbon (courtesy of Heshbon Archaeological Expedition)*

must be analyzed and compared with similar burial contexts within a site. The investigation then broadens to include parallel burial sites at the regional level and those found in more distant locations.

The recovery of a large number of undisturbed burials at a site provides the best information for social and political reconstructions. Unfortunately, Palestinian rock-cut tombs have been easy prey for tomb robbers, both ancient and modern. Tombs that were reused over a long period of time also suffered various types of disturbance leaving assemblages incomplete. In such situations, a number of questions about cultural dynamics and funerary practices at a particular site remain unanswered. Although tombs were robbed and their stratigraphy disturbed, it is sometimes possible to locate sectors within the tomb that remain untouched and therefore provide stratigraphic information as to the tomb's use.

Analysis and correlation of human bone materials is most important for understanding the population at the site. While tomb robbers may remove artifactual materials, they rarely take bone materials. The specific morphological character of the bones are often clues as to whether a tomb was utilized by a single family or by the ancient community at large. The presence or absence of fetal or infant bone materials can also provide testimony as to certain social or religious traditions. Even the presence of certain animal bones provides valuable evidence of the existence of special mortuary traditions.

In conclusion, burial excavation in Palestine can be one of the most interesting and rewarding aspects of archaeological fieldwork. The value of cultural, social, and religious data recovered from burials, however, will depend solely on the discipline and breadth of observation exercised during the excavation process.

BIBLIOGRAPHY

Abercrombie, J. R.
  1979   *Palestinian Burial Practices from 2100–600 B.C.E.* Unpublished Ph. D. dissertation, University of Pennsylvania.
Aitken, M.
  1963   Magnetic Location. Pp. 555–568 in *Science in Archaeology: A Comprehensive Survey of Progress and Research*, eds. D. Brothwell and E. Higgs. New York: Basic Books.
Anati, E.
  1963   *Palestine Before the Hebrews.* New York: Knopf.
Baikie, J.
           A Century of Excavation in the Land of the Pharaohs. New York: Revell.
Belzoni, G. B.
  1966   A Cache of Mummies at Thebes. Pp. 140–42 in *Hands on the Past*, ed. C. W. Ceram. New York: Knopf.

Bennett, C. M.
    1965   Tombs of the Roman Period. Pp. 516–545 in *Excavations at
                Jericho II, ed. Kathleen Kenyon. London: BSAJ.
Binford, L. R.
    1971   Mortuary Practices: Their Study and Potential. Pp. 6–29 in
                Approaches to the Social Dimensions of Mortuary Practices, ed J. A.
                Brown. Memoirs of the Society for American Archaeology, No.
                25. Washington, D.C.: Society for American Archaeology.
    1972   *An Archaeological Perspective*. New York: Seminar.
Callaway, J. A.
    1963   Burials in Ancient Palestine: From the Stone Age to Abraham.
                BA 26: 74–91.
Childe, V. G.
    1956   *A Short Introduction to Archaeology*. London: Muller.
Clark, A.
    1963   Resistivity Surveying. Pp. 569–581 in *Science in Archaeology: A
                Comprehensive Survey of Progress and Research*. eds. D. Brothwell
                and E. Higgs. New York: Basic Books.
Crawford, O.
    1966   Archaeology from the Air. Pp. 387–93 in *Hands on the Past*, ed.
                C. W. Ceram. New York: Knopf.
Davis, J. J.
    1974   Tekoa Excavations: Tomb 302. *NEASB* 4: 27–49.
    1978   Heshbon 1976: Areas F. and K. *AUSS* 16: 129–148.
    1983   Abila Tomb Excavations. *NEASB* 21: 30–58.
    1985   Abila Tomb Excavations: 1984. *NEASB* 24: 65–92.
Deiss, J. J.1966 *Herculaneum*. New York: Crowell.
de Vaux, R.
    1961   *L'Archaeologie et les manuscrits de la Mer Morte*. London: Oxford
                University.
Free, J. P.
    1956   The Excavation of Dothan. *BA* 19: 43–48.
Goodenough, E. R.
    1953   The Archaeological Evidence from Palestine. *Jewish Symbols in
                the Greco-Roman Period*, Vol. 1. New York: Pantheon.
Hammond, P. C.
    1974   Magnetometer/Resistivity Survey at Petra, Jordan—1973.
                BASOR 214: 39–41.
Hertz, R.
    1960   *Death and the Right Hand*. Trans. R. Needhan and C. Needham.
                Glenco, IL: Free.
Irion, P. E.
    1968   *Cremation*. Philadelphia: Fortress.
James, E. O.
    1957   *Prehistoric Religion*. London: Thames and Hudson.
Kenyon, K.
    1957   *Digging up Jericho*. London: Benn.
Kroeber, A. L.
    1937   Archaeology. *Encyclopedia of the Social Sciences*, Vol. 2.
Kurtz, D. C. and Boardman, J.
    1971   *Greek Burial Customs*. Ithaca, NY: Cornell University.
Lapp, P. W.
    1968   Bâb edh-Dhrâ⁽ Tomb A 76 and Early Bronze I in Palestine.
                BASOR 189: 14–17.

Loffreda, S.
1968   Iron Age Rock-Cut Tombs in Palestine. *Liber Annuus* 18: 244–287.
Macalister, R. A. S.
1902   *Excavations in Palestine, 1898–1900.* London: PEF.
Mason, O. T.
1893   The Birth of Invention. *Annual Report Smithsonian Institution for 1892.* Washington, D.C.: Smithsonian Institution.
McKenzie, J. L.
1965   *Dictionary of the Bible.* New York: Bruce.
Meyers, E. M.
1970   Secondary Burials in Palestine. *BA* 33: 2–29.
Meyers, E. M., and Kraabel, A. T., and Strange., J. F.
1972   Archaeology and Rabbinic Tradition at Khirbet Shemaᶜ 1970 and 1971 Campaigns. *BA* 35: 2–31.
Swauger, J. L.
1966   Dolmen Studies in Palestine. *BA* 29: 106–114.
Thompson, H. O.
1966   Science and Archaeology. *BA* 29: 114–125.
Toynbee, J. M. C.
1971   *Death and Burial in the Roman World.* Ithaca, NY: Cornell University.
Waterhouse, S. D.
1973   Heshbon 1971: Areas E and F. *AUSS* 11: 113–125.
Waterhouse, S. D. and Ibach, R., Jr.
1975   Heshbon 1973: The Topographical Survey. *AUSS* 13: 217–233.
Wheeler, M.
1954   *Archaeology from the Earth.* Baltimore: Penguin.

10
ARCHAEOLOGICAL SURVEYS

JAMES R. KAUTZ, III

Louisiana Department of Health and Human Resources

It may come as a surprise to some people to learn that archaeologists do not recover all of their information by digging into the earth. Important archaeological data can be found on the surface of a site, even though the archaeologists do not dig up a trowel of soil. As surface surveyors they are involved in a discipline that is older than excavation, is experiencing a resurgence in interest, but is little-known or appreciated by the casual reader or beginner.

Even seasoned archaeologists occasionally infer that surface archaeology is in some way inferior to the excavation of a site.[1] The author was present at a session chaired by Joseph Callaway in which a scholar had explained the values of surface exploration and had given a detailed report of one such project. In the discussion that followed, a professor of archaeology sincerely and unmaliciously contrasted surface work with what he termed "real archaeology" (i.e., excavation). (Those who know Callaway can effortlessly envision his wry smile at the moment in which he saw a scholarly controversy brewing.)

The objective of this essay is to help the reader to understand the values, methods and limitations of surface survey. A brief history of the discipline will be followed by a discussion of prominent theories, designs and methods of survey. While the focus is archaeology in Palestine, New World developments in this discipline will be presented, because it is here that most of the leading theorists and practitioners have worked.

✓ DEFINITION

Archaeological survey is the work of discovering attributes of human cultures from the features (e.g., buildings, hearths, caves, cisterns) and artifacts (e.g., sherds, worked stone, bone, tiles) that lie exposed on the surface. The surveyor's "universe" (his isolated field of study) may be a single site, such as a *tell* or *khirbet* (ruin) or a defined region, such as the

---

[1] *Israel Exploration Journal* reports "Notes and News" of surveys under "Excavations."

Valley of the Sorek. His attention will be focused on what is in this universe (its "population"), the spatial distribution of the cultural elements in this area, and the physical attributes (floral, faunal, geologic) of the area. Published results may include maps, photographs and descriptions of sites and artifacts, but they should also include hypotheses and theories concerning the history of the area and the cultural makeup of those who inhabited it.

I. ARCHAEOLOGICAL SURVEY WORK IN PALESTINE

The earliest archaeological work in Palestine was surface survey. The reports of travelers and explorers discussed in Miller's essay in this volume included maps and descriptions of regions. Often explorers attempted to relate the towns and ruins that they discovered to sites mentioned in the Bible and other ancient texts.

Antiquarian and religious interests dominate these reports, but their value to geographers and students of culture is also significant. The explorers covered territory that was remote. Many sites that they reported have not been mentioned in later geographical and historical literature. Their work, coming, as it did, long before the current period of massive industrial and agribusiness disturbance of the land, identified sites that may now be buried under cities or bulldozed for road development.

Both the value and inadequacy of their work are illustrated by the story of the "Shihan Warrior Stele." In 1851, F. de Saulcy found a relief of a warrior in Transjordan. His report of the find-spot is obscure, but later explorers recall that it was at Rujm el-Abd near the village of Faqu‘a. Modern villagers recall the legend of a "negro statue" taken from their village—probably the same stele. Yet the Central Moab Survey found that Rujm el-Abd has long since disappeared. Its location is now covered with simple homes and dusty streets. No doubt within the crude masonary walls of Faqu‘a are the stones that once were piled around the ancient stele. Whatever sherds and other chronometric clues there may have been to suggest the historical and cultural context of the "Warrior" have now been swept away.

In short, de Saulcy salvaged a valuable treasure. But his lack of maps and scientific reporting prevent our knowing where he found it, and the fact that he did his work more than six decades before the pottery chronology of Palestine was developed, leaves us with few clues as to the period of the stele's deposition.

Until quite recently, the methods of surface archaeologists skewed their results to an unusual degree. Explorers commonly employed local guides, who led them along beaten paths or took them aside to sites known by the local population. Thus, they tended to note the larger sites or those situated in locations that are useful under limited historical or climatic conditions. Furthermore, those sites that were discussed in their publications were most often ones that fit into the picture of the world already known. We may read pages about a battle site such as Jericho, for instance, but find rare footnotes about a cluster of farm villages and a few stone dams in the nearby valley of Buqeʿah (Stager 1976). (Ironically, the ruins of Buqeʿah provide more positive information about life and history in the biblical age than does Tell es-Sulṭan [Jericho].)

Surface exploration from the earliest days until World War II should not be belittled, however. The work of Nelson Glueck in Transjordan and the Negeb, for instance, expanded the horizons of biblical scholars and stirred a valuable series of hypotheses. Martin Noth's reconstruction of Israelite history was founded largely on his knowledge of surface discoveries.

Recent developments in archaeological theory and method offer promise of a better understanding of the peoples and cultures of Palestine, however. Three forces have converged to spark the current revolution of survey archaeology.

1. *Scholary interest.* Most writers of the history of archaeology trace the current interest in surface survey to the theories of Julian Steward, an American social anthropologist. Steward's work in the Great Basin led him to investigate the ways in which spatial relationships reflect "laws" of cultures. After all, one of humankind's primary ways of relating to its environment is its settlement or migration patterns. (One can readily see the significance of this in 20th century America by observing the growth of communities in the "sunbelt" and the petroleum-rich regions in recent years or by analyzing housing patterns in the light of school redistricting in urban America.)

Gordon Willey listened to Steward and embarked upon a wide-ranging regional survey in the Virú Valley of Peru. (For a review of the significance of Steward and Willey, see Thomas 1979:271–74.)

Willey's lead was soon followed by North American archaeologists who formulated and tested hypotheses of site function, demography, seasonal settlement, and land-use policy (Parsons 1972:127–34). This interest was not confined to the western side of the Atlantic, however, and has resulted in field applications in the Near East. (Note especially Adams 1965; Braidwood 1937; Price-Williams 1973.)

2. *Political developments.* Changes of military and political boundaries in Palestine have been followed by archaeological surveys. Most notable are the surveys of territories occupied after the War of 1967 (Kochavi 1972; Cohen 1972) and the Sinai Survey (Beit-Arieh 1979).

3. *Economics.* Economics affect survey archaeology in two ways. First,

the industrial and urban expansion of modern society has threatened numbers of archaeological sites, large and small. Thousands of sites are bulldozed or flooded annually.

In Egypt and on both sides of the Jordan, settlements spring up precisely where the Byzantine communities marketed their goods.

Impounded waters cover terraces where Neolithic farmers invented agriculture. Even such seemingly modest disturbances as field irrigation or the building of a one-land road take their toll. Governments—both Israeli and Arab—are conscious of the fact that the ancient locations are cultural resources. Consequently, efforts are undertaken to survey regions that will be impacted and, when possible, to mitigate the damages.

Second, the economics of archaeological fieldwork have pressed change upon the practitioner. When the bounty of United States government "counterpart funds" was supplying hundreds of thousands of dollars per year, excavators uncovered wide areas to bedrock. Funding has been reduced. The necessity of lower-cost methods of research has been the mother of the rediscovery of surface survey. Survey can be small-scale and low-destruction archaeology and is, therefore, attractive under present circumstances.

From the past 15 years of survey have come an increased understanding of the land beyond the great cities and battle sites and, indeed, an awareness that the history of those sites is little appreciated without a knowledge of their environments.

Among the discoveries have been Roman, Byzantine and Early Islamic agricultural sites in an area of the coastal plain long thought to be uncultivated (Roll and Ayalon 1981), small Iron Age I villages in the mountains where Samuel once presided (Mazar 1981), and Late Bronze Age settlements in Moab, which Glueck thought was vacant during that period (Miller 1979:50–51). Debir, once thought by consensus to be Tell Beit Mirsim, is now placed by many at Khirbet Rabud, a site redisvovered in a post-June 1967 War survey (Kochavi 1974).

II. THE DESIGN OF SURFACE SURVEY

Archaeologists currently employ surface techniques in two basic research designs. Often the surface project is supplemental to an excavation. Since there was some controversy over the identification of Ai, Callaway's staff spent several afternoons collecting sherds at locally known sites, such as Khirbet Haiy. From these expeditions it was concluded that no other site than et-Tell could be considered a candidate for the site of the famous Israelite battle at Ai.

Since the early 1970s, surveys of the environments of tells have often been carried on more systematically and with more research questions or hypotheses, however. The Lahav (Tell Ḥalif) Research Project gave several weeks to intensive surveys of selected areas around Tell Ḥalif. Concern for such questions as how intensively the area was settled, and what use had been made of the land led not only to discoveries of dams, building remains and farming terraces but also to some tentative conclusions about why and under what political conditions the area and the mound were occupied.

Similar searches have been carried out around Tell el-Ḥesi (O'Connell and Rose 1980), and in association with the synagogue excavations in Galilee (Meyers and Strange 1978), and the Heshbon Excavation (Ibach 1978 a,b). The Yoqneam Regional Project shows a modified form of this approach. Tel Yoqneam was the focal pont of a survey in the western valley of Jezreel. Yoqneam and other sites were excavated or tested (Ben-Tor 1980). Research questions range from the environmental interests exhibited by the Lahav and Bab ed-Draʿ staffs (Rast and Schaub 1974) to the identification of sites and settlement patterns noted by the Shechem area survey (Campbell 1968).

The second generic research plan identifies an area, independent of any central site or mound. Selection of the area may be determined by such considerations as a scholar's interest in a region's history. J. Maxwell Miller initiated the Central Moab survey when he became aware that in spite of the fact that the actual field research on the plateau between the Arnon (Wadi Mojib) and the Zered (Wadi Ḥesa) had been quite limited, an important historical reconstruction had been based upon that research. His survey has underscored some of Glueck's conclusions, seriously challenged others, and provided a vastly increased understanding of the human use of the plateau since Upper Palaeolithic (Miller 1979).

In the case of a survey of palaeolithic sites in southern Jordan, an area was targeted on the basis of its geomorphology. Donald Henry, the director of this survey, recognized that palaeolithic localities are often found in such areas as the Ras en-Naqb basin and he designed a project to search the area (Henry 1979).

Cohen and Dever selected the Central Negeb Highlands because of Dever's long-term interest in the enigmatic period that bridged the high Early Bronze and Middle Bronze Ages. Earlier surveys had contributed to theories about the use and settlement of the Negeb in the so-called "EB IV—MB I" or "Intermediate Bronze Age," and some of these theories included the placement of the Hebrew patriarchs in that place and time. While the archaeological evidence says nothing about the patriarchs, it does demonstrate that, while the area seldom held a sedentary population, it was farmed in the Intermediate Bronze (EB IV) Age. The extent of the survey was severely limited because of a shift in the deployment of Israeli troops, but Dever and Cohen contributed a great deal toward an explanation of the little-known transitional age (Dever 1970; 1973; Cohen and Dever 1979).

Other projects receive their primary impetus from the need to salvage as much as possible from the onslaught of industrial and agricultural expansion (e.g., the East Jordan Valley Survey [Ibrahim, Sauer, Yassine 1976]; the survey of the Central Coastal Plain [Gophna 1977]). The fact that "salvage" or "mitigation" is the immediate cause for a project does not imply that scholarly care and research design are neglected, however. Economic and time constraints influence most field archaeologists, whether excavators or surface workers. As will be shown below, it is possible to design a project to answer the research questions properly, even in the face of such limitations.

Research Design: Theory

In some sciences, researchers have the luxury of selecting a single question or hypothesis and then performing experiments that are directed toward answers to questions or toward rejections of hypotheses. For example, one might ask, "will children who ingest large quantities of sugar behave erratically?" or "does the water in this river contain toxic levels of mercury?"

Such singular, limiting questions can be asked of a region: "does this area's pottery contain local clays?" or "did the Iron Age inhabitants of this plateau live in walled villages only?" Since the archaeologist will exhaust almost as much time, energy, and money covering the area in the quest for the answer to one research question as for 20, it is necessary to develop a wide range of questions at the outset. Indeed, the first step toward a successful survey must be the acknowledgement of the potential value of surface survey. R. Ruppe once complained that the low view that has been held of surface study makes it "probable that many investigators have failed to extract as much information from a survey as they could have" (1966:13).

New World Archaeologists have sought to remedy such narrowness. Chided and inspired by the advocates of "the New Archaeology" (e.g., Binford 1964), they have set high goals of explaining—not merely describing—culture processes (Judge 1973:7; Martin and Plog 1973:10). While few projects in the Near East have as yet shown published results of such thinking, recent scholarly discussions indicate that the attempt is being made. The beginning student will do well to become acquainted with the theoretical literature (Thomas 1979 would be a good first step) and to watch for the results of this trend in Palestinian archaeology.

Simply stated, the more optimistic and inquisitive one becomes before starting the engine on the survey vehicle, the more productive one will be at the time of publication. Research questions that are likely to generate meaningful conclusions from field survey include those concerned with population density, natural resources, site functions, communication and transportation routes, continuity over an extended period of time, and to family, tribal or national relations.

Where does one find a good list of questions? The anthropologist will usually turn to ethnography—the descriptive study of contemporary cultures. Suppose an archaeologist knows that shepherds of recent times maintain homesteads, inhabited by women year-round, as well as all-male pasture camps that are used seasonally. If archaeologists are studying a climatically-similar area, they may frame hypotheses that will drive them to look for signs of such patterns in the ancient artifacts and assemblages.

Historians—or those whose primary interest is historical reconstruction—may turn to history for their hypotheses. But most workers in the Near East attempt to combine historical questions with cultural questions. For example, since the Bible shows a conflict between Israel and the Philistines, what can archaeology show about the nature of both peoples and their interaction? What constitutes a Philistine village or an Israelite village? Where do these come into territorial conflict? Why? Was there a shift in settlement technology after the conflict was resolved? Why?

Once archaeologists begin to think about such theoretical questions, the next step is the formulation of a list of observations that may provide answers. These may follow a deductive track: "If Early Bronze Age populations were politically related to local chiefs, then we should find small settlements clustering within 4 km radii of larger, walled towns." Archaeologists may elect a more inductive approach: "Let us see what assemblages are present at the mountain Iron-Age-I sites and note any distinctiveness from the sites found in the valley." These are, of course, simplistic examples of research questions, but they demonstrate the sorts of questions that may be posed when setting out on a project.

Some of these questions will be unanswerable within the limits of present knowledge and technology or without excavation. The available resources—time, personnel, and money—will also limit the pool of questions.

While one may learn a great deal from patterns of spatial distribution of artifacts at each site, the process of collecting, measuring, and mapping at each site—or at even the larger sites only—on an area-wide survey, is exhausting. Jack Pinkerton, an architectural engineer who helped plan and direct the Central Moab Survey, regularly provoked discussions on the subject of "diminishing returns." Perhaps every survey needs continuing dialogue between a theoretician and an engineer. In any event, there will be need, from the planning stage through the daily operations of a survey project, for decisions about what should be observed, collected, and recorded. Such decisions are best made on the basis of scientific theory and optimism about the utility of surface survey.

Research Design: Field Method

Theoretically, every square meter of a region should be examined by the survey team before statements about the region's ancient history and culture are made. Unfortunately, surveys do not always have this option. Even the survey that claims to cover 100 percent of an area usually ends up missing locations because of rugged terrain and inaccessibility. Furthermore, cost factors militate against such total-area surveys. If the details are to be observed in the field, some method of sampling must be used.

Although random sampling was applied by Harold S. Gladwin in the 1930s (Martin and Plog 1973:7), the technology of sampling and spatial analysis has developed most rapidly in the past two decades. One purpose of sampling is to permit precise, careful observation of a few portions of a region. If the archaeologist carefully studies an unrepresentative sample, it is likely that false conclusions about the region will be reached. Consequently, field archaeologists have turned to statisticians to develop the archaeological application of "probability sampling" (Read 1975).

Traditional, intuitive procedures of survey, some of which are still used, led workers to survey the "most likely" areas of a region or to excavate "the best" part of a tell. A skilled archaeologist may, indeed, choose more "productive" sites by virtue of experience and intuition than would be chosen by random selection. The probablistic archaeologist argues that when the traditional archaeologist finishes the work, the latter can speak only of the sites actually surveyed or areas actually excavated. The probablist wants to be able to *infer* from the few spots selected for study (the "sampled population") what *should be* found over the field of study (the "universe").

In order to be able to infer confidently, the worker must employ a sampling strategy that eliminates biases and allows for idiosyncrasies in geography and the settlement patterns of the inhabitants. Consciously or not, surface surveys may introduce worker bias by looking for prominent sites, avoiding logistically different areas, or collecting only "diagnostic" sherds or lithics.

Even random sampling may be biased. Suppose a region is largely unknown, archaeologically. The researcher might divide it into 200 squares (quadrats) of equal size. The archaeologist numbers each of these and uses a table of random numbers (found in the back of a statistics text) to select 80 of these (a 0.4 sample) for intensive survey. No bias? There probably is. Let us assume that 90 percent of the settlements are in the valleys and mountain-pass areas of the region. Then suppose that the random method selected a greater number of ridge tops than valleys or passes. It would be possible, under these circumstances, to conclude that the region was sparcely populated and that the population was evenly distributed between the valleys and ridges.

For this reason, several alternative strategies have been developed (Mueller 1974). Among these are *transects* and *stratified random quadrats*. A *transect* is a long, narrow rectangle that may be laid out across an area in such a way as to cut through all types of terrain. If transects are selected randomly, each has an equal probability of being selected and every archaeological location and zone has an equal chance of being discovered and described.

Stratified random quadrats are grid areas selected randomly from horizontal strata. Horizontal strata are natural zones in a region, such as ridge tops, slopes and natural terraces (where, in Palestine, springs are often located), stream courses, dry lake beds, and distinct vegetation habitats. The archaeologist planning a project would lay out the topographical maps and, if available, aerial or satellite photographs. Drawing upon the information of the geology and biology of the area, the archaeologist would divide the area into its strata. A grid of equal-sized quadrats is then superimposed on the stratified map and a sample of quadrats is selected by a random method.

Using either of these methods—or any other probablistic method— the field team covers each quadrat or transect thoroughly, noting all archaeological features and artifacts. Even within a quadrat, probablistic sampling may be used. Large sites, densely covered with sherds, might be divided into small areas and a thorough collection made from a statistically significant number of them. Few projects take such extreme pains, however.

At least two major arguments are leveled against this type of surveying. First, while it eliminates the need to cover 100 percent of the area, it is still costly in terms of money, time, and transportation. Among the added costs are planning and computer time, measuring instruments, and costs of driving over areas that are not randomly selected. Second, the method may easily miss the large or unique sites. Imagine a survey that covered step-by-step the east side of the Mount of Olives but missed Jerusalem.

To these challenges the advocates of probablistic sample surveying reply:

1. sampling is not designed to find *all* the sites or the unique ones. It is designed to obtain a representative sample of sites if one cannot go after every spot in an area (Flannery 1976:132–135);

2. the best research design should incorporate two or more field plans, especially if an area is largely unknown. The first would seek to determine the distribution of sites and the second would aim for the

desired level of precision, based on the distributional data of the first phase (Read 1975:53–60; Judge, Ebert and Hitchcock 1975:121–22).

David Thomas used a combination of quadrats and linear and circular transects in his survey of the Toquima Mountains near Gatecliff Shelter. The quadrats were randomly spaced; the transects were focused upon known water sources (1979:294–99).

III. THE FIELD TECHNIQUES

Once the team is in the field, ingenuity and resourcefulness are joined to the careful planning of the previous months. Artifacts are collected, sorted, and counted. Some are processed (drawn, described, photographed) just as if they had been excavated. Site and environment photographs are used for recording (and for jogging the memory of a team that may have charted 30 sites and localities in a week). Forms, carefully prepared to elicit as much observation as the team has decided to attempt, are filled out on site and are completed as soon as possible in camp.

Mapping is essential. Most expeditions obtain the latest maps and aerial and satellite photographs available. In the Near East, these are expensive and often restricted for military purposes. Devices for aiding the surveyor in plotting sites on map range from hand-held compasses to distance meters that use laser technology and computers to measure elevations and triangulate locations. Whereas explorers even as late as Glueck described site locations with estimated distances and directions (e.g., "five minutes north of er-Riha we came to Mehattet el-Hajj;" or "Majdalein is located 1 km west of Qasr, on the edge of a precipice"), there is no longer an excuse for a location that does not cite a standard map grid (such as the Palestine Grid). Supplementing the grid locator number will be a thorough description and any names given the site by local residents.

More sophisticated technologies such as infrared aerial photography, photogrammetry (Beale 1982), computer-assisted mapping (Dudnick 1971) and cesium magnetometry (McGovern 1981) are in the arsenal for those whose objectives can be met by their use and whose resources can provide them.

IV. OF CAVEATS AND DREAMS

For all the statistical and technological efforts in the past two decades, surface archaeology remains an inexact science. Arguments over "systematic random sampling," "cluster analysis," the "efficiency" of transects versus quadrats and other seemingly esoteric and scholastic issues are as heated—and as unresolved—as the debates in the 1960s over the "Wheeler-Kenyon" method. We still understand far too little about the way in which a cultural item becomes an archaeological artifact. We also need to understand more about the ways the surface of the earth transforms itself over millennia (O'Connell and Rose 1980; Bar-Yosef and Goren 1980) and the ways artifacts are redistributed through the generations (Baker 1978).

While the author has argued for an optimistic approach to discovery, it is also important to argue for humility in drafting theories and conclusions. What is *not* found by survey is precisely that: not *found*. It is not, necessarily, nonexistent. Worker biases, which may be minimized by planning and corrected by statistics, are not yet eliminated. Recovery is incomplete and our knowledge of Palestine lags behind our curiosity.

Still, the advent of the most highly developed research designs and technologies has hardly begun to dawn upon Palestinian archaeology. It is to be hoped that the work of the past three generations of archaeologists will be merely the lower strata in a multilayered mound.

BIBLIOGRAPHY

Adams, R. McC.
1965   *Land Behind Baghdad: A History of Settlement on the Diyala Plains.* Chicago: University of Chicago.
Aharoni, Y.
1957   *The Settlement of Israelite Tribes in Upper Galilee.* Jerusalem: Magnes (Hebrew).
Alon, D., and Levy, T. E.
1980   Preliminary Note on the Distribution of Chalcolithic Sites on the Wadi Beersheba—Lower Wadi Besor Drainage System. *IEJ* 30: 140–47.
Baker, C. M.
1978   The Size Effect: An Explanation of Variability in Surface Artifact Assemblage Context. *Am Ant* 43: 288–93.
Bar-Yosef, O., and Goren, N.
1980   Afterthoughts Following Prehistoric Surveys in the Levant. *IEJ* 30: 1–16.
Beale, T. W.
1982   ASOR to Introduce New Photogrammetric Recording and Mapping System for Field Archaeologists and Epigraphists. *ASOR Newsletter* 7: 1–3.
Beit-Arieh, I.
1979   Notes and News: Sinai Survey. *IEJ* 29: 256–57.
Ben-Tor, A.
1980   The Regional Study—A New Approach to Archaeological Investigation. *BAR* 6/2: 30–44.
Binford, L. R.
1964   A Consideration of Archaeological Research Design. *Am Ant* 29: 425–41.
1972   *An Archaeological Perspective.* New York: Seminar.

Braidwood, R. J.
    1937   *Mounts in the Plain of Antioch: An Archaeological Survey.* Oriental
                Institute Publications, No. 48 Chicago: University of Chicago.
Campbell, E. F., Jr.
    1968   The Shechem Area Survey. *BASOR* 190: 19–41.
Cohen, R.
    1972   Surveys in the Negev. *Hadashot Arkheologiyot* 41–42: 39–40
    1979   The Negev Archaeological Emergency Project. *IEJ* 29: 250–51.
Cohen, R., and Dever, W.
    1979   Notes and News: Be'er Resisim, 1979. *IEJ* 29: 254–55.
    1981   Notes and News: Be'er Resisim, 1980. *IEJ* 30: 228–31.
Dever, W.
    1970   The Middle Bronze I Period in Syria and Palestine. Pp. 132–63
                in *Near Eastern Archaeology in the Twentieth Century: Essays in
                Honor of Nelson Glueck,* ed. J.A. Sanders. Garden City, NY:
                Doubleday.
    1973   The EB IV-MB I Horizon in Transjordan and Southern Pal-
                estine. *BASOR* 210: 37–63.
Dudnick, E. E.
    1971   *SYMAP User's Reference Manual for Synagraphic Computer Map-
                ping. Chicago: University of Illinois at Chicago Circle.*
Flannery, K. V.
    1976   The Trouble with Regional Sampling. Pp. 159–60 in *The Early
                Mesoamerican Village,* ed. K.V. Flannery. New York: Academic.
Glueck, N.
    1934   Explorations in Eastern Palestine, I. *AASOR* 14: 1–113.
    1935   Explorations in Eastern Palestine, II. *ASSOR* 15: 1–202.
    1939   Explorations in Eastern Palestine, III. *AASOR* 18–19: 1–287.
    1951   Explorations in Eastern Palestine, IV. *AASOR* 25–28: 1–423.
Gophna, R.
    1977   Archaeological Survey of the Central Coastal Plain. *TA* 5: 136–
                47.
Gophna, R., and Ayalon, E.
    1980   Survey of the Central Coastal Plain, 1978–1979; Settlement
                Pattern of the MB II A. *TA* 7: 147–50.
Goring-Morris, A. N., and Gilead, I.
    1981   Notes and News: Prehistoric Survey and Excavations at Ramat
                Matred, 1979. *IEJ* 31: 132–33.
Goring-Morris, A.N., and Gopher, A.,
    1981   Notes and News: Har Harif, 1980. *IEJ* 31: 133–34.
Henry, D. O.
    1979   Paleolithic Sites Within the Ras en Naqb Basin, Southern Jor-
                dan. *PEQ* 111: 79–85.
Hester, T. R.; Heizer, R. F.; and Graham, J. A.
    1975   *Field Methods in Archaeology.* Palo Alto, CA: Mayfield.
Ibach, R., Jr.
    1976   Archaeological Survey of the Hesban Region. *AUSS* 14: 119–26.
    1978a   Expanded Archaeological Survey. *AUSS* 16: 201–13.
    1978b   An Intensive Surface Survey at Jalul. *AUSS* 16: 215–22.
Ibrahim, M.; Sauer, J.A.; and Yassine, K.
    1976   The East Jordan Valley Survey, 1975. *BASOR* 222: 41–66.
Judge, J. W.
    1973   *Paleoindian Occupation of the Central Rio Grande Valley in New
                Mexico.* Albuquerque: University of New Mexico.

Judge, J.W.; Ebert, J. I.: and Hitchcock, R. K.
1975   Sampling in Regional Archaeological Survey. Pp. 82–123 in *Sampling in Archaeology*, ed. J. W. Mueller. Tucson: University of Arizona.

Kautz, J. R.
1981   Tracking the Ancient Moabites. *BA* 44: 27–35.

Kennedy, D. L.
1982   *Archaeological Explorations on the Roman Frontier in North-East Jordan.* Oxford: British Archaeological Reports.

Kochavi, M., Ed.
1972   *Judaea, Samaria and the Golan: Archaeologial Survey, 1967–1968.* Jerusalem: Carta (Hebrew).

Kochavi, M.
1974   Khirbet Rabud-Debir. *Ta* 1: 2–33.

McGovern, P.
1981   Notes and News: Baq'ah Valley Project 1980. *BA* 44: 126–28.

Marfoe, L.
19779   The Intergrative Transformation: Patterns of Sociopolitical Organization in Southern Syria. *BASOR* 234: 1–42.

Martin, P. S., and Plog, F.
1973   *The Archaeology of Arizona: A Study of the Southwest Region.* Garden City, NY: Doubleday.

Mattingly, G. L.
1983a   Nelson Glueck and Early Bronze Age Moab. *ADAJ* 27: 481–89.
1983b   The Natural Environment of Central Moab. *ADAJ* 27: 597–605.

Mazar, A.
1981   Giloh: An Early Insraelite Settlement Site Near Jerusalem. *IEJ* 31: 1–36.

Meyers, E. M.; Strange, J. F.; and Groh, D. E.
1978   The Meiron Excavation Project: Archaeological Survey in Galilee and Golan, 1976. *BASOR* 230: 1–24.

Miller, J. M.
1979   Archaeological Survey of Central Moab: 1978. *BASOR* 234: 43–52.

Mueller, J. W.
1974   *The Use of Sampling in Archaeological Survey.* Memoirs of the Society for American Archaeology 28. Salt Lake City: Society for American Archaeology.

O'Connell, K., and Rose, G.
1980   Tell el-Hesi, 1979. *PEQ* 112: 73–91.

Ohel, M. Y., and Bruder, G.
1980   Upper Dishon Basin Project: The First Season 1979. *IEJ* 30: 34–51.

Parsons, J. R.
1972   Archaeological Settlement Patterns, *ARA* 1: 280–85.

Portugali, Y.
1982   A Field Methodology for Regional Archaeology (The Jezreel Valley Survey, 1981). *TA* 9: 169–78.

Price-Williams, D.
1973   Preliminary Report of the Environmental Archaeological Survey of Tell Fara, 1972. Pp. 193–216 in *Archaeological Theory and Practice,* ed. D. E. Strong. New York: Seminar.

Rast, W. E., and Schaub, R. T.
    1974   Survey of the Southeastern Plain of the Dead Sea, 1973. *ADAJ*
                19: 5–53.
Read, D. W.
    1975   Regional Sampling. Pp. 45–60 in *Sampling in Archaeology*, ed.
                J. W. Mueller. Tucson: University of Arizona.
Redman, C. L. And Watson, P. J.
    1970   Systematic, Intensive Surface Collection. *Am Ant* 35: 279-91.
Roll, I., and Ayalon, E.
    1981   Two Large Wine Presses in the Red Soil Regions of Israel. *PEQ*
                113: 111–25.
Ruppe, R. J.
    1966   The Archaeological Survey: A Defense. *Am Ant* 31: 181–88.
Thomas, D. H.
    1979   *Archaeology.* New York: Holt, Rinehart and Winston.
Urman, D.
    1971   *Announcement of Historical Sites (Golan Heights), 1.* Jerusalem:
                Israel Army.
Vescelius, G. S.
    1960   Archaeological Sampling: A Probelm of Statistical Inference.
                Pp. 457–70 in *Essays in the Science of Culture,* ed. G. E. Dole and
                R. Carniero. New York: Crowell.
Willey, G. R.
    1953   *Prehistoric Settlement Patterns in the Virú Valley, Peru.* Washington,
                D.C.: Bureau of Ethnology.

11
CERAMIC DATING

ODED BOROWSKI
Emory University

One of the characteristic elements of an ancient Near Eastern site is potsherds, which are broken pieces of clay vessels. Once a vessel is broken, potsherds are virtually indestructible. They do not rust or corrode, melt or evaporate. Potsherds are hard evidence of the ancient culture which produced the vessels to which they originally belonged and, as such, they maintain within them some of the characteristics of the original vessel. By this virtue they can be helpful in tracing that ancient culture which produced them, especially in providing its date.

The first one to recognize that pottery and potsherds are the key to dating the different strata (layers) which make up a tell was W. M. Flinders Petrie, an Englishman who came to excavate at Tell el-Ḥesi in 1890 after excavating for several years in Egypt. By finding parallels between the pottery at Tell el-Ḥesi and the Egyptian pottery with which he was already familiar, Petrie laid the foundations for "ceramic typology," the study of changes in pottery styles which can be used as a clue to chronology (Dever 1980:42). Following Petrie, archaeologists started using pottery in the disentanglement of strata in ancient mounds. The greatest contribution to Palestinian pottery chronology was made by William F. Albright through his excavations at Tell Beit Mirsim in southern Judah during the late 1920s and early 1930s. Albright established the framework for the pottery chronology of the Bronze and Iron Ages in Palestine. His work had been refined by one of his students, G. Ernest Wright, and with periodic modifications is still being used. A detailed study of pottery chronology from prehistoric times through the Iron Age was assembled and published by Ruth Amiran (1970) and has been consulted by most biblical archaeologists and students.

What does pottery have that makes it essential for dating? Like many other things, such as clothing and housing, pottery styles and manufacturing techniques change over the course of time. But the durability of pottery makes it unique. When a specific pottery style can be associated with an historical period and a geographical region, this indicator becomes a key indicating similar occurrences. In order to utilize pottery for dating purposes, comparative studies have to be conducted. These include comparisons of pottery from different strata and from different sites. There are certain elements which make the comparative study of pottery possible. In addition to style they include the tradition in which the vessel was shaped and the technique used for its manufacture. Although our knowledge of pottery comes from whole vessels, potsherds which are in abundance at every ancient site are used for dating because they are more readily available than whole or repairable vessels.

Certain parts of a vessel are more useful for dating because they maintain stylistic elements. These parts, sometimes referred to as diagnostic sherds, include bases, rims, handles, and spouts. They can indicate the size, shape, and function of the vessel. The pieces coming from the body of the vessels can also be useful because they contain clues to the technique used in manufacturing the vessel. By studying body sherds one can tell whether the vessel was made on a wheel or was shaped by hand and what type of inclusions were added to the clay, such as straw, ground pottery, and crushed stones. The mixture used in the production of the vessel was part of the pottery tradition in which the vessel was made. Body sherds also yield information concerning the temperature in the kiln when the vessel was fired. Lower temperatures usually indicate early traditions, while higher temperatures reflect later historical periods. The ability to reach high temperatures helped potters produce stronger and more durable vessels which could have thinner bodies.

Another important element in the study of pottery for dating is decoration. There were many ways in which pottery was decorated throughout the ages. Besides the style, the technique is very important. Pottery was decorated directly on the clay before or after firing. At times, the vessel was dipped in a thin mixture containing pigments, then painted and fired, or it was dipped after firing and then decorated. Another way of decorating a clay vessel was by burnishing. The vessel was covered with a thin layer of liquefied clay and then smoothed over with a hard object such as a bone or pebble and then fired. Besides producing a decorative effect, the vessel became sealed and less porous. Most of the information used in pottery dating comes from common vessels which can be compared one to another. Pottery which is uncommon cannot be used for dating unless its relationship to common pottery can be established. One example of such pottery is the Iron Age Negeb pottery which, when discovered, could not be used for dating until its chronology was established by the common pottery found with it. Now pottery from the Negeb can be used to a certain degree for dating.

How can pottery be used for dating? To be able to use pottery for dating it has to be collected in a meaningful manner which will make dating a find possible. The basic principle in pottery dating is that finds are dated by the latest pottery associated with them. To explain the use of this principle, a simple example will suffice. Coins found in one's pocket or purse have different denominations and were minted at different dates. The date of the pocket or purse is established by the date of the latest coin; it cannot be earlier than the latest coin, but it can be later than the earliest and the latest coin in the purse. To make sure that the pottery is not contaminated (i.e., that it was not mixed with pottery which does not belong with a certain grouping), special efforts have to be made in its collection.

How is pottery collected?

Most American archaeological projects use the "Wheeler-Kenyon" method of excavation, sometimes known by its popular name, the "Gezer method," since it is named after the site in Israel where it was modified and taught to many archaeologists-in-training. Today, many archaeological projects place such importance on methodology that they prepare special manuals in which a prominent place is given to the means of collecting and processing pottery (Seger 1971:34–41; 1980:34–41; Blakely and Toombs 1980:87–95; Dever and Lance 1978:108–138).

The heart of the Gezer System is the locus; the locus is a unit with three dimensions—length, width, and height. There are two types of loci: the "artificial" and the "authentic." The artificial locus is a means by which the archaeologist tries to reach the authentic locus and identify it. An artificial locus is a creation of the archaeologist, while an authentic locus is an entity which can be identified and labeled, like a wall, an oven, a floor, or a foundation trench. Sherds can help date authentic loci if they are collected in a controlled manner. Sherds are collected into a bucket, which is not only a physical entity but also a unit of control, like a mini-locus. While a locus gets a number connecting it with the excavated square, the bucket gets a number relating it to the locus. Thus, every bucket contains sherds from a certain locus. The location of the bucket in the square is plotted on the top plan. This enables the archaeologist to know the exact origin of the sherds and to what layer they belong. If we refer to the example of the coins in the pocket, we can understand why it is so important to control the collection of sherds: the date of the locus is determined by the latest sherd found in it. An Early Bronze Age sherd can be found in an Iron Age locus, but it is highly unlikely for it to be the other way around, unless some means of contamination, such as pits or rodent activity, can be identified. Special care has to be taken when excavating architectural remains, such as walls, floors and installations, because these are the elements later combined into strata and phases. These are also the type of remains which might be reused in different periods; thus it is important to be able to tell at what time each of them was constructed and when each went out of use. The pottery coming from under a floor should be earlier than that which comes from on top of it. Likewise, pottery coming from a foundation trench should be earlier than that which comes from the floor sealing it. Pottery related to an installation should be collected in the context of this feature to help date it. By carefully collecting pottery a sequence or a chronology can be developed. To use pottery for precise dating, its context has to be related to historical events, such as wars and destructions, events that can be dated at times by written records.

What happens after the pottery is collected?

To date a locus by its pottery, the archaeologist has to be able to identify the sherds and assign them to the proper period in which they were made. Since the sherds are dirty when they come out of the soil, first they have to be cleaned. Cleaning the sherds with a brush is done after they have soaked in water for a short time. This process is very important, not only for loosening the dirt, but also for enabling the archaeologist to determine whether the sherds bear inscriptions made with ink. In antiquity body sherds were used for writing receipts, letters, and other things. Brushing the sherd before examining it for an inscription might erase the writing. The examination of the sherd is possible after it has been soaked. After the sherds are washed and allowed to dry, they are identified or "read." The different periods represented by the sherds in each locus are registered, and certain sherds, mostly diagnostic, are then chosen for further study and are published as part of the excavation report.

After selecting the sherds, each one of them is marked with the locus number. Each sherd is numbered, thereby enabling the archaeologist to keep track of the data. To enable other archaeologists to study the results of the excavation, the information and conclusions have to be published. Part of the supporting evidence is the pottery recovered from the different loci. In addition to actual examination of the sherds and reconstructed vessels, pottery can be studied from drawings (figs. 1 & 2) and photographs (figs. 3 & 4), two ways of making it available to those who were not actually digging the site. Through the years, certain conventions for publishing pottery were developed and they are now followed by almost every archaeologist. Pottery sherds are drawn in profile, a practice which enables comparison. Pottery vessels are also drawn in profile, but the right half shows the vessel in section and the left shows its exterior. All drawings are made to scale. Accompanying the drawings are descriptions of the color and content of the clay.

As mentioned above, certain features are characteristic of certain periods; these include form, decoration, and technique. Let us take a look at some of the characteristics which help archaeologists use pottery for dating, and let us examine a few characteristic examples from different periods. As we begin this discussion, it is important to remember

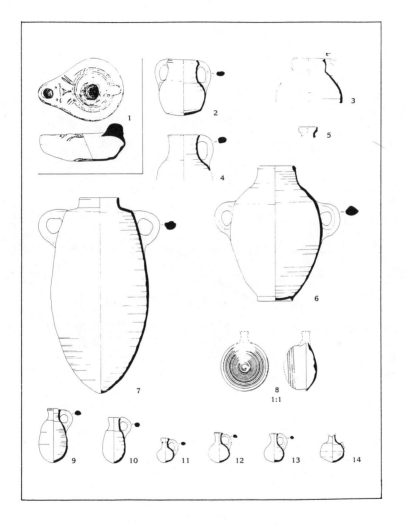

FIG. 1   *Examples of pottery vessels drawn in profile, showing sections and
exteriors (courtesy of the Lahav Research Project)*

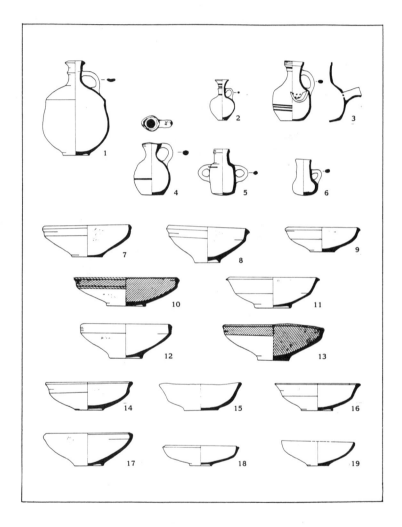

FIG. 2 *Examples of pottery vessels drawn in profile, showing sections and exteriors (courtesy of the Lahav Research Project)*

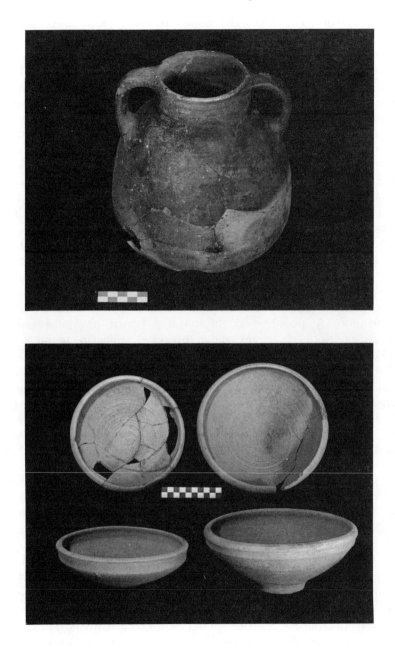

FIG. 3

FIG. 4 *Iron Age II pottery vessels photographed for publication (courtesy of the Lahav Research Project)*

that one sherd does not make a chronological period; the archaeologist is looking for an assemblage, a group of vessels or their sherds, to date a stratum.

The use of clay for making vessels was introduced in the Neolithic period, but until the introduction of the potter's wheel in the Early Bronze Age, pottery was formed by hand in several ways. A small vessel was produced by using a ball of clay and shaping it into the desired vessel. A larger vessel was made by first forming long coils or rings and then joining them one on top of the other to form a vessel. The separate coils were smoothed to form one unit. Often, shaping the vessel was done on a mat, the imprints of which can still be seen on the bottoms of vessels (Amiran 1963:17–21). Neolithic pottery is decorated with incised and painted chevrons and zigzag lines, sometimes creating triangular designs (Amiran 1970:17–21).

The Chalcolithic period produced a variety of vessels, some of which can be grouped according to the first site in which they were discovered. The first one, the Ghassulian, includes bowls, chalices, goblets, and cornets, some of which are painted and have lug handles. The second, the Beer-sheba culture, includes small and large bowls, cooking pots, jars, and more. A special vessel, the so-called "churn," is typical to the Chalcolithic period. It is suggested that this vessel, appearing to imitate a goat-skin, was used for making butter (Amiran 1970:33).

The Early Bronze Age is represented by a large variety of vessels. Typical to the Early Bronze are ledge-handles, which are shelf-like handles sometimes decorated by being pinched either up or down to create a wave effect. Pottery dated to EB I includes vessels decorated with red or grey burnish and with diagonal or net painting. Another characteristic feature, mostly on large jars, is a raised rope-like decoration. Also typical in this period are "teapot" vessels with long spouts and loop-handles, and flat, shallow platters (Amiran 1970:35–57). A group of vessels characteristic of EB II is Abydos ware, named after the site in Upper Egypt in which it was first discovered. This ware was imported from Canaan to Egypt during the time of the First Dynasty. Characteristic to this group are the elongated jugs with long necks and a loop-handle from the rim to the top of the shoulder (Amiran 1970:59–66).

A group diagnostic of EB III is Khirbet Kerak ware, named after the site at the southeastern tip of the Sea of Galilee where this pottery was first discovered. There are several elements which make this group different from other Early Bronze pottery: the clay mixture is of inferior quality; it was not made on a potter's wheel; both inside and outside the vessels are covered with a heavy slip and are burnished to a high gloss; the firing produced a partly-black and partly-red vessel (Amiran 1970:68–75). The decorations include incised and raised lines and knobs.

To a certain degree, the transitional period of EB IV/MB I continues the tradition of earlier periods. This can be seen in vessels like the "teapot" and features like the ledge-handle. typical to this period is the four-sprouted oil lamp, which is a transitional form between the earlier saucer-like one and the later one-spouted lamp.

The MB II A-B introduces new features, some of which are carinated bowls and goblets, deep kraters, storage jars with rounded shoulders, and elongated juglets (dipper juglets) with pointed bottoms. A group unique to the MB II period is Tell el-Yahudiyeh ware, named after a site on the Nile Delta where it was first observed. A common vessel in this style is the gray or light brown juglet with a long neck and a loop-handle, which is sometimes doubled. The juglets are burnished with gray, black or yellow slip and decorated with punctured zigzag or diagonal lines that are filled with white chalk. This group is tentatively associated with the Hyksos who ruled Canaan and Egypt during this period (Amiran 1970:118–120).

During the Late Bronze period, certain bowls continue with their carination, which gradually degenerates and disappears at the end of the period. Round and straight bowls are very prominent, as well as kraters and one-spouted oil lamps. At the beginning of the Late Bronze Age, the cooking pot continues the tradition of the rounded-rim pot of the Middle Bronze, but some start to exhibit a tendency toward the everted triangular rim, which becomes very pronounced during LB IIB. Storage jars continue in the tradition of the Middle Bronze, but they gradually develop a button-like base and shoulders. Several groups of vessels from the Late Bronze Age are characterized by their decoration, (e.g., bichrome ware, "chocolate-on-white" ware, and those with a palm-tree and ibex motif) (Amiran 1970:152–65). A new type of vessel, the pilgrim flask, appears on the scene in the Late Bronze. Typical of this period are Syrian, Cypriot, and Mycenaean imported vessels. Most noticeable are the Syrian elongated flasks, the Cypriot "milk bowls" with their wishbone handle, the Cypriot bilbil jugs with their leaning neck, and the Mycenaean pyxis. Most of these forms were imported and imitated by local artisans in ancient Palestine.

While pottery is used for dating throughout the history of the Near East and even up to our present time, as the Gaza and Hebron wares of the 20th century exemplify, this essay will conclude with a few examples from the Iron Age. Typical of the beginning of the Iron Age in the Coastal Plain and the southern Shephelah is Philistine pottery, which is distinct by its form and decoration, showing both Mycenaean and Aegean influences. One of the forms introduced in Palestine at the time is the "beer jug" which has a perforated spout like a strainer. A decoration typical of this pottery is that of a bird looking forward or pluming its wings; this pottery is decorated with black or red paint on white slip. The cooking pots of the Iron Age start in the tradition of the Late Bronze, but they soon develop pronounced shoulders and, still later, exhibit a ridged or stepped rim. During this period, a different type of cooking pot developed in the south; this vessel has a deep body and a long, ridged neck (Amiran 1970:227–32). The kraters or large bowls also develop a distinct form; examples from the north usually have two handles, while examples from the south have four or more handles. Starting in Iron Age I, there are changes in the forms of storage jars; the collared-rim jar which is, at first, large and round evolves into the elongated type with a short neck and pronounced shoulders. The oil lamps in the Iron Age start out following the Canaanite tradition of a one-spout lamp with a round bottom and a wide lip. At the end of the Iron Age, we find that the lamps are smaller and have a high and pronounced base. The common black juglet, which starts at the beginning of the Iron Age with a long neck and a loop-handle attached to its middle and shoulder, appears at the end of this period with a rounded body, a short neck and a loop-handle attached to its rim and shoulder.

There is much more to say about pottery dating, but continuous refinements in ceramic analysis prevent the final word from being spoken. As long as archaeologists continue to excavate, changes will be made in the pottery chronology. Therefore, the most important element is control over the process of pottery retrieval; even if our interpretations change, we have to be sure that the ceramic data were obtained in a reliable manner.

BIBLIOGRAPHY

Amiran, R.
      1963   *The Ancient Pottery of Eretz Yisrael from its Beginnings in the Neo-lithic Period to the End of the First Temple.* Jerusalem: Bailik Institute and the Israel Exploration Society (Hebrew).

      1970   *Ancient Pottery of the Holy Land from its Beginnings in the Neolithic Period to the End of the Iron Age.* New Brunswick, NJ: Rutgers University.

Blakely, J. A., and Toombs, L. E.
      1980   *The Tell el-Hesi Field Manual,* Cambridge, MA: ASOR.

Cole, D. P.
      1984 .   *Shechem I: The Middle Bronze IIB Pottery.* ASOR Excavation Reports. Winona Lake, IN: Eisenbrauns/ASOR.

Dever, W. G.
      1980   Archaeological Method in Israel: A Continuing Revolution. *BA* 43: 40–48.

Dever, W. G., and Lance, H. D., eds.
      1978   *A Manual of Field Excavation: Handbook for Field Archaeologists.* New York: HUC-JIR

Duncan, J. G.
      1930   *Corpus of Dated Palestinian Pottery.* London: British School of Archaeology in Egypt.

Glock, A. E.
   1975   Homo Faber: The Pot and the Potter at Taanach. *BASOR* 219: 9–28.

Gonen, R.
   1973   *Ancient Pottery.* Cassell's Introducing Archaeology Series, Book 2. London: Cassell.

Johnston, R. H.
   1974   The Biblical Potter. *BA* 37: 86–106.

Lapp, P. W.
   1961   *Palestinian Ceramic Chronology 200 B.C.–A.D. 70.* ASOR Publications of the Jerusalem School, Vol. 3. New Haven, CT: ASOR.

Rast, W. E.
   1978   *Taanach I: Studies in the Iron Age Pottery.* ASOR Excavation Reports. Cambridge, MA: ASOR.

Sauer, J. A.
   1973   *Heshbon Pottery 1971: A Preliminary Report on the Pottery from the 1971 Excavations at Tell Ḥeshbân.* Berren Springs, MI: Andrews University.

Seger, J. D.
   1971   *Handbook for Field Operations.* Jerusalem: Hebrew Union College Biblical and Archaeological School.

   1980   *Field Operations Guidebook.* Omaha, NE: Lahav Research Project.

Shepard, A. O.
   1956   *Ceramics for the Archaeologist.* Carnegie Institution of Washington Publication NO. 609. Washington, D.C.: Carnegie Institution of Washington.

12
RADIOCARBON DATING

James M. Weinstein
Cornell University

Radiocarbon (carbon-14) dating is a method of estimating the absolute age of a carbon-bearing material by comparing its radioactivity with that of a modern sample. It is currently applicable to carbonaceous substances up to 70,000 years old, and it may soon be capable of dating materials up to 100,000 years in age. The method was developed at the University of Chicago in the late 1940s, principally through the efforts of W. F. Libby and two co-workers, E. C. Anderson and J. R. Arnold. Libby himself was awarded the Nobel Prize for chemistry in 1960 for his fundamental contributions to the development of this chronometric technique. Radiocarbon dating has revolutionized the study of prehistory and the rise of civilization and has even produced valuable chronological information on archaeological remains from historical periods. More than a hundred laboratories throughout the world now date carbon-14 samples on a regular basis. Some of these facilities also engage in research designed to improve the accuracy, precision, and usefulness of the radiocarbon technique.

Radiocarbon dating has been of inestimable value for establishing the absolute chronology of Palestine from ca. 50,000 B.C. down to the end of the fourth millennium B.C., i.e., from late Middle Palaeolithic times to the beginning of the Early Bronze Age. It has also had some impact on the chronological framework of the Early Bronze Age, and in a small number of cases it has contributed to the dating of archaeological materials from more recent periods. More than 500 archaeological samples from the southern Levant have been carbon-dated since 1951, and, on average, 20–30 new dates are published annually.

I. RADIOCARBON DATING: PRINCIPLES, METHODOLOGY, AND CALIBRATION[1]

There are three naturally occurring isotopes of carbon: carbon-12, -13, and -14. There are approximately 1,000,000,000,000 carbon-12 atoms for each 100 atoms of carbon-13 and 1 atom of carbon-14. Carbon-12 and -13 are stable, while carbon-14 is not. This radioactive carbon-14 is formed in the upper atmosphere, where cosmic rays produce neutrons which react with nitrogen (^{14}N) to create carbon-14 (^{14}C):

$$^{14}N + neutron \rightarrow {}^{14}C + {}^{1}H$$

This ^{14}C in turn combines with oxygen; as $^{14}CO_2$ it is assimilated by plants through the mechanism of photosynthesis and ingested by animals which eat the vegetation. Atmospheric carbon dioxide also enters the hydrosphere as dissolved carbonate, so ^{14}C is taken in by marine and freshwater plants and animals. Thus all elements of the biosphere contain ^{14}C. The production of ^{14}C through cosmic radiation stays essentially in balance with its depletion through radioactive disintegration.

When an organism dies, it no longer takes in ^{14}C and its current store of ^{14}C decays back to nitrogen, emitting a beta particle in the process:

$$^{14}C \rightarrow {}^{14}N + e^{-}$$

This decay takes place at a measureable rate: half of the ^{14}C atoms disintegrate in 5730 ± 40 years. It thus becomes possible to determine the age of virtually any carbon-containing material by comparing its ^{14}C activity with that of a modern sample.

The 5730-year "half-life" of ^{14}C is the mean of three independent laboratory determinations published in 1962 (Godwin 1962). A second half-life measurement is also quoted for ^{14}C: 5568 ± 30 years. This represents the weighted average of three earlier determinations and was the best estimate available to Libby in 1951, when he and Arnold published the first date-list from the University of Chicago radiocarbon laboratory (Arnold and Libby 1951). Since carbon-14 assays published in the 1950s and early 60s employed the "Libby half-life," scientists have agreed to continue using this value as the basis for calculating the ages of all samples rather than recalculate the old dates. However, conversion of the radiocarbon age of a sample from the 5568-year half-life is easily accomplished by multiplying the former measurement by 1.03.

Most carbon-containing substances are suitable for radiocarbon dating. Carbon-14 samples are classified as being either short-lived or long-lived. A short-lived material such as bone, nuts, olive pits, or grain is

[1] Details of the radiocarbon dating technique appear in Aitken 1974: 26–84; Browman 1981; Goffer 1980; 298–314; Michels 1973: 148–67; Ralph 1971; and Taylor 1978.

likely to have been deposited in an archaeological context within a short period of time after being removed from the life cycle; its radiocarbon determination should therefore correspond closely with the event that the excavator wishes to date. A long-lived material (wood) may have grown for hundreds of years, and the radiocarbon assay will give only the date of the tree rings measured. The inner rings provide a date that represents the formative stage of the tree's growth, while the outer rings give a determination closer to the time when the tree was cut down. The significance of wood dates is further complicated by the fact that wood architectural elements may have been in use in a building for a considerable length of time before the structure was destroyed or abandoned. Also, driftwood could lie around for many years before being thrown in a hearth, while large pieces of wood could easily be reused. The date obtained from a long-lived material may therefore have little or no relevance for dating the sample's archaeological context.

Charcoal is generally classified with wood, i.e., as a long-lived material, and the same difficulties concerning the temporal relationship between a sample and its context that apply to wood normally apply to charcoal. However, if charcoal comes from shrubbery which has only a few years' growth, it is essentialy short-lived. Therefore, when a radiocarbon "sample" is put together from tiny pieces of charcoal collected over a large area, such as a courtyard or the floor of a large room, it could contain wood of varying ages, e.g., fragments from a large roof beam mixed with twigs from a hearth. Since the ^{14}C date from such a sample would be of questionable chronological value, this method of collecting radiocarbon samples is not encouraged.

The minimum amount of pure carbon needed for dating is 1 gram. The size of a sample needed to yield this amount varies by type of material and from one laboratory to another. An archaeologist should consult the laboratory to which the samples are to be sent to find out how large a sample the facility requires for each type of material. In general, a minimum of 10 grams of wood, charcoal, and many short-lived samples should be submitted, and at least twice that amount is desirable because much of the sample may be lost during pretreatment. Bone and shell call for significantly larger amounts—in some cases as much as a kilogram of the former and several kilograms of the latter. Such quantities may be needed because the carbon in bone and shell is mostly in the form of carbonate. Since this mineral fraction is easily contaminated with older or younger carbon from a sample's surrounding environment, radiocarbon laboratories prefer to date the small organic portion, which is called collagen in bone and teeth, conchiolin in shell. To extract this component, a large initial sample may be required.

The sampling procedure for radiocarbon materials follows a fairly standard sequence of events. The archaeologist picks up the sample with a clean instrument such as a pair of tweezers or a knife. The sample, which should not be treated with a preservative or other chemical, is wrapped in alumnium foil or put in a small glass or metal jar or securely sealed polyethylene bag. Each sample is clearly labeled with a number or letter, the identification tag being inserted between the foil, jar, or polyethylene bag and an outer container, commonly a second plastic bag. Large charcoal fragments are shipped or, preferably, hand-carried to the radiocarbon laboratory in a box which is carefully filled with packing material to minimize crumbling. Special submission forms on which the pertinent data about each specimen are recorded, such as the name of the site, the context of the sample, possible sources of contamination, and the purpose in submitting the item for radiocarbon dating are also sent to the laboratory.[2]

At the dating facility, each sample is tagged with the laboratory's letter code and unique number, e.g., BM-1328 for the 1328th item processed at the British Museum Research Laboratory. The sample is weighed, and steps are then taken to remove any older or younger carbon contaminants whose presence could alter the radiocarbon measurement. Mechanical cleaning comes first; tiny rootlets can be picked out with tweezers, while bones are scraped to clean off surface contaminants. The sample is subsequently given one or more chemical washings; a sodium hydroxide (NaOH) treatment removes humic acid, while hydrochloric acid (HCl) eliminates inorganic carbon.[3]

The next step is to convert the sample to a form suitable for counting its radioactivity. The technique used at Chicago and several other dating facilities in the late 1940s and early 50s was to measure the sample as solid carbon. The dates obtained by this approach were erratic for various reasons. For one thing, carbon samples were easily contaminated by the radioactive fallout from the atmospheric nuclear and thermonuclear weapons tests then being conducted by the United States and the Soviet Union. A second critical problem was the inefficiency of the counting equipment; only about five percent of the beta-particle disintegrations could be counted. This meant that a large initial sample was required for dating, something that archaeologists could not always provide. Between counting inefficiency and sometimes inadequate sample size (the latter resulting in a smaller number of counts), the statistical errors accoompanying solid-carbon dates were frequently rather large

[2] These forms should be obtained in advance from the laboratory and filled out in the field. An example of one of these submission forms, that used by the British Museum Research Laboratory, is published in Kinnes et al. 1982: fig. 1.

[3] Various contaminants, their effects on radiocarbon dates, and the techniques and problems of removing them are described in Olsson 1974; 1979; Ralph 1971: 11–16. Although pretreatment can reduce the size of a sample by up to 90 percent, the amount lost is usually much less than that.

(on the order of ± 200–500 years). This put a severe limitation on the chronological usefulness of these dates.

In the early 1950s, the solid-carbon technique was superseded by the proportional-gas counting and liquid scintillation methods. In the former, the sample is burned in a chemical train and converted to a gas, either carbon dioxide, methane, or acetylene. The gas is subsequently purified in the train for removal of various electronegative impurities and radon (a radioactive element), and the activity of the sample is measured in a proportional counter. In the liquid scintillation method, which is the one most often used by laboratories today, the sample is converted to a liquid, usually benzene, which becomes the solvent for a scintillation counter.

The activity of a sample is measured for up to ca. 24 hours—the exact length of time varies in different dating facilities—and then a second time several weeks later. This second counting reduces the possibility of error due to contamination by radon, whose half-life is 3.82 days. By comparing the ^{14}C remaining in the ancient sample with that found in a modern reference standard—oxalic acid provided by the National Bureau of Standards in Washington, D.C.—the "conventional radiocarbon age" of the sample is calculated.[4]

Radiocarbon ages are expressed in terms of years "Before Present

---

[4] The National Bureau of Standards (NBS) supplies this oxalic acid as an international reference. The radiocarbon measurement of an individual sample is related directly to this NBS standard or indirectly via a secondary laboratory standard whose activity vis-à-vis the NBS reference is known. The secondary standard employed in many dating facilities is mid-19th century wood. Ninety-five percent of the ^{14}C activity of the NBS standard is taken as the modern-day value for A.D. 1890 wood, before the biosphere was contaminated with old carbon from the burning of enormous quantities of fossil fuel (coal and oil) and recent carbon from the fallout associated with atmospheric weapons testing.

A small adjustment to the age measurement may be required in order to correct for isotopic fractionation (an increase or decrease in ^{14}C which can occur during various chemical reactions as well as during sample preparation). The correction is accomplished by measuring a sample's $^{13}C{:}^{12}C$ ratio in a mass spectrometer and then doubling the result to obtain an estimate of the $^{14}C{:}^{12}C$ ratio. (Previous research has shown that the fractionation of ^{14}C is about twice that of ^{13}C.) This indirect approach is necessitated by the fact that the amount of ^{14}C in a sample is too small to measure directly in the mass spectrometer. The international reference for ^{13}C is a NBS limestone standard, though formerly it was belemnite obtained from a South Carolina source known as the Peedee belemnite formation (hence the term—PDB standard). While severe fractionation may require correcting the radiocarbon date by up to several hundred years, most corrections are less than ± 50 years. Most radiocarbon dates, especially those produced in the 1950s, have not been corrected for fractionation; even today many laboratories do not adjust their age measurements for fractionation effects. This adds to the difficulty in using published ^{14}C assays for dating events of historical periods. (Another reason for caution in using ^{14}C dates for this purpose is that systematic discrepancies seem to occur in the replicate measurements of dendrochronologically-dated wood by different laboratories [Baxter 1983]. This means that it can be very dangerous to rely on the results of any individual laboratory for the precise dating of a specific archaeological event.)

(abbreviated B.P.), with A.D. 1950 being the reference point for this figure. A sample dated in 1985 will therefore have 35 years subtracted from the initial age measurement to obtain the appropriate B.P. value. Subtraction of 1950 years from this figure yields the 5568-year half-life A.D./B.C. date. The statistical uncertainty (σ) accompanying every radiocarbon date is based on the random nature of the nuclear disintegrations in a sample. Some laboratories also include in this tolerance the uncertainties involved in the count rates for the background radiation and the modern standard. The statistical uncertainty is expressed in terms of either one or two standard deviations. A one-sigma (1σ) standard deviation means that there is a 68.27 percent chance that the date falls within the stated limits; a two-sigma (2σ) tolerance means that there is a 95.45 percent chance that the date falls within the indicated limits.[5]

A new radiocarbon dating system in use at several laboratories in Europe and North America employs high-energy particle accelerators as mass spectrometers to detect ^{14}C atoms directly.[6] This technique is of considerable interest to archaeologists because it has the potential to extend the limit of radiocarbon dating back to ca. 100,000 years from the current 50,000–70,000 years, and to reduce the size of the statistical error accompanying a mean date.[7] Moreover, only milligram rather than gram samples are required for the procedure.[8] However, the equipment used for accelerator dating systems is much more expensive than that employed in conventional setups; hence most laboratories will

[5] For example, a 1σ date of 2500 ± 150 B.C. means there are about 2 out of 3 chances that the true date lies between 2650 and 2350 B.C. The corresponding 2σ date, 2500 ± 300 B.C., means there are about 19 out of 20 chances that the true date falls between 2800 and 2200 B.C. Conventional radiocarbon ages published in *Radiocarbon* are cited with ± 1 standard deviation. A recent study by Scott, Baxter, and Aitchison (1983) concludes that the standard deviations reported with most ^{14}C dates need to be doubled to provide more realistic error values.

[6] The literature on radiocarbon dating with accelerators is growing rapidly. A few general works to be consulted include: Bennett 1979; Browman 1981: 281–86; Hedges 1981; 1983; Taylor et al. 1984. The proceedings of the 10th and 11th International Radiocarbon Conferences (published in *Radiocarbon* 22 [1980] and 25 [1983] respectively) include numerous papers on this new approach to carbon-14 dating.

[7] The outside limit for radiocarbon dating using conventional methods is ca. 50,000 years because the number of ^{14}C atoms in a sample older than that is too small to detect relative to counter background radiation. Through isotopic enrichment of the sample, it is possible to extend this range back to ca. 70,000 years. Artificial enrichment may allow accelerators to push the limit beyond 100,000 years (Hedges 1981: 8).

[8] Because the samples dated by accelerators (and the new, small gas counters) are so little, even a tiny amount of contamination can have a significant effect on a ^{14}C measurement. Accordingly, improved sampling and sample-preparation techniques are being created for these systems: Gillespie and Gowlett (1983); Wand, Gillespie, and Hedges (1984); Gillestpie, Hedges, and Wand (1984).

continue using the proportional-gas and liquid scintillation methods, sometimes with special setups to yield high-precision dates (see e.g., Pearson 1979; Tans and Mook 1979).

Not long after the initial development of radiocarbon dating, it was found that one of the basic assumptions of the method, namely, that the atmospheric inventory of ^{14}C has remained constant over time, was incorrect.[9] Because of short-term variations in the ^{14}C content (known as the De Vries effect), which may be due to solar fluctuations, radiocarbon assays of archaeologically well-dated objects (particularly from Egypt) were consistently turning out younger than expected.[10] To "correct" the conventional radiocarbon dates, ^{14}C measurements have been made of dendrochronologically dated wood (sequoias [*Sequoia gigantea*] and bristlecone pines [*Pinus aristata* and *Pinus longaeva*]) to obtain a tree-ring "calibration" of the radiocarbon determinations.[11] By dating many wood samples, it gradually became possible to construct a calibration curve which provides a systematic correction for conventional ^{14}C dates. More than a dozen calibration curves have been published since 1970.[12] The one used for this article is the "CRD-1σ" calibration. It has a 1σ tolerance and uses the same data base and statistical methods as the "CRD-2" calibration published by Klein et al. (1982).[13] A CRD-σ or -2σ date is expressed in terms of a "range" (e.g., 2905–2760 B.C.) rather than a midpoint plus statistical uncertainty. At the present time, the CRD-1σ table covers radiocarbon determinations between 7230 and 940 years B.P., while the CRD-2σ table gives calibrated dates for radiocarbon ages

[9] In fact, most of the fundamental assumptions on which the radiocarbon dating method is based have been modified or corrected to some degree: see Browman (1981) and Taylor (1978).

[10] Long-term variations, which affect dates more than ca. 6,000 years old, also occur. These are thought to be due to changes in the intensity of the earth's magnetic field, which affects the number of cosmic rays entering the upper atmosphere, and thus the amount of ^{14}C which is created.

[11] For dendrochronology and its application to radiocarbon dating, see Baillie (1982); Eckstein, Wrobel, and Aniol (1983); Ottaway (1983). In addition to the 8681-year bristlecone pine sequence, there is now a 7272-year European oak *(Quercus petraea* and *Quercus robur)* sequence (Pilcher et al. 1984). A high-precision calibration of the radiocarbon timescale based on the European oak chronology is currently in preparation (Pearson, Pilcher, and Baillie 1983; Pearson and Baillie 1983). The implications of a high-precision calibration for both normal and high-precision ^{14}C dates are discussed in Baillie and Pilcher (1983); Harkness (1983); Watkins (1983).

[12] Suess (1970; 1979) and Ralph, Michael, and Han (1973) have produced the two most widely used calibrations in Near Eastern archaeology. The Suess curve emphasizes the short-term variations (the "wiggles") in the atmospheric inventory of ^{14}C while the Ralph, Michael, and Han curve (better known as the "MASCA curve") smoothes them out. A third calibration, one that is especially popular with British archaeologists, is that of Clark (1975).

[13] The CRD-1σ table had not been published as of February 1985. However, a copy was kindly given to the writer by Jeffrey Klein, the principal author of this new table.

between 7240 and 10 years B.P. Conventional ^{14}C ages of less than 940 years B.P. can be corrected, with a 1σ standard deviation, by the use of Stuiver's (1982) high-precision calibration.

II. HISTORY OF RADIOCARBON DATING IN PALESTINIAN ARCHAEOLOGY

The first Palestinian ^{14}C date came from a piece of linen cloth that was probably used as wrapping for one for the Dead Sea Scrolls (Sellers 1951a; 1951b; Crowfoot 1955:27). The sample was processed with the laboratory tag C-576 in the Institute for Nuclear Studies at the University of Chicago and was published in 1951 (Libby:291). The ^{14}C determination, 1917 ± 200 B.P., which translated into A.D. 33 ± 200 on the 5568-year half-life and has a calibrated range of 175 B.C.-A.D. 245, is reasonably good when one considers that it was obtained by the solid-carbon method.

A second solid-carbon date was published in 1954 (Libby: 734). This time the sample (C-919) was charcoal from Stratum III at the Late Chalcolithic site of Horvat Beter. Unfortunately, the radiocarbon age, 7420 ± 520 B.P. (= 5470 ± 520 B.C.), is much too early for the archaeological context and is even too old for any calibration table. Inadequate sample size may have been responsible for this anomalous determination (M. Dothan 1956: 113, n. 4). In 1956 (Rubin and Suess: 448; M. Dothan), a somewhat better date was obtained from another Stratum III charcoal sample (W-245) by the proportional-gas technique: 5280 ± 150 B.P.(= 3330 ± 150 B.C.), with a calibrated range of 4385-3880 B.C.

In the second half of the 1950s, single dates were published from such sites as Dibon (Reed 1957), Dothan (Free 1957), and Timnaᶜ (de Vries and Waterbolk 1958: 1555). Also in the late 1950s and into the early 60s, ^{14}C assays became available from several sites located on the west side of the Dead Sea, specificially, Qumran, the Cave of Horror in Naḥal Ḥever, and the caves in the Wadi Murrabbaᶜat. The dates obtained from these samples—GL-25, -47, Q-621, -771, I-616, GL-37, Gro(GrN)-940, Gro(GrN)-943, and Gro(GrN)-965 (Weinstein 1984: table 1)—like those from Dibon, Dothan, and Timnaᶜ, vary considerably in accuracy, and today they are rarely mentioned in the archaeological literature.

The first "series" of Palestinian ^{14}C dates was a group of nine radiocarbon determinations from Kathleen Kenyon's excavations at Jericho.[14] The samples were processed in 1953 at the Davy-Faraday Research Laboratory of the Royal Institution of London (laboratory

---

[14] If each of the two published measurements for GL-30, an MB II sample, is counted as a separate date, then there are actually 10 dates in this new series.

code: F), subsequently designated the Geochronological Laboratory of the University of London (GL). Three of the dates (GL-5, -6, -24) were published in 1955 in the *Eleventh Annual Report of the University of London Institute of Archaeology,* and these and three additional assays (GL-38, -30, -38) appeared a year later in *Antiquity* in a paper entitled "The Radiocarbon Age of Jericho," by F. E. Zeuner. This article was the first prominent publication in the field of Palestinian radiocarbon dating; one of its most memorable features was the claim (supported by Kenyon [1956] but disputed by Robert Braidwood [1958: 1426–27] and others) that "the pre-pottery Neolithic City of Jericho is . . . the oldest city in the world" (Zeuner 1956: 197). The remaining three dates in the Jericho series (GL-33, -41, -42) did not recieve formal publication until 1967 (Deevey, Flint and Rouse: 31). Altogether, this series includes 4 Early Neolithic II (= Kenyon's Pre-Pottery Neolithic B), 1 Early Bronze IA (= Kenyon's Proto-Urban), and 4 Middle Bronze II (= Albright's MB IIB) dates.

In 1957 (Broecker and Kulp: 1330), a small piece of charcoal from an Upper Levalloiso-Mousterian level in Kebara Cave became the first Palaeolithic sample from Palestine to be carbon-dated. The measurement (L-336D: 28,050 B.C.) proved to be much too young for the latter part of the Middle Palaeolithic period, perhaps because of contamination or inadequate sample size. Nonetheless, this assay is important from an historical standpoint because it was one of the earliest attempts to give an absolute dating to Pleistocene activities in the Near East.

The role of radiocarbon dating in Palestinian archaeology expanded significantly in the 1960s. During this decade, several major series of ^{14}C dates became available. These included determinations for the Early Neolithic period at Beidha and Jericho; the Bronze Age and Iron Age at Gibeon; the Iron Age at Tell es-Saidiyeh; and the Byzantine period at the Monastery of St. Catherine in southern Sinai (see Weinstein 1984: table 1). The most active laboratories for the processing of Palestinian archaeological materials were those at the British Museum (BM), the University of Michigan (M), and the University of Pennsylvania (P).

The 1970s and early 80s have witnessed a virtual explosion in the processing and publishing of radiocarbon materials from the southern Levant. This situation is attributable to several factors:

1. The opening of numerous radiocarbon laboratories in Europe and the United States as well as at one research facility in Israel (the Weizmann Institute in Rehovot [RT]).

2. A great increase in the number of excavations undertaken by pre-historians. The effect such activity has had on the production of ^{14}C dates has been extraordinary. For example, the number of Palaeolithic dates had increased nearly ninefold since 1970, from 9 to 78, and whereas only four ^{14}C dates existed for the entire Epipalaeolithic period

prior to 1970, by late 1984 there were more than 50 such dates (Weinstein 1984: table 1).

3. The growing recognition by archaeologists that an acceptable radiocarbon chronology for ancient Palestine requires numerous series of dates rather than single assays. More than a dozen such series have been published in the last 15 years.

4. The continued processing of radiocarbon samples from Jericho, which has probably yielded more dates (76) than any other site in the ancient Near East.

5. The development of calibration systems. This has made it possible for archaeologists to secure useful chronometric information from samples relating to events of historical periods.

Although the number of Palestinian ^{14}C dates has grown remarkably in recent years, there has not been a similar increase in the number of synthetic studies of this material. The most comprehensive publication is a recent article written by the present author (Weinstein 1984). This paper includes a corpus of 474 ^{14}C assays from Israel, Jordan, the West Bank, Golan Heights, Gaza Strip, and Sinai[15] and offers a brief analysis of the data on a period-by-period basis. It also notes some of the principal current problems in the field of Palestinian radiocarbon dating. Several other publications provide corpora and general discussions of the Palaeolithic, Epipalaeolithic, and Early Neolithic data, e.g., Henry and Servello (1974), Valla (1975: 19–22), Bar-Yosef (1981a: 405; 1981b: 566–67), and Henry (1983: 104–5), but of these, only the article by Henry and Servello includes an evaluation of the individual assays. The analytical studies of the Chalcolithic ^{14}C dates by Lee (1976) are unpublished. The radiocarbon determinations for Shiqmim and other Chalcolithic sites along the Naḥal Beer-sheba have been published by Levy and Alon (1985:74). The only other synthetic papers are several pertaining to the Early Bronze Age radiocarbon materials (Callaway and Weinstein 1977; Mellaart 1979; Weinstein 1980).

III. PRACTICAL CONSIDERATIONS IN PALESTINIAN RADIOCARBON DATING

There are four stages in the radiocarbon dating process: (1) collection and submission of the sample, (2) laboratory processing, (3) analysis

---

[15] After Weinstein (1984) went to press, 14 additional dates, from Lachish, became available (Ussishkin 1983: 164–65, tables 2–3). The author is aware of the existence of ca. 35–40 more, still-unpublished assays.

and interpretation of the data, and (4) publication. The excavator is responsible for what happens in stage 1, rarely participates in the activities of stage 2, and handles many or all of the tasks in stages 3 and 4. Laboratory processing errors do occur on occasion, but they are not the principal cause of difficulties with problematic radiocarbon dates. Most of the problems that arise do so because (1) the archaeologist fails to give adequate consideration to what type of sample material should be collected, and from which context(s), to date a particular event, and (2) the excavator records and publishes insufficient or incorrect information about the sample and its stratigraphic context to make the ^{14}C date of any value. In this section of the paper, we will consider some guidelines for the archaeologist to follow in collecting and submitting radiocarbon samples and interpreting the final dates.[16]

1. *A radiocarbon sample shold only be submitted to a dating facility if there is a clear archaeological/historical need for the ^{14}C assay.*

A ^{14}C sample is worth collecting and submitting if its date can provide a time estimate at least as precise as the date obtainable through stratigraphic or typological methods. If an event cannot be given an absolute date by archaeological or historical methods, then a ^{14}C determination is essential. An assay may also be useful if it provides a temporal estimate as accurate as that obtainable on archaeological grounds. In this case the determination can offer independent support for the archaeological date or force the excavator to reconsider the available evidence. However, if conditions are such that a ^{14}C determination for a sample will automatically be less precise than an archaeological date, then the sample should not be submitted for radiocarbon dating.[17] For example, in view of the present level of precision of conventional radiocarbon dating setups, Palestinian archaeological and historical evidence generally provides more accurate dates for most cultural remains and stratigraphic phases after ca. 2000 B.C. than can be obtained through carbon-14 dating. Thus it is inappropriate to submit samples

[16]Burleigh (1974) and Harkness (1975) have written convenient summaries of the practical aspects of carbon-14 dating. Waterbolk's (1971; revised version published in 1983) discussion of some of the problems involved in interpreting the radiocarbon data is fundamental.

[17]Of course, both long-lived and short-lived organic materials should be saved for other purposes, such as dendrochronological analysis of large wood and charcoal samples, and investigations of ancient dietary habits and environment through isotopic fractionation studies (Browman 1981: 268–79). Short-lived samples should also be saved for the time when accelerator systems are able to measure ^{14}C with sufficient precision to reduce the standard deviation to a fraction of what it is today. As for dendrochronology, although there is no tree-ring sequence yet for the Levant, it is important that samples possessing 50 or more rings be preserved for eventual correlation with a master sequence.

from Iron IB (ca. 1000–900 B.C.) or IIA (ca. 900–800 B.C.) contexts, or from a late LB IIB/early Iron IA destruction, since the resultant dates, even if derived from short-lived and well-stratified samples, will be superfluous at best.

2. *There should be a direct chronological relationship between the sample collected and the event to be dated.*

Abuse of this principle is commonplace in archaeology. It manifests itself most often in a failure to recognize that a piece of wood or charcoal will normally yield a determination older than the event being dated, and the difference in time between the age of the rings mesured and this event could be considerable (Coles and Jones 1975). The results obtained from such material can be extremely misleading, even when one is dealing with a large number of dates from a well-stratified site (e.g., Willkomm 1983). Because wood and charcoal exhibit this trait, short-lived materials are generally preferable for Bronze Age and more recent periods. Otherwise, as can be seen in the examples cited below, the radiocarbon results may provide little or no help in dating a particular event.

Hel-809, a sample of charred wood from Level VIII at Lachish (Ussishkin 1978: 90), comes from destruction debris assigned to the end of the Middle Bronze Age. The calibrated date for the sample is 1945–1675 B.C. This determination may well be accurate if it results from the measurement of the inner rings of an older tree, but because a date obtained from a wood architectural element (if that is what this sample derives from) can at best reflect the construction, rather than destruction, of a structure, it is irrelevant for estimating when the final Middle Bronze Age city at Lachish was destroyed. Moreover, the imprecision of the radiocarbon method vis-à-vis the archaeologically established chronology for the Middle Bronze Age and later periods means that any ^{14}C date, even if from a short-lived sample, will (as noted above) almost certainly have too wide a range to be of any archaeological value; hence there is little to be accomplished right now by submitting any radiocarbon samples from Middle or Late Bronze Age or Iron Age destruction debris.

GrN-4553, a piece of charred wood from a ceiling beam in the Late Bronze Age sanctuary at Deir ʿAllah (Vogel and Waterbolk 1967: 140), yielded a calibrated measurement of 1550–1360 B.C. This date is again valid only for the age of the tree-rings measured, and since there is no published information as to whether these rings originate in the inner or outer part of the trunk (the same is true for the Lachish sample), the precise significance of the determination for estimating even the time of the sanctuary's erection is uncertain. Since this assay has no significance for dating the destruction of the building, its citation—in an uncalibrated form, 1180 ± 60 B.C.—as providing "confirmation" for the destruction of the Deir ʿAllah sanctuary at ca. 1200 B.C. (T. Dothan 1982: 84, 94) is incorrect.[18] As with the Lachish sample, even short-lived material would not have provided an archaeologically useful result.

3. *The sample should come from a chronologically homogeneous deposit.*

Single-burial tombs and occupational floors on one-phase sites provide the optimum contexts for ^{14}C samples because they were in use for only a short period of time, and little difficulty exists in relating any given sample to the artifacts from the same locus. Conversely, trash pits, leveling and glacis fills, and most burial caves provide the worst samples because these deposits contain jumbled archaeological materials from several periods, and the radiocarbon samples generally cannot be related to the artifacts of any one period. Such a situation is unfortunate, since trash pits, for example, are among the best sources of datable materials (e.g., human and animal waste, charcoal, bones, uneaten food) on Near Eastern sites.

Four ^{14}C dates from Charnel House A 55 at Bab ed-Draʿ illustrate what can easily happen when samples are collected from mixed deposits (see Weinstein 1984). This large funerary structure was in use from EB II until its abandonment in early EB IV (Rast and Schaub 1978: 24). Three samples from A 55 (SI-2499, -2501, and -2874) were of charcoal, while the fourth (SI-2497) was a mixture of burned fabric, charcoal, and ash. The assays cover a wide range (2660–2530 B.C., 3365–2925 B.C., 3150–2895 B.C., and 2305–1905 B.C. respectively), but there is nothing inherently wrong with any of them. Since it is not known when any of the samples got into the charnel house, the chronological range of all of the archaeological materials in A 55 must be taken into account in evaluating these dates. In so doing, one could easily hypothesize that SI-2501 and -2874 predate A 55's construction or pertain to its initial use in EB II, SI-2499 relates to the tomb's EB III use-phase, and SI-2497 belongs to the EB IV phase. Such an interpretation may be entirely wrong, but there is nothing in the archaeological record to refute it.

A similar phenomenon can be seen in a date obtained from a piece of poplar wood found in the lower of two pre-Ghassulian levels at Tell

---

[18] Two other archaeological samples whose ^{14}C dates have similar chronological problems are: (1) a charcoal sample (GX-1718) from the late MB III destruction at Shechem, which yielded a date of 2000–1700 B.C. (Seger 1972: 31; Weinstein 1984); and (2) a piece of charred wood (Hel-1026) from Level III at Lachish, which gave a date of 1360–1030 B.C. (Ussishkin 1978: 90; Weinstein 1984). In an interesting study, Willkomm (1983) showed that the use of numerous wood and charcoal samples led to the systematic misdating of the stratified remains of a medieval German village.

Tsaf, a Jordan valley site located ca. 11 km south of Beth-shan. The measurement, 6125–5485 B.C. (RT-number unpublished), is too early for the Chalcolithic period, but the reported occurrence in this level of "Dark Faced Burnished Ware" along with a Chalcolithic flint industry (Gophna and Kislev 1979: 112–13) suggests a mixed Late Neolithic/ Early Chalcolithic assemblage. The ^{14}C date may therefore be connected with the Late Neolithic rather than Chalcolithic finds.[19] Unfortunately, there is no way to be sure, at least with the evidence at hand.

4. *Sources of sample contamination must be aggressively looked for.*

Sample integrity can be a real problem with radiocarbon materials from archaeological sites. Natural contaminants are not uncommon in such circumstances, and the excavator has to be diligent in searching them out. The most significant sources of natural contamination in the Near East probably are humic acids, modern rootlets, inorganic carbonates, bitumen, and animal dung. Contamination can also be created artificially if the excavator accidentally drops cigarette ash on a sample, packages the material improperly, or applies chemical preservatives to an artifact from which a ^{14}C sample is later taken.[20] Laboratories make every effort to decontaminate samples, but pretreatment is most successful when advance warning has been given that a contaminant is likely to be present.

Unless a contaminant has been identified on the site or in a laboratory, it is often hard to decide whether a particular ^{14}C date is anomalous because of sample contamination: there are too many other possible explanations for aberrant determinations, e.g., the statistical probability of error associated with every ^{14}C date, accidental mislabeling (e.g., K-1083 from Beidha; see Weinstein 1984: table 1), or even stratigraphic misassociation (e.g., Belfer-Cohen and Bar-Yosef 1982: 38). However,

[19] This hypothesis is based on the assumption that the Late Neolithic and Early Chalcolithic materials are indeed stratigraphically mixed. Andrew Moore (personal communication, 1983) has suggested to the writer that the red-slipped pottery at Tell Tsaf may be Late Neolithic II (= Pottery Neolithic B or Wadi Rabah phase) in date, while some of the painted ceramics could be comparable to the Late Neolithic-Early Chalcolithic material from ʿAin el-Jarba, Anati's Hazorea site, or possibly even Ghrubba.

[20] E.g., a measure of 6200 ± 300 B.C. (BM-2114) for a horse bone of Late Middle Bronze Age date from Tell el-ʿAjjul may be the result of the paraffin wax preservative on the bone not having been removed completely (Burleigh, Ambers, and Matthew 1984: 69). Also, grain found at Tell Siran inside a bronze bottle inscribed for Amminadab I gave a date (P-2207: 440–395 B.C.) ca. 200 years too recent for this Ammonite king (Fishman, Forbes, and Lawn 1977: 211). Although it is possible that the grain was put in the bottle during the Persian period (the bottle itself came from a mixed stratigraphic context; see Thompson 1973), it is equally likely that moisture and corrosion products inside the bottle contaminated the sample material (Thompson 1983; cf. Helbaek 1974).

since most contaminants contain younger carbon, one good indication is a well-stratified sample whose ^{14}C date is much too recent based on the archaeological evidence. To cite an extreme example, carbonized wood from the EB II Stratum I at Arad yielded a date of 805–380 B.C. (I-number unpublished: Aharoni 1964: 159; 1967: 238; Weinstein 1984: table 1). Perhaps this sample, which derives from a context close to the surface of the site, was contaminated by rootlets. Another inordinately low date is Lv-358, which comes from a sample of bones found in an Early Neolithic II (= Pre-Pottery Neolithic B) context at El-Khiam (Gilot 1970: 158). The assay, 1540–1010 B.C., again suggest the presence of a contaminant.

Contamination can affect entire series of dates. For example, the majority of the ^{14}C dates associated with the Palaeolithic caves of Amud, Kebara, and Tabun are extraordinarily low, oftentimes by tens of thousands of years (Weinstein 1984). These caves contain numerous possible sources of contamination, e.g., bat guano in Kebara Cave, roof collapse with subsequent inflow of water at Tabun Cave, and groundwater and alternating layers of humus and calcium carbonate at Amud Cave. Since even a small amount of contamination can have a significant impact on the date of an extremely old sample (because there is so little ^{14}C in the sample to start with), great care is needed in pretreating old samples whose environments are so unfavorable.

Many samples processed during the 1950s have unacceptably low ^{14}C dates, which must be evaluated with great care. Laboratory pretreatment was then in an early stage of development, and the contaminants present in many archaeological samples were not always completely removed (Waterbolk 1971: fig. 3, legend). For example, there are 22 Early Neolithic I (= Kenyon's Pre-Pottery Neolithic A) radiocarbon dates from Jericho (Burleigh 1981: 502-4; 1984; 762–63). The uncalibrated measurements for most of them fall within the period of ca. 7800–7200 B.C. However, four dates produced back in 1956, three from charcoal and one from humic extract, are consistently low: 6820 ± 150 B.C. (GL-39), 6740 ± 150 B.C. (GL-40), 6945 ± 150 B.C. (GL-43), and 5350 ± 200 B.C. (GL-46). For the succeeding Early Neolithic II (= Kenyon's Pre-Pottery Neolithic B) period, 18 of whose 21 dates range from ca. 7200 to 6600 B.C., there are three anomalously young assays, again produced in 1956: 6250 ± 200 B.C. (GL-28), 6440 ± 200 B.C. (GL-36), and 5850 ± 160 B.C. (Gl-38) (Burleigh 1981: 502).

5. *The amount of material collected for each sample should be in excess of the laboratory's minimum requirement.*

If possible, more material should be collected for each sample than the laboratory's minimum requirement. This will generally insure that the datable portion of the sample, i.e., the fraction remaining after pretreatment, will be adequate for the counting procedure. It also makes it possible for the dating facility to redate traditional portions of the same sample material if the first measurement appears to be aberrant.

Four dates from grain found in Stratum II at Early Bronze Age Arad illustrate the advantage of having enough sample material for replicate measurements (Fishman, Forbes, and Lawn 1977: 210–11). P-2054 (barley) and -2055 (wheat) yielded results of 3375–3135 B.C. and 3860–3650 B.C. respectively. Because these dates were so inconsistent, and the second sample was much too early for the EB II period, the Pennsylvania laboratory ran additional portions of the same samples. The new assays, 2970–2795 B.C. (P-2054A) and 2805–2545 B.C. (P-2109) respectively, are overlapping and generally supportive of the archaeologically expected date for EB II (though the lower limit of P-2109 is too recent).

6. *Wood and charcoal samples should be identified by species.*

Botanical analysis of wood and charcoal samples is an essential element in the radiocarbon dating process. Some Levantine woods such as poplar have a relatively short life-span, while others, such as oak, juniper, and cedar live for hundreds of years. Because of their excellent building properties, woods like cedar and oak were frequently employed in ancient Palestine for major architectural elements such as roof beams, columns, and door panels. Since cedar *(Cedrus libani)* in particular may possibly survive for a thousand years or more (Bryant Bannister, personal communication), a ^{14}C date from a piece of this wood could easily be hundreds of years earlier than the event that the archaeologist wishes to date.[21] Moreover, unless the excavator is fortunate enough to find a piece of wood that still contains the sapwood (the outmost rings) of a tree, which is unlikely to occur unless one is dealing with a tree trunk or large architectural piece (such as the roof truss fragment from the Monastery of St. Catherine dated as BM-1222: Burleigh and Matthews 1982: 164), there is little chance of estimating how many years separate the rings that were carbon-dated from the time when the tree was felled. It is therefore essential that all wood and charcoal samples be identified botanically in order to determine whether one is dealing with a relatively short-lived or long-lived species of wood.

---

[21] E.g., a cedar wood sample (Hel-1025; Ussishkin 1978: 90; Weinstein 1984) from Level II at Lachish has yielded a calibrated date of 1125–835 B.C. Another cedar wood sample from Lachish (Hel-1028:Ussishkin 1978:90; Weinstein 1984), derivng perhaps from door paneling in the 13th century B.C. temple in Level VI, has produced a date of 2000–1700 B.C.

7. *Samples should be collected in a series and, if they come from a stratified site, should be stratigraphically related.*

Single samples are to be avoided at all costs. Too many possibilities of a counting error or contamination by older or more recent carbon exist with any given sample to allow an archaeologist to trust a single determination as anything more than an approximate guide to the absolute date of a particular event. A single date requires additional support from archaeological or other sources before it can be given serious consideration.

Series of dates can be consistent or inconsistent. In the latter situation, one may be at a loss to decide whether some dates should be accepted and others rejected, or all dates should be disregarded. Three assays from charcoal samples found at different levels of a midden at the Harifian site of Abu Salem in the central Negeb form a remarkable little series (Buckley 1973: 296). The homogeneity of the dates—8020 ± 150 B.C. (I-5498), 8280 ± 150 B.C. (I-5499), and 8280 ± 150 B.C. (I-5500)— is extraordinary and adds weight to the argument based on archaeological grounds (Scott 1977) that the Harifian industry of the late Epipalaeolithic period overlaps with the beginning of the Neolithic era. On the other hand, in a miniseries of three dates from EB I tombs at Bab ed-Dra', the results are as heterogeneous as one could possibly imagine. Two samples of powdery wood from the transitional EB IA/B tomb A 100 produced one excellent date, 3545–3345 B.C. (SI-3310A) and one date two millennia too early (SI-3310B: 5480–5220 B.C.), while a powdery wood and ash sample from the EB IA tomb A 78 gave a "modern" reading (Weinstein 1984). An explanation for the chaotic nature of this collection of dates is not yet available.

Carbon-14 dates obtained from a stratified series of samples covering different phases of a single period can sometimes provide a reasonable estimate of the length of that period. For example, a series of seven EB III samples of charcoal from Trench III at Jericho (BM-548 to -554: Burleigh, Hewson, and Meeks 1977: 152–53; Weinstein 1984) yielded dates whose ranges cover the period from 2925 to 2305 B.C. The dates are, with one exception, internally consistent and support the archaeological evidence that EB III was an exceptionally long period in ancient Palestine. The one anomaly in the series is BM-554, which, although it derives from the stratigraphically latest sample in the series, gave a measurement of 2905–2760 B.C. Whether this date is out of line because of sample contamination, laboratory error, or the dating of the inner rings of an older tree is beyond our knowledge. However, the compatibility of the other assays with the stratigraphic succession of the samples allows us to discount BM-554 as possessing any significance for dating the end of the EB III period.

Sometimes apparently anomalous results in series of dates can be chronologically significant. In the case of some 13 radiocarbon dates from the Monastery of St. Catherine that were processed at the British Museum and University of Michigan laboratories (Weinstein 1984), nearly all were in agreement with a Byzantine dating of this monastery. Wood from two windows, however, gave results that are much too recent (M-1812: "modern" date; M-1814; A.D. 1630–1850). Such young measurements suggest that restoration work was carried out in those window areas in recent times.

Series of dates have other advantages over individual assays, e.g., the ability to yield statistically and archaeologically meaningful mathematical and graphic treatments.[22] Also, a series derived from both short-lived and long-lived samples may assist the excavator in determining whether any early measurements from long-lived samples are chronologically meaningful or are due to the dating of the inner rings of older trees or the reuse of older wood. Altogether, series of ^{14}C dates have much more value than isolated dates, and today few archaeologists make the mistake of submitting only one or two samples from a stratified site.

IV. PUBLICATION OF RADIOCARBON DATES

Most ^{14}C dates initially appear in *Radiocarbon*. This scientific periodical, which is published by the *American Journal of Science*, has served since 1959 as the principal medium for the dissemination of radiocarbon date-lists from laboratories around the world. Each archaeological entry in a laboratory's date-list is cited by its unique identifier and includes the sample material, radiocarbon age with standard error (the A.D./B.C. figure was formerly included as well, but this item was dropped in 1977), provenience and stratigraphic context, date of collection and name(s) of collector(s) and submitter(s), and appropriate references to the excavation from which the sample came. Brief comments on the significance of individual or related dates are frequently included. Since most of the stratigraphic and ceramic facts are reserved for more detailed publication in the excavator's final report, the archaeological information presented in *Radiocarbon* is kept to a minimum. This can have unfortunate consequences, since the archaeological details relating to about a third of all Palestinian ^{14}C dates never appear anywhere else, generally because the excavator fails to follow through with a final report on his or her site. Hence the limited information published in *Radiocarbon* is often all that other archaeologists and radiocarbon specialists ever

[22] For different methods of averaging and grouping ^{14}C dates, see Long and Rippeteau (1974); Ward and Wilson (1978); Wilson and Ward (1981). For ways of displaying dates in graphic form, see Waterbolk (1971); Ottaway (1973); Geyh and de Maret (1982).

get to see. It is therefore essential that an excavator work with the dating facility to insure that as much information as possible is inserted in the *Radiocarbon* entries regarding the provenience, context, and integrity of each sample, the reason the samples were submitted, and possible sources of contamination. This will enhance the value of the assays considerably, even if no final excavation report ever appears.

The basic rule in publishing radiocarbon dates anywhere is that the author should *always* provide the laboratory letter code and number for each date being discussed. Moreover, in all secondary citations of a ^{14}C date, a cross-reference should be given either to the original publication of the assay or to a reference where the original publication is cited. Because ^{14}C determinations are frequently published in places other than in *Radiocarbon,* it can take hours or even days to track down the archaeological and technical data relating to a given assay if the original publication is not cited in a secondary discussion.[23]

It is an unfortunate fact of archaeology that some radiocarbon dates do not get published at all. This situation arises most often when assays turn out to be incompatible with what an excavator believes the date(s) should be on scientific or stratigraphic grounds. It should go without saying that if a radiocarbon sample is worth collecting and processing, then the resultant assay should be published, even if it is in complete disagreement with the excavator's well-considered and archaeologically secure date. Wildly erroneous ^{14}C determinations can indicate the presence of contaminants not noticed at the site; mistakes in the collection, storage, or shipping of the samples; equipment problems in the dating facility; or errors in the archaeologist's analysis and interpretation of the data. By publishing supposedly "bad" dates, the archaeologist can help others to avoid similar difficulties with their own carbon-14 materials.

BIBLIOGRAPHY

Aharoni, Y.
1964   The Second Season of Excavation at Tel Arad (1963). *Yediot* 28: 153–75 (Hebrew).
1967   Excavations at Tel Arad: Preliminary Report on the Second Season, 1963. *IEJ* 17: 233–49.
Aitken, M. J.
1974   *Physics and Archaeology.* 2nd ed. Oxford: Clarendon.
Arnold, J. R.; and Libby, W. F.
1951   Radiocarbon Dates. *Science* 113: 111–20.

---

[23] Unfortunately, some radiocarbon laboratories do not publish date-lists on a regular basis. Bibliographical references to an individual assay from one of these dating facilities can be difficult to locate when a secondary publication fails to cite its source of information. Computerized data base systems (see e.g., Gulliksen 1983; Moffett and Webb 1983) will eventually simplify the task of collecting and retrieving ^{14}C dates considerably.

Baillie, M. G. L.
1982   *Tree-Ring Dating and Archaeology.* Chicago: University of Chicago.
Baillie, M. G. L.; and Pilcher, J. R.
1983   Some Observations on the High-Precision Calibration of Routine Dates. Pp. 51–63 in *Archaeology, Dendrochronology and the Radiocarbon Calibration Curve,* ed. B. S. Ottaway. Occasional Paper 9. Edinburgh: University of Edinburgh.
Bar-Yosef, O.
1981a   The Epi-Palaeolithic Complexes in the Southern Levant. Pp. 389–408 in *Préhistoire du Levant.* Colloques Internationaux du Centre National de la Recherche Scientifique 598. Paris: Centre National de la Recherche Scientifique.
1981b   The Pre-Pottery Neolithic Period in the Southern Levant. Pp. 555–69 in *Préhistoire du Levant.* Colloques Internationaux du Centre National de la Recherche Scientifique 598. Paris: Centre National de la Recherche Scientifique.
Baxter, M. S.
1983   An international tree ring replicate study. *PACT* 8: 123–32.
Belfer-Cohen, A.; and Bar-Yosef, O.
1981   The Aurignacian at Hayonim Cave. *Paléorient* 7/2: 19–42.
Bennett, C. L.
1979   Radiocarbon Dating with Accelerators. *American Scientist* 67: 450–57.
Braidwood, R.
1958   Near Eastern Prehistory. *Science* 127: 1419–30.
Broecker, W. S.; and Kulp, J. L.
1957   Lamont Natural Radiocarbon Measurements IV. *Science* 126: 1324–34.
Browman, D. L.
1981   Isotopic Discrimination and Correction Factors in Radiocarbon Dating. Pp. 241–95 in Vol. 4 of *Advances in Archaeological Method and Theory,* ed. M. B. Schiffer. New York: Academic.
Buckley, J.
1973   Isotopes' Radiocarbon Measurements X. *Radiocarbon* 15: 290–98.
Burleigh, R.
1974   Radiocarbon Dating: Some Practical Considerations for the Archaeologist. *Journal of Archaeological Science* 1: 69–87.
1981   Radiocarbon Dates. Pp. 501–4 in Vol. 3 of *Excavations at Jericho,* by K. M. Kenyon. London: BSAJ.
1984   Additional Radiocarbon Dates for Jericho (with an Assessment of all the Dates Obtained). Pp. 760–65 in Vol. 5 of *Excavations at Jericho,* by K. M. Kenyon and T. A. Holland. London: BSAJ.
Burleigh, R.; Ambers, J.; and Matthews, K.
1984   British Museum Natural Radiocarbon Measurements xvii. *Radiocarbon* 26:59–74.
Burleigh, R.; Hewson, A.; and Meeks, N.
1977   British Museum Natural Radiocarbon Measurements IX. *Radiocarbon* 19: 143–60.
Burleigh, R.; and Matthews, K.
1982   British Museum Natural Radiocarbon Measurements XIII. *Radiocarbon* 24: 151–70.

Callaway, J. A.; and Weinstein, J. M.
1977   Radiocarbon Dating of Palestine in the Early Bronze Age.
            BASOR 225: 1–16.
Clark, R. M.
1975   A Calibration Curve for Radiocarbon Dates. *Antiquity* 49: 251–
            66.
Coles, J.; and Jones, R. A.
1975   Timber and Radiocarbon Dates. *Antiquity* 49: 123–25.
Crowfoot, G. M.
1955   The Linen Textiles. Pp. 18–38 in *Discoveries in the Judaean Desert
            I: Qumran Cave I*, by D. Barthelemy and J. T. Milik. Oxford:
            Clarendon.
Deevey, E. S.; Flint, R. F.; and Rouse, I., eds.
1967   *Radiocarbon Measurements: Comprehensive Index, 1950–1965.* New
            Haven: American Journal of Science.
Dothan, M.
1956   Radioactive Examination of Archaeological Material from Is-
            rael. *IEJ* 6: 112–14.
Dothan, T.
1982   *The Philistines and Their Material Culture.* New Haven: Yale Uni-
            versity.
Eckstein, D.; Wrobel, S.; and Aniol, R.W .
1983   *Dendrochronology and Archaeology in Europe.* Mitteilungen der
            Budesforschungsanstalt für Forst- und Holzwirtschaft, Ham-
            burg 141. Hamburg: Max Wiedebusch.
Fishman, B.; Forbes, H.; and Lawn, B.
1977   University of Pennsylvania Radiocarbon Dates XIX. *Radiocar-
            bon* 19: 188–228.
Free, J. P.
1957   Radiocarbon Date of Iron Age Level at Dothan. *BASOR* 147:
            36–37.
Geyh, M. A.; and der Maret, P.
1982   Histogram evaluation of ^{14}C dates applied to the first complete
            Iron Age sequence from West Central Africa. *Archaeometry* 24:
            158–63.
Gillespie, R.; and Gowlett, J. A. J.
1983   Archaeological Sampling for the New Generation of Radiocar-
            bon Techniques. *Oxford Journal of Archaeology* 2: 379–82.
Gillespie, R.; Hedges, R. E. M.; and Wand, J. O.
1984   Radiocarbon Dating of Bone by Accelerator Mass Spectrometry.
            Journal of Archaeological Science 11: 165–70.
Gilot, E.
1970   Louvain Natural Radiocarbon Measurements VIII. *Radiocarbon*
            12: 156–60.
Godwin, H.
1962   Half-life of Radiocarbon. *Nature* 195: 984.
Boffer, Z.
1980   *Archaeological Chemistry: A Sourcebook on the Applications of Chemis-
            try to Archaeology.* Chemical Analysis 55: New York: Wiley.
Gophna, R.; and Kislev, M.
1979   Tel Saf (1977–1978). *RB* 86: 112–14.
Gulliksen, S.
1983   Radiocarbon Database: A Pilot Project. *Radiocarbon* 25: 661–66.

Harkness, D. D.
   1975   The Role of the Archaeologist in C-14 Age Measurement. Pp.
                 128–35 in *Radiocarbon: Calibration and Prehistory*, ed. T. Watkins.
                 Edinburgh: Edinburgh University.
   1983   High-Precision C14 Calibration: A Reconnaissance of the Ad-
                 vantages and Potential Dangers. Pp. 25–36 in *Archaeology,
                 Dendrochronology and the Radiocarbon Calibration Curve*, ed. B. S.
                 Ottaway. Occasional Paper 9. Edinburgh: University of Edin-
                 burgh.
Hedges, R. E. M.
   1981   Radiocarbon dating with an accelerator: review and preview.
                 Archaeometry 23: 3–18.
   1983   14C Dating by the Accelerator Technique. *PACT* 8: 165–75.
Helbaek, H.
   1974   Grain from the Tell Siran Bronze Bottle. *ADAJ* 19: 167–68.
Henry, D. O.
   1983   Adaptive Evolution within the Epipalaeolithic of the Near East.
                 Pp. 99–160 in Vol. 3 of *Advances in World Archaeology*, eds. F.
                 Wendorf and A. E. Close. New York: Academic.
Henry, D. O., and Servello, A. F.
   1974   Compendium of Carbon-14 Determinations Derived from
                 Near Eastern Prehistoric Deposits. *Paleorient* 2: 19–44.
Kenyon, K. M.
   1956   Jericho and its Setting in Near Eastern Prehistory. *Antiquity* 30:
                 184–95
Kinnes, J., et al.
   1982   Radiocarbon Dating and Archaeological Research Policy. *Antiq-
                 uity* 56: 209–12.
Klein, J., et al.
   1982   Calibration of Radiocarbon Dates: Tables Based on the Con-
                 sensus Data of the Workshop on Calibrating the Radiocarbon
                 Time Scale. *Radiocarbon* 24:103–50.
Lee, J. R.
   1976   The Correction of Carbon-14 for the Pre-Urban ("Chal-
                 colithic") Period. Paper delivered at the Fourth Archaeological
                 Conference in Israel, March 17–18, 1976.
Levy, T. E. and Alon, D.
   1985   Shiqmim: A Chalcolithic Village and Mortuary Centre in the
                 Northern Negev. *Paléorient* 11: 71–83.
Libby, W. F.
   1951   Radiocarbon Dates, II. *Science* 114: 291-96.
   1954   Chicago Radiocarbon Dates V. *Science* 120: 733–42.
Long, A.; and Rippeteau, B.
   1974   Testing Contemporaneity and Averaging Radiocarbon Dates.
                 Am Ant 39: 205–15.
Mellaart, J.
   1979   Egyptian and Near Eastern Chronology: A Dilemma? *Antiquity*
                 53: 6–18
Michels, J.
   1973   *Dating Methods in Archaeology*. New York: Seminar.
Moffett, J. C., and Webb, R. E.
   1983   Database Management Systems, Radiocarbon and Archaeology.
                 Radiocarbon 25: 667–68.

Olsson, I. U.
1974   Some problems in connection with the evaluation of C^{14} dates. *Geologiska Föreningens i Stockholm Förhandlingar* 96: 311–20.
1979   The Importance of the Pretreatment of Wood and Charcoal Samples. Pp. 135–46 in *Radiocarbon Dating*, eds. R. Berger and H. E. Suess. Berkeley: University of California.

Ottaway, B.
1973   Dispersion diagrams: A new approach to the display of carbon-14 dates. *Archaeometry* 15: 5–12.

Ottaway, B. S., ed.
1983   *Archaeology, Dendrochronology and the Radiocarbon Calibration Curve*. Occasional Paper 9. Edinburgh: University of Edinburgh.

Pearson, G. W.
1979   Precise ^{14}C measurement by liquid scintillation counting. *Radiocarbon* 21: 1–21.

Pearson, G. W.; and Baillie, M. G. L.
1983   High-Precision ^{14}C Measurement of Irish Oaks to Show the Natural Atmospheric ^{14}C Variations of the AD Time Period. *Radiocarbon* 25: 187–96.

Pearson, G. W.; Pilcher, J. R.; and Baillie, M. G. L.
1983   High-Precision ^{14}C Measurement of Irish Oaks to Show the Natural ^{14}C Variations from 200 BC to 4000 BC. *Radiocarbon* 25: 179–86.

Pilcher, J. R., et al.
1984   A 7,272-year tree-ring chronology for western Europe. *Nature* 312: 150–52.

Ralph, E. K.
1971   Carbon-14 Dating. Pp. 1–48 in *Dating Techniques for the Archaeologist*, eds. H. N. Michael and E. K. Ralph. Cambridge: MIT.

Ralph, E. K.; Michael, H. N.; and Han, M. C.
1973   Radiocarbon Dates and Reality. *MASCA Newsletter* 9, No. 1.

Rast, W. E.; and Schaub, R. T.
1978   A Preliminary Report of Excavations at Bâb edh-Dhrâ^c. *AASOR* 43: 1–32.

Reed, W. L.
1957   A Recent Analysis of Grain from Ancient Dibon in Moab. *BASOR* 146: 6–10.

Rubin, M.; and Suess, H. E.
1956   U. S. Geological Survey Radiocarbon Dates III. *Science* 123: 442–48.

Scott, E. M.; Baxter, M. S.; and Aitchison, T. C.
1983 ^{14}C Dating Reproducibility: Evidence from a Combined Experimental and Statistical Programme. *PACT* 8: 133–45.

Scott, T. R.
1977   The Harifian of the Central Negev. Pp. 271–322 in Vol. 2 of *Prehistory and Paleoenvironments in the Central Negev, Israel*, ed. A. E. Marks. Dallas: Southern Methodist University.

Seger, J. D.
1972   Shechem Field XIII, 1969. *BASOR* 205: 20–35.

Sellers, O. R.
1951a   Date of Cloth from the ʿAin Feshka Cave. *BA* 14: 29.

1951b   Radiocarbon Dating of Cloth from the ʿAin Feshka Cave. *BASOR* 123: 24–26.

Stuiver, M.
1982   A High-Precision Calibration of the AD Radiocarbon Time Scale. *Radiocarbon* 24: 1–26.

Suess, H. E.
1970   Bristlecone-pine calibration of the radiocarbon time-scale 5200 B.C. to the present. Pp. 303–11 in *Radiocarbon Variations and Absolute Dating*, ed. I. U. Olsson. New York: Wiley.
1979   A Calibration Table for Conventional Radiocarbon Dates. Pp. 777–84 in *Radiocarbon Dating*, eds. R. Berger and H. E. Suess. Berkeley: University of California.

Tans, P. P.; and Mook, W. G.
1979   Design, Construction, and Calibration of a High Accuracy Carbon-14 Counting Set Up. *Radiocarbon* 21: 22–40.

Taylor, R. E.
1978   Radiocarbon Dating: An Archaeological Perspective. Pp. 33–69 in *Archaeological Chemistry—II*, ed. G. F. Carter. Advances in Chemistry Series 171. Washington, D.C.: American Chemical Society.

Taylor, R. E., et al.
1984   Radiocarbon Dating by Particle Accelerators: An Archaeological Perspective. Pp. 333–56 in *Archaeological Chemistry—III*, ed. J. B. Lambert. Advances in Chemistry Series 205. Washington, D.C.: American Chemical Society.

Thompson, H. O.
1975   1973
            The Excavations of Tell Siran (1972). *ADAJ* 18: 5–14.
1983   The Tell Siran Bottle: An Additional Note. *BASOR* 249: 87–89.

Ussishkin, D.
1978   Excavations at Tel Lachish—1973–77, Preliminary Report. *TA* 5: 1–97.
1983   Excavations at Tel Lachish 1978–1983: Second Preliminary Report. *TA* 10: 97–175.

Valla, F. R.
1975   *Le Natoufien: une culture préhistorique en Palestine.* Cahiers de la Revue Biblique 15. Paris: Gabalda.

Vogel, J. C.; and Waterbolk, H. T.
1967   Gronigen Radiocarbon Dates VII. *Radiocarbon* 9: 107–55.

de Vries, H.; and Waterbolk, H. T.
1958   Groningen Radiocarbon Dates III. *Science* 128: 1550–56.

Wand, J. O.; Gillespie, R.; and Hedges, R. E. M.
1984   Sample Preparation for Accelerator-based Radiocarbon Dating. *Journal of Archaeological Science* 11: 159–63.

Ward, G. K.; and Wilson, S. R.
1978   Procedures for Comparing and Combining Radiocarbon Determinations: a Critique. *Archaeometry* 20: 19–31.

Waterbolk, H. T.
1971   Working with Radiocarbon Dates. *Proceedings of the Prehistoric Society* 37, part 2: 15–33.
1983   Ten Guidelines for the Archaeological Interpretation of Radiocarbon Dates. *PACT* 8: 57–70.

Watkins, T.
1983   The Archaeological Application of High-Precision Radiocarbon
        Dating. Pp. 74–82 in *Archaeology, Dendrochronology and the
        Radiocarbon Calibration Curve*, ed. B. S. Ottaway. Occasional Pa-
        per 9. Edinburgh: University of Edinburgh.
Weinstein, J.
1980   Palestinian Radiocarbon Dating: A Reply to James Mellaart.
        Antiquity 54: 21–24.
1984   Radiocarbon Dating in the Southern Levant. *Radiocarbon* 26:
        297–366.
Wilkomm, H.
1983   The Reliability of Archaeologic Interpretation of [14]C Dates.
        Radiocarbon 25: 645–46.
Wilson, S. R.; and Ward, G. K.
1981   Evaluation and Clustering of Radiocarbon Age Determinations:
        Procedures and Paradigms. *Archaeometry* 23: 19–39.
Zeuner, F. E.
1956   The Radiocarbon Age of Jericho. *Antiquity* 30: 195–97.

13
PALYNOLOGY

Avraham Horowitz
Tel Aviv University

I. INTRODUCTION

Palynology (from παλυνος, Greek, meaning "dust") is a rather new branch of the natural sciences, and its extensive application to archaeology is only a matter of recent years. The discipline pertains mainly to pollen grains ("pollen" means originally "fine flour" and signifies the substance; therefore, it should not be used in the plural), but it also deals with some other microscopic fossils and organisms that remain in an analyzed sample after the extraction of the pollen. These are of lesser value to archaeology and will not be dealt with in the present context. However, this essay will deal with the wider meaning of "pollen," which includes spores.

Palynology is divided into three distinct categories:

1. Study of the pollen grains, their anatomy, physiology and functions in the plant's life. This branch will be entirely left to botanists.

2. Study of fossil pollen grains in geologically younger deposits, in which the pollen could be traced to their parent plants and therefore represent the actual vegetation. This branch is called "Quaternary Palynology," and here lies the real interest of archaeologists.

3. Study of fossil grains which are too old to be allocated with certainty to any known plants, most of which are now extinct. This branch of palynology will be left to geologists, stratigraphers and other specialists.

It should be noted that palynology has a role in allergiology, honey production, and many other fields.

In the discipline of archaeology, the intelligent use of palynological techniques can yield useful information regarding palaeoclimates, natural vegetation, agriculture, and other aspects of the natural environment. The study of a sequence of sites in an area could yield information about changing climatic conditions and environments. In recent years, archaeologists have also become aware of the possibility of following the reverse, namely, the influence of human activity on the environment.

The present account will mainly deal with two points: a general discussion of palynology is a necessary background for any archaeologist who would attempt to make use of it, and several case studies that illustrate palynology's value in archaeology. Since the application of palynology to archaeological studies is a recent development, no doubt the examples are far from representing all the possibilities; future collaboration will certainly produce additional results.

II. THE POLLEN GRAIN

The pollen grain is the male sperm cell of the plant and is formed by a complex process in the anther, which is part of the male flower or the male part of bisexual flowers. Some male flowers consist only of anthers, while other flowers have petals and other organs. The process is more or less similar in the flowering plants, angiosperms, and gymnosperms which have no real flowers to speak of, like the conifers and others. Some palynologists refer to the pollen of gymnosperms as "prepollen," since they are not produced by a real flower, the prefix "pre" designating the fact that these plants appeared earlier in the geological record.

Spores, produced by cryptogamous plants, such as ferns and moss, are not sperm cells, but rather the distribution units of these plants. The spores germinate and grow a prothalim; it is during this stage in the life of cryptogamous plants that sex organs are produced.

Both pollen grains (including of course the "prepollen") and spores have their role in palynology, because of two virtues they have in common: both are produced in great quantities and dispersed by the vegetation, although for different reasons, and both can be preserved in sediments, recovered, and identified, thereby providing evidence of their parent plants. Therefore, the term "Pollen Analysis" normally includes both pollen and spores as parts of almost any palynological study.

Both pollen and spores are made of two major parts: (1) the internal protoplasm, which is the living matter and is so important in the plant's life; (2) the shell, which is the only part that gets fossilized and is so important in palynological research. This essay will not deal with the protoplasm, however interesting it may be.

The shell of pollen grains and spores is made of one of the most resistant natural organic substances, called sporopollenin. This substance is resistant to almost all acids and many bases, except for oxidation. This fact enables the pollen and spores to become fossilized quite easily in almost any kind of soil or rock, except for those that are highly oxidized. Oxidation can occur in two cases: (1) while soil or sediment is deposited, in which case the preservation of pollen is rare; (2) in outcrops, which could be remedied by digging further or sampling a drillhole. The resistivity of pollen and spores to almost any chemical makes their recovery from samples quite simple, since all other matter can be dissolved with strong reagents.

Both pollen and spores fall within the size range of tens of microns, mostly in the range of 20–80; this makes it very easy to observe them under an ordinary microscope. A good quality microscope is necessary for detailed and extended palynological studies. Most types of pollen and spores shells bear many structural and morphological characteristics, and every plant species produces its own pollen or spore with respect to shape, size, and ornamentation. Fig. 1 gives some examples of the different morphologies of various grains. When more details are necessary for the study of a grain, the scanning electron microscope comes into the picture, but this apparatus can only show the external features of the grain. The transmitted light of an ordinary microscope can show both the external details and cross sections in the shell, which are sometimes indispensable for identification. Although the photographs taken by a scanning electron microscope are much more impressive than those taken by the ordinary microscope (compare the samples in Fig. 1), the routine work is almost always done with a light microscope. Indeed, careful work with the latter gives no less information on the morphology of the grains and much more on the shell's structure. Counting the grains, a standard procedure in any palynological study, is much more easily done under the light microscope.

III. DISPERSION

Pollen and spores are produced in great quantities by plants and, when ripe, they are discharged for dispersion. Pollen grains have to arrive at the female organs of the plants and fertilize them to make seeds, which again have to be dispersed to propagate the plants. With the ferns it is somewhat simpler; the only stage of dispersion is that of the spores. Dispersion is accomplished through three main agents; insects (and rarely other animals like hummingbirds), winds, and water. Insect-pollinated plants mostly produce smaller quantities of pollen, and some of them are specially adapted to the insect on which they depend for pollination. Fortunately for palynologists, most of the insect-pollinated plants produce little pollen, and this sticks to the insects and never comes to the soil and sediments; consequently they do not have to include these pollen types in their studies. One of the rare exceptions to this rule is the case where a digging bee or wasp chooses to lay its eggs in an archaeological site. However, some of the insect-pollinated plants (e.g., eucalyptus and olive trees) produce rather large quantities of pollen grains, and these pollen do appear in the soil and sediments and need to be examined.

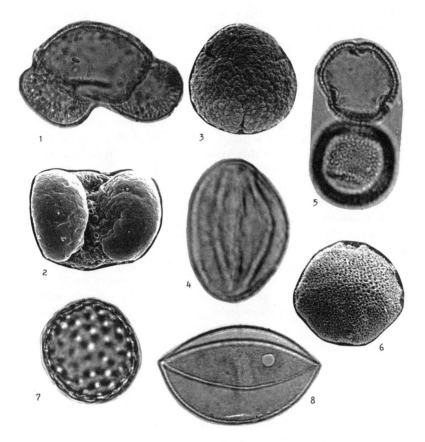

FIG. 1:   *Microphotographs of some pollen grains from Israel, taken from the*
reference collection. Scanning Electron photographs by Mr. M. Dvorachek, Geo-
logical Survey of Israel, Jerusalem.
1. *Pine* (Pinus halepensis), *length 70 micron.*
2. *Same as 1, SEM.*
3. *Oak* (Quercus ithaburensis), *length 45 micron (SEM).*
4. *Evergreen oak* (Quercus calliprinos), *length 35 micron.*
5. *Olive* (Olea europaea), *length ca. 30 micron, in two different foci.*
6. *Pistachio* (Pistacia atlantica), *length 38 micron (SEM).*
7. *Goosefoot* (Chenopodium album), *diameter 52 micron.*
8. *Cereal, length ca. 80 micron.*

The wind-pollinated plants are by far the most important contributors to the pollen spectra of terrestrial sediments, which constitute the bulk of samples collected during archaeological research. It should be noted, though, that each species produces a different amount of pollen per individual plant. Therefore, the pollen count in a sample needs to be corrected so that the palynologist can see the true relationships of the various plant species within the surrounding vegetation. Another complication is that different pollen types travel in different ways. Some pollen is rather heavy and travels only short distances, while other pollen is lighter, like most conifers' pollen which is equipped with air bladders that aid transport in the winds. As a result, plants which have heavier pollen would be represented only if they grew near the site, while those with lighter pollen might be represented even if they grew far away.

Pollen and spores carried by water, such as streams, rivers, and sea currents, can be divided into two groups: (1) those which are initially discharged into the water which is their means of dispersal, like many fern and moss spores or true water plants; (2) those which discharge their pollen initially into the air. A considerable amount of pollen from this latter group could reach the water by rain and air movements and then be carried by the water, sometimes to a rather distant place in which it is deposited. This group, naturally, is less important in the study of most archaeological sites, but it could be of great importance when analyzing lakeshore sites or when inferring from a sediment core the general environmental conditions.

Following its transport, a portion of the pollen is deposited and embedded within the site's sediments. Most of the pollen which arrives at a site is deposited from the winds, and indeed there is a never-ending pollen rain almost everywhere around the world. The major question in analyzing an archaeological site, in fact any deposit, is the ratio between the quantities of sediment and pollen in a given sample. The failure to recognize this fact hindered the application of pollen analysis to archaeology for years.

When pollen analysis began in northwestern Europe, pollen grains were traditionally recovered from peat bogs. Peat is rich in pollen and spores, because it is an organic sediment composed mainly of plant remains. Most of the western European peat bogs are in heavily forested areas, where the amount of dust in the air is negligible. As a result, the ratio of pollen versus sediment in peat bogs is very high (most of these trees are wind pollinated and produce large quantities of pollen), and pollen analysts in Europe used to collect very small samples to obtain acceptable pollen spectra, in the order of one gram or less. In archaeological sites, and especially in the Levant, the picture is quite different: the amount of dust carried by the wind is considerable, while the amount of pollen is rather small because of the scarce vegetation in this region.

Consequently, when one takes only a gram of sediment, one hardly finds any pollen. Indeed, investigators who applied the traditional techniques to extract pollen from archaeological sites failed, for the most part, and it was believed that Near Eastern sites were unacceptable for palynological research. A group of palynologists from the southwestern United States, who would not give up so easily, developed extraction techniques in which the sample used was in the order of 200–300 grams, and indeed succeeded in obtaining acceptable pollen spectra. These techniques have been further refined, and treatment of samples in the order of 2–3 kilograms is not a rare procedure in the laboratory. As a result, almost any sample proved to yield pollen spectra sufficient for study.

After the pollen grains have been deposited and embedded in the soil or sediment, they become fossilized. Normally this process does not involve any change in the grain, and grains are preserved as their original chemical substance, sporopollenin, for any length of time. Pollen grains and spores have been recovered from sedimentary rocks that date to the appearance of plants on the earth. Spores maintaining their chemical characteristics have been recovered from strata as early as the beginning of the Middle Precambrian era. However, not all pollen grains and spores are equally preserved in the sediments, and several species of plants which produce large quantities of airborne pollen are known to be almost absent from the fossil pollen spectra. One of the examples in our region is pollen of pistachio, which is very common in the airborne pollen spectra but very rare in the sediments.

The pollen and spore content of a sample would therefore depend on several factors:

    Mode of pollination (wind-pollinated plants are best represented);

    Amount of pollen produced by each plant;

    Ability of each kind of pollen to be transported;

    Differential preservation of different pollen and spores;

    Quantitative ratio of pollen and spores versus sediment.

The result is that the pollen spectrum does not represent a one-to-one correspondence between pollen and ancient vegetation, since the pollen spectrum results from a complexity of intervening factors.

IV. METHODOLOGY

Any regional palynological study, even when finally focused on a single site, should include four procedures to be of significance:

1. A working knowledge of the pollen grains and spores occurring in the region. This is done by collecting pollen and spores from the actual plants that are common to the region and preparing a reference collection. This procedure could, of course, make use of herbarium specimens. The reference collection should be as complete as possible,

and it should be studied in detail. Failing to do so would result in identifications on a family level, which could be of some importance, but much of the information would be lost.

2. A thorough study of the recent pollen and sediment transport and deposition processes. This is done by collecting recent sediment samples from many localities and comparing the pollen spectra with the actual vegetation, wind directions and, where applicable, river courses and sea currents. Palynologists have discovered that the study of air-borne pollen, trapped on sticky glass, is of lesser importance because of differential preservation. Many pollen types which encompass a considerable part of the airborne spectrum do not appear at all in the sediments and soils.

3. A detailed study of several sediment cores, deposited continuously in several localities in the region under investigation; it is preferable to have cores that were deposited in somewhat different environments (e.g., cores drilled in lake sediments, marshes, loess accumulations, and marine sediments). The cores should extend in time from the present day down to layers older than the sites that will be studied. The cores should then be dated. Apparently, the best dating method as far as archaeology is concerned remains radiocarbon dating. It is also essential to date all samples collected with the same method, and preferably in the same laboratory.

4. An analysis of samples from the archaeological site itself. Collection of the samples should be done with care to prevent any possibility of contamination by recent pollen. This is done by sampling only freshly cut outcrops, using clean tools, and sealing the samples in plastic bags or jars, accurately marked. But the most important consideration is the choice of samples; the main concern is the exact stratigraphic location of the samples. This presents some problems; for instance, if a sample is taken from a layer covering a floor, is it known exactly how long it took to accumulate? A hundred years difference, which is not much for sediment accumulation, may cause us to analyze a period of devastation instead of a period of settlement.

Palynologists learned quite recently that the best material suitable for pollen analysis on archaeological sites is mudbricks that have not been burned, either when they were prepared or as as result of later fires. Mudbricks are very common in most sites and are expendable; their stratigraphic context is usually clear. Pollen samples from mudbricks are easily obtained. One could arrive at most sites even after the excavation was finished and collect a decent sample by simply cleaning some of the remaining brick walls. This makes life easy for the interested archaeologists, and the situation is even better in terms of palynology. We learned by observing people who still make mudbricks in the Levant, Africa, Mexico and the Far East that they all use more or less similar methods. A mud pool is prepared at the end of the rainy season, and the bricks are cut and left to dry. In most cases the end of the rainy season is also the flowering season, and the rain water which is used to make the mud contains a substantial amount of contemporaneous pollen. When the mudbricks are dried, they are completely sealed against further contamination; consequently, the pollen spectra recovered from mudbricks have a definite stratigraphic context.

The mudbricks are also very easy to prepare for the pollen analysis, because they are made of silty sediments. The pollen grains are relatively well preserved since, in most cases, the dry sealing protects against oxidation, and there is practically no limit to the amount available for experiments and repetitions, if these are found necessary.

Preparation of the samples for pollen analysis involves several stages: dissolving the cement material of the sample, eliminating all remains of minerals, getting rid of the organic material which is not pollen, and mounting the sample on glass slides for transmitted light microscope examination (or on aluminum stubs for the scanning electron microscope).

Since pollen grains are acid resistant, most palynologists tend to use a variety of strong acids in their analyses. We found out that this method is time-consuming, expensive, and must be done with great care, since some of the acids may be fatal (e.g., hydrofluoric acid used to dissolve silicates). Furthermore, some of the pollen can be destroyed by the acids. Consequently, a method which makes use of very little acid was developed in our laboratory; it saves time, money, labor, and pollen grains. This method involves dissolving the carbonates in hydrochloric acid and spinning the material in a centrifuge. The differential settling allows for the removal of the coarser grains. Then the organic material is floated in a heavy liquid. The pollen and spores are separated by differential sieving, a process that removes most of the other organic substances. The pollen is mounted in glycerin jelly and sealed with paraffin. Almost any amount of material can thus be treated and the results are impressive; many sites for a long time considered barren (in both archaeological and prehistoric periods) yielded rich pollen spectra.

The slides are then put under the microscope, pollen grains are identified and counted, the results are plotted, and the pollen spectrum is compared for discussion and conclusions. Ideally, the pollen should be counted until at least 200 grains are identified and recorded. This number is accepted by many investigators as a reliable basis for statistical treatment. However, experience shows that sometimes this number is difficult to achieve, and approximately 100 grains still form a good basis. Once again, this sampling number is part of traditional palynology. In Western Europe and North America, where forests are widespread, it is customary to count samples until one has at least 150 arboreal pollen.

This comprises a good basis for determining the composition of the forest. In the Levant however, where forests are rarely the major element in a vegetation natural environment, the total number of counted pollen could be smaller and still represent well the composition of the flora. In fact, several plant groups which have similar environmental demands can be grouped together. Thus, the total number of variables is relatively small, and less pollen is required to obtain a relevant meaning.

Presentation of the palynological results is also somewhat different in the Levant and other desert border areas. There is hardly any point in making a separate arboreal pollen diagram, since sometimes these grains are so rare or even totally absent that their significance is minimal. We tend to present the pollen spectra of archaeological sites in our region as percentages of the constituents of the total number of identified and counted grains.

The next stage is to define the environmental groups that are best represented and relate them to a specific problem. For example, if the general climatic conditions are of interest, we would compare the distribution of arboreal versus non-arboreal pollen (see Fig. 2). Other environmental groups could be set apart and compared (e.g., desert vegetation, steppe vegetation, water plants, and marsh vegetation).

Since we are dealing with human settlements, special emphasis is placed on pollen grains of cultivated plants, which can sometimes form a considerable part of the spectrum. These could be of two types: first, plants that have been cultivated (e.g., cereals), whose pollen is different from the pollen of their wild ancestors; second, plants which grow wild in the region and are only planted in or around the site (e.g., cypress and pine). There is no way to differentiate their pollen from those of the wild trees, but abnormal concentrations would give a clue. For instance, if we know from pollen diagrams of continuous drillholes in the region that a particular pollen type occupies a certain part of the natural spectrum, and samples from a site are much richer in this pollen type, it gives us a clue for possible planting. A problem arises sometimes with cultivated plants whose pollen cannot be differentiated from pollen of wild plants of the same or closely related species. Such problems occur with olives, cherub, rosaceous fruit trees, leguminosase and others, and here it is only our judgment, based on what we know from the natural conditions, that can help. This is also a situation in which palaeobotanical analyses of the site can yield valuable information. In some other cases plants are not really cultivated, but a large amount of a certain type is collected in the wild and stored in the site, like some of the Malvaceae. Once again, abnormally high percentages of "strange" or "exotic" plants call for an explanation.

Another group of pollen grains usually found in archaeological sites

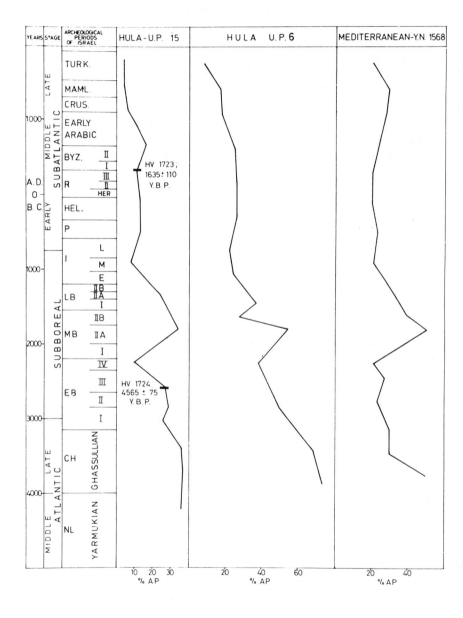

FIG. 2   *Percentages of arboreal pollen grains from three boreholes, which serve as good indications of water availability for plant life in the Mediterranean domain. The curves are correlated according to radiocarbon datings with the important archaeological cultures.*

are those originating from the ruderal flora. The flora includes plants which are essentially of no use to humans, and some of them are troublesome weeds. Occurrences of pollen from ruderal plants only indicate the phase of settlement of a site, and their total absence from analyzed site-samples may indicate that those have not been collected properly. The most important family of these plants is the Chenopodiaceae; the presence of their pollen should not be given too much environmental significance, since in nature they occur almost always in saline conditions.

An occurrence quite common to pollen spectra recovered from archaeological sites is the appearance of pollen lumps. These are groups of pollen, all of which derived from the same species and apparently even the same plant. Lumps can sometimes comprise tens of pollen grains sticking together; they seem to have originated in plants that grew in the immediate vicinity of the soil or sediment accumulation. When pollen grains are ripe and leave their parent plant they are usually covered with an oily, sticky substance. The grains cannot travel in large groups for any considerable distance, and they break apart quite soon. Consequently, the occurrence of pollen lumps is regarded as an indication that the plants grew very close to the sampling site. This may sometimes be a useful piece of information.

V. CASE STUDY—ISRAEL

Palynological studies of archaeological sites in Israel are at present in a preliminary state. The first three stages in the process are complete: (1) accumulation of a reference collection, (2) analysis of present-day depositional processes (and the relationship of recent pollen spectra to the vegetation and transporting agents), and (3) analysis of dated sediment cores. We are now ready to refine the boreholes analyses and datings, together with the routine analyses of archaeological sites. This is all done at the Palynology Wing of the Archeometric Laboratory of the Institute of Archaeology, Tel Aviv University, in collaboration with other institutions.

The amount of work that remains is incredible, since human habitation is known in Israel almost continuously for the last million years or so. The study is divided into two major parts: first, a more general investigation of the Quaternary period and the prehistoric settlements; second, a more detailed study of the last 10,000 years since the beginning and development of agriculture. The state of the art is fully presented, up to 1978, in *The Quaternary of Israel*, Chapter 6 (Horowitz 1979), but there has been some advance since then.

Recent Pollen Spectra

The distribution of the natural constituents in recent pollen spectra over Israel is rather consistent, as seen from analyses of recent sediments and soils. The arboreal pollen is dominated by oak in the north, with some occurrences of other Mediterranean elements (e.g., olive, cypress, and pistachio pollen). The percentage of arboreal pollen within the total spectrum decreases gradually southwards, until in the central and southern Negeb it is not encountered at all. In the northern Negeb the arboreal pollen comprises only 2–5 percent of the total. This picture changes in the Jordan Valley, where arboreal pollen is some 15 percent to the north, increasing up to 25–30 percent to the south, in the Dead Sea region. This phenomenon is a combined result of the poor vegetation cover in the south and the considerable transport of pollen by northern winds. Arboreal pollen is much better distributed by the wind, and the results are its better representation in regions poor in natural vegetation. Pollen of Mediterranean trees, even cedars from the Lebanon, are represented as far south as the Bay of Elath (in recent sediments), hundreds of kilometers from their provenance. Other effects of wind transport can also be seen in the distribution of pine versus oak pollen. Pine pollen is better represented in the coastal plain, where it arrives with the eastern winds that prevail in the region during its flowering season, while oak grains are much better represented in the Jordan Valley, where they are carried with western winds. Here we could see the influence of local winds during different flowering seasons (see detailed discussion by Weinstein, in Horowitz, 1979). Another contribution of the winds was found in considerable amounts of desert elements brought by dust storms, such as Chenopodiaceae and *Artemisia* pollen deposited all over the country, with percentages decreasing to the north. This contribution is quite important in archaeological sites, where most of the sediment arriving and covering the site is of an aeolian origin. Long distance transportation of pollen, which is of less importance to archaeology, is encountered in the marine sediments, both of the Mediterranean and the Bay of Elath, which include pollen grains and spores brought by the Nile and sea curents from Tropical Africa.

It seems that oak is the most important pollen when drawing conclusions as to the climate and vegetation cover of the northern part of Israel. Indeed, the arboreal vs. non-arboreal pollen ratio seems to be the best climatic indication in the Mediterranean domain. To the south, in the Negeb and Sinai, where arboreal pollen is rare, the environmental conclusions should be drawn according to the distribution of pollen of non-arboreal origin. This poses a problem of accuracy, since most of the non-arboreal pollen cannot be classified more specifically than to the family level. Different plants of the same family can grow in different environments, and in this case only the prominent distribution could be taken as representative. There is also a time lag in the response of the flora to climatic change: the first phase of a climatic amelioration in the desert would result in a much better distribution of the desert elements, only later to be followed by other plants of different environmental significance.

Care should also be taken while drawing environmental conclusions based on Mediterranean arboreal pollen recovered from archaeological sites, since some of the Mediterranean trees have been planted (e.g., olives and cyrpess). Therefore, the oak pollen is a much more reliable source of information, as it was never found to be planted by humans.

Another important issue related to the distribution of pollen in recent sediments concerns the validity of conclusions drawn from a drillhole. Since the recent pollen spectra are quite uniform over a considerable area, a sequence recovered from a drillhole is reliable for the entire region. Proof for that assumption was found while analyzing drillhole cores from various parts of Israel (Fig. 2) which yielded almost identical results.

Continuous Sequences

We shall discuss briefly the Pleistocene sequence but more attention will be given to the last 6000 years of occupation.

When *The Quaternary of Israel* (Horowitz 1979) was written, we did not have a continuous pollen diagram for the entire period, and the information came from piecing together fragmentary evidence from many boreholes and outcrops that had been palynologically analyzed during the last 20 years or so. Only recently have we completed pollen analysis of two deep boreholes from the Huleh Valley and the Dead Sea Basin, both of which span the entire Quaternary. The conclusions drawn from these continuous pollen diagrams (Horowitz 1982a; 1982b) seem to corroborate the picture presented earlier (Horowitz 1979), a picture of alternating pluvial and interpluvial climates through the Glacial Pleistocene. Human habitation took place in Israel as early as the beginning of the Glacial Pleistocene and, until the end of this period some 12,000 years ago, it was entirely dependent on the natural conditions. The pluvial climates, of which four major phases are known, were the result of a shift in the present day climatic belts of the Levant some 200–300 km southwards; this allowed for the occupation of the entire area of Israel, sometimes even considerable parts of Sinai. High percentages of oak pollen were recovered from prehistoric sites as far south as southern Sinai. In general, the pollen spectra demonstrated that whenever climatic conditions ameliorated, prehistoric occupation was pushed more to the south, while during the dry interpluvials people inhabited only the northern part of the country, sometimes being pushed north to the Lebanon and Syria. This simple pattern of prehistoric occupation of Israel which emerged from pollen analyses enabled us to predict the location of and find many other sites, thereby increasing our knowledge of the prehistory of Israel and adjacent areas.

This rather basic pattern was somewhat changed at the beginning of the Holocene some 12,000 years ago, when agriculture and husbandry enabled settlement in areas which were just on the borderline of occupational zones in earlier times. Neolithic and Chalcolithic sites are less dependent on the natural vegetation and fauna, and in general their pollen spectra show quite poor environments, especially in the south of Israel and in Sinai. Such environments could not supply enough food in earlier periods, but the ever-increasing quantity of pollen grains of cultivated plants prove that those people began to take some active control of their natural surroundings. The difference between the prehistoric and protohistoric settlement pattern of Israel is quite striking then. During the interpluvials, prehistoric people almost deserted this region and lived far to the north, while during the last interpluvial, the Holocene, with the development of agriculture, people remained in this area and culture flourished. The slight climatic oscillations found during the Holocene explain some northward and southward movements during several phases of the protohistoric settlement (see detailed discussion in Chapter 8 of Horowitz 1979).

Detailed pollen analyses of several cores covering the last 6000 years, of which only the arboreal versus non-arboreal pollen ratios are presented in Fig. 2, indicate that climatic oscillations have occurred through the period. Plotting these oscillations against the settlement pattern of Israel allows us to see the influence of environment on the habitation in the various periods; it also gives some information concerning the influence of people, both direct and indirect, on the natural surroundings. A detailed discussion of the subject is presented by Gophna in Chapter 8 of Horowitz 1979.

The Ghassulian Chalcolithic culture flourished in Israel during the fourth millennium B.C. and enjoyed the warm and humid climate of the Atlantic stage, in mid-Holocene times. The pollen spectra indicate that the natural Mediterranean forest was widespread, and pollen analyses of sites show oak pollen in the Negeb and even in southern Sinai. The result of this optimal climate was the spreading of great numbers of large and small settlements all over the country. The inhabitants cultivated the soil, but to a great extent they were seminomadic shepherds of sheep, goats, and cattle. Settlements of this period were very abundant in the northwestern Negeb, and the Beer-sheba—Arad loess regions, which are presently semiarid, were then the most densely populated areas of Israel. Less extensive habitation is known from other lowland regions of Israel, and there are few settlements in the mountainous areas. We try to explain this pattern by the flourishing of the Mediterranean forest in the higher regions, which prevented their exploitation for pasture.

The Early Bronze occupation of Israel occurred during the third millennium B.C., when the high arboreal pollen percentages of the preceding Atlantic stage began to decrease; the modern-day percentage was reached towards the end of the third millennium B.C. This probably caused some northward shift of Early Bronze people, but here palynology serves to show that the shift in economy and lifestyle between the seminomadic Chalcolithic and the large Early Bronze agricultural villages and towns is primarily of a cultural nature. No change observed in the natural environments could be responsible for such an abrupt and essential difference. Indeed, the agricultural techniques established in the Early Bronze people continued in the Levant until almost the present day. The "break" between the Early and the Middle-Late Bronze Ages could well be the result of a deteriorating climate recorded at the end of the Early Bronze Age by a sharp decrease of arboreal pollen. The population also changed because of the worsening climate, and the intrusion of nomadic tribes, which are known to have invaded the country at this time.

During the Middle Bronze Age, the climate became favorable once again, and settlements flourished in the country. A slow deterioration began in the Late Bronze Age, but at the beginning of the Iron Age Israel was still regarded as a country "of milk and honey." The further deterioration, which is so clearly marked in the pollen diagrams, forced the people to develop new agricultural techniques to cope with the environment, and the great development of this time was terrace cultivation. This technique, which quickly spread around the entire region, enabled farmers to make use of the soil in hilly areas and to conserve what little rain there was. The terraces also prevented soil erosion, which became an acute problem in the dry climate.

Thus we can see that the environmental information indicated by pollen analyses of continuous cores and drillholes could clarify some important points in the settlement pattern of Israel through the protohistoric and historic periods. It should be noted, though, that we are still in a preliminary stage of our knowledge and are now analyzing more sequences from different regions, establishing a much more detailed and reliable radiometric time scale, and studying the sections in much more detail, mainly by closer sampling intervals.

VI. POLLEN ANALYSIS OF ARCHAEOLOGICAL SITES—SOME SPECIFIC PROBLEMS

One of the more serious problems confronting both archaeologists and palynologists who seek to apply pollen analysis techniques in excavations is the interpretation of the results. In the general environment (as opposed to the site), vegetation and climate in the time of occupation could better be studied in sediment cores which should, of course, be appropriately dated. The main difficulty is that a site could hardly ever yield a complete continuous sequence, which is essential for studying the natural environment. Human activities (e.g., fire, deforestation, pasturage, plant introduction, and the local development of ruderal vegetation) help to mask the natural environment. Samples collected from archaeological sites should therefore be regarded primarily as sources of knowledge about the sites themselves, not the environment in general.

Another point which an archaeologist should bear in mind when submitting samples collected from a site is the importance of a sample which represents the present-day conditions. Preferably, several such samples should be submitted. These are not always the best representatives of the present-day conditions, since human interference also plays a role here. This is, however, an indispensable source of information and a relatively good point of reference.

As stated above, mudbricks are probably the best source of reliable pollen spectra in an archaeological site. If by good luck people in the vicinity still make them, one of the modern mudbricks would serve as a good reference for the recent pollen spectrum. Since oxidation destroys pollen grains, sediments and soils in which oxidation has occurred are to be avoided. This applies mainly to layers, burnt horizons and, in general, reddish or yellowish colored soil or sediment samples. Another sort of sample should be avoided, though it is sometimes tempting to collect: a sample exceedingly rich in organic material. The excess organic matter, which is very hard to get rid of during a standard preparation procedure, would most probably mask the pollen grains in the slide. It would probably be possible to eliminate most of the organic masking substances by complex chemical treatment, but there is a good chance that one would also destroy some or most of the pollen grains in the process.

Pollen analyses of samples from archaeological sites are a good source for knowledge of agriculture. The oldest site to yield cereal pollen is Rosh Horesha in the western central Negeb. The culture is late Natufian, and the radiocarbon 11,140 B.C. ± 200 (Bar Yosef 1980; Horowitz 1979). The pollen spectrum is:

Arboreal pollen (total 9.5%):
Juniperus—3%
Pinus alepensis—2%
Pistacia—2%
Olea europaea—1%
Acacia—1%
Non-arboreal pollen (total 90.5%):
Cereals—6%
Gramineae and Cyperaceae—56%
Chenopodiaceae—19%
Compositae—5%

Occurrences of *Ephedra, Atemisia,* Malvacae and Cruciferae.
For comparison, the recent pollen spectrum from this area is:
Gramineae and Cyperaceae—91%
Chenopodiaceae—6%
Papilionaceae—2%
Occurrences of *Zygophyllum, Artemisia* and Compositae.

A comparison of the late Natufian and the recent spectra, besides the interesting cereal pollen, shows almost 10 percent arboreal pollen at the site; this indicates a much better rain regime than at present, with no arboreal pollen at all. It is impossible to say whether the olive was already planted at the site or grew wild. Only a comparison of sediments of similar age and not connected to habitation in the same area could give a clue, but such analysis has not yet been done. This is just an example; in fact, cereal pollen is quite common in almost any archaeological site anlayzed.

A sample collected from the Chalcolithic site of Tell Zaaf in the Beth-shan Valley by Gophna yielded as much as 23 percent cereal pollen; a pre-Pottery Neolithic site in southern Sinai, Nebi Salah B, excavated by Beit-Arieh, yielded 12 percent cereal pollen. Cereal pollen were found in many Iron Age sites, like Beer-sheba, Lachish, Ai, Masos, and Tel ʿIra

The olive was probably cultivated at many sites. Drori (1979) found their pollen in abundance in the Middle Bronze, Late Bronze and Iron Age mudbricks from Tell Lachish. Baruch, according to communication with the writer, found a considerable peak of olive pollen in sediments of similar age from Lake Kinneret. Pollen of rosaceous fruit trees, probably almonds, was recovered from the Iron Age layers at Beer-sheba, Masos, and other sites.

Cypress was probably planted at least in two sites—Masos, where it takes up 24 percent of the Iron Age I spectrum, and Ganei Hataʿarukha, where it comprises 40 percent of proto-Urban samples and 48 percent of the MB IIA. Pollen grains of Malvaceae were found in abundance in the Iron Age samples from Masos (14 percent) and Beer-sheba (9 percent). These pollen are rather large and heavy and never travel far, so their provenence must be close. They could have grown on the site itself, but I tend to doubt it. It seems that these pollen were brought to the site when the Malvaceae plants were collected in the vicinity and then brought for storage. This is done also by present-day bedouins of the northern Negeb, who collect *Malva nicaeensis* during the flowering season, dry the plants at home, and keep them the year round for use in soups or as a cooked vegetable.

Pollen analysis could be used also with respect to other problems arising in excavation, such as determining the contents of jars. A sample of black, asphalt-like substance was found in one of the jars excavated at the Roman site of En Bokeq, near the Dead Sea. The material was dissolved, and the pollen spectrum comprised grains of a wide variety of wild flowers; this clearly indicated that the substance was honey. The black lining of large jars from another Roman site, Caesarea, was found to contain pollen of the grapevine together with large amounts of wild yeast. Here is proof that the jars were used to store wine. However, the pollen spectra were also very rich in pine grains, an indication that pine resin was used to line the jars. Pine resin, because of the considerable amount of phenol it holds, serves as a preserving agent for wine, seals the ceramic jars, and even adds to the taste of wine. In other words, it seems that those jars held retsina, which is still widely used in Greece today.

BIBLIOGRAPHY

Bar-Yosef, O.
1981   The Epi-Palaeolithic Complexes in the Southern Levant. Pp. 389–408 in *Préhistoire du Levant*. Colloques Internationaux du Centre National de la Recerche Scientifique 598. Paris: Centre National de la Recerche Scientifique.
Butzer, K. W.
1971   *Environment and Archaeology*, 2nd ed. Chicago: Aldine.
Dimbeby, G. W.
1985   *The Palynology of Archaeological Sites*. Orlando, FL: Academic.
Drori, I.
1979   *Tell Lachish: Subsistence and Natural Environments in the Middle Bronze, Late Bronze and Iron Age*. Unpublished M.A. thesis, Tel Aviv University (Hebrew).
Evans, J. G.
1978   *An Introduction to Environmental Archaeology*. Ithaca, NY: Cornell.
Faegri, K., and Iversen, J.
1964   *Textbook of Pollen Analysis*. Copenhagen: Munksgaard.
Horowitz, A.
1979   *The Quaternary of Israel*. New York: Academic.
1982a   Palynostratigraphy of Notera 3 borehole. Unpublished report.
1982b   Palynostratigraphy of Amazyahu 1 borehole. Unpublished report.

14
REMOTE SENSING

THOMAS L. SEVER

National Space Technology Laboratories

I. FOREWORD

I was surprised. Dr. Joseph Callaway had driven to the National
Space Technology Laboratories on the Mississippi coast with his wife,
Sarah, to learn about advanced remote sensing capabilities, particularly
about how the capabilities could be applied to archæological research. I
say surprised, because for three years I had been trying to communicate
the potential of remote sensing in archæology and had met with minimal success. After Callaway's visit it would be different. I did not know at
the time that this scholar, respected for his thorough excavation and
research, was also a visionary who gazed upon the technological horizon.
In the twilight dark of the computer building, I displayed hundreds of
visual representations that were generated through the combination of
sophisticated imaging systems and computer intelligence. What he saw
on the television-like screen seemed to confirm his suspicions: there was
a wealth of research capability and archæologists were simply unaware
of it. Eventually he would invite me to make presentations in Atlanta and
Dallas at the ASOR meetings. He would also put me in contact with
leading Middle Eastern archæologists such as Dr. Joe Seger who would
be the first to incorporate advanced remote sensing analysis into his
research design. Later on, things blossomed when several prominent
archæologists became involved in applying NASA's remote sensing
technology to archæology. But it all began in a Mississippi swamp in
1982 where NASA tests its Space Shuttle engines. Whatever success
remote sensing will have in the field of archæology is attributable in
large measure to Callaway's vision. This chapter is a non-intensive discussion of the fundamentals and capabilities of the evolving field of
remote sensing—a field which holds great potential for the discipline of
archæology.

II. REMOTE SENSING: A TOOL FOR ARCHAEOLOGICAL RESEARCH

Remote sensing technology may represent the kind of scientific breakthrough for archaeology in the second half of the 20th century that radiocarbon dating was in the first half of the century. The potential that remote sensing, combined with advanced computer analysis, holds for the study of prehistoric cultures is at present beyond measure. Advances in the field are now occurring at a phenomenal rate as satellite systems of increasing capability are launched into orbit. It is clear, at least, that basic archaeological survey will be radically altered in the future by remote sensing, and interdisciplinary programs of broader scope are now possible. In time, remote sensing could prove to be the most important benefit of humanity's giant venture into space.

The rapid advancement of remote sensing technology promises to provide reliable and inexpensive information that can be employed for intensive archaeological and ethnographic investigations. While archaeologists have employed remote sensing analysis in the form of aerial photography and ground-based instruments in the past, they remain relatively unfamiliar with the state of the art technology that is now opening the doors to new frontiers in archaeological investigation. This newer remote sensing technology received little attention with its inception in the mid 1960s. Today, articles and news releases abound, while organizations such as the National Aeronautics and Space Adminisration (NASA) have libraries of research reports on remote sensing. While the average archaeologist is only vaguely familiar with the concept of remote sensing, its application is creating the potential for a revolution in many areas of prehistoric research.

Many archaeological sites are hidden six inches to five feet below the surface, while others manifest themselves by soil discoloration, prolific vegetation growth, or spatial anomalies against homogeneous land cover patterns. Because of their characteristics, archaeological features often elude ground survey methodologies. For instance, in a region suspected of prehistoric habitation, traditional survey requires that exploratory trenches be dug which cover only a small percentage of the total area, thereby reducing the chance of discovery. Remote sensing promises to improve this methodology by rendering baseline understanding of the study area before expensive survey and excavation strategies are initiated. This a priori knowledge is of major importance in a scientific discipline which destroys its own data. Based on the cultural features under investigation and the environment in which they occur, remote sensing instruments covering a broad range of the electromagnetic spectrum offer unlimited possibilities for archaeological research. While remote sensing technology is only in the pioneering stages for archaeology, it promises to become a fundamental part of its scientific methodology in the future.

Remote sensing instruments, collectively referred to as sensors, are able to detect information in wavelengths of the electromagnetic spectrum which cannot be detected by the human eye or by conventional photography. These sensors are mounted on satellites, the space shuttle, and aircraft. The data collected by these instruments are recorded in a numeric format and stored on magnetic tape. The numeric data can then be analyzed with the aid of sophisticated computer software and processed to create images which can be reviewed on a computer screen.

The relationship of an ancient society to its environment is an important aspect in the study of prehistory. How a culture interacted with its environment not only tells us much about the culture itself, but also has ramifications in understanding modern-day society. Researchers are interested in the surface cover of the prehistoric landscape, the hydrology, routes of travel, the mineral resources that were available, the optimum locations for settlement, and other information relative to human activity. In the past this information has been acquired through expensive and time-consuming surveys performed over several field seasons and painstakingly analyzed in the laboratory.

Recent remote sensing instrumentation can provide information both about the surface cover of a large region and the precise location of various types of resources. Anomalies can be detected in the digital imagery which can be attributed to subsurface cultural remains, even when the anomalies are not visible from ground level. The digital surface cover imagery can be combined with other ancillary data such as topography, soils, and meteorological information to form a data base. This information can be interactively processed to understand the relationships between the various planes of data. The combination of the archaeological ground truth information with the data base can be used to construct predictive models for settlement and activity. For example, by taking the known locations of prehistoric sites and placing their coordinates into the data base, it is possible to extract the physical variables that typify each site. In this way, one may learn that the sites are located between 300 m to 800 m above sea level, on slopes between 2° and 5°, with aspects ranging from 160° to 210°, on a specific type of soil, within 100 m to 300 m of a stream of a specific water carrying capacity. From this information a map can be produced which outlines all the other potential areas in a region which fulfill these characteristics. This predictive model can subsequently be verified through ground survey and archaeological excavation.

Before 1972, archaeologists were basically limited to the use of black-and-white, color, and color infrared (CIR) aerial photography which assisted them in the detection, examination, and recording of sites. While black-and-white or color film provides the greatest capability in terms of versatility and high resolution of detail, they nevertheless possess certain liabilities. For instance, they are limited to seeing only what the human eye can see. In order to produce an optimum product, the camera must operate in daylight, during clear weather, on days with minimal atmospheric haze.

Colored infrared (CIR) film has improved upon the eye's visible range by detecting wavelengths beyond the red end of the light spectrum. Initially employed during World War II to differentiate artificially camouflaged objects, CIR can be successfully used in studies dealing with vegetational differences. It is subject, however, to the limitations indigenous to conventional camera systems.

While photographic systems are the most common types of sensor systems used in archaeological remote sensing investigations to date, they cannot obtain information about the thermal characteristics (temperature and emissivity) of vegetation, soil, and water on the earth's surface. Remote sensors, on the other hand, are capable of simultaneously collecting data in the visible, infrared, and thermal portions of the electromagnetic spectrum.

Aerial photography was first used for archaeological interpretation in England by J. E. Capper who published an aerial image of Stonehenge in 1907. Better known, however, were the combined efforts of Leonard Woolley, T. E. Lawrence, and S. F. Newcombe during the 1914 Sinai expedition. British archaeologists working as photographic interpreters during World War I discovered that archaeological features manifested themselves as "features of long-obliterated structures in the terrain, soil formations, and vegetative cover . . . that are either invisible or easily overlooked in surface reconnaissance." Moreover, "some features, invisible to the eye at any angle, may be recorded for study by the use of special combinations of films and light filters", and overlapping photographs produce stereoscopic vision so that even the slightest undulation produced by surface remains may be accurately measured and described (Schorr 1974:163).

The importance of aerial photography increased and was employed in many investigations that were undertaken in both the tropical rain forests and highland deserts of Middle and South America (Ford and Willey 1949; Johnson and Platt 1930; Kosok 1965; Schaedel 1951; Shippee 1933; and Willey 1959). Other areas of investigation included the location of campsites in the Arctic (Harp 1974), Middle Age sites in England (St. Joseph 1966), and ruins in Chaco Canyon (Lyons 1976; Lyons and Avery 1977; Lyons and Hitchcock 1977; Lyons and Ebert 1978; and Lyons and Mathien 1980).

After the launch of the first Landsat satellite in 1972, many new uses were made of the remotely sensed digital data which acquired information beyond the visible portions of the electromagnetic spectrum. Applications of Landsat imagery were employed to study agrarian systems in Niger and Upper Volta (Reining 1973; 1974a; 1974b), population data and migration practices of the Sonrai in West Africa (Reining 1973), and Navajo ethnological factors in New Mexico (Fanale 1978). The 80-m resolution, however, limited the application to large scale analysis and empirically based sampling designs.

Improved remote sensing instruments with greater resolution and more precise bandwidths are now opening the doors to new frontiers in archæological investigations. These instruments, whether from aerial or space platforms, are just beginning to receive recognition within the archæological community. An investigation utilizing L-band radar data found indications of ridged field systems in the Belize and Peten areas of the Yucatan (Adams, Brown, and Culbert 1981) which have revised notions regarding Maya subsistence economy. Through the detection of prehistoric subsurface river systems, another investigation using Shuttle Imaging Radar (SIR-A) data has made a dramatic contribution to archæology by discovering the existence of prehistoric man who occupied the Sudanese desert around 200,000 B.C. (Elachi 1982) (fig. 1). In Chaco Canyon, New Mexico, remote sensing was employed to record and prioritize the area for archæological survey and analysis, detect a number of features resulting from prehistoric occupation and, more particularly, to determine the location of prehistoric roadways (fig. 2). This was the first application of digital thermal infrared multispectral data in detecting archæological phenomena which were not visible in the simultaneously acquired CIR photography (Sever 1983). Remotely sensed data has also successfully detected both historic and prehistoric features at Poverty Point, Louisiana (Gibson 1984) (fig. 3).

A few other projects have made use of the recent remote sensing technology, but in general the technology, until recently, has had little impact on the discipline of archæology. Since 1983, however, a number of steps have been taken to incorporate the new technology into archæological methodology. A small committee created by the united action of all the national archæological organizations met with Dr. S. G. Tilfod, Director of NASA's Earth Science and Application Division and other representatives of NASA in December, 1983. The purpose of this meeting was to explore the possibilities of expanding research activities in the field of archæology to bring together NASA's remote sensing technology with the expertise of the archæology community in cooperative studies.

As a result of the meeting, NASA agreed to fund the remote sensing analysis of a few research projects. In addition, a Conference entitled "Conference on Remote Sensing: Potential for the Future" was held on March 1 and 2, 1984, at the Earth Resources Laboratory (ERL) located at

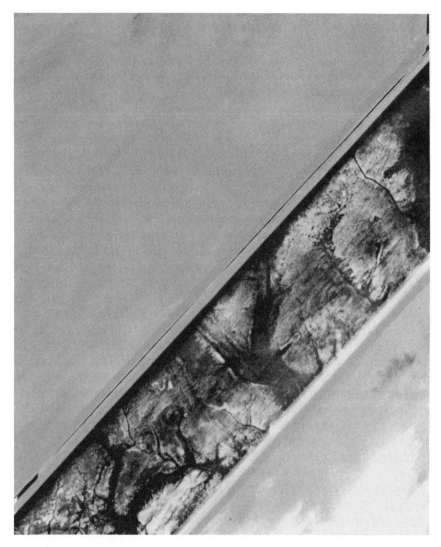

FIG. 1   *Prehistoric riverbeds buried beneath the sands of the Sahara as detected by SIR-A*

FIG. 2   *Pseudocolor composite image used to detect the location of prehistoric roadways in Chaco Canyon, New Mexico*

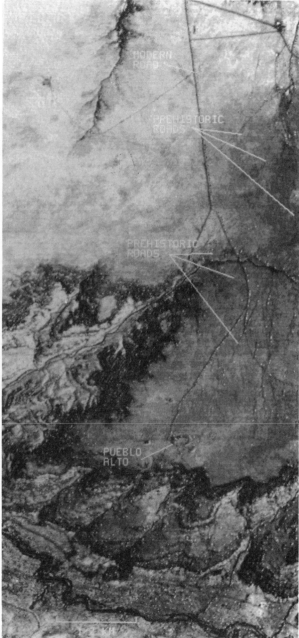

HACO CANYON, NEW MEXICO
rchaeological Investigation

Pseudocolor composite image from TIMS high-pass filtered data, low-pass filtered data, and raw Channel 3 (9.0–9.4 micrometers) data, assigned to the blue, green, and red colors, respectively. The TIMS data were acquired at 5-meter resolution in August 1982. This image reveals prehistoric roads in Chaco Canyon, New Mexico, which were constructed by the Anasazi culture around 900 A.D. Although these prehistoric roads are not visible from ground level, they demonstrate the ability of high-pass filters to extract information along one axis of an image using digital data.

◄ *Chaco Canyon National Monument*
  • *Santa Fe*
  ● *Albuquerque*

NEW MEXICO

Prehistoric Road Detection

FIG. 3   *Remote sensing used to detect historic and prehistoric features at Poverty Point, Louisiana*

the National Space Technology Laboratories (NSTL), Mississippi. Twenty-two archaeologists representing the major professional institutions in the United States convened to learn of the current capabilities in remote sensing technology and to discuss a policy that would serve as a guide for the immediate future of remote sensing in archaeology. The results of the Conference have been published in a final report (Sever and Wiseman 1985).

III. THE ELECTROMAGNETIC SPECTRUM

All materials in the universe at temperatures above absolute zero ($-270°C$) produce electromagnetic radiation in the form of waves. The electromagnetic spectrum is a continuum of electric and magnetic wavelengths that extend from the short cosmic rays of high frequency to long radio waves of low frequency at the other end. The limits of the electromagnetic spectrum are not known below the cosmic waves or above the radio waves (fig. 4).

While the limits of the electromagnetic spectrum may lie at infinity, the known portions of the spectrum have been divided into various sections which are referred to as the ultraviolet, visible, near infrared, thermal, microwave, etc. If the known span of the electromagnetic spectrum were conceived of as being analogous to the circumference of the earth, the human eye and conventional film would be able to see only that portion of it that is equal to the diameter of a pencil.

While humans are relatively blind to their universe, they are now constructing instruments which can see objects or phenomena in the various regions of the electromagnetic spectrum. By the use of computer algorithms, the information seen in those select portions of the spectrum can be transferred to the visible regions for analysis and interpretation. In this way, information such as plant disease can be detected long before the disease manifests itself to the human eye. Similarly, archaeological phenomena, such as the location of prehistoric agricultural fields, may be detected because of soil moisture or chemical composition, even though the fields are not visible from either ground level or aerial photography. Using remote sensing technology, the archaeologist can now see features and patterns that the eyes cannot see.

IV. DIGITAL DATA AND PIXELS

As opposed to photography where images are exposed onto film and processed chemically, remotely sensed images are recorded in a digital or numeric format and processed electronically by the use of various computer algorithms. A typical scanner system, whether from a satellite or airborne platform, collects energy from the earth's surface and passes

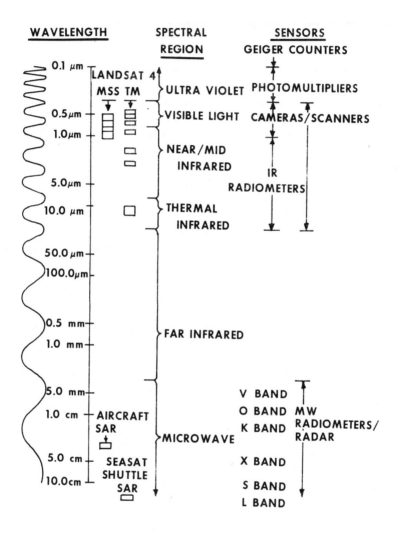

FIG. 4   *Diagram of the Electromagnetic Spectrum*

the energy through an optical system. This incoming energy is spectrally dispersed and optically focused on various detectors that are sensitive to various portions of the electromagnetic spectrum. The smallest area that a sensor can detect is called a resolution element or pixel (picture element).

Depending on the sensor's design, an element can range dramatically in size. For instance, the Advanced Very High Resolution Radiometer (AVHRR) satellite has a 1-km resolution, while the MOMS airborne sensor produces a 1-foot resolution.

As the platform passes above the landscape, the ground surface is scanned in successive strips or scan lines. Each scan line is composed of a row of elements with the energy of each element having been individually measured and assigned a digital brightness value between 0 and 255 (256 total) by each detector.

Brightness values range from dark (0) to bright (255) because there are eight binary bits in a byte. The system is related to the base 2 numerically; therefore, $2^8 = 256$. The energy received by each detector varies in signal strength as each pixel of the landscape varies in character. The composite of all elements and scan lines renders an image similar to a photo. Thus, if a scanner system has 15 different detectors, each resolution element on the ground is "seen" 15 different ways. Each of the 15 different detectors therefore produces its own image which is sensitive to a special region of the electromagnetic spectrum. In this way, images are constructed that would normally be beyond the range of human vision.

The human eye can discriminate only about 20 to 30 shades of gray under normal viewing situations. Under the same conditions, it can discriminate a much larger number of color hues. Since remote sensing instruments can gather up to 256 shades of gray in numeric format for each channel of its detection array, literally thousands of pieces of gray scale information are available for analysis. The same numeric data from a scanner system can be combined to produce millions of color hues of which the human eye can only separate a small proportion. In short, there is more information available than the investigator can "see," however, electronic manipulation of the data allows investigators to extract much of the information in a form that can be visualized.

The objective of digital image analysis is to identify features or areas of interest in an image. In this regard, numeric data are essential in obtaining accurate quantitative information. Computer manipulation of the data can selectively extract features of interest from the total area, increase or decrease emphasis of the selected features, determine their spectral signatures, and examine data characteristics not immediately visible in the imagery. Sophisticated computer analysis techniques have been developed to analyze both single channel and multichannel data sets. The images can be viewed on a television-like computer screen to enhance the image and to diagnose the information. The image can then be photographed in black-and-white or in color to produce photographic prints, slides, or maps.

The use of techniques designed to analyze signal channel data is straightforward and simple. These techniques enhance an image in order to illustrate features within the data that are of special interest to the investigator. Some of these enhancement techniques include sun-angle correction, density slicing, band ratioing, edge enhancement, synthetic color assignment, and filtering. These techniques can be used to minimize the effects of scattered wavelengths of radiation in the atmosphere. They can also be employed to determine the edge or boundary of a specific feature as well as to isolate linear and curvilinear patterns.

Techniques which draw from more data, however, are capable of yielding better information. Thus multichannel analysis can often provide greater investigative capability by combining several different bands of data into one multispectral image. In this manner, abstract images can be processed into one classified image to accentuate features of interest that can be more readily interpreted by the specialist and non-specialist alike.

Multichannel analysis is based upon the fact that a given pixel is perfectly registered spatially on the ground in the matrices of all the other spectral channels. The brightness value of each pixel varies from channel to channel and consequently produces a spectral signature. By definition, a spectral signature is a quantitative measurement of the properties of an object at one or several wavelength intervals. Thus all the pixels of water in an image will have similar spectral signatures and differ from all the pixels of vegetation. The signatures can be more discriminantly analyzed to separate the water into pond water, lake water, or river water; the vegetation into forests, grasslands, or agricultural fields. The analysis can continue by breaking the agricultural fields into wheat, soybeans, or corn. Finally, extensive analysis can even break the corn into various stages of maturity. The finer analysis techniques require more computer processing time and are subsequently more expensive. In addition, finer analysis techniques are dependent upon such factors as computer hardware and software available to the investigator, the type of sensor data being analyzed, season of the year and time of day for data acquisition, the atmospheric haze conditions, and even the wind conditions upon the ground surface.

In the classified image, spectral signatures are developed to produce various "classes" of information. In the classification technique, each pixel or group of pixels (depending on the window size selected by the investigator) is analyzed and assigned a spectral signature. Homogeneous signatures are grouped in various categories that are referred to as spectral "classes." By assigning a different color for each class, an image is produced that represents different types of ground information, e.g., water, forest, urban complex. The development of numeric data in an image format not only allows for a visual representation of the results of analysis; it also provides the investigator with easy access to the acreages, percentages, and correlation of the features within the image.

V. LANDSAT

Since 1972, Landsat satellites have been collecting data over the earth's surface. These unmanned satellites are in nearly polar, sun-synchronous orbits at an altitude of 920 km. They circle the earth every 103.3 minutes (14 times a day), with each successive path occurring 26° to the west. The Landsat paths are at azimuths of about 191° measured from true north. After 252 orbits, or every 18 days, Landsat passes over the same place on earth. Because Landsat 1 and 2 were 180° in an oppositional phase, every place on earth came under a Landsat vehicle every 9 days. The data acquired by Landsats 1, 2, and 3 are at an 80-m resolution.

The Landsat vehicles are solar panel-studded space observatories, each weighing 953 kilograms (2,100 lbs.). Each satellite has a height of 3 m and a width of about 4 m when the solar cells, which provide the power source for the mechanical systems, are extended. The Multispectral Scanner (MSS), the primary sensor aboard Landsat, provides a continuous series of images of 185-km-wide sections of the earth's surface. The MSS measures reflected sunlight from objects on earth in the following four wavelength bands: 0.5 to 0.6 micrometer (green), 0.6 to 0.7 micrometer (red), and 0.7 to 0.8 and 0.8 to 1.1 micrometers (both near-infrared). Values of radiance are recorded in each of these four bands for every surface picture element scanned, and they collectively comprise a multispectral data set which is the basis for analysis.

Each target produces its own characteristic spectral signature because of the different materials of which it is composed. Green vegetation reflects more green light than red light, it also reflects heavily in the near infrared. Dry soils reflect more radiation in the red, while moist soils reflect less in all bands because of the absorption properties of water. Water absorbs all wavelengths of light and thus there is no return to the sensor which records a 0 count value or a black feature on the MSS image. The four radiance values for each pixel are used to develop statistics input to a maximum likelihood classifier. The resulting classes are labeled and integrated into a surface cover category classification. The accuracy of this classification is verified through photographic interpretation and ground truth missions.

Although each MSS band produces images which are of value in themselves, the classified image produces the optimum interpretation of surface cover features. Band 4 of the Landsat is particularly useful in the analysis of water characteristics whose depth and turbidity affect the reflectance signal. Band 5 distinguishes topographic and man-made features as well as bedrock and snow. Band 6, measuring infrared reflectance beyond the limits of human vision, can detect stress in vegetation. Band 7 is well suited for distinguishing drainage systems, shorelines, wetlands, and urban areas.

The predicted lifespan of the Landsat satellites had been a year in space. Landsat 1, however, operated for five and a half years before technical problems shut it down on January 6, 1978. Landsat 2 was finally retired on February 25, 1982. Landsat 3 remains an operational satellite.

The area covered by a single Landsat frame would require over 1000 pictures to image the same area using conventional aerial surveying techniques. With Landsat, we can view a host of features upon the earth's surface. Recent advances in satellite technology are dramatically increasing our analysis capabilities in space. Geophysical information, which was once too costly or impossible to gather, can now be easily acquired virtually overnight.

On July 16, 1982, a second generation earth-sensing satellite, designated Landsat 4, was launched; it culminated nearly a decade of development effort. This launch inaugurated a new era in satellite technology. After mechanical failure, a similar satellite, Landsat 5, was launched on March 1, 1984. Landsat 5 contains modern sophisticated sensors such as the proven multispectral scanner (MSS) and the thematic mapper (TM). The Thematic Mapper (TM) is the experimental sensor onboard Landsat 4 and 5 and offers improved spectral and spatial resolution, geometric fidelity, and radiometric accuracy. In addition, the TM sensor's eight-bit data precision offers improvements in data quantification as compared to the six-bit data received from Landsat 1, 2, and 3. This increased performance presents new opportunities for the discrimination of landcover, particularly with respect to small surface features. The TM consists of seven precise spectral bands which gather data at 30-m resolution as compared to the 80-m resolution of Landsats 1, 2, and 3 (Table 1). One band of the TM, however, the thermal band, acquires data at 120-m resolution because of optical and cooling limitations of the current scanner technology.

The TM was placed into a circular, near polar, sun-synchronous orbit similar to Landsats 1, 2, and 3. The TM orbits at an altitude of 705 km and images the same area on the earth every 16 days as opposed to the 18 day cycle of the previous satellites. Data are relayed directly to a

TABLE 1

SPECTRAL CHARACTERISTICS OF THE THEMATIC
MAPPER (TM) SATELLITE

TM Spectral Data

Band	*Spectral Range, m*	*Radiometric Resolution*	*Principal Applications*
1	0.45 to 0.52	0.8% NE	Coastal water mapping Soil/vegetation differentiation Deciduous/coniferous differentiation
2	0.52 to 0.60	0.5% NE_p	Green reflectance by healthy vegetation
3	0.63 to 0.69	0.5% NE_p	Chlorophyl absorption for plant species differentiation
4	0.75 to 0.90	0.5% NE_p	Biomass surveys Water body delineation
5	1.55 to 1.75	1.0% NE_p	Vegetation moisture measurement
6	10.4 to 12.5	0.5K NETD	Plant heat stress measurement Other thermal mapping
7	2.08 to 2.35	2.4% NE_p	Hydrothermal mapping

NE_p = noise equivalent reflectance
NETD = noise equivalent temperature difference

ground receiving station at either White Sands, New Mexico or Goddard
by way of the Tracking Data Relay Satellite System (TDRSS).
The seven narrow bands of the TM provide improved data for
information extraction and analysis. The spectral band ranges for the
TM and some of the applications for each band are listed in Table 1. The
TM provides access to new areas of the electromagnetic spectrum and
combines with increased spatial resolution so that new phenomena relating to archaeological research can now be explored.

New satellite systems of unparalleled capability are scheduled for
launch in the next few years which will represent a quantum leap for
remote sensing technology in space. These instruments will be launched
by both United States and foreign governments. NASA is designing a
satellite which will have a ten-m resolution or greater and a pointable
field of view which among other advantages will allow for next day
coverage of an area. NASA is also developing the Shuttle Imaging
Spectrometer Experiment (SISEX) which will be carried by the Shuttle
and converted to a satellite shortly thereafter. SISEX will acquire data in
128 bands simultaneously and will have a major impact in the disciplines
of archaeology, geology, forestry, and agriculture. When one considers
the four spectral bands of Landsat compared to the 128 bands of SISEX,
one can appreciate the rapid advancement in satellite technology.

The French will launch two satellites (called SPOT), one in 1985 and one in 1987. Two more will be launched around 1990. The European Space Agency plans to launch a remote sensing craft in 1987 that uses microwave sensors. The Japanese, Germans, and Russians also have remote sensing instruments scheduled for launch in the next three to five years. The National Oceanic and Atmospheric Administration (NOAA) of the United States plans to launch 19 remote sensing platforms into space between 1985 and 1992 which will represent a dramatic range of analysis capability. In addition, commercial interests are also emerging which will culminate in the construction of even more advanced remote sensing systems. These systems may operate as free-flyers of the upcoming Space Station.

As we enter a new era in remote sensing capability, it is important that archaeologists apprise themselves of this technology before they find themselves too far behind and unable to catch up. For better or worse, satellite imaging brings all of our far flung physical and cultural resources under the scrutiny of the professional and amateur alike. If serious minded investigators do not educate themselves now, they may find in the immediate future that the pothunters have once again beaten them to the field.

VI. RADAR DATA

Clouds, which often encompass much of the earth's surface, particularly in the tropics, prevent acquisition of satellite data. Radar, however, sends out microwave signals that penetrate not only cloud layers but will also penetrate, using certain bands, surface cover such as jungle canopy or desert sand. Radar data are considered to be that electromagnetic energy ranging between 0.1 cm and 200 cm of the microwave region. Most microwave sensors operate in one portion of the microwave region and are identified by a letter code. These letters were designated for security purposes during World War II and have remained a part of the remote sensing vocabulary. The following is a list of Radar Bands and Frequencies:

Radar Frequency Band	Wavelength (λ)	Frequency Range
P	136–77 Cm	220–390 MH_z
UHF	100–30 Cm	300–1000 MH_z
L	30–15 Cm	1000–2000 MH_z
S	15–7.5 Cm	2000–4000 MH_z
C	7.5–3.75 Cm	4000–8000 MH_z
X	3.75–2.40 Cm	8000–12,500 MH_z
Ku	2.4–1.67 Cm	12,500–18,000 MH_z
K	1.67–1.18 Cm	18,000–26,500 MH_z
Ka	1.18–0.75 Cm	26,500–40,000 MH_z

Microwave sensors promise to make significant contributions to archaeological analysis not only because of their cloud and surface penetration power, but also because they are particularly effective in the detection of linear or geometric patterns. In addition, microwave data can be acquired anytime of the day or night since radar is an active remote sensing system. An active system is one that sends out its own energy signal and measures the strength of the signal as it returns from the surface cover objects. Passive sensors like the Landsat satellite sense only the energy provided by nature.

Radar (Radio Detection and Ranging) uses microwave energy rather than light energy to image an object. This is accomplished by releasing short powerful pulses of microwave energy at regular intervals in a certain direction. When these pulses illuminate a target, they are reflected to the source and recorded on a receiving antenna. In this way the time and distance to the target and the intensity of reflection can be measured and displayed as an image. The microwave signal is affected by the surface roughness of the target, the angle at which the object is viewed (angle of incidence), and the polarization of the received radiation. Roughness of the terrain is relative to the wavelength of the radar signal and angle of incidence. As a result, water provides little or no return, vegetation provides a variety of returns, and man-made objects provide a very strong or bright return.

X and C band radar systems can be used to locate prehistoric wall structures, canals, and roadway systems in tropical environments. L-band radar systems are preferable in desert environments where the lack of moisture prevents the signal returns and thus allows the signal to penetrate the sand until it strikes subsurface features. As mentioned previously, data gathered by aircraft borne radar were used by R.E.W. Adams and his colleagues to detect ridged agricultural fields attributable to the prehistoric Maya in Central America.

A dramatic example of the potential that radar remote sensing holds for archaeology was demonstrated by the Shuttle Imaging Radar (SIR-A) mission over the Sudanese desert in 1982. The 50-km wide path of SIR-A penetrated 1-4 m beneath the desert sand to reveal subsurface prehistoric river systems as well as the underlying geology. Here human artifacts dating back to 200,000 B.C. were located along with the shells of Zootecus insularis, a land snail indicative of formerly moist soil and vegetation. The second Shuttle Imaging Radar mission (SIR-B) and the third (SIR-C) are scheduled. Airborne radar data are currently being used for an archaeological investigation in Costa Rica while SIR-B data will be merged with TM satellite data to detect geological strata conducive to early hominid remains in Kenya. Both the Costa Rica and Kenya projects are cooperative efforts between NASA and the National Science Foundation (NSF).

VII. AIRBORNE SENSORS

Airborne sensors are another valuable resource tool for archaeological investigation because they can provide data ranging from 30- to 3-m resolution. NASA's Earth Resources Laboratory has two operational airborne sensors, the Thematic Mapper Simulator (TMS) and the Thermal Infrared Multispectral Scanner (TIMS), which are flown in the NASA/NSTL Learjet 23 aircraft at altitudes ranging from 6500 feet to 40,000 feet. During daylight missions CIR photography is simultaneously acquired, with 60 percent overlap for stereoscopic viewing to aid in digital data analysis. The TMS was initially designed to evaluate the applicability of 30-m ground resolution and the seven Thematic Mapper spectral bands for various remote sensing applications in anticipation on the operational status of the Landsat 4 TM satellite. TMS data allowed users to understand data characteristics and develop data analysis techniques prior to the availability of data from the satellite-borne system. Although the Landsat TM is now operational, the TMS continues to be used to acquire high-resolution data and to collect data within narrow acquisition windows. Many research investigations at ERL have successfully used TMS data to detect and analyze factors that are immediately transferrable to archaeological research. These investigations include discrimination of small heterogeneous features, soil delineation, geological mapping, geobotanical mapping, vegetational stress assessment, and urban studies.

Perhaps the most promising sensor for future archaeological remote sensing research is the TIMS. The TIMS is a six-channel thermal infrared multispectral scanner capable of measuring target radiation in 400-nanometer intervals from 8.2 through 9.4 micrometers, and in 800- and 1000-nanometer intervals from 9.4 through 12.2 micrometers. Under laboratory conditions, noise equivalent temperature differentials of 0.05° to 0.30° are achievable.

TIMS' uniqueness lies not only in its thermal IR capability, but also in its multispectral nature. Each of the six bands measures thermal radiation as temperature in degrees centigrade, of the target. If thermal radiation were the only contributor to the detected energy, all six bands would produce the same results. The emissivity of the target being overflown, however, is also a contributor to the measured return. Emissivity is the ratio of radiant emission of a source to that of a blackbody at the same temperature. Essentially a measure of the capability of a source to release absorbed energy, emissivity is a function of the type of material and its surface geometry and can vary with both wavelength and the temperature of the material. (Consider an earth scene that absorbs the sun's energy during the daylight hours and emits this energy during night hours.) Since the emissivity of any given object is not constant, slight variations in signal levels, primarily attributable to target emissivity, are in the output data. These small variations allow investigators to determine, by remote means, the apparent spectral emissivity differences of selected features.

A secondary benefit of TIMS results from its very high thermal sensitivity. High sensitivity was designed into the system because of the small emissivity contribution. With a thermal sensitivity of 0.3°C or less, apparent spectral emissivity detection would be virtually impossible. Consequently, the TIMS consistently produces sensitivities less than or equal to 0.1° C. This capability allows single-band usage for detecting very subtle thermal variations. Detection of boat wakes, thermal effluents, thermal shadows, and archaeological phenomena are examples of this secondary aspect of TIMS.

Airborne TMS and TIMS data were successfully employed at Chaco Canyon, New Mexico, and Poverty Point, Louisiana, in an archaeological context. In Chaco Canyon, TIMS data revealed subterranean walls, agricultural fields, and both excavated and unexcavated sites. Filtering techniques were developed to accentuate prehistoric roadways that are visible neither from ground level nor in the aerial photography.

Airborne data were also applied at the massive 400-acre site of Poverty Point, Louisiana. Analysis of the digital data revealed anomalies that can be attributed to both historic and prehistoric time periods. Areas of prehistoric barrow pits, fill deposits, a ramp entrance, historic cemeteries, and a corridor extending to an outlying storage area are some of the anomalies that have been verified by both archaeological survey and excavation.

VIII. MICROTOPOGRAPHIC DATA

Both desert and forest environments often prevent the acquisition of detailed topographic data through standard data collection methods. A solution to this situation, however, incorporates the use of laser or lidar profiling instruments. These airborne instruments are potentially capable of producing contour intervals of less than 1 meter. It has been demonstrated, for instance, that the energy pulses generated from these instruments are able to penetrate forest canopy that is 99 percent dense. The signal reflected to the aircraft can be processed to produce ground level terrain as well as the tree heights upon that terrain.

Several profiling instruments are currently in operation which are capable of acquiring the topographic information needed for archaeological research. One of these instruments is referred to as the Airborne Oceanographic Lidar (AOL) which was developed in 1977 by the NASA Wallops Facility. The AOL was flown in 1979 in a Massachusetts State Forest where excellent canopy penetrations were attained. Recently, the U.S. Geological Survey at NSTL developed a terrain profiler that has an accuracy of better than 15 cm. at flight altitudes up to 900 m. It is clear that profiling instruments are now available that can produce the microtopographic data needed for intensive site specific analysis.

IX. SATELLITE POSITIONING TECHNOLOGY

Let us presume that an important archaeological feature is detected in the imagery. The feature lies within a pixel whose resolution is 5 m. How does the archaeologist find that five-m area either in an unmapped desert region of the Sudan or a dense tropical forest in Brazil? Previously this position could only be located using precise theodolites and electronic distancing instruments for angle and distance measurements. These instruments required highly skilled observers and technicians and clean lines-of-sight between adjacent survey points. This expensive time-consuming effort is cost prohibitive for the archaeologist, especially in forested or mountainous terrain. New satellite technology promises to revolutionize surveying methods by eliminating the need for highly-skilled field operators and by producing accurate measurements at a fraction of the cost.

The NAVSTAR GLOBAL Positioning System beams continuous signals to users anywhere on earth. The satellites contain a radio system that broadcasts continually on two frequencies. The heart of the system is a set of atomic clocks that loses less than one second every 70,000 years. Ground receivers can be installed in ships, airplanes, automobiles, and backpacks. Using a portable backpack receiver, an archaeologist can press a button and receive an immediate reading of his or her position on earth to within 5 cm. The unit weighs only 15 pounds and uses a disposable lithium battery; it may be quickly adapted for employment in ground vehicles.

X. DATA BASE

A final area of technological advancement which has implications for archaeology is the continuing development of geographic information systems or data bases. These systems are capable of handling a variety of data types, primarily in a digital format, so that the interactions between elements of the environment may be modeled and analyzed. For example, the ability to register geographically satellite acquired data with digital terrain data, soils data, meteorological data, and hydrological data has resulted in the capability to model the potential locations of archaeological sites.

Environmental factors influence the location, distribution, and mode of human adaptation. The interaction between culture and environment has resulted in settlement patterns that isolate a culture's preference for particular niches in the physical environment. By reconstructing the environment it is possible therefore to outline the locations in the environment that share common characteristics. These characteristics may include soil, slope, elevation, rainfall, and distance from water. The ability to predict accurately the location of archaeological sites in a region can streamline and prioritize survey techniques.

A danger exists, however, that officials and agencies might place excessive reliance on predictive modeling and unjustifiably conclude that since no sites exist in a particular area of the data, then no sites exist in the region. Until accurate predictive models have been proven to be reliable, it is important that they be used only to identify areas for investigation and not be used as a statement of fact upon which to base cultural resource management decisions.

XI. CONCLUSION

Technological advances in remote sensing and data base analysis are providing archaeologists with rapid, inexpensive methods for acquiring and analyzing data. In the future, archaeologists may be able to secure digital satellite data, as well as terrain data, soils data, hydrology data, etc., and commence their analysis projects using sophisticated computers and modeling techniques. Not only will their vision be increased along the broad stretch of the electromagnetic spectrum, they will also possess a better understanding of cultural and environmental relationships before survey and excavation strategies are initiated. By "seeing" the invisible, analyzing its importance, and navigating themselves to precise locations, archaeologists will be able to uncover the secrets in understanding the past as well as charting the future.

Beyond the few examples of remote sensing instruments and analysis capabilities cited in this chapter lies the unknown. One can only speculate as to the capabilities that rest on the technological horizon. Archaeologists can play an instrumental role in the development of that technology. To keep pace, they must begin now; for remote sensing is advancing at a logarithmic proportion. Five years ago digital remote sensing could help archaeologists very little. Today the capabilities are spectacular; five years from now they will be unbelievable.

ACRONYMS AND ABBREVIATIONS

1. AOL: Airborne Oceanographic Lidar
2. AVHRR: Advanced Very High Resolution Radiometer
3. CIR: Color Infrared

4. EM: Electromagnetic
5. ERL: Earth Resources Laboratory
6. GPS: Global Positioning System
7. MSS: Multispectral Scanner
8. NASA: National Aeronautics and Space Administration
9. NOAA: National Oceanic and Atmospheric Administration
10. NSTL: National Space Technology Laboratories
11. SIR-A: Shuttle Imaging Radar (A-stands for first mission)
12. TIMS: Thermal Infrared Multispectral Scanner
13. TM: Thematic Mapper
14. TMS: Thematic Mapper Simulator

GLOSSARY OF TERMS

Absorption: The process by which radiant energy is absorbed and converted into other forms of energy.

Active system: A remote sensing system that transmits its own electromagnetic emanations at an object(s) and then records the energy reflected or refracted to the sensor.

Active microwave: Ordinarily referred to as a radar.

Aerial photograph, vertical: An aerial photogaph made with the optical axis of the camera approximately perpendicular to the earth's surface and with the film as nearly horizontal as is practicable.

Algorithm: (1) A fixed step-by-step procedure to accomplish a given result; usually a simplified procedure for solving a complex problem; also a full statement of a finite number of steps. (2) A computer-oriented procedure for resolving a problem.

Ancillary data: In remote sensing, secondary data pertaining to the area or classes of interest, such as topographical, demographic, or climatological data. Ancillary data may be digitized and used in the analysis process in conjunction with primary remote sensing data.

Anomaly: An area on an image that differs from the surrounding normal area. For example, a concentration of vegetation within a desert scene constitutes an anomaly.

Band: (1) A selection of wavelengths. (2) Frequency band. (3) Absorption band. (4) A group of tracks on a magnetic drum. (5) A range or radar frequencies, such as X-band, Q-band, etc.

Camera, multiband: A camera that exposes different areas of one film, or more than one film, through one lens and a beam splitter, or two or more lenses equipped with different filters, to provide two or more photographs in different spectral bands.

Category: Each unit is assumed to be of one and only one given type. The set of types is called the set of "classes" or "categories," each type being a particular category. The categories are chosen specifically by the investigator as being the ones of interest to him or her.

Class: A surface characteristic type that is of interest to the investigator, such as forest by type and condition, or water by sediment load.

Classification: The process of assigning individual pixels of a multispectral image to categories, generally on the basis of spectral reflectance characteristics.

Color infrared film: Photographic film sensitive to energy in the visible and near-infrared wavelengths, generally from 0.4–0.9 μm; usually used with a minus-blue (yellow) filter, which results in an effective film sensitivity of 0.5–0.9 μm.

Color infrared film is especially useful for detecting changes in the condition of the vegetative canopy which are often manifested in the near-infrared region of the spectrum. Note that color infrared film is not sensitive in the thermal infrared region and therefore cannot be used as a heat-sensitive detector.

Cultural features: All map detail representing man-made elements of the landscape.

Data processing: Application of procedures—mechanical electrical, computation, or other—whereby data are changed from one form into another.

Detector (radiation): A device providing an electrical output that is a useful measure of incident radiation. It is broadly divisible into two groups: thermal (sensitive to temperature changes), and photodetectors (sensitive to changes in photon flux incident on the detector), or it may also include antennas and film. Typical thermal detectors are thermocouples, thermopiles, and thermistors; the latter is termed a bolometer.

Digitization: The process of converting an image recorded originally on photographic material into numerical format.

Display: An output device that produces a visible representation of a data set for quick visual access; usually the primary hardware component is a cathode ray tube.

Electromagnetic radiation (EMR): Energy propagated through space or through material media in the form of an advancing interaction between electric and magnetic fields. The term radiation, alone, is commonly used for this type of energy, although it actually has a broader meaning. Also called electromagnetic energy.

Electromagnetic spectrum: The ordered array of known electromagnetic radiations extending from the shortest cosmic rays, through gamma rays, X-rays, ultraviolet radiation, visible radiation, infrared radiation, and including microwave and all other wavelengths of radio energy.

Element: The smallest definable object of interest in the survey. It is a single item in a collection, population, or sample.

Emissivity: The ratio of the radiation given off by a surface to the radiation given off by a blackbody at the same temperature; a blackbody has an emissivity of 1, other objects between 0 and 1.

Filtering: In analysis, the removal of certain spectral or spatial frequencies to highlight features in the remaining image.

Frame: Complete tape of a single or multidrive Landsat frame covering roughly an area about 100 nautical miles square.

Gray Scale: A monochrome strip of shades ranging from white to black with intermediate shades of gray. The scale is placed in a setup for color photographs and serves as a means of balancing the separation of negatives and positive dye images.

Image Enhancement: Any one of a group of operations that improve the detectability of the targets or categories. These operations include, but are not limited to, contrast improvement, edge enhancement, spatial filtering, noise supression, image smoothing, and image sharpening.

Infrared: Pertaining to energy in the 0.7–100 μm wavelength region of the electromagnetic spectrum. For remote sensing, the infrared wavelengths are often subdivided into near infrared (0.7–1.3 μm), middle infrared (1.3–3.0 μm), and far infrared (7.0–15.0 μm). Far infrared is sometimes referred to as thermal or emissive infrared.

Map: A representation in a plane surface, at an established scale, of the physical features (natural, artificial, or both) of a part of the earth's surface, with the means of orientation indicated.

Maximum likelihood rule: A statistical decision criterion to assist in the classification of overlapping signatures; pixels are assigned to the class of highest probability.

Microwave: Electromagnetic radiation having wavelengths between 1 m and 1 mm or 300–0.3 GH_z in frequency, bounded on the short wavelength side by the far infrared (at 1 mm) and on the long wavelength side by very high-frequency radio waves. Passive systems operating at these wavelengths are sometimes called microwave systems. Active systems are called radar, although the literal definition of radar requires a distance-measuring capability not always included in active systems. The exact limits of the microwave region are not defined.

Multichannel system: Usually used for scanning systems capable of observing and recording several channels of data simultaneously, preferably through the same aperture.

Orbit: The path of a satellite around a body under the influence of gravity.

Passive system: A sensing system that detects or measures radiation emitted by the target. Compare active system.

Photogrammetry: The art or science of obtaining reliable measurements by means of photography.

Pixel: (Derived from "picture element.") A data element having both spatial and spectral aspects. The spatial variable defines the apparent size of the resolution cell (i.e., the area on the ground represented by the data values), and the spectral variable defines the intensity of the spectral response for that cell in a particular channel.

Radar: Acronym for radio detection and ranging. A method, system or technique, including equipment components, for using beamed, reflected, and timed EMR to detect, locate, and (or) track objects, to measure altitude and to acquire a terrain image. In remote sensing of the earth's or a planetary surface, it is used for measuring and, often, mapping the scattering properties of the surface.

Radiation: The emission and propagation of energy through space or through a material medium in the form of waves; e.g., the emission and propagation of EM waves or of sound and elastic waves. The process of emitting radiant energy.

Remote sensing: In the broadest sense, the measurement or acquisition of information of some property of an object or phenomenon, by a recording device that is not in physical or intimate contact with the object or phenomenon under study; e.g., the utilization at a distance (as from an aircraft, spacecraft, or ship) of any device and its attendant display for gathering information pertinent to the environment, such as measurements of force fields, electromagnetic radiation, or acoustic energy. The technique employs such devices as the camera, lasers, and radio frequency receivers, radar systems, sonar, seismographs, gravimeters, magnetometers, and scintillation counters.

Resolution: The ability of an entire remote sensor system, including lens, antennae, display, exposure, processing, and other factors, to render a sharply defined image. It may be expressed as line pairs per millimeter or meter or in many other ways. In radar, resolution usually applies to the effective beamwidth and range measurement width, often defined as the half-power points. For infrared line scanners the resolution may be expressed as the instantaneous field of view. Resolution may also be expressed in terms of temperature or other physical property being measured.

Sensor: Any device that gathers energy, EMR or other, converts it into a single scale and presents it in a form suitable for obtaining information about the environment.

Signature: Any characteristic or series of characteristics by which a material may be recognized in an image, photo, or data set. See also spectral signature.

Spectral regions: Conveniently designated ranges of wavelengths subdividing the electromagnetic spectrum; e.g., the visible region, X-ray region, infrared region, middle-infrared region.

Spectral signature: Quantitative measurement of the properties of an object at one or several wavelength intervals.

Target: (1) An object on the terrain of specific interest in a remote sensing investigation. (2) The portion of the earth's surface that produces by reflection or emission the radiation measured by the remote sensing system.

Thermal infrared: The preferred term for the middle wavelength range of the IR region, extending roughly from 3 μm at the end of the near infrared, to about 15 or 20 μm, where the far infrared begins. In practice the limits represent the envelope of energy emitted by the earth behaving as a gray body with a surface temperature around 290°K (27°C).

Visible wavelengths: The radiation range in which the human eye is sensitive, approximately 0.4–0.7 μm.

Wavelength (symbol λ): Wavelength = velocity/frequency. In general, the mean distance between maxima (or minima) of a roughly periodic pattern. Specifically, the least distance between particles moving in the same phase of oscillation in a wave disturbance. Optical and IR wavelengths are measured in nanometers (10^{-9} m), micrometers (10^{-6} m) and Angstroms (10^{-10} m).

BIBLIOGRAPHY

Adams, R. E.; Brown, W. E., Jr.; and Culbert, T. P.
    1981   Radar Mapping Archaeology and Ancient Maya Land Use. *Science* 213: 1457–63.

Elachi, C.
    1982   Radar Images of the Earth from Space. *Scientific American* 247: 54–61.

Fanale, R.
    1978   *Ethnographic Stratification of the San Juan Basin, Report No. 2, San Juan Basin Ethnographic Project.* Albuquerque: National Park Service.

Ford, J. A., and Willey, G. R.
    1949   *Surface Survey of the Virú Valley, Peru.* Anthropological Papers of the American Museum of Natural History, Vol. 43. New York: American Museum of Natural History.

Gibson, J. L.
    1984   *The Earthen Face of Civilization: Mapping and Testing at Poverty Point, 1983.* Baton Rouge: Louisiana Division of Archeology,

Harp, E., Jr.
    1974   Threshold Indicators of Culture in Air Photo Archeology: A Case Study in the Arctic. Pp. 14–27 in *Aerial Photography in Anthropological Field Research,* ed. E. Z. Vogt. Cambridge: Harvard University.

Johnson, G. R., and Platt, R. R.
  1930   *Peru from the Air*. Washington, D.C.: American Geographical Society.
Kosok, P.
  1965   *Life, Land and Water in Ancient Peru*. New York: Long Island University.
Lyons, T. R., ed.
  1976   *Remote Sensing Experiments in Cultural Resource Studies: Non-Destructive Methods of Archeological Exploration, Survey, and Analysis: Reports of the Chaco Center, No. 1*. Albuquerque: National Park Service and University of New Mexico.
Lyons, T. R., and Avery, T. E.
  1977   *Remote Sensing: A Handbook for Archeologists and Cultural Resource Managers*. Washington, D.C.: National Park Service.
Lyons, T. R., and Ebert, J. E., eds.
  1978   *Remote Sensing and Non-Destructive Archeology*. Washington, D.C.: National Park Service.
Lyons, T. R., and Hitchcock, R. K., eds.
  1977   *Aerial Remote Sensing Techniques in Archeology: Reports of the Chaco Center, No. 2*. Albuquerque: National Park Service and University of New Mexico.
Lyons, T. R., and Mathien, F. J., eds.
  1980   *Cultural Resources Remote Sensing*. Washington, D.C.: National Park Service.
Reining, P.
  1973   *Utilization of ERTS-1 Imagery in Cultivation and Settlement Site Identification and Carrying Capacity Estimates in Upper Volta and Niger*. Springfield, VA: National Technical Information Service.
  1974a   *Human Settlement Patterns in Relation to Resources of Less Developed Countries*. Proceedings: COSPAR Meetings, Sao Paulo, Brazil. (On file at International Office, American Association for the Advancement of Science, Washington, D.C.)
  1974b   *Use of ERTS-1 Data in Carrying Capacity Estimates for Sites in Upper Volta and Niger*. Paper presented at the 1974 Annual Meeting of the American Anthropological Association, Mexico City. (On file at International Office, American Association for the Advancement of Science, Washington, D.C.)
Schaedel, R. P.
  1951   The Lost Cities of Peru. *Scientific American* 185: 18–23.
Schorr, T. S.
  1974   Aerial Ethnography in Regional Studies: A Reconnaissance of Adaptive Change in the Cauca Valley of Columbia. Pp. 40–53; 163–88 in *Aerial Photography in Anthropological Field Research*, ed. E. Z. Vogt. Cambridge: Harvard University.
Sever, T. L.
  1983   *Feasibility Study to Determine The Utility of Advanced Remote Sensing Technology in Archeological Investigations*. National Space Technology Laboraties, MS: NASA.
Sever, T. L., and Wiseman, J.
  1985   *Conference of Remote Sensing: Potential For the Future*. National Space Technology Laboratories, MS: NASA.

Shippee, R.
    1933   Air Adventures in Peru. *National Geographic* 63: 81–120.
St. Joseph, J. K. S., ed.
    1966   *The Uses of Air Photography, Nature and Man in a New Perspective.*
              London: Baker.
Willey, G. R.
    1959   *Aerial Photographic Maps as Survey Aids in Virú Valley: The Arch-
              eologist at Work.* New York: Harper.

15
COMPUTERS AND ARCHAEOLOGICAL RESEARCH

JAMES F. STRANGE
University of South Florida

Before 1970 the application of the computer to problems in ancient Near Eastern archaeology was hardly more than a dream. Yet, as we shall soon see, in the decade from 1970–80 the use of computer-assisted analyses of various kinds, not to mention data base management, graphics, and other applications, has moved from the realm of possibility to that of necessity.

It might be of some interest to speculate about the specific reasons for turning to the machine for information storage, retrieval, and analysis. However, the purpose of this essay is simply to describe some of the major applications to which the computer has been put in the field of ancient Near Eastern archaeology. Therefore, many intriguing and fascinating computer applications in European and classical archaeology will not appear. Rather, the limited aim here is simply to be instructive and pragmatic. The goal is to review some of the major uses of the computer in ancient Near Eastern archaeology in three areas: (1) data base establishment, (2) data base management, and (3) data analysis. This eliminates some important possibilities, as many readers will know, but perhaps we can save these for another place.

I. DATA BASES IN ANCIENT NEAR EASTERN ARCHAEOLOGY

A leader in establishing a data base in ancient Near Eastern archaeology was the Expedition to Caesarea Maritima, under the direction of Robert J. Bull of Drew University. Bull was interested in using the computer for data recording as early as 1970, when he was Director of the W. F. Albright Institute of Archaeological Research in Jerusalem. He was then planning the first field season at Caesarea and was exploring various alternatives in registration systems and recording systems. It was fairly obvious that a site of such enormous size as ancient Caesarea would likely be a mine of the material culture of the Roman and Byzantine

Periods: coins, sculpture, pottery, oil lamps, and small finds of every kind. If the computer was not relied upon simply to record this massive amount of information, then the sheer volume of the data threatened to overwhelm any traditional registration system.

Bull found ready assistance from Dr. Donald Fisher, then Professor and Chairman of Computer and Information Science at Oklahoma State University, in Stillwater. Fisher devised the information system or data base design, using the pottery encoding system developed by Lawrence Toombs of Wilfrid Laurier University in Ontario (Fisher 1974; Toombs 1971; Fisher and Yates 1972). The Expedition to Caesarea Maritima developed this immense data base over several seasons, but it was never used by the archaeologists.

The present author was in Jerusalem with Robert Bull at the same time that the latter was first thinking about and planning the first season of excavations at Caesarea Maritima. Those first discussions of possible encoding and registration systems with Bull resulted in the adoption of a computerized data base by another archaeological expedition in Israel, namely, the Joint Expedition to Khirbet Shemaᶜ, directed by Eric M. Meyers of Duke University.

I became an Associate Director of this expedition in 1971. In that year I learned to program in Fortran IV and developed a mini-data base from the artifact registration of the first season's work in square B.1 at Caesarea, the square I had directed. In the course of learning to program, it had become abundantly clear to me that computers would soon be a *sine qua non* for data analysis for archaeologists, though the seemingly insurmountable problem was cost effectiveness. Computer time was expensive.

One of the duties of successive artifact Registrars of the Joint Expedition to Khirbet Shemaᶜ was therefore to see to it that they always recorded artifacts in an identical format. This system did not use the expensive, specially printed IBM keypunch forms used by Fisher and his assistants at Caesarea. Thus, after the field season a series of keypunch operators at the Computer Center at the University of South Florida read the registration records directly from spiral notebooks—though not without protest—and typed ("keyboarded") the data onto IBM punchcards. These cards were then read immediately into computer memory with a card reader and printed out in lists. These lists remained, therefore, the primitive data base of the Khirbet Shemaᶜ project until its end in 1972 (Meyers, Kraabel, and Strange 1976:269–80).

The successor to the Joint Expedition to Khirbet Shemaᶜ was the Meiron Excavation Project, also directed by Eric M. Meyers, and with largely the same staff. The Registrars again made sure in successive excavation seasons to use the same registration format in the familiar spiral notebooks. This did not in itself represent an advance. However, we also began to amass two other data bases; namely, pottery field readings and coin readings. At the time of analysis of the data, then, it became clear that we needed file merging. That is, in order to produce the Locus List, which is important to all archaeologists, it would be necessary to merge the coin list, pottery reading list, and locus descriptions. This was accomplished in a pilot run in 1977 as the senior staff completed the final report.

The next advance for the Meiron Excavation Project was the use of the terminal "in the field." This was certainly not a new idea, as it had been tried in the early 1970s by a variety of archaeologists (Buckland 1973; Gaines 1974; Wilcock 1973; Chenhall 1971:24). Our idea was to make it economically feasible by bringing a *microcomputer* into camp and building files there. In effect we would be moving the data base out of the university office and making it available to the archaeologists in the field.

During the 1980 excavations at Nabratein, Israel, the Meiron Excavation Project used the Radio Shack TRS-80 Model I with 32K Random Access Memory (RAM), two cassette recorders for mass storage, and a printer. Staff members J. F. Strange and Thomas R. W. Longstaff wrote the software for building and updating the artifact and coin registration files and the pottery reading files (Strange 1981).

This system had its difficulties ("bugs"), but one effect was to make clear to the staff of the Expedition that such immediate access to the data base is simply a necessity for intelligent field decisions. Recent advances in field methods have resulted in recovery of ever greater amounts of information. The archaeologist is therefore continually confronted with a mass of data too large to digest, and therefore may make poor field decisions. Even the simple making of lists helps the field archaeologist know where certain types of artifactual material come from, and therefore which areas to pursue, in terms of the objectives of the excavation.

A somewhat different application of a computer generated data base was that of Z'ev Yeivin of the Department of Antiquities of Israel. In this case, Yeivin decided to store all published Iron Age pottery of ancient Israel and the lands adjoining Israel. His objective was to shorten the search time of the scholar poring through publications to look for parallels to his or her pottery. Yeivin skirted the problem of directly encoding profile drawings by the simple expedient of encoding the name of the vessel, as there is fair unanimity among archaeologists as what to call each vessel. It was also necessary, of course, to store the name of the publication, the site, locus identification, and many other categories, including a description of the pot itself.

Yeivin took advantage of the state of the art by having special forms printed for an optical reader. That is, a machine read the file cards, which were prepared by Yeivin and his assistants, directly into computer memory. This is an important innovation, as it meant there was only one clerk entering the data into the machine (ignoring for the moment the second clerk who verified the cards against the original publications). It is a rule in electronic data processing that the fewer clerks who handle the data, the fewer errors which will creep into the data base.[1]

Yeivin accessed his data base via about 29 categories or combinations of categories. That is, he could query the data base to print out all instances of chalices associated with Gezer bowls, or all instances of cooking pots with specific types of rim, or any other way he chose. The only constraint on the system was the complexity of the search program and the organization of the data within the data base. This became an invaluable aid for the archaeologist preparing his or her pottery for publication.[2]

Yet another approach to a similar data base was provided by Thomas McClelland, a doctoral candidate at the University of Pennsylvania. McClelland's objective was no less than the complete reseriation of the published Iron Age pottery of ancient Palestine, relying on modern, sophisticated statistical techniques. To realize this aim he needed an accurate data base of all published Iron Age pottery from the area (McClelland 1975).

McClelland's data base was, in fact, a completely uniform reclassification of the data. McClelland discovered five problems in assembling his data base: (1) There are internal discrepancies in vessel counts and classifications in the catalogues from any given site. (2) Not all interpreters of the Iron Age classify their pottery the same way. (3) Certain categories overlap, as, for example, the chalice or goblet (Amiran 1969:213). (4) Stratum and locus descriptions use not only different numbers and letters for the same thing but also presuppose different definitions of the smallest unit of excavation. (5) The site publications and Duncan's *Corpus* may disagree about the number of vessels and types found at any given site (McClelland 1975:Appendix 5).

Thus, McClelland's strategy was to develop a uniform system of classification of all published Iron Age vessels, to resolve the discrepancies in the vessel counts and classifications at a given site, and to preserve the "locus" and provenience designations translated into Arabic numerals in each site report. For example, Megiddo stratum VIIA is reported as stratum 7-1 (McClelland 1975:815). This allowed him to develop five

---

[1] Yeivin's work remains unpublished.

[2] Thus Yeivin was able to accomplish on the computer in a few minutes what would have taken a team of graduate students days or weeks to accomplish. This approximates Chenhall's second reason for using the computer in archaeology: ". . . analyses can be performed on the computer that, from a practical standpoint, cannot be accomplished any other way" (1981:8).

regional occupational sequences that seemed to have meaning: (1) Hazor, (2) Megiddo/ʿAmal/Beth-shan, (3) Lachish/Tell Beit Mirsim, (4) Jemmeh/Zuwayid/Tell el-Farʿah (S), and (5) Tell Deir ʿAllah (McClelland 1975: 190–229).

The most controversial aspect of McClelland's research is his new chronological seriation of Iron Age pottery in ancient Palestine (McClelland 1979). Be that as it may, his storage of ancient Iron Age ceramics in an accurate, easily revisable data base provided him with a research tool that would have been simply impossible before the advent of the computer. With the development of huge amounts of permanent storage on microcomputers and of sophisticated software for the microcomputers, we will likely see extensions of McClelland's research on much more compact machines than he used.

Another recent use of the computer for assembling a data base from a single site has been that of the Heshbon Excavation Project in Jordan under the direction of Lawrence Geraty, formerly of Andrews University. In this case the staff, particularly Øystein LaBianca and Lawrence Geraty, became convinced of the value of computerizing the existing locus descriptions, artifact registration, and other related information. They began after the fact, but managed to encode all the information they deemed relevant, to verify the data, to update the data base, and continued to enlarge it up to and including their last season in the field, 1980 (Geraty 1980).

This was very much an "in-house" project, using the Andrews University computer and the services of James Brower, Director of the Computer Center. The result included the production of an encoding manual written by Lawrence Mitchell in 1978 and subsequently updated (Mitchell 1978). The complete system allowed the encoding, storage, and retrieval of information keyed to the excavated unit, including data on soil descriptions, architecture, stratigraphy, artifacts, pottery, coins, biodata, and photographs and other records (Mitchell 1978:14–37). The result was probably the most complete computerized data base of field information ever assembled in ancient Near Eastern archaeology.

Still another equally ambitious application of the computer for onsite and off-site recording and retrieval of excavation data was that developed by Debra F. Katz Price for use at Tell Michal, Israel, a project under the general direction of Zeʾev Herzog (Katz Price 1982; cf. Patton and Holoien 1981: 160). Use of this system began in 1978 at Tell Michal during the second season of excavation and continued through the summer of 1979. The follow-up at the Tel Aviv University Computation center continued through 1980.

The data base management system that the project used was again System 2000. This set of programs had the advantages of being in use world-wide, of handling textual as well as numeric data, and of using "natural-like" language (Katz Price 1982:4). Besides, Price was from the University of Minnesota, where the Computer Center had experience in using System 2000 with archaeological data.[3]

The design of the data base relied on the explicit recording system already in use. This system was based on forms already used for data recording by hand. The computer system, then, preserved as many existing terminologies and formats as possible, which made the system more "friendly" to the user. Since computerized systems do not rely on redundancy in the recording systems, and since manual systems generally do, Price found it possible to simplify the forms and perhaps avoid some confusion.

The focus of the recording system at Tell Michal was the locus. Price identified 125 distinct attributes related to locus descriptions. "These attributes included excavation history, location, detailed artifactual data concerning type, characteristics, provenance, location by measurements, chronological assignments and related documented references" (Katz Price 1982:4). In the actual system, then, the "Basket List" was linked to locus descriptions, and "Objects" were related to the Basket List. "Object Notes" described the artifacts. "Publications" stored article and book references to the objects in question. Finally, the attribute "Museum Storage Analysis" allowed the staff to keep track of the location of any given artifact (Katz Price 1982:4–5).

The test of any computerized data system is its success in the field. In this case, the system did all that anyone hoped it could, that is, storing detailed, accurate information about loci, artifacts, publications, provenance, and non-archaeological information that the staff needed (name of Area Supervisor, dates excavated, etc.). The system also revealed missing and erroneous data. That is, it was successful in its error-trapping routines. Errors are a major area of concern for any recording system, and this system did not escape that concern. Its success in calling attention to missing and erroneous data contributed to the overall usefulness of the system.

The Tell Michal computerized data base generated "reports" on demand, which were generally detailed locus lists, basket lists, and artifact lists. The computer easily tallied these lists with artifact and provenance descriptions, according to the needs of the staff. Some experimentation with graphics helped the staff recognize artifact distribution patterns that would not have been so readily detected otherwise. These reports were actually plots of the find-spots of artifacts on a

---

[3] Note that many of the computer projects reported in Patton and Holoien (1981) rely on the System 2000, which is a commercial system developed and marketed by the Intel Corporation (formerly MRI Systems Corporation).

plan of the excavated area, though without drawings of the architecture (Katz Price 1982:9–11).

The major limitation of the system was the slow response time of the computer. The ensuing data backlog could not be handled by the system in a timely manner. The decision of the staff was to change the computerized system from an immediate-access system to a research-oriented system. System personnel continued to enter data daily from one area to test potential computer applications, but the immediate response for the entire expedition had to be given up (Katz Price 1982:10–11). Nonetheless, this was an important step in the use of the computer in "real time" in the field from which we have much to learn.

Finally, it seems proper to mention here the computer-assisted cataloging system developed for artifacts from Tell Akhmim, Egypt by Sheila McNally and Vicki Walsh (McNally and Walsh 1984; Patton and Holoien 1981:160; cf. Katz *et al.* 1985, Bennett, 1974; Loy and Powell 1977; Joukowsky 1980; Rouse 1960; Redman 1973; Dever and Lance 1977:108–38). In this case, the data base is designed to allow for efficient processing of the great quantities of artifacts, and to support cross-cultural comparisons. In other words, the data base allowed for sorting and classification of large numbers of artifacts rapidly and accurately. On the other hand, the same system also enabled the archaeologists to make intra-cultural and cross-cultural inferences from artifact characteristics.

McNally and Walsh devised a pottery and artifact classification and encoding system that was clear and simple, yet used objective, global definitions of artifacts so that artifacts from different cultures could be compared. To this end, the cataloging system was divided into several stages so that the first stage was simple and global. The second stage of cataloging was more specific and included the simplification and reduction of variables. The result of the cataloging system was a set of encoding sheets from which the data could be entered by keyboarding directly into the computer.

McNally also turned to the same commercially available data base management system as Katz, the System 2000 (McNally and Walsh 1984). This package was also already available at her host institution, the University of Minnesota (MRI, Inc. 1974). System 2000 contains a feature called "Report Writer" that enables the user to call up data in whatever format the user desires. System 2000 can sort through the data bank of virtually any number of variables and print out the results according to the user's needs. This is a normal feature of a good data base management package.

Another example of the use of the System 2000 for a data base application in ancient Near Eastern archaeology is also from the University of Minnesota. In this case a team of scholars entered into the computer all available cuneiform documents from the second millenium Old Babylonian town of Kutalla. This required transliteration of 102 documents into a Roman alphabet, identification of 88 components of the economic transactions thus recorded (buyer, seller, item, data, etc.) and, eventually, a search of the data base for a series of variables relative to the aims of the project. In this case, the researchers were asking for the economic history of Kutalla. (Ward and Holoien 1981).

For the sake of introducing some comparative data, certain documents from ancient Ur and Dilbat were also entered into the data base. The entire file was then searched with a concordance command ("Tally"). Other special reports were generated with the Report Writer command, which could and did retrieve entire documents. Finally, the entire data base was searched to produce a tabulation of all sales of land, and the price of each piece of property was printed.

This study provided some important insights into the economic history of an Old Babylonian site, but it also illustrates the utility of such computerized investigations. In this case, the computer made possible what traditional scholarly approaches would regard as untenable. This is the value of such a computerized data base.

Most archaeologists, unlike those in the previous cases, have approached a computerized data base with limited plans in mind. For example, the staff of the Joint Expedition to Khirbet Shemaᶜ originally had very limited goals in mind when we turned to the computer. After we had labored with encoding the artifact registration into the computer, we asked for no more than a comprehensive artifact list. However, very shortly we looked at that list and instantly realized that the computer could just as easily print out all the artifacts by *material*. This would help us answer questions like, "Where are all these iron nails coming from?" The next step is rather obvious, namely, have the computer search by material, but also by field, square, and locus and print out the report in the same sequence. What seems so obvious now was only the beginning to be understood in the early 1970s. The final step, data base management, became a reality only ten years later.

II. DATA BASE MANAGEMENT

Early users of the data bases generally thought of the electronic file of archaeological information in much the same way they thought of their 3 × 5 cards in the past. In other words, the information so stored was regarded essentially as a static, unchanging well of information from which one dipped from time to time in order to trace an artifact or to review some information relative to an isolated problem. Notice, however, that even with 3 × 5 cards any researcher finds that he or she must do at least three things: (1) Correct the information. (2) Enter new information. (3) Delete irrelevant information. These are important processes in effective data base or data bank management.

Users of an artifact file system may also find it necessary to present the same information in different ways. For example, art historians will probably find it necessary to discuss whatever art motifs are found on the artifacts in question, while the historians of technology may treat the same motifs solely in terms of the ancient methods of manufacture. The choice of organization of the data may change from presentation to presentation, even though the file itself may not change. We may identify any machine-supported capacity to change either the content or organization of a file as a kind of data base management (Chenhall 1981).

The reader may realize that those data bases treated in section 1 of this essay were probably examples of data base management as much as they were simply of data base establishment. The staff of the Caesarea Maritima expedition would probably find it necessary to update their computer files to the extent that they used them. It was certainly the case that the data base established by the Joint Expedition to Khirbet Shemaᶜ and by its successor, the Meiron Excavation Project, had to be managed, and is still being managed as changes are necessary. This element of relative permanence is the mark of a true data bank, which may be defined as a large file of information that will be accessed or used by (ordinarily) a group of researchers.

One need not use expensive or complicated programs for data base applications in archaeology. In 1983, the Expedition to Sepphoris, Israel, had planned to use a large, student-written data base program, but found that it could not. The program in question had a bug that seemed impossible to correct, even though it had worked well in the United States. The staff fell back on two commercial programs that had been brought along for other purposes. The programs were SuperScripsit (C), marketed by Radio Shack, and Enhanced VisiCalc (TM), written by Software Arts, Inc. for Radio Shack.

VisiCalc is one of the original electronic spreadsheets so popular in business applications. In this case, we stored (among other things) the entire set of pottery readings, pail by pail. Keyboard operators typed the data from specially prepared IBM-type encoding sheets originally developed for the 80-column card.

Enhanced VisiCalc allows one to print all or selected records, thereby generating a report. It is also possible to edit any given value or label, which is a method of updating and correcting the records. One can also count or tally columns or rows, gaining more information than simple inspection could afford.

SuperScripsit (C) is Radio Shack's word processor program. In this case we stored a variety of records electronically. The largest electronic document was "Artifact Registration," though it was quite small by most standards. We stored only 434 artifact descriptions (the sum total from four, 5 × 5-m squares), though we did so quickly and accurately. It is also possible to use the "Global Search" and "Replace" feature of Super-Scripsit (C) to execute an automatic count of the number of coins, needles, etc., in the data base or replace automatically certain terms with more satisfactory descriptors.

The use of commercial packages is likely the direction archaeologists will move in the future. After all, the idea is imposition of control on the whole array of data that the archaeologist has unearthed, whether that be through special programs or commercially available ones (Chenhall 1981:2). The issue, then, is not the source of the program, but the effectiveness of the machine and its software in managing or controlling the huge amounts of information that advanced excavation methods force upon us.

Data bank management, then, is as necessary in classical and ancient Near Eastern archaeology as it is in European and American archaeology. However, our colleagues in Europe and North America have responded to the need first. Therefore, it may be a surprise for some to hear that the first conference in data banks in archaeology was held at the University of Arkansas in 1971, about the time that practioners in the ancient Near East were evaluating the situation and experimenting with machine storage of their data (Gaines 1971). The second conference took place in 1972 in France (Gardin 1974). By 1981, Sylvia Gaines could report that European archaeologists had access to no less than 33 archaeological data banks in 17 countries (Gaines 1981a; cf. Verhaeghe 1979). The American situation is somewhat more restricted, for *Data Bank Applications in Archaeology* reports on seven archaeological data banks, of which only four are from the United States, though that is hardly an exhaustive list (Gaines 1981b).[4]

In this essay we have reported on seven data bases (or data banks). These include that of the Caesarea Maritima project, housed at Oklahoma State University. The data bank associated with the Joint Expedition to Khirbet Shema᷾ and the Meiron Excavation Project is located at the University of South Florida. Some of the later material from the Meiron Excavation Project is both at the University of South Florida and Colby College in Waterville, Maine. Yeivin's data are at Hebrew University in Jerusalem. McClelland's data base is at the University of Pennsylvania, where it was developed. The Heshbon Project's data

[4] The American systems mentioned are ADAM (Archaeological Data Management) at Arizona State University, AMASDA (Automated Management of Archaeological Survey Data in Arkansas) at the University of Arkansas, AZSITE (apparently Arizona Sites) at the Arizona State University Museum, and ORACLE at Indiana University.

bank is at Andrews University, while the Tell Michal, Israel, data are at the University of Minnesota. This last university also houses the data bank from the Akhmim, Egypt, excavations, as well as the file of Kutalla's Old Babylonian records.

III. DATA ANALYSIS

By far one of the most powerful uses of the computer is in data analysis, which need not always be the use of powerful and sophisticated statistical programs. Yet one of the first uses of the computer for data analysis for ancient Near Eastern archaeology is just such a detailed analysis. In this case, the data were recovered from Ksar Akil in Lebanon and amounted to about 15,000 palaeolithic stone cores, blanks, and tools that needed description and interpretation. Use of the computer as an interpretive aid was more or less inevitable, in view of the sheer volume of data (Azoury 1971; Azoury and Hodson 1973; cf. Doran and Hodson 1975:257–64).

The site of Ksar Akil, near Beirut, is a palaeolithic rock shelter with carbon-14 dates between 40,000 and 30,000 BP. The mass of recovered lithic materials that was recovered offered a large enough data sample that it appeared feasible to infer in some detail the development of a set of lithic industries at a single site over several thousands of years. To this end Azoury tried a new, exciting system of description and developed a specialized set of analyses (Bordes 1961).

Azoury classified the 15,000 stone artifacts hierarchically according to the system of F. Bordes. Level One of this system classifies all lithic artifacts as either (1) cores, (2) tools, (3) blanks, or (4) waste flakes. In Level Two, the Bordian system separates cores into seven types, tools into three types, and blanks into two types. Azoury did not consider waste flakes. Each of the classifications in Level Two were further refined into Level Three's subtypes (de Sonneville-Bordes and Perrot 1954–56). Thus, all stone artifacts were classified in a system that used three levels.

In practice this meant that one described each piece individually by making two or three strokes on a worksheet, checking off only a few of the 128 attributes listed. In this way the 14 stone tool assemblages from the 14 strata at Ksar Akil were inserted into a data matrix of 14 rows and 128 columns. This could be printed out as a suitably labeled matrix. The data were also treated by "constellation analysis" (Newcomer and Hodson 1973).

Constellation analysis is a statistical method that looks for structures within the data beyond the three dimensions to which the human mind is accustomed (Doran and Hodson 1975:205–9). In this case, Azoury identified eight general groups or "constellations" of artifacts that he thought helped to isolate major trends in lithic industries at Ksar Akil over the ten millennia at the site. He next calculated the mathematical "difference" between each constellation. When all such calculations were completed, he had a picture of lithic industry development at the site, though he had to combine both typological and technological data on the artifacts to do so. He also found that a reduced type-list of butts, blanks, and cores correlated +89 percent with the results of an exhaustive type list. This is an important methodological discovery, for it implies that less descriptive detail, when developed properly, allows the researcher to discover the structure within the data, as well as an exhaustive list, saving much time and money.[5]

Many scholars trained in ancient Near Eastern archaeology do not have the statistical knowledge to undertake such an analysis as that of Azoury. This was true of the Joint Expedition to Khirbet Shema[c], whose staff was trained in textual studies, field archaeology, and ancient history. Therefore, under the tutelage of George G. Levenbach, the staff made use of the computer, but they did not have to earn new degrees in computer science (Meyers, Kraabel and Strange 1976:99–102, 243–47).

During the 1970s, one of the most promising methods in automatic classification of archaeological data was cluster analysis (Doran and Hodson 1975:175–85). Some archaeologists had experimented with a number of types of such analyses, though few were engaged in ancient Near Eastern archeology. Guided by George Levenbach, I stepped into this vacuum with some trepidation. The result was an attempt to classify the squares (the smallest excavated plot) from the excavations at Khirbet Shema[c] by comparing the distributions of various kinds of artifacts. It was possible to classify the squares in this manner, though it was not clear what the resulting dendrogram actually meant (Meyers, Kraabel, and Strange 1976:101).[6]

Meanwhile, Levenbach addressed various statistical problems in ancient Near Eastern archaeology, including an analysis of the pottery from ancient Mycenae. In this case, Mertz and Levenbach (1978) asked how much information about dates is lost when one reduces the number of variables used to describe ancient pottery. This may be particularly important when examining the data from a series of sites in order to deduce the distribution of pottery types chronologically.

Mertz and Levenbach used the Mycenaean pottery studies of Furumark (1941), which are well known among ancient Near Eastern archaeologists. They used Furumark's counts of pottery forms, which are described by type, site, context, decorative motif, and date. They then used a computer program to construct a series of two-way contingency

---

[5] But no attention was here paid to the question of the proportion of information thereby lost.

[6] A dendrogram is a tree-like diagram showing classification into groups.

tables. This means that they compared all 336 types to all 80 decorative motifs, then all types to all sites, then all types to all contexts, etc. As one can see, this is a complicated task and is best accomplished by a computer.

A major problem in comparing such tables is the zeros entered at any point. For specific mathematical reasons, zeros are very troublesome in some comparative statistics. However, in the case of information theory, it is easy to handle such information. The authors of this study ordered the sites from richest to poorest in each table, using the zeros as important information for such ordering. The computer then calculated the interdependence of rows and columns. In its next run, the computer calculated the interdependence of rows and columns with the "pottery poor" sites eliminated.

The result was similar to what Azoury had deduced in his study, but in a different analysis and for a different reason. Levenbach and Mertz concluded that, if the eight "poorest" site groups are discarded from a distribution analysis, only five percent of the pottery evidence would be missing, but 12 percent of the chronological information is lost. Although there is still a relatively large amount of information remaining, the effect on the analysis is two and one half times greater than one might predict. Therefore, with respect to information theory, it would be prudent to include the "pottery poor" sites, if chronological inferences are desired.

It is also possible to use far less sophisticated computerized procedures for exploratory purposes. For example, the Meiron Excavation Project recently published its preliminary report of the 1980 season of excavation at Nabratein, Israel (Meyers, Strange, and Meyers 1981). In the coin report, authored by Joyce Raynor, the staff provided some computer-generated calculations of the Pearson Coefficient of Correlation (Meyers, Strange, and Meyers 1981:16).[7] The reader can discover the meaning of this calculation in any elementary statistical text. Our objective was to arrive at a quantitative estimate of the difference between the distribution of the coins at Nabratein and their distribution at the three other ancient villages we had excavated. Our impression from the number of coins found was that Nabratein stood out from the other three, but the calculation of the coefficient helped sharpen and confirm that intuition. It was also possible to convert the Pearson Coefficient into a mathematical distance simply by subtracting the coefficient from 1.0000 and multiplying it by 100, like deriving a percentage. This calculation was also easily accomplished on the computer. The calculations

---

[7] Pearson's Moment assumes the linear relationship of the data, but on occasion it is useful to violate the assumptions of a statistical procedure *knowingly* in order to gain a mathematical perspective on an archaeological intuition.

demonstrated that our perceptions could be supported mathematically, though we knew no statistician would regard our calculations as rigorous.

Recently, archaeologists discovered the color graphics capabilities of computers in manipulating data and have produced some stunning results.[8] Other archaeologists have stayed with the simpler scatter diagrams available in the *Statistical Package for the Social Sciences* (Nie *et al.* 1975), or have discovered how to sketch on the screen, sometimes in three dimensions.[10] Some, following the lead of McClelland, are working on seriation, though the last great unexplored area, according to Sabloff (1981) is modelling.[11] Archaeologists working in the Near East will certainly continue to build and manage data bases, engage in data analysis of increasingly sophisticated order, and discover the graphics and modelling capabilities of these ever more reliable machines.

BIBLIOGRAPHY

Aharoni, Y., *et al.*,
1976　　　Methods of Recording and Documenting. Pp. 119–32 in *Beer-Sheba I: Excavations at Tel Beer-Sheba, 1969–1971 Seasons*, eds. Y. Aharoni *et al.* Tel Aviv: Tel Aviv University.

Aharoni, Y., *et al.*, eds.
1976　　　*Beer-Sheba I: Excavations at Tel Beer-Sheba, 1969–1971 Seasons.* Tel Aviv: Tel Aviv University.

Amiran, R.
1969　　　*Ancient Pottery of the Holy Land.* Jerusalem: Massada.

Arnold, J. B., III.
1982　　　Archaeological Applications of Computer Graphics. Pp. 179–216 in *Advances in Archaeological Method and Theory*, ed. M. B. Schiffer, vol. 5. New York: Academic.

Azoury, I.
1971　　　A Technological and Typological Analysis of the Transitional

[8] The least known and perhaps most sophisticated application of color graphics to archaeological data is in Badler and Badler 1978. All of the illustrative material in this article is from Troy. The authors cite their own system: Badler and Badler (1977a). See also Badler and Badler 1977b. One of the most recent discussions of archaeological computer graphics is in Arnold 1982.

[9] This is a highly developed package of statistical routines designed, as its name implies, for use with social sciences data.

[10] Interactive graphics system, as they are called, are now simply legion. The American Institute of Architects (AIA) schedules seminars on computers and computer graphics at its annual meeting. These seminars focus on issues such as computer graphics, systems drafting (by computer), and computerized design. In addition, the capability of digitizing a two or three dimensional image for rotation, scaling, and merging with other images is now available on relatively inexpensive microcomputers. Someone should soon discover how to use this capability in a cost effective and timely manner in archaeology.

[11] Sabloff's study is one of the most important books to appear on this subject.

and Early Upper Palaeolothic Levels of Ksar Akil and Abu Halka. Unpublished Ph.D. dissertation, London University.

Azoury, I.; and Hodson, F. R.
1973   Comparing Palaeolothic Assemblages: Ksar Akil, A Case Study. *WA* 4: 292–306.

Badler, N. I.; and Badler, V. R.
1977a   *SITE: A Color Computer Graphics System for the Display of Archaeological Sites and Artifacts.* Dept. of Computer and Information Science, Technical Report No. 76–77. Philadelphia: University of Pennsylvania.
1978   Interaction with a Color Computer Graphics System for Archaeological Sites. *Computer Graphics* 1/11: 12–18.

Badler, V. R.; and Badler, N. I.
1977b   A New Analysis of Thermi. P. 38 in *Archaeological Institute of America 79th Annual Conference Abstracts.* Atlanta: Archaeological Institute of America.

Bennett, A.
1974   Basic Ceramic Analysis. *Eastern New Mexico University Contributions in Anthropology* 6: 1–183.

Bordes, F.
1961   *Typologie du Paléolithique Ancient et Moyen.* Bordeaux: Delmas.

Buckland, P.
1973   An Experiment in the Use of a Computer for On-Site Recording of Finds. *Science and Archaeology* 9: 22–24.

Chenhall, R. G.
1971   *Computers in Anthropology and Archaeology.* IBM Data Processing Application. White Plains, NY: IBM Corporation.
1981   Computerized Data Bank Management. Pp. 1–8 in *Data Bank Applications in Archaeology*, ed. S. W. Gaines. Tucson: University of Arizona.

Dever, W. G.; and Lance, H. D., eds.
1977   *A Manual of Field Excavation: Handbook for Field Archaeologists*, New York: HUC-JIR.

Doran, J. E.; and Hodson, F. R.
1975   *Mathematics and Computers in Archaeology.* Cambridge: Harvard University.

Duncan, J. G.
1930   *Corpus of Dated Palestinian Pottery.* London: British School of Archaeology in Egypt.

Fisher, D. D.
1974   An Information System for the Joint Caesarea Maritima (Israel) Excavations. Pp. 191–204 in *Computers in the Humanities*, ed. J. L. Mitchell. Minneapolis: University of Minnesota.

Fisher, D. D.; and Yates, K. M., Jr.
1972   *Artifact and Pottery Coding Manual*, Stillwater, OK: Oklahoma State University.

Furumark, A.
1941   *The Chronology of Mycenaean Pottery.* Stockholm: Pettersons.

Gaines, S. W.
1974   Computer Use at an Archaeological Field Location. *Am Ant* 39: 454–62.
1981a   Computerized Data Banks in Archaeology: The European Situation. Computers and the Humanities 15: 223–26.

Gaines, S. W. ed.
1971   Conferences. *Newsletter for Computer Archaeology*, 6/4: 1–2.
1981b   *Data Bank Applications in Archaeology*. Tucson: University of Ari-
            zona.
Gardin, J. C.
1974   *Les Banques de Données Archéologique*. Paris: Centre National de la
            Recherche Scientifique.
Geraty, L. T.
1980   Computer-Assisted Management of Heshbon Data: Coding
            Stratigraphic And Typological Data. Paper presented at the
            Annual Meeting of the American Schools of Oriental Research,
            Dallas (November, 1980).
Ginouves, R.; and Guimier-Sorbets, A. M.
1978   *La Constitution des Données en Archéologie Classique*. Paris: Centre
            National de la Recherche Scientifique.
Hodson, F. R.; Kendall, D. G.; and Tautu, P., eds.
1973   *Mathematics in the Archaeological and Historical Sciences*. Edin-
            burgh: Edinburgh University.
Joukowsky, M.
1980   *A Complete Manual of Field Archaeology*, Englewood Cliffs: Pren-
            tice-Hall.
Katz, D. *et al.*
1978   System 2000 Applications in Ancient Studies. Paper presented
            at a System 2000 Users' Conference, Austin.
Katz Price, D. F.
1982   The Tel Michal Computer Project, unpublished manuscript, 18
            pp., 14 figures.
Laflin, S., ed.
1978   *Computer Applications in Archaeology 1978*. Proceedings of the
            (Sixth) Annual Conference at the Computer Center, University
            of Birmingham. Birmingham: University of Birmingham.
Loy T.; and Powell, G. R.
1977   *Archaeological Data Recording Guide*, British Columbia Museum
            Heritage Records 3. Victoria, British Columbia: Provincial Mu-
            seum.
Lusignan, S.; and North, J. S., eds.,
1977   *Computing in the Humanities: Proceedings of the Third International
            Conference on Computing in the Humanities*. Waterloo, Ontario:
            International Conference of Computing in the Humanities.
McClelland, T. L.
1975   Quantitative Studies in the Iron-Age Pottery of Palestine. Un-
            published Ph.D. dissertation, University of Pennsylvania.
1979   Chronology of the "Philistine" Burials at Tell el-Farʿah (South),
            Journal of Field Archaeology 6:57–73.
McNally, S.; and Walsh, V.
1984   The Akhmim Data Base: A Multi-Stage System for Computer-
            Assisted Analysis of Artifacts. *Journal of Field Archaeology* 11:
            47–59.
Mertz, R. R.; and Levenbach, G. J.
1978   An Information Theory Approach to Mycenean Pottery. Pp.
            23–33 in *Computer Applications in Archaeology 1978*, ed. S. Laflin.
            Birmingham: University of Birmingham.

Meyers, E. M.; Kraabel, A. T.; and Strange, J. F.
1976   *Ancient Synagogue Excavations at Khirbet Shema, Upper Galilee, Israel, 1970–72. AASOR,* Vol. 42. Durham, NC: Duke University.

Meyers, E. M.; Strange, J. F.; and Meyers, C. L.
1981   Preliminary Report on the 1980 Excavations at En-Nabratein, Israel. *BASOR* 244: 1–25.

Mitchell, J. L., ed.
1974   *Computers in the Humanities.* Minneapolis: University of Minnesota.

Mitchell, L.
1978   *User's Manual: Heshbon Data Entry Forms.* Anguin, CA.: Pacific Union College.

MRI, Inc.
1974   *System 2000 Reference Manual.* 2nd rev. ed. Austin: MRI Systems Corporation.

Newcomer, M. H.; and Hodson, F. R.
1973   Constellation Analysis of Burins from Ksar Akil. Pp. 87–104 in *Archaeological Theory and Practice,* ed. D. E. Strong. New York: Seminar.

Nie, N. H., *et al.*
1975   *Statistical Package for the Social Sciences,* 2nd ed., New York: McGraw-Hill.

Patton, P. C.; and Holoien, R. A.
1981   *Computing in the Humanities.* Lexington Books Series in Computer Science. Lexington, MA: Heath.

Redman, C. L.
1973   Multistage Fieldwork and Analytic Techniques. *Am Ant* 38: 61–69.

Rouse, I.
1960   The Classification of Artifacts. *Am Ant* 25: 324–29.

Sabloff, J. A., ed.
1981   *Simulations in Archaeology.* Albuquerque: University of New Mexico.

Schiffer, M. B. ed.
1982   *Advances in Archaeological Theory and Method,* vol. 5. New York: Academic.

de Sonneville-Bordes, D.; and Perrot, J.
1954–56 Lexique typologique du Paléolithique superieur. *Bulletin de la Societe Prehistoire Française* 51: 327–35; 52: 76–79; 53: 408–12, 547–59.

Strange, J. F.
1981   Using the Microcomputer in the Field: The Case of the Meiron Excavation Project. *Newsletter of the American Schools of Oriental Research* 4: 8–11.
1984   Recent Computer Applications in Ancient Near Eastern Archaeology. Pp. 129–46 in *The Answers Lie Below: Essays in Honor of Lawrence Edmund Toombs,* ed. H. O. Thompson. Lanham, MD: University Press of America.

Strong, D. E., ed.
1973   *Archaeological Theory and Practice.* New York: Seminar.

Toombs, L. E.
1971   Coding Pottery in the Field. Pp. 25–28 in *Coding & Clustering*

Pottery by Computer, ed. N. E. Wagner, Waterloo, Ontario: Waterloo Lutheran University.

Verhaeghe, F., ed.
1979   *Archaeology, Natural Science and Technology: The European Situation,* 3 vols. Strasbourg: European Science Foundation.

Wagner, N. E.
1971   *Coding and Clustering Pottery by Computer.* Waterloo, Ontario: Waterloo Lutheran University.

Ward, R. D.; and Holoien, R. A.
1981   A Computer Data Base for Babylonian Economic Documents. Pp. 163–79 in *Computing in the Humanities,* eds. P. C. Patton and R. A. Holoien. Lexington, MA: Heath.

Wilcock, J. D.
1973   The Use of Remote Terminals for Archaeological Site Records. *Science and Archaeology* 9: 22–25.

16
PUBLICATION OF ARCHAEOLOGICAL REPORTS

ROGER S. BORAAS
Upsala College

In a recent discussion of "Archaeological Publications and Their Use," H. Darrell Lance (1981:47–66)[1] classified the written reports of archaeological work into three main types: (a) primary reports, (b) criticism, and (c) synthesis (1981:53). The primary materials are in turn subdivided into "current reports, preliminary reports, and final reports" (1981:53). The initial publication of archaeological fieldwork is an important step in any project, but as Lance rightly cautions, "if a researcher finds a piece of information in an early preliminary report, he or she dare not cite that datum without checking all subsequent, current, preliminary, or final reports to make sure that it has withstood the test of later seasons of excavation or more detailed study" (1981:54–55). As a form of scientific inquiry, archaeological fieldwork suffers a unique limitation properly noted by Lance: ". . . the excavation of any particular piece of archaeological data can occur only once. There is no way to repeat the experiment, as it were, even if it was done incompetently" (1981:49). This fact sets archaeological fieldwork apart from most scientific disciplines; the non-repeatable nature of excavation points to the importance of proper field methods and recording techniques.

While Lance's analysis was prepared primarily for the sake of readers who are interested in the relation of archaeological work to biblical studies, I will attempt to view the problems from the side of the excavator/reporter. My perspective has been conditioned by four different forms of the task. Work has been in progress for some years on "final reports" materials pertaining to the excavations at Shechem and Hesban.[2] "Current reports" were written in connection with my work at

---

[1] See also the review by Currid 1984.

[2] Final report responsibilities have comprised modest efforts regarding early Iron Age materials from Shechem and a review of excavation strategy and tactics for the Hesban project, both still in preparation.

Rujm el-Malfuf and Khirbet Iskander (Boraas 1971:35–41, figs. 1–41; and Richard and Boraas 1984:63–87). The writer was involved in the production of a "preliminary report" for each of the five seasons of the Tell Ḥesban excavations (Boraas and Horn 1969; 1973; and 1975; Boraas and Geraty 1976; 1978). Some of this writer's archaeological reporting falls into the "criticism" category.[3] From such involvement one claims not the wisdom of the expert, but perhaps the scars of a sometime warrior.

As with all writing, there are preliminary decisions which affect the entire enterprise, some of which are hidden from the reader except by indirect observation, and some of which ought, I would argue, to be stated at the outset in order to minimize confusion or misunderstanding. One of the first choices faced by the excavator/reporter is the selection of audience for the types of reporting that will make the results known. Usually required by the Antiquities Law of the country in which excavation has occurred, the early release of a brief summary of a season's work, whether surface exploration, preliminary soundings, scientific environmental data-gathering or full-scale excavation, is seldom a problem because the publication vehicle is also selected. The official journal or annual of the host government's Department of Antiquities and the host country's local press provide both an official scholarly and a popular audience for the first releases on a project's work. These reports most often comprise only the most conspicuous or "newsworthy" results and will not include any technical data for cross-examination. The chief merit of such releases is their speed of dissemination following completion of the work, but there is no attempt to present an exhaustive account at this point.

More difficult is the choice of audience for a preliminary report. If fund-raising for future seasons is partly dependent on wide dissemination and popular understanding of the project, the audience must be broadened beyond one's scholarly colleagues who are more interested in the integrity and range of the archaeological investigations. This figured quite strongly in the decision about the form and content of the reports on the first three seasons of the excavations at Ḥesban. The format chosen for reporting the final two seasons was governed more by the effort to provide scholarly colleagues with sufficient detail to allow for a cross-checking of conclusions. Whatever one judges to be the success of either effort, there was a clear shift in the intended audience, and it had its effect on the contents of the initial Ḥesban reports.

In final reports, one writes primarily for scholarly colleagues, for both contemporary and future generations of students; this requires a report with a full range of details, comparisons, conclusions and syn-

[3] This item and Boraas 1984.

theses which the data allow. Consequently, the choice of genre for reporting beyond the earliest releases is also important. Here the
economics of data-processing, publication-fund planning, and writing
time of the scholars compete with the kinds of publications that might be
available. As Lance (1981:54) correctly notes, preliminary reports "can
be found scattered throughout the journals that specialize in Palestinian
archaeology or in separate volumes, monographs, or annuals." The cost
of preparation, access to a particular vehicle for publication, and time-
delay involved in the backlog of a particular journal may all affect the
choice an archaeologist makes. One clear reason for the prompt publication of the Ḥesban preliminary reports was the fact that the first excavation director, Siegfried Horn, served as editor of a denominational
quarterly journal *(Andrews University Seminary Studies)* which provided an
immediately available medium for releasing such reports, both articles
and monographs. Most archaeologists cannot rely on such dependable
publishing support, and the uncertainties of genre follow, especially in a
period when costs of producing and publishing photographs, line drawings, or other illustrations continue to escalate. Both the scope of materials planned for a preliminary report and the schedule of writing times
to be allocated are related to the genre decision. The choice of genre
may sometimes be decided by the editorial policy of the journal. It may
wish to emphasize conclusions at the price of the supporting details, for
instance. Archaeologists should have such choices in mind prior to
launching the fieldwork. Such decisions will aid those responsible for
summarizing the results even during field operations. A clear choice of
genre for the preliminary report form can carry even into the shaping of
weekly summaries by field supervisors and can condition the forms of
recording documents used to mark the progress of excavation from day-
to-day.

Different choices need to be made in any form of reporting beyond
the "current reports" stage of publication. These choices concern the
data being sought, the terminology adopted, the excavation strategy
involved in the project, and the modes of recording being used. Such
decisions show respect for one's readers and an interest in bringing the
earliest and best possible criticism to bear on the studies under way.

In times of increasingly narrow research designs, it is necessary for a
reader to comprehend as precisely as possible what sort(s) of information
were being sought in an excavation. It is no longer possible to assume
that this is self-evident in terms of a general historical interest or comparative cultural analyses. If there are specific goals motivating the
excavation, they will affect both excavation and recording practices, and
they deserve to be declared "up front." This is all the more important in
excavations conducted over several seasons, since goals may shift after
developments in the earlier seasons. For example, the choice of proceed-

ing beyond the initially planned three seasons of work at Tell Ḥesban was governed in part by the architectural remains discovered by the end of the third season and the assessment that at least two additional seasons of work would be needed to complete the excavation of those features (Boraas and Geraty 1976:6). A description of such presuppositions and goals gives the reader a basis for measuring the adequacy of the procedures employed and allows a collegial and responsible reflection on the relation between objectives and results. The more technical and narrowly defined the project's goals are, the more vital it is that the presuppositions concerning them be made clear from the beginning.

Another presupposition that should be declared is the choice of terminology adopted for the expedition's work and reporting. The most casual glance at almost any group of reports on archaeological fieldwork underscores the truth of Lance's comment that "excavators systematize and present their evidence in quite different styles. Systems of numbering squares and loci and of recording and referring to objects and architecture are idiosyncratic to each archaeological publication" (Lance 1981:51). While one might bemoan this situation and wish that excavators would develop a standardized terminology, it is not likely in the foreseeable future. One of the obvious difficulties is that scholars tend to be individual in their modes of perception as well as expression. While that has the merit of allowing freedom in the ways in which data are recovered from the ground, it has produced a cloud of terminological confusion that can be next to impenetrable. Consider the fact that the term "fill" has become next to useless, since it is applied to practically any soil layer of indiscriminate function or uncertain character. Whatever terminology an excavator might adopt, it is helpful to have it in place so that one may attempt to be consistent in the recording documents and in all forms of reporting. Imagine the writer's dismay when he discovered that a square supervisor's preliminary report had used a single term in seven different ways on a single page of manuscript. Adopting a basic set of terms for regularly recurring items may produce less scintillating prose in reports, but it will have the merit of allowing clarity whenever the terms appear. Even a modest standard glossary adopted by an expedition can help (Boraas and Horn 1969:112–13).[4]

Perhaps the most important of the presuppositions that must be declared is the pair of primary considerations concerning method, i.e., excavation strategy and tactics and recording procedures. The critical nature of these considerations rests on a fact already mentioned: the excavation of a given datum can occur only once. The unrepeatable nature of the recovery of an archaeological datum requires that the

---

[4] Usage cited was employed both in the field recording instruments, field summaries, and published preliminary reports.

method by which it was excavated and the medium by which it was recorded be clearly stated. It will be most important for the reader to know whether the archaeological datum in question was central or peripheral to the excavation aims. Within the current conventions of verbal description and scientific illustration, the more clarity which can be provided the reader concerning standard procedures employed the better. As for excavation strategy, the reason for the choice between pursuing maximum stratigraphic penetration as opposed to broad exposure should be identified. Similarly helpful is an explanation of the reasons particular zones of a site were chosen for excavation. Any changes in tactics ought to be explained; tactics almost always change in excavations reaching beyond a single season's work. Even within a single season, shifts of tactics are sometimes brought on by such elementary considerations as staff health. If such explanations can be provided at the beginning of a report, the reader will be in a better position to assess the results both realistically and sympathetically. It also allows for critical discussion among informed peers at an early stage of a complex or long-term project, the benefit of which will be in the integrity of results obtained in the long-run.

When one has stated the nature of the task as fully as possible, there are still important issues that should be discussed in the preparation of an archaeological report. Three of these issues will be discussed below: (1) degree of coverage, (2) level of interpretation imposed, and (3) the problem of drawing historical conclusions.

The degree of coverage may be established by the organ of publication used. Length of report, limits of illustrative material to be included, or an editorial policy restricting the quantity of specific details included in a report may settle the matter for a writer. Behind such judgments concerning preliminary reports is the assumption that the excavation field recording documents are the most complete records on the excavated materials. As any field supervisor knows, that assumption may or may not be true. Whether the mode of field recording is a "diary" style, a "locus sheet" style or any combination of daily observations and measurements, there are always gaps and missing elements, the need for which may not appear until some later interpretive question raises the need for them. Moreover, the initial observations of many scientific data are by definition briefest in the field, and they only become complete following various laboratory analyses.

The implication of these facts, I suggest, is that more detailed descriptive material should accompany the initial conclusions. The publisher may rightly observe that not everyone is interested in every locus description which lay behind an excavator's conclusion, and that it may waste a journal's space to record such material. One device which might alleviate this problem is to divide the material into descriptive and analytical segments, allowing readers to follow the presentation at the level of their interest. Unfortunately, the only other option is that the serious reader examine the field records directly or wait however many years it takes for the final reports to appear. Lance rightly identifies the danger of the latter choice: "Unfortunately, too many excavation projects never advance beyond the preliminary report. In fact, some digs have published nothing beyond brief current reports" (Lance 1981:55). The ideal from this writer's perspective is a preliminary report published promptly after a season's fieldwork but which offers full descriptive material and tentative conclusions. This would require close cooperation among all staff members, and the successful completion of such reports would stand as a tribute to the commitment and good will of all staff involved.

As for the level of interpretation imposed, it must be recognized from the outset that all preliminary report interpretations are tentative and subject to revision. In view of the normal processes of archaeological criticism (Lance 1981:56–57), one needs to remember that even final report interpretations are subject to revision (Lance 1981:57).[5] Both the methods and presentation of results will undergo a careful scrutiny. That primary attention ought to be given to stratigraphic matters perhaps goes without saying, but it raises a difficult question about the use of illustrations. Balk photos, especially if not taken quite promptly after soil exposures, are notoriously difficult to reproduce and publish with sufficient clarity to convey the fine relations of layers sometimes involved. Wall fragments may be conspicuous and clear, but closely packed soil, ash, or organic layers will be next to invisible because of their size, if not their coloration. The alternative of using a balk section drawing is usually where the critical question arises. Shall one present the actual drawing of the layer relations, or shall one schematize the relations so as to highlight the conclusions asserted in the text? While one may argue that *every* drawing is an interpretation, it is clear that schematized drawings are even more interpretive and can be used or abused to support conclusions. There is the question as to whether it is more important for an excavator to appear to be right or more important for the excavator to present uninterpreted evidence for common scrutiny and critique. The temptation doubles if the excavator's chosen interpretation tends to be more striking or unique for the period or phenomena being investigated. The desire to present "distinctive" or "revolutionary" finds will certainly assault the excavator's judgment on this decision.

On the other hand, ceramic interpretation is more easily affected by the selection of what is to be drawn and published than by the nature of

---

[5] See especially the comments on the Megiddo publications.

the illustrations themselves. Once again, there is a need for more stan-
daridzation in the manner of illustration and verbal description of pottery. One of the most conspicuous omissions from preliminary reports is
the discussion and presentation of odd or exceptional pieces of pottery,
comparative studies of which might produce some of the most helpful
criticism of tentative findings. In this writer's judgment, one of the main
weaknesses of the final three volumes in the Hesban report series was
the lack of clear and detailed illustrations of pottery, except for occasional photos of groups of vessels or the odd whole vessel. Given the long
delay in the publication of the final report on the Hesban ceramic
collection, the inaccessibility of ceramic information from this site is
detrimental to the study of other sites in the region.

The variety and forms of scientific studies which can be included
vary with the types of materials retrieved and the necessary analysis
times for reports to be drawn up. Beyond that, however, is the degree of
interpretive impact such studies could have on the overall report. Attempts to integrate such studies are at their infancy[6] and require all the
imaginative ingenuity which the archaeologists and scientific specialists
can muster. It may be a relatively simple thing to note the presence of a
major pathology in burial evidence from a given period, but to relate
that to the studies on food sources in the area is a complicated task. The
integration of such information with weather, erosion, or other discernible patterns requires an overview not always easy to reach. In principle,
therefore, it would seem that the level of interpretation imposed ought
to be guided by the amount of integration possible in the time frame that
the publication allows. The fact that *all* conclusions are tentative should
encourage excavators to offer interpretive options boldly.

The final issue discussed in this essay is the process by which historical conclusions about a site are derived from excavated data. There are
two factors which determine what can be accomplished in this endeavor.
The first limitation is the nature and extent of historical knowledge on
the period and site under investigation. The level of historical understanding of a particular time and place can vary from little or none[7] to
extensive. New historical and archaeological data may supplement or
modify the understanding established by previously known data, sometimes calling longstanding theories into question.[8]

The second outside limit is the type and range of new data available

[6] See Dever 1981, especially section g, p. 18 and n. 20.
[7] See the problem of Eblaite materials, e.g., in articles by Biggs (1981), Pettinato
(1980), and Archi (1981).
[8] See the theory of Amorite migration under review in Richard 1980.

on a site at the end of an excavation season. The discovery of substantial defense walls and of extensive stone domestic architecture in the 1981 and 1982 seasons at Khirbet Iskander already calls for a modification of the previously held belief that the final stage of the Early Bronze Age was characterized by a nomadic society. Even at an early period in the excavations, it became possible to view "the Iskander evidence—impressive domestic structures, multiple phasing, the monumentality of the defensive structures, and a year-round, agriculturally-based settlement—as presenting a portrait of EB IV society more akin to the urban EB III peoples than to the pastoral-nomadic elements of the EB IV population who are best known by their burial customs" (Richard and Boraas 1984:84–5).

New information that brings revision to old theories is just one side of the picture. Equally important are the archaeological data which agree with prior historical knowledge. The primary danger with the former, contradictory evidence is the way in which it is used by some to jump to conclusions. This is vividly portrayed by Lance in relation to the history of Israelite occupation of ancient Canaan (Lance 1981:64).[9] The effort to assert precise historical identifications may founder on the lack of any known historical data pertaining to the site.[10] The prompt publication of preliminary reports on archaeological work is desirable, but historical conclusions based on these early interpretations must be viewed as tentative. While the final preliminary report of the Hesban series offered a site-wide sequence of 24 occupation strata (Boraas and Geraty 1976:15–16), the surest historical conclusion came in the form of negative evidence on the site. The anticipated evidence of Israelite occupation in a major site in the Transjordan, as reflected in the Book of Numbers, simply was not present in anything but two dump accumulations on the west and south sides of the site. What was there was non-architectural. It comprised pottery mixed with soil which had been used to fill a rock-cut trench or was scattered on bedrock. Such negative evidence challenged the identification of Tell Hesban as biblical Heshbon and caused the excavators to make plans to work at the neighboring site of Jalul, thought by some to offer a solution to this historical problem.

Archaeologists must accept the tension between their desire to propose theories on the basis of available evidence and the need to control speculation that is based on limited data. Even tentative conclusions require a certain amount of evidence, but such proposals are valuable because they bring about a critical examination of excavated results. This delicate balance is, after all, the purpose of archaeological reports.

[9]See especially Lance's references to recent criticism by J. Maxwell Miller in nn. 17 and 18.
[10]As in recent salvage work by Donald Wimmer at Tell Safut, Jordan, in 1982 and 1983.

BIBLIOGRAPHY

Archi, A.
  1981   Further Concerning Ebla and the Bible. *BA* 44: 145–154.
Biggs, R.
  1981   The Ebla Tablets: An Interim Perspective. *BA* 43: 76–88.
Boraas, R.
  1971   A Preliminary Sounding at Rujm el-Malfuf, 1969. *ADAJ* 16: 31–45.
  1984   Some Aspects of Archaeology—Tactics and Strategy. Pp. 39–50 in *The Answers Lie Below: Essays in Honor of Lawrence Edmund Toombs*, ed. H. O. Thompson. Lanham, MD: University Press of America.
Boraas, R., and Geraty, L. T.
  1976   *Heshbon 1974: The Fourth Campaign at Tell Hesban.* Andrews University Monographs 9. Berrien Springs, MI: Andrews University.
  1978   *Heshbon 1976: The Fifth Campaign at Tell Hesban.* Andrews University Monographs 10. Berrien Springs, MI: Andrews University.
Boraas, R. and Horn, S. H.
  1969   *Heshbon 1968: The First Campaign at Tell Hesban.* Andrews University Monographs 2. Berrien Springs, MI: Andrews University.
  1973   *Heshbon 1968: The First Campaign at Tell Hesban.* Andrews University Monographs 6. Berrien Springs, MI: Andrews University.
  1975   *Heshbon 1973: The Third Campaign at Tell Hesban.* Andrews University Monographs 8. Berrien Springs, MI: Andrews University.
Currid, J. D.
  1983   Review of H. D. Lance, *The Old Testament and the Archaeologist. JBL* 102: 291–92.
Dever, W. G.
  1981   The Impact of the "New Archaeology" on Syro-Palestinian Archaeology. *BASOR* 242: 15–29.
Lance, H. D.
  1981   *The Old Testament and the Archaeologist.* Philadelphia: Fortress.
Pettinato, G.
  1980   Ebla and the Bible. *BA* 43: 202–16.
Richard, S.
  1980   Toward a Consensus of Opinion on the End of the Early Bronze Age in Palestine-Transjordan. *BASOR* 237: 5–34.
Richard, S., and Boraas, R. S.
  1984   Preliminary Report on the 1981–82 Seasons of the Expedition to Khirbet Iskander and Its Vicinity. *BASOR* 254: 63–87.

PART THREE

INTEGRATIVE
ARCHAEOLOGICAL STUDIES:
THE SYNTHESIS

17
IMPACT OF THE "NEW ARCHAEOLOGY"

WILLIAM G. DEVER

University of Arizona

In a recent popular survey of the development of Syro-Palestinian archaeology (Dever 1980a), I sought to chart the growth of our discipline by distinguishing four "revolutions." These were turning points that characterized: (1) the exploratory phase (1838–1914); (2) the beginning of large-scale fieldwork and the evolution of a basic chronological-cultural framework (1918–40); (3) the introduction of modern stratigraphic methods (1948–70); and (4) an incipient revolution caused by the rise of the "new archaeology" (1970—).

In a festschrift honoring Joseph A. Callaway, whose own career epitomizes for many the remarkable growth of biblical and Syro-Palestinian archaeology, I have been asked to expand on the idea of the latter revolution. I shall attempt to do so by reflecting on what the newer approach consists of, how it differs from the old, and what more it is capable of achieving.

I. THE INITIAL IMPACT OF THE "NEW ARCHAEOLOGY"

A Model for Assessing Methodological Change

Before we treat the newer approaches of the 1970s that have been regarded by some as revolutionary, let us adopt a model from the work of a distinguished philosopher and historian of science, Thomas S. Kuhn, whose seminal work *The Structure of Scientific Revolutions* (1970) should be required reading for all in our field. Although our branch of historical and humanistic archaeology cannot yet (and perhaps should not) claim to be scientific in the same sense that the natural or "hard" sciences are, Kuhn's analysis, in my opinion, provides an analogy for virtually any branch of inquiry that considers itself a professional or

[1] I am indebted to my student Nephi Bushman for calling to my attention certain passages of Kuhn utilized here.

academic discipline, as our branch of archæology is beginning to do (cf. Dever 1982; 1985).

For our purposes, Kuhn's arguments may be summarized briefly (and very simplistically) as follows. (1) What holds any intellectual discipline together is not a set of rules, much less the verbalization of theories that students absorb and that supposedly qualify them for practice, but rather acknowledged models of past achievements, research from which new problems and theories derive. Such "shared paradigms," as Kuhn terms them, can be "prior to, more binding, and more complete than any set of rules for research that could be unequivocally abstracted from them" (1970:46). (2) The shared paradigm is thus basically not a deliberate program based on a well-defined theoretical platform, but a practical consensus among a group of practitioners who come to be acknowledged as successful and therefore dominate a particular phase in the development of a discipline. The shared paradigm comprises a set of problems that are deemed worthy of interest and capable of being solved, together with a way of viewing the evidence and working toward a solution. (3) As long as a single such paradigm appears to be more successful than others competing with it (i.e., it "works" better), it will persist—whether all practitioners agree on the rules or not, and despite a characteristic neglect (or even disinterest) in articulating abstract theory. These integrative stages of research in a developing discipline may be regarded as phases that are mature, i.e., that provide the foundations upon which further advance may build. This is what Kuhn describes as "normal science," or the commitment to and continuation of a particular research tradition (1970:11). (4) When, however, the paradigm shifts, as it does periodically, an intervening phase occurs that Kuhn calls a "scientific revolution." These alternating shifts are largely pragmatic: they usually take place when certain problems do not yield to a solution, despite ever more persistent and ingenious applications of the method. Since science aims at all-embracing explanations of "laws," any anomaly that persists violates the integrity of the paradigm. When that happens a crisis begins to take shape; the stage is then set for a change of paradigm, or a "revolution." (The crisis may also be provoked, of course, by new developments in other, related disciplines.) In time a new paradigm will replace the old, and after the interruption normal science will again proceed apace until the next revolution.

Paradigms Old and New

Using Kuhn's provocative model, it seems apparent that Syro-Palestinian (and "biblical") archaeology since about 1970 has indeed undergone changes that constitute at least a revolution in the making. A brief comparison of the older and the newer paradigms will confirm this.

(1) *1918–70.* Let us look first at both fieldwork and publication

before about 1970, during our second and third revolutions (above, and Dever 1980a). While there was little research design in the modern sense, and virtually no explicit statements of what is properly meant by archaeological theory (below), it is possible to extrapolate from the literature something of what the excavators of that period thought they were doing. Thus a paradigm can be reconstructed, for instance, from the methods employed and the problems chosen for investigation.

It is clear that "method," where discussed at all, dealt principally not with archaeological theory of interpretation but with technique: how to dig, record, and analyze certain aspects of the material culture. In this formative period the objective was to disentangle and place in correct relative sequence the levels of the major tells in Syria-Palestine; to establish an absolute chronology on the basis of local and international synchronisms; then finally to correlate the dated remains with known texts, especially biblical, so as to corroborate certain fixed events in what I would call "political history" (see below).[2] In practice, this paradigm meant concentration on building up the skills of stratigraphy and comparative ceramic typology, almost to the exclusion of any other methodical concern, although with notable success. In results, it led to the triumph of the *Kulturgeschichte* school, now generally discredited but nonetheless a movement that provided the fundamental building block for all future progress in understanding the actual cultural history of the area.

In retrospect, all this seems commendable but somewhat parochial. The older paradigm dealt largely with what historians of the Annales School call history's upper plane. To use the analogy of Braudel's three tiers, discussed in his monumental study of the Mediterranean world in the age of Philip II (1972), earlier archaeologists in our field sought to portray largely the "history of events." These, however, are but rapid, essentially superficial fluctuations in the stream of history, caused by public figures and political happenings, only "surface disturbances, crests of foam that the tides of history carry" (1972:21). This approach largely ignored Braudel's middle plane, the slower-moving yet dynamic "social history" of interacting groups, a "swelling current of collective destinies." And it was oblivious to the still lower, almost timeless and impersonal undercurrent of the daily life of countless individuals, conditioned by the relation between human society and the environment, "the deeper reality of history."[3]

---

[2] I had originally used this term almost intuitively (cf. 1974:13; 1982:105) before the analogy from Braudel employed below (p. 3) came to mind. Whether such "political history" was a product of the Calvinist mentality of many of the practitioners of biblical archaeology, or of the general intellectual climate in America in the 1920s–30s, is an intriguing question but beyond our scope here. Cf. further Dever 1980c; 1985.

[3] Braudel's overview can best be seen in the Preface to the first French edition of 1949,

For example, the earlier school of biblical archaeology in the 1930s–60s proceeded by trying to locate and clear the public sectors of the large tells, investigating monumental architecture such as palaces and temples, but especially city fortifications and their destructions. The focus was almost exclusively on affairs of the state, where dominant personalities, political conflict, and religious ideas were assumed to be the principal agents that shaped events. Ideological factors in cultural change, other than politics and religion, were either overlooked or minimized, as were the effects of the natural environment, the economy, or social structure—in short, the role of culture. The general objective was usually to reconstruct larger historical episodes such as the "Israelite conquest of Canaan." The secular school of the period did not, of course, take its agenda so narrowly from problems of biblical history, but its overall paradigm was much the same, as will be seen, for instance, from an examination of the Megiddo or Beth-shan projects.[4]

(2) *1970 to the present.* It is now evident that the paradigm has been changing since about 1970. It would appear that the crisis Kuhn describes as precipitating a revolution was brought on partly by the failure of the older approach to solve some of the most fundamental historical problems. A brief perusal of the current literature will show, for example, how intractable certain problems have proven, such as the exact nature of the early Israelite settlement of Canaan or the proper historical and cultural milieu in which the Patriarchal narratives are to be set (see the most recent surveys of Miller 1977, Dever 1977, with full references to the earlier literature, and also below on the Israelite "conquest").

There were also external factors that forced a change beginning about 1970. Already in 1972, it was possible to list factors in what I perceived then as the "coming of age" of Syro-Palestinian archaeology as a discipline independent of what had formerly been called by consensus "biblical archaeology" (Dever 1974). Among the developments already evident were trends toward multidisciplinary staffs and research designs; increasing resort to public funding; growing competition from the burgeoning, secularist "national schools" in the Middle East; and finally, what was then only dimly foreseen, the impact of the "New Archaeology" on the American academic scene.

More recently (1981), as it gained momentum in the mid-1970s, I analyzed the theory of the new archaeology and its relevance to our

---

reprinted in English in the second English edition (1972:17–22). Here I have freely paraphrased Braudel, which scarcely does justice to either the fecundity of his thought or the richness of his prose. In thinking about the Annales School I have profited from Stager's important essay (1985), as well as from the application of this model to southern Syria and Lebanon by his student Leon Marfoe (1979).

[4] This succinct critique may not do justice to earlier schools, but see more extended and balanced treatments in Dever 1974; 1980a; 1982; and especially 1985.

branch of archaeology, showing that most of our new paradigms have been borrowed—belatedly and often uncritically—from New World archaeology and anthropology. The intellectual movement in American archaeology in the 1960s and 1970s popularly known as the new archaeology is, of course, too diverse and still too controversial to be readily characterized. But there is a consensus on the major emphases of the movement, the most significant of which for our purposes are: (1) The use of cultural-evolutionary paradigms; (2) a multidisciplinary orientation; (3) the necessity for a holistic approach; (4) the adoption of scientific methods for the formulation and testing of laws of cultural change; (5) the value of ethnography and modern material culture studies; and (6) the potential of archaeology for elucidating patterns of human thought and action.[5] As Willey and Sabloff have succinctly summarized the newer thinking in American archaeology, it is marked by "the concern with artifacts as behavior, with cultural ecology in its broadest sense, with systematic analysis, and with process as a central concept in cultural history" (1980:246).

II. THE REVOLUTION TAKES HOLD

As we shall see, the above approach is beginning to be widely adopted in Syro-Palestinian archaeology today, precisely as a paradigm, i.e., in the literature as a working blueprint for current fieldwork and research, even though there may be as yet little evidence of the underlying theory. In that sense a Kuhnian "revolution" may be said to be in the making. Indeed, it would be possible to take the diagnostic features of the "new archaeology" outlined above as criteria for assessing how far the "old archaeology" in our field has changed, were it not for two difficulties.

First, the impact of American new archaeology of the 1960s and 1970s is only now beginning to be felt fully in our field, so it is premature to speak of anything more than general trends. Second, the real test of archaeological theory and method lies in results, as seen in final reports of specific field projects, and obviously only preliminary reports, if those, are available from the most up-to-date projects. A listing of the penultimate or final report volumes of the past decade or so would only serve to underline the fact that all these works reflect essentially the archaeology of the 1960s, rather than current trends, and are in that sense "prerevolutionary." That would include American reports on Ai, Beth-shan, Gezer, Pella, Khirbet Shemaʿ and Meiron, Sarepta, Taanach, Tell el-Ful, and Tell es-Saidiyeh; Israeli reports on Arad, Ashdod, Azor and Tell

---

[5] See further the excellent survey of the new archaeology in Willey and Sabloff 1974:178–211; and cf. the critique in Dever 1981, with full references to the literature.

Yarmuth, Beer-sheba, Beth-shan, Deir el-Balaḥ, Lachish, Mevorakh, and Tell el-Qasileh; and European reports on Tell Deir ʿAllah, Jericho, and Tell Keisan.[6]

How, then, can we assess the strength and utility of this incipient revolution in our field? We can do so only by looking at the most current trends, as these are reflected primarily in: (1) recent field projects, (2) newer research designs, and (3) preliminary reports and papers in the journals and at national meetings.

(1) Here we can only single out what appear to be some of the most innovative of recent and reasonably well-published sites in Israel and Jordan—harbingers of things to come.[7]

In Israel, there is a growing tendency to concentrate on survey and settlement pattern analysis, on regional studies, on one-period sites, and on "problem-solving" archaeology, in comparison with the older large-scale tell excavations. In many cases natural scientists and collaborators from allied disciplines are being employed, both in prehistory and in historical archaeology, in order to reconstruct the total environmental and cultural context as far as possible (Bar-Yosef and Mazar 1982). One may cite as examples of recent Israeli projects the work of the Tel Aviv University Institute of Archaeology in the Negeb-Sinai and the Sharon Plain (1973—),[8] and the Yoqneam Regional Project of the Hebrew University of Jerusalem (1977—) in the Jezreel Valley.[9] American work in the newer mode would include the Galilee Synagogue Project directed by Eric M. Meyers and his colleagues (1970–1980), which thus far has excavated synagogues and Jewish towns at Khirbet Shemaʿ, Meiron, Gush Halav, and Nabratein.[10] The Lahav Project (1976—) has an inter-

[6] Here we cannot analyze these more conventional report volumes in detail, nor would it be helpful except as a point of departure. I have attempted a partial critique in the forthcoming paper referred to below in n. 21.

[7] There are, of course, other significant new projects in the field, but I can document only those that have begun substantial publication. This resume deliberately excludes prehistory, which is best considered a separate discipline and confines itself therefore to the Bronze-Iron Ages and Classical periods. Israel and Jordan are the focus here because of the extent and variety of fieldwork; Syria is excluded because in our view there are not published projects in the historical periods that signify the newer approach we are analyzing.

[8] On the Sinai, see Beit-Arieh and Gophna 1976; Beit-Arieh 1974; 1981a; 1981b. On Tel Aphek and the Sharon Plain, see Kochavi 1975; Kochavi, Beck, and Gophna 1979; Gophna and Ayalon 1980; Gophna and Beck 1981. The now completed excavations at Tell Michal (Herzog et al. 1980) and the successor of this project at Tell Jerisheh (1981—) are also part of the Tel Aviv's Institute regional project. This regional approach began with the late Yohanan Aharoni in the Negeb.

[9] See Ben-Tor and Rosenthal 1978; Ben-Tor 1979; Ben-Tor, Portugali, and Avissar 1979; 1981. On recent trends in Israeli archaeology, see further Bar-Yosef and Mazar 1982.

[10] See Meyers, Kraabel, and Strange 1976; Meyers, Strange, and Groh 1978; Meyers et al. 1979; Meyers, Strange, and Meyers 1981; 1982a; 1982b.

disciplinary staff and also has a strong ethnoarchaeological component.[11] The joint American-Israeli, multidisciplinary investigation in
archaeology and arid lands studies, the "Central Negev Highlands Project" (1978–1980), was deliberately planned around an attempt to apply
the newer methods experimentally at one-period EB IV—MB I sites in
the Negeb.[12]

In Jordan, the American excavations at Ḥesban (1968–1976), at Bab
ed-Draʿ (1975—), and in the Beqʿah Valley (1977—) have already produced impressive preliminary reports that attest to strong environmental and interdisciplinary orientation.[13] Thus to judge from excavations
already underway in Israel and Jordan, the newer approach seems here
to stay. However, despite greatly expanded potential, it is too early to see
how successful these projects may be in achieving results that will differ
substantially from those of more traditional projects.

(2) We have already implied that the best indicator of change so far
available may be the research design lying behind the newer projects.
Statements of objectives and strategy, however, are still rarely spelled out
explicitly in the published preliminary reports. Research design is thus
accessible largely in "behind-the-scenes" grant proposals that many of us
review for the National Endowment for the Humanities, or in the
proposals for ASOR affiliation that come before the Committee on
Archaeological Policy.[14] There is no doubt that these research designs—
which scarcely even existed a decade ago in American Syro-Palestinian
archaeology—are rapidly becoming much more sophisticated. The best
of these proposals are now compatible with the approach and the standards of mainstream New World archaeology—not that this necessarily
the only criterion, but it is clearly superior to the lack of criteria that
characterized our field until recently.[15] Seminar papers and current
projects of the graduate students in our more progressive programs also
reveal similar research interests, closer to American anthropology than

[11] See Seger 1983.

[12] See Cohen and Dever 1978; 1979; 1981; Dever 1980b.

[13] On Bab ed-Draʿ, see Rast and Schaub *et al.* 1978; 1980; 1981; 1984; on the Beqʿah
Valley Project, see McGovern 1980; 1981. The Ḥesban project, with its five published
volumes of preliminary reports, is in my opinion the best example yet in our field of the
potential of environmental archaeology—this despite the fact that it is a church-related
project that normally I would place in the category of the older biblical archaeology school;
see below and n. 22. See Boraas and Horn 1969; 1973; 1975; Boraas and Geraty 1976;
1978.

[14] I cannot document these statements, since the proposals are confidential. Part of
the basis of my overview, however, is the unique opportunity I have had as Chairman of
ASOR's Committee on Archaeological Policy to review research design and to make on-site
inspections for more than 35 archaeological projects annually in Israel, Jordan, Syria,
Cyprus, Tunisia, Egypt, and Yemen.

[15] As noted in the conclusion below, the necessity for developing *explicit* criteria for
aims and methods has been perhaps the most beneficial aspect of the new archaeology. See
further Dever 1981:16.

former biblical archaeologists would ever have imagined. Thus there is a growing consensus, a sort of "oral tradition" among professional workers at all levels in our field, and it clearly reflects a new paradigm.

Finally, we must look at the journals and professional meetings in this country to see how far and how rapidly American Syro-Palestinian archaeology has moved beyond the traditional boundaries. A survey of the last several years of *BASOR*—always a bellwether for our field—reveals that alongside conventional site reports, epigraphy, and discussion of general historical problems, there is a whole new array of topics. One now finds articles on theory and method, New World archaeology, cultural anthropology, prehistory, survey, ethnoarchaeology, geology, climatology, laboratory analyses of various kinds, palaeobotany and palaeozoology, systems theory, spatial analysis, demography, and other subjects.[16]

Similar trends are seen at national professional meetings, especially good places to "take the pulse" of an evolving discipline. At the annual SBL-ASOR meetings, the same, or still broader, topics are presented in numerous papers, or even in workshops and seminars totally devoted to a single such subject. More significantly, younger scholars are also attending and giving papers at meetings of the Archaeological Institute of America, the Society for American Archaeology, the American Anthropological Association, and elsewhere where they feel very much at home.

Thus, while there may be disagreement on much of the theory behind the newer experimental methods and their application in our field, there is a new paradigm. New ideas are being tried, in both fieldwork and research, and there is a growing forum for their discussion.

III. WHERE DO WE GO FROM HERE

We might begin this inquiry by abandoning the sterile debate about whether Near Eastern archaeology as it is developing today should remain "historical" or become more "anthropological." Let us begin instead with the concept of "culture," assuming that archaeology is unique simply as that branch of inquiry that seeks to investigate and explain this universal human phenomenon in the past. The newer methods in archaeology are simply the latest attempts, and we hope the best to date, to do that. It is no coincidence that the watchwords of archaeology today, as summarized above, are exactly parallel to the essentials of culture. Culture is: (1) adaptation to the environment ("ecological"),

---

[16] As Editor of *BASOR* from 1978–84, I can attest that there was no attempt to establish quotas: the published manuscripts represent a typical cross-section of what the majority of archaeologists were currently doing (or at least publishing).

(2) patterned individual and social response ("behavioral," "systemic"), and (3) ever-changing ("processual").

The newer approach will be broad enough to encompass all of culture. It will be more capable than ever of helping to write "political history" on a grand scale, but its processual and environmental thrusts will enable it also to begin to grasp Braudel's deeper planes of social and even of individual history. The newer archaeology will thus be more complex but also more challenging, more productive, more relevant.

Two examples may serve to illustrate the potential of the new approach.

A. *The Israelite Settlement of Canaan.*

As we have already noted, the previous generation of archaeologists concentrated largely on LB/Iron I destruction levels in an attempt to corroborate an Israelite conquest of Canaan as envisioned in the book of Joshua. This rather simplistic approach failed, however, because it proved incapable of comprehending the mounting data. The emergence of ancient Israel now appears to have been part of a gradual and exceedingly complex process of socioeconomic change in ancient Palestine, stretching over some two centuries, with many regional and cultural variations. Recently, numerous biblical historians have reopened the discussion, employing models drawn from anthropology, sociology, and the history of religions. But the debate remains inconclusive, in part, in my judgment, because it makes too little or too inept use of archaeology.[17]

A more fruitful approach would consider what Syro-Palestinian archaeology today, conceived in truly interdisciplinary fashion, can contribute to the discussion. For instance, Lawrence Stager (1985) has illuminated early tribal history of the period of the Judges by coupling more conventional textual, historical, and archaeological studies with new models utilizing settlement history, ecology, demography, sociology of religion, and ethnoarchaeology. The result is a much more richly textured tapestry, and surely one more consistent with the reality (and also with the account in Judges). This is only a single, provisional example of the new archaeology at work, but it demonstrates the potential.[18]

---

[17] For the literature and the discussion until recently, see Miller 1977; add now Freedman and Graf 1983. The treatment of M. Chaney in the latter, as well as the earlier analysis of Gottward 1979, makes an admirable attempt to include archaeological data but suffers from the increasing difficulty the nonspecialist has in obtaining critical, up-to-date syntheses. See below and n. 18.

[18] Stager's work (1985) is a prolegomenon to the full publication of the early Iron I material from Ai and Khirbet Radannah, which is in his hands. See also the similar approach of Carol Meyers 1983. Israeli archaeologists have been particularly active in survey and excavation of transitional LB/Iron I sites; see, for example A. Mazar 1981 and references there.

B. *Religion and Cult.*

Traditionally, archaeology in the Holy Land has been preoccupied with confirmation of ancient religion. But as I have attempted to show in a recent programmatic essay (1983), despite this obsession, archaeological investigation has scarcely augmented our understanding of the cult in ancient Israel in any specific or fundamental way. Much of *Religionsgeschichte* was in reality an analysis of the literary tradition. It resulted, not surprisingly, in a history of the formation of the literary corpus, but not of early religious belief, much less practice.[19] To be sure, the "myth and ritual" school attempted the latter but largely in ignorance or defiance of the accumulating archaeological data, apart from texts. The "biblical theology" movement arose partly in reaction against these deficiencies, and in some versions, such as that of G. E. Wright, it sought to make use of archaeological data. But it defined religion essentially in terms of thought, i.e., theology rather than cult.

All schools underestimated the significance of the fact that the literary tradition in the Hebrew Bible is not only later but elitist. The tradition idealizes "normative" religion, as conceived by the Jerusalem priestly establishment, but it does not adequately portray folk religion, i.e., actual, popular religious practice. Only archaeology, in uncovering the material remains of the cult, is capable of penetrating behind the facade to get at the latter. And only archaeology can provide the essential basis for the comparative studies that are necessary to comprehend ancient Israelite religion in the larger setting of the religious life and institutions of greater Canaan. Such an application of archaeology to biblical studies has yet to be attempted, but it is now within the realm of possibility.[20]

IV. CONCLUSION

So exciting are the prospects outlined above that it is tempting to be overly sanguine about the revolution taking place in our field. Elsewhere, however, I have outlined in detail both theoretical objections and practical difficulties in adapting the new archaeology, much of which was pioneered on one-period New World sites, to the complex tell-sites of the Middle East (Dever 1981). In addition, Sabloff's recent survey of American new archaeology a decade later has pointed out that even here the revolution has only begun (1981). He argues that this is largely

[19] The work of F. M. Cross on Canaanite and early Israelite religion is a notable exception, but even this construes the contribution of archaeology as consisting almost exclusively of epigraphic, rather than material, remains. Cf. n. 20 below.

[20] See the detailed, programmatic strategy for fieldwork and research in Dever 1983. I expect to attempt an initial synthesis myself in a forthcoming article on the archaeological background of Canaanite and early Israelite religion.

because "new theoretical interests had not led to concomitant methodological and conceptual growth" (1981: 3). Therefore, he and American archaeologists have recently moved somewhat away from pure theory, advocating a "back-to-basics" approach that will start with a meticulous interpretation of the archaeological record in order to build theory from the ground up, what may be called "lower-level interpretation and middle-range theory" (Willey and Sabloff 1980: 249–54; see also Binford 1977 on "bridging theory").

Never having gone to the extremes of the new archaeology in the first place, we may profit from this caution as we proceed in Syro-Palestinian archaeology. There our stress on data and on the working out of a detailed stratigraphic and chronological framework for the material culture, our best achievements, provide a firm foundation on which to build new theory and method.

In summary, there *is* a new paradigm in Syro-Palestinian archaeology, an orientation and *modus vivendi* so heuristically powerful that it has changed our discipline irrevocably. Perhaps the most significant and persistent aspect of the change has been in forcing us: (1) to ask new questions; and (2) to make explicit what we are trying to learn in archaeology and how we propose to go about it.[21] The revolution came about not primarily as a negative (i.e., "secular") reaction to the older-style biblical archaeology, as some detractors think. Nor has it been forced on the field by an avant-garde minority.[22] It is rather the inevitable and beneficial evolution of a branch of archaeology that is maturing as a discipline. This emerging discipline builds on the best of the older or biblical archaeology, but it adds new dimensions as altogether new questions are raised. It presumes the traditional skills of stratigraphy and typology, as well as competence in ancient Near Eastern languages and history, but it also requires thorough grounding in new scientific and anthropological methods. It remains interested in a dialogue with biblical studies, but it also forms new research strategies and academic align-

---

[21] See my forthcoming paper "Major Problems of Excavating Stratigraphic Tell-sites in Syria-Palestine," read at the Second International Symposium on the Archaeology of Ancient Syria-Palestine in Tübingen in 1982. This is a preliminary attempt at an archaeological hermeneutic for our field; New World archaeologists have been concerned for some time now with what may be termed "archaeological epistemology."

[22] This statement alone would be sufficient to refute the charges of Shanks 1983. The simple fact is that the new archaeology is the natural outgrowth of biblical archaeology, as G. E. Wright himself foresaw in his last published article in 1975, and as I have maintained all along (1974, and especially 1980c: 9–15). I have also noted that while some former biblical archaeologists resisted the newer developments, others have been in the forefront of the revolution described here (cf. n. 13 above). Finally, it should be observed that Classical archaeology—traditionally closely aligned with Near Eastern archaeology—has been undergoing a similar revolution (see Dyson 1981; Coulsen, Sonkowsky and Wilkie 1984).

ments with many other fields, especially with the maturing discipline of general archaeology in America.[23]

Perhaps we may conclude by quoting Kuhn once more on the nature of "revolutions" in academic disciplines:

> I would argue, rather, that in these matters neither proof nor error is at issue. The transfer of allegiance from paradigm to paradigm is a conversion experience that cannot be forced. Lifelong resistance, particularly from those whose productive careers have committed them to an older tradition of normal science, is not a violation of scientific standards but an index to the nature of scientific research itself. The source of resistance is the assurance that the older paradigm will ultimately solve all its problems, that nature can be shoved into the box the paradigm provides. Inevitably, at times of revolution, that assurance seems stubborn and pigheaded as indeed it sometimes becomes. But it is also something more. That same assurance is what makes normal or puzzle-solving science possible. And it is only through normal science that the professional community of scientists succeeds, first, in exploiting the potential scope and precision of the older paradigm and, then, in isolating the difficulty through the study of which a new paradigm may emerge. . . . Though some scientists, particularly the older and more experienced ones, may resist indefinitely, most of them can be reached in one way or another. Conversions will occur a few at a time until, after the last holdouts have died, the whole profession will again be practicing under a single, but now a different, paradigm (Kuhn 1970: 151–52).

BIBLIOGRAPHY

Bar-Yosef, O.; and Mazar, A.
1982   Israeli Archaeology. *WA* 13: 310–25.
Beit-Arieh, I.
1974   An Early Bronze II Settlement at Nebi Salah in Southern Sinai. *TA* 1: 144–56.
1981a   An Early Bronze Age II Site near Sheikh ʿAwad in Southern Sinai, *TA* 8: 95–127.
1981b   A Pattern of Settlement in Southern Sinai and Southern Canaan in the Third Millennium B.C. *BASOR* 243: 31–55.
Beit-Arieh, I.; and Gophna, R.
1976   Early Bronze II Site in Wadi el-Qudeirat (Kadesh-barnea). *TA* 3: 142–50.
Ben-Tor, A.
1979   Tel Qiri—A Look at Village Life. *BA* 42: 105–13.

---

[23] On the possibility of archaeology emerging as an independent (although still very interdisciplinary) discipline, see J. Wiseman 1980; and, on our branch of archaeology, cf. Dever 1982; 1985.

Ben-Tor, A.; and Rosenthal, R.
1978   The First Season of Excavations at Tel Yoqneᶜam, 1977: Prelimi-
            nary Report. *IEJ* 28: 57–82.
Ben-Tor, A.; Portugali, Y.; and Avissar, M.
1979   The Second Season of Excavations at Tel Yoqneᶜam, 1978: Pre-
            liminary Report. *IEJ* 29: 65–83.
1981   The First Two Seasons of Excavations at Tel Qashish, 1978–
            1979. *IEJ* 31; 138–64.
Binford, L. R.
1977   General Introduction. Pp. 1–10 in *For Theory Building in Archae-
            ology; Essays on Faunal Remains, Aquatic Resources, Spatial Analysis,
            and Systemic Modelling*, ed. L. R. Binford. New York: Academic.
Boraas, R.; and Geraty, L. T.
1976   *Heshbon 1974: The Fourth Campaign at Tell Ḥesban*. Andrews
            University Monographs 9. Berrien Springs, MI: Andrews Uni-
            versity.
1978   *Heshbon 1976: The Fifth Campaign at Tell Ḥesban*. Andrews Uni-
            versity Monographs 10. Berrien Springs, MI: Andrews
            University.
Boraas, R.; and Horn, S. H.
1969   *Heshbon 1968: The First Campaign at Tell Ḥesban*. Andrews Uni-
            versity Monographs 2. Berrien Springs, MI: Andrews
            University.
1973   *Heshbon 1971: The Second Campaign at Tell Ḥesban*. Andrews
            University Monographs 6. Berrien Springs, MI: Andrews Uni-
            versity.
1975   *Heshbon 1973: The Third Campaign at Tell Ḥesban*. Andrews Uni-
            versity Monographs 8. Berrien Springs, MI: Andrews
            University.
Braudel, F.
1972   *The Mediterranean and the Mediterranean World in the Age of Philip
            II*. 2 vols. Trans. from the French second edition of 1966. New
            York: Harper & Row.
Cohen, R.; and Dever, W. G.
1978   Preliminary Report of the Pilot Season of the "Central Negev
            Highlands Project." *BASOR* 232: 29–45.
1979   Preliminary Report of the Second Season of the "Central Negev
            Highlands Project." *BASOR* 236: 52–71.
1981   Preliminary Report of theThird and Final Season of the "Cen-
            tral Negev Highlands Project." *BASOR* 243: 57–77.
Coulsen, W. D. E.; Sonkowsky, R. D.; and Wilkie, N. C.
1984   *Contributions to Aegean Archaeology: Studies in Honor of William A.
            McDonald*. Minneapolis: University of Minnesota.
Dever, W. G.
1974   *Archaeology and Biblical Studies: Retrospects and Prospects*. The
            1972 Winslow Lectures at Seabury-Western Theological Semi-
            nary. Evanston: Seabury-Western Theological Seminary.
1977   The Patriarchal Traditions. Palestine in the Second Millennium
            B. C. E.: The Archaeological Picture. Pp. 70–120 in *Israelite and
            Judean History*, eds. J. H. Hayes and J. M. Miller. Philadelphia:
            Westminster.
1980a   Archeological Method in Israel: A Continuing Revolution. *BA*
            43: 41–48.

1980b   New Vistas in the EB IV ("MB I") Horizon in Syria-Palestine. *BASOR* 237: 35–64.
1980c   Biblical Theology and Biblical Archaeology: An Appreciation of G. Ernest Wright. *HTR* 73: 1–15.
1981   The Impact of the "New Archaeology" on Syro-Palestinian Archaeology. *BASOR* 242: 15–29.
1982   Retrospects and Prospects in Biblical and Syro-Palestinian Archaeology. *BA* 45: 103–7.
1983   Material Remains and the Cult in Ancient Israel: An Essay in Archaeological Systematics. Pp. 571–87 in *The Word of the Lord Shall Go Forth: Essays in Honor of David Noel Freedman*, eds. C. L. Meyers and M. O'Connor. Winona Lake, IN: ASOR.
1985   Syro-Palestinian and Biblical Archaeology. Pp. 31–74 in *The Hebrew Bible and Its Modern Interpreters*, eds. D. A. Knight and G. M. Tucker, Chico, CA: Scholars.

Dyson, S. L.
1981   A Classical Archaeologist's Response to the "New Archaeology." *BASOR* 242: 7–13.

Freedman, D. N.; and Graf, D. F., eds.
1983   *Palestine in Transition: The Emergence of Ancient Israel.* Sheffield: Almond.

Gophna, R.; and Ayalon, E.
1980   Survey of the Central Coastal Plain, 1978–1979: Settlement Pattern of the Middle Bronze Age IIA. *TA* 7: 147–51.

Gophna, R.; and Beck, P.
1981   The Rural Aspect of the Settlement Pattern of the Coastal Plain in the Middle Bronze Age II. *TA* 8: 45–80.

Gottwald, N. K.
1979   *The Tribes of Yahweh: A Sociology of the Religion of Liberated Israel, 1250–1050 B. C. E.* Maryknoll, NY: Orbis.

Herzog, Z., *et al.*
1980   Excavations at Tell Michal 1978–1979. *TA* 7: 11–51.

Kochavi, M.
1975   The First Two Seasons of Excavations at Aphek-Antipatris. *TA* 2: 17–42.

Kochavi, M.; Beck, P.; and Gophna, R.
1979   Aphek-Antipatris, Tel Poleg, Tel Zeror and Tel Burga: Four Fortified Sites of the Middle Bronze Age IIA in the Sharon Plain. *ZDPV* 95: 121–65.

Kuhn, T. S.
1970   *The Structure of Scientific Revolutions.* 2nd ed. Chicago: University of Chicago.

Marfoe, L.
1979   The Integrative Transformation: Patterns of Socio-Political Organization in Southern Syria. *BASOR* 243: 1–42.

Mazar, A.
1981   Giloh: An Early Israelite Settlement Site Near Jerusalem. *IEJ* 31: 1–36.

McGovern, P. E.
1980   Explorations in the Umm ad-Dananir Region of the Baqʿah Valley. 1977–1978.) *ADAJ* 24: 55–67.
1981   The Baqʿah Valley Project. *ADAJ* 25: 356–57.

Meyers, C.
1983   Of Seasons and Soldiers: A Topological Appraisal of the Pre-
        monarchic Tribes of Galilee. *BASOR* 252: 47–59.
Meyers, E. M.; Kraabel, A. T.; and Strange, J. F.
1976   Ancient Synagogue Excavations at Khirbet Shemaʿ, Upper
        Galilee, Israel, 1970–1972. *AASOR* 42. Durham, NC: Duke
        University.
Meyers, E. M.; Strange, J. F.; and Groh, D.
1978   The Meiron Excavation Project: Archaeological Survey in
        Galilee and Golan, 1976. *BASOR* 230: 1–24.
Meyers, E. M.; Strange, J. F.; and Meyers, C. L.
1981   *Excavations at Ancient Meiron, Upper Galilee, Israel, 1971–72,
        1974–75, 1977.* Cambridge: ASOR.
1982a   Preliminary Report of the 1980 Excavations at en-Nabratein,
        Israel. *BASOR* 244: 1–25.
1982b   Second Preliminary Report on the 1981 Excavations at en-
        Nabratein, Israel. *BASOR* 246: 35–54.
Meyers, E. M., *et al.*
1979   Preliminary Report on the 1977 and 1978 Seasons at Gush
        Halav (el-Jish). *BASOR* 233: 33–58.
Miller, J. M.
1977   The Israelite Occupation of Canaan. Pp. 213–84 in *Israelite and
        Judean History,* eds. J. H. Hayes and J. M. Miller. Philadelphia:
        Westminster.
Rast, W. E.; and Schaub, R. T.
1978   A Preliminary Report of Excavations at Bab edh-Dhraʿ, 1975.
        Pp. 1–32 in *Preliminary Excavation Reports: Bab edh Dhraʿ, Sardis,
        Meiron, Tell el-Hesi, Carthage (Punic). AASOR* 43, ed. D. N. Freed-
        man, Cambridge: ASOR.
1980   Preliminary Report of the 1979 Expedition to the Dead Sea
        Plain, Jordan. *BASOR* 240: 21–61.
1981   *The Southeastern Dead Sea Plain Expedition: An Interim Report of the
        1977 Season. AASOR* 46, ed. J. A. Callaway. Cambridge: ASOR.
1984   Preliminary Report of the 1981 Expedition to the Dead Sea
        Plain, Jordan. *BASOR* 254: 35–60.
Sabloff, J. A.
1981   When the Rhetoric Fades: A Brief Appraisal of Intellectual
        Trends in American Archaeology During the Past Two Decades.
        BASOR 242: 1–6.
Seger, J. D.
1983   Investigations at Tell Halif, Israel, 1976–1980. *BASOR* 252: 1–
        28.
Shanks, H.
1983   Whither ASOR? Identity Crises over Biblical Archaeology Af-
        fects Scholarly Organization. *BAR* 9/5: 76–81.
Stager, L. E.
1985   The Archaeology of the Family in Ancient Israel. *BASOR* 260:
        1–35.
Wiley, G. R.; and Sabloff, J. A.
1974   *A History of American Archaeology.* San Francisco: Freeman.
1980   *A History of American Archaeology,* rev. ed. San Francisco: Free-
        man.

Wiseman, J.
1980   Archaeology in the Future: An Evolving Discipline. *AJA* 84: 279–85.
Wright, G. E.
1975   The "New Archaeology." *BA* 38: 104–17.

18
HISTORICAL GEOGRAPHY*

ANSON F. RAINEY
Tel Aviv University

The necessary link between archaeology and history is what we call historical geography (Rainey 1982). Its goal is the synthesis between the information retrieved from the ground that deduced from the historical sources.

The abundant research being conducted today in the Land of the Bible has its roots in the historical and religious interest inherent in the Judaeo-Christian tradition. According to Halakhic Judaism, one cannot fully express one's faith by living out all the commandments unless one lives on the soil of the "Land of Israel." The Christian concern for geography of the "Holy Land" is motivated by the desire to see and in some way relive the experiences of the Scriptures at the places where they occurred. The biblical tradition itself is predicated on a certain amount of geographical knowledge. Israel's constitution as a nation is firmly linked with its occupation of the "Land of Canaan." The historical and religious experience of Israel took place in a specific geographical context. The various narratives allude to topographical details on occasion, but often take for granted a knowledge of the terrain and its geopolitical significance. Genesis 14 is a prime example of concern by an ancient Hebrew author for geography (Aharoni 1979:82, 140). Many of the place names in this narrative are double, e.g., "Bela (that is Zoar) . . . the Valley of Siddim (that is, the Salt Sea) . . . En-mishpat (that is, Kadesh) . . ." (Gen. 14:2–7). An older tradition of toponymy was known to the writer, as elsewhere in the "historical books (e.g., Judg. 1:10, 11, 23), and it was deemed worthy of preservation. But such an antiquarian

---

*Place names in the following essay will be cited in their biblical or other ancient form, and in their Arabic or modern Hebrew form according to the method adopted by the present writer for the two leading text books on the subject, cf. Aharoni 1979:429 and Rainey *apud* Avi-Yonah 1977: 225–27. The choice of the Arabic or the Modern Israeli name was governed by the familiarity of scholars with the site in question. Usually, the Arabic form is preferred with the Modern Hebrew name added for convenience. Consistency in citing place names is neither possible nor desirable.

interest was secondary to the main concern that the Israelite reader should have the benefit of geographical orientation; thus, all the pre-Israelite toponyms in that chapter are equated with their Iron Age counterparts.

The study of the historical geography of Bible lands, especially as applied to the Levant in modern research, may be compared to the discipline of "coordination" as practiced in other countries, e.g., in Great Britain (Dymond 1974:159–63; Wainwright 1962). The information of *all* relevant disciplines is brought to bear in order to create a synthesis of the daily life and the historical events in a particular place or area. The goal is a three-dimensional picture within time and space of ancient society and human experience. Beyond this secular approach, many would also hope to understand better the culture and religion. That can best be achieved by first formulating the earthly dimensions as background for the spiritual.

There is no short cut to the realization of an historical-geographical synthesis. Several academic disciplines must be brought to bear on the problem (Rainey 1976b). These are: (1) Physical Geography, the description of the terrain in all its aspects and its accurate depiction in graphic form (i.e., maps); (2) Historical Philology, the analysis of the original sources containing geographical information; (3) Toponymics, the linguistic interpretation of the modern (i.e., Arabic 19th century C.E.) place names and the attempt to identify them with toponyms in the ancient sources; (4) Archaeology, the delineation of the actual site(s) and artifacts of everyday life. The ensuing discussion will concentrate on the first three of these disciplines. Since the present volume deals with the many facets of archaeology, we will only touch on the relation between field research and historical-geographical interpretation. When treating the various specialties that make up historical geography, specific illustrations will be given, taken almost at random from the accumulated data now available. As background reading in methodology, one should consult: Aharoni 1979:3–130; Rainey 1976b; 1978; 1982; also Dymond 1974 and Wainwright 1962.

I. WRITTEN SOURCES

A useful fact about geographical details in ancient sources is that they can usually be counted reliable. At least it was not a practice to invent topographical elements. A biased source, such as pharaonic propaganda, might make unwarranted claims about victories and conquests, but the geographical framework will be based on actual situations.

Biblical

There is a variety of geographical information in the Bible (Aharoni 1979:81–92). When dealing with these passages, one must grapple with the textual problems, utilizing the LXX and all other relevant versions.

On occasion, the Arabic toponym helps to decide between ancient manuscript readings, e.g., the Adadah of Josh. 15:22 must be rejected in favor of Aroer in 1 Sam. 30:28 because the Arabic name is Khirbet ʿArʿarah (Aharoni 1979: 117). Biblical sources for geography may be classified under three headings: (1) purely geographical composition, e.g., the Table of Nations (Genesis 10), the List of Conquered Kings (Joshua 12), of the "land that remains" (Josh. 13:1–6); (2) administrative texts, the only avowed document being 1 Kgs. 4:7–19, though many other passages manifest the characteristic features of official lists. A classic example is the roster of towns in Josh. 15:21–62; its organization by regions with subdivisions according to local districts, and the recurrent subtotals, make it obvious that the passage is dependent upon official records (Alt 1925a; Noth 1953:92–100). In turn, the text proves that a similar origin may be posited for the other town lists in Joshua and Nehemiah. The tribal genealogies, replete with place names, must also reflect the census lists compiled by the monarchial administration (cf. 1 Chr. 5:17). Boundary descriptions are taken from real life administrative documents, even though they have been incorporated into the idealized picture of the tribal inheritances in the Book of Joshua. The record of towns fortified by Solomon (1 Kgs. 9:15–19; 2 Chr. 8:1–6) and Rehoboam (2 Chr. 11:5–12) have the stamp of archival material. (3) accounts of military campaigns, both actual and predicted (as in the political oracles of some of the prophets).

Epigraphic

Among the plethora of documents from the cuneiform and hieroglyphic cultures, there are some texts of specific geographical import (Aharoni 1979:92–97). The topographical lists of various pharaohs, in particular Thutmose III and Shishak, furnish detailed information about towns in Canaan. Political correspondence such as the el-Amarna tablets and the New Assyrian letters makes it possible to deduce the relative significance of various towns and regions as they interacted with one another and with the "great powers" of Mesopotamia and Egypt. Royal annals of pharaohs and Mesopotamian kings frequently describe, albeit tersely, the military campaigns conducted in the Levant.

From Transjordan and Cisjordan, the epigraphic finds have been meager; apart from one display inscription, the Mesha stela, the texts with geographical details are administrative records such as the Lachish and Arad letters and the Samaria ostraca. The latter are especially illuminating as examples of record keeping with regard to local towns and their respective administrative districts (Aharoni 1979:356–68).

Post-biblical

The profound interest in the Land of Israel as the basis for Halakha led to numerous discussions on geographical points among the Rabbis.

The search for Holy Places led to extensive compilations of geographical materials on the part of the Church Fathers. The Graeco-Roman world also saw the composition of strictly geographic works such as those of Strabo, Ptolemy *et al.* Historians of the Hellenistic and Roman kingdoms and the Hellenic-style histories of the Jews and their wars by Josephus Flavius are replete with geographical details. These documents generally reflect the situation in the Hellenistic-Roman period, after certain drastic changes in the settlement patterns and populations had taken place. Nevertheless, they are an essential link between the modern and the biblical world (Avi-Yonah 1977). Sometimes they are the only witness we have to the location of a biblical site. Of particular value is the *Onomasticon* of Eusebius. His mileages and directions are proving to be highly accurate within the framework of his method; the latter simply has to be properly understood. However, it should be remembered that many settlements had moved from their original OT site to a location more suitable to the conditions of the Graeco-Roman Age. But at least the indications given by the Rabbis and the Church Fathers serve to point us to the immediate vicinity of the biblical town, if not always to the exact spot.

Medieval

Not much credence can be given to the many pilgrim itineraries or to the geographical opinions expressed in the Crusader historians. By that time the true memory of many biblical locations was buried in a mass of local superstition and tradition. However, the most rational study to come from the Middle Ages is the 13th century work of Estori Haparhi (Elbaum 1972). His knowledge of the classics and of Arabic made it possible for him to identify properly a great many OT towns. The Arab geographers, though not having a specific biblical interest, do give accurate accounts of the land as they saw it, on the basis of their firsthand contact with the local population (Le Strange 1890).

II. TOPONYMICS

An important aspect of any ancient culture is its corpus of geographical names. These reflect many aspects of local psychology, society, and religion (Wainwright 1962:38–55).

Arabic

During its rediscovery of the "Holy Land" in the wake of Napoleon's campaign to the Middle East, the western scholarly world was surprised by the number of ancient names still preserved in the Arabic toponymy of the country. Explorers, adventurers, scholars and finally tourists, began to collect and publish these Arabic names during the course of the

19th century. The monumental contributions of that era were by Robinson and Smith (1867), Guérin (1868; 1874; 1880) and the Survey of
Western Palestine (Conder and Kitchener 1881–83). Robinson and
Smith had been the first to establish biblical geography as a scholarly
discipline. Their explorations in 1838 and 1853 led to dozens of identifications of biblical place names. The Survey of Western Palestine provided the first complete topographical map of the entire country based
on modern survey methods. Their list of toponyms (Palmer 1881) is still
the basic tool for researching the place names of the Arabic society that
developed after the Moslem conquest.

By the end of the 19th century, it was possible to formulate the main
linguistic shifts from Hebrew and Aramaic to Arabic (Kampfmeyer
1892–93). Though many names were obvious, e.g. Esdud = Ashdod,
Yafa = Joppa, etc., others were not so clear; note, for example, Zerʻin
= Jezreel, el-Jib = Gibeon. A few Hebrew names were taken over by the
newly arrived Moslems directly, that is phonetically, as Mukhmas from
Michmas (Heb. *Mikmas)*, but most of the other names became Arabized
as the indigenous population adopted Arabic culture and language. The
resultant forms reflect the phonetic differences between the two languages, e.g., Heb. *s* becomes Ar. *sh* while Heb. *sh* becomes Ar *s*, etc. The
situation is even more complicated when the biblical name has been
supplanted by a Graeco-Roman appelation: Sebastieh preserves the
name given by Herod to Samaria (Heb. *Shomron)* and Lejjun comes from
Legio, the military base that grew up beside the abandoned ruins of
Megiddo. In such cases, a study of the later sources (Rabbinic and
Ecclesiastical) usually has led to the equation of the Graeco-Roman with
the OT city. Sometimes the biblical name has been "transformed" into a
Moslem saint whose grave is venerated on or beside the site; ancient
Rehob became Tell eṣ-Ṣarem, "Mound of the Sharp Sword" (Palmer
1881:169), while the old name was preserved there as the tomb of
Sheikh er-Riḥab.

On occasion the biblical name, in Arabic dress, moved away from the
original site with the removal of the settlement to a more convenient
locale. Beisan, the reflex of ancient Beth-shan, was found at the village
on the ridge opposite the mound that had been the biblical city. Excavations at the latter gave the final proof by the discovery of a stela of Seti I
mentioning Beth-shan (cf. *infra*).

Ancient

The study of the place names in the ancient sources, including the
Bible, is a field of social research in its own right (Rainey 1978). The
psychology of the people as reflected in their attitude to their land and to
their settlements, is reflected in the names they gave to the towns and
also to hills, valleys, creeks, wells, springs, prominent rocks and trees and

other topographical features. If one is to understand fully a place name, one must analyze it for its linguistic form by comparing all the different spellings in the Hebrew, Greek, Egyptian and Akkadian (Assyrian-Babylonian) inscriptions.

III. TOPOGRAPHY

Physiography

The geology and natural history of the Holy Land were the subject of scientific inquiry from the beginning of modern exploration (Ben-Arieh 1979). Today there are greatly improved methods for analyzing the flora and fauna and the surface morphology of the country (cf. the relevant chapters in this volume). However, the concern of the historian is with society and its environment, how it affected mankind and how mankind affected it. To achieve this goal, accurate *recording* of the topography is essential. Ever since the first modern mapping project, published after the campaign by Napoleon as the Jacotin Maps in 1810 (Karmon 1960), cartography has steadily improved (Schattner 1972). Keippert in Berlin constructed a map based on the compass readings taken by Robinson and Smith (1867). But the Survey of Western Palestine map produced by a team of British Royal Engineers (Conder and Kitchener 1881–83) gave complete coverage to Cisjordan "from Dan to Beer-sheba." Schumacher (1886; 1888; 1889) provided the northern part of Transjordan, and one section of the Moabite plateau was done by the British team (Conder 1892) before Turkish suspicions brought an end to the project. With the establishment of the Mandate, new maps began to be published on the metric scale; these have been continued and improved by the Survey Departments of Israel and Jordan.

The historian must use the 19th century maps for toponymic detail and frequently for roads and trails in use before the introduction of 20th century road building (e.g., Rainey 1981; Dorsey 1981). On the other hand, the most up-to-date maps must be scrutinized for this accurate recording of physical features and soil types.

Nomenclature

One of the first tasks to confront the historical geographer is the correct delineation of topographical features and their ancient names (Rainey 1976b). One must establish what is meant by terms such as Negeb, Shephelah, or Galilee. Ever since the beginning of modern research there has been a sloppy use of biblical Hebrew terms. G. A. Smith (1931) made a valiant effort and often was successful in defining the Bible's geographical terms in relation to the terrain, but even he led us astray with a misunderstanding of Jezreel Plain (Smith 1931:249–50), which resulted in the false distinction between Esdraelon and Jezreel (Rainey 1976a:635).

There is a varying degree of certainty as to the proper identification of such features as the Brook Besor, which is assumed to be the Wadi Ghazzeh, or the (River) Yarkon, which might be either the Wadi el-ʿAujeh or the Wadi Musarah. Today's maps confidently place both these water courses where our *assumption* has led us. The location of hills and cliffs is often difficult, although a visit to the scene of some biblical event may lead to its identification (e.g., Bozez and Seneh, 1 Sam. 14:4).

When the biblical references are not sufficiently precise, one may find more detailed allusions in the Rabbinic or the Ecclesiastical sources (Avi-Yonah 1976). Naturally, one must then try to estimate just how knowledgeable these later sources may be about the earlier period. Generally speaking, Rabbinic texts show a high degree of accuracy in reflecting the OT topographical nomenclature. Christian writers are frequently dependent ultimately on Jewish sources and, thus, may share the benefit of firsthand knowledge. Crusader texts, on the contrary, are more often based on idle fancy and folklore.

Complete certainty in defining the ancient geographical terms cannot be attained with the sources available. But one must make the effort in any serious historical research. The modern geographers must not be allowed to apply the biblical terms in any manner that suits their fancy without reference to the ancient sources (Rainey 1976a). Furthermore, maps for biblical atlases should be based on the best in modern topographical recording, i.e., on the latest scientific maps (Baly 1982).

Site Identification

The fundamental step in historical geography is, of course, the location of biblical towns (Rainey 1976b). Out of approximately 475 place names in the OT (taking account of doublets and doubtful cases), only about 262 have been identified with any degree of certainty, viz. 55 percent. There are 190 of these based on the preservation of the ancient name, 40 percent of the overall total. Of these latter, only 158, i.e. one third, are sites still bearing an Arabic reflex of the Hebrew name, while 32 more (6.7 percent) have the ancient toponym located nearby. There are only 72 proposed identifications where the ancient name is not to be found anywhere in the vicinity; only about half of these carry any degree of conviction, and the rest are more or less conjectural (Aharoni 1979:128–29).

Even the presence nearby of a likely Arabic toponym may not be decisive if the proposed location contradicts the indications of the written sources. For example, there is a site called Khirbet ʿAjlan not far from Tell el-Ḥesi (modern Hebrew Tel Ḥasi); this led Albright (1924:7–

8) to identify the latter with the biblical Eglon. It is most likely that the Arabic toponym is named after a freedman of ʾAmr, the Moslem general who had an estate in the district of Beit Jibrin (Le Strange 1890:413). Elliger (1934:66–67) had noted that placing Eglon far out to the west at Tell el-Ḥesi makes nonsense out of the itinerary of Josh. 10:34–37. Eusebius (*Onom.* 84:22) also indicated that Eglon should be east of Beit Jibrin (= Eleutheropolis) rather than west of it.

With or without the proper Arabic reflex of the old name, one must collect all the references to the town being sought and analyse them for their geographical testimony. This applies to biblical and nonbiblical texts, including postbiblical. The specific allusions must then be separated from the more generalized statements; only the former can carry any weight. Rarely are there detailed topographical points in the ancient text (e.g., Josh. 8:9–13 and 1 Sam. 14:4–5) which facilitate an on-the-spot analysis. Some passages, such as the individual groupings according to districts in Josh. 15:21–63; 18:21–28, place the town being sought in logical proximity to other towns, the identifications of which may be certain. For example, Makkedah has to be in the same vicinity as Lachish (Josh. 15:37–40; Dorsey 1980). Accounts of military clashes sometimes give further specific information; Azekah is placed at Tell ez-Zakariyeh because it is just west of Khirbet Shuweikeh along Wadi es-Sanṭ. Shuweikeh preserves the name of biblical Socho, and the Sanṭ is a type of tree, probably an echo of the Hebrew Elah (LXX terebinth). So, the Vale of Elah is confirmed by the presence of Socho, and together they point to Tell ez-Zakariyeh as the site of Azekah (1 Sam. 17:2; Schwarz 1850:2).

The application of the post-biblical sources to OT site identifications may be fruitful, if proper controls are exercised. The classic text is that of Eusebius' *Onomasticon,* a geographical catalogue composed in the 4th century C.E. (Wolf 1964). Directions and distances from the nearest Roman administrative center are usually given by Eusebius, who was evidently working from a schematic road chart of the Roman administration (Wolf 1964:77–78). When he says the Makkedah is "eight miles east from Eleutheropolis" (*Onom.* 126:22–25), he is obviously pointing to the Byzantine ruin of Khirbet Beit Maqdum, but the biblical Makkedah may be located at nearby Khirbet el-Qom (Dorsey 1980). Scholars have not always taken seriously Eusebius' intentional deviations from his simple formula. When he says that Bethel is on the left side of the road as one comes from Neapolis (modern Nablus) to Ailia (Jerusalem), "somewhere near" (Gk. *amphi* + accusative) the 12th milestone, he is clearly indicating that Bethel is *not* exactly 12 miles from Jerusalem but off the road to the east. In fact, the turnoff from the Jerusalem-Nablus road that leads to Beitin is 12 Roman miles from the Damascus Gate. (Rainey 1971). Furthermore, when Eusebius says that Gath *(Geth)* of the Philistines is even to the present time a village as one passes from Eleutheropolis to Diospolis near (*peri* + accusative) the fifth milestone of Eleutheropolis (*Onom.* 68:4–17),

he is clearly indicating that Gath is not at Khirbet Dhikhrin, which is five Roman miles from Beit Jibrin (Eleutheropolis), but rather at a site nearby (Rainey 1975:65*).

The 19th century explorers often had only a vague concept of what an ancient site really comprised (Conder 1878:II, 46–47). They usually assumed that the village bearing the Arabic reflex of a biblical name must be the actual site of the ancient town. In many cases, they were correct, of course. For example, Esdud, Yafa and Arad were all identical with the antiquity mounds from the biblical period, viz. Ashdod, Joppa, Arad. But this was not always the case, and only with the demonstration of stratigraphy by Flinders Petrie at Tell el-Hesi in 1890 did it become clear beyond doubt that the pre-Hellenistic settlements were usually on tells, artificial mounds built up of the debris of successive occupations. A few brilliant pioneers, such as J. L. Porter, Charles Warren, and Selah Merril, had already sensed this, perhaps under the inspiration of Layard at Nineveh. Porter, by intelligently analyzing his ancient sources, went out into the field on horseback and successfully identified Gath at Tell eṣ-Ṣafi, today Tel Zafit (Porter 1858:252–54; Rainey 1975), Hazor with Khirbet Waqqas = Tell Qedah (Porter 1875:415), and he even sensed the importance of Tell el-Mutesellim beside Lejjun, which later turned out to be the site of biblical Megiddo (Porter 1858:386; 1865:255).

Today, the historical geographer has the results of nearly a century of excavation in the Holy Land. Sites of many periods, from prehistoric to Crusader, have been exposed. When looking for an appropriate antiquity mound, one now has some idea of what to expect. If it is a Canaanite city state, an Israelite administrative center, a Graeco-Roman *polis*, or a Byzantine village, one knows that the shape of such a settlement should have left a certain kind of ruins. Even if the building stones have been largely plundered by medieval peasants, there is usually a general resemblance between the existing mound and the kind of settlement depicted in the sources. It is not idle to stress once again that one must first analyze carefully all the sources before going into the field to look for a site.

One of the indicators of the chronological periods represented on a site is the pottery strewn about the surface. Nevertheless, factors can distort the complete correlation between sherds and texts. Even in excavation, whole occupation periods may be missing from a site, although the location seems indisputable. The heavy building operations of one period may obliterate the traces of historically well-documented occupation that preceded. On the other hand, a clear correspondence between the periods represented archaeologically and attested historically is only a proof in favor of an identification when the other factors are in accord. Albright claimed to have all the proper archaeological periods for biblical Debir at Tell Beit Misrim (1967:209), but his site was in the Shephelah while the Bible places Debir in the Hill Country (Josh. 15:49; Elliger 1934:66–67). Therefore, the alleged "archaeological confirmation" was only an irrelevant myth.

Some classic examples of the modern site now being some distance removed from the OT mound are: Acco = ʿAkko, with nearby Tell el-Fukhkhar; Beisan = Beth-shan, with nearby Tell el-Ḥuṣn; ʿAin Shems = Beth-shemesh, with nearby Tell er-Rumeileh; Nablus (Neapolis) = Shechem, with Tell Balaṭa. In other cases, the modern town has grown so much larger than the ancient site that it has swallowed it up. Jerusalem is the most famous in this category; the extent of the OT town is small in contrast to the Herodian and later Byzantine city. Gaza is another case in point; the ancient tell is in the heart of the modern town. The OT site of Lod (Lydda), within the Arab town (Gophna 1969:80), is scarcely known from an archaeological point of view. And only in 1968 was it determined that the Iron Age site of Bethlehem is, in fact, on the hill occupied by the Church of the Nativity (Kloner 1971:237; Avi-Yonah 1975:200). Until then, everyone had taken for granted the identification without even asking the question, "Where is the Iron Age tell?"

The number of sites where an epigraphic discovery has confirmed an identification are relatively few. Most of them are mounds bearing the ancient name in Arabic form. Such was Tell Jezer, surrounded by bilingual inscriptions in the rock saying "precinct of Gezer" (Clermont-Ganneau 1899:86–87, 224–75). A stela referring to Beth-shan was found in the excavations at Tell el-Ḥuṣn (Rowe 1980:I, 24–29, Pl. 41), but the adjacent village was Beisan. At Tell Arad, inscriptions mention the name of the site (Aharoni 1981:112), but the identification was never in doubt anyway. The Mesha stela clearly identifies its find spot as biblical Dibon, but the village there is Dhiban. Doubts about the identification of el-Jib with Gibeon (Alt 1926:11–12) were dispelled when Pritchard (1959:1–17) found a collection of jar handles in the water shaft incised with the biblical name gbʿn, Gibeon. In the case of Lachish, however, the name was found on an ostracon which strongly infers that the find spot was Lachish, even though the mound was called Tell ed-Duweir after a nearby village. So the identification, proposed on the basis of Eusebius and the Sennacherib reliefs (Albright 129:3, n. 2), was confirmed by an inscription discovered *in situ*. Hazor was properly identified by Porter (cf. *supra*) and by Garstang (1927), the former starting from the ancient texts, the latter from the giant size of the mound. This identification has now been confirmed by the surface find of a Middle Age cuneiform tablet, a judicial document mentioning the name Hazor (Hallo and Tadmor 1977).

IV. SYNTHESIS

Coming now to the final step, we must stress that information from one discipline, such as Palestinian ceramics, should not be mixed indiscriminately with evidence from some other field. A difficult biblical passage cannot be solved by reference to potsherds. Neither can a knotty stratigraphical problem be solved by recourse to a verse of the Bible. The material from each discipline must be collected and evaluated independently before the various lines of evidence can be brought together. Even then, there is no guarantee that gaps will not remain in the final picture. The steps in achieving a synthesis may be roughly classified as source analysis, regional history and, finally, geopolitical summary.

Text Analysis

In effect, the geographical study of ancient documents, especially the biblical, is a specialized kind of Form Criticism *(Formgeschichte)*. This term is applied by biblical scholars to the study of pericopes in relation to their form and literary context. It attempts to understand the original form and purpose of the passage before it was incorporated into a large narrative. The geographical lists of Joshua are a case in point. Another typical kind of geographical text is the reference to the military successes and failures by the kings of Israel and especially Judah. References to the Judaean control over Philistia (under Uzziah, 2 Chr. 26:5–6; under Hezekiah, 2 Kgs. 18:8) and the southern trade route (under Solomon, 1 Kgs. 9:26; under Jehoshaphat 1 Kgs. 22:47–48; 2 Chr. 20:35–37; under Uzziah, 2 Kgs. 14:22 = 2 Chr. 26:2) functioned as weathervanes of Judah's geopolitical strength. That this situation fluctuated can be seen in the counter-attack of Philistines, Edomites, and Arabs in these same areas (under Jehoram, 2 Chr. 21:16–17; under Ahaz, 2 Chr. 28:17–18).

The individual passages which pertain to a particular problem must be gathered, studied individually, and then compared with one another. Then we are ready to integrate our results with the evidence from other disciplines.

Territorial History

There will be many instances when an antiquity site cannot be identified. Such may be the case with several sites in the same area, e.g. those between Arad and Beer-sheba in the biblical Negeb (Tell el-Milḥ = Tel Malḥata, Tell el-Meshash = Tel Masos, Khirbet Gharrah = Tel 'Ira, and Khirbet Ghuzzah = Ḥorvat ʿUzza). Even here, historical geography can make a contribution. The cornerstone of all modern historical geographical research is the "history of territorial divisions" *(Territorialgeschichte)*, inaugurated by Albrecht Alt (1925:2; 1966:136). It is simply the study of territorial units in the light of their own respective occurrences in the historical sources. The administrative district called the Negeb of Judah has a long and checkered history (Aharoni 1967:394, 400–401). When all the historical evidence is assembled, we can note when the region was attacked by enemies and when it was restored by a strong Judean king (cf. references *supra*). This may provide us with a chronological framework by which to date, at least tentatively, some of the archaeological remains on the unidentified sites.

The modern scholar enjoys a distinct advantage which Alt and his disciples did not have at the beginning. The physical morphology of any given region can now be studied intensively with all the tools of modern geology. Soil patterns, hydrology, flora and fauna can be analysed to give a picture of the ecological framework within which the historical events of the texts can be placed. Archaeological surveys and excavations can correlate the occupation sites with the physiology, showing how the ancient population chose to favor certain areas for settlements while utilizing others for agriculture. A striking example is the study of the antiquity sites in the Nahal Ayyalon basin (Gophna 1969) paralleled by the soil distribution study (Dan 1969). When the sites were recorded on the soil map (Gophna 1969:85), it was revealed that they clung to the edge of the rich alluvial soil in the central basin, leaving it open for cultivation. The territory in question can probably be equated with the "Valley of Ono," in Neh. 6:2.

The territorial history, then, is a coordination of data from texts, archaeological survey, and ecological study.

Geopolitics, Economics, and Society

The ultimate goal of all these disciplines is to understand ancient society. The political and social information derived from written sources (e.g., the feudal society of the Canaanite vassal states as against the national states of Israel, Judah, Aram and others) can be "brought down to earth," so to speak, when the geographical pegs have been secured. To illustrate, we learn from Egyptian sources about the sites along a great trunk route connecting Egypt with Damascus, the Beqʿah Valley and, ultimately, with North Syria and Mesopotamia. Pharaoh was deeply concerned that caravans be enabled to move safely along this route, and the local vassals were charged with that responsibility (Rainey 1968:8–9). Towns along the route can be plotted by the following the march of Thutmose III, Amenhotep II, and even Shishak in the 10th century B.C.E. Many of them can be identified by the preservation of the ancient name, even though some of them never appear in the Bible. Especially prominent is the line of towns along the eastern margin of the Sharon Plain (the "Land of Hepher," 1 Kgs. 4:10), viz. Aphek (Tell Ras el-ʿAin), Socho (Khirbet Shuweket er-Ras), Yaḥam (Khirbet Yemma), Gath-padalla (Jett), Borim (Khirbet Burin), also ʿArrabu (ʿArrabeh) and Burquna (Burqin) in the Valley of Dothan (Rainey 1968:1–3, 7).

Ironically, this trunk route has no biblical name, nor is it ever called by any name in non-biblical sources. The popular notion that it was ever called Via Maris or in Hebrew, *derek hayyam*, "Way of the Sea," has been thoroughly disproved (Meshel 1973; Rainey 1981:146–49). However, the caravan that took Joseph to Egypt obviously was following this route (Gen. 37:25). Solomon's fortification of Hazor, Gezer, and Megiddo (1 Kgs. 9:15) is evidently related to the same route; it was imperative that Israel have strong points along the way to control the caravan traffic. In fact, the chief economic strength of the Israelite state was control over this vital trunk route. Though specific reference is never made to this international highway in any monarchial context, knowledge of its geographical character and its geopolitical significance helps us to understand why the Plain of Sharon and the Valley of Jezreel were so crucial to the survival of Israel as a viable power. The same can be said for the Negeb as a crossroads on the routes to Arabia and Egypt. Judah needed the Negeb (cf. the passages cited above) as Israel needed the Jezreel Valley. Control of the trade routes was the major source of foreign income for both states.

Many other illustrations of the geographical contributions to our understanding of ancient Israel could be mentioned. The more we succeed in putting the Bible on the map, the more we may empathize with the trials and the challenges in the life of ancient Israel.

BIBLIOGRAPHY

Aharoni, Y.
1967 The Negeb. Pp. 384–403 in *Archaeology and Old Testament Study*, ed. D. W. Thomas. Oxford: Clarendon.
1979 *The Land of the Bible*. Revised and enlarged ed., trans. and ed. A. F. Rainey. Philadelphia: Westminster.
1981 *Arad Inscriptions*. Jerusalem: Israel Exploration Society and Bialik Institute.
Albright, W. F.
1924 Researches of the School in Western Judaea. *BASOR* 15: 2–11.
1929 The American Excavations at Tell Beit Mirsim. *ZAW* N.F. 6 (47): 1–17.
1967 Debir. Pp. 207–20 in *Archaeology and Old Testament Study*, ed. D W. Thomas. Oxford: Clarendon.
Alt, A.
1925a Judas Gaue unter Josia. *PJ* 21: 100–16. Reprinted 1953 in *Kleine*

Schriften zur Geschichte des Volkes Israel, II: 276–88. München: Beck'sche Verlagsbuchhandlung.

1925b   Die Landnahme der Israeliten in Palastina. Reformations Program der Universitat Leipzig. Reprinted 1953 in *Kleine Schriften zur Geschichte des Volkes Israel.* I: 89–125. Munchen: Beck'sche Verlagsbuchhandlung.

1926   Gibeon und Beeroth. *PJ* 22: 11–21.

1966   *Essays on Old Testament History and Religion.* Trans. R. A. Wilson. Oxford: Blackwell.

Avi-Yonah, M.

1975   Bethlehem. Pp. 198–206 in *EAEHL,* Vol. 1, eds. M. Avi-Yonah and E. Stern. Englewood Cliffs, NJ: Prentice-Hall.

1976   *Gazetteer of Roman Palestine.* Qedem 5. Jerusalem: Institute of Archaeology, Hebrew University and Carta.

1977   *The Holy Land from the Persian to the Arab Conquest (536 B.C–A.D. 640). A Historical Geography.* Rev. by A. F. Rainey. Grand Rapids: Baker.

Baly, D.

1982   What to Look for in a Biblical Atlas. *BA* 45: 61–62.

Ben-Arieh, Y.

1979   *The Rediscovery of the Holy Land in the Nineteenth Century.* Detroit: Wayne State University.

Clermont-Ganneau, Ch.

1899   *Archaeological Researches in Palestine.* London: PEF.

Conder, C. R.

1878   *Tentwork in Palestine,* 2 vols. London: Bentley.

1892   *Survey of Eastern Palestine.* London: PEF.

Conder, C. R., and Kitchner, H. H.

1881–3   *Memoirs of the Survey of Western Palestine,* 3 vols. London: PEF. Reprinted Jerusalem: Kedem, 1970.

Dan, J.

1969   Soils of the Western Basin. Pp. 64–74 in *The Western Basin of Nahal Ayyalon,* ed. Sh. Marton. Tel Aviv: Hakkibutz Hameuchad (Hebrew).

Dorsey, D. A.

1981   *The Roads and Highways in Israel during the Iron Age.* Unpublished Ph.D. dissertation, Dropsie University.

Dymond, D. P.

1974   *Archaeology and History: A Plea for Reconciliation.* London: Thames and Hudson.

Elbaum, Y.

1972   Estori (Israel ben Moses) Ha-Parhi. Cols. 918–19 in vol. 6 of *Encyclopedia Judaica.* Jerusalem: Keter.

Elliger, K.

1934   Josua in Judaa. *PJ* 30: 47–71.

Garstang, J.

1927   Hazor. *PEFQS* 111:224–25.

Gophna, R.

1969   The Occupation in the Biblical Period. Pp. 75–88 in *The Western Basin of Nahal Ayyalon,* ed. Sh. Marton. Tel Aviv: Hakkiburtz Hameuchad (Hebrew).

Guérin, V.

1868   *Description géographique, historique et archéologique de la Palestine.*

Priemière partie: Judée. 3 vols. Paris. Reprinted Amsterdam: Oriental, 1969.

1874   *Description géographique, historique et archéologique de la Palestine. Deuxième partie: Samaria.* 2 vols.

1880   *Description géographique, historique et archéologique de la Palestine. Troisième partie: Galilee.* 2 vols.

Hallo, W. W., and Tadmor, H.
1977   A Lawsuit from Hazor. *IEJ* 27: 1–11.

Kampfmeyer, G.
1982–3   Alte Namen in heutigen Palästina und Syrien. *ZDPV* 15: 1–33, 67–116; 16: 1–71.

Karmon Y.
1960   An Analysis of Jacotin's Map of Palestine. *IEJ* 10: 157–73, 241–54.

Kloner, A.
1971   Archaeological Survey of Israel. *IEJ* 21: 235–37.

Le Strange, G.
1890   *Palestine under the Moslems.* Reprinted Beirut: Khayats, 1965.

Meshel, Z.
1973   Was there a "Via Maris"? *IEJ* 23: 162–66.

Noth, M.
1953   *Das Buch Josua.* Handbuch zum Alten Testament, erste Reihe, 7. 2nd ed. Tübingen: Mohr (Paul Siebeck).

Palmer, E. H.
1881   *Arab and English Name Lists: The Survey of Western Palestine.* London. Reprinted Jerusalem: Kedem, 1970.

[Porter, J. A.]
1858   *A Handbook for Travellers in Syria and Palestine.* London: Murray. 2 vols.

1875   *A Handbook for Travellers in Syria and Palestine,* 2nd ed. London: Murray.

Porter, J. A.
1865   *The Giant Cities of Bashan and Syria's Holy Places.* London: Nelson.

Pritchard, J. B.
1959   *Hebrew Inscriptions and Stamps from Gibeon.* Philadelphia: University of Pennsylvania.

Rainey, A. F.
1968   Gath-Padalla. *IEJ* 18: 1–14.
1971   Bethel is still Beitin. *WTJ* 33: 175–88.
1975   The Identification of Philistine Gath. *EI* 12: 63*–76*.
1976a   Review of Baly, D., *The Geography of the Bible,* 2nd ed. *JBL* 64: 634–35.
1976b   Sites, Ancient, Identification of. Pp. 825–27 of *IDB Supp,* ed. K. Crim *et al.* Nashville: Abingdon.
1978   The Toponymics of Eretz-Israel. *BASOR* 231: 1–17.
1981   Toponymic Problems (cont.). *TA* 8: 146–51.
1982   Historical Geography—The Link between Historical and Archaeological Interpretation. *BA* 45:217–23.

Robinson, E., and Smith, E.
1867   *Biblical Researches in Palestine and the Adjacent Regions,* 3rd ed. 3 vols. London. Reprinted Jerusalem: Universitas, 1970.

Rowe, A.
1930   *The Topography and History of Beth-Shan.* Philadelphia: University of Pennsylvania.
Schattner, I.
1972   Maps of Erez Israel. Cols. 918–32 in vol. 2 of *Encyclopaedia Judaica.* Jerusalem: Keter.
Schumacher, G.
1886   *Across the Jordan.* London: PEF.
1888   *The Jaulan.* London: PEF.
1889   *Abila, Pella and Northern ʿAjlun.* London: PEF.
Schwarz, J.
1850   *Descriptive Geography and Brief Historical Sketch of Palestine.* Trans. I. Laeser. Philadelphia: Hart. Reprinted New York: Harmon, 1964.
Smith, G. A.
1931   *Historical Geography of the Holy Land,* 25th ed. Reprinted London: Collins, 1966.
Wainwright, F. T.
1962   *Archaeology and Place Names and History: An Essay on Problems of Co-ordination.* London: Routledge and Kegan Paul.
Wolf, C. U.
1964   Eusebius of Caesarea and the Onomasticon. *BA* 27:66–96.

19
SOCIOCULTURAL ANTHROPOLOGY AND SYRO-PALESTINIAN ARCHAEOLOGY

ØYSTEIN S. LaBIANCA
Andrews University

This essay will explore some of the mutual benefits which could result from a closer cooperation between sociocultural anthropologists and Syro-Palestinian archaeologists. After a brief introduction to the rise of anthropological theory in Europe and America, the essay concentrates on the rapprochement which has occurred within the general field of anthropology between sociocultural anthropologists and archaeologists; this rapprochment results from the emergence of a unifying theoretical framework, namely the cultural adaptationist's perspective. The first part of the essay suggests that the richness of both the archaeological and the literary record of Syro-Palestine makes it possible for scholars to understand the role of historical and environmental processes in the origin, persistence, and change of cultural features.

In the second part of the essay, it is suggested that sociocultural anthropology offers Syro-Palestinian archaeology two things: (1) master concepts that can help to integrate the results of multidisciplinary investigations and (2) models which may prove helpful in conceptualizing the dynamic cultural processes to which changes in the observed archaeological record may be attributed. To illustrate this, attention is focused on the experience of the Heshbon Expedition team. The master concept used to integrate the data recovered in the Tell Ḥesban excavations and surveys was the "food system." As models for use in conceptualizing dynamic cultural processes, the team has utilized research by anthropologists on the processes of sedentarization and nomadization.

I. THE RAPPROCHEMENT BETWEEN SOCIOCULTURAL ANTHROPOLOGY AND ARCHAEOLOGY

The rise of anthropology and sociology postdates a number of great social upheavals which followed in the wake of the industrial revolution, the first phase of which began in England in the middle of the 18th century (Lenski and Lenski 1982:244). Among the immediate con-sequences of this revolution was the disruption of traditional ties of kinship and friendship which had formed the social and economic support for most people until that time (Lenski and Lenski 1982:258). As a result of the twin processes of industrialization and urbanization, rural households were broken up as the young and able-bodied adults were drawn to jobs in factories located in the rapidly growing towns and cities, and the old and infirm were left behind to manage on their own. Thus, both groups were separated from the traditional sources of social and economic security. The Lenskis write about this period: "It was an uprooted, extremely vulnerable mass of people who streamed into the towns and were thrown into situations utterly foreign to them, and into a way of life that often culminated in injury, illness, or unemployment. A multitude of social ills—poverty, alcoholism, crime, vice, mental and physical illness, personal demoralization—were endemic" (1982:258).

These were the circumstances which led to the establishment of the helping professions and the social bureaucracy which the industrialized nations today take for granted. Instead of depending on the bonds of mutual obligation and assistance, which had for centuries tied kinfolk and villagers to each other, the ill, the unemployed, and the destitute gradually came to depend on a new group of helpers (i.e., nurses, social workers, insurance agents, counselors, union organizers). Along with these professions came a whole host of modern estalishments—hospitals, insurance agencies, welfare agencies, labor unions,—devoted to helping people cope without having to depend on these traditional kinship-based ties of mutual obligation and support. These are the arrangements which make possible the sense of personal freedom which, from our cultural perspective today, is regarded as our natural right.

The social transformations which were observed in the wake of each phase of the industrial revolution stimulated much thinking about the gains and the losses which each new machine or manufacturing process had brought. In just a few generations—indeed, within the lifetime of many adults—obvious alterations in the customary ways of thinking and behaving became apparent. These rapid changes in the customary ways of thinking and behaving made social processes much more visible, and they became the object of curiosity and systematic investigation. The rise of sociology and anthropology can be attributed to a large degree, then, to a heightened sense of self-consciousness which was experienced by people in the rapidly transforming societies of Western Europe and North America during the 19th century.

The problems which most interested the founders of the social sciences had to do, in one way or another, with the changes which occurred in the bonds that tie indviduals together in groups and so-cieties. Among the early sociologists, much attention was given to the

social problems which arose in the wake of industrialization and urbanization. As Goldthorpe (1969:10) has noted:

> The Marxian theme of the alienation of the industrial worker, the quest
> of Comte and of Durkheim to discover new bases of social consensus
> amid economic conflict and moral diversity, Weber's preoccupation with
> the necessary evil of bureaucracy—all these are aspects of a deeply felt
> concern with the human and social costs of material progress.

These are themes which to this day remain important to sociologists.

While sociologists were concentrating on the social costs of the industrial revolution, the founders of modern social anthropology, (e.g.,
Lewis Henry Morgan, William Halse Rivers-Rivers, Bronislaw Malinowski, Alfred Reginald Radcliffe-Brown) were beginning to examine
the social bonds of peoples whose social support systems had as yet not
been drastically disrupted by this great transformation. What they discovered, of course, was the importance of kinship as the principal
mechanism of bonding people in social groups in non-Western societies
(Langham 1981). Thus, if one wished to understand the customary ways
of thinking and behaving of an Iroquois Indian or an Andaman Is-
lander, one had to first come to grips with their rules of kinship and
descent.

Since the peoples in whom anthropologists were interested were
located on the frontiers of European expansion, anthropologists wishing
to obtain firsthand information left their home countries and lived
among the "primitives" they wished to study. Out of this necessity developed the tradition of "doing fieldwork"—which remains to this day a
rite of passage for graduate students in anthropology—and a curiosity
about and an acquaintance with a wide variety of languages and customs
(cf. Jarvie 1967; Nash and Wintrob 1972; Levine 1973; Whiting and
Whiting 1973; Spradley 1980). The task of explaining why different
cultures vary so much, yet also have so many things in common, remains
one of the central problems of sociocultural anthropology.

Several of the early British anthropologists, however, thought that
accounting for the persistence of social institutions was a more pressing
concern than explaining cultural variation and change. Having witnessed great upheavals in their own societies, fieldworkers like Malinowski and Radcliffe-Brown sought to understand how a particular
culture managed to remain "in balance." While Malinowski failed to
offer a solution to this problem, his quest for an answer led him to an
idea which has remained central to much anthropological thought. His
idea was that cultures, like biological organisms, consist of a large
number of interrelated parts and that, as Firth explains (1975:5), "the
definition and the meaning of any selected item of culture or social

behavior was to be understood first in terms of its relationship to other items." This meant that in doing fieldwork an anthropologist would need to identify the various parts of the culture (e.g., general features of the language, organization of family life, settlement patterns, political and economic systems, religion, styles of art and dress) and then attempt to show how all of these fit together into a whole. While it is almost impossible for the student of modern complex societies to attempt such "complete description," it was not beyond the reach of these early field-workers, since the groups studied were typically very small, consisting in many instances of only a few hundred individuals. The "holistic" approach remains, therefore, one of the central principles guiding modern cultural anthropological inquiry.

While the British functionalists—as Malinowski, Radcliffe-Brown, and others in the British tradition are often called—were refining their techniques of analyzing the social organization of various primitive groups, Franz Boas and his students—Edward Sapir, Robert Lowie, Alfred Kroeber, Ruth Benedict, Margaret Mead and others—were laying the foundation for what is sometimes referred to as the American, or Boasian, tradition of cultural anthroplogy. This was a more diverse tradition, simultaneously emphasizing investigations of languages, art and technology, race and culture, and culture and personality. In their attempts to account for the similarities and diversities in the languages, customs, and technologies encountered in their fieldwork, these American investigators, along with some European anthropologists, began to examine the role of the local environment and historical factors in explaining the differences and similarities they had observed (Harris 1968; Hatch 1973; Stocking 1968).

The wide range of concerns and approaches of contemporary "sociocultural" anthropology emerged out of these and other American and European traditions (Hunter and Whitten 1976; Harris 1980; Haviland 1981; Ember and Ember 1981; Keesing 1981). Specifically, the current concerns with the problem of human ecology and adaptive dynamics are derived from the American emphasis on the comparative study of social organization and the interrelationships between various cultural parts (Newman 1970; Thompson 1972; Stini 1975; Vayda and McCay 1975; Yellen and Lee 1976; Haas and Harrison 1977; Hardesty 1977; Burton, Kates, and White 1978; Hill 1978; Thomas, Winterhalder, and McRae 1979; Bartlett 1980; Rappaport 1968; 1971; 1977; Ortner 1983). While other theoretical orientations have gained momentum in more recent decades (Keesing 1974), the movement toward viewing cultures as adaptive systems, which was spearheaded by Julian Steward (1955), has become the vehicle of rapproachement between sociocultural anthropologists and archaeologists (Binford 1962; 1964; 1965; 1983; Adams 1965; 1966; 1974; 1978; Flannery 1965; 1967a; 1967b; 1972;

1976; Deetz 1970; Trigger 1968; 1971; Angel 1972; Leone 1972; Redman 1973; 1976; Sterud, Straus, and Abramovitz 1980; Sabloff 1981; Butzer 1982; Price 1982).

Keesing (1974) has identified four broad assumptions shared by most "cultural adaptationists." First, "cultures are systems (of socially transmitted behavior patterns) that serve to relate human communities to their ecological settings" (cf. Redman 1978:1–15). Second, "cultural change is primarily a process of adaptation" (cf. Thomas, Winterhalder, and McRae 1979). Third, "technology, subsistence economy, and elements of social organization directly tied to production are the most adaptively central realms of culture. It is in these realms that adaptive changes usually begin and from which they usually ramify" (cf. Steward 1955). Fourth, "the ideational components of cultural systems may have adaptive consequences—in controlling population, contributing to subsistence, maintaining the ecosystem, etc."

An example of cultural adaptationist reasoning is Marvin Harris' (1974) account of India's sacred cows. Lenski and Lenski (1982:45) explain this perspective by noting that Harris

> rejected the view that an ideology evolves arbitrarily, unrelated to the rest of societal life or to the experiences of its members in the past. Rather, he suspected that any belief that has been as widespread and as persistent as the Indian taboo against cow slaughter must have significant adaptive value for the society. . . . He found, first of all, that the cow is of enormous value to the members of Indian society in meeting their basic needs. A peasant's cow is, in effect, a factory that provides food (milk, butter); fertilizer; fuel for cooking (dried manure is excellent for this purpose, producing a clean, low heat); flooring material (a paste of manure and water hardens into a smooth surface that holds down dust and can be swept clean); and, most important of all, oxen to pull the peasant's plow. Harris also found that less than 20 per cent of the food consumed by Indian cattle is edible by humans. In short, the cow converts substances of little worth to the peasant into extremely valuable products.
>
> Although Indian peasants recognize that a living, productive cow is vastly more valuable to them and to their children than the same cow consumed as food, it would be only natural for them to ignore this fact when they are desperately hungry. The religious taboo against killing cows is a powerful cultural mechanism that serves to protect these animals even in times of famine and thereby preserve an invaluable resource. In short, Hinduism's conception of the cow as sacred is based on the experience of countless generations of the Indian people.

To date, the majority of anthropological studies involving adaptationist reasoning have been carried out either by ethnographers interested primarily in the adaptive dynamics of selected contemporary populations or by prehistoric archaeologists interested in reconstructing ancient socities. Largely untouched by anthropologists is the problem of the adaptive dynamics of complex civilizations such as those of Europe and the ancient Near East. Study on this problem is found in the writings of a group of French social historians who are members of the Annales School of historical analysis, e.g., Marc Bloch (1973) and Fernand Braudel (1973; 1981). Although not strictly "adaptationists" in their approach, these historians acknowledge an explicit concern with every-day material life; they are interested in the complex and long-term undercurrents that account for the continuities and changes which characterize the complex societies of Europe and Asia. A closer look at the ideas of these scholars can benefit both anthropologists and Syro-Palestinian archaeologists.

In Braudel's schema (1973:xii; cf. 1981:23–26), it is the everyday material life, the labors and exchanges of innumerable forgotten town and country folk, which make up the deepest undercurrents of history. Anchored in people's quest for food, clothing, and shelter, this life is made up of "repeated actions, empirical processes, old methods and solutions handed down from time immemorial." Economic life is one of the fastest moving undercurrents in the stream of events that make up history. This aspect of life is a matter of daily activity and concern.

The fastest moving current in this stream of events is the superficial history of the social hierarchies that have the power to "manipulate exchange to their advantage and disturb the established order." This is the history of rulers and wealthy merchants, of wars and treaties, of foreign exchanges and monopolies. It is the zone of activity which hovers above the market economy and constitutes its upper limit. It represents the "favoured domain of capitalism" (Braudel 1981:24).

Of all the regions in the world where the problem of sociocultural change is being investigated, few, if any, offer greater potential for illuminating the causal interactions of these historical and environmental processes than does the region of Syro-Palestine. In addition to having a rich and well-preserved archaeological record, the area is well known from literary records. This situation has the potential of making Syro-Palestine the proving ground for novel and significant theoretical ad-vances in our understanding of culture change; it is here that the new syntheses offered by sociocultural anthropologists and historians can be evaluated. The second half of this paper is offered as an initial step toward this end.

II. MASTER CONCEPTS FOR INTEGRATING THE RESULTS OF ARCHAEOLOGICAL INVESTIGATIONS

Over the two decades since the first strata were excavated at Tell Ḥesban, a site located on the edge of the highland which rises to the north and east of the northern tip of the Dead Sea, the goals of the excavators have expanded from an initial concern with the nature and date of a biblical event, namely the settlement of Hebrews in this vicinity, to its present broader concern with cultural processes (LaBianca 1978; Geraty and LaBianca 1985). Because of a desire to understand the entire occupational history of the site and its surrounding region and because of a commitment to integrate all of the data recovered in the excavations and surveys, this conceptual evolution was inevitable. The seriousness with which this commitment was carried out is to the credit of Siegfried Horn and Lawrence Geraty, directors of the project's five seasons, and to Roger Boraas, its chief archaeologist.

The integrative concept which has offered the best solution to the problem of understanding the various data from Tell Ḥesban and its vicinity is the ancient food system. Originally developed in the course of ethnoarchaeological fieldwork in the vicinity of Ḥesban (LaBianca 1983), the following discussion of the ancient food system reflects the influence of a number of different theorists, the majority of whom are sociocultural anthropologists. Particularly worthy of acknowledgement are Steward (1955), Dyson-Hudson and Dyson-Hudson (1970), Duckham and Masefield (1971), Murdoch and Wilson (1972), Barth (1973), Holling (1973), Kates, Johnson, and Haring (1977), Adams (1974; 1978), Cox and Atkins (1979), and Gilbert, Norman, and Winch (1980). As a master concept for integrating the finds from a Syro-Palestinian excavation such as Tell Ḥesban, the study of the ancient food system has been particularly useful for the following reasons.

First, the food system concept provides a framework for analyzing the majority of daily activities carrried out by the ancient and modern populations in the lands of the Middle East. Representing a fundamental concern of all peoples throughout history, this concept offers an important point of contact between the past and the present. Because many of the activities involved in the quest for food pertain to material life (as discussed above), and because this material life reflects some of the deepest and slowest moving undercurrents in history, the food system concept provides an important focus for ethnoarchaeological research. These investigations are conducted by archaeologists-turned-ethnographers who study selected aspects of present-day material life in order to arrive at hypotheses for interpreting the material remains of past societies.

Second, the food system concept focuses attention on all of the purposive, patterned, and interconnected activities carried out by a group of individuals in their quest for food (Dyson-Hudson and Dyson-Hudson 1970). In the case of human populations, this includes a multitude of social institutions, economic activities, and technological developments. As has been discussed elsewhere (LaBianca 1983; Geraty and LaBianca 1985), land use, settlement pattern, operational facilities, and diet represent components of the food system particularly suitable for archaeological investigation.

Third, the focus on "food" directs attention to the interaction between populations and their local environments, since the latter are exploited for the purposes of gathering or producing food. It also directs attention to interactions between populations located in outlying geographical regions insofar as these are involved in competition over land resources, food surpluses, and technological know-how.

Fourth, the "system" perspective focuses attention on the dynamic interrelationships which exist between the various components of the local food system, the local environment, and impinging outlying systems. For example, archaeologically attested changes in settlement at Tell Hesban and vicinity have been found to be systematically related to local variability in the availability of water, land fertility, and topography. These changes in settlement, in turn, were related to changes in other components of the food system, e.g., land use, operational facilities, diet. Furthermore, the temporal variability of this food system was related to synergistic interactions between the local population, the natural habitat, and factors having their origins in impinging, outlying systems. Thus, the instability which has characterized the food system of Hesban and vicinity over the past three millennia is attributable to the relationship between multiple factors, the total effect of which is greater than the sum of any two or more factors taken independently (cf. Geraty and La-Bianca 1985).

Fifth, the food system concept avoids the sedentary bias which often results from conceptualizations based on the term "agriculture." To most Europeans and North Americans, except perhaps those who are experts in the field of agricultural development, "agriculture" implies village-based farming. In the case of the Middle East, however, village-based farming is only part of the picture, the other part being the food production activities of nomadic pastoralists. The food system concept lends itself equally well to an analysis of food production activities of both village farmers and bedouins. Furthermore, this concept includes the "infrastructure" which lies behind agricultural practices themselves, i.e., all those political, economic, social, religious, educational, and technological arrangements which support the strategies of food procurement.

Sixth, the food system concept, in contrast to the "food production," "farming," or "agriculture" concepts, includes hunting and gathering as components of a food system. In the case of both villagers and nomadic pastoralists, hunting and gathering have traditionally played a much greater role than hitherto acknowledged. Furthermore, hunting and gathering were during prehistoric times the primary means of obtaining food.

Seventh, the food system concept provides a framework for consideration of a food web that extends beyond its human part. For example, wildlife encountered in villages and towns, as well as in archaeological excavations in the form of animal remains, can in most cases be readily accounted for when the feeding habits of particular species represented are considered. In the case of dogs, cats, and certain species of rodents and reptiles, their entire lives are lived within the confines of human settlements. Other species are frequently linked with human society— animals that belong either to cereal or grassland ecosystems, or scavangers feeding upon the organic wastes which abound in and around human settlements. Thus, the large majority of animals found in association with human populations can be accounted for when considered in the light of the food system concept.

Eighth, the food system concept is capable of dismantling the walls which divide academic disciplines and frustrate attempts to integrate the results of various kinds of research (e.g., epigraphy, ethnoarchaeology, ceramic analysis, metallurgy, faunal analysis, palaeobotany, geology, human osteology). Each of these lines of evidence illuminates one or more of the components or processes in the food system. Once the food system is accepted as a master concept for integrating various lines of evidence, members of a multidisciplinary team are in a much better position to relate their data to the overall picture. Without such a master concept, their results will, understandably, be offered as contributions to a particular discipline rather than as contributions to an interdisciplinary project.

While the food system concept helps to integrate diverse lines of evidence resulting from multidisciplinary investigations, additional concepts are needed to explain the dynamic processes at work in a particular food system throughout its history. In the region surrounding Tell Ḥesban, there are marked changes from one cultural period to another in the location and quantity of settlements, in the kinds of animals raised and eaten, in the types of dwellings built or reused, in the sorts of water collection and storage installations constructed or reused, and in the kinds of transport and food storage arrangements maintained, and so on. How are such changes to be explained? How does sociocultural anthropology help explain such changes?

In our continuing attempts to understand the history of these shifting patterns of human settlement, land use, operational facilities, and diet, we have begun to focus on the role of two complementary processes which, we believe, represent fundamental cultural processes in this region. These are the processes of sedentarization and nomadization.

Much attention has been devoted by anthropologists to the process of sedentarization, the process by which nomadic groups abandon their migratory existence in favor of settled life in villages and towns (Barth

1961; Marx 1967; Bates 1971, 1973; Nelson 1973; Bates and Rassam 1983). Indeed, anthropologists have also been active in Jordan in studying this process (Glubb 1938; Peake 1935; 1958; Gubser 1973; Chatty 1978; LaBianca 1983). The process of sedentarization in the vicinity of Ḥesban during the three millennia since the beginning of the Iron Age (ca. 1200 B.C.) has been discussed elsewhere (Geraty and LaBianca 1985). We have concluded from the archaeological evidence that the process of sedentarization in antiquity resembled in many respects the process of sedentarization in Jordan over the past three centuries. Glubb (1938:448–49) has offered an insightful proposal regarding this recent process based on his experience as a British army officer in Jordan during the 1930s:

> All the Arab countries—Trans-Jordan, Syria, Palestine and Iraq—have for centuries past been recruited by nomadic tribes which have migrated from Central Arabia. These tribes at first continue their nomadic lives in the deserts bounding the cultivated area; they gradually reduce the distance of their annual migration, and increase the numbers of their sheep at the expense of the camels. Later they become . . . complete agriculturalists; they retain their tents probably for a considerable time. The process of transformation of a pure nomadic camel tribe from Central Arabia into a group of agriculturalists still living in tents occupied in the past an average period of about three hundred years. But many such tribes continue to live in tents for several centuries longer. Indeed, the tribe itself and the tribal organization usually disappear before the members abandon tents and take to stone villages.
>
> Certain factors have made the last twenty years a period of exceptionally rapid change, not indeed in Trans-Jordan alone, but likewise in Asia, Europe and America. But the gradual transformation of camel nomads into sheep breeders, sheep breeders into tribal cultivators and tribal cultivators into non-tribal villagers has been going on for thousands of years. At all times, therefore, tribes have existed in Trans-Jordan in every stage of this metamorphosis, from the completely nomadic camel breeder to the completely sedentary cultivator. Indeed, the different sections and families of the same tribe may often be seen in different stages of sedentarization. To divide the inhabitants of Trans-Jordan into rigid groups of nomads, semi-nomads or settled is therefore difficult, for all these types of life shade off imperceptibly one into the other.

Much less is known about the complementary process of nomadization or bedouinization, whereby populations abandon their settled ways in favor of various types of nomadic livelihoods (LaBianca 1985). One reason for the neglect of this topic is the fact that sedentarization is presently a ubiquitous phenomenon throughout much of the Middle East, but nomadization is less common and perhaps more subtle.

Neither "nomadization" nor "bedouinization" are terms which are in common use in the literature dealing with sociocultural aspects of the Middle East. Whereas the term "nomadization" has been used by Aubin (1974), Bonte (1975), and Vryonis (1975), thus far only one article has come to my attention which uses specifically the term "bedouinization." Written in 1954 by Werner Caskel, who was at the time a Professor of Oriental Philology at the University of Cologne, the article is relevant to the present study because it makes specific reference to the fact that in Arabia and the countries of the Fertile Crescent "the process of de-Bedouinization and re-Bedouinization can be traced fairly exactly." Indeed, Caskel (1954:45) even notes that "in Transjordan these processes can even be proved by archaeological evidence."

While the terms themselves have not been used much in the English literature, the processes to which they refer have been examined by a number of English-speaking anthropologists (Salzman 1978). For example, Haaland (1969) has suggested that one reason why people return to nomadic pastoralism is that it is notably responsive to inputs of labor, thus making it an attractive alternative when sedentary agriculture becomes more difficult. This economic advantage of pastoralist production has also been noted by Barth (1973).

Regarding the origin of nomadic pastoralism, Lees and Bates (1974; cf. Bates 1971) have suggested that this specialized lifestyle was a consequence of agricultural expansion into arid regions; this process meant that increasing numbers of households turned to full-time herding to find adequate food for their animals. This view represents a refinement of earlier proposals by Robert McC. Adams (1974; 1978).

In addition to these economic perspectives that help explain why people become nomads, there are also political factors at work. Historians, for example, are inclined to view the rise and fall of nomadic societies as a direct consequence of the strengthening or weakening of the administrative grasp and military power of state governments (Reifenberg 1955; Caskel 1954; Mayerson 1964; Rowton 1974; Hutteroth 1975; Sharon 1975). Anthropologists like Irons (1971; 1974), on the other hand, have argued that nomadism can be viewed as a defensive adaptation to the state machinery, as in the case of the Yomut Turkmen.

To stimulate research on the process of nomadization in Jordan, several proposals follow which may serve as a point of departure for future investigations. First, pastoral nomadism has played a role on the sociopolitical stage of this region during the cultural periods investigated by the Heshbon Expedition. At this point, this would take us back to the Late Bronze Age (ca. 1550–1200 B.C.). This statement is supported by historical sources dealing with the cultural history of this region (Kirk 1944; Rowton 1974), and this state of affairs is reflected in numerous ways in the archaeological evidence from Tell Ḥesban and vicinity.

Second, various types of coexisting pastoral nomadic strategies may emerge as the end product of this nomadization. This is particularly apparent during the latter part of the Ottoman or Turkish period in Jordan (ca. 1800–1917 A.D.), when the region located within a 10 km radius of Ḥesban was exploited by means of at least three different pastoralist strategies: (1) Camel-and-horse-breeding Beni Sakhr bedouin visited the highland region to the south and east of Ḥesban during the spring and summer. Having gradually pushed their way northward from their traditional home territories in the Arabian desert over the past 300 years, this group was described by Tristram (1873:247) as the rulers of this highland area. Although they avoided tilling the fertile soils of this plateau, their slaves, the Abu Endi, did so in exchange for protection. (2) In contrast to the horizontal migration pattern followed by the Beni Sakhr, the Adwan tribe followed a vertical or transhumant pattern of migration, grazing their herds of sheep, goats, and cattle on the hills and slopes to the north and west of Ḥesban. During the fall and winter, they returned to their cultivated fields in the Jordan valley. (3) A similar pattern was followed by members of the Hamideh tribe along the slopes leading from the highland plateau to the shores of the Dead Sea. Unlike both the camel and horse breeding Beni Sakhr and the cattle and sheep breeding Adwan, the Hamideh Arabs herded a particular breed of small, black cattle (resembling the Scotch kylo, according to Tristram 1873:266) and donkeys. Theirs was also a position of subservience to the Beni Sakhr.

Third, the process of nomadization appears to gain increasing momentum during periods of weakening military and administrative control by state governments. This was the case during the 6th century B.C., when the Babylonian invasion of the kingdoms of Ammon, Moab, and Edom brought an end to these local Transjordanian governments (Hashemite Kingdom of Jordan 1978:25). Over the ensuing centuries, a process of nomadization occurred and led to the establishment in this region during early Hellenistic times (332–200 B.C.) of a group of nomads practicing vertical or transhumant pastoralism. This suggestion is based on the fact that the political boundaries established by the Hellenistic overlords ran along the highland region of the Transjordanian plateau rather than along the Jordan-Dead Sea basin (Ministry of Labour 1970). The small number of settlements in the highlands during this period and the semisedentary ways of transhumants explain the location of this border.

The process of nomadization which followed the withdrawal of Byzantine military defenses east of the Jordan rift valley during the 6th century A.D. (Mayerson 1964; Vyronis 1975) attests to the importance of the political dimension. Instead of a predominantly vertical or transhumant form of pastoralism, a horizontal type of nomadism appears to have emerged in this region; the latter involved horses and camels and commitments to the ways of desert tribes (Caskel 1954; Mayerson 1964; Hill 1975). This appears also to have been the case following the demise of the brief Ayyubid-Mamluk occupation of this area (1260–1400 A.D.), as shown by recent studies of the Ottoman or Turkish period in Palestine (Hutteroth 1975; Sharon 1975). Indeed, according to Ottoman tax records from the 16th century, the horse-and-camel- breeding Beni Sakhr may already have established themselves in Transjordan by this time (Hutteroth 1975:8).

III. CONCLUSION

This essay has focused on the sociocultural concepts and approaches that the Hesban project has accepted and developed to guide its researchers in the task of integrating a large body of data. We readily acknowledge, however, that in addition to the ones we have found helpful many others could be added. For example, much work has been done by sociocultural anthropologists on the problem of ancient trade (Polanyi, Arensberg, and Pearson 1957; Renfrew 1969; Lamberg-Karlovsky 1972; Tourtellot and Sabloff 1972; Flannery 1976; Bates and Lees 1977; Hirth 1978). Whereas commerce and trade were activities which account for only a small proportion of the activities of inhabitants at ancient Tell Hesban, the opposite may have been the case in urban centers and harbor sites now under excavation by Syro-Palestinian archaeologists. To understand these sites, commercial models proposed by sociocultural anthropologists may be useful.

This example from the experience of the Hesban team illustrates the way in which certain concepts and approaches of sociocultural anthropologists and other social scientists may prove useful to Syro-Palestinian archaeologists. Although many questions remain unanswered, it is clear that the perspective of the sociocultural anthropologist is especially useful in the process of integrating a wide range of data. This perspective emphasizes the interconnected nature of the various parts of sociocultural systems and focuses attention on the processes whereby such systems originate, maintain themselves, and change.

BIBLIOGRAPHY

Adams, R. McC.
  1965   *Land Behind Baghdad: A History of Settlement on the Diyala Plains.* Chicago: University of Chicago.
  1966   *The Evolution of Urban Society.* Chicago: Aldine.
  1974   The Mesopotamian Social Landscape: A View from the Frontier. Pp. 1–20 in *Reconstructing Complex Societies,* ed. C. B. Moore. Supplement to *BASOR,* No. 20. Cambridge: ASOR.

1978   Strategies of Maximization, Stability, and Resilience in Meso-
              potamian Society, Settlement, and Agriculture. *Proceedings of the
              American Philosophical Society* 122: 329–35.
Angel, J. L.
1972   Ecology and Population in the Eastern Mediterranean. *WA* 4:
              88–105.
Aubin, F.
1974   Anthropologie du Nomadisme. *Cahiers Internationaux de So-
              ciologie* 56: 79–90.
Barth, F.
1961   *Nomads of South Persia: The Basseri Tribe of the Khamseh Con-
              federacy.* Boston: Little, Brown.
1973   A General Perspective on Nomad-Sedentary Relations in the
              Middle East. Pp. 11–21 in *The Desert and the Sown,* ed. C. Nelson.
              Institute of International Studies Research Series, No. 21.
              Berkley: University of California.
Bartlett, P. F.
1980   Adaptive Strategies in Peasant Agricultural Production. *ARA*
              545–73.
Bates, D. G.
1971   The Role of the State in Peasant-Nomad Mutualism. *Anthrop Q*
              109–31.
1973   *Nomads and Farmers: A Study of the Yoruk of Southeastern Turkey.*
              Anthropological Papers, No. 52, Ann Arbor: Museum of An-
              thropology, University of Michigan.
Bates, D. G., and Lees, S. H.
1977   The Role of Exchange in Productive Specialization. *Am Anthrop*
              79: 824–41.
Bates, D. G., and Rassam, A.
1983   *Peoples and Cultures of the Middle East.* Englewood Cliffs: Pren-
              tice-Hall.
Binford, L. R.
1962   Archaeology as Anthropology. *Am Ant* 28: 217–25.
1964   A Consideration of Archaeological Research Design. *Am Ant* 29:
              425-41.
1965   Archaeological Systematics and the Study of Culture Process.
              Am Ant 31: 203–10.
1983   *In Pursuit of the Past.* New York: Thames & Hudson.
Bloch, M.
1973   *French Rural History: An Essay on its Basic Characteristics.* Trans. J.
              Sondhiem from French. Berkeley: University of California.
Bonte, P.
1975   Review of E. Bernus, *Atlas des structures agraries au sud du Sahara.*
              Etudes Rurales 60: 117–18.
Braudel, F.
1973   *Capitalism and Material Life 1400–1800.* Trans. Miriam Kochan
              from French. New York: Harper & Row.
1981   *The Structures of Everyday Life.* Trans. Sian Reynolds from
              French, Vol. 1 New York: Harper & Row.
Burton, I.; Kates, R. W.; and White, G. F., eds.
1978   *The Environment as Hazard.* New York: Oxford University.

Butzer, K. W.
1982   *Archaeology as Human Ecology.* Cambridge: Cambridge University.
Caskel, W.
1954   The Bedouinization of Arabia. In Studies in Islamic Cultural History, ed. G. E. Grunebaum. *Am Anthrop* 56: 36–46.
Chatty, D.
1978   *The Current Situation of the Bedouin in Syria, Jordan and Saudi Arabia and their Prospects for the Future.* Amman: University of Jordan.
Cox, G. W., and Atkins, M. D.
1979   *Agricultural Ecology: An Analysis of World Food Production Systems.* San Francisco: Freeman.
Deetz, J. F.
1970   Archaeology as a Social Science. *Bulletin of the American Anthropological Association* 3: 115–25.
Duckham, A. N., and Masefield, G. B.
1971   *Farming Systems of the World.* London: Chatto & Windus.
Dyson-Hudson, R., and Dyson-Hudson, N.
1970   The Food Production System of the Semi-Nomadic Society: The Karimojong, Uganda. Pp. 93–123 in *African Food Production Systems: Cases and Theory,* ed. P. F. M. McLoughlin. Baltimore: Johns Hopkins University.
Ember, C. R., and Ember, M.
1981   *Cultural Anthropology,* 3rd rev. ed. Englewood Cliffs: Prentice-Hall.
Firth, R.
1975   An Appraisal of Modern Social Anthropology. *ARA* 4: 1–25.
Flannery, K. V.
1965   The Ecology of Early Food Production in Mesopotamia. *Science* 147: 1247–55.
1967a   Culture History v. Cultural Process: A Debate in American Archaeology. *Scientific American* 217: 119–22.
1967b   Vertebrate Fauna and Hunting Patterns. Pp. 132–77 in *The Prehistory of the Tehuacan Valley,* vol. 1, ed. D. S. Byers. Austin: University of Texas.
1972   The Cultural Evolution of Civilizations. *Annual Review of Ecology and Systematics* 3: 399–426.
1976   *The Early Mesoamerican Village.* New York: Academic.
Geraty, L. T., and LaBianca, Ø. S.
1985   Food-Procuring System in Jordan: The Case of Tell Ḥesban and its Surrounding Region. Pp. 323–330 in *Studies in the History and Archaeology of Jordan,* vol. 2, ed. A. Hadidi. Amman: Department of Antiquities.
Gilbert, E. H.; Norman, D. W.; and Winch, F. E.
1980   *Farming Systems Research: A Critical Appraisal. MSU Rural Development Paper, no. 6.* Lansing: Michigan State University Department of Agricultural Economics.
Glubb, J. B.
1938   The Economic Situation of the Trans-Jordan Tribes. *Journal of Central Asian Studies* 25: 448–59.

Goldthrope, J. H.
1969   Introduction. Pp. 9–16 in *The Founding Fathers of Social Science*, ed. T. Raison. Baltimore: Penguin.
Gubser, P.
1973   *Politics and Change in Al Karak, Jordan.* Oxford: Oxford University.
Haaland, G.
1969   Economic Determinants in Ethnic Process. Pp. 58–73 in Ethnic Groups and Boundaries, ed. F. Barth. Boston: Little, Brown.
Haas, J. D., and Harrison, G. G.
1977   Nutritional Anthropology and Biological Adaptation. *ARA* 6: 69–101.
Hardesty, D. L.
1977   *Ecological Anthroplogy.* New York: Wiley.
Harris, M.
1968   *The Rise of Anthropological Theory.* New York: Crowell.
1974   *Cows, Pigs, Wars, and Witches.* New York: Random House.
1980   *Culture, People, Nature,* 3rd rev. ed. New York: Harper & Row.
Hashemite Kingdom of Jordan
1978   *Archaeology of Jordan.* Amman: Ministry of Information.
Hatch, E.
1973   The Growth of Economic, Subsistence, and Ecological Studies in American Anthropology. *JAR* 29: 221–43.
Haviland, W. A.
1981   *Cultural Anthropology,* 3rd rev. ed. New York: Holt, Rinehart, & Winston.
Hill, D. R.
1975   The Role of the Camel and the Horse in the Early Arab Conquests. Pp. 32–43 in *War, Technology and Society in the Middle East,* ed. V. J. Parry and M. E. Yapp. Oxford: Oxford University.
Hill, J. H.
1978   Language Contact Systems and Human Adaptions. *JAR* 34: 1–26.
Hirth, K. G.
1978   Interregional Trade and the Formation of Perhistoric Gateway Communities. *Am Ant* 43: 35–45.
Holling, C. W.
1973   Resilience and Stability of Ecological Systems. *Annual Review of Ecology and Systematics* 4: 1–23.
Hunter, D. E., and Whitten, P.
1976   *The Study of Anthropology.* New York: Harper & Row.
Hutteroth, W.
1975   The Patterns of Settlement in Palestine in the Sixteenth Century. Pp. 3–10 in *Studies on Palestine during the Ottoman Period,* ed. M. Maˤoz. Jerusalem: Magnes.
Irons, W. G.
1971   Variation in Political Stratification Among the Yomut Turkmen. *Anthrop Q* 44: 143–56.
1974   Nomadism as a Political Adaptation: The Case of the Yomut Turkmen. *American Ethnologist* 1: 635–58.
Jarvie, I. C.
1967   On Theories of Fieldwork and the Scientific Character of Social Anthropology. *Philosophy of Science* 34: 223–42.

Kates, R. W.; Johnson, D. L.; and Haring, K. J.
 1977 Population, Society and Desertification. Pp. 261–317 in *Desertification: Its Causes and Consequences*, ed. Secretariat of the United Nations Conference on Desertification. New York: Pergamon.
Keesing, R. M.
 1974 Theories of Culture. *ARA* 3: 73–97.
 1981 *Cultural Anthropology: A Contemporary Perspective*, 2nd ed. New York: Holt, Rinehart & Winston.
Kirk, M. E.
 1944 An Outline of the Ancient Cultural History of Transjordan. *PEQ* 76: 180–98.
LaBianca, O. S.
 1978 Man, Animals, and Habitat at Hesban—An Integrated Overview. *AUSS* 16:229–52.
 1983 Objectives, Procedures, and Findings of Ethnoarchaeological Research in the Vicinity of Hesban in Jordan. *ADAJ* 27: 269–87.
 1985 The Return of the Nomad: An Analysis of the Process of Nomadization in Jordan. *ADAJ* 29: 251–54.
Lamberg-Karlovsky, C. C.
 1972 Trade Mechanisms in Indus-Mesopotamian Interrelations. *JAOS* 92: 222–29.
Langham, I.
 1981 *The Building of British Social Anthropology*. Vol. 8 in *Studies in the History of Modern Science*, eds. R. S. Cohen, E. N. Hiebert, E. I. Mendelsohn. Dordrecht: Reidel.
Lees, S. H., and Bates, D. G.
 1974 The Origins of Specialized Nomadic Pastoralism: A Systemic Model. *Am Ant* 39: 187–93.
Lenski, G. and Lenski, J.
 1982 *Human Societies: An Introduction to Macrosociology*, 4th rev. ed. New York: McGraw-Hill.
Leone, M. P., ed.
 1972 *Contemporary Archaeology: A Guide to Theory and Contributions*. Carbondale: Southern Illinois University.
Levine, R. A.
 1973 Research Design in Anthropological Field Work. Pp. 183–95 in *A Handbook of Method in Cultural Anthropology*, eds. R. Naroll and R. Cohen. New York: Columbia University.
Marx, E.
 1967 *Bedouin of the Negev*. Manchester: University of Manchester.
Mayerson, P.
 1964 The First Muslim Attacks on Southern Palestine (A.D. 633–34). *American Philological Association Transactions* 95: 155–99.
Ministry of Labour
 1970 *Atlas of Israel*. Jerusalem: Ministry of Labour.
Murdock, F. P., and Wilson, S. F.
 1972 Settlement Patterns and Community Organization: Cross-Cultural Codes 3. *Ethnology* 11:254–95.
Nash, D., and Wintrob, R.
 1972 The Emergence of Self-Consciousness in Ethnography. *CA* 13: 527–42.

Nelson, C., ed.
1973   *The Desert and the Sown.* Institute of International Studies Research, no. 21. Berkeley: University of California.
Newman, R. W.
1970   Why Man Is Such a Sweaty and Thirsty Naked Animal: A Speculative Review. *Human Biology* 42: 12–17.
Ortner, D. J., ed.
1983   *How Humans Adapt: A Biocultural Odyssey.* Washington: Smithsonian Institution.
Peake, F. G.
1935   *The History of East Jordan.* Jerusalem.
1958   *A History of Jordan and Its Tribes.* Coral Gables: University of Miami.
Polanyi, K.; Arensberg, C. M.; and Pearson, H. W., eds.
1957   *Trade and Market in the Early Empires.* New York: Free.
Price, B. J.
1982   Cultural Materialism: A Theoretical Review. *Am Ant* 47: 709–41.
Rappaport, R. A.
1968   *Pigs for the Ancestors.* New Haven: Yale University.
1971   The Flow of Energy in an Agricultural Society. *Scientific American* 225: 116–32.
1977   Ecology, Adaptation and the Ills of Functionalism. *Michigan Discussions in Anthoropology* 2: 138–90.
Redman, C. L., ed.
1973   *Research and Theory in Current Archaeology.* New York: Wiley.
Redman, C. L.
1976   Anthropological Archaeology in the Near East. Pp. 213–18 in *The Study of the Middle East,* ed. L. Binder. New York: Wiley.
1978   *The Rise of Civilization.* San Francisco: Freeman.
Reifenberg, A.
1955   *The Struggle between the Desert and the Sown.* Jerusalem: Jewish Publishing Department of the Jewish Agency.
Renfrew, C.
1969   Trade and Culture Process in European Prehistory. *CA* 10: 151–69.
Rowton, M.
1974   Enclosed Nomadism. *Journal of the Economic and Social History of the Orient.* 17: 1–30.
Sabloff, J. A.
1981   When the Rhetoric Fades: A Brief Appraisal of Intellectual Trends in American Archaeology During the Past Two Decades. *BASOR* 242: 1–6.
Salzman, P. C.
1978   The Study of "Complex Society" in the Middle East: A Review Essay. *International Journal of Middle East Studies* 9: 529–57.
Sharon, M.
1975   The Political Role of the Bedouins in Palestine in the Sixteenth and Seventeenth Centuries. Pp. 11–30 in *Studies on Palestine during the Ottoman Period,* ed. M. Maʿoz. Jerusalem: Magnes.
Spradley, J. P.
1980   *Participant Observation.* New York: Holt, Rinehart & Winston.

Sterud, E. L.; Straus, L. G.; and Abramovitz, K.
1980   Recent Developments in Old World Archaeology. *Am Ant* 45: 759–86.
Steward, J. H.
1955   *Theory of Culture Change*. Urbana: University of Illinois.
Stini, W. A.
1975   What is Adaption? Pp. 1–13 in *Ecology and Human Adaption*, ed. W. A. Stini. New York: Brown.
Stocking, G. W.
1968   *Race, Culture, and Evolution*. New York: Free.
Thomas, R. B.; Winterhalder, B.; and McRae, S. D.
1979   An Anthropological Approach to Human Ecology and Adaptive Dynamics. *Yearbook of Physical Anthropology* 22: 1–46.
Thompson, S. I.
1972   From Functionalism to Cultural Ecology: Plus Ca Change, Plus C est La Meme Chose. *Steward Anthropological Journal* 4: 56–67.
Tourtellot, G., and Sabloff, J. A.
1970   Exchange Systems Among the Ancient Maya. *Am Ant* 37: 126–35.
Trigger, B. G.
1968   Major Concepts of Archaeology in Historical Perspective. *Man* 3: 527–41.
1971   Archaeology and Ecology. *WA* 2: 320–26.
Tristram, H. B.
1873   *The Land of Moab*. New York: Harper.
Vayda, A. P., and McCay, B. J.
1975   New Directions in Ecology and Ecological Anthropology. *ARA* 4: 292–306.
Vryonis, S.
1975   Nomadization and Islamization in Asia Minor. In *Dumbarton Oaks Papers*, No. 29. Washington: Dumbarton Oaks Center for Byzantine Studies.
Whiting, B., and Whiting, J.
1973   Methods for Observing and Recording Behavior. Pp. 282–315 in *A Handbook of Method in Cultural Anthropology*, eds. R. Naroll and R. Cohen. New York: Columbia University.
Yellen, J. E., and Lee, R. B.
1976   The Dobe-/Du-da Environment. Pp. 28–46 in *Kalahari Hunters-Gathers*, eds. J. E. Yellen and R. B. Lee. Cambridge: Harvard University.

20
SETTLEMENT PATTERNS AND
SOCIOCULTURAL RECONSTRUCTION

Gerald L. Mattingly
Cincinnati Christian Seminary

As Dever points out in his contribution to this collection of essays, Syro-Palestinian archaeology is currently undergoing a transformation, a "revolution" created by a new understanding of the nature and scope of archaeological inquiry. Although the interrelationships between archaeology and other disciplines are still being identified and defined, it is already clear that the connection between archaeology and cultural anthropology is particularly close. In a discussion of the goals of these two fields of study, Fagan (1978: 19) writes

> Anthropology is a discipline for the study of humankind in the widest possible sense, both in the past and in the present. . . . Archaeologists are anthropologists as well; their goals are the same as those of their colleagues. But their concern is with ancient societies, with cultures that existed in the past and are now extinct or in existence only in modified form.

This equation has enormous implications for the development of archaeological theory and method. In particular, if archaeology is truly interested in the study of ancient society, archaeological reports must begin showing a decided shift from the descriptive to the synthetic. To be sure, artifacts must still be classified and described, but an anthropologically oriented archaeology looks beyond the artifacts, always seeing the recovered materials as pieces of a larger sociocultural mosaic, not just another group of "lifeless catalogue items" (Fagan 1978:19). Once archaeologists arrive at this understanding of their task, the specific goal of archaeology becomes nothing less than the reconstruction of ancient society.

The viewpoint espoused in the preceding paragraph helps to explain the purpose of this essay. The following pages contain an examination of some of the assumptions, methods, and limitations involved in reconstructing the economic, social, and political systems of an ancient society. Special attention is given to the ways in which settlement patterns can help the archaeologist arrive at a better understanding of the ecological and cultural variables at work in a given region.

As an illustration of how this approach can be used in Syro-Palestinian archaeology, this essay presents a hypothetical reconstruction of the Early Bronze Age cultural patterns in part of Jordan's Kerak district. Since the writer participated in two seasons of Emory University's "Archaeological Survey of Central and Southern Moab" (i.e., the Kerak plateau) and wrote his doctoral dissertation on the subject treated in this case study (Mattingly 1980),[1] he is familiar with the archaeological data from this region *and* with the uncertainties attached to this kind of study. This essay displays an attitude of cautious optimism in its advocacy and application of this integrative approach.

I. THE POSSIBILITY OF RECONSTRUCTING SOCIOCULTURAL SYSTEMS

The possibility of reconstructing non-material aspects of extinct societies was only recently acknowledged in archaeological circles. Desiring to maintain a high level of objectivity, advocates of a more traditional archaeology insisted that discussions of artifacts alone increase the reliability of the archaeologist's conclusion (Binford 1968: 20). As recently as 1967, Chang (13) suggested that "those who want to make inferences and to step beyond the limitations of archaeological remains can do so and engage in the fancy game of socio-cultural reconstruction." Of course, Chang's perspective had been around for some time, as is evident from a glance at Hawkes' "ladder of reliability." By means of the following series of propositions, Hawkes (1954: 161–62) claimed to measure the degree to which a sociocultural feature could be investigated archaeologically:

1. To infer from the archeological phenomena to the techniques producing them I take to be relatively easy.
2. To infer to the subsistence-economics of the human groups concerned is fairly easy.
3. To infer to the social/political institutions of the groups, however, is considerably harder.
4. To infer to the religious institutions and spiritual life . . . is the hardest inference of all.

---

[1] This essay is an abbreviated version of part of the writer's doctoral dissertation. In 1982, Emory University's Archaeological Survey of Central and Southern Moab examined the sites between the Kerak-Qatrana highway and Wadi Hesa; the data from this season must still be integrated into the picture provided by the 1978 and 1979 seasons.

Although he said that only sociopolitical and religious institutions are more difficult to reconstruct, Hawkes' emphasis on the ease with which categories one and two could be approached by archaeology seemed to indicate that "the discipline would be forever concerned with the mundane aspects of society" (Redman *et al.* 1978: 3). Many prophetic voices were raised in opposition to such restrictions.[2] One of the earliest and most significant exhortations came from Steward and Seltzer (1938: 7), who observed

> Often ten pages are devoted to the minutiae of pottery types . . . while one page or less describes subsistence and the relationship of the culture to the geographical environment. . . . Even less space is usually accorded data concerning social groups and population distribution and concentration which are indicated by such elements as house remains and village locations.

Obviously, Steward and Seltzer were calling for inquiry into some of the very categories that Hawkes seemed to discourage, including information that can be extracted from settlement patterns.

Archaeologists have now responded to the critique of Steward, Seltzer, and other scholars, and the task of archaeology is recognized as going far beyond the collection and description of artifacts. In the course of his discussion on cultural materialism and cultural ecology, Harris (1969: 684–85) summarizes the current interests in archaeology:

> The demands of the moment are to be met by data on population size, density, minima and maxima in short and long-time runs; seasonal and climatic cycles; response of settlement pattern; rate of population increase; food production techniques; total exploited habitat; short- and long-run changes in natural biota; techno-environmental effects; size of food producing and non-food producing groups; incidence of warfare; contribution of disease vectors to mortality; nature of social organization defined in terms of house groups, village or town units; and intercommunity organization.

Trigger (1968: viii) condenses this extensive list into a single, yet extremely complex question: "What are the relationships among sociopolitical complexity, subsistence techniques, and environment?"

It is clear by now that the task of reconstructing extinct sociocultural patterns is quite demanding. Unfortunately, only a fraction of the issues enumerated by Harris and only bits and pieces of the question posed by Trigger can be approached with the data presently available on Early

---

[2] Some of the objections to a restricted view of archaeology are found in Binford 1968; see also Redman *et al.* 1978: 1–17.

Bronze Age Moab. If the goal of an integrated synthesis is to be even partially achieved, it will be necessary to use various types of information and methods. Not only must all of the available evidence come under consideration, but investigators must exploit these data with every means of analysis and interpretation at their disposal.

II. METHODOLOGY USED IN SOCIOCULTURAL RECONSTRUCTION

A prerequisite for this type of study is an explicit delineation of the methods to be employed. Naturally, the approach that will be followed in this reconstruction of Early Bronze Age Moab's sociocultural patterns is largely determined by the information available on this period and region, but the essential tools of any such reconstruction are included in the approach outlined below.

While the data pertaining to Central Moab were not collected under the aegis of the "New Archaeology,"[3] the methodological steps utilized in this study are aligned with the ambitions and techniques of what Willey and Sabloff (1974: 131–77) refer to as the "Classificatory-Historical Period: The Concern with Context and Function." The context-and-function movement dominated American archaeology from 1940 to 1960, but many of the theoretical concepts and techniques of data retrieval and analysis have been used in Syro-Palestinian fieldwork only in the last several years.[4]

The contextual-functional approach may be characterized by three fundamental presuppositions: (1) artifacts are the material remains of sociocultural behavior; (2) settlement patterns reflect socioeconomic adaptations and sociopolitical organization; (3) a dynamic relationship exists between a culture and its natural environment. A clarification of the role of the natural sciences in archaeological research also began during the heyday of the context-and-function movement. It is obvious that a

[3] The New Archaeology is one of the most recently developed schools of thought in American archaeology. Willey and Sabloff (1974: 183–89) describe this movement by listing its three basic tenets: (1) adherence to cultural evolutionary theory; (2) utilization of systems theory; and (3) belief in the supreme value of logico-deductive reasoning. The basic theoretical orientation of the New Archaeology was set forth in Watson, LeBlanc, and Redman 1971. An early critique of this movement is found in Wright 1975, and a more recent and important assessment is found in Dever 1981.

[4] While the context-and function movement dominated American archaeology from 1940–60, many of its theoretical concepts and methods of data retrieval and analysis have been used in Syro-Palestinian fieldwork only in recent years. Gaster (1979: 186–89) indicates that an awareness of this theoretical orientation was quite visible during the 1978 meeting of ASOR. Dever (1982: 104) observes that in some respects Syro-Palestinian archaeologists "are approximately where American archaeology was in the 1930s (as a brief reading of Willey and Sabloff's *A History of American Archaeology* will show)."

consideration of these factors alone should force archaeological research beyond the descriptive level.

Although the context-and-function avenue fails to yield detailed information about cultural process (Binford 1968: 14–27), much more can be said about the economic, social, and political aspects of the past with this approach than through the earlier preoccupation with chronology and classification. This is not to belittle the importance of archaeology's development of sophisticated means of dating and artifact analysis. But once a large quantity of data has been accumulated and can be dated with a relatively high degree of precision, it is time to move into additional areas of inquiry.

The contextual-functional approach makes reconstruction of non-material aspects of culture feasible, since tentative conclusions can be attained by means of analogy, inference, conjecture, and imagination.[5] Of course, these interpretative steps must be tightly regulated by using primary archaeological data from the area and time under investigation, comparative archaeological materials from surrounding regions, historical sources, and ethnographic reports. Thus, the methodology used in a contextual-functional study, including this examination of Central Moab, may be described as an inductive approach, i.e., as moving from the available particulars to a general synthesis.

For this essay to contribute to a broad understanding of the Early Bronze Age culture of the Kerak plateau, the archaeological data gathered by the Emory University survey team will be analyzed from three perspectives: (1) environmental setting, (2) historical-cultural context, and (3) settlement pattern. The information derived from these lines of evidence will ultimately yield a synthetic, albeit largely hypothetical, picture of the basic sociocultural patterns of the period and region under consideration. It should be noted that this order of investigation allows the process of reconstruction to move from the concrete aspects of the picture to the more abstract. Indeed, the third avenue of inquiry, the mapped settlement patterns, forms the basis of speculation about economic, social, and political systems.

Environmental Setting

An interest in the environmental context of ancient cultures is one of the most pervasive features of contemporary archaeological research (Willey and Sabloff 1974: 151–56, 189–91). Clarke (1972: 1–60) suggests that today's archaeological scene may be described by reference to its morphological, anthropological, ecological, and geographical paradigms. Of these four models, the ecological approach has become closely

---

[5] Discussion of these speculative steps can be found in Anderson 1969; Ascher 1961; Thompson 1956; Watson 1976.

associated with the present emphasis on the use of systems thinking in the formulation of archaeological theory (Clarke 1968).

A discussion of the environmental setting of archaeological sites within a particular region should include a description of geography, topography, geology, rainfall, climate, flora, and fauna. More important, however, is the determination of what these conditions were like in the specific period of time being investigated, since the level of development of many sociocultural features is partially explained by these environmental factors. Several comments about Central Moab's environmental setting will suffice as background for this brief study.[6]

The hostility of Transjordan's natural environment is often exaggerated, a fact that results in a misunderstanding of the ancient and modern lifestyles followed in this area. Certainly, the climatological, hydrological, and biological conditions on the Moabite plateau placed restrictions on the sociocultural development of the region's inhabitants, but apparently even the Early Bronze Age population was able to exploit the available resources with remarkable success. Although the eastern side of the plateau borders the desert, most of Central Moab has arable soil and an adequate level of precipitation. The annual rainfall, which generally ranges between 200 mm and 400 mm, is sufficient to allow the modern villagers to raise a variety of crops, and the detrimental effects of dry years are offset by the addition of pastoral activities to an agricultural susbistence base.

That there have been frequent, small-scale fluctuations in the climate and rainfall patterns of the Middle East appears likely, but the occurrence of a major climatological change during or since the Early Bronze Age remains a debatable issue.[7] To be sure, the flora and fauna of Central Moab have been altered by human activity, a fact demonstrated dramatically by the extensive deforestation of Transjordan's tableland. In spite of such alterations, the inhabitants of this region have constantly adapted themselves to the changing environment, as evidenced in the continuous occupational history of Central Moab.

Historical/Cultural Context

The study of ecology is interested in far more than the natural restrictions imposed on a society by its geographical location. Indeed, "cultural ecologists" understand human culture as a subsystem that interacts with the total ecosystem. An ecosystem includes the physical environment, the biotic community, and other human cultures (Fagan

---

[6] For more details on Central Moab's environmental setting, see Mattingly 1980: 40–63; 1980: 40–63; 1983.

[7] For a brief examination and bibliography on the possibility of climatic change during or since the Early Bronze Age, see Mattingly 1980: 64–69.

1978: 126–27). Thus, the reconstruction of a territory's cultural history calls for a narrow focus upon that area's internal development and a consideration of the region's position within a much larger context. No part of the ancient world existed in a cultural vacuum (Hole 1968:246), and even Central Moab, which was somewhat isolated from other regions by natural barriers, must have shared in the material and social developments that took place beyond its boundaries. Since so little specific information is available on Early Bronze Transjordan and its connections with other lands, the historical-cultural context of the Moabite plateau can only be established through broad generalizations and comparisons with Early Bronze Age Palestine.

Dornemann (1983: 5–7) describes the area between Wadi Mojib and Wadi Hesa, Central and Southern Moab, as a distinct unit in terms of natural boundaries and historical geography. This geographical unit did not, however, have a wholly distinctive culture. Dornemann maintains that the borders of Transjordan's various subdivisions played only a minor role in producing distinguishable archaeological assemblages. Although more formidable topographical barriers separate Palestine from Transjordan, the cultural diffusion and commercial contacts between Early Bronze populations on both sides of the Dead Sea brought about a similar repertoire of material culture.[8]

Although opinions on the subject differ, it is likely that the history of Early Bronze Age Palestine and Transjordan will be told largely in terms of a series of people movements from the northern and eastern frontiers of the Levant. The impact of these recurrent population increments is well attested in the history and archaeology of Palestine, and it is probable that the highlands of Moab were not exempt from these incursions and the accompanying cultural ramifications.

Influences from the major urban centers of the third millennium also made their way into Palestine and Transjordan. Although southern Transjordan was not situated at the center of ancient Near Eastern trade, the major transit corridor that passes through the heart of the Kerak plateau, the so-called "King's Highway," must have allowed contacts between this region and Egypt, Syria, and Mesopotamia. At present, the Transjordan evidence for such international trade and influence is not abundant, but it will undoubtedly increase with additional excavations.[9]

Settlement Patterns

Ever since Gordon R. Willey published his *Prehistoric Settlement Patterns in the Virú Valley, Peru* (1953), the settlement pattern approach has

---

[8] An important study of the continuity and unity of Palestine's Early Bronze Age culture is found in de Vaux 1971.

[9] Sauer (1982: 76) speaks about the oscillation between Egyptian and Syrian influence in Transjordan.

been a standard feature of archaeological research (Willey and Sabloff 1974:148–51). The preparation of maps that display the spatial-temporal configurations of human settlement in a particular region is one of the most fundamental and informative techniques in archaeology. The vital role of this approach in the reconstruction of economic and sociopolitical systems is identified by Adams (1969: 122): "What we are concerned with, after all, is not the abstract geometry of lines and circles on a map, as they shift over time, but with the interplay of natural and social forces that has shaped the course of historical development."

Willey (1956: 1) proposes that the study of settlement patterns is not a method in itself; instead, a mapped settlement pattern should be viewed as uninterpreted data that can be used in a variety of ways. Trigger (1970: 238) expresses a similar viewpoint: "The value of settlement patterns for reconstructing prehistoric cultures is seen as a result of the variety of institutions that are 'reflected' in the settlement pattern." In a series of steps leading from the level of description to synthesis, the study of settlement patterns may be seen as a transitional stage. While the completed maps, which display the distribution of sites from each archaeological period, remain in the realm of uninterpreted data, the information that comes to light upon examination of the patterns on these maps points to conclusions about sociocultural systems that functioned at the sites themselves. In other words, a knowledge of the region's ecology and historical/cultural context provides the necessary background for speculation about human activity in the region, but this human behavior is actually reflected in the settlement patterns. Thus, the primary sources for this reconstruction of Early Bronze culture in Central Moab are the data recovered in the regional survey, i.e., the site reports (provided in capsule summaries in Table 1), the pottery evidence (Table 2), and the Early Bronze Age settlement pattern of this territory (Fig. 1).

Since the settlement pattern approach holds great potential for Syro-Palestinian archaeology, where so many regions are known only through surface surveys, the writer would like to refer to some important bibliographic sources on the subject. General works on the use of settlement patterns include Willey (1953), Chang et al. (1968), Ucko, Tringham, and Dimbleby (1972), Trigger (1965; 1967; 1968; 1970; 1971; 1975), and Butzer (1982). Of major importance for their use of a settlement pattern approach in a Near Eastern setting are the works of Robert McC. Adams (1965; 1969; 1974; 1981) and Adams and Nissen (1972). Indeed, because of his painstaking concern for the details of history and settlement patterns and his ecological vision, Wright (1974: 124) suggests that Adams' *Land Behind Baghdad* (1965) has become a model for subsequent surveys in the Near East.

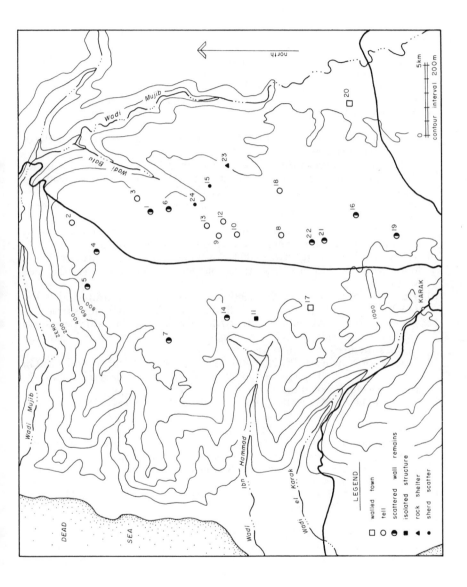

FIG. 1   *Map of Early Bronze Age Sites in Central Moab*

TABLE 1
BRIEF DESCRIPTIONS OF EARLY BRONZE AGE SITES
IN CENTRAL MOAB

1. Balu𝑐 on the northern rim of Wadi Qurri (PG 245/860): scattered wall remains covering an area ca. 100 m north-south × 750 m east-west.
2. Rujm Umm el-Qleib (PG 233/920): wall remains partially surrounding a central tower-like structure, which measures 7 m × 7 m.
3. Ruins on Wadi Suwar (PG 255/879): small mound of tumbled stones surrounded by wall remains; ruins have a diameter of ca. 25 m.
4. Mis𝑐ar (PG 215/900): scattered wall remains within and south of a modern village.
5. Rujm Umm 𝑐Awarwareh (PG 190/914): several wall remains in the middle of a large sherd scatter.
6. Balu𝑐 on the southern rim of Wadi Qurri (PG 245/855: enormous complex of ruins extending ca. 1 km east-west; a few Early Bronze sherds scattered among the Iron Age and post-Iron Age remains.
7. Imra𝑐 (PG 153/845): several wall remains visible in the dump of a modern village.
8. el-Misna𝑐 (PG 223/767): low mound which measures ca. 80 m north-south X 110 m east-west; many wall remains visible on the site's surface.
9. Humeimat Northwest (PG 226/803): low mound which measures ca. 275 m north-south × 175 m east-west; complex of wall remains covers the site's surface.
10. Humeimat Southwest (PG 227/798): low mound which measures ca. 300 m north-south × 115 m east-west; wall remains visible on the site's surface.
11. Dolmen north of ed-Dimnah (PG 167/794): stone structure which measures ca. 3 m on each side and is ca. 1.5 m high; Early Bronze Age sherds gathered in the structure's immediate vicinity.
12. Humeimat Northeast (PG 235/799): low mound which measures ca. 150 m north-south × 200 m east-west; a few Early Bronze sherds scattered among the later complex of ruins on the site's surface.
13. Umm el-Habaj (PG 230/810): low mound which measures ca. 300 m north-south × 150 m east-west; wall remains visible on the site's surface.
14. Khirbet Harzia (PG 180/792): heavy concentration of ruins which measures ca. 75 m north-south × 150 m east-west; scarcity of sherds from any period probably due to site's location on steep, easily-eroded slope.
15. Karyyah (PG 264/815): large sherd scatter which measures ca. 225 m north-south × 200 m east-west.
16. Hujfa (PG 244/710): scattering of wall remains and stone rubble which measures ca. 225 m north-south × 200 m east-west.
17. Khirbet Birjes (PG 172/737): low mound which measures ca. 75 m north-south × 150 m east-west; wall remains are visible on site's perimeter.
18. Rujm Mensahlat (PG 258/773): low mound which measures ca. 150 m. north-south × 140 east-west; few remains are visible on the site's surface.
19. Ader (PG 225/685): large scatter of remains and sherds now covered by rapidly-growing modern village.
20. el-Lejjun (PG 317/719): enormous site which measures ca. 250 m north-south × 700 m east-west; remains of walls and towers clearly visible along much of the site's perimeter.
21. Muharakat South (PG 217/729): scattering of wall remains which measure ca. 200 m north-south × 75 m east-west.

22. Muharakat North (PG 216/733): several wall remains spread over an area which measures ca. 35 m north-south × 25 m east-west.
23. Rock Shelter on the upper Wadi Mujib (PG 315/803): long line of overhanging stone that forms a low chamber; located on a steep hillside overlooking the wadi.
24. Balu‘ South (PG 257/843): large sherd scatter which measures ca. 150 m north-south × 150 m east-west.

TABLE 2

EARLY BRONZE AGE SITES IN CENTRAL MOAB,
WITH PERCENTAGE OF EARLY BRONZE SHERDS

1. Balu‘ on the northern rim of Wadi Qurri (81% EB): 136 EB IV
2. Rujm Umm el-Qleib (88% EB): 7 EB I, 187 EB II–III, 95 EB IV
3. Ruins on Wadi Suwar (56% EB): 5 EB IV.
4. Mis‘ar (18% EB): 54 EB
5. Rujm Umm ‘Awarwareh (33% EB): 20 EB
6. Balu‘ on the southern rim of Wadi Qurri (1% EB): 2 EB, 5 EB II–III, 1 EB IV
7. Imra‘ (8% EB): 13 EB II–III, 20 EB IV
8. El-Misna‘ (15% EB): 18 EB II–III, 15 EB IV
9. Humeimat Northwest (41% EB): 1 Chal/EB I, 17 EB, 59 EB IV.
10. Humeimat Southwest (4% EB): 7 EB, 1 EB IV.
11. Dolmen north of ed-Dimnah (61% EB): 39 EB II–III, 1 EB IV
12. Humeimat Northeast (2% EB): 4 EB
13. Umm el-Habaj (17% EB): 2 EB I, 3 EB II–III, 106 EB IV
14. Khirbet Harzia (15% EB): 1 EB I, 6 EB II–III
15. Karyyah (61% EB): 35 EB II–III, 24 EB IV
16. Hujfa (13% EB): 2 EB I, 5 EB II–III
17. Khirbet Birjes (82% EB): 6 EB I, 209 EB II–III, 14 EB IV
18. Rujm Mensahlat (92% EB): 6 Chal/EB I, 6 EB II–III, 9 EB IV
19. Ader (57% EB): 67 EB II–III, 99 EB IV
20. el-Lejjun (50% EB): 2 Chal/EB I, 6 EB II–III, 28 EB IV
21. Muharakat South (25% EB): 14 EB IV
22. Muharakat North (32% EB): 5 EB II–III, 18 EB IV
23. Rock Shelter on the upper Wadi Mujib (96% EB): 68 EB I
24. Balu‘ South (64% EB): 9 EB I, 8 EB II–III, 39 EB IV

The major published reports of Nelson Glueck's survey of the Transjordan (1934; 1935, 1939; 1951) must be singled out has having special significance for students for Syro-Palestinian archaeology. Many of Glueck's conclusions have stood the test of time, although some of

Glueck's historical reconstruction is open to criticism and correction.[10] Glueck's pioneering efforts in archaeological survey and the interpretation of his recovered data are directly related to the present study, since Central Moab was one of the first regions he explored.

Thomas L. Thompson's studies of settlement patterns in Palestine and Transjordan (1974a; 1974b; 1975; 1978; 1979) should also be mentioned as having special value, both for their explicit use of a settlement pattern approach and for their geographical scope. Although Thompson's endeavors have also received much criticism, the value of his approach and his tentative conclusions should not be overlooked.[11]

Many other studies, though less comprehensive than these, could be cited as helpful examples of the ways in which the settlement pattern approach can be used to increase our understanding of ancient Syro-Palestinian cultural patterns.[12] The fact that this integrative approach is being used by so many archaeologists in the Middle East is encouraging. More encouragement is found in the increasing awareness of concepts borrowed from the "New Geography," especially the so-called "central place theory."[13]

III. THE ECONOMIC SYSTEM OF EARLY BRONZE AGE CENTRAL MOAB

Smith (1976: 435) suggests that the most significant reconstructions taking place in archaeology today are those concerned with the economic system of a particular region. Since an economy is directly related to its environmental setting and the surrounding sociopolitical developments, a useful and natural starting point for the present reconstruction is a summary of Moab's Early Bronze economy. Although scholars have not given this territory's Early Bronze culture much attention, it is generally assumed that Transjordan's Early Bronze Age inhabitants were pastoral nomads.[14] Such an ambiguous designation may be sufficient, if it is recognized that this lifestyle manifests itself in a wide variety of ways, some of which include a degree of sedentarization and agriculture (Dever 1980: 56–57). Because of the available archaeological and ethnographic evidence, it appears likely that Central Moab's Early Bronze

[10] For bibliographical references to critiques of Glueck, see Mattingly 1980: 74, n. 13.

[11] For evaluations of Thompson's works, see Cohen and Dever 1978: 43, nn. 8, 18; idem 1979: 59, nn. 5, 21; Dever 1980: 56, 60, nn. 48, 49; Geraty 1982: 306–9; Prag 1984:58–68.

[12] See Cohen and Dever 1978; idem 1979; Ibrahim, Sauer, and Yassine 1976; Marfoe 1979; Mittmann 1970; Parr 1972; Prag 1974; Strange 1982.

[13] For discussion and bibliography on these concepts, see Mattingly 1980: 31–32; Strange 1982.

[14] This position was advocated by Albright and Glueck, whose opinions on this issue went unquestioned for many years; see Mattingly 1980: 153–55.

population was involved in a whole range of "occupations," including farming, trade and industry, and hunting, as well as livestock breeding. This diverse economy was probably pursued in a variety of settlement types, including some permanent towns and villages. The Moabite plateau is quite capable of supporting a sizeable population; the existence of some 275 archaeological sites in this small area indicates that the Kerak district has always been well suited for human occupation, including sedentary occupation. In this recent reevaluation of the archaeological materials from Transjordan, Dornemann (1983: 4–5) objects to the traditional description of this territory as an unsettled backwater. Dornemann would probably surprise many readers when he states that the fertile highlands of Ammon, Moab, and Edom "were as inviting and as capable of sustaining a population as most areas of Palestine."

In his early writings, Glueck emphasized the EB IV-MB I occupation of the Moabite plateau and made virtually no reference to EB I-III. Glueck's later studies not only included discussion of Moab's EB I-III occupation, and it is also clear that Glueck's revised perspective allowed for a more sedentary population engaged in agriculture.[15] Similar acknowledgement of the existence of agricultural settlements in this region is found in Prag's synthesis of evidence on the Intermediate Early Bronze-Middle Bronze Age (1974: 96–103) and in Thompson's studies on Bronze Age Transjordan (1974b; 1978; 1979). Thompson (1974b: 69-70) notes that "Jordan can, by no stretch of the imagination, be understood as an agricultural 'fringe' area. The central Jordanian plateau is *sui generis*, and the hill country, even far to the south of Karak, has more in common with the hill country of Palestine that it does with the Negev and Sinai." Thompson's conclusion on the role of farming in the Bronze Age villages of this region is quite daring:

> . . . the typical Bronze Age settlement of both Palestine and eastern Jordan can be characterized as that of small village agriculture. This type of settlement seems to be continuous throughout this entire area from the Late Chalcolithic period through the Late Bronze period (1974b: 70).

Although the available evidence does not offer an indisputable case for a largely sedentarized population in Early Bronze Age Moab, at least the assumption that this area was occupied exclusively by pastoral nomads has been challenged.

During the summers of 1978 and 1979, the Emory University survey team examined 24 sites that yielded sherds from the Early Bronze Age.

---

[15] This is quite obvious when one compares the 1940 and 1970 editions of Glueck's *The Other Side of the Jordan.*

Twenty-one of these locations were classified as "A" sites when they were intially mapped, i.e., the majority of these sites were described as significant villages or towns. This does not mean that all of the surface (or subsurface) ruins at these sites date to the Early Bronze Age. It is possible, however, that some of these sites, which yielded large numbers of Early Bronze sherds and smaller quantities of later sherds, were occupied primarily during the Early Bronze Age. This is the case with Balu' on the northern rim of Wadi Qurri (Site 1), Rujm Umm el-Qleib (Site 2), Khirbet Birjes (Site 17), Rujm Mensahlat (Site 18), Ader (Site 19), and el-Lejjun (Site 20). Furthermore, if there is a relation between settlement size and economy (Gabel 1967: 19), it seems likely that some of these larger sites were dependent on both stockbreeding and farming. Since all of these Early Bronze settlements had access to agriculturally suitable land, which is located in an adequately watered region, there is no compelling reason to insist that whatever agriculture was practiced in Early Bronze Moab was secondary. If pastoral, hunting, and trading activities are added to the practice of dry farming, we are probably arriving at a realistic understanding of the economic structure of this time and place.

With regard to the role of interregional trade in Moab, reference should be made to the relation of Early Bronze Age sites to the King's Highway. Out of the 275 sites examined by the Emory team in the 1978 and 1979 seasons, only a handful of settlements were located near the present highway, which is usually thought to follow the ancient route. Although no one has suggested that the King's Highway was the major thoroughfare in every era of Moab's ancient history, the recent survey fails to indicate that many settlements were situated along this road in any period. This does not mean that there was no major highway across the plateau; the distribution of sites simply points to the fact that water and tillable soil played more important roles in determining regional settlement patterns, including those of the Early Bronze Age.

Since Prag (1974: 74) points to the importance of the Jordan Valley as a trade route, it is also helpful to indicate the most of the ancient Near East displayed a "vertical economy" (Flannery 1969: 73). This means that Central Moab could have been involved in trade with other regions of Transjordan (by means of the King's Highway), with the highlands to the west of the Jordan (via routes along and ascending out of the Jordan rift), and with the settlements located below the plateau in the Dead Sea basin (Thompson 1979: 15; Harlan 1981; 162–63; McCreery 1981; 168).

Even simple agrarian societies included settlements that required local products or services they could not provide for themselves; this resulted in the development of intraregional trade. Certain strategically located villages and towns, which we can refer to as "service centers," gained economic and political ascendancy over the other settlements in the same region. This hierarchy of settlements often developed according to the principle of "effort minimization," i.e., a central place serviced in an encircling group of dependent sites. Of course, the application of spatial analytical techniques to a particular region is fraught with difficulties. First, since archaeologists must work with broad chronological divisions, the contemporaneity of the archaeological sites in a given region is difficult to demonstrate. Obviously, this places great restrictions on any analysis of the relationships between sites in a settlement configuration (Parr 1972: 807; Hodder and Orton 1976: 18–19). Second, the hierarchical and horizontal organization of sites in a region may be disrupted by rough terrain or other geographical factors (Hodder 1972: 916–17).

The data from Central Moab are further impaired by two additional factors. First, a group of unclassified Early Bronze Age sites in this region complicates the effort to bring precision to the settlement analysis. Second, since none of the Early Bronze sites on the Moabite plateau was occupied in only one period, the actual size of any site in a particular phase of the Early Bronze Age is impossible to determine.

In light of the limitations just mentioned, the following observations about the intraregional connections of Central Moab are only tentative generalizations. Once again, hypotheses of this kind, if recognized as such, are better than total silence about this area. Furthermore, these tentative observations are always subject to refinement, especially that which might result from further archaeological excavations on the plateau. Although the Central Moab Survey did not make systematic, intensive collections of sherds at the 24 Early Bronze sites in this region,[16] perhaps some significance can be attached to the large numbers of Early Bronze Age sherds that were found at particular sites.

The only EB I site that yielded a sizeable quantity of sherds is the rock shelter on the upper Wadi Mujib (Site 23), but this site can hardly be thought of as an important ancient settlement. In fact, this rock shelter may have been used as a burial place. EB I sherds were found at several other sites, but they were not recovered in large number, perhaps an

[16] This technique is described in Redman and Watson 1970. For an informative study of survey design, see Schiffer, Sullivan, and Klinger 1978. With regard to methodology, the Moab Survey team simply attempted to retrieve most of the diagnostic sherds from each of the 585 archaeological sites within the boundaries of the survey. It is recognized that many variables may have skewed the thoroughness of such a survey technique, but the urgent nature of this survey seemed to warrant this approach. With this explanation in mind, the reader should note that the percentages of Early Bronze Age sherds in Table 2 are intended to show the relative number of sherds from this period, not a scientific estimate of population density in a certain era.

indication that EB I occupation in this region was quite limited. It is also possible that Central Moab's EB I population was more nomadic and has left only ephemeral remains.

The sherd count for EB II-III leads to a different conclusion. Apparently, Khirbet Birjes (Site 17), Rujm Mensahlat (Site 18), and Ader (Site 19) were the most important settlements on the plateau during this phase. Appropriately, each of these sites is widely separated from the others, and each could have served as the hub of the remaining clusters of EB II-III settlements in this area. Relatively large numbers of EB II-III sherds were recovered at Rujm Umm el-Qleib (Site 2), the Dolmen north of ed-Dimnah (Site 11), and Karyyah (Site 15), but these sites could not have been major market centers.

Finally, the collections of EB IV sherds from Central Moab indicate that there were a number of important centers of activity on the plateau during this period: Baluʿ on the northern rim of Wadi Qurri (Site 1), Humeimat Northwest (Site 9), Umm el-Habaj (Site 13), Ader (Site 19), and el-Lejjun (Site 20). Since Baluʿ on the northern rim of Wadi Qurri, along with its counterpart on the southern side of the wadi, comprised the largest settlement in Central Moab, it is important to notice that many of the EB IV sites were located in the vicinity of Baluʿ. As in the EB II-III period, Rujm Umm el-Qleib (Site 2) yielded a large quantity of EB IV sherds. Although this site was not a large population center, it may have served as a checkpoint, or military station, in much the same way as el-Lejjun (Site 20) functioned on the eastern limit of the plateau.

IV. THE SOCIOPOLITICAL SYSTEM OF EARLY BRONZE AGE CENTRAL MOAB

Now that some attention has been given to the natural environment, historical-cultural context, and economic activities of Early Bronze Age Central Moab, it is time to turn to the less tangible sociopolitical organization of this time and region. Human society cannot be described exclusively in terms of ecological context, technological capabilities, and economic activities. Instead, a proper understanding of the ancient Moabites' cultural history is based upon the recognition that "social" factors often take precedence over the material aspects of life (Hole and Heizer 1973: 352–53). While environment and technology set the limitations on mankind's need and ability to adapt, a population's adaptability is largely influenced by factors from the social, political, and religious realms.[17]

---

[17] Although the writer's original study included a section on Early Bronze Age religion (see Mattingly 1980: 225–40), a reconstruction of Moabite religion in this period is beyond the scope of this essay.

The Social Structure of Early Bronze Age Central Moab

Although the writer's original study of Early Bronze Moab included an investigation of the relationship between site size and population (Mattingly 1980: 193–201), little will be said about this subject in the present essay. As Stager (1975: 185–86) observes, population estimates obtained from anepigraphic archaeological sources are "notoriously unreliable," since the determination of ancient population figures is filled with known and unknown variables (Sumner 1979: 165–73). It should be noted, however, that the maximum areas covered by Central Moab's Early Bronze sites indicate that almost all of these settlements fall into the category of "village."

It is not surprising to learn that the village was the dominant type of settlement on the plateau in this early period, since the village is still a major component in all Near Eastern societies. Undoubtedly, the village community constituted the "social space" for most of Moab's ancient population. In other words, each village was a microcosm of the whole society, and it is likely that most of the plateau's inhabitants had few direct contacts beyond their own village or a neighboring cluster of villages.[18] Naturally, such isolation had profound effects on the social structure of this region. For example, there were economic and soicopolitical bonds between villages and towns, but there can be no doubt that the household was the most important socioeconomic unit on the plateau. The centrality of the individual household is still maintained in much of the Middle East, especially when compared to involvement in national life (Watson 1979: 217).

Like the towns and villages of ancient Palestine, the settlements of Transjordan were little more than accretions of households that were based on family affiliations (Anati 1963: 330). In his discussion of the Early Bronze Age towns of Palestine, Anati (1963: 329) suggests that ancient family life was probably similar to that of Near Eastern villages of today. The traditional character of this area's culture, especially the conservatism displayed in social institutions, makes Anati's hypothesis plausible. Thus, it is possible that the ancient, pre-Islamic Transjordanian family was much like today's Muslim Arab family, which Patai (1958: 136–39) has characterized with six descriptive terms: (1) extended, (2) patrilineal, (3) patrilocal, (4) patriarchal, (5) endogamous, and (6) occasionally polygynous. Any further discussion of Early Bronze Age Moabite family structure would be even more speculative, but an analysis that acknowledges the continuity of Near Eastern kinship patterns will not be far from the truth.

Although there is no direct evidence of social stratification from the

[18] Van Nieuwenhuijze (1962: 295) refers to the village as a microcosm that is normally embedded in a cosmos of villages.

region under investigation, it can be assumed that future excavation will recover such information by studying the construction and furnishing of tombs and houses (Mattingly 1980: 207–19). The examination of numerous tombs at Jericho and Bab ed-Draʿ clearly demonstrates that socioeconomic differentiation was found in these ancient societies. Even without this comparative data from sites near to the Moabite plateau, it is well known that all societies contain social divisions which, according to Mair (1970: 48–61), are based on six criteria: (1) differentiation by sex, (2) differentiation by age, (3) rank, hierarchy, or stratification, (4) caste, (5) moieties or dual divisions, and (6) associations. Van Nieuwenhuijze (1962: 303–5) has pointed out that present-day Near Eastern villages normally exhibit a plurality of stratification criteria (e.g., descent, learning, wealth, occupation); it should be expected that such criteria were operative in ancient Transjordan as well.

The Political Organization of Early Bronze Age Central Moab

No society has a political organization that is based solely on kinship (Lienhardt 1969: 51–52). Although political activities may not always be professionalized or institutionalized, even the simplest societies regulate their affairs by means of political processes. For example, the political system of early Bronze Age Central Moab had to take into account such issues as foreign relations, defense from external attack, and maintenance of internal order. While it is obvious that the inhabitants of each village or town had to consider these matters in relation to its own local settlements, an inquiry into the political organization of the Central Moabite plateau must also seek to determine the presence or absence of an intercommunity political system.

Because of the complexity of social phenomena, Trigger (1975: 96–104) suggests that five different approaches should be used when attempting to reconstruct political organization: (1) demographic, (2) cultural, (3) societal, (4) geographical, (5) iconographic. With the exception of Trigger's fifth approach, the iconographic, data are available for each of these avenues to contribute to an understanding of Early Bronze Age Moab's political system of Early Bronze Palestine with that of Transjordan.

Inferences about the intracommunity government of ancient Moab can be made on the basis of population estimates. Naroll (1956: 690) suggests that communities with less than 300 inhabitants do not need authoritative officials, but populations exceeding 500 seem to need the appointment of such officials. Since the overwhelming majority of Early Bronze Age Moab's settlements probably had populations of less than 500, village leaders, other than heads of families or tribal chiefs, may not have been present. Several larger villages may have been ruled by councils of chiefs.

A scholarly consensus refers to Palestine's Bronze Age political organization as a disunited configuration of city-states.[19] The city-state was
composed of a central town and its surrounding agricultural lands and
dependent villages. Since each city-state was largely self-supporting and
autonomous, these feudal-like kingdoms were often at war with one
another (Kenyon 1960: 103; Lapp 1970: 112–13; de Vaux 1971: 113).[20]
Such rivalry and its resultant intrigue are well known from the Late
Bronze Age correspondence that took place between Tell el-Amarna and
Palestine (Lapp 1970: 113). Kenyon (1960: 102–3) was probably correct
when she suggested that the city-state system began in the Proto-Urban
period and continued into Iron Age I. It is likely that Palestine's system
of city-states was paralleled by a similar political organization in Transjordan (Glueck 1970: 157; Kirk 1944: 185; Van Zyl 1960: 104).
    While the subordinate villages of a city-state were ruled by tribal
headmen, the entire political unit was under the control of a council
chief or a petty king, whose orders were dictated from a major settlement in the center of his tiny kingdom. The existence of this city-state
form of government precluded a political system that united all of
Transjordan. Nevertheless, it is likely that one or two towns wielded
more power and influence in Central Moab during each phase of the
Early Bronze Age, creating centers of political activity, not just market
towns.
    Trigger's geographical approach to the study of ancient government
is based on the assumption that the distribution of settlement types in a
particular region can be explained by locational theory (Trigger 1975:
101). As already mentioned, several towns in Central Moab could have
served as regional centers of trade and market. However, when the
economic, military, and demographic factors are brought together, only
one Early Bronze Age site in Central Moab, el-Lejjun (Site 20), exhibits
all of the qualifications of a city-state (e.g., surrounding agricultural land,
evidence of fortifications, potential for sizeable population). It is important to note that the Early Bronze Age site of el-Lejjun is located immediately to the west of the Roman fortress with the same name; both
settlements served as regional centers on the eastern edge of the fertile
plateau, controlling and protecting the local population, water resources,
and access route to the heart of the district. Other settlements, notably
Baluʿ (Site 1), Humeimat Northwest (Site 9), Umm el-Habaj (Site 13),
Khirbet Birjes (Site 17), Rujm Mensahlat (Site 18), and Ader (Site 19),

---

[19] On the city-states of Bronze Age Palestine, see Aharoni 1967: 122–23; Amiran
1970: 96; Anati 1963: 43, 325–27; Kenyon 1960: 102–3; Lapp 1970: 112–13; de Vaux
1971: 234–35; Wright 1961: 81.
    [20] Of course, the towns of Transjordan also had to protect themselves from common
enemies, e.g., bedouin and Egyptians; see Lapp 1970: 114.

were probably important settlements, but they may not have attained the prominence that would have enabled them to function in the city-state capacity. Since most of these sites are located in separate regions of the plateau, they could have served as economic, sociopolitical, and religious centers for the surrounding population. There is, however, a notable concentration of sites in the vicinity of Baluᶜ (Site 1), perhaps indicating that this area had special importance throughout Moab's Early Bronze history.

Another of Trigger's approaches to the study of ancient political organization, the cultural approach, simply recognizes that the inventory of material culture exceeds the boundaries of any one government (Trigger 1975: 98–99). This means that the ancient city-states were involved in intraregional trade, a situation requiring some measure of political contact. While the towns and villages to the north of Wadi Mojib were geographically separated from those in Central Moab, both sides of this great canyon shared in a common material culture. The southern portion of the Moabite plateau (i.e., the region between the Kerak-Qatrana highway and Wadi Hesa) was obviously in more contact with the settlements in Central Moab. Between these two regions there was un-doubtedly much direct economic and political contact, both cooperation and competition.[21] Moreover, commercial and military connections with other regions of the Levant helped to mold a small number of city-states into political and economic centers.

Finally, Trigger's societal approach may provide additional aid in the reconstruction of the political organization of this region. Since community leadership is often directly related to social position, the vested interests of the wealthy and socially prominent can lead to a correlative development of social stratification and political organization (Trigger 1975: 99–101). In other words, the status holders in Early Bronze Age Moabite society could have guarded their positions through political advancement, thereby contributing to the development of political organization in this region.

CONCLUSION

It is obvious that one encounters many difficulties in reconstructing the sociocultural patterns of human groups that have left no written records. Trigger's attempts to solve some of the problems in Nubian history convinced him that

---

[21] A preliminary examination of the site descriptions and ceramic evidence from the 1982 season of the Moab Survey indicates that there were significant Early Bronze Age settlements in the southern portion of the plateau; cf. Mattingly 1984.

the reconstruction of prehistory is frequently more difficult than one would care to admit and that prehistorians rarely keep in mind the full range of alternative explanations to which their data may be susceptible. In a discipline where interpretations are fraught with uncertainity, it is important to be sophisticated about these alternatives (Trigger 1968: xi).

Even when historical documents are available to inform archaeological research, the interpretations can still be plagued by uncertainties. That difficulties abound in this study of Early Bronze Age Central Moab is obvious; it has already been acknowledged that the conclusions reached in this essay are inevitably subject to change. This does not mean that this reconstruction should be put off "until the uncertain future when 'sufficient' data are at hand."[22] In light of the tentative nature of his conclusions, the writer is aware of four major factors that detract from the accuracy and comprehensiveness desired in this study. The first major limitation to the approach advocated in this essay is the reconstruction's heavy dependence on data obtained by archaeological survey. While the value of surface reconnaissance has been adequately demonstrated, the surface of an archaeological site is not always a microcosm of its subsurface contents.

In addition to the incomplete coverage provided by archaeological survey, the small amount of stratigraphic evidence from Central Moab imposes a second limitation on this reconstruction. In fact, the excavation of so few stratified, chronologically-identifiable deposits of Early Bronze Age cultural material makes it impossible to obtain a reliable picture of the nature and extent of Central Moab's Early Bronze occupation. No amount of comparative archaeological data from surrounding regions of information obtained through surface survey can overcome this deficiency. Excavation is the pressing need in Moab; the recovery of additional archaeological data from this region will be welcomed.

A third limitation is found in the writer's decision to focus upon such a small section of Transjordan. The narrow boundaries of this study were chosen for two reasons. First, the writer is more familiar with the geography and sites of Central Moab, having spent many weeks in the summers of 1979, 1982, and 1983 roving over its terrain and examining its ancient settlements. Second, because of the recent work of the Archaeological Survey of Central and Southern Moab, the ceramic evi-

[22] This phrase was borrowed from Adams and Nissen 1972: 17, which goes on to say that "it is quite unlikely that certainties will generally be substituted for probabilities in any reasonable future; our task, in fact, is not to avoid probabilistic statements, but to make explicit the evidence and asumptions on which they are based." This writer is in complete agreement with this line of reasoning.

dence and site descriptions for this part of the plateau are far more exhaustive and reliable than for the other regions of Moab.

The constant use of methods that are highly speculative is recognized as a fourth limitation of this study. Because of the small amount of archaeological investigation conducted in Central Moab, the writer has attempted to exploit every archaeological datum. It is hoped that this has been accomplished without overstating what the evidence reasonably allows.

During the oral defense of this writer's dissertation, Professor Callaway noted that theoretical reconstructions, such as the one presented in this essay, can never replace the hard work of "dirt archaeology." Naturally, Callaway is right in placing this emphasis on the necessity of fieldwork, but he is also in sympathy with any approach that holds promise of increasing our understanding of the ancient world. Callaway's emphasis on the importance of excavation serves as a corrective to those who do all of their archaeology while sitting behind a desk. Appropriately, this warning comes from one who has demonstrated, through many years of fieldwork and publication, that he is vitally interested in the discoveries and methodological development of Syro-Palestinian archaeology. Since this volume is intended to acknowledge Joseph A. Callaway's contributions to this discipline, it has been a privilege to participate in its production.

BIBLIOGRAPHY

Adams, R. Mc.
1965   *Land Behind Baghdad: A History of Settlement on the Diyala Plains.* Chicago: University of Chicago.
1969   The Study of Ancient Mesopotamian Settlement Patterns and the Problems of Urban Origins. *Sumer* 25: 111–24.
1974   The Mesopotamian Social Landscape: A View from the Frontier. Pp. 1–20 in *Reconstructing Complex Societies: An Archaeological Colloquium*, ed. C. B. Moore. Supplement to *BASOR*, No. 20. Cambridge: ASOR.
1981   *Heartland of Cities: Surveys of Ancient Settlement and Land Use on the Central Floodplain of the Euphrates.* Chicago: University of Chicago.
Adams, R. Mc., and Nissen, H. J.
1972   *The Uruk Countryside: The Natural Setting of Urban Societies.* Chicago: University of Chicago.
Aharoni, Y.
1967   *The Land of the Bible: A Historical Geography.* Trans. A. F. Rainey from Hebrew. Philadelphia: Westminster.
Amiran, R.
1970   The Beginnings of Urbanization in Canaan. Pp. 83–100 in *Near Eastern Archaeology in the Twentieth Century: Essays in Honor of Nelson Glueck*, ed. J. A. Sanders. Garden City, NY: Doubleday.

Anati, E.
1963   *Palestine Before the Hebrews: A History from the Earliest Arrival of Man to the Conquest of Canaan.* New York: Knopf.
Anderson, K. M.
1969   Ethnographic Analogy and Archaeological Interpretation. *Science* 163: 133–38.
Ascher, R.
1961   Analogy in Archaeological Interpretation. *SJA* 17: 317–25.
Binford, L. R.
1968   Archaeological Perspectives. Pp. 5–32 in *New Perspectives in Archaeology,* ed. S. R. Binford and L. R. Binford. Chicago: Aldine.
Butzer, K. W.
1982   *Archaeology as Human Ecology.* New York: Cambridge University.
Chang, K. -C.
1967   *Rethinking Archaeology.* New York: Random House.
Chang, K. -C., *et al.*
1968   *Settlement Archaeology.* Palo Alto, CA: National.
Clarke, D. L.
1968   *Analytical Archaeology.* London: Methuen.
1972   Models and Paradigms in Contemporary Archaeology. Pp. 1–60 in *Models in Archaeology,* ed. D. L. Clarke. London: Methuen.
Cohen, R., and Dever, W. G.
1978   Preliminary Report of the Pilot Season of the "Central Negev Highlands Project." *BASOR* 232: 29–45.
1979   Preliminary Report of the Second Season of the "Central Negev Highlands Project." *BASOR* 236: 41–60.
Dever, W. G.
1980   New Vistas on the EB IV ("MB I") Horizon in Syria-Palestine. *BASOR* 237: 35–64.
1981   The Impact of the "New Archaeology" on Syro-Palestinian Archaeology. *BASOR* 242: 15–29.
1982   Retrospects and Prospects in Biblical and Syro-Palestinian Archaeology. *BA* 45: 103–7.
Dornemann, R. H.
1983   *The Archaeology of the Transjordan in the Bronze and Iron Ages.* Milwaukee: Milwaukee Public Museum.
Fagan, B. M.
1978   *Archaeology: A Brief Introduction.* Boston: Little, Brown.
Flannery, K. V.
1969   Origins and Ecological Effects of Early Domestication in Iran and the Near East. Pp. 73–100 in *The Domestication and Exploitation of Plants and Animals,* ed. P. J. Ucko and G. W. Dimbleby. London: Duckworth.
Gabel, C.
1967   *Analysis of Prehistoric Economic Patterns.* Studies in Anthropological Method. New York: Holt, Rinehart and Winston.
Glaster, L. M.
1979   Colloquia. *BA* 42: 186–89.
Geraty, L. T.
1982   Review of Thomas L. Thompson, *The Settlement of Palestine in the Bronze Age. CBQ* 44: 306–9.
Glueck, N.
1934   Explorations in Eastern Palestine, I. *AASOR* 14: 1–113.

1935	Explorations in Eastern Palestine, II. *AASOR* 15: 1–202.
1939	Explorations in Eastern Palestine, III. *AASOR* 18–19: 1–287.
1940	*The Other Side of the Jordan.* New Haven: ASOR.
1951	Explorations in Eastern Palestine, IV. *AASOR* 25–28: 1–423.
1970	*The Other Side of the Jordan,* rev. ed. Cambridge: ASOR.

Harlan, J. R.
1981   Natural Resources of the Southern Ghor. *AASOR* 46: 155–64.

Harris, M.
1969   *The Rise of Anthropological Literature: A History of Theories of Culture.* New York: Crowell.

Hawkes, C.
1954   Archaeological Theory and Method: Some Suggestions from the Old World. *Am Anthrop* 56: 155–68.

Hodder, I. R.
1972   Locational Models and the Study of Romano-British Settlement. Pp. 887–909 in *Models in Archaeology,* ed. D. L. Clarke. London: Methuen.

Hodder, I. R., and Orton, C.
1976   *Spatial Analysis in Archaeology.* Cambridge: Cambridge University.

Hole, F.
1968   Evidence of Social Organization from Western Iran, 8000–4000 B.C. Pp. 245–65 in *New Perspectives in Archaeology,* ed. S. R. Binford and L. R. Binford. Chicago: Aldine.

Hole, F., and Heizer, R. F.
1973   *An Introduction to Prehistoric Archaeology,* 3rd ed. New York: Holt, Rinehart and Winston.

Ibrahim, M.; Sauer, J. A.; and Yassine, K.
1976   The East Jordan Valley Survey, 1975. *BASOR* 221: 41–66.

Kenyon, K.
1960   *Archaeology in the Holy Land,* 3rd ed. London: Benn.

Kirk, M. E.
1944   An Outline of the Ancient Cultural History of Transjordan. *PEQ* 76: 180–98.

Lapp, P. W.
1970   Palestine in the Early Bronze Age. Pp. 101–31 in *Near Eastern Archaeology in the Twentieth Century: Essays in Honor of Nelson Glueck,* ed. J. A. Sanders. Garden City, NY: Doubleday.

Lienhardt, G.
1969   *Social Anthropology,* 2nd ed. London: Oxford.

Mair, L.
1970   *An Introduction to Social Anthropology.* New York: Oxford.

Marfoe, L.
1979   The Integrative Transformation: Patterns of Sociopolitical Organization in Southern Syria. *BASOR* 234: 1–42.

Mattingly, G. L.
1980   *A Reconstruction of Early Bronze Age Cultural Patterns in Central Moab.* Unpublished Ph.D. dissertation, Southern Baptist Theological Seminary.
1983   The Natural Environment of Central Moab. *ADAJ* 27: 597–605.
1984   The Early Bronze Age Sites of Central and Southern Moab. *NEASB* 23: 69–98.

McCreery, D. W.
1981   Flotation of the Bab edh-Dhraᶜ and Numeira Plant Remains. *AASOR* 46: 165–69.

Mittman, S.
1970   *Beiträge zur Siedlungs- und Territorialgeschichte des nördlichen Ostjordanlandes.* Abhandlungen des Deutschen Palästina-Vereins. Wiesbaden: Harrassowitz.

Naroll, R.
1956   A Preliminary Index of Social Development. *Am Anthrop* 58: 687–715.

van Nieuwenhuijze, C. A. O.
1962   The Near Eastern Village: A Profile. *The Middle East Journal* 16: 295–308.

Parr, P. J.
1972   Settlement Patterns and Urban Planning in the Ancient Levant: The Nature of the Evidence. Pp. 805–10 in *Man, Settlement and Urbanism,* ed. P. J. Ucko, R. Tringham, and G. W. Dimbleby. London: Duckworth.

Patai, R.
1958   *The Kingdom of Jordan.* Princeton: Princeton University.

Prag, K.
1974   The Intermediate Early Bronze-Middle Bronze Age: An Interpretation of the Evidence from Transjordan, Syria, and Lebanon. *Levant* 6: 69–116.

1984   Continuity and Migration in the South Levant in the Late Third Millennium: A Review of T. L. Thompson's and Some Other Views. *PEQ* 116: 58–68.

Redman, C. L., and Watson, P. J.
1970   Systematic, Intensive Surface Collection. *Am Ant* 35: 279–91.

Redman, C. L., *et al.*
1978   Social Archaeology: The Future of the Past. Pp. 1–17 in *Social Archaeology: Beyond Subsistence and Dating,* ed. C. L. Redman et al. New York: Academic.

Sauer, J. A.
1982   Prospects for Archaeology in Jordan and Syria. *BA* 45: 73–84.

Schiffer, M. B.; Sullivan, A. P.; and Klinger, T. C.
1978   The Design of Archaeological Surveys. *WA* 10: 1–28.

Smith, J. W.
1976   *Foundations of Archaeology.* Beverly Hills: Glencoe.

Stager, L. E.
1975   *Ancient Agriculture in the Judaean Desert: A Case Study of The Buqeᶜah Valley in the Iron Age.* Unpublished Ph.D. dissertation, Harvard University.

Steward, J. H., and Seltzer,
1938   Function and Configuration in Archaeology. *Am Ant* 4: 4–10

Strange, J. F.
1982   New Developments in Greco-Roman Archaeology as a Discipline. *BA* 45: 85–88.

Sumner, W. H.
1979   Estimating Population by Analogy: An Example. Pp. 164–74 in *Ethnoarchaeology: Implications of Ethnography for Archaeology,* ed. C. Kramer. New York: Columbia University.

Thompson, R. H.
1956   The Subjective Element in Archaeological Inference. *SJA* 12: 327–32.
Thompson, T. L.
1974a   *The Historicity of the Patriarchal Narratives: The Quest for the Historical Abraham.* Beiheft zur Zeitschrift für die alttestamentliche Wissenschaft. Berlin: de Gruyter.
1974b   Observations on the Bronze Age in Jordan. *ADAJ* 19: 63–70.
1975   *The Settlement of Sinai and the Negev in the Bronze Age.* Beihefte zum Tübinger Atlas des Vorderen Orients Reihe B, Nr. 8. Wiesbaden: Ludwig Reichert.
1978   The Background of the Patriarchs: A Reply to William Dever and Malcolm Clark. *JSOT* 9: 2–43.
1979   *The Settlement of Palestine in the Bronze Age.* Beihefte zum Tübinger Atlas des Vorderen Orients Reihe B, Nr. 34. Wiesbaden: Ludwig Reichert.
Trigger, B. G.
1965   *History and Settlement in Lower Nubia.* Yale University Publications in Anthropology, No. 69. New Haven: Yale University.
1967   Settlement Archaeology—Its Goals and Promise. *Am Ant* 32: 149–60.
1968   *Beyond History: The Methods of Prehistory.* Studies in Anthropological Method. New York: Holt, Rinehart and Winston.
1970   Settlement Patterns in Archaeology. Pp. 237–62 in *Introductory Readings in Archaeology,* ed. B. M. Fagan. Boston: Little, brown.
1971   Archaeology and Ecology. *WA* 2: 321–36.
1975   The Archaeology of Government. *WA* 6: 95–106.
Ucko, P. J.; Tringham, R.; and Dimbleby, G. W.
1972   *Man, Settlement and Urbanism.* London: Duckworth.
Vaux, R. de
1971   Palestine in the Early Bronze Age. Pp. 208–37 in *The Cambridge Ancient History,* 3rd rev. ed., Vol. I, Part 2. Cambridge: Cambridge University.
Watson, P. J.
1979   *Archaeological Ethnography in Western Iran.* Viking Fund Publications in Anthropology, No. 57. Tucson: University of Arizona.
Watson, P. J.: LeBlanc, S. A.; and Redman, C. L.
1971   *Explanation in Archaeology: An Explicitly Scientific Approach.* New York: Columbia University.
Watson, R. A.
1976   Inference in Archaeology. *Am Ant* 41: 58–66.
Willey, G. R.
1953   *Prehistoric Settlement Patterns in the Virú Valley, Peru.* Washington, D.C.: Bureau of American Ethnology.
1956   *Prehistoric Settlement Patterns in the New World.* Viking Fund Publications in Anthropology, No. 23. New York: Johnson Reprint.
Willey, G. R., and Sabloff, J. A.
1974   *A History of American Archaeology.* London: Thames and Hudson.
Wright, G. E.
1961   The Archaeology of Palestine. Pp. 73–112 in *The Bible and the Ancient Near East: Essays in Honor of William Foxwell Albright,* ed. G. E. Wright. Garden City, NY: Doubleday.

1974   The Tell: Basic Unit for Reconstructing Complex Societies of the Near East. Pp. 123–43 in *Reconstructing Complex Societies: An Archaeological Colloquim,* ed. C. B. Moore. Supplement to *BASOR,* No. 20. Cambridge: ASOR.

1975   The "New Archaeology." *BA* 38: 104–15.

Van Zyl, A. H.

1960   *The Moabites.* Pretoria Oriental Series, No. 3. Leiden: Brill.

21
EPIGRAPHY AS A DATING METHOD

JOEL F. DRINKARD, JR.
Southern Baptist Theological Seminary

I. INTRODUCTION

The relative dating of pottery by a typological analysis has been a mainstay of Palestinian archæology since the pioneering work of Petrie at Tell el-Ḥesi. (See the article on pottery dating by Oded Borowski in this volume.) Albright and Wright trained successive generations of American ceramics specialists who were skilled in the typological analysis of pottery. In terms of pottery, typological study involved first the classification of objects by use or function. Thus, lamps are classified separately from bowls, store jars, juglets, and other types of vessels. Then the individual class is studied to find the development of significant features. For a store jar, these features might include the rim, handle, foot, as well as size and shape. By noting changes in the development over time (as indicated by appearance in more recent strata of an excavation), a relative chronology of the individual class of objects at that site can be determined. Then by a comparison of similar objects at other sites, the typological development over a wider geographic area and time span can be determined.[1]

Albright also pioneered the early study of a similar typological approach to inscriptions.[2] The consonants in an inscription would be

---

[1] For a brief discussion of typology, see Lance 1981: 37–46.

[2] Albright's contributions cannot be overstated. For a full bibliography of his works see Wright 1961:363–89 and Malamat 1969:1–5. Just to list a few articles concerning epigraphy, one should include:
"The Early Alphabetic Inscriptions from Sinai and Their Decipherment" (1948).
"The Gezer Calendar (1943).
"Notes on Early Hebrew and Aramaic Epigraphy" (1926).
"The Oldest Hebrew letters: the Lachish Ostraca" (1938).
"Ostracon C1101 of Samaria" (1936).
The Proto-Sinaitic Inscriptions and Their Decipherment (1966).
"A Reexamination of the Lachish Letters" (1939).

analyzed by epigraphic form into types. These type forms could then be put into a relative chronology. By a comparison with inscriptions of known date (or approximate date) a more exact dating could be proposed. Cross has continued the work of Albright in this field and has provided the analysis for dating many of the inscriptions recovered in the past 30 years.[3]

As with pottery typology, the typological study of inscriptions presupposes a clear stratigraphic context in order to date properly each inscription. The inscriptions can then be placed in a relative chronology on the basis of stratigraphy, that is, the inscriptions of the more recent (upper) strata are newer than the inscriptions of the earlier (lower) strata, with the exception of intrusions. Thus at a typical Palestinian site one would expect to find ancient Hebrew inscriptions in earlier strata than Persian-Aramaic ones. Similarly, later strata might have Greek, Roman, and Arabic inscriptions successively. More to the point, even within the Hebrew inscriptions, one might well find epigraphic changes from the earliest to the latest inscriptions.

One simple example of this typological development may be mentioned from the inscriptions at Arad. In the Stratum VI inscriptions, dated by Aharoni (1981: 9) to ca. 595 B.C., the *yod* has a figure seven shape, while in the Stratum VIII inscriptions which date to ca. 700 B.C. (Aharoni 1981: 9), the *yod* has a tail from the base of the vertical stroke (see Table 1, *Yods*). From this data, one would assume that the *yod* with the tail is earlier typologically than the figure seven *yod*. From similar evidence based on other consonants, one could form a relative dating of the epigraphic forms from Arad. One would then compare the forms from Arad with other inscriptions and begin to develop a relative dating from all Hebrew inscriptions. The evidence of inscriptions of known date, or whose date is widely accepted by scholars, would then give a more exact chronology of epigraphic forms. As the typological analysis is refined and more inscriptions are studied, unstratified inscriptions can be dated on the evidence of epigraphic form. As mentioned above, Cross has provided much of the evidence for such dating of preexilic Hebrew

[3] Among Cross' articles, the following are representative:
"Early Alphabetic Scripts (1969a).
"Epigraphic Notes on Hebrew Documents of the Eighth-Sixth Centuries B.C.: I. A New Reading of a Place Name in the Samaria Ostraca" (1961); ". . . II. The Murabbaᶜat Papyrus and the Letter Found Near Yabneh-Yam" (1962a); ". . . III. The Inscribed Jar Handles from Gibeon" (1962b).
"Epigraphic Notes on the Amman Citadel Inscription" (1969b).
"The Evolution of the Proto-Canaanite Alphabet" (1954).
"Inscribed Javelin-heads from the Period of the Judges: A Recent Discovery in Palestine," by Frank Cross, Jr. and M. T. Milik (1954).
"The Origin and Early Evolution of the Alphabet" (1967).
"An Ostracon from Heshbon" (1969c).

TABLE 1
TYPE FORMS OF SELECTED CONSONANTS

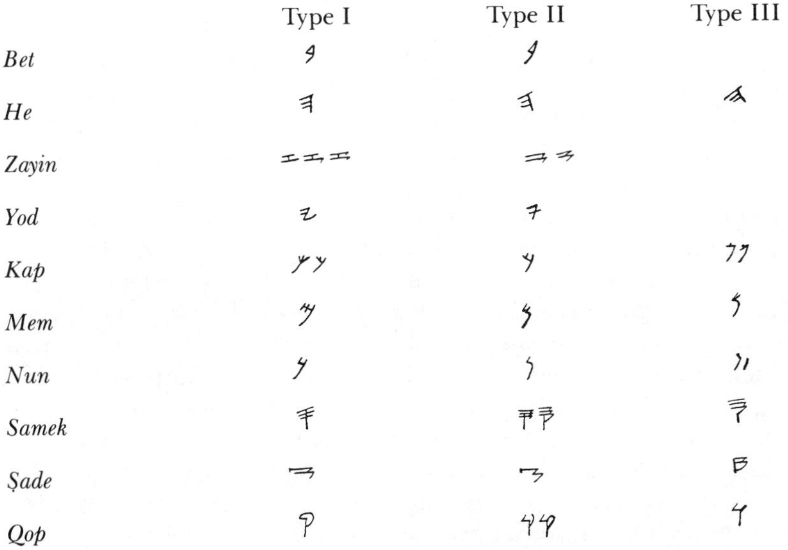
Type I
Type II
Type III
Bet
He
Zayin
Yod
Kap
Mem
Nun
Samek
Ṣade
Qop

inscriptions. Several other major contributors of epigraphic studies on preexilic Palestinian inscriptions include Avigad,[4] Naveh,[5] Lemaire,[6] Gibson,[7] and Herr,[8] as well as Diringer[9] and Birnbaum[10] of an earlier generation. Hanson (1976: 561–76) has an excellent article on the study of Jewish palaeography, the terminology and techniques used, and the major scholars who are involved in this kind of investigation. Although

[4] Avigad's articles on epigraphy include:
"The Epitaph of a Royal Steward from Siloam Village" (1953).
"The Second Tomb-Inscription of the Royal Steward" (1955).
"Some Notes on the Hebrew Inscriptions from Gibeon" (1959).
In addition, Avigad has contributed numerous articles on seals and seal impressions from Palestine.

[5] Among Naveh's works on epigraphy are:
"The Date of the Deir ʿAlla Inscription in Aramaic Script" (1976).
The Development of the Aramaic Scripts (1970a).
"A Hebrew Letter from the Seventh Century B.C." (1960).
"Old Hebrew Inscriptions in a Burial Cave" (1963).
"The Scripts in Palestine and Transjordan in the Iron Age" (1970b).

[6] André Lemaire, *Inscriptions Hébraïques*, Vol. I (1977).

[7] John C. L. Gibson, *Textbook of Syrian Semitic Inscriptions*, Vol. 1 (1971).

[8] Larry G. Herr, *The Scripts of Ancient Northwest Semitic Seals* (1978).

[9] David Diringer, *Le iscrizioni antico-ebraiche palestinesi*. (1934).

[10] Solomon A. Birnbaum, *The Hebrew Scripts*, 2 Vols. (1954–57 and 1972).

his work deals with inscriptions of a later period than those mentioned in this article, the same methodology applies.

Several inscriptions whose dates are widely accepted may be compared to show the general development of ancient Hebrew epigraphic forms. The Mesha stele, fig. 1, is usually dated ca. 835 B.C. The Siloam tunnel inscription, fig. 2, is dated ca. 700 B.C. and the Lachish letters, figs. 3 and 4, ca. 587 B.C. In fig. 5, a comparison of selected epigraphic forms from these inscriptions will show a typological progression for a number of consonants.

Two comments need to be made concerning this typological progression. First, the consonants did not all change at the same time. And second, the rate of change in the consonants is not constant. Certain epigraphic forms continued in use for centuries with little change, while others underwent significant change in a short period of time. Cross' approach of carefully determining the change of individual consonants over time and then making a comparative study of inscriptions represents the current state-of-the-art of epigraphic studies. Yet even Cross' approach leaves one area of the study of epigraphic forms untouched (at least this is true in the articles Cross has published). That area is a frequency analysis of the appearance of various forms of the same consonant in the same inscription or in inscriptions dated to the same time period. A major aspect of the typological analysis of pottery is the study of the frequency of a given form. A frequency analysis helps determine when a form was introduced, when it became dominant and when it was replaced by another form. A study of the relative frequency of different forms can pinpoint dating with more accuracy. A similar frequency analysis of epigraphic forms should prove invaluable in the dating of inscriptions of unknown date.

The remainder of this essay will propose such a methodology of epigraphic dating based on the frequency of occurrence of epigraphic forms of selected consonants. Such an analysis will be made on several inscriptions whose date is widely accepted by scholars. Then an analysis will be made of some inscriptions whose dating is disputed in an attempt to suggest an appropriate date for them. The inscriptions of known date include the Siloam tunnel inscription, the Shebna burial inscription, and the Murabbaʿat papyrus, each of which is dated ca. 700 B.C.[11] The Meṣad Ḥashavyahu inscription is used as an example of an inscription of ca. 625 B.C.[12] The Lachish Letters are used as examples of inscriptions

---

[11] All the epigraphic forms mentioned in this essay have been studied from the photographs as listed in this and the following three footnotes.

Siloam—Birnbaum 1954–57: pl. 14; and Diringer 1934: tav. XI.

Shebna—Avigad 1953: pls 8–10; and Avigad 1955: pl. 24.

Murabbaʿat—Benoit, Milik, and deVaux 1961: pl. XXVIII.

[12] Naveh 1960: pl. 17; Yeivin 1962: pl. 1; and Naveh 1962: pls. 5 and 6.

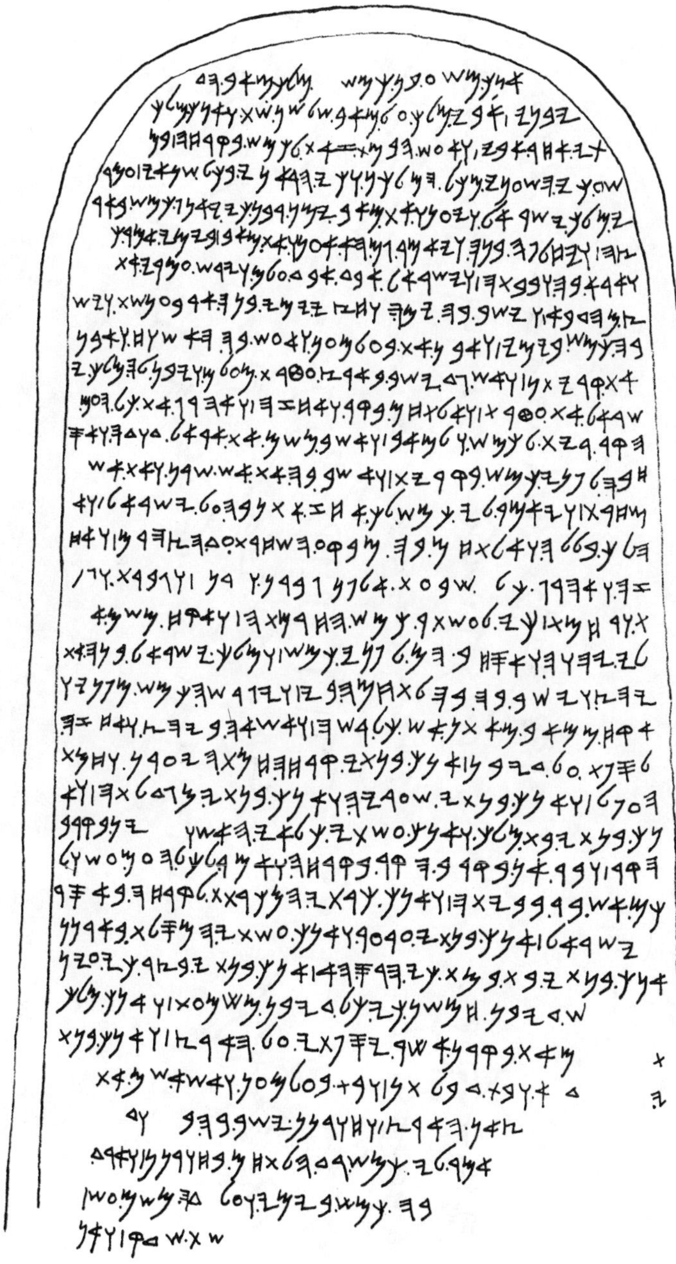

FIG. 1 *The Mesha Stele*

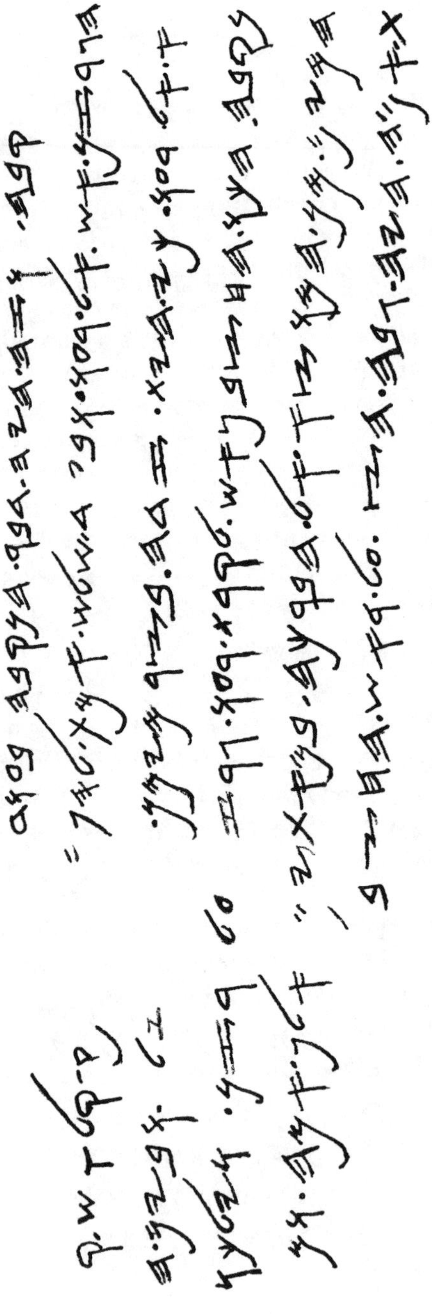

FIG. 2   *The Siloam Tunnel Inscription*

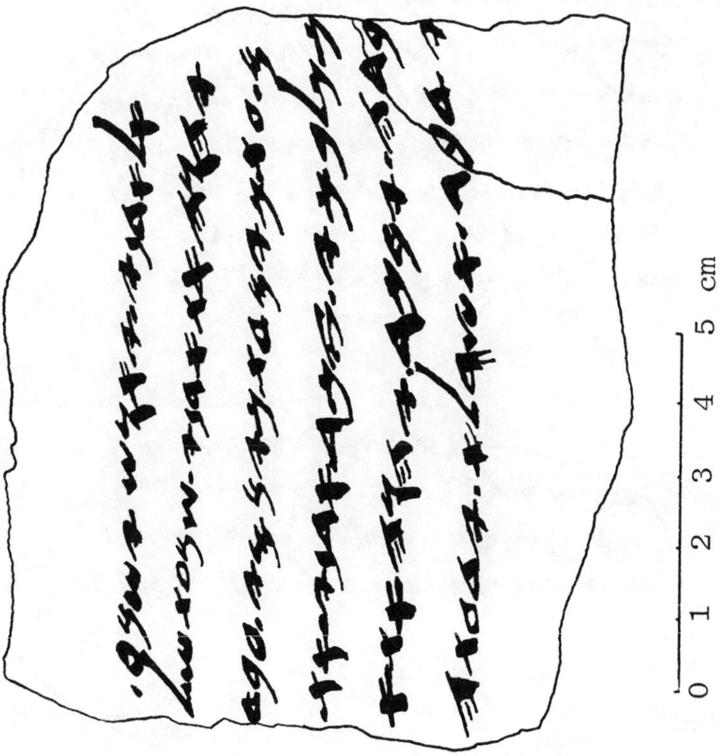

FIG. 3 *Lachish Letter No. 2*

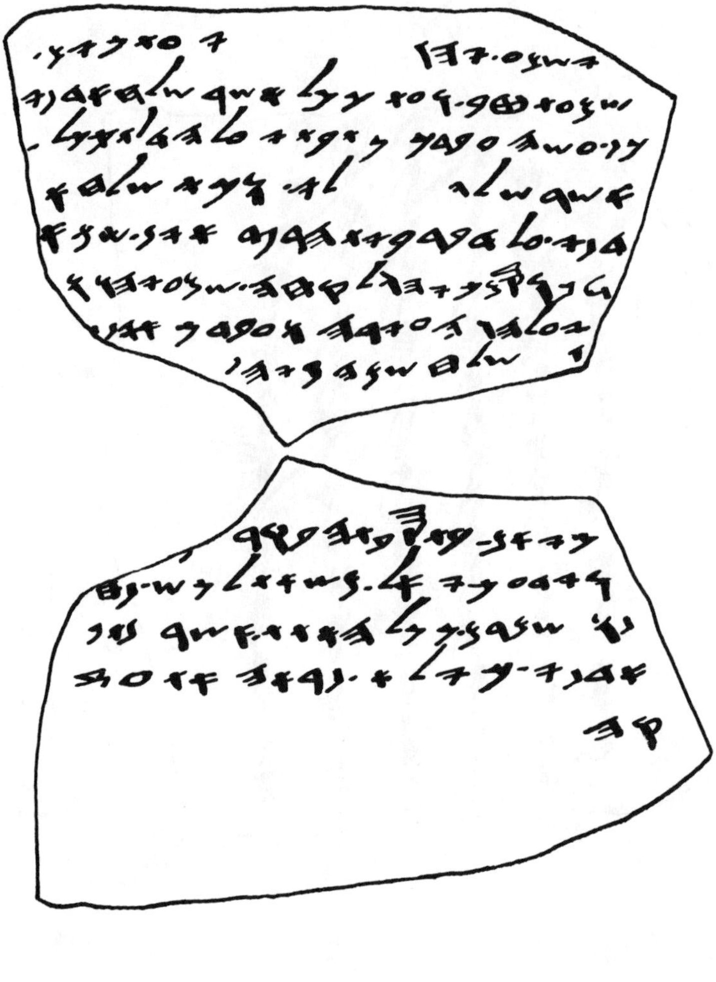

FIG. 4 *Lachish Letter No. 4*

FIGURE 5
COMPARISON OF SELECTED CONSONANTS FROM MESHA, SILOAM,
AND LACHISH TEXTS

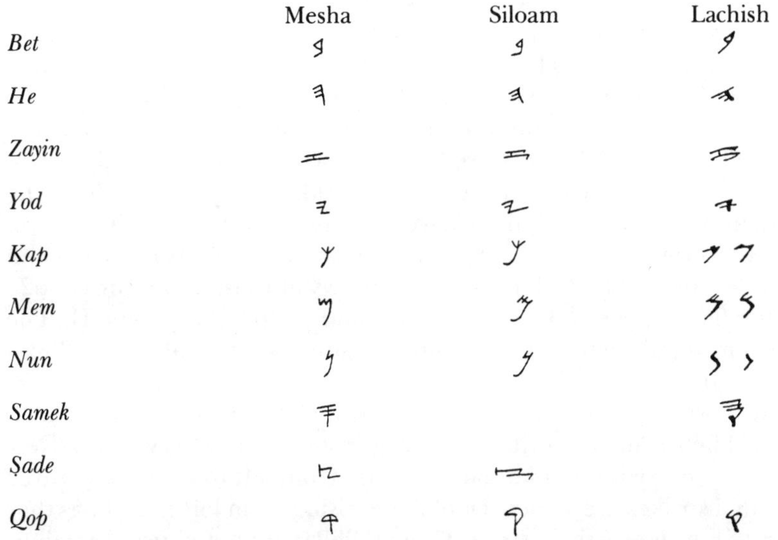

	Mesha	Siloam	Lachish
Bet	[glyph]	[glyph]	[glyph]
He	[glyph]	[glyph]	[glyph]
Zayin	[glyph]	[glyph]	[glyph]
Yod	[glyph]	[glyph]	[glyph]
Kap	[glyph]	[glyph]	[glyph] [glyph]
Mem	[glyph]	[glyph]	[glyph] [glyph]
Nun	[glyph]	[glyph]	[glyph] [glyph]
Samek	[glyph]		[glyph]
Ṣade	[glyph]	[glyph]	
Qop	[glyph]	[glyph]	[glyph]

dating ca. 587 B.C.[13] The frequency of appearance of selected consonants from these inscriptions will be analyzed to note patterns of development. It must be recognized that the Siloam and Shebna inscriptions are lapidary; as such the epigraphy tends to be more conservative than inscriptions of ink on sherd or papyrus. As a result, the lapidary inscriptions may preserve a more archaic epigraphy than other inscriptions from the same period.

Cross (1962a, 1962b) adopts in his articles the more technical terminology to describe epigraphic forms (e.g., formal, cursive, semi-formal, vulgar). In this essay, the epigraphic forms will be classified into types and identified only by type.

The Arad inscriptions of Strata VI, VII, and VIII will then be compared with the inscriptions listed above. The Arad inscriptions were selected because of the continuing debate concerning the date of both inscriptions and strata, especially strata VII and VIII.[14]

II. THE EPIGRAPHIC FORMS

It will not be possible here to study all consonants to show the epigraphic development. Some consonants changed very little over time,

[13]Torczyner 1938: photos; and Torczyner 1940: photos.
[14]On the photos, see Aharoni 1981: photos. For the debate as to date, see note 15 below.

the *taw* for example. The consonants which have been selected are those listed in Table 1. Each does show typological development, and the whole gives a good representation of the Hebrew alphabet.

Bet. One distinctive feature Cross (1962b: 19) noted for the *bet* of the eighth to the sixth centuries B.C. was its leg. The leg was angular in the older formal type (which will be designated Type I), and was gently curved in the newer cursive, Type II (Cross 1962b: 19). The form of *bet* and succeeding consonants are shown by type in the accompanying tables. The Type II *bet* appeared as early as the Murabbaʿat Papyrus, where two of the three *bets* have a curved rather than angular leg. The Siloam and Shebna inscriptions have only the Type I *bet*. In the control inscriptions for ca. 700 B.C., 18 *bets* are present; 16 (89%) are Type I and two (11%) are Type II. The Meṣad Ḥashavyahu inscription of ca. 625 B.C. has 24 *bets*; eight (33%) are Type I and 16 (67%) are Type II. The Lachish materials demonstrate a similar pattern with 17 of 61 *bets* (28%) Type I and 44 (72%) Type II. Thus one can see that *bet* showed a shift toward more Type II forms from ca. 700 B.C. to 587 B.C. See Table 2.

He. The formal *he* of the eighth century B.C. (Type I) was relatively upright. The vertical stroke slants slightly from left to right. The three horizontal strokes are somewhat oblique, rising from left to right as they connect with the vertical stroke. Cross (1962a: 38) noted two directions in which the *he* developed during the eighth to sixth centuries B.C.: the top horizontal developed a breakthrough to the right (Type II) and the stance became more oblique with the vertical shaft tending to shorten (Type III). In the inscriptions dated ca. 700 B.C., ten of the 29 *hes* (34%) are Type I while the remainder (66%) are Type II. The formal *he* (Type I) has fallen out of use completely in the Meṣad Ḥashavyahu inscription; 11 of the 13 *hes* (85%) are Type II, and the remaining two (15%) are Type III. In the Lachish inscriptions, the progression in form continues. Of 104 *hes*, seven (7%) are Type I, 41 (40%) are Type II and 56 (53%) are Type III. Table 3 shows the pattern of *hes*.

Zayin. The formal *zayin* of the eighth century B.C. was formed with two horizontal strokes joined by a short vertical stroke near the middle. Usually the lower horizontal had a tic from the right tip back leftward; the upper horizontal often also had such a tic (Cross 1962a: 39). This formal *zayin* is Type I. The Type II *zayin* lacked the vertical stroke in the middle but usually retained the two tics on the horizontal strokes. This

TABLE 2
DEVELOPMENT OF *BET* IN CONTROL INSCRIPTIONS

	Siloam	Shebna	Murabbaʿat	ca. 700	Meṣad Ḥashavyahu	Lachish
Type I	13	2	1	16 (89%)	8 (33%)	17 (28%)
Type II			2	2 (11%)	16 (67%)	44 (72%)

TABLE 3
DEVELOPMENT OF *HE* IN CONTROL INSCRIPTIONS

	Siloam	Shebna	Murabbaʿat	ca. 700	Meṣad Ḥashavyahu	Lachish
Type I	8	2		10 (34%)		7 (7%)
Type II	13	4	2	19 (66%)	11 (85%)	41 (40%)
Type III				0	2 (15%)	56 (53%)

latter form may have been written at times in one stroke without lifting the pen.

Only the Type I *zayin* is found in the inscriptions of ca. 700 B.C. and at Meṣad Ḥashavyahu. In the Lachish materials, seven of the 12 *zayin*s (58%) are Type I and five (42%) are Type II. Table 4 gives the result of an analysis of the *zayin*s. It must be noted that the small number of *zayin*s makes any conclusion based on *zayin* alone tenuous.

TABLE 4
DEVELOPMENT OF *ZAYIN* IN CONTROL INSCRIPTIONS

	Siloam	Shebna	Murabbaʿat	ca. 700	Meṣad Ḥashavyahu	Lachish
Type I	5	2	1	8 (100%)	1 (100%)	7 (58%)
Type II						5 (42%)

Yod. The formal *yod* of ca. 700 B.C. was formed with two near horizontal strokes, rising slightly from left to right, joined to a near vertical oblique stroke. From the bottom of the oblique line, a tail was drawn to the right. This *yod* is Type I. In a cursive form of the *yod* which developed late in the seventh century B.C., the second horizontal stroke broke through the oblique stroke and replaced the tail (Cross 1962a: 39). This cursive *yod* is Type II.

In the inscriptions of ca. 700 B.C., all the *yod*s (21) are Type I. In the Meṣad Hashavyahu materials, 26 of 28 *yod*s (93%) are likewise Type I and two (7%) are Type II. But by the final years of the monarchy, the Type II *yod* was dominant; in the Lachish materials, 63 of 76 *yod*s (88%) are Type II. The *yod* is a particularly important letter for this analysis because it is a common letter and it undergoes a typological progression during the time period under study. Table 5 shows the frequency of occurrence of the two types of *yod*.

TABLE 5
DEVELOPMENT OF *YOD* IN CONTROL INSCRIPTIONS

	Siloam	Shebna	Murabbaʿat	ca. 700	Meṣad Ḥashavyahu	Lachish
Type I	9	3	9	21 (100%)	26 (93%)	13 (12%)
Type II					2 (7%)	63 (88%)

Kap. The formal *kap* of the eighth century B.C. was composed of three strokes: a long diagonal stroke drawn downward from right to left, often with a gentle "S" curve, and two short strokes to the left which join the diagonal about one-third down from the top. The upper of these short strokes was nearly vertical, the lower a diagonal from left to right. The upper stroke attached at or just to the left of the juncture of the other two strokes. This formal *kap* is Type I. Two cursive tendencies occurred in the seventh and sixth centuries B.C. Following one tendency, the lower stroke dropped to a near-horizontal position and the upper stroke moved to the left away from the juncture (Type II). In the other development, the lower stroke moved upward as well as horizontally to join the long diagonal at the top. In the extreme development of this form, the left stroke dropped well below the horizontal (Cross 1962a: 39). This form of *kap* is Type III.

TABLE 6

DEVELOPMENT OF *KAP* IN CONTROL INSCRIPTIONS

	Siloam	Shebna	Murabba'at	ca. 700	Meṣad Ḥashavyahu	Lachish
Type I	4	2	3	9 (100%)	1 (7%)	9 (13%)
Type II					14 (93%)	26 (46%)
Type III						23 (41%)

Only the Type I *kap* appears in the inscriptions of ca. 700 B.C. In the Meṣad Ḥashavyahu materials, 14 of 15 *kaps* are Type II (93%) and the other one is Type I (7%). The formal Type I *kap* occurs nine times (13%) in the Lachish ostraca, while the Type II *kap* occurs 26 times (46%), and the Type III form appears 23 times (41%). See Table 6 for the development of the *kap*.

Mem. Cross (1962b:22) noted that the formal *mem* of the late eighth century B.C. was made with two "Vs" or check marks attached to the diagonal leg drawn downward from right to left. By ca. 700 B.C., the upstroke of the two Vs became nearly horizontal and was often only a vestigial tic (Type I). At the same time, the right shoulder tended to drop, the two Vs moved upward to join the leg at the top, and the juncture often became rounded (Type II). Finally, the upstrokes of the Vs were lost completely, with the two downstrokes joining at a point with the now rounded main leg, or the left downstroke joined directly to the curved leg and the right downstroke became a diagonal cutting through the rounded shoulder (Type III).

In the inscriptions of ca. 700 B.C., 17 of the 19 *mems* (89%) are Type I and two (11%) are Type II. The Meṣad Ḥashavyahu *mems* are all Type II (11). Of the 60 *mems* at Lachish, 15 (25%) are Type I, 25 (42%) are Type II, and 20 (33%) are Type III. Table 7 describes the frequency of the *mems* in the various inscriptions.

TABLE 7
DEVELOPMENT OF *MEM* IN CONTROL INSCRIPTIONS

	Siloam	Shebna	Murabbaʿat	ca. 700	Meṣad Ḥashavyahu	Lachish
Type I	12		5	17 (89%)		15 (25%)
Type II		2		2 (11%)	11 (100%)	25 (42%)
Type III						20 (33%)

TABLE 8
DEVELOPMENT OF *NUN* IN CONTROL INSCRIPTIONS

	Siloam	Shebna	Murabbaʿat	ca. 700	Meṣad Ḥashavyahu	Lachish
Type I	6		2	8 (100%)	8 (80%)	13 (26%)
Type II					2 (20%)	16 (32%)
Type III						21 (42%)

Nun. The development of the *nun* is similar to that of the *mem* during this period. It was formed with a single "V" or "check-mark" attached to a diagonal leg. As with the *mem,* the upstroke of the V often shortened and dropped to a near horizontal position, Type I. As the *nun* continued to develop, the V moved upward and joined the leg at its top, and the juncture often became rounded, Type II. Toward the end of the seventh century B.C., a *nun* appears without the downstroke of the V as well as a "headless" form. These are Type III *nuns.*

All eight *nuns* from ca. 700 B.C. are Type I, while in the Meṣad Ḥashavyahu materials, eight (80%) are Type I and two (20%) are Type II. In the Lachish Inscriptions, 13 *nuns* (26%) are Type I, 16 (32%) are Type II, and 21 (42%) are Type III. See Table 8.

Samek. Very few *samek*s appear in the inscriptions under study. There is, however, a noticeable development in the *samek.* Only one example of the *samek* occurs in the ca. 700 B.C. inscriptions, and that one in the Shebna materials. It has much the same form as the *samek* in the Gezer calendar and the Mesha stele, with three horizontal strokes across a vertical leg, Type I. Type II appeared as early as the Samaria ostraca. It is characterized by tics on the right end of the horizontals; also the vertical stroke may not reach the top horizontal.

This second form continues to develop further through the seventh century B.C., with the vertical stroke dropping to reach only the lower horizontal and the tic on the lower horizontal increasing in size to become a dominant feature. Type III *samek* is a more cursive form in which the tic on the top horizontal may disappear. The verticle leg drops further, to the point that it begins at the base of the tic from the lower horizontal. The vertical leg may have been drawn continously from that lower tic in a single stroke.

The Type I *samek* is found in the one example from ca. 700 B.C. The Type II *samek* is the only form found in the Meṣad Ḥashavyahu materials (four occurrences). In the Lachish ostraca, nine of the *samek*s are Type II (69%) and four are Type III (31%). Table 9 shows the frequency distribution of the *samek*s.

TABLE 9
DEVELOPMENT OF *SAMEK* IN CONTROL INSCRIPTIONS

	Siloam	Shebna	Murabbaʿat	ca. 700	Meṣad Ḥashavyahu	Lachish
Type I	1			1 (100%)		
Type II					4 (100%)	9 (69%)
Type III						4 (31%)

Ṣade. The *ṣade* from Gezer and Mesha appeared almost as a letter "Z" drawn from a vertical stroke on the left. In the Samaria ostraca, the *ṣade* developed a tic at the end of the lower horizontal of the Z. In the inscriptions of ca. 700 B.C., the vertical stroke of the *ṣade* shortened and the two horizontals lengthened and were closer together. The horizontals were made in two separate strokes, Type I. During the seventh century B.C., a form of *ṣade* appeared which resembled the numeral "3" (Cross 1962a: 40). This is Type II. In the early sixth century B.C., the vertical stroke of the *ṣade* lengthened and the whole form came to resemble the letter "B", Type III.

All five occurrences of *ṣade* in the Siloam inscription are Type I, while the one occurrence from Shebna and the one from Murabba'at are Type II. Thus 71% of the ca. 700 B.C. *ṣade*s are Type I and 29% are Type II. All seven *ṣade*s from Meṣad Hashavyahu are Type II, though the form is stretched horizontally somewhat more than typical. At Lachish, one *ṣade* is Type II (20%) and four are Type III (80%). Table 10 shows the occurrence of the types of *ṣade*.

TABLE 10
DEVELOPMENT OF *SADE* IN CONTROL INSCRIPTIONS

	Siloam	Shebna	Murabbaʿat	ca. 700	Meṣad Ḥashavyahu	Lachish
Type I	5			5 (71%)		
Type II		1	1	2 (29%)	7 (100%)	1 (20%)
Type III						4 (80%)

Qop. The formal *qop* of the eighth and seventh centuries B.C. had a vertical leg; from the top of this leg was a horizontal stroke to the left, then a circular stroke upward, to the right, and downward, resulting in a 270° arc (Cross, 1962a: 41). This *qop* is Type I. A second form of the *qop* had the head made in two strokes from the top. The left portion of the head formed an acute angle; the right portion was a curved stroke from near the top of the head to the leg. Later the right portion of the head dropped so that it began from the top of the vertical, formed an oval shape and rejoined the vertical lower. These two forms are designated Type II. A third *qop* appeared in the late seventh century B.C. in which the right portion of the head was reduced to a diagonal stroke, Type III. From the ca. 700 B.C. inscriptions, five *qops* appear, all in the Siloam inscription. All five are Type I. The Meṣad Ḥashavyahu materials preserve eight *qops* of Type II (89%) and one of Type III (11%). The Lachish inscriptions have eight *qops* of Type II (62%) and five of Type III (38%). Table 11 describes the *qops*.

A few caveats are necessary before presenting the combined analysis of the forms. It is true that the term "typology" is not in favor in some circles. However, that term does indicate a development in form. Such a development in the form of the Hebrew consonants is all that is being suggested by the use of the word typology. It is also admitted that setting forth "static" types is somewhat artificial, since many examples of form seem to fall along a continuum. Yet in order to clarify the chronological development of the characters, it is necessary to "freeze" certain forms as "type" forms. Such forms are no more important than intermediate forms along the continuum. But such type forms do permit one to catalogue and analyze the development of forms.

In no way is it suggested that the development of certain consonants is to be associated with the development of other consonants, nor does Type I of a given consonant necessarily correspond chronologically with Type I of another consonant. Each consonant developed independently, although certain traits do appear on several consonants at approximately the same time. As an example, Cross (1962a: 36) mentioned a flourish or tic that appeared on the right end of horizontal strokes in the eighth century B.C. (especially on the *alep, zayin, yod, samek,* and *ṣade*).

Finally, it must be admitted that the numbers of individual consonants studied in several cases are too small to permit significant analysis. However, a pattern based on the combined evidence of several consonants should provide much stronger support for the comparative dating of the inscriptions.

TABLE 11
DEVELOPMENT OF *QOP* IN CONTROL INSCRIPTIONS

	Siloam	Shebna	Murabbaʿat	ca. 700	Meṣad Ḥashavyahu	Lachish
Type I	5			5 (100%)		
Type II					8 (89%)	8 (62%)
Type III					1 (11%)	5 (38%)

III. ANALYSIS

The following consonants underwent significant typological developments during the period from ca. 700 B.C. to the end of the monarchy, 586 B.C., developments which should prove useful in relative dating of inscriptions: *bet, he, zayin, yod, kap, mem, nun, samek, ṣade,* and *qop.* Table 12 shows the percentage of occurrence by type for each consonant in ca. 700 B.C. inscriptions, in the Meṣad Ḥashavyahu materials of ca. 625 B.C. and in the Lachish ostraca of 586 B.C. In each case, we note a progression from older (Type I) to newer forms (Type II or III), as we move to the end of the monarchy.

It is possible to make one further comparison of the typological progression shown by the consonants in Table 12. The changes from one type to another are evident. But how much change is necessary for it to be considered significant? For present purposes, a change of less than 15 percentage points is not considered significant; 15 or more percentage points is considered significant. In Table 13, the forms from 700 B.C. inscriptions are compared with Meṣad Ḥashavyahu (ca. 587 B.C.). The comparisons are plotted as being typologically older, newer, or the same.

IV. THE ARAD INSCRIPTIONS

The final section of this essay will look at the Arad inscriptions ascribed to Strata VI, VII, and VIII. Because the date of both the inscriptions and the strata have been seriously debated,[15] a typological analysis of forms could help date the inscriptions epigraphically. The Stratum VI inscriptions are generally dated to the end of the monarchy, contemporary with the Lachish Letters.[16] Although the date of these inscriptions is not disputed, they will be analyzed to determine if their epigraphic forms fit that time period. It is particularly the Stratum VII and VIII inscriptions whose date is disputed.[17] Therefore, their epigraphic forms are more significant for this study.

The Arad inscriptions which comprise this study are as follows:

Stratum VI—Inscriptions 1–23
Stratum VII—Inscriptions 31–34, 36, 47, 105–8
Stratum VIII—Inscriptions 40–46, 49–53, 64, 89–91, 109.

[15] See among others, Aharoni 1967; Aharoni and Amiran 1964; Holladay 1976; Aharoni and Aharoni 1976; Pardee 1978; Zevit 1980.
[16] Aharoni dates them specifically to ca. 595 B.C. (1981: 9). Most scholars agree on the date of Stratum VI material.
[17] Note especially Holladay 1976: 281; Pardee 1978: 323 and 327.

As with the other inscriptions, the Arad inscriptions will be studied by epigraphic form of the same selected consonants. Instead of providing a separate table for each consonant, the results will be combined into one, Table 14.

Bet. Like the *bet*s of the control inscriptions, the *bet*s of Arad inscriptions showed a progression toward more Type II forms as one moves from Stratum VIII to Stratum VI. In the Stratum VIII inscriptions, half

TABLE 12

DEVELOPMENT OF SELECTED CONSONANTS IN
CONTROL INSCRIPTIONS

		ca. 700	*Meṣad Ḥashavyahu*	*Lachish*
Bet	Type I	89%	33%	28%
	Type II	11%	67%	72%
He	Type I	34%		7%
	Type II	66%	85%	40%
	Type III		15%	53%
Zayin	Type I	100%	100%	58%
	Type II			42%
Yod	Type I	100%	93%	12%
	Type II		7%	88%
Kap	Type I	100%	7%	13%
	Type II		93%	46%
	Type III			41%
Mem	Type I	30%		25%
	Type II	60%	100%	42%
	Type III	10%		33%
Nun	Type I	100%	80%	26%
	Type II		20%	32%
	Type III			42%
Samek	Type I	100%		
	Type II		100%	69%
	Type III			31%
Ṣade	Type I	71%		
	Type II	29%	100%	20%
	Type III			80%
Qop	Type I	100%		
	Type II		89%	62%
	Type III		11%	38%

TABLE 13
TYPOLOGICAL COMPARISON OF SELECTED CONSONANTS IN
CONTROL INSCRIPTIONS

	700 vs 625 B.C.	*625 vs 586 B.C.*
Bet	o	s
He	o	o
Zayin	s	o
Yod	s	o
Kap	o	o
Mem	o	o
Nun	o	o
Samek	o	o
Ṣade	o	o
Qop	o	o

Summary:

	8 = o	9 = o
	2 = s	1 = s

o = older typologically
s = same typologically
n = newer typologically

the *bet*s (five of ten) are Type I. There is no significant difference in the Stratum VII inscriptions, where nine of 17 *bet*s (53%) are Type I. The Stratum VI inscriptions have only 20 of 58 *bet*s Type I (34%), a pattern not significantly different from the Lachish Letters.

He. In the Arad VIII inscriptions, seven of 21 *he*s (33%) are Type I, and 14 (67%) are Type II. The Arad VII *he*s are relatively close to the Arad VIII forms; seven are Type I (44%) and nine are Type II (56%). The Arad VI *he*s show a significant development of form. Three (6%) are Type I, 31 (61%) are Type II, and 17 (33%) are Type III.

Zayin. The only form of zayin that appears in the Arad VIII and VII incriptions is Type I, and only three of these. Similarly, the Arad VI inscriptions only preserve three clear *zayin*s; two are Type I (67%) and one is Type II (33%).

Yod. The form of the *yod* at Arad is strikingly like that of the control inscriptions. All the *yod*s from Arad VIII inscriptions (22) are Type I. Fifteen of the 16 *yod*s from Arad VII inscriptions are Type I (94%). And all *yod*s from Arad VI (74) are Type II.

Kap. Only the Type I *kap* appears in the Stratum VIII inscriptions from Arad. No clear *kap*s appear in the Arad VII inscriptions. The Arad VI inscriptions do not show quite the same pressure toward the cursive form as do the Lachish Letters: 21 of the 26 *kaps* (81%) are Type I, one (4%) is Type II, and four (15%) are Type III.

Mem. The Arad VIII inscriptions preserve ten clear *mems*. Three (30%) are Type I, six (60%) are Type II, and one (10%) is Type III. The Arad VII *mems* (ten total) are all Type II. Seventy-two *mems* occur in the Arad VI materials. Four (5%) are Type I, 66 (92%) are Type II, and two (3%) are Type III.

TABLE 14

DEVELOPMENT OF SELECTED CONSONANTS FROM ARAD

		Arad VIII		Arad VII		Arad VI	
Bet	Type I	5	(50%)	9	(53%)	20	(34%)
	Type II	5	(50%)	8	(47%)	38	(66%)
He	Type I	7	(33%)	7	(44%)	3	(6%)
	Type II	14	(67%)	9	(56%)	31	(61%)
	Type III					17	(33%)
Zayin	Type I	2	(100%)	1	(100%)	2	(67%)
	Type II					1	(33%)
Yod	Type I	22	(100%)	15	(94%)		
	Type II			1	(6%)	74	(100%)
Kap	Type I	5	(100%)			21	(81%)
	Type II					1	(4%)
	Type III					4	(15%)
Mem	Type I	3	(30%)			4	(5%)
	Type II	6	(60%)	10	(100%)	66	(92%)
	Type III	1	(10%)			2	(3%)
Nun	Type I	3	(33%)	5	(36%)	3	(5%)
	Type II	6	(67%)	5	(36%)	55	(92%)
	Type III			4	(28%)	2	(3%)
Samek	Type I						
	Type II			1	(100%)	3	(60%)
	Type III					2	(40%)
Ṣade	Type I	2	(67%)				
	Type II	1	(33%)			10	(91%)
	Type III					1	(9%)
Qop	Type I						
	Type II	3	(100%)	1	(100%)	10	(91%)
	Type III					1	(9%)

Nun. The Arad ostraca show the *nuns* had developed somewhat more in form than some of the other consonants. Three of the Arad VIII *nuns* are Type I (33%), and six are Type II (67%). Arad VII has five Type I *nuns* (36%) and a like number of Type II forms, but also has four Type III *nuns* (28%). In the Arad VI inscriptions, one finds three Type I *nuns* (5%), 55 Type II (92%), and two Type III (3%).

Samek. No *samek* appears in the Arad VIII materials. The one Arad VII occurrence is Type II. In the Arad VI inscriptions, three *sameks* are Type II (60%) and two are Type III (40%).

Sade. Two of the Arad VIII *sades* are Type I (67%) and one is Type II (33%). No *sade* appears in the Arad VII inscriptions. From Arad VI ten of the 11 examples are Type II (91%) and only one is Type III (9%).

Qop. The Arad VIII and VII inscriptions preserve only the Type II *qop*, three and one respectively. The Arad VI ostraca have ten Type II (91%) *qops* and one Type III example (9%).

From Table 14, it is apparent that the Arad inscriptions show a development of form from Stratum VIII to Stratum VI. It now remains to compare these forms with the control inscriptions of 700 B.C., 625 B.C., and 586 B.C. to find the "best fit" of a date for the Arad materials. To accomplish this, the data of Table 14 will be compared with Table 12. The results are shown in Table 15.

It seems clear from Table 15 that the Arad VIII epigraphic forms, while falling between the 700 B.C. and 625 B.C. forms, are typologically closer to the 700 B.C. forms. When it is remembered that the 700 B.C. forms consisted primarily of lapidary inscriptions which might be expected to preserve more conservative forms, the closeness to 700 B.C. forms is even stronger. The Arad VIII forms are definitely older typologically than the 625 B.C. forms. The Arad VII forms fit well with the 625 B.C. inscriptions; they are definitely newer than the 700 B.C. forms and older than the 586 B.C. forms. The Arad VI forms are older typologically than the 586 B.C. forms but newer typologically than the 625 B.C. forms. In general, this study has offered some additional support for Aharoni's dating (1980: 9) for the Arad inscriptions of Strata VIII to VI. His dates for the destruction of the Strata, and for the inscriptions are:

> Stratum VIII—destroyed ca. 701 B.C.
> Stratum VII—destroyed ca. 609 B.C.
> Stratum VI—destroyed ca. 595 B.C.

In summary, this essay has suggested a typological analysis of epigraphic forms as an added dating technique. In no way is it suggested that such a technique should be primary when other dating methods are available. However, when no other stratigraphic or artifactual technique

TABLE 15

TYPOLOGICAL COMPARISON OF SELECTED CONSONANTS FROM ARAD WITH CONTROL INSCRIPTIONS

	Arad VIII vs 700 B.C.	Arad VIII vs 625 B.C.	Arad VII vs 700 B.C.	Arad VII vs 625 B.C.	Arad VII vs 586 B.C.	Arad VI vs 625 B.C.	Arad VI vs 586 B.C.
Bet	n	o	n	o	o	s	s
He	s	o	n	o	o	n	o
Zayin	s	s	s	s	o	n	o
Yod	s	s	s	s	o	n	s
Kap	s	o				o	o
Mem	n	o	n	s	o	s	o
Nun	n	n	n	n	s	n	o
Samek			n	s	o	n	s
Ṣade	s	o				s	o
Qop	n	s	n	s	o	s	o

Summary:

5 = s	5 = o	2 = s	2 = o	7 = o	1 = o	7 = o
4 = n	3 = s	6 = n	5 = s	1 = s	4 = s	3 = s
	1 = n		1 = n		5 = n	

o = older typologically
s = same typologically
n = newer typologically

is applicable, a typological analysis could prove helpful in dating an inscription. In addition, it could give supporting evidence in disputed cases, such as the Arad inscriptions.

BIBLIOGRAPHY

Aharoni, M., and Aharoni, Y.
    1976   The Stratification of Judahite Sites in the 8th and 7th Centuries B.C.E. *BASOR* 224: 73–90.
Aharoni, Y.
    1967   Excavations at Tel Arad, Preliminary Report on the Second Season, 1963. *IEJ* 17: 233–49.
    1981   *Arad Inscriptions.* Jerusalem: Israel Exploration Society.
Aharoni, Y., and Amiran, R.
    1964   Excavations at Tel Arad, Preliminary Report on the First Season, 1962. *IEJ* 14: 131–47.
Albright, W. F.
    1926   Notes on Early Hebrew and Aramaic Epigraphy. *JPOS* 6: 75–102.
    1936   Ostracon C1101 of Samaria. *PEQ* 68: 211–15.

1938   The Oldest Hebrew Letters: The Lachish Ostraca. *BASOR* 70: 11–17.
1939   A Reexamination of the Lachish Letters. *BASOR* 73: 16–21.
1943   The Gezer Calendar. *BASOR* 92: 16–26.
1948   The Early Alphabetic Inscriptions from Sinai and Their Decipherment. *BASOR* 110: 6–22.
1966   *The Proto-Sinaitic Inscriptions and Their Decipherment.* Cambridge: Harvard University.

Avigad, N.
1953   The Epitaph of a Royal Steward from Siloam Village. *IEJ* 3: 137–52.
1955   The Second Tomb-Inscription of the Royal Steward. *IEJ* 5:163–66.
1959   Some Notes on the Hebrew Inscriptions from Gibeon. *IEJ* 9: 130–33.

Benoit, P.; Milik, J. T.; and de Vaux, R.
1961   *Les Grottes de Murabbaʿat.* Discoveries in the Judaean Desert, II, part 1. Oxford: Clarendon.

Birnbaum, S. A.
1954–57   *The Hebrew Scripts*, 2 vols. London: Paleographia.
& 1972

Cross, F. M., Jr.
1954   The Evolution of the Proto-Canaanite Alphabet. *BASOR* 134: 15–24.
1961   Epigraphic Notes on Hebrew Documents of the Eighth-Sixth Centuries B.C.: I. A New Reading of a Place Name in the Samaria Ostraca. *BASOR* 163: 12–14.
1962a   Epigraphic Notes on Hebrew Documents of the Eighth-Sixth Centuries B.C.: III. The Murabbaʿat Papyrus and the Letter Found Near Yabneh-Yam. *BASOR* 165: 34–46.
1962b   Epigraphic Notes on Hebrew Documents of the Eighth-Sixth Centuries B.C.: II. The Inscribed Jar Handles from Gibeon. *BASOR* 168: 18–23.
1967   The Origin and Early Evolution of the Alphabet. *EI* 8: 8–24.
1969a   Early Alphabetic Scripts. Pp. 97–123 in *Symposia,* ed. F. M. Cross. Cambridge: ASOR.
1969b   Epigraphic Notes on the Amman Citadel Inscription. *BASOR* 193: 13–19.
1969c   An Ostracon from Heshbon. *AUSS* 7: 223–29.

Cross, F. M., Jr., and Milik, J. T.
1954   Inscribed Javelin-heads from the Period of the Judges: A Recent Discovery in Palestine. *BASOR* 134: 11–14.

Diringer, D.
1934   *Le iscrizioni antico-ebraiche palestinesi.* Florence: Felice Le Monnier.

Gibson, J. C. L.
1971   *Textbook of Syrian Semitic Inscriptions*, Vol. 1. Oxford: Clarendon.

Hanson, R. S.
1976   Jewish Palaeography and Its Bearing on Text Critical Studies. Pp. 561–76 in *Magnalia Dei: The Mighty Acts of God*, eds. F. M. Cross, W. E. Lemke, and P. D. Miller, Jr. Garden City, NY: Doubleday.

Herr, L. G.
1978   *The Scripts of Ancient Northwest Semitic Seals.* Harvard Semitic Monograph Series 18. Missoula, MT: Scholars.

Holladay, J. S., Jr.
1976   Of Sherds and Strata: Contributions Toward An Understanding of the Archaeology of the Divided Monarchy. Pp. 253–93 in *Magnalia Dei: The Mighty Acts of God*, eds. F. M. Cross, W. E. Lemke, and P. D. Miller, Jr. Garden City, NY: Doubleday.

Lance, H. D.
1981   *The Old Testament and the Archaeologist.* Philadelphia: Fortress.

Lemaire, A.
1977   *Inscriptions Hébraïques*, Vol. I. Paris: Les Editions du Cerf.

Malamat, A., ed.
1969   *Eretz Israel, Volume 9: W. F. Albright Volume.* Jerusalem: Israel Exploration Society.

Naveh, J.
1960   A Hebrew Letter From the Seventh Century B.C. *IEJ* 10: 129–39.
1962   More Hebrew Inscriptions from Meṣad Ḥashavyahu. *IEJ* 12: 27–32.
1963   Old Hebrew Inscriptions in a Burial Cave. *IEJ* 13: 74–92.
1970a   *The Development of the Aramaic Scripts.* Jerusalem: Israel Academy of Sciences and Humanities.
1970b   The Scripts in Palestine and Transjordan in the Iron Age. Pp. 277–83 in *Near Eastern Archaeology in the Twentieth Century: Essays in Honor of Nelson Glueck*, ed. J. A. Sanders. Garden City, NY: Doubleday.
1976   The Date of the Deir ʿAlla Inscription in Aramaic Script. *IEJ* 17: 256–58.

Pardee, D.
1978a   Letters from Tel Arad. *UF* 10: 289–336.
1978b   An Overview of Ancient Hebrew Epistolography. *JBL* 97: 321–46.

Torczyner, H.
1938   *Lachish I: The Lachish Letters.* London: Oxford University Press.
1940   *The Lachish Ostraca: Letters of the Time of Jeremiah* (Hebrew). Jerusalem: Jewish Palestine Exploration Society.

Wright, G. E., ed.
1961   *The Bible and the Ancient Near East: Essays in Honor of William Foxwell Albright.* Garden City, NY: Doubleday.

Yeivin, S.
1962   The Judicial Petition From Meṣad Ḥashavyahu. *Bibliotheca Orientalis* 19: 3–10.

Zevit, Z.
1980   *Matres Lectionis in Ancient Hebrew Epigraphs.* ASOR Monograph Series 2. Cambridge: ASOR.

22
THE FUTURE OF "BIBLICAL ARCHAEOLOGY"

J. KENNETH EAKINS
Golden Gate Baptist Theological Seminary

Confusion. Transition. Identity Crisis. Such terms are often used to describe the current condition of biblical archaeology. This unsettled state of affairs is not a phenomenon restricted to biblical archaeology alone, but is shared by other branches of archaeology as well.[1]

The purpose of this essay, however, is not to comment on the present state of the discipline, but rather to look to the future. The title selected reflects the author's conviction that biblical archaeology does have a future. Its past, mostly honorable, and its present, characterized not only by confusion, but also by numerous active and skilled archaeologists supported by a base of enthusiastic lay persons, mandate a future. But what kind of a future? The title is perhaps too ambitious at this point. Can one really hope to predict the future of the discipline? Perhaps not. An attempt will be made in this essay to sketch one possible future—a picture that will be a blend of what the author thinks will most likely happen along with that which he believes should and may occur. This exercise in prediction can be approached best by considering three interrelated elements: purpose, practice, and problems.

I. PURPOSE

The first subject for attention, one often ignored, is that of purpose. Why should there be a discipline of biblical archaeology? What is its purpose? The question cannot be evaded. A healthy future requires at least some measure of agreement in this matter. The following is proposed as a working statement of purpose: *The purpose of biblical archaeology is the clarification and illumination of the biblical text and content through archaeological investigation of the biblical world.

---

[1] To sample some of the discussion see the Spring 1982 issue of *BA*. See also Dever 1974; Dyson 1981; Eakins 1983; Renfrew 1980; Sabloff 1981; Sauer 1982; and Wiseman 1980.

Now, there are several facets of this seemingly simple statement that need amplification. First, note the words "clarification" and "illumination." One must insist, emphatically, that the purpose of biblical archaeology is not to "prove the Bible." Those who have used archaeology in this futile and misguided manner have not been leaders in the discipline, but they have been highly vocal and sufficiently numerous to cause many to regard the field of biblical archaeology with disdain. Legitimate archaeology has been damaged by such efforts. Dever is surely correct when he states that any attempt to use archaeology to prove the Bible is "bad archaeology—and even worse theology" (1974:34). Callaway has noted that the problem is often not a case of someone attempting to prove that the Bible is true, but rather that a particular belief *about* the Bible is true (1966:206). All such approaches must be resisted. "Archaeology can take one into the historical, cultural, and religious context of the Bible, but it must stand at a distance from the revelation because this is the realm of faith, not science, of theology, not archaeology" (Callaway 1961:172).

Earlier attempts to articulate a legitimate role for archaeology in relation to biblical studies, as in G. Ernest Wright's "What Archaeology Can and Cannot Do" (1971:70–76) and Roland de Vaux's "On Right and Wrong Uses of Archaeology" (1970:64–80) need to be reviewed and updated periodically and, of course, much of that is now being done. An important and valid contribution can be made by archaeology in the realm of clarification and illumination of the Bible, and this objective can be pursued with integrity.

Second, the words "text" and "content" are envisioned in very broad terms. With reference to text one remembers the proven value of biblical archaeology not only in helping establish a more exact text, but also its contribution to an understanding of why and how a certain text is there at all—in other words, the matters of canon and canonization. As far as content is concerned, one thinks of form (e.g., poetic devices, literary genres, structural patterns) and subject matter (e.g., patterns of culture, world views, historical data, religious instruction). Among the many outstanding examples of help that have been received in these areas would be the Ugaritic texts from Ras Shamra and the Dead Sea Scrolls. Today the student of the Bible approaches, by necessity, the content of Scripture from a time and culture far removed from the original *Sitz im Leben*. Archaeology has had, and will continue to have, an important role to play in breaking down barriers of time and culture.

Archaeological investigation will be discussed later, under practice, but let it be acknowledged now that this is only one of several valid and desirable ways to approach the biblical text and content. It should also be noted that the writer does not have in mind any kind of independent methodology as far as biblical archaeology is concerned.

Finally, in this statement of purpose, the term "biblical world" is vague and is subject to changing definitions. Albright's well-known geographic and temporal limits (1969:1–2)—or lack of them—has caused unnecessary consternation among many. Although it is undesirable, even impossible, to establish limits more narrow than those set by Albright, there is no need to expect a biblical archaeologist to master the archaeology of the entire biblical world. That is impossible, and it is ludicrous to imagine that a biblical archaeologist can or should have that kind of encylopedic expertise.

II. PRACTICE

What will be the nature of the practice of biblical archaeology in the future? There is no reason to doubt that many men and women will continue to participate in this well-established discipline. For the most part they will be better trained and equipped than their industrious and resourceful predecessors, and they will be committed to a multidisciplinary approach to the archaeological task. How will they fit into the broad discipline of archaeology?

The Discipline of Biblical Archaeology

Much of the theory and most, if not all, of the method of biblical archaeology will be the same as that held and practiced by the best of nonbiblical archaeologists working in any given region. Much basic work remains to be done with reference to theory and method, and biblical archaeologists need to participate with others in this endeavor. There are many unanswered questions. For example, what actually constitutes a representative sample of any particular segment of the past? What does it include and how much is required in order to make a valid synthesis? Can it be obtained at all? Certainly one cannot determine a fully satisfactory methodology until the kinds of information needed are known. One shudders to think of all the evidence that has been unsought and unrecognized while archaeologists have concentrated on architecture, pottery, and other artifacts. While today's archaeologists are aware of the importance of many other items (e.g., botanical, geological, osteological, ethnological, ecological), important windows to the past are probably still being missed.

Biblical archaeology has not been, will not be, and should not be a totally independent discipline. The question is whether in the future the endeavor will be a branch of biblical studies or of archaeology. Actually, since biblical archaeology overlaps each of these, the question is where will the emphasis be placed? Although biblical archaeology has been pursued in most cases by biblical scholars, it can and should be regarded as a branch of archaeology. After all, in the name "biblical archaeology" (whether or not this is an appropriate name for the discipline is discussed later) it is the word biblical which functions as the adjective, and it is the word archaeology which stands as the noun.

This traditional combination of the two words reflects an underlying realism. Archaeology as pursued by biblical scholars embraces a theory, follows a methodology and employs a vocabulary that is more at home in the discipline of archaeology than it is in the usual biblical fields (literature, theology, history, languages). "Obviously, biblical archaeology is not one of the traditional Biblical disciplines. Its genealogy is found outside the Bible. Instead, it is one of the sciences which has been adopted by Biblical studies and invited to share in the sacred inheritance" (Callaway 1961:155). Callaway (1961:172) suggests that biblical archaeology "remains a scientific instead of a theological discipline."

Perhaps it is instructive to note that at the annual SBL/ASOR meetings, biblical archaeologists tend to find that most of their time is spent in the archaeological sessions sponsored by ASOR. Many of these scholars also belong to and attend meetings of other archaeological societies on a regular basis. It is difficult to escape the conclusion that biblical archaeologists are best regarded as archaeologists, but also as persons who are competent in biblical studies as well.

Biblical archaeology is that branch of archaeology which pursues the purpose stated above and whose practitioners are usually biblical scholars. While all biblical scholars will be interested in archaeology and the Bible, some, perhaps not a large group in the future, will also be biblical archaeologists. What sets these apart from other biblical scholars? First, they will have a broad, general knowledge of the theory, practice, and results of archaeological work in the biblical world. This will require effort to gain and maintain, but it can be accomplished. General knowledge of this type provides a critically important foundation to more specialized interests. Second, they will have real expertise in some limited phase of archaeological endeavor in this sphere. Specialization is not an option but a requirement. It is to be disparaged only when it does not have a broad, general foundation. The biblical archaeologist will find himself or herself as part of a team, utilizing whatever unique skills he or she possesses. Field experience will be an absolute necessity and at least some of the working time in the field, regardless of job description, should be spent "in the dirt." Even members of the specialty staff must not spend all their time in a field laboratory. Since the data are being recovered from the soil (e.g., bones, botanical substances), those with primary responsibility for its study (e.g., the osteologist, botanist) need to have a firsthand acquaintance with this matrix and the excavation procedures being employed. "When archaeology is being itself, and not masquerading as a branch of history, linguistics, religion, or cultural anthropology, it is always as Sir Mortimer Wheeler described it, 'archaeology *from the earth*' " (Toombs 1982:89).

Biblical archaeologists are needed to help ask the right questions, formulate appropriate strategy, devise proper methodology, and participate in the analysis, synthesis, and publication of data. These tasks must not be left solely to the Egyptologist, to the specialist in Mesopotamian or Syro-Palestinian archaeology or to archaeologists working elsewhere in the biblical world. It is not enough for the biblical archaeologist merely to interpret and apply the work of others. Although there may be merit in Lance's suggestion (1982:100) that a dig staff might well include a member whose primary task would be to interpret the results for biblical scholars, this should not be the model of a "biblical archaeologist." The present writer does not share the view that biblical archaeology is merely the dialogue between the two disciplines, biblical studies and archaeology.[2]

A third distinguishing feature of these scholars is that they will spend at least some of their time teaching courses in archaeology and a significant part of their research and writing time will be in this field. The author rejects the concept that one cannot truly be an "archaeologist" without working full-time in archaeology. That draws the circle far too small. The biblical archaeologist needs continued involvement in biblical studies but can still be fully professional in archaeology.

Characteristics of Future Practice

The practice of archaeology in the land of the Bible will continue to be influenced by concepts drawn from the "new archaeology." One result will be the growing recognition of the value of a team approach to the total task of archaeology. Geologists, botanists, physical anthropologists, cultural anthropologists and other specialists will play an increasingly important role.[3] One does not have a team, however, just because persons of diverse interests and responsibilities are on the staff. In fact, their presence could pose a threat to unity. Technical jargon can confuse and mislead the uninitiated, and the interface of several distinct disciplines is not always readily apparent. The various specialists and archaeologists

---

[2] This concept of biblical archaeology as dialogue has been promoted by Dever (1982:103).

[3] Although Callaway's fine work at Ai (Callaway 1972; 1980) preceded the period where the full value of a multidisciplinary staff was apparent, he has been quick to acknowledge the importance of this approach. In a recent interview, reported in the alumni bulletin of The Southern Baptist Theological Seminary, he spoke of the "new day" in archaeology which is now dawning because of a team approach (Knox and Wilkinson 1982:12). Unfortunately, costs sometime preclude having all the specialists one would desire present on the staff (Joukowsky 1980:25–34).

will need to learn one another's vocabulary and devise improved ways of working together as a unit in the development of theory and method, the planning of strategy, the analysis of data, and the publication of preliminary and final reports. Certainly it is not sufficient for specialists to work in isolation and to submit reports that end up as appendixes. Synthesis is the responsibility of the staff and must not be left solely to a reader confronting a bewildering array of complex data. This common error of the past must not be carried into the future.

Although the day is rapidly passing when a field archaeologist with a strong personality can dominate a dig, the need for persons with skills in traditional field archaeology is by no means diminished. No team can function responsibly without the presence of those who have mastered the intricacies of stratigraphic excavation and pottery analysis. These skills will continue to be honed and developed, with old approaches being reevaluated and new methods being formulated. As an example of a technique that field archaeologists need to investigate further, one can cite the use of the so-called "moving balk," which appears to have significant value in selected cases.

The future will probably witness a reduction in the size of most excavation projects (Dever 1980:47). There are at least two compelling reasons for this. The first is the matter of cost. The cost of conducting an excavation has escalated relentlessly in recent years. Even if world inflation cools with some amelioration in the cost of food, vehicles, and other required supplies, other factors will continue to push the budget upward. For example, there is the expense of processing data which are increasingly varied and numerous. Then there is the matter of site preservation which in some cases will be quite expensive. Also, money for publication will be necessary. This pressing concern will be discussed later.

The other compelling reason for the reduction in project size is the dawning realization that digging has outstripped the archaeologist's ability to process, analyze, and publish. Recent decades have been characterized by a kind of euphoria as archaeologists discovered the wealth of information available through a multidisciplinary staff, and an all-out assault was made on numerous sites. Unfortunately, the full implications of the expanded work were not always recognized. It has been fashionable to lament that archaeologists in the past dug "too much, too fast." Now it is painfully clear that present-day archaeologists have tended to fall into the same trap. The data recovered from every square meter have increased enormously, and the abundance and complexity of these data mandate a deceleration of the whole process.

The use of volunteer workers will certainly continue in the future, but only those expeditions that provide a quality educational experience will attract many applicants. Persons anticipating careers in archaeology need an opportunity to participate in high-quality field experiences, and the educational aspects of a project must be stressed. In addition, these experiences should continue to be made available to other interested persons who do not plan careers in the discipline. Archaeology must resist becoming an esoteric enterprise practiced by fewer and fewer persons speaking an increasingly unintelligible language to an ever constricting readership. The good will of a non-professional volunteer can result in greater community understanding of archaeology with a number of significant benefits, including, at times, those of a financial nature.

In the future, more and more volunteers may have an opportunity to experience archaeology through special field schools in their own country. There they will participate in the processing of material culture items that have been brought home from dig sites. By means of seminars, illustrated lectures, and actual handling of artifacts, they can gain a significant exposure to archaeology without actually participating in excavation or survey work. At the same time, the work of getting material ready for publication will be facilitated.

The future of archaeology in the biblical world will be increasingly characterized by a greater emphasis upon regions as opposed to single sites. The world of a volunteer on a dig tends to be very small, since much of the field experience is restricted to a square that measures 5 m to a side. The world of a dig staff also tends to be small, since it is normally confined to the site being excavated. This results in distortion. Cooperation and coordination of effort between teams working at locations in the same region need to be increased. The present custom of making one or two hasty tours of neighboring sites each season has only limited value. Dialogue and cooperation at all stages, though obviously not easy to achieve, would be exceedingly helpful. Better use of funds and more appropriate strategy should result. This kind of cooperation can probably not be achieved consistently unless and until it is required by the Department of Antiquity of the country in which the work is being done.

Finally, the future practice of biblical archaeology will be characterized by a better record in the area of publication. The scandal of the discipline in this regard is well known and widely lamented.

III. PROBLEMS

Thus far the focus has been on purpose and practice. Now a few of the problems confronting biblical archaeologists need to be examined. The future of the discipline will certainly be shaped by the solutions devised to these and other questions.

First, there are the interrelated problems of name and image. In

recent years, some have suggested that the designation "biblical archaeology" should be abandoned.[4] The writer has been somewhat am-
bivalent about this question in the past but now is convinced that the
name biblical archaeology is neither irrational nor inappropriate, if
considered in light of the picture just sketched concerning purpose and
practice. The name embodies a long tradition and there seems to be no
very satisfactory alternative, although numerous substitute names have
been suggested. The name will probably be retained by most. The
problem of "image," admittedly present in some quarters (but perhaps
this problem has been exaggerated), will not be solved by changing the
name, but rather by the pursuit of worthy goals in a thoroughly professional manner. Biblical archaeologists must avoid isolationism and seek
dialogue and involvement in the larger archaeological community, as
well as maintain contact, where appropriate, with professional groups in
the natural and physical sciences.

Second, there is the problem of scope. In the past, the name biblical
archaeology has been misleading. The practitioners of the discipline
have been mainly concerned with only a portion of the Bible, that part of
the canon called the Old Testament by Christians, and consequently the
major focus has been on a limited part of the biblical world. This
becomes immediately apparent when one examines the standard books
and periodicals in the field and when one notes the departments in
which biblical archaeologists teach.

Vitality in the future will be greatly enhanced if increased attention is
given to the New Testament. It is rather amazing that the majority of
New Testament scholars have continued to pay so little attention to the
discipline of archaeology. The time is ripe to correct this deficiency, with
a resultant strengthening of both disciplines. The full contribution of
the Dead Sea Scrolls and of the Nag Hammadi Codices to New Testament study is far from assimilated. Recent excavations in a number of
cities in Israel, including Caesarea and Jerusalem, have revealed a wealth
of new information pertaining to the New Testament period. The whole
Graeco-Roman world of Paul and the early church awaits the attention of
those who have an interest in the New Testament. Here, biblical archaeologists need to align themselves with classical archaeologists working in
the region.

The discipline has also been, as others have noted (Dever 1974:12;
Shanks 1982), primarily a North American and a Protestant movement.
This type of parochialism has almost certainly introduced a degree of
distortion in the acquisition and interpretation of evidence. Vision limited in this way will not be adequate for the broad horizons to be

[4] For the view that the name is a handicap, see Dever 1974; Holland 1974. For an
opposing view, see Shanks 1981.

encountered in the future. There is a real need for greater participation by persons from various religious backgrounds and for biblical archaeology to become a more international endeavor.

Another problem concerns the training of biblical archaeologists in the future. What should their education include and where and how can this be received? These scholars will probably continue to receive a significant portion of their formal education in seminaries and schools of religion. Here they will be well trained in biblical studies, including biblical and other ancient Near Eastern languages, and may receive at least some training in archaeology. This training will need to be supplemented in most cases, however, by a significant exposure to university programs in anthropology and archaeology. Some may well pursue studies in statistics, computer science, and in certain physical and biological sciences, such as geology and botany. Classroom studies will not be enough, however. The budding biblical archaeologist must become engaged in a program of archaeological fieldwork. While the percentage of the archaeologist's time spent in the field in relation to other important tasks, especially publication work, will decline, there will always be a need for more survey and excavation. Much, but not all of this will probably continue to be conducted under the umbrella of ASOR, with its opportunity for field experience plus the provision of an organizational structure, a forum for discussion and a channel for publication.

The ties of ASOR with biblical studies are longstanding and strong. Consider that one of its sponsoring institutions, from the beginning, is the Society of Biblical Literature; consider that a large number of the institutions forming the Corporation of ASOR from 1900 to the present are institutions with some kind of religious affiliation. Consider, also, the fact that many of the great leaders of ASOR through the years have been biblical scholars, as well as archaeologists.

Biblical archaeologists must continue to be represented in the membership and the leadership of ASOR, although some may choose to work through other organizations. Those within ASOR will find a growing number in the membership whose interests are not biblical in nature. There is room for all persons, regardless of orientation, who are committed to quality practice. ASOR deserves the enthusiastic support of all its members during this exciting but difficult period of introspection and planning for the future. Biblical archaeologists must also continue to publish worthy manuscripts in all of ASOR's journals, as well as in other professional archaeological publications.

This introduces a fourth problem, the publication dilemma. There are numerous reasons for the poor publication record in the past. For one thing, few archaeologists enjoy the detailed labor involved in the preparation of a final report. Also, at this stage all of the deficiencies and errors in the fieldwork push their way forcefully to the front. One needs to remember that no work is ever complete (i.e., a "final" report is not really final) and that no work is without its share of error.

In defense of archaeologists one should acknowledge that many have simply found it very difficult to obtain time for writing lengthy reports. While institutions may permit a professor to be away for a summer's excavation, they seldom realize the need for adequate time for the processing of material culture and the preparation of reports. Any major archaeological expedition today is a year-round venture, although the digging time may be relatively minimal. "The tendency in the past has been for a highly organized field operation to disintegrate into a hundred or more pieces as personnel return home following the dig. Much harm has resulted. The analysis of data has been unsatisfactory. Publication has lagged" (Eakins 1983:39). A better job of educating institutions about the true nature of the work of archaeologists must be accomplished in the future.

There is a further difficulty in the realm of publication. What should be the nature of a final report? Surprisingly little attention appears to have been paid to this important question. What may have been adequate in the past will not be satisfactory in the future in light of the rapidly evolving nature of archaeology. Everyone seems to agree that it is necessary to move to a greater emphasis on synthesis and explanation. But the implications of this are yet to be realized fully and worked out in actual practice. The present legitimate concern for archaeologists to get about the work of publication should be accompanied by serious reflection and dialogue about the form and content of final reports suitable to the changing state of the discipline. The reports must be written, but scholars need to help one another learn the best way to proceed.

The dearth in publication also extends to textbooks. The books presently available tend to be out of date and restricted in scope. Weaknesses due to the inability of a single author to understand and present biblical archaeology in its present breadth are apparent. Although the cutting edge will always be found in the scholarly, professional journals, there is an obvious need to find ways in the future of producing useful textbooks despite the difficulties posed by the rapid accumulation of knowledge and the changing character of the discipline. Is it not time for some workshops concentrating on the strategy necessary to produce suitable reports and textbooks? Certainly it would appear that the writing of textbooks in the future will have to be a team effort just as fieldwork has become a team project.

In addition, archaeologists should continue to write reliable articles in a popular style for interested lay readers.[5] The *Biblical Archeologist* has

_____
[5] For an attempt by the present author to report highly technical data in a popular style, see Eakins 1980.

played an important role in this regard in the past, and its possibilities for the future are almost unlimited. A large base of supportive lay persons is exceedingly beneficial to the discipline.

Finally, the vexing problems of institutional support and funding must be addressed creatively. Individuals will need to interpret the value of biblical archaeology to administrators who are often skeptical and who are always, in these days, hard-pressed financially. There is a real need for more institutions, including institutions with religious affiliations, to develop and support sound programs in archaeology. This will cost money, of course, and these funds will have to be justified in terms of the yield to the school. No one can provide the necessary information interpretation for administrators and trustees except those who understand biblical archaeology and who are willing to expend their energy for its future—in the boardroom as well as in the field. This is not a time for timidity. Fortunately, it can be demonstrated, the author believes, that money spent for programs in biblical archaeology has been and will be a good investment for many institutions.

Support means more than money, however. Time is a key ingredient in the commitment. Not a few biblical archaeologists in the past have practiced without full institutional support with reference to time. For some it has been a summertime activity, squeezed out of vacation time and personal funds. Frequently, no credit has been given toward teaching load, even in those cases where students from the archaeologist's own school have been present at the site. And certainly all too few institutions have recognized the archaeologist's need for additional time after the fieldwork is complete.

The funding of archaeological work has become increasingly difficult. This is partially due to the rapidly increasing costs, but there is another aspect to be considered also. As archaeology has become more complex and productive, it has also tended to become more remote and less attractive to many. Some of the luster, even "glamor" is gone. Although the museum mentality of an earlier time is often decried, and rightly so, it is still true that a search for treasure is a potent stimulus to raising funds.

Funds will have to be sought increasingly from the private sector in the future, most likely, and this must be done with integrity with reference to purpose and expected results. The public must be educated to the true values of archaeological research and stimulated to support the work on the basis of a realistic understanding of expected results. Fortunately, a large reservoir of good will toward biblical archaeology still exists, and this can be tapped by those who are willing to make the effort. Certainly the majority of lay persons interested in the discipline are sophisticated enough to appreciate the exciting possibilities inherent in the practice of archaeology as it is now maturing.

One other item with reference to fund raising needs to be stressed. In the past, the appeal has tended to be for financial support for fieldwork. In the future it will be essential to explain that archaeological projects require support through the publication phase as well. Final reports are becoming more and more expensive to publish, and donors need to understand that no project is complete until this final stage of the work has been accomplished.

This whole effort of education and communication would be facilitated, if there were a more structured way to proceed. ASOR would benefit from the establishment and growth of more regional branches, both on a professional and on a popular level. There has always been a bit of the egalitarian spirit in ASOR, and this should be promoted in the future. This need not pose a danger or threat to professional standards. Rather, it will help provide a firm base for the practice of the discipline.

IV. CONCLUSION

Most persons who are interested in biblical archaeology do care where the discipline is going. Biblical archaeologists in the past were a determined and resourceful lot. Their descendants are no less capable and committed, and they are resolved to seek and find answers to the numerous problems confronting the discipline. They are determined to learn from the errors of the past, but not to let those mistakes cast too dark a shadow over the solid achievements of previous investigators. They are willing to modify or relinquish positions held in the past when new evidence indicates the need. They are committed to a thoroughly reputable and professional practice in the future.

There is reason for optimism. The current period of reassessment, which is necessary and healthy, should result in the taking of paths leading to a bright future. The yield of benefits for students of the Bible will be great.

BIBLIOGRAPHY

Albright, W. F.
    1969   The Impact of Archaeology on Biblical Research—1966. Pp. 1–14 in *New Directions in Biblical Archaeology*, eds. D. N. Freedman and J. C. Greenfield. Garden City, NY: Doubleday.
Callaway, J. A.
    1961   Biblical Archaeology. *Rev Exp* 58: 155–72.
    1966   The Emerging Role of Biblical Archaeology. *Rev Exp* 63: 199–209.
    1972   *The Early Bronze Age Sanctuary at Ai (et-Tell)*. London: Quaritch.
    1980   *The Early Bronze Age Citadel and Lower City at Ai (et-Tell)*. Cambridge: ASOR.

Dever, W. G.
1974   *Archaeology and Biblical Studies: Retrospects and Prospects.* Evanston, IL: Seabury-Western Theological Seminary.
1980   Archeological Method in Israel: A Continuing Revolution. *BA* 43: 40–48.
1981   The Impact of the "New Archaeology" on Syro-Palestinian Archaeology. *BASOR* 243: 15–29.
1982   Restrospects and Prospects in Biblical and Syro-Palestinian Archeology. *BA* 45: 103–7.
Dyson, S. L.
1981   A Classical Archaeologist's Response to the "New Archaeology." *BASOR* 242: 7–13.
Eakins, J. K.
1980   Human Osteology and Archeology. *BA* 43: 89–96.
1983   Biblical Archaeology in Transition. *Perspectives in Religious Studies* 10: 33–39.
Holland, D. L.
1974   "Biblical Archaeology": An Onomastic Perplexity. *BA* 37: 19–23.
Joukowsky, M.
1980   *A Complete Manual of Field Archaeology: Tools and Techniques of Field Work for Archaeologists.* Englewood Cliffs, NJ: Prentice-Hall.
Knox, M., and Wilkinson, D. R., eds.
1982   "New Day" Dawns for Archaeology. *The Tie* 51: 12.
Lance, H. D.
1981   *The Old Testament and the Archaeologist.* Philadelphia: Fortress.
1982   American Biblical Archeology in Perspective. *BA* 45: 97–101.
Renfrew, C.
1980   The Great Tradition versus the Great Divide: Archaeology as Anthropology? *AJA* 84: 287–98.
Sabloff, J. A.
1981   When the Rhetoric Fades: A Brief Appraisal of Intellectual Trends in American Archaeology During the Past Two Decades. *BASOR* 242: 1–6.
Sauer, J.
1982   Syro-Palestinian Archeology, History, and Biblical Studies. *BA* 45: 201–9.
Shanks, H.
1981   Should the Term "Biblical Archaeology" Be Abandoned? *BAR* 7/3: 54–57.
1982   In America, Biblical Archaeology Was—And Still Is—Largely a Protestant Affair. *BAR* 8/3: 54–56.
Toombs, L. E.
1982   The Development of Palestinian Archeology as a Discipline. *BA* 45: 89–91.
Vaux, R. de
1970   On Right and Wrong Uses of Archaeology. Pp. 64–80 in *Near Eastern Archaeology in the Twentieth Century: Essays in Honor of Nelson Glueck,* ed. J. A. Sanders. Garden City, NY: Doubleday.
Wiseman, J.
1980   Archaeology in the Future: An Evolving Discipline. *AJA* 84: 279–85.

Wright, G. E.
1959   Is Glueck's Aim to Prove that the Bible is True? *BA* 22: 101–8.
1969   Biblical Archaeology Today. Pp. 149–65 in *New Directions in Biblical Archaeology*, eds. D. N. Freedman and J. C. Greenfield. Garden City, NY: Doubleday.
1971   What Archaeology Can and Cannot Do. *BA* 34: 70–76.

EPILOGUE

Joseph A. Callaway

23
BIOGRAPHICAL SKETCH OF JOSEPH A. CALLAWAY: CHRISTIAN MINISTER, OLD TESTAMENT PROFESSOR, AND FIELD ARCHAEOLOGIST

Eric C. Rust
Southern Baptist Theological Seminary

Joseph Callaway was born in Warren, Arkansas, in 1920. His roots go back on his father's side to three generations of farmers in the Warren community and, beyond that, to a long line of ancestors in the area around Athens, Georgia. Growing up on a farm, Joseph was accustomed to hard work—a good training for one who later was to spend his days excavating in Palestine and investigating the communal life of a largely agricultural culture. When depression hit in the 1930s, Joseph's father managed to maintain his farm, and Joseph himself was able to stay in school, graduating from high school at the age of seventeen.

After selling farm machinery for a short time, Joseph married Sarah Fuller and returned to farming. Meantime, his religious convictions were pointing him in the direction of some form of Christian service. Sarah and Joseph sold the farm and assets and entered Ouachita University in 1948.

In a short time, Joseph got over the lapse of ten years in his education, and he graduated in three and a half years. He majored in English language and literature, a valuable training for his future task, as well as a natural result of his avid love of reading and writing.

The family, including by now a son and a daughter, moved to Louisville, Kentucky, in 1951. Joseph entered The Southern Baptist Theological Seminary as a ministerial student and, in order to provide financial support, also undertook a full-time pastorate of the Baptist Church at Worthington, Indiana. As a seminarian, he was especially interested and gifted in the subject of Hebrew, Old Testament, and archaeology. Joseph was especially stimulated by William Morton, Professor of Biblical Archaeology, and he took advanced elective courses in this area and easily headed the list of achievement in it.

With his Master of Divinity behind him, it was natural for Joseph to enter the graduate school in 1954 and pursue a doctorate in Old Testament studies. Those of us who formed his committee recognized that there was in this man both a capacity for painstaking research and a perceptive insight into what was essential in the data which he was studying. He was instructor in Old Testament Hebrew as well as grading fellow in Old Testament Archaeology, and thus he began to serve his apprenticeship in teaching Old Testament studies.

During Joseph's graduate work, Morton was off campus for much of the time, studying at the American School of Oriental Research in Jerusalem and participating in an excavation in Moab. In consequence, Joseph's seminar work had to be replaced by a heavy spate of reading in the field of archaeology. His real insight and integrative vision came when he read Albright's *From the Stone Age to Christianity.* Callaway's major professor was Clyde Francisco, and it was under his direction that Joseph wrote a dissertation entitled "An Introductory Study of the Basis and Nature of Messianism in the Old Testament."

Callaway joined the religion faculty of Furman University in 1957, but within a year he was back at Southern Seminary. In 1958, Joseph was invited to return and take the position vacated by Morton's move to Midwestern Baptist Theological Seminary. He taught Old Testament studies with a special concern for Biblical Archaeology, and this has been his role ever since.

This, however, only marked the beginning of Callaway's career in archaeological studies. He now had the opportunity to move out from his "armchair" position to an active participation in archaeological investigations. In 1960, Joseph became a staff member of the Shechem Excavations under the direction of G. Ernest Wright, and this determined his future bent.

It was during this Shechem dig that Callaway developed his interest in the technique of stratigraphic excavation. He was assigned an out-of-the-way test trench in front of the Canaanite temple; the preliminary report indicated that the trench had been cut through hard-packed soil. Joseph had recently read the description of stratigraphic excavation in Sir Mortimer Wheeler's *Archaeology from the Earth,* and this provided him with the hunch that the trench might have been dug through several strata. Starting at the top of the trench, he began to clear away the top soil and soon discovered a cobblestone pavement. Digging deeper, he discovered more such pavements and developed a steplike pattern at the side of the trench in which successive layers of cobblestone streets were exposed in the balk. In all he found nine such streets superimposed upon one another. Joseph's discovery proved to be the key to the structure of the temple, since he had laid bare the stratigraphy of the "courtyard temple" precinct which had preceded the construction of the massive Canaanite temple itself.

Back at the Seminary, Joseph was encouraged to seek further training in excavation techniques. His teaching competence had already made
him a valuable member of the faculty, and he was granted early sabbatical leave to study with Mortimer Wheeler and Kathleen Kenyon at
the Institute of Archaeology of the University of London: Callaway and
his family went to London for the academic year 1961–62. In the
summer of 1961, he had already participated with Kathleen Kenyon in
the first season of the Jerusalem excavations. In London he studied in
one seminar led by her, unfortunately her last year at the Institute. His
fellow post-graduate students included his friends, Lawrence E.
Toombs, Claire Epstein, and Rafik Dajani. During this term, he was
required to study the unpublished material on the Early Bronze Age
Tombs at Ai, a task that proved rewarding in two ways. He was able to
produce a monograph *Pottery from the Tombs at ʿAi (et-Tell)*, published in
1964. In addition, he had found an area of excavation and research on
which he has now become the acknowledged expert. For the years ahead
he was to devote his energies as Director of successive excavations at et-
Tell.

With the second term at the Institute completed, Joseph returned to
Jerusalem to share a second time in these excavations. Beginning in
April, 1962, he worked six days a week for three months. In that same
summer, he worked at Shechem for another two months under the
direction of Wright.

Meantime, Joseph had not neglected his responsibilities as a teacher
and scholar at Southern Baptist Theological Seminary. A grant from the
Nicol family had enabled him to plan and organize the Nicol Museum of
Biblical Archaeology, which he housed in a section of the Seminary
Library. This Museum, of which he at once became Curator, was opened
in 1960 and has proved, not only a valuable adjunct for archaeological
teaching at the Seminary, but also a source of information and biblical
enlightenment to the many interested laypeople and school children of
the area.

In addition to this, Joseph also produced a revised and considerably
rewritten edition of the book entitled *Biblical Backgrounds*, originally
written by one of his predecessors at Southern Seminary, J. McKee
Adams. For all practical purposes, he wrote a new book, and it is still in
use at the Seminary and elsewhere, although it is now in need of revision.

In 1964, Joseph again turned his attention to Shechem and enrolled
as a field supervisor under the direction of Wright. He and Lawrence
Toombs planned, however, to undertake another project before joining
the Shechem excavation. His aroused interest in Ai led him to plan an
expedition to that site and complete the work undertaken 30 years
before by Judith Marquet-Krause. When Toombs had to withdraw be-

cause of illness in his family, Callaway still carried on with his project. He planned a six week dig at Ai, before proceeding from there to Shechem. The successful consequences of this dig at et-Tell set the direction for all of Joseph's future activities. On this occasion, he was able to make major discoveries concerning the stratigraphic history of the site and the Early Bronze Age sanctuary. Ai now became a continuing project. After the excavations in 1966, he was able to secure a Smithsonian Institution grant of foreign currency funds for the successive years of 1968, 1969, 1970, 1971 and 1972.

Thus, across a continuing series of excavations, interrupted only by the War of 1967, this team of excavators has been able to survey the various strata of Ai (et-Tell). As a result, a descriptive account has become available of the site in the Early Bronze Age. By 1972, Joseph phased out the actual field work and turned his attention to collating and publishing the archæological data which the excavations had provided. Thousands of pottery drawings, hundreds of photographs, innumerable technical descriptions of artifacts and a large number of architectural drawings and sections had accumulated by 1972. These required completion in Jerusalem. This was made possible by grants from the National Endowment for the Humanities, which matched those from the Littauer Foundation in New York. Processing of the materials for the final reports continued through 1976. When the entire project was completed, all the drawings, plans, sections, technical descriptions, and photographs were shipped to Louisville.

From vast accumulation of data, Callaway has been hard at work producing a series of final reports. The first dealt in detail with the Early Bronze Age sanctuary at Ai and was published in 1972 under the title *The Early Bronze Age Sanctuary at ʿAi (et-Tell)*. A second final report was published in 1980, *The Early Bronze Age Citadel and the Lower City at Ai (et-Tell)*. Further final reports are either in the press or in advanced stages of preparation. Many would agree that these volumes on Ai have set a new standard for archæological reports on excavation projects in Palestine.

Along with these authoritative books, one has only to look at the many contributions to learned journals to realize the solid contribution which Joseph Callaway has made and will continue to make to archæological scholarship. The large gaps in our knowledge of the culture and life of ancient Palestine have been lessened by his work. He has been busy collating his data, working through the levels of stratification from the Bronze Age to the Iron Age. In this he was aided by a Guggenheim grant for personal research during a sabbatical leave in 1974.

In his study of the Iron Age, Joseph is venturing out beyond pure description and attempting to reconstruct the cultural life of the agricultural community at ancient et-Tell. He has thus left behind the older archæological methods associated with the Albright school and moved into the approach commonly labeled "New Archaeology." Joseph's willingness to move beyond the approach which he employed in his earlier work is to be commended.

In addition to this archaeological fieldwork and literary output, Joseph Callaway did not neglect his work at The Southern Baptist Theological Seminary. From 1978 to 1980 he undertook the task of Director of Graduate Studies and he continued his work in seminars and colloquia. The seminarians, both graduate and undergraduate, who have studied with Callaway have found him an inspiring teacher. Many of Joseph's former students are now professors, and they are indebted to his capacity to awaken a vital interest in archaeology and biblical study. He has left a lasting mark upon Southern Seminary and, now that he has retired, we are especially grateful for his commitment to the mission of the school.

Joseph has never lost his initial vision which brought him into the ministry. He has been a loyal churchman, a committed Christian, and a preacher of the gospel. He has supported his local church and taught in its Sunday School. Always he has been concerned about the impact of his archaeological research upon the Bible and its message.

Joseph Callaway has received many honors and been elected to many important offices. He has been vice-president and president of the Southeast Region of the Society of Biblical Literature. His special relationship, however, has been with the American Schools of Oriental Research. With this body he has served as trustee, and then successively as trustee, second vice-president, secretary-treasurer, first vice-president, and president of the Albright Institute in Jerusalem. He also served as Editor of the *Annual of the American Schools of Oriental Research* from 1978–1982, as well as being a member of the Project Review Panel of the National Endowment for the Humanities since 1978.

In all of his labors and accomplishments, Joseph has been much helped by the unselfish cooperation and practical assistance of his wife, Sarah. To her is due a large measure of his success, as he would acknowledge. We can be grateful for the work that has been accomplished and we can look forward to much fruitful research and writing in the years ahead.

24
JOSEPH A. CALLAWAY: SELECT BIBLIOGRAPHY

Compiled by Joel F. Drinkard Jr. and John M. Gibson

1960 Corinth. *Rev Exp* 57: 381–88.

1961 Biblical Archaeology. *Rev Exp* 58: 155–72.

1962 Gezer Crematorim Re-examined. *PEQ* 94: 104–17.

1963 Burials in Ancient Palestine: From the Stone Age to Abraham. *BA* 26: 74–91.

1964 *Pottery from the Tombs at ʿAi (el Tell).* Colt Archaeological Institute. Monograph Series. London: Quaritch.

1965 Ai (et-Tell), *RB* 72: 409–15.

  Biblical Backgrounds. By J. M. Adams. Revised by J. A. Callaway. Nashville: Broadman.

  The Fifth Campaign at Balâṭah (Shechem). R. J. Bull, J. A. Callaway, E. F. Campbell, Jr., *et al. BASOR* 180: 7–41.

  The 1964 ʿAi (et-Tell) Excavations. *BASOR* 178: 13–40.

1966 The Emerging Role of Biblical Archaeology. *Rev Exp* 63: 199–209.

  A Guide to Biblical Backgrounds. (Study Guide for Seminary Extension). Nashville: Seminary Extension Department of Southern Baptist Seminaries.

  A Sounding at Khirbet Haiyan. J. A. Callaway and M. B. Nicol. *BASOR* 183: 12–19.

1968 Isaiah in Modern Scholarship. *Rev Exp* 65: 397–407.

  New Evidence on the Conquest of ʿAi. *JBL* 87: 312–20.

1969 Archaeology and the Bible. Pp. 41–48 in *The Broadman Bible Commentary,* vol. 1, ed. C. J. Allen. Nashville: Broadman.

  The 1966 ʿAi (et-Tell) Excavations. *BASOR* 196: 2–16.

1970 The 1968–69 ʿAi (et-Tell) Excavations. *BASOR* 198: 7–31.

  Et-Tell (Ai). *RB* 77: 39–94.

  Khirbet Raddana (el-Bire). *IEJ* 20: 230–32.

  The 1968 ʿAi (et-Tell) Excavations. *PEQ* 102: 42–44.

1971 A Salvage Excavation at Raddana, in Bireh. J. A. Callaway and R. E. Cooley. *BASOR* 201: 9–19.

  The Significance of the Iron Age Village at Ai (et-Tell). Pp. 56–61 in *Proceedings of the Fifth World Conference of Jewish Studies,* 1969.

1972 The Early Bronze Age Citadel at ʿAi (et-Tell). J. A. Callaway and K. Schoonover. *BASOR* 207: 41–53.

  The Early Bronze Age Sanctuary at Ai (et-Tell), I. J. A. Callaway with the assistance of W. W. Ellinger. London: Quaritch.

1974   Khirbet Raddana. *RB* 81: 91–94.

A Re-examination of the Lower City at Ai (et-Tell) in 1971, 1972. J. A. Callaway and N. E. Wagner. *PEQ* 106: 147–55.

A Second Ivory Bull's Head from Ai. *BASOR* 213: 57–61.

1975   Ai. Pp. 36–52 in *EAEHL*, vol. 1, ed. M. Avi-Yonah. Jerusalem: Israel Exploration Society and Massada Press.

1976   Excavating Ai (et-Tell): 1964–72. *BA* 39: 18–30.

Review of A. Ben-Tor, *Two Burial Caves of the Proto-Urban Period of Azor and The First Season of Excavations at Tell Yarmuth. JBL* 95: 515–16.

1977   Radiocarbon Dating of Palestine in the Early Bronze Age. J. A. Callaway and J. M. Weinstein. *BASOR* 225: 1–16.

Review of W. G. Dever, *et al., Gezer II: Report of the 1967–70 Seasons in Fields I and II. JBL* 96: 279–81.

1978   New Perspectives on Early Bronze III in Canaan. Pp. 46–58 in *Archaeology in the Levant: Essays for Kathleen M. Kenyon*, eds. P.R.S. Moorey and P. J. Parr. London: Warminster.

1979   Dame Kathleen Kenyon, 1906–1978. *BA* 42: 122–25.

1980   *The Early Bronze Age Citadel and Lower City at Ai (et-Tell). A Report to the Joint Archaeological Expedition to Ai (et-Tell); No. 2.* J. A. Callaway with the assistance of K. Schoonover and W. W. Ellinger, III. ASOR Excavation Reports. Cambridge: ASOR.

Die Grabungen in Ai (et-Tell) 1964–1972. *Antike Welt. Zeischrift fur Archaeologie und Kulturgeschichte* 11: 38–46.

Sir Flinders Petrie, Father of Palestinian Archaeology. *BAR* 6/6:44–55.

1981   Rebel Leaders of Judea. *Biblical Illustrator* 7/2: 17–23.

The Southeastern Dead Sea Plains Expedition. Eds. W. E. Rast and R. T. Schaub. *AASOR* 46. J. A. Callaway, series editor.

1982   Review of R. Amiran, *Early Arad: The Chalcolithic Settlement and Early Bronze City. BASOR:* 247: 71–79.

1983   *The Excavations at Araq el-Emir*, Vol. I. Ed. N. L. Lapp, *The Amman Airport Excavations*, 1976. Ed. L. Herr. *AASOR* 47–48. J. A. Callaway, series editor.

A Visit with Ahilud. *BAR* 9/5: 42–53.

1984   Review of T. Dothan, *The Philistines and Their Material Culture. JBL* 103: 625–27.

Village Subsistence at Ai and Raddana in Iron Age I. Pp. 51–66 in *The Answers Lie Below: Essays in Honor of Lawrence Edmund Toombs*, ed. H. O. Thompson. Lanham, MD: University Press of America.

1985   Was My Excavation of Ai Worthwhile? *BAR* 11/2: 68–69.

GLOSSARY

Compiled by Joel F. Drinkard, Jr. and John M. Gibson

ACROPOLIS: Literally "high town"; normally a defensible hilltop that constituted the fortified center of an ancient city on which temples, the king's residence, and a place of assembly were located.

AKKADIAN: The culture and particularly the language of the ancient city or region of Akkad near modern Baghdad. Its linguistic representatives include the closely related Semitic dialects of Assyrian and Babylonian.

ARABAH: The arid rift valley bordered by the Dead Sea and the Gulf of Elath to the north and south and by the Transjordanian plateau and the Negeb to the east and west.

ARCHAEOLOGY: The systematic excavating, recovery, analysis, and study of ancient civilizations. The analysis should include not only artifacts, but also consideration of such evidence as climatic conditions, sociocultural patterns, religion, and historico-political conditions.

ASHLAR MASONRY: Masonry used as building stone which has been cut precisely into squared blocks to give a very tight fit.

BALK (BAULK): An unexcavated strip, usually one meter in width, between trenches or squares of an excavation site. The balk provides visual evidence of the stratigraphy of the square on its vertical face.

BURNISH: A pottery finish created by buffing the semi-hardened surface of the clay with a tool such as bone, shell, or other instrument prior to firing the vessel.

CARBON DATING: A relative dating technique based on the radioactive decay of carbon-14 in organic matter. The inherent uncertainties in this technique favor its application to prehistoric periods (ca. 50,000 to 3000 B.C.) rather than historic periods.

CARINATION: The ridge on a piece of pottery formed by an abrupt change in the slope of the external surface.

CARDO: Major north-south street of a Roman city.

CASEMATE WALL: An ancient fortification formed with a double wall having a narrow interstitial space interrupted by transverse partitions creating small chambers, some of which were used as storerooms or living spaces.

CHALCOLITHIC: The copper-stone age when both copper and stone tools and weapons were used.

CUNEIFORM: Literally, "wedge-shaped." The characteristic ancient writing techniques of Mesopotamia and surrounding areas in which characters were impressed in clay tablets or cones before firing.

DECUMANUS (s.) DECUMANI (pl.): Major east-west street of a Roman city.

DOLMEN: A tomb structure consisting of two or more massive upright stones with a horizontal cap stone.

EPIGRAPHY: The study of ancient written remains incised in stone and metal, such as monuments, statues, and coins; also the classification, dating, and interpretation of such inscriptions.

FILL: Tell debris or virgin soil deposited by ancient inhabitants of a site in their effort to level uneven ground during new construction.

GLACIS: A sloping bank, often plastered, below the external wall of an ancient fortification. Its purpose was to make attack more difficult because it left attackers exposed, could not be easily undermined, nor could battering rams or chariots approach the wall closely.

IN SITU: Literally "in place"; undisturbed; an artifact found in its original location.

KHIRBET: Arabic for "ruin," referring to an ancient site where ruins are visible on the surface. Often used of a site with few occupation levels in contrast to the "tell" which has many occupation levels.

KRATER: A large ceramic bowl or vessel, often used for mixing liquids.

LAYER: The compressed debris and occupational artifacts that constitute one level of build-up in a tell. It may constitute a stratum or a phase of a stratum.

LOCUS (s.), LOCI (pl.): The smallest distinguishable stratigraphic unit—e.g., layer, surface, wall, floor, feature.

MESOLITHIC: Middle Stone Age, between the Palaeolithic and Neolithic Periods when cultural development included settled village sites, animal domestication, cultivation of crops, and the use of polished stone implements.

MOUND: Usually means the same as tell.

NECROPOLIS: Literally "city of the deal"; referring to a large ancient burial ground or cemetery.

NEGEB: The arid region south of Beer-sheba from Wadi Arabah in the east and extending west to Gaza on the Mediterranean.

OFFSET-INSET: An ancient city-wall construction with alternating sections of the wall set slightly anterior or posterior in relation to adjacent sections. This construction was designed to confine damage to the wall, as well as strengthening it.

OSSUARY: A receptable for bones of the dead.

OSTRACON (s.) OSTRACA (pl.): Pieces of pottery used as writing surfaces on which letters, lists, receipts, and so on were incised or written in ink.

PALAEOGRAPHY: The study of typologies and evolutionary development of ancient scripts.

PALAEOLITHIC: Old Stone Age, marked by the use of stone implements and food gathering activities.

PHASE: An interval within a coherent development observed in an occupation level. A stage within a stratum.

POTSHERD (SHERD): A piece of broken pottery.

SARCOPHAGUS: An ancient coffin constructed of stone, terra cotta, lead, or wood.

SECTION: A vertical cut made through a mound to reveal its internal structure. Scale drawings of sections reveal the stratification of the mound as seen in the face of a balk.

SHEPHELAH: The plain which lies between the Mediterranean coast on the west and the Judaean hill country on the east.

SLIP: A thin layer of fine clay applied as a glaze to the pot before firing.

SOUNDING: A trial excavation, often used to establish the stratigraphy of a site before large-scale digging takes place.

STELE (STELA): A stone with carved decoration, inscription, or both, which was erected as a monument, legal statement, or for cultic purposes.

STRATIGRAPHY: The sequence of layers or strata of a tell. The stratigraphic method involves a careful excavation and analysis of one occupation layer at a time.

STRATUM (s.) STRATA (pl.): A layer of occupational debris which is internally coherent and usually separated from earlier and later strata by layers of fill or destruction.

TELL (TEL): A mound or small hill with a flat top which is indicative of many ancient sites, especially in Palestine. It is built up by successive layers or strata of occupational debris.

TERMINUS AD QUEM (TERMINUS ANTE QUEM): Literally "limit to which (limit before which)." The latest possible date.

TERMINUS A QUO (TERMINUS POST QUEM): Literally "limit from which (limit after which)." The earliest possible date.

TRANSHUMANCE: Seasonal movement of livestock by pastoral peoples between the highland and lowland pastures.

TUMULUS: A mound of earth over a tomb.

TYPE: A collection of artifacts or other cultural features classified together because they share certain important characteristics.

TYPOLOGY: The study and classification of types.

WADI: The bed of a stream in arid regions that remains dry except in the rainy season.

THE ARCHAEOLOGICAL PERIODS OF SYRIA-PALESTINE*

Paleolithic	700,000 — 14,000 B.C.
Epipaleolithic	14,000 — 8000 B.C.
Neolithic	8000 — 4200 B.C.
Chalcolithic	4200 — 3300 B.C.
Early Bronze	3300 — 2000 B.C.
EB I	3300 — 3000 B.C.
EB II	3000 — 2800 B.C.
EB III	2800 — 2400 B.C.
EB IV	2400 — 2000 B.C.
Middle Bronze	2000 — 1550 B.C.
MB I (formerly MB IIA)	2000 — 1800 B.C.
MB II (formerly MB IIB)	1800 — 1650 B.C.
MB III (formerly MB IIC)	1650 — 1550 B.C.
Late Bronze	1550 — 1200 B.C.
LB I	1550 — 1400 B.C.
LB II	1400 — 1200 B.C.
Iron	1200 — 539 B.C.
Iron I	1200 — 930 B.C.
Iron IIA	930 — 721 B.C.
Iron IIB	721 — 605 B.C.
Iron IIC	605 — 539 B.C.
Persian	539 — 332 B.C.
Hellenistic	332 — 63 B.C.
Early Hellenistic	332 — 198 B.C.
Late Hellenistic	198 — 63 B.C.
Roman	63 B.C. — A.D. 324
Early Roman	63 B.C. — A.D. 135
Late Roman	A.D. 135 — 324
Byzantine	A.D. 324 — 640
Early Byzantine	A.D. 324 — 491
Late Byzantine	A.D. 491 — 640
Early Islamic	A.D. 640 — 1174
Umayyad	A.D. 661 — 750
Abbasid	A.D. 750 — 878
Fatamid	A.D. 969 — 1174
Crusader	A.D. 1099 — 1291
Late Islamic	A.D. 1174 — 1918
Ayyubid	A.D. 1174 — 1250
Mamluk	A.D. 1250 — 1516
Ottoman	A.D. 1516 — 1918

*These dates are only approximate. Scholars disagree about these dates which are constantly being refined in the light of new archaeological evidence. For this reason there are some differences between the dates within the text and those on this table.

Copied with permission from Philip J. King, *American Archaeology in the Mideast* (Philadelphia: ASOR, 1983)

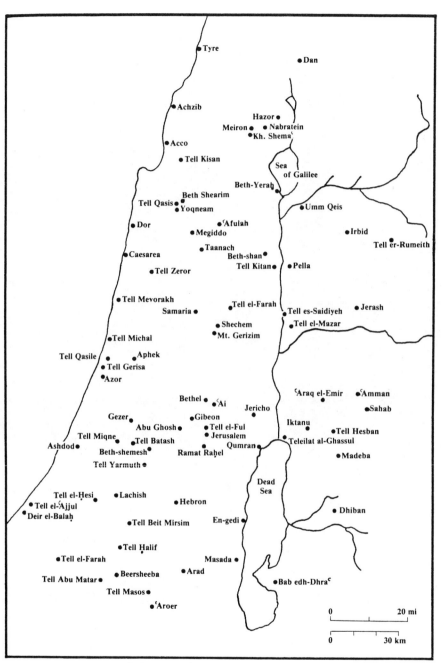

Tyre

Dan

Achzib

Hazor
Meiron • • Nabratein
• Kh. Shema⁽

Acco

Tell Kisan

Sea
of Galilee

Beth-Yeraḥ

Beth Shearim
Tell Qasis •
Yoqneam

Umm Qeis

Dor

⁽Afulah
Megiddo

Irbid

Tell er-Rumeith

Caesarea

Taanach
Beth-shan
Tell Kitan • • Pella

Tell Zeror

Tell Mevorakh

Tell el-Farah

Samaria •

Tell es-Saidiyeh   Jerash

Shechem
Mt. Gerizim

Tell el-Mazar

Tell Michal

Tell Qasile
Aphek
• Tell Gerisa
Azor

Bethel • • ⁽Ai
Jericho

⁽Araq el-Emir   ⁽Amman

Gezer •
Abu Ghosh •
Gibeon
Tell el-Ful

Sahab

Tell Miqne •
Tell Batash
Ashdod •
Beth-shemesh
Jerusalem
Qumran
Ramat Raḥel

Iktanu

Tell Hesban

Teleilat al-Ghassul

Madeba

Tell Yarmuth •

Dead
Sea

Tell el-Ḥesi
• Tell el-⁽Ajjul
• Deir el-Balaḥ

Lachish

Hebron

Tell Beit Mirsim

En-gedi •

Dhiban

Tell Ḥalif

Tell el-Farah •

Masada •

Tell Abu Matar •
Beersheeba
Arad

Tell Masos •

Bab edh-Dhra⁽

⁽Aroer

0   20 mi

0   30 km

Archaeological Sites in Palestine—Transjordan

INDEX OF AUTHORS

INDEX OF SITES